FUNDAMENTALS OF
MARKETING

FOURTH CANADIAN EDITION

FUNDAMENTALS OF
MARKETING

FOURTH CANADIAN EDITION

William J. Stanton
Professor of Marketing
University of Colorado

Montrose S. Sommers
Chairman
Department of Consumer Studies
University of Guelph
Ontario

James G. Barnes
Dean
Faculty of Business Administration
Memorial University
Newfoundland

McGraw-Hill Ryerson Limited

Toronto   Montreal   New York   Auckland   Bogotá   Cairo
Guatemala   Hamburg   Johannesburg   Lisbon   London
Madrid   Mexico   New Delhi   Panama   Paris   San Juan
São Paulo   Singapore   Sydney   Tokyo

FUNDAMENTALS OF MARKETING
Fourth Canadian Edition

Copyright © McGraw-Hill Ryerson Limited, 1985, 1982. All rights reserved. No part of this publication may be reproduced, stored in a retrieval system, or transmitted, in any form or by any means, electronic, mechanical, photocopying, recording, or otherwise, without prior written permission of McGraw-Hill Ryerson Limited.

ISBN 0-07-548915-5

2 3 4 5 6 7 8 9 0   JDC   4 3 2 1 0 9 8 7 6 5

Printed and bound in Canada by John Deyell Company Limited

Care has been taken to trace ownership of copyright material contained in this text. The publishers will gladly take any information that will enable them to rectify any reference or credit in subsequent editions.

Canadian Cataloguing in Publication Data
Stanton, William J., date
  Fundamentals of marketing

Includes index.
ISBN 0-07-548915-5

1. Marketing.   I. Sommers, Montrose S., date.
II. Barnes, James G.   III. Title.

HF5415.S745   1985   658.8   C85-098496-3

William J. Stanton is a Professor of Marketing at the University of Colorado. He received his Ph.D. and M.B.A. degrees from Northwestern University and his B.S. degree from the Illinois Institute of Technology. His prior college teaching experience was at the Universities of Washington, Utah, and Alabama. For close to 30 years, Professor Stanton has worked extensively with both undergraduate and graduate students at Colorado. He has been involved in developing teaching-learning materials as well as in developing curricular programs for those students. As an extension of his teaching interests through the years, Professor Stanton has been involved in several ways with the business community and the government. He has worked in business and has taught in several management development programs for marketing executives, some of which were in Europe, Mexico, and Canada. He has also served as a consultant for several business organizations and has engaged in research projects for the federal government.

Montrose S. Sommers is Professor of Consumer Studies and Chairman of the Department of Consumer Studies at the University of Guelph. He received his D.B.A. from the University of Colorado, his M.B.A. from Northwestern University and his B.Comm. from the University of British Columbia. He has taught at the Universities of British Columbia, Texas, Toronto, and Nairobi (Kenya) where he has been involved in teaching and program development for undergraduate as well as graduate students. Over the years, Professor Sommers has been a consultant to both business and government in Canada and abroad on such topics as consumer research, marketing management and strategy, and international marketing.

James G. Barnes is Professor of Marketing and Dean of the Faculty of Business Administration, Memorial University of Newfoundland. He received his Bachelor of Commerce and Bachelor of Arts (Economics) degrees from Memorial University of Newfoundland and his M.B.A. from the Harvard Business School. He completed his Ph.D. at the University of Toronto. He has been on faculty at Memorial University since 1968 and has been a visiting faculty member at Queen's University and the University of Bath, England.

Professor Barnes has been teaching Marketing courses for seventeen years, particularly in the areas of Consumer Behaviour, Marketing Research, Current Topics in Marketing, and Fundamentals of Marketing. He has also developed a considerable amount of material relating to various seminars that he regularly delivers for management audiences, particularly in the area of Not-for-Profit Marketing. He serves as a seminar leader in management programs and as a consultant in Marketing Research to some of Canada's largest corporations and to various departments of government at the federal and provincial levels.

Contents

Preface

As we move through the late 1980s, the socioeconomic setting is different from what it was not so long ago. Both our economic growth rate and our birthrate have slowed down. We are faced with high-cost energy, the threat of recurring recession and inflation, and increased social complexity. Many industries face intensive foreign competition, and others are perplexed by the value of the Canadian dollar and still high interest rates. People's values are changing. There is a growing demand for a better quality of life. There is concern about our social and physical environment.

These social and economic changes pose major challenges to business in general and to marketing in particular. Marketing executives must develop a societal orientation and an awareness of their social responsibilities. At the same time, they must satisfy increasing consumers' wants and generate profits for their firms. A textbook in marketing should change to reflect social and economic challenges and to offer some strategic guides to marketing executives. Consequently, several changes have been made in this edition to keep it up to date, to introduce recent developments and new concepts, and to reflect the importance of societal dimensions of marketing.

Changes also have been made to improve this edition as a teaching and learning tool — which, after all, is what a basic textbook is. The treatment of strategic marketing planning has been revised and developed at a level, and in a manner, that is appropriate for a beginning marketing course. Strategic planning is introduced in Chapter 2, and then discussed in further detail near the end of the book (Chapter 24). The theme of strategic planning is carried throughout the book.

A glossary has been added to this edition. A new chapter—a societal appraisal of marketing and a look into the future — combines and condenses the final two chapters of the previous edition. There is an expanded treatment of market segmentation and target-market selection. Several other chapters have been substantially rewritten. Twelve of the twenty-nine cases are new, and all material has been updated wherever possible. The five-part Bentley Tea Case has been retained due to its success as a teaching vehicle.

A major feature in this edition is the editorial "fine tuning" of the entire text. Considerable time and effort have been devoted to editing the book to make it clearer and more readable. Illustrations — charts, drawings, and photographs — were carefully developed to strengthen understanding of the text material.

Fundamentals of Marketing, Fourth Canadian Edition, is intended for use as the basic text in an introductory course in marketing. It is designed for students who plan to specialize in marketing and for those who will be taking only one course in the field. Both these groups are provided with a realistic treatment of marketing as it operates in Canadian business today.

Those who are familiar with the earlier editions of this book will find that the basic theme, approach, and organization have been retained. The central theme is that marketing is a total system of business action rather than a fundamental assortment of functions and institutions, as it has often been treated in marketing literature and in practice. While some attention is directed to the role of marketing in our socioeconomic system, the book is written largely from the viewpoint of marketing executives *in an individual firm*. This firm may be a manufacturer or a middleman, a business or a nonbusiness (not-for-profit) organization, and it may be marketing products or services.

The marketing concept is a philosophy that stresses the need for a marketing orientation compatible with society's long-run interests. A company's managerial planning and operations should be directed toward satisfying the customers' long-run wants, considering societal interests, and obtaining profitable sales volume. In short, marketing is recognized as an all-pervasive ingredient of the system of business management. And all managerial activity in a firm should be directed toward making the marketing process more effective.

This philosophy is evident in the framework of the strategic marketing planning process. A company sets its marketing objectives, taking into consideration the environmental forces that influence its marketing effort. Management next selects target markets. The company then has four strategic elements — its product, price structure, distribution system, and promotional activities — with which to build a marketing program to reach its markets and achieve its objectives. An effective marketing program requires an effective marketing mix—that is, the best possible strategic combination of these four elements. Throughout these four areas, especially in channel structure and promotion, management makes extensive use of another element—the human factor. In all stages of the marketing process, management should use marketing research as a tool for problem solving and decision making.

This framework for the strategic marketing planning process is reflected generally in the organization of the book's content. The text is divided into eight parts. Part 1 serves as an introduction and includes chapters on the marketing environment and marketing information systems. Part 2 is devoted to the analysis and selection of target markets—either consumer or industrial markets.

Parts 3 through 6 deal with the development of a marketing program, and each of these parts covers one of the abovementioned components of the strategic marketing mix. In Part 3 various topics related to the product are discussed. The company's price structure is the subject of Part 4, and Part 5 covers the distribution system, including the management of physical distribution. Part 6 is devoted to the total promotional program, including advertising and personal selling.

The major portion of the book pertains to the domestic marketing of manufactured goods. In the interest of completeness, however, Part 7 is devoted to marketing fundamentals as they are applied to three special fields—the marketing of services, marketing in nonbusiness organizations, and international marketing. Part 8 deals with the strategic planning and evaluation of the total marketing effort in an individual firm. Part 8 also includes an appraisal of the role of marketing in our *society*, including the subjects of consumer criticisms and the social responsibility of an organization. Following Part 8 are two appendixes. One is on marketing arithmetic, and the other is a discussion of careers in marketing and how to get a job.

Special attention has been devoted to the preparation of the discussion questions found at the end of each chapter. These questions generally cannot be answered "right out of the book." Instead, they are intended to be thought-provoking and to serve as an aid in applying the material in the chapter. Some of the questions require outside fieldwork, and they thus have the merit of introducing students to practical business applications of the textbook fundamentals.

Another feature of *Fundamentals of Marketing, Fourth Canadian Edition*, is the inclusion of short cases after each of the eight parts in the text. Each case focuses on a specific issue related to a topic covered in the text. In line with the managerial approach in this book, the cases provide an opportunity for problem analysis and decision making by the student.

To complement this book as a teaching and learning tool, the *Study Guide*, prepared by Professor Tom Clift of Memorial University of Newfoundland has been revised and expanded. It contains a series of current examples and workbook exercises that serve to provide the student with more experience in, and exposure to, real-life marketing situations.

Many people — business executives, publishers, students, present and past colleagues, and other teachers — have contributed greatly to this book. Several of the cases were written by other professors, and in each instance the authorship is identified. The assistance provided by Chris Vaughan and Corinne Burry at Memorial University of Newfoundland and Ian Murray at the University of Guelph was much appreciated.

Finally, sincere thanks to one of the best sponsoring editors in the business, Henry Klaise. If it had not been for our delay in meeting deadlines, Henry would have seen this project completed before receiving his much-deserved promotion. We wish him continued success. We look forward very much to working with our new editor, Jim Saunders, and with the always-supportive editorial staff at McGraw-Hill Ryerson.

William J. Stanton
Montrose S. Sommers
James G. Barnes

Modern Marketing

AN INTRODUCTION TO MARKETING, THE MARKETING ENVIRONMENT, STRATEGIC PLANNING, MARKETING RESEARCH, AND THE ROLE OF MARKETING IN BUSINESS TODAY

The first part of this book is an introduction to the field of marketing. In Chapter 1 we explain what marketing is, how it has developed, and how it is continuing to develop. We look at the role of marketing both in our overall socioeconomic system and in the individual organization. This individual organization may be a business firm or a nonprofit organization; it may be marketing products, services, ideas, people, or places; and it may be marketing them domestically or internationally.

In Chapter 2 we examine the external, uncontrollable environment within which marketing executives must work. We also discuss the management process in marketing and introduce the concept of strategic marketing planning. Chapter 3 explains the role of marketing information systems and describes the procedure in a marketing research investigation. Marketing information systems and marketing research are major tools used in strategic planning, problem solving, and decision making.

Chapter 1

The Field of Marketing

CHAPTER GOALS

This chapter is an answer to the question "What is marketing?"—and the answer may surprise you. After studying the chapter, you should understand:

1. *The meaning of marketing—its societal definition and business system definition*
2. *The difference between selling and marketing*
3. *The present-day importance of marketing both in the total economy and in the individual firm*
4. *The marketing concept*
5. *The four-stage evolution of marketing management*
6. *The broadened view of the marketing concept*

NATURE AND SCOPE OF MARKETING

Not long ago, a young man rented a large billboard and used it to express his love for a certain young woman. Whether he realized it or not, he was engaging in marketing. At the other end of the size scale, De Havilland also engages in marketing when it recognizes that the airlines need quieter, more fuel-efficient planes with short-distance take-off and landing capabilities and then develops, sells, and delivers the planes to fill that need.

In a business firm, marketing generates the revenues that are managed by the financial people and used by the production people in creating products or services. The challenge of marketing is to generate those revenues by satisfying consumers' wants at a profit and in a socially responsible manner.

Societal Dimensions of Marketing

But marketing is not limited to business. Whenever you try to persuade somebody to do something—donate to the Red Cross, refrain from littering the highways, save energy, vote for your candidate, accept a date with you (or maybe even marry you)—you are engaging in marketing. Thus marketing has a broad societal meaning. In fact, the societal view is more truly descriptive of marketing today. Moreover, modern business marketing activities are, to a large extent, a consequence of the societal view of marketing.

Any interpersonal or interorganizational relationship involving an exchange (a transaction) is marketing. That is, **the essence of marketing is a transaction — an exchange — intended to satisfy human needs or wants.**[1] Consequently, marketing occurs any time one social unit strives to exchange something of value with another social unit. Marketing consists of all the activities designed to facilitate that exchange.[2]

Within this societal perspective, then, (1) the marketers, (2) what they are marketing, and (3) their potential markets all assume broad dimensions. The category of **marketers** might include, in addition to business firms, such diverse social units as (a) a political party trying to market its candidate to the public, (b) the director of an art museum providing new exhibits to generate greater attendance and financial support, (c) a labour union marketing its ideas to members and to the company management, and (d) professors trying to make their courses interesting for students.

In addition to the range of items normally considered as products and services, **what is being marketed** might include (a) *ideas*, such as reducing air pollution or contributing to the Red Cross; (b) *people*, such as a new professional football coach or a political candidate; and (c) *places*, such as industrial plant sites or a place to go for a vacation.

In a broad sense, **markets** include more than the direct consumers of products, services, and ideas. Thus a university's market includes the legislators who provide funds, the citizens living near the university who may be affected by university activities, and the alumni. A business firm's market may include federal and provincial government regulatory agencies, environmentalists, and local tax assessors.

In the broad sense, this book is marketing *marketing*. What is being exchanged? What activities are designed to facilitate that exchange? What is the target market?

Business Dimensions of Marketing

But this book is about business, so let's look at marketing in a business context. Many people think they already know a good bit about the business of marketing. After all, they watch television commercials that attempt to persuade them to buy. They purchase products on a self-service basis in supermarkets. They observe personal selling activities when they buy clothes. Some have friends who "can get it for them wholesale." But in each of these examples, we are talking about only one part of the totality of marketing activities.

---

[1] In this book the terms *needs* and *wants* are used interchangeably. In a limited physiological sense, we might say that we "need" only food, clothing, and shelter. Beyond these requirements we get into the area of "wants." More realistically in our society today, however, many people would say they "need" a telephone or they "need" some form of mechanized transportation.

[2] See Philip Kotler, "A Generic Concept of Marketing," *Journal of Marketing*, April 1972, pp. 49–54. Also see Philip D. Cooper and William J. Kehoe, "Marketing's Status, Dimensions, and Directions," *Business*, July-August 1979, pp. 14–20.

Systems Definition of Business Marketing

Marketing is the creation and delivery of a standard of living. Marketing involves:

- finding out what consumers want,
- then planning and developing a product or service that will satisfy those wants,
- and then determining the best way to price, promote, and distribute that product or service.

Stated more formally, **marketing** is a total system of business activities designed to plan, price, promote, and distribute want-satisfying goods and services to present and potential customers.

MARKETING IS:

a system:	of business activities
designed to:	plan, price, promote, and distribute
something of value:	want-satisfying goods and services
to the benefit of:	the market — present and potential household consumers or industrial users

---

This definition has several implications:

1. It is a managerial, systems definition.
2. The entire system of business activities must be market- or customer-oriented. Customers' wants must be recognized and satisfied effectively.
3. The definition suggests that marketing is a dynamic business process — a total, integrated process — rather than a fragmented assortment of institutions and functions. Marketing is not any one activity, nor is it exactly the sum of several. Rather, it is the result of the *interaction* of many activities.
4. The marketing program starts with the germ of a product idea and does not end until the customer's wants are completely satisfied, which may be some time after the sale is made.
5. The definition implies that to be successful, marketing must maximize profitable sales over the *long run*. Thus, customers must be satisfied in order for a company to get the repeat business that ordinarily is so vital to success.

Marketing and Related Terms

Sometimes marketing is confused with other business terms, especially selling, merchandising, and distribution. Marketing is the comprehensive concept. Each of the others is only one part — one activity — in the total marketing system.

MARKETING IS: THE TOTAL OF WHAT WE ARE TALKING ABOUT.

Selling is:	One part of promotion, and promotion is one part of the total marketing system.
Merchandising is:	Product planning — the internal company planning to get the right product or service to the market at the right time, at the right price, and in the right colours and sizes.
Distribution is:	Market coverage — the retailing and wholesaling structure — the channels used to get the product to its market.
Physical distribution is:	Materials-flow activities such as transportation, warehousing, and inventory control.

HISTORICAL DEVELOPMENT OF MARKETING

Marketing develops as a society and its economy develop. The need for marketing arises and grows as a society moves from an economy of individual and household self-sufficiency to an economy built around division of labour, industrialization, and urbanization.

In an agrarian or a backwoods economy, the people are largely self-sufficient. They grow their own food, make their own clothes, and build their own houses and tools. There is no marketing because there are no surpluses and therefore nothing to exchange. As time passes, however, the concept of division of labour begins to evolve. People concentrate on producing the items that they produce best. This results in their producing more than they need of some items, and less than they need of others. *Whenever people make more than they want or want more than they make, the foundation is laid for trade, and trade (exchange) is the heart of marketing.*

At first the exchange process is a simple one. The emphasis is largely on the production of basics, which usually are in short supply. Little or no attention is devoted to marketing, and exchanges are very local — among neighbours or perhaps among neighbouring villages.

In the next step in the evolution of marketing, small producers begin to manufacture their goods in larger quantities, in anticipation of future orders. Further division of labour occurs, and a type of business develops to help sell the increased output. This business — which acts as an intermediary between producers and consumers — is called a middleman. To facilitate communication and buying and selling, the various interested parties tend to settle near each other. Trading centres are thus formed. Some nations are today going through these earlier stages of economic development.

Modern marketing in Canada, as in other western countries, was born with the Industrial Revolution. Concurrent with, or as a by-product of, the Industrial Revolution, there was a growth of urban centres and a decline in rural population. Home handicraft operations moved into factories, and people came to the cities to work in the factories. Marketing remained an infant during the last half of the nineteenth century and the first two decades of the twentieth. Emphasis was on the growth of manufacturing enterprises, because the market demand generally exceeded the available supply of products. Since about 1920, however, this situation has been reversed, and supply generally has exceeded demand. Thus the stage was set to shift the spotlight from production to marketing.

PRESENT-DAY IMPORTANCE OF MARKETING

Today most nations—regardless of their degree of economic development or their political philosophy—are recognizing the importance of marketing. Economic growth in developing nations depends greatly upon those nations' ability to develop effective distribution systems to handle their raw materials, and upon their agricultural and industrial output. Canadian crown corporations, as well as similar ones in countries with some major state-owned industries (Great Britain, Sweden, Italy), are looking to modern marketing practices as a way to improve their economic health. Even communist countries (Russia and other Eastern European nations) are using advertising, pricing, and other marketing activities to improve their domestic distribution systems and to compete more effectively in international trade.

Importance of Marketing in Our Socioeconomic System

Aggressive marketing practices have been largely responsible for the high material standard of living in Canada. Today, through mass, low-cost marketing, we enjoy products that once were considered luxuries and that are still so classified in many countries. Even nonprofit organizations (universities, churches, political parties, hospitals) are recognizing that marketing can aid them in dealing with their various publics — their "target markets."

In Canada, modern marketing came of age after World War I, when the words *surplus* and *overproduction* became an important part of the economics vocabulary. Since about 1920, except during World War II and the immediate postwar period, a strong *buyers' market* has existed. That is, the available supply of products and services has far surpassed effective demand. There has been relatively little difficulty in producing most goods. The real problem has been in marketing them. During recession periods, businesspeople soon realize that it is a slowdown in marketing that forces cutbacks in production. It becomes evident that "nothing happens until somebody sells something."

The importance of marketing in the business world might be more easily understood in quantitative terms. Between one-fourth and one-third of the civilian labour force is estimated to be engaged in marketing activities. This includes all employees in retailing, wholesaling, transportation, warehousing, and the communications industries. It also includes the people employed in marketing departments of manufacturers, as well as those engaged in marketing activities for financial, service, agricultural, mining, and other so-called nonmarketing industries. Furthermore, over the past century, jobs in marketing have increased at a much more rapid rate than jobs in production. The great increase in the number of marketing workers is a reflection of marketing's expanded role in the economy and the increased demand for marketing services.

Another measure of the importance of marketing is its cost. On the average, about *50 cents of each dollar we spend at the retail level goes to cover marketing costs*. These costs should not be confused with marketing profits, however. Nor should it be assumed that products and services would cost less if there were no marketing activities.

An Economy of Abundance

A brief comparison of the Canadian economy with those found elsewhere in the world further demonstrates the importance of marketing. The type of economy we have largely explains why marketing is so much a North American phenomenon, both in practice and as a field of study. Unlike other economies, ours is an economy of abundance. This means that as a nation, we produce and consume far beyond our subsistence needs. Although marketing exists in every type of *modern* economy, it is especially important for successful business performance in a highly competitive economy of abundance.

Marketing activity in Canada has the task of encouraging the consumption of the vast output of our industrial, agricultural, and service sectors. Although modern marketing has been successful, its success has not been greeted with joy in all quarters. Many social and economic resources are scarce and are becoming more so. A number of respected students of social and economic systems have raised serious questions concerning the influence that marketing has on the allocation of these resources. The question they raise is whether too much marketing is leading to a misallocation of resources. Is marketing accepting its responsibility to guide our use of economic resources toward socially desirable goals? We may be so successful in promoting the consumption of automobiles and fashionable clothing that we overlook more basic issues, such as an education, care for the elderly, sewage disposal, and the elimination of pollution. In other words, are we marketing the wrong things?

Marketing is the link between production and consumers — as important during shortages as in periods of abundance.

Marketing in an Era of Uncertainty

In the 1970s, many industries in countries around the world were suddenly faced with an unusual economic situation — shortages of materials with which to make their products and operate their businesses. To some people, this meant that the most advanced Western economies had reached the end of an era — an era characterized by the philosophy of unlimited resources, in which people could use products and waste them as they pleased.

The oil shortage in 1973 also triggered the so-called energy crisis. However, by the mid-1970s, shortages also occurred in many industries not directly affected by the availability of oil. The inflationary period that then ensued, and which appears to have been eased by the mid-1980s, created very uncertain conditions for business and industry. Will inflation return, will consumer demand return — these questions create the current era of uncertainty. The answers to them are not clear.

Earlier we said that for most products the real problem is selling them, not producing them. In some industries today, that statement must be modified. Management is worried about how to *make* some products.

At the same time, in most of these industries, management still has to worry about how to *market* the output. Industries faced with shortages will not find their marketing task any easier. Most firms still face substantial challenges in marketing. Competition within industries and between industries is still intense in most cases. Essentially, however, Canada is still an economy of abundance. Consumers in total still have considerable disposable income, in spite of the recession, inflation, and the unemployment of the last several years.

Since the economic climate is changing and the future is uncertain, a company must be alert to adapt its marketing program to the changes. In the 1950s and 1960s, for example, a guiding marketing strategy was to expand the product assortment—that is, to market a wide range of products. In an abrupt about-face in the 1970s, companies began to eliminate low-profit products and concentrate on the more profitable items. The current situation calls for an emphasis on increasing the productivity of marketing.

Management must continually examine its marketing program with an eye toward pruning out unprofitable, wasteful parts. Management also might remember that shortages also create new marketing opportunities. Less building heat means people want more sweaters, and high-priced gasoline means a demand for more bicycles. Uncertain conditions cause changes in consumer behaviour. These must be monitored carefully so that programs can be adjusted.

Importance in the Individual Firm

No matter what the economic climate is, marketing considerations are the most critical factors in planning and decision making in a company. As the National Association of Manufacturers expressed it:[3]

> *In this exciting age of change, marketing is the beating heart of many operations. It must be considered a principal reason for corporate existence. The modern concept of marketing recognizes its role as a direct contributor to profit, as well as sales volume.*
>
> *No longer can a company just figure out how many widgets it can produce and then go ahead and turn them out. To endure in this highly competitive change-infested market, a company must first determine what it can sell, how much it can sell, and what approaches must be used to entice the wary customer. The president cannot plan; the production manager cannot manage; the purchasing agent cannot purchase; the chief financial officer cannot budget, and the engineer and designer cannot design until the basic market determinations have been made.*

---

[3]As quoted in "An Historic Marketing Paper," *Sales Management*, March 20, 1959, p. 7. These statements are every bit as true today as when they were first stated many years ago.

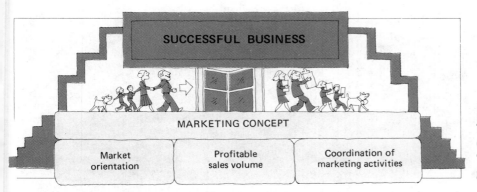

Figure 1-1
THE MARKETING
CONCEPT IS BUILT ON
THREE FOUNDATION
STONES.

Too often, unfortunately, business is oriented toward production. Products are designed by engineers, manufactured by production people, priced by accountants, and then given to sales managers to sell. Just *building* a good product will not result in a company's success, nor will it have much bearing on consumer welfare. The product must be *marketed* to consumers before its full value can be realized.

Many organizational departments in a company are essential to its growth, *but marketing is still the sole revenue-producing activity*. This fact sometimes is overlooked by the production managers who use these revenues and by the financial executives who manage them.

THE MARKETING CONCEPT

As businesspeople have come to recognize that marketing is vitally important to the success of a firm, an entirely new way of business thinking—a new philosophy—has evolved. It is called the *marketing concept*, and it is based on three fundamental beliefs (see Fig. 1-1):

1. All company planning and operations should be *customer-oriented*.

2. The goal of the firm should be *profitable sales volume*, not just volume for the sake of volume alone.

3. All marketing activities in a firm should be *organizationally coordinated*.

In its fullest sense, the **marketing concept** is a philosophy of business that states that the customers' want-satisfaction is the economic and social justification for a firm's existence. Consequently, all company activities must be devoted to finding out what the customers want and then satisfying those wants, while still making a profit over the long run (see Fig. 1-2).

What Business Are You In?

The marketing concept calls for a management reorientation regarding what business a company is in. Typically, when an executive is asked, "What business are you in?" the answer is, "We make this," or "We sell that." These executives must start thinking in terms of what *benefits they market — what needs (wants)* they are satisfying.

As marketing requested it   As sales ordered it   As engineering designed it

As manufactured   As installed   What the customer wanted

Figure 1-2
A MARKETING
MANAGEMENT
PROBLEM.

We hope that management will not implement the marketing concept the way this company did.

WHAT BUSINESS ARE YOU IN?		
Company	Production- Oriented Answer	Marketing- Oriented Answer
Universal Studios	We make movies.	We market entertainment.
Revlon Cosmetics — its president said:	"In the factory we make cosmetics."	"In the drugstore we sell hope."
Bell Canada	We operate a telephone company.	We provide a communications system.
Lennox	We make furnaces and air conditioners.	We provide a comfortable climate in the home.
Head Ski	We make skis.	We market recreation, exercise, ego-building, and a chance to meet fun people.
Canadian Pacific	We run a railroad.	We offer a transportation and materials-handling system.

Unfortunately, even today many people, including some business executives, still do not understand the difference between selling and marketing. In fact, many people think the terms are synonymous. Instead, these concepts actually have *opposite* meanings.

Under the *selling* concept, a company makes a product and then uses various selling methods to persuade customers to buy the product. In effect, the company is bending consumer demand to fit the company's supply. Just the opposite occurs under the *marketing* concept. The company finds out what the customer wants and then tries to develop a product that will satisfy that want and still yield a profit. Now the company is bending its supply to the will of consumer demand.

We can summarize the contrasts between selling and marketing as follows:

Difference Between Marketing and Selling

SELLING	MARKETING
1. Emphasis is on the product.	1. Emphasis is on customer's wants.
2. Company first makes the product and then figures out how to sell it.	2. Company first determines customers' wants and then figures out how to make and deliver a product to satisfy those wants.
3. Management is oriented to sales volume.	3. Management is profit-oriented.
4. Planning is oriented to short-term results, in terms of today's products and markets.	4. Planning is oriented to the long run, in terms of new products, tomorrow's markets, and future growth.

STAGES IN THE EVOLUTION OF MARKETING MANAGEMENT

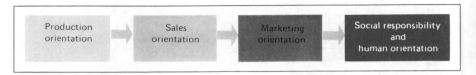

MARKETING MANAGEMENT AND ITS EVOLUTION

For a business enterprise to realize the full benefits of the marketing concept, that philosophy must be translated into action. This means that (1) the marketing activities in the firm must be fully coordinated and well managed, and (2) the chief marketing executive must be accorded an important role in company planning. As these two moves occur, marketing management begins to develop. **Marketing management** is the marketing concept in action.

Since the Industrial Revolution, marketing management has evolved through three stages of development, and a fourth one is emerging. However, many companies are still in the earlier stages. And as yet only a few firms exhibit the managerial philosophies and practices characteristic of the most advanced developmental period.

Production-Orientation Stage

In this first stage, a company typically is production-oriented. Executives in production and engineering shape its planning. The function of the sales department is simply to sell the company's output, at a price set by production and financial executives. This is the "build a better mousetrap" stage. The underlying assumption is that marketing effort is not needed to get people to buy a product that is well made and reasonably priced.

During this period, manufacturers have sales departments — marketing is not yet recognized — headed by sales managers whose main job is to operate a sales force. This form of organization predominated in Canada until about the start of the Great Depression in the 1930s.

Sales-Orientation Stage

The Depression made it clear that the main problem in the economy no longer was to make or grow enough products, but rather to *sell* the output. Just *producing* a better mousetrap brought no assurance of market success. The product had to be sold, and this called for substantial promotional effort. Thus, there evolved a period when selling and sales executives were given new respect and responsibilities by company management.

Unfortunately, it was also during this period that selling acquired much of its bad reputation. This was the age of the "hard sell" — pictured in terms of the unscrupulous used-car salesperson or the door-to-door encyclopedia salesperson. What is more unfortunate is that even today many organizations — both business and nonbusiness groups — still believe that they must operate with a "sales stage" (that is, a "hard-sell") philosophy to prosper. And as long as there are companies operating with a "sales stage" philosophy, there will be continued (and justified, in the authors' opinion) criticisms of selling and marketing.

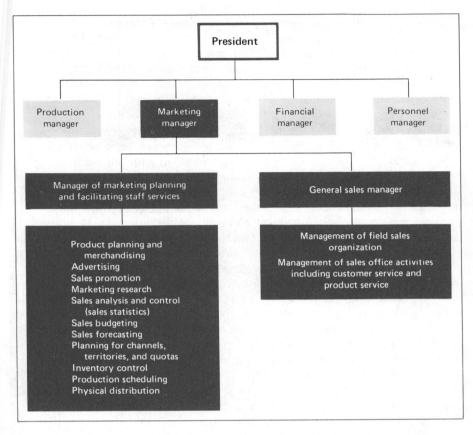

Figure 1-3
COMPANY
ORGANIZATION
EMBRACING THE
MARKETING
CONCEPT.

At this point all
marketing activities
have been inte-
grated under a
single marketing
manager. Organi-
zationally, the
company has
adopted the
"marketing
concept."

Two significant organizational changes typically occur during the sales
stage. First, all marketing activities such as advertising and marketing research are grouped under one executive, still typically called a sales manager or vice president of sales. Second, activities such as sales training and
sales analysis, formerly performed by other departments, now are handled in the sales department. The sales era generally extended from the
1930s well into the 1950s, although no specific dates sharply define any of
the four stages.[4]

In the third stage, companies embrace the concept of coordinated marketing management, directed toward the twin goals of customer orientation
and *profitable* sales volume. Attention is focused on marketing, rather than
on selling, and the top executive in this area is called a marketing manager
or a vice president of marketing. In this stage, several activities that tradi-

Marketing-Orientation Stage

[4]The conceptual foundations for scientific sales management and modern marketing management actually were laid in the literature of the 1920s and earlier. There we find a direct
application of Frederick W. Taylor's scientific management concepts to early sales management.
See Bernard J. LaLonde and Edward J. Morrison, "Marketing Management Concepts Yesterday and Today," *Journal of Marketing*, January 1967, pp. 9–13.

tionally were the province of other executives become the responsibility of the marketing manager (see Fig. 1-3). For instance, inventory control, warehousing, and aspects of product planning are often turned over to the marketing manager. These managers should be introduced at the *beginning*, rather than at the end, of the production cycle. In this way they can integrate marketing into each stage of the company's operations. Marketing should influence all short-term and long-range company policies.

The key to implementing the marketing concept successfully is a favourable attitude on the part of top management. As a senior bank executive stated: "Marketing begins with top management. Only top management can provide the climate, the discipline, and the leadership required for a successful marketing program."[5] And a top marketing executive at International Minerals and Chemical Corporation warned: "But a company cannot become customer-conscious by edict. Since all organizations tend to emulate their leader, it is most important that the head of the business be thoroughly customer-conscious. . . . He can develop a mood, an atmosphere, and an esprit de corps reflecting the preeminence of the customer that permeates every nook and corner of the company."[6]

We are *not* saying that marketing executives should hold the top positions in a company. The marketing concept *does not* imply that the president of a firm must come up through the marketing department. We say only that the president must be marketing-oriented.

Many firms are now in the third stage in the evolution of marketing management. The marketing concept has generally been adopted by both large and medium-sized companies. The president of Burroughs Corporation caught the spirit of firms that have fully embraced the marketing concept when he said, "Any company is nothing but a marketing organization." The president of Pepsi-Cola said, "Our business is the business of marketing."

How well many companies have actually implemented the marketing concept, however, is still questionable. We know that there are many forms and degrees of market orientation. Many companies are using the appropriate titles and other external trappings but are paying little more than lip service to the concept. Unfortunately, in many instances the misunderstanding endures that marketing is merely a fancy name for selling.

| Social Responsibility and Human-Orientation Stage | Social and economic conditions in the 1970s led to the fourth stage in the evolution of marketing management—a stage characterized by its societal orientation. It is increasingly obvious that marketing executives must act in a socially responsible manner if they wish to succeed, or even survive. External pressures — consumer discontent, a concern for environmental problems, and political-legal forces — are influencing the marketing programs of countless firms. |

---

[5]"The Marketing Executive: Industry's New Crown Prince," *News Front*, August 1963, p. 30.

[6]Anthony E. Cascino, "Organizational Implications of the Marketing Concept," in Eugene J. Kelley and William Lazer (eds.), *Managerial Marketing: Perspectives and Viewpoints*, 3d ed., Richard D. Irwin, Inc., Homewood, Ill., 1967, p. 346.

Many people are realizing that there are limits to our natural resources. We have already experienced shortages of several resources. Consequently, this fourth period might be viewed as a "survival" stage. Marketers must be supply-oriented — whether we mean the supply of raw materials, of energy resources, of clean air and water, or of just the "good life" in general.

Perhaps this fourth stage may also be viewed more broadly as a human-orientation period — a time in which there is a growing concern for the management of human resources in marketing. We sense a change in emphasis from materialism to humanism in our society. One mark of a relatively affluent, economically well-developed society is a shift from consumption of products to consumption of services, and a shift in cultural emphasis from things to people. In this fourth stage, marketing management must be concerned with creating and delivering a better quality of *life*, rather than only a material standard of *living*.[7]

BROADENING THE MARKETING CONCEPT

The wave of consumer protests starting in the late 1960s — the rise of *consumerism* — was an indication to some people that there had been a failure to implement the marketing concept.[8] Others went so far as to suggest that the traditional marketing concept is an operational philosophy that *conflicts* with a firm's social responsibility.

From one point of view, these charges are true. A firm may totally satisfy its customers (in line with the marketing concept), while at the same time be adversely affecting society. To illustrate, a steel company in Ontario might satisfy its customers in Manitoba with the right product, reasonably priced, and at the same time pollute the air and water at home.

The marketing concept and a company's social responsibility can be quite compatible. They need not conflict. The key to compatibility lies in extending the *breadth* and *time* dimensions in the definition of the marketing concept.

Regarding *breadth*—let us assume that a company's market includes not only the buyers of the firm's products, but also any other people directly affected by the firm's operations. Then, under this broader definition of customers, the marketing concept and the social responsibility of the firm can indeed be compatible. In our example, the Ontario steel mill has several "customer" groups to satisfy. Among these are (1) the Manitoba customers of the steel shipments, (2) the consumers of the air that contains impurities given off by the mill, (3) the recreational users of the local river affected by waste matter from the mill, and (4) the community affected by employee traffic driving to and from work.

This broadening of the marketing concept is consistent with our previously stated, broader societal definition of marketing. There we recognized that a given marketer may have several different target markets.

---

[7]See Leslie M. Dawson, "Marketing for Human Needs in a Humane Future," *Business Horizons*, June 1980, pp. 72–82.

[8]Peter Drucker (a professor and management consultant and certainly not unfriendly toward business) referred to consumerism as "the shame of the total marketing concept."

Regarding the extended *time* dimension—we must view consumer satisfaction and profitable business as goals to be achieved *over the long run*. If a company prospers in the long run, it must be doing a reasonably good job of satisfying its customers' current social and economic demands.

Thus, the marketing concept and a company's social responsibility are compatible, if management strives *over the long run* to balance its efforts to (1) satisfy the wants of product-buying customers, (2) satisfy the societal wants affected by the firm's activities, and (3) meet the company's profit goals.

Consumerism and marketing's social responsibility are discussed in more detail in the final chapter of this book.

SUMMARY

In a societal sense, marketing is any exchange activity intended to satisfy human wants. In this context we need to look broadly at (1) who should be classed as marketers, (2) what is being marketed, and (3) who are the target markets. In a business sense, marketing is a system of business action designed to plan, price, promote, and distribute want-satisfying goods and services to markets.

Historically, marketing developed as societies moved from agrarian self-sufficiency to an exchange economy. Trade developed when there was division of labour, factory industrialization, and urbanization of the population. Marketing is practised today in all modern nations, regardless of their political philosophies. One of every three or four people is employed in marketing, and about half of what consumers spend goes to cover the costs of marketing.

The philosophy of the marketing concept holds that a company should (1) be customer-oriented, (2) strive for profitable sales volume, and (3) coordinate all its marketing activities. Marketing management is the vehicle that business uses to activate the marketing concept. Our socioeconomic structure—and marketing management is a part of it—has evolved:

- from an agrarian economy in a rural setting,
- through a production-oriented, subsistence-level economy in an urban society,
- and then through a sales-oriented economy,
- into today's customer-oriented economy, featuring a society of abundance with discretionary purchasing power.

Looking to the future, our attention is shifting to societal relationships:

- to the quality of our life and environment
- to the conservation and allocation of our scarce resources
- to a concern for people

These point up the need to broaden the marketing concept to include satisfaction of *all* a company's markets, while generating profits *over the long run*.

KEY TERMS
AND
CONCEPTS*

1. For each of the following, describe (1) what is being marketed and (2) who is the target market.
   a. B.C. Lions professional football team
   b. Automobile workers' labour union
   c. Professor teaching a first-year sociology course
   d. Police department in your city

2. What is the difference between marketing and selling?

3. In line with the broader, societal concept of marketing, describe some of the ways in which nonbusiness organizations to which you belong are engaged in marketing activities.

4. One way of explaining the importance of marketing in our economy is to consider how we would live if there were no marketing facilities. Describe some of the ways in which your daily activities would be affected under such circumstances.

5. One writer has stated that any business has only two functions — marketing and innovation. How would you explain this statement to a student majoring in engineering, accounting, finance, or personnel management?

6. In what ways do shortages and inflation increase the importance of marketing activities in our society? In the individual firm?

7. In what ways do recession and high unemployment rates increase the importance of marketing activities in our society? In the individual firm?

8. Using a marketing approach (benefits provided or wants satisfied), answer the question, "What business are you in?" for each of the following companies:
   a. Polaroid (cameras)
   b. *Playboy* magazine
   c. Bank of Nova Scotia
   d. Petro-Canada
   e. Canadian Pacific Air Lines

9. Distinguish between the sales era and the marketing era in the development of marketing management.

10. Name some companies that you believe are still in the production or sales stage. Explain why you choose each of them.

11. "The marketing concept does not imply that marketing executives will run the firm. The concept requires only that whoever is in top management be marketing-oriented." Give examples of how a production manager, company treasurer, or personnel manager can be marketing-oriented.

QUESTIONS
AND
PROBLEMS

---

*The numbers refer to pages on which the terms and concepts are defined. In addition, see the glossary at the back of the book.

Chapter 2 | *The Marketing Environment and Marketing Management*

CHAPTER GOALS

A variety of environmental forces impinge on an organization's marketing system. The marketing system must be managed — and its activities must be planned — for effective operation within its environment. After studying the chapter, you should understand:

1. *The systems approach to marketing — what a marketing system is*
2. *The influences of environmental forces on a firm's marketing system*
3. *The management process as it applies to marketing*
4. *The meanings of some fundamental management terms*
5. *The basic framework of strategic planning*
6. *The concept of the marketing mix*

The major responsibility of marketing executives is to plan, implement, and evaluate their organization's marketing system — in other words, to *manage* this system. This marketing system performs its functions within an external environment that is continually changing and that generally cannot be controlled by an individual organization. At the same time, there is a set of marketing and nonmarketing resources *within* the organization, and these variables generally *can* be controlled by its executives.

Effective management normally involves the strategic planning of the total organizational effort, followed by strategic planning in the organization's various functional divisions, including marketing. The success of a company's marketing effort depends largely upon management's ability to strategically plan a marketing program within the framework of the company's environment, and then to carry out that plan. Thus, management must strive (1) to forecast the direction and intensity of changes in the external environment, and (2) to respond to these changes through (3) effective utilization of its controllable resources.

We begin our discussion of the marketing environment and marketing management with a brief discussion of the concept of a marketing system.

An increasing number of companies are adopting (1) a fact-based approach to solving their marketing problems and (2) a coordinated effort in the management of their marketing programs. In effect, these companies are applying systems theory and analysis to their marketing activities.

Webster's New Collegiate Dictionary defines **system** as a "regularly interacting or interdependent group of items forming a unified whole." A series of flows connects the items and is the means by which these items interact. The human body, for example, is a total organic system with interacting digestive, circulatory, and muscular subsystems. In our natural environment, we recognize the food chain as an ecological system.

Now let's relate this "system" definition to marketing activities. In marketing, the "interacting or interdependent group of items" includes the following:

1. The entire organization doing the marketing job.
2. The product, service, idea, or person being marketed.
3. The target market.
4. Intermediaries helping in the exchange (the flow) between the marketing organization and its market. These are the retailers, wholesalers, transportation agencies, financial institutions, and so on.
5. Environmental constraints—demographic factors, economic conditions, social and cultural forces, political and legal forces, technology, and competition.

The simplest marketing system consists of two interacting elements: the marketing organization and its target market. In business, these two elements are connected by two sets of flows (Fig. 2-1). One set of flows

SYSTEMS APPROACH TO MARKETING

What Is a Marketing System?

Figure 2-1

In the simplest marketing system, the interacting elements—the marketing organization and the target market—are connected by two sets of flows.

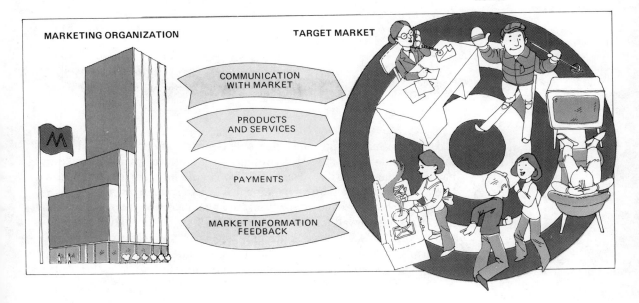

MARKETING ORGANIZATION   TARGET MARKET

COMMUNICATION WITH MARKET

PRODUCTS AND SERVICES

PAYMENTS

MARKET INFORMATION FEEDBACK

consists of a company distributing a product or service to its customers in exchange for some kind of payment. The other flow is an information flow. The company uses its sales force or advertising to communicate with its market. Then the market, in return, provides informational feedback to the firm.

In a real-life setting, however, a company's marketing system is rarely as simple as that shown in Fig. 2-1. Some or all of the other elements listed above enter the system to make it far more complex. In addition, management usually has multiple (and often conflicting) goals, and alternative courses of action do exist. Within the marketing organization, there are sybsystems that must be carefully related to the basic (external) system. This complexity introduces risk and uncertainty. The systems approach — a coordinated, fact-based approach — is an orderly method for dealing with the complexity and the uncertainty.

Think back for a moment to Chapter 1, where we emphasized that marketing is not limited to business. This concept of a marketing system is also perfectly applicable to any nonbusiness organization, such as a social club, a labour union, or a political party.

Synergism and Marketing Systems

The idea of *synergism* is useful in understanding the benefits of the systems approach in marketing. *Webster's* defines **synergism** as the "cooperative action of discrete agencies such that the total effect is greater than the sum of the effects taken independently." In other words, the effectiveness of a company's marketing activities is increased substantially by carefully coordinating (synchronizing) the actions of the separate parts to form a system. Thus, the effectiveness of packaging and labelling is enhanced if a manufacturer's sales force can persuade retailers to give the product a good display location. A pricing structure coordinated with the firm's promotional program optimizes the results of both. In essence, the systems approach allows management to draw the most benefit from each marketing activity.

> The elements in a marketing system are like the components of a stereo system. They do very little separately. But when properly connected, they can fill the air with beautiful music. That is **synergism**.

ENVIRONMENT OF A MARKETING SYSTEM

A company's marketing system must operate within the framework of forces that constitute the system's environment. These forces are either external or internal to that firm. The *internal forces* are inherent in the organization and are controlled by management. The *external forces*, which generally *cannot* be controlled by the firm, may be divided into two groups. The first is a set of broad (*macro*) influences such as culture, laws, and economic conditions. The second group we shall call (for lack of a better term) the firm's *micro*environment. This group includes suppliers, marketing intermediaries, and customers. These microelements, while external, are

Figure 2-2
EXTERNAL ENVIRONMENT OF A COMPANY'S MARKETING SYSTEM.

Six uncontrollable macroenvironmental forces impinge upon a company's marketing system. Three other external forces also tend to shape that system, but the company can influence these forces to some degree.

closely related to a specific company and are included as part of the company's total marketing system. Figure 2-2 shows the external forces, which we now discuss.

External Macroenvironment

The following six interrelated macroenvironmental forces have considerable effect on any company's marketing system. Yet, they generally are not controllable by management.

1. Demography
2. Economic conditions
3. Social and cultural forces
4. Political and legal forces
5. Technology
6. Competition

If there is one similarity among these forces, it is that they are subject to change—and at an increasing rate. The 1970s saw the end of an era during which we experienced unparalleled economic prosperity, a high rate of economic growth, and a population boom. We also experienced dissenting movements among students, consumers, and environmentalists. Near the end of this era, we had price inflation, an energy crisis, and a recession.

And now in the mid-1980s, we have a new set of macro forces. Our social and economic goals are being shaped by a realization that:

- Our population is aging.
- Our birthrate is declining.
- Our reserves of natural resources are shrinking.
- The cost of energy remains very high.
- The inflation rate, though low, is still higher than in the 1950s and 1960s and remains a threat.
- The rate of economic growth is at a low level.
- We may be developing different sets of social values.
- Unemployment remains high.

Truly, these factors present a set of strong challenges to business management, and especially to marketing executives.

Demography

Demography is the statistical study of human population and its distribution. It is especially important to marketing executives, because people constitute markets. Demography will be discussed in greater detail in Chapter 4. So at this point we shall mention just a few examples of how demographic factors influence marketing systems.

Our population now is growing at a very slow rate, and the marketing implications of this trend are substantial. Fewer babies mean smaller markets for baby clothing, furniture, and toys. (As a result, many companies are adjusting their marketing programs. Johnson & Johnson, for example, now promotes the sales of baby hair shampoo to adults.) Then, a few years later, a low birthrate translates into fewer children in grade schools and a decreased demand for schools, school books and supplies, and teachers.

Economic Conditions

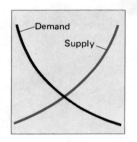

Economic
Conditions

People alone do not make a market. They must have money to spend and be willing to spend it. Consequently, the condition of the economy (the economic environment) is a significant force that affects the marketing system of just about any organization — whether business or nonbusiness.

Perhaps the most pervasive macroeconomic element affecting marketing is economic growth. In the 1950s and 1960s, we enjoyed an unprecedented period of high economic growth. But in the mid-1970s, it became a whole new ball game. Our birthrate began to decline, the cost of energy soared, and we finally became concerned about the shrinking supply of our irreplaceable resources. The net result has been a slower rate of economic growth. And the high growth rates of former years are not likely to return very soon.

Marketing programs are also strongly affected by other economic factors such as interest rates, money supply, price inflation, the unemployment rate, and credit availability. Consider how increases in interest rates have hurt the housing market. In international marketing, the exchange rates and currency devaluation policies (also a political-legal force) have a major impact on exports and imports.

The level of personal disposable income (take-home pay), particularly in relation to price levels and inflation, affects marketing systems very much. Here we also see the factor of consumer psychology at work. Many employed Canadians may have adequate income to buy a particular item but, fearing job loss, may put the money in the bank. Some may decide to spend the money, fearing either that inflation will eat up the savings or that the product will cost more next year anyway. Either way, the marketing of both the item and the savings account is affected.

Social and Cultural Forces

The social-cultural environment really encompasses the economic, political-legal, and technological forces we are talking about in this section. That is, people and their sociocultural customs and beliefs are fundamentally what shape the economy, the political-legal system, and technology. Social pressures against air and water pollution, for instance, led to legislation and government regulation, which in turn stimulated new technology to reduce pollution. To add to the complexity of the task facing marketing, cultural patterns — life-styles, social values, beliefs, desires — are changing — much faster than they used to.

The impact of the sociocultural environment on marketing systems is reflected in several sections of this book. Two chapters (5 and 25) are devoted entirely to the topic. For now, as examples, we shall only highlight three sets of social forces that have significant marketing implications.

The first set involves the personal life-styles and social values of individuals. Many values — even some basic ones — have been shifting over the past few years. Consider just a few of these:

Social and
Cultural Forces

- From a thrift-and-savings ethic to spending freely and buying on credit, and back to thrift-and-savings
- From a work ethic to self-indulgence and having fun, and some signs of a shift back to a work ethic
- From sexual chastity to sexual freedom, to sexual conservatism again
- From a husband-dominated family to equality in husband-wife roles; or, in a broader context, the changing role of women
- From emphasis on *quantity* of goods to emphasis on *quality* of goods and quality of life
- From self-reliance to reliance on government and other institutions, to more self-reliance again
- From postponed gratification to immediate gratification, to some postponing again
- From the artificial to the natural

The second type of social forces involves broader, nonpersonal social problems, including a concern about:

- The pollution of our natural environment
- Safety in our products and occupations
- The conservation of irreplaceable resources
- The maintenance of an ethical and socially responsible position in marketing

Any *one* of these elements poses tremendous challenges to marketing executives. Yet various segments of society are demanding marketing action on *all* of them.

The third aspect of the social environment is called **consumerism**, the name given to the popular movement of consumer discontent starting in the mid-1960s. Fed by unrealized expectations and perceived injustices in the marketplace, a wave of consumer dissatisfaction swept through society.

Political and
Legal Forces

It attracted the attention of legislators and government regulatory agencies, once they saw the movement was genuine. Since then, management has more routinely made many adjustments in its marketing programs in response to this sociocultural force.

Political and Legal Forces

To an increasing extent, every company's conduct is influenced by the political-legal processes in society. Legislation at all levels exercises more influence on the *marketing* activities of an organization than on any other phase of its operations.[1]

Here we should note an exception to the generalization that macro-environmental forces are not controllable by management. A large firm or an industry, working through its lobbyists and trade association, may have some influence in shaping a piece of legislation or a regulation from some government agency.

The political-legal influences on marketing can be grouped into five categories. In each, the influence stems both from legislation and from policies established by the maze of government regulatory agencies. The categories are:

1. *General monetary and fiscal policies.* Marketing systems obviously are affected by the level of government spending, the money supply, and tax legislation.

2. *Broad social legislation and accompanying policies set by regulatory agencies.* Human-rights laws and programs fall in this category. Also included is legislation controlling the environment — antipollution laws, for example, and related regulations established by various governmental agencies and boards.

3. *Governmental relationships with individual industries.* Here we find subsidies in agriculture, shipbuilding, passenger rail transportation, and other industries. Tariffs and import quotas affect specific industries.

4. *Legislation specifically related to marketing.* Marketing executives do not have to be lawyers. But they should know something about these laws, especially the major ones — why they were passed, what are their main provisions, and what are the current ground rules set by the courts and regulatory agencies for administering these laws.

    Such marketing-related legislation is designed primarily to regulate and maintain competition, and to protect the consumer. Table 2-1 is a summary of the legislation administered by Consumer and Corporate Affairs Canada. We shall not continue our discussion of marketing legislation at this point. Instead, we shall cover the relevant legislation in our discussion of particular marketing activities (pricing, promotion, and so on).

---

[1]See "When Lawyers Dictate the Limits of Marketing," *Business Week*, July 14, 1980, p. 76.

Table 2-1   LEGISLATION ADMINISTERED BY CONSUMER AND
CORPORATE AFFAIRS CANADA

1. Fully Administered by Department of CCA

- Bankruptcy Act and Bankruptcy Rules
- Boards of Trade Act
- Canada Cooperative Associations Act
- Canada Corporations Act
- Combines Investigation Act
- Consumer Packaging and Labelling Act
- Copyright Act
- Department of Consumer and Corporate Affairs Act
- Electricity Inspection Act
- Farmers' Creditors Arrangement Act
- Gas Inspection Act
- Hazardous Products Act
- Industrial Design Act
- National Trade Mark and True Labelling Act
- Patent Act
- Precious Metals Marking Act
- Textile Labelling Act
- Timber Marking Act
- Trade Marks Act
- Weights and Measures Act

2. Administered Jointly With Other Departments

- Canada Agricultural Products Standards Act (with Agriculture)
- Canada Dairy Products Act (with Agriculture)
- Fish Inspection Act (with Environment)
- Food and Drugs Act (with Health and Welfare)
- Maple Products Industry Act (with Agriculture)
- Shipping Conferences Exemption Act (with Transport)
- Winding-up Act (with Finance)

5. *The provision of information and the purchase of goods.* This fifth area of government influence in marketing is quite different from the other four. Instead of telling marketing executives what they must do or cannot do — instead of the legislation and regulations — the government is clearly helping them. The federal government, through Statistics Canada and other agencies, is the largest source of secondary marketing information in the country. And the government is the largest single buyer of goods and services in the nation.

Technology

Technology has a tremendous impact on our lives — our life-styles, our consumption patterns, and our economic well-being. Just think of the past effects of major technological developments like the automobile, airplane, television, computer, antibiotics, and birth control pills. Except perhaps

Technology

for the automobile, all these technologies reached the large-scale marketing stage only in your lifetime or your parents' lifetime. Think how your life in the future might be affected by the new information technology, cures for cancer and the common cold, the development of energy sources to replace fossil fuels, low-cost methods for making ocean water drinkable, or even commercial travel to the moon.

Major technological breakthroughs carry a threefold market impact. They can:

- Start entirely new industries, as computers and airplanes have done.

- Radically alter, or virtually destroy, existing industries. Television caused major restructuring of the radio and movie industries, and information technology is causing it again; wash-and-wear fabrics hurt commercial laundries and dry cleaners.

- Stimulate other markets and industries not related to the new technology. New home appliances and frozen foods gave homemakers additional free time to engage in other activities, and further appliance and food refinements facilitate the working couple.

Technology is a mixed blessing in other ways, also. A new technology may improve our lives in one area, while creating environmental and social problems in other areas. The automobile made life great in some ways, but it also created traffic jams and air pollution. Television provided built-in baby-sitters, but it also had an adverse effect on family discussions and on children's reading habits. It is a bit ironic that technology is strongly criticized for creating problems (air pollution, for example), but at the same time we look to technology to solve these problems.

Competition

Competition

As we noted in Chapter 1, people basically buy want-satisfaction in the form of product or service benefits. Let's say we are manufacturers of wooden tennis rackets. We face direct competition from three sources. Our potential customers might derive their want-satisfaction from (1) wooden rackets made by other firms, (2) metal or fibreglass rackets, or (3) substitute products in the sporting goods field. In addition, our company, like any other firm, is competing for the consumer's limited buying power. So our competition also might be a new pair of slacks, a garden tool, or a car repair bill. Whatever its source, the fact is that competition is a very strong force in the marketing environment.

External Microenvironment

Three environmental forces are a part of a company's marketing system but are external to the company. These are the firm's market, suppliers, and marketing intermediaries. While generally classed an noncontrollable forces, these external elements can be influenced to a greater degree than the macro forces. A marketing organization, for example, may be able to exert some pressure on its suppliers or middlemen. And, through its advertising effort, a firm can have some influence on its present and potential market (see Fig. 2-2).

The Market

As both an external force and a key part of every marketing system, *the market* is really what marketing and this book are all about — how to define it and how to reach it and serve it efficiently, profitably, and in a socially responsible manner. The market is (or should be) the focal point of all marketing decisions in an organization. We stressed this in Chapter 1, and you can see this focus in several of the illustrations in this chapter. This tremendously important factor is the subject of Part 2 (Chapters 4 to 7), and it crops up frequently throughout the text.

Suppliers

You can't sell a product if you can't first make it or buy it. So it is probably rather obvious that suppliers of products and services are critical to the success of any marketing organization. In our economy a buyer's market exists for most products. That is, there is no problem in making or buying a product; the problem is usually how to market it.

Marketing executives often do not concern themselves enough with the supply side of the exchange transaction. But the importance of suppliers in a company's marketing system comes into focus sharply when shortages occur. We saw this in the mid-1970s when suddenly there were critical shortages of several basic commodities. Many of these shortages were related to energy-supply problems and the huge price increases imposed by the major oil-exporting nations. Normal supply-channel relationships for oil and other products were disrupted and had to be modified.

But shortages only highlight the importance of cooperative relationships with suppliers. Suppliers' prices and services are a significant influence on any company's marketing system. At the same time, these prices and services can very often be influenced by careful planning on the part of the buying organization.

Suppliers

Marketing Intermediaries

Marketing intermediaries are independent business organizations that directly aid in the flow of products and services between a marketing organization and its markets. These intermediaries include two types of institutions: (1) resellers — the wholesalers and retailers — or the people we call "middlemen," and (2) various "facilitating" organizations that provide transportation, warehousing, financing, and other supportive services needed to complete exchanges between buyers and sellers.

These intermediaries operate between a company and its markets, and between a company and its suppliers. Thus they complete what we call "channels of distribution" or "trade channels."

In some situations it may be more efficient for a company to operate on a "do-it-yourself" basis without using marketing intermediaries. That is, a firm can deal *directly* with its suppliers or sell *directly* to its customers and do its own shipping, financing, and so on. But marketing intermediaries do perform a variety of services. They are specialists in their respective fields. Typically, they justify their economic existence by doing a better job at a lower cost than the marketing organization can do by itself.

Internal Nonmarketing Environment

An organization's marketing system is also shaped to some extent by a set of *internal* forces that are largely controllable by management. These internal factors are the organization's resources in nonmarketing areas. For example, a company's marketing system is influenced by its production, financial, and personnel capabilities. If management is considering adding a new product, it must determine whether existing *production facilities and expertise* can be used. If the new product requires a new plant or machinery, *financial capability* enters the picture.

Other nonmarketing forces are the *company's location*, its *R&D strength* as evidenced by the patents it holds, and the overall *image* the firm projects to its public. Plant location often determines the geographic limits of a company's market, particularly if high transportation costs or perishable products are involved. The R&D factor may determine whether a company will lead or follow in the industry's technology and marketing.

MANAGING A MARKETING SYSTEM

Within the environment that we have just discussed, a company must plan, implement, and evaluate its marketing system. That is, the organization must *manage* its marketing effort—and must do this effectively. An effective marketing program is important to a firm's well-being, but who is responsible for this program? The answer is the firm's *management*. A company's success depends mainly on the calibre of its management.

The "marketing" part of the term "marketing management" was defined in Chapter 1, but what about the "management" part? The terms **management** and **administration** are used synonymously here. They may be defined as the process of planning, implementing, and evaluating the efforts of a group of people toward a common goal. Through management, the combined group output surpasses the sum of the individual outputs.

The Management Process

The management process, as applied to marketing, consists basically of (1) planning a marketing program, (2) implementing it, and (3) evaluating its performance. The **planning** stage includes setting the goals and selecting the strategies and tactics to reach these goals. The **implementing** stage includes forming and staffing the marketing organization and directing the actual operation of the organization according to the plan. The **performance evaluation** stage is a good example of the interrelated, continuing nature of the management process. That is, evaluation is both a look back and a look ahead—a link between past performance and future planning and operations. Management looks back to analyse performance in light of organizational goals. The findings from this evaluation of past performance then are used to look ahead in setting the goals and plans for future periods (see Fig. 2-3).

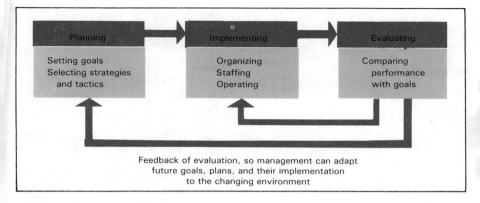

Figure 2-3
THE MANAGEMENT
PROCESS IN
MARKETING SYSTEMS.

Plans are implemented, and performance results are evaluated to provide information used to plan for the future. The process is continuous and allows for adapting to changes in the environment.

Several basic terms continually appear in discussions of the management of a marketing system. These terms sometimes are used carelessly, and they may mean different things to different people. Consequently, at this point let's look at the way these terms will be used in this book.

Some Basic Management Terminology

Objectives and Goals

We shall treat these two terms — objectives and goals — as synonymous, to be used interchangeably in all our discussions. An **objective** (or **goal**) is something that is to be attained. Effective planning must begin with a series of objectives that are to be reached by carrying out the plans. The objectives are, in essence, the reasons for the plans. Furthermore, the objectives should be stated in writing, to minimize (1) the possibility of misunderstanding and (2) the risk that managerial decisions and activities will not be in accord with these goals.

To be effective, the goals also should be stated as specifically as possible:

Too Vague, Too General	More Specific
1. Increase our market share.	1. Next year, increase market share to 25 percent from its present 20 percent level.
2. Improve our profit position.	2. Generate a return on investment of 15 percent next year.

Strategies

A **strategy** is a broad, basic plan of action by which an organization intends to reach its goal. The word "strategy" (from the Greek word *strategia*) originally was related to the science or art of military generalship. A strategy is a grand plan for winning a battle as a step toward achieving the objective of winning the war.

In marketing, the relationship between goals and strategies may be illustrated as follows:

Goals	Possible Strategies
1. Reduce marketing costs next year by 15 percent below this year's level.	1a. Reduce warehouse inventories and eliminate slow-moving products.
	1b. Reduce number of sales calls on small accounts.
2. Increase sales next year by 10 percent over this year's figure.	2a. Intensify marketing efforts in domestic markets.
	2b. Expand into foreign markets.

Two companies might have the same goal, but use different strategies to reach that goal. For example, two firms might each aim to increase their market share by 20 percent over the next three years. To reach this goal, one firm's strategy might be to intensify its efforts in the domestic markets. The other company might select the strategy of expanding into foreign markets.

Conversely, two companies might have different goals but select the same strategy to reach them. As an illustration, suppose one company's goal is to increase its sales volume next year by 20 percent over this year's sales. The other company wants to earn a 20 percent return on investment next year. Both companies might decide that their best strategy is to introduce a major new product next year.

Tactics

A **tactic** is an operational means by which a strategy is to be implemented or activated. A tactic typically is a more specific, detailed course of action than is a strategy. Also, tactics generally cover shorter time periods—they are more closely oriented to short-term goals—than are strategies.

Let's look at some examples:

Strategies	Tactics
1. Direct our promotion to males, age 25–40.	1a. Advertise in magazines read by this market segment.
	1b. Advertise on television programs watched by these people.
2. Increase sales-force motivation.	2a. Conduct more sales contests.
	2b. Increase incentive features in pay plans.
	2c. Use more personal supervision of salespeople.

To be effective, the tactics selected must parallel or support the strategy. It would be a mistake, for example, to adopt a strategy of increasing our sales to the women's market—and then advertise in men's magazines or use advertising messages that appeal to men.

Policy

A **policy** is a method or course of action adopted by management to routinely guide future decision making in a given situation. Policies typically are used on all levels in an organization—from the presidential suite down to new workers. It may be company *policy*, for example to have a union leader on the board of directors. Sales managers may follow the *policy* of hiring only university graduates for sales jobs. In the office, our *policy* may be that the last person leaving must turn off the lights and lock the door.

A policy typically is an "automatic decision-making mechanism" for some situation. That is, once a course of action is decided upon in a given situation, then that decision becomes the *policy* that we follow every time the same situation arises. For example, to reach the goal of a certain sales volume in our company, suppose we decided on a strategy of offering quantity discounts in pricing. The relevant tactic we selected was a certain detailed discount schedule. Now, once those decisions have been made, we can follow the pricing *policy* of routinely granting a quantity discount according to our predetermined schedule.

Control

Many writers and business executives refer to the management process as consisting of planning, implementation, and *control*. In this book we use the term *performance evaluation* to represent the third activity in the management process. To speak of *control* as only one part of the management process seems to these authors to be a misleading and unduly restricted use of the term.

Control is not an isolated managerial function—it permeates virtually all other managerial activities. For example, management *controls* its company operations by virtue of the goals and strategies it selects. The type of organizational structure used in the marketing department determines the degree of *control* over marketing operations. Management *controls* its sales force by means of the compensation plan, the territorial structure, and so on.

Levels of Goals and Strategies

When discussing objectives, strategies, and tactics, it is important to identify the organizational level we are talking about. Otherwise, we run the risk of creating confusion and misunderstanding, for a very simple reason: What is an *objective* for an executive on one organizational level may be a *strategy* for management on a higher level.

As an illustration, suppose one executive says, "Our goal is to enter the four-province Western market next year and generate a sales volume of at least $1 million." A second executive says, "No — entering that new market is only a strategy. Our goal is to increase our market share to 15 percent next year." A third executive says that the second is wrong. "Increasing our market share is our strategy," is this person's argument. "Our goal is to earn a 20 percent return on investment."

Actually, all three executives are correct. They simply are speaking from the perspectives of different organizational levels in their firm. These relationships may be summarized as follows:

- *Company goal:* To earn a 20 percent return on investment next year.
- *Company strategy (and marketing goal):* To increase our share of the market to 15 percent next year.
- *Marketing strategy (and sales-force goal):* To enter the four-province Western market next year and generate a minimum sales volume of $1 million.

And so on down to an individual sales representative. This person's goal may be to exceed quota by 15 percent, and the proposed stategy may be to average three more sales calls per day.

In any case, for a particular *level of objective*, a *strategy* is a plan of action designed to reach that objective. *Tactics* then are the operational details that activate or implement this plan.

STRATEGIC PLANNING

We now are ready to talk about the design of a marketing program within the environmental framework discussed earlier in this chapter. To do an effective job in developing a marketing program, management should plan first at the total-company level and then for the marketing department. In this section, we introduce the concept of strategic planning, which is implicit in the next six parts of this book. We then return to the topic in Part 8, after you have an understanding of marketing fundamentals, institutions, and activities.

Nature of Strategic Planning

There's an old saying to the effect that if we don't know where we are going, then any road will take us there. That is, we need a plan. If we don't have a plan, we cannot get anything done — because we don't know what needs to be done or how to do it.

The essence of planning is simply to study the past to decide in the present what to do in the future. This leads us to the more formal concept of *strategic planning*. Strategic planning is a total-company concept that involves a long-run orientation.

Strategic planning may be defined as the managerial process of matching an organization's resources with its marketing opportunities over the long run. The strategic planning process consists of (1) defining the organization's mission, (2) setting organizational objectives, and (3) selecting the strategies and tactics that will enable the organization to reach its goals.

Defining an organization's *mission* means answering the question, "What business are we in?" Here we urge management to take a marketing point of view rather than a production orientation. Clairol is marketing hair care rather than making shampoo or hair colouring. Xerox is marketing automated office systems — not making copiers, typewriters, etc. You may recall other examples from the "What business are you in?" box in Chapter 1.

In a large, diversified organization that markets many different products, total-company strategic planning may be extremely broad and general — too much so to provide sufficient guidance to the executives responsible for the various products. For more effective planning and operation, the organization may be divided into major product divisions, and a separate strategic plan can be prepared for each division. These divisions are called **strategic business units (SBUs)**. They are, in effect, separate "businesses." Each of them (1) is assigned profit responsibility and (2) produces and markets a group of similar products or services.

Some possible SBU divisions are as follows:

Insurance company. Life insurance; fire, casualty, auto insurance

Appliance manufacturer. White goods (refrigerators, washers, etc.); electronic products (television, radio, video equipment); sound equipment (stereos, etc.)

University. Different schools (engineering, business, education, law, etc.) *or* different teaching methods (on-campus courses, television courses, correspondence courses)

Strategic Business Units

Once strategic planning is completed for the company as a whole and perhaps for each strategic business unit, then management can do the planning for marketing, production, and other major functional areas. Strategic *marketing* planning obviously should be integrated with total-company planning. As we indicated in our discussion of management terminology, the goals and strategies at the marketing level are closely related to those at the company level. Thus, a company strategy often translates into a marketing goal. For example, to reach a company goal of a 20 percent return on investment next year, one company strategy might be to reduce marketing costs by 15 percent. This company strategy would then become a marketing goal.

The **strategic marketing planning** process consists of these steps:

1. Conducting a situation analysis. This step involves an analysis of the company's existing situation — its markets, competition, products, distribution systems, and promotional programs. This step also includes

Strategic Marketing Planning

an analysis of the company's future marketing opportunities. These opportunities obviously should be compatible with the predetermined company mission. They also are shaped by external environmental influences and the company's nonmarketing resources, discussed earlier in this chapter.

2. Setting the marketing objectives.

3. Selecting and analysing the target market. This step is the subject of Part 2 (Chapters 4 to 7) in this book.

4. Designing and developing a strategic marketing mix that will enable the organization to satisfy its target markets and achieve its marketing goals. The concept of the marketing mix is introduced in the next section, and it also is the subject of the bulk of this book—Parts 3 to 6 (Chapters 8 to 20).

The Marketing Mix

Marketing mix is the term that is used to describe the combination of the four inputs that constitute the core of an organization's marketing system. These four elements are the product offerings, the price structure, the promotional activities, and the distribution system. While the marketing mix is largely controllable by company management, the mix still is constrained by external environmental forces. The mix also is both influenced and supported by a company's internal nonmarketing resources. Figure 2-4 reflects a company's total marketing system as being a combination of these environmental and internal forces.

Figure 2-4
A COMPANY'S
COMPLETE
MARKETING SYSTEM.

A framework of internal resources operating within a set of external forces.

The four "ingredients" in the marketing mix are interrelated. Again we see the *systems* concept; decisions in one area usually affect actions in the others. Also, each of the four contains countless variables. A company may market one item or several—related or unrelated. They may be distributed

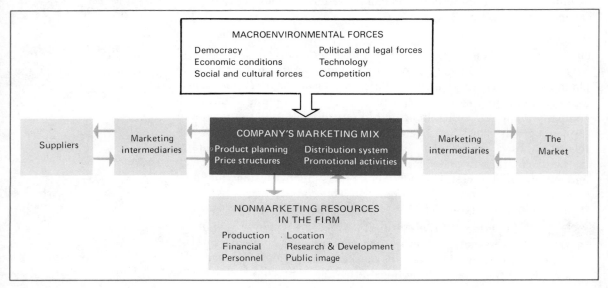

through wholesalers or directly to retailers, and so on. Ultimately, from the multitude of variables, management must select the combination that will best adapt to the environment. In terms used earlier, management is seeking the mix that will lead to the optimal *synergistic* results.

Product

Managing the product ingredient includes planning and developing the right products and/or services to be marketed by the company. Strategies are needed for changing existing products, adding new ones, and taking other actions that affect the assortment of products carried. Strategic decisions are also needed regarding branding, packaging, and various other product features.

Price

In pricing, management must determine the right base price for its products. It must then decide on strategies concerning discounts, freight payments, and many other price-related variables.

Promotion

Promotion is the ingredient used to inform and persuade the market regarding a company's products. Advertising, personal selling, and sales promotion are the major promotional activities.

Distribution

Even though marketing intermediaries are primarily a noncontrollable environmental factor, a marketing executive has considerable latitude when working with them. Management's responsibility is (1) to select and manage the trade channels through which the products will reach the right market at the right time, and (2) to develop a distribution system for physically handling and transporting the products through these channels.

Nonbusiness Marketing Mix

The concept of the marketing mix is also applicable to nonbusiness and/or nonprofit organizations. To illustrate, the marketing mix for an art museum might include:

- *"Product."* An exhibition of paintings and sculptures providing customer benefits of education, enjoyment, and use of leisure time.
- *Price.* Public donations and admission charges.
- *Distribution.* Direct from museum to its market. No marketing intermediaries (middlemen) used. The Art Gallery of Ontario, at one point, developed mobile displays for showing in communities where people could not easily visit the main gallery.
- *Promotion.* Advertisements in the media and elsewhere about a new exhibit. Signs at the entrance.

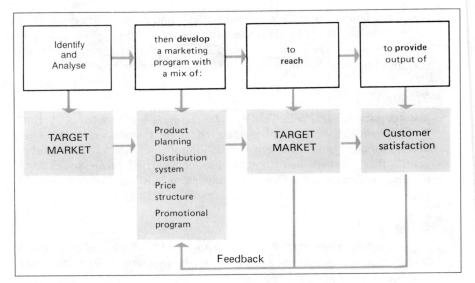

Figure 2-5
MARKETING IN THE
FIRM BEGINS AND
ENDS WITH THE
CUSTOMERS.

In conclusion, an organization's marketing effort should start and end with its customers (Fig. 2-5). Management should select its target markets, analyse them carefully, and then develop a program to reach those markets. Permeating the planning and operation of this model is the company's marketing information system — a key marketing subsystem intended to aid management in its decision making. The next chapter is devoted to the subjects of marketing information systems and marketing research.

SUMMARY

Today, business management is increasingly realizing the wisdom and benefits of applying the systems concept to marketing. A marketing system is an interacting set of institutions, activities, and flows designed to facilitate exchange transactions between an organization (business or nonbusiness) and its market. A company operates its marketing system within a framework of ever-changing forces that constitute the system's environment. Some of these forces are external variables that generally cannot be controlled by the executives in a firm. These macroenvironmental influences include demography, economic conditions, sociocultural factors, political-legal constraints, technology, and competition. Another set of environmental factors — suppliers, marketing intermediaries, and the market itself — is also external to the firm, but is clearly a part of the firm's marketing system.

At the same time, a set of nonmarketing resources *within* the firm (personnel, finance, and so on) influence its marketing system. These variables generally are controllable by management.

Within this external and internal environment, a company must develop and operate its marketing system. That is, the organization must *manage* its marketing effort. The management process, as applied to marketing, involves (1) *planning* the company's goals and strategies, (2) *implementing* these plans by organizing, staffing, and operating in the field, and (3) *evaluating* the marketing performance. Executives need to understand the management concepts of objectives, strategies, tactics, and policies. These are usually established for each major level in the organizational hierarchy.

An organization's marketing effort is more likely to be successful if the firm engages in strategic marketing planning. Marketing planning should be done within the context of the organization's overall strategic planning. Strategic marketing planning involves (1) setting marketing goals, (2) selecting target markets, and (3) developing a strategic marketing mix to satisfy these markets and achieve these goals. A company's marketing mix is the core of its marketing system. The mix is a combination of the company's product offerings, price structure, distribution system, and promotional activities.

KEY TERMS AND CONCEPTS

Marketing System   19

Synergism   20

Macroenvironmental forces influencing marketing systems   21

External microenvironment of a firm   26

Marketing intermediaries   27

Nonmarketing resources in a firm   28

Management and administration   28

The management process: planning, implementing, evaluating   28

Basic management terminology: objectives, goals, strategies, tactics, policies   29–31

Levels of goals and strategies   32

Strategic planning   32

Strategic business unit (SBU)   33

Strategic marketing planning   33

Marketing mix: product, price, promotion, distribution   34

QUESTIONS AND PROBLEMS

1. How does the systems approach to marketing differ from the more traditional approaches?

2. Explain how the concept of synergism is related to the systems approach to marketing.

3. It is predicted that college enrolments will decline during the next several years. What marketing measures should your school take to adjust to this forecast?

4. What are the growth prospects for the following industries in the late 1980s? As a chief marketing executive in a firm in each of these industries, what ideas do you have to counteract a declining trend or to capitalize on a rising trend?
   a. Suede and leather clothing
   b. Breakfast cereals
   c. Chemical products
   d. Cigarettes
   e. Home appliances
   f. Home video game cartridges

5. What should be the role of marketing in treating the following major social problems?
   a. Air pollution
   b. The depletion of irreplaceable resources

6. Give some examples of the effects of marketing legislation in your own buying, reading, recreation, and other everyday activities. Do you believe these laws are effective? If not, what changes would you recommend?

7. Using examples other than those in this chapter, explain how a firm's marketing system can be influenced by the environmental factor of technology.

8. Explain how each of the following resources within a company might influence that company's marketing program.
   a. Plant location   c. Financial resources
   b. Company image   d. Personnel capability

9. Specify some internal environmental forces affecting the marketing program of:
   a. Your school   c. A supermarket
   b. A local barbershop   d. Pepsi-Cola

10. Explain the component stages of the management process as this process might be applied to an organization's marketing system.

11. a. Define the terms "strategy" and "tactics," using examples.
    b. What is the difference between a strategy and a policy in marketing management?

12. Using examples, explain the concept of a "strategic business unit."

13. What is the difference between strategic planning and strategic marketing planning?

14. Explain how the concept of the marketing mix might be applied to:
    a. The Canadian Red Cross
    b. The fire department in your hometown
    c. Your school

Marketing Information Systems and Marketing Research

CHAPTER GOALS

A marketing system runs on current, accurate information — about the market, the macroenvironment, and internal and external operations. This chapter is concerned with the sources and uses of such information. After studying the chapter, you should understand:

1. *Marketing information systems — what they are, why they are needed, and how they are used*
2. *The difference between a marketing information system and marketing research*
3. *The procedure in marketing research investigations*
4. *The current status of marketing research*

"To manage a business well is to manage its future, and to manage the future is to manage information."[1] In the preceding chapter, we noted that marketing executives must be future-oriented. That is, they must (1) anticipate changes, (2) forecast the direction and intensity of these changes, and then (3) adjust their strategic marketing planning in line with these changes.

To do these things, management needs information — lots of it — about potential markets and the environmental forces discussed in Chapter 2. In fact, *one essential requirement for success in strategic marketing planning is information — effectively managed.* Today, a mass of information is available both from external sources and from within a firm. The problem, however, is to sort it out and use it effectively — to manage it. This is the role of a marketing information system.

A marketing information system is the major tool used by management to aid in problem solving and decision making. Marketing research is a major component in a marketing information system. The use of this tool should permeate every phase of a company's marketing program. For this reason, we discuss information management early in this book. We shall be referring to this tool throughout our discussions of the planning, operation, and evaluation of marketing programs.

[1]Marion Harper, Jr., "A New Profession to Aid Management," *Journal of Marketing*, January 1961, p. 1.

NEED FOR A MARKETING INFORMATION SYSTEM

Today, many environmental forces make it imperative that every firm manage its marketing information as effectively as possible. Let's consider just a few of these forces and their relationship to information management.

1. *There is a shortening of the time span allotted to an executive for decision making.* Product life-cycles frequently are shorter than they used to be. Also, companies are being forced to develop and market new products more quickly than ever before. Most companies are facing increasingly competitive markets.

2. *Marketing activity is becoming more complex and broader in its scope.* Companies are expanding their markets, even to the point of engaging in multinational marketing. Our insights into buyer behaviour, while limited, are still sufficient to tell us there is a world of behavioural data we need to acquire and understand.

3. *Shortages of energy and other raw materials and demands for improved productivity* mean that we must make more efficient use of our resources and labour. A company needs to know which of its products are profitable and which ones should be eliminated.

4. *Consumer discontent* is often intensified because management lacks adequate information about some aspect of its marketing program. Consumers are more discerning and are demanding better quality and service. Maybe the firm does not realize that its product is not up to consumer expectations, or that its middlemen are not performing adequately.

5. *The knowledge explosion (the information explosion)* is fantastic. We have more than an adequate supply of information. We simply need to figure out what to do with it — how to manage it. Fortunately, with the continued improvement of computers and other data processing equipment, management has a fast, inexpensive means of processing masses of marketing information.

Without a marketing information system, management is blind to the constantly changing effects of the market forces discussed in Chapter 2.

A marketing information system can help marketers to cope with each of these dynamic forces. Yet, many firms seem to be doing little or nothing toward managing information in a sophisticated manner. Even today, many firms do not have a marketing research department.

WHAT IS A MARKETING INFORMATION SYSTEM?

A **marketing information system (MkIS)** is an interacting, continuing, future-oriented structure of people, equipment, and procedures. It is designed to generate and process an information flow to aid decision making in a company's marketing program.[2]

---

[2]Definition adapted from Samuel V. Smith, Richard H. Brien, and James. E. Stafford, "Marketing Information Systems: An Introductory Overview," in Samuel V. Smith, Richard H. Brien, and James E. Stafford (eds.), *Readings in Marketing Information Systems*, Houghton Mifflin Company, Boston, 1968, p. 7.

A Marketing Information System Is:

1. The systems concept applied to information handling, to:
   a. determine what data you need for decision making.
   b. generate (gather) this information.
   c. process the data (with the aid of quantitative analytical techniques).
   d. provide for the storage and future retrieval of the data.
2. Future-oriented. It anticipates and prevents problems as well as solving them. It is preventive as well as curative medicine for marketing.
3. Operated on a continuing basis, not a sporadic, intermittent one.
4. Wasted if the information isn't used.

A marketing information system to some extent resembles a military or diplomatic intelligence operation. It gathers, processes, and stores potentially useful information that currently exists in fragmented — but open and available — form in several locations inside and outside the company. In an MkIS, however, we are *not* suggesting the use of undercover intelligence methods such as industrial espionage or hiring competitors' personnel to learn their secrets. In most cases a company does not need to rely on such clandestine methods. The information a company needs is usually available by socially acceptable means, if the firm will just establish a reasonably simple marketing information system.

A marketing information system is especially characterized by its use of a computer and personnel possessing quantitative analytical capabilities. A modern MkIS is not possible without a computer, because of the masses of data to be handled. Fortunately, the wide variety in types and prices of computer hardware and software available today brings an MkIS capability to almost any organization.

An organization generates and gathers much information in its day-to-day operations, and much more information is available to it. But unless the company has some system to retrieve and process this information, it is unlikely that it is using its marketing information effectively. Without such a system, information flowing from these sources is frequently lost, distorted, or delayed.

In contrast, a well-designed MkIS can provide a faster, less expensive, and more complete information flow for management decision making. Executives can receive more frequent and more detailed reports. The storage and retrieval capability of an MkIS allows a wider variety of data to be collected and used. Management can continually monitor the performance of products, markets, salespeople, and other marketing units in greater detail.

A marketing information system is of most obvious value in a large company, where information is likely to get lost or distorted as it becomes widely dispersed. However, experience also tells us that integrated information systems can also have beneficial effects on management's performance in small and medium-sized firms.

BENEFITS AND USES OF AN MkIS

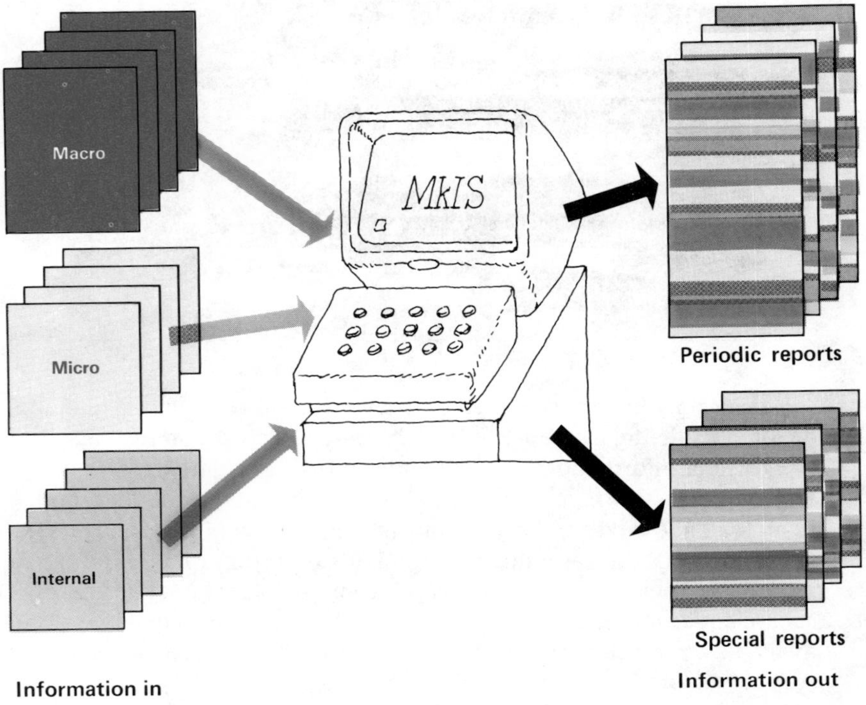

Activity ↓ Goal	Information needed (typically)	The MkIS
1. Sales forecasting ↓ Accurate sales forecasts	a. Forecasts of business conditions b. Data on customers' industries: current situation, trends, etc. c. Competitors' products, promotion, sales, etc.	Collects Accepts Processes Reports Stores Makes available for future use
2. Evaluating territorial sales performance ↓ Identify strong and weak sales territories	a. Sales reports in detail b. Territorial potential c. Changes in competitors' activities	

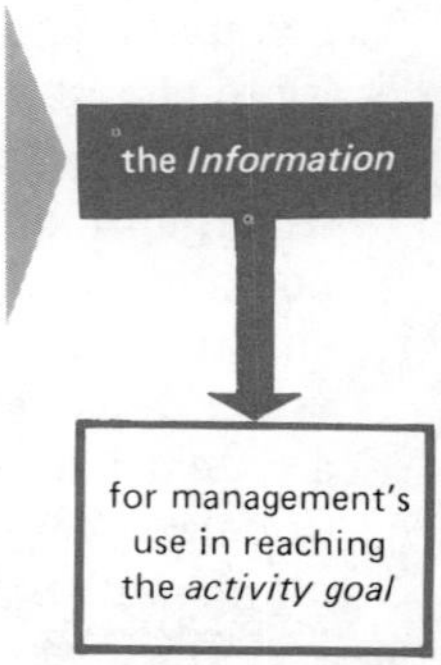

the *Information*

for management's use in reaching the *activity goal*

Figure 3-1
A MARKETING
INFORMATION
SYSTEM, WITH
TWO EXAMPLES
OF ITS USE.

Figure 3-1 illustrates the use of an MkIS in connection with two marketing activities — sales forecasting and the evaluation of territorial sales performance. In Table 3-1 we see how two companies have actually used a marketing information system.

Table 3-1   EXAMPLES OF COMPANY USES OF MARKETING
INFORMATION SYSTEMS

Merck & Company

The Merck Sharp & Dohme division is responsible for the production and marketing of prescription drugs and vaccines. Subsystems of sales and marketing information include its:

1. *Call-reporting system* that provides information covering company representatives' calls on physicians and dispensing outlets (wholesale, retail, and institutional customers).
2. *Sales-reporting system* that provides information about actual sales to all customers.
3. *External marketing information system* that monitors marketing activities of competitors. Merck uses outside computer services that consolidate a number of external data sources.
4. *Branch-operations information system* that provides financial and accounting information flows.

Vulcan Materials Company

Vulcan is a major producer of construction aggregates (sand, gravel), chemicals, aluminum, tin, and steel scrap. The company's 711 marketing information system for sales forecasting ("It improves our forecasting odds like loaded dice improve a crapshooter's odds") is a currently updated, detailed sales-forecasting system. It includes realistic sales targets and feedback for self-correction by the field sales force. It also provides information about:

1. Reasons for lost business
2. Competitors' pricing and other actions
3. Customers' end-use application
4. Shipping
5. Special customer or marketing developments

Source: Stanley J. Pokempner, *Information Systems for Sales and Marketing Management,* report no. 591, The Conference Board, New York, 1973, pp. 24–74.

RELATIONSHIP OF MARKETING INFORMATION SYSTEMS AND MARKETING RESEARCH

The relationship between marketing information systems and marketing research is perceived quite differently by various people. Some see an MkIS as simply a logical, computer-based extension of marketing research. (The first marketing information systems were developed in the 1960s, while marketing research as a separate activity predates this by some 40 years.) Others see the two as distinctly different activities, related only to the extent that they both deal with the management of information. Firms without an MkIS will perceive a broader role for their marketing research group. If a company has a formal MkIS, then the marketing research activity is probably treated as just one part of this information system.

The essence of what we mean by marketing research is contained in Richard Crisp's definition of the term. He called **marketing research** "the systematic, objective, and exhaustive search for and study of the facts relevant to any problem in the field of marketing."[3] This definition suggests a

[3]Richard D. Crisp, *Marketing Research*, McGraw-Hill Book Company, New York, 1957, p. 3.

Table 3-2   CONTRASTING CHARACTERISTICS OF MARKETING
RESEARCH AND A MARKETING INFORMATION SYSTEM

Marketing Research	Marketing Information System
1. Emphasis is on handling external information.	1. Handles both internal and external data.
2. Is concerned with solving problems.	2. Is concerned with preventing as well as solving problems.
3. Operates in a fragmented, intermittent fashion—on a project-to-project basis.	3. Operates continuously—is a system.
4. Tends to focus on past information.	4. Tends to be future-oriented.
5. Need not be computer-based.	5. Is a computer-based process.
6. Is one source of information input for a marketing information system.	6. Includes other subsystems besides marketing research.

systematic activity, thus sounding like the essence of an MkIS. Yet, as traditionally practised, marketing research has tended to be *unsystematic* (see Table 3-2 for a comparison of the two activities as they are usually practised).

Much marketing research tends to be conducted on a project-to-project basis, with each project having a starting point and an end. Projects often seem to deal with unrelated problems on an intermittent, almost "brushfire" basis. This is in contrast to the continuous information flow in a marketing information system. Marketing research tends to stress the collection of past data to solve problems. Information systems perform future-oriented activities designed to prevent problems from arising.

In recent years, users of marketing research have begun to use research studies not merely to address problems that may arise, but to identify problems as well. One of the most valuable marketing research tools is the *tracking* study, which is conducted by many consumer-products companies on a regular basis to monitor certain markets. Such studies may be undertaken annually or semi-annually and provide information on trends in market size, usage patterns, market share, and other important indicators.

We should recognize that many marketing research practitioners would not agree with the distinctions we have drawn between marketing research and an MkIS. They would contend that they already are doing much of what we have attributed to an MkIS. And they may be correct *if* the firm has no formal MkIS. Then the scope of the marketing research activity is likely to be much broader. It may well include some sales-volume analysis, marketing cost analysis, demand forecasting, and so on.

In firms that have an MkIS, a separate marketing research activity can be extremely valuable. Marketing research projects are a significant source of data for an MkIS. Consequently, at this point we turn to the subject of marketing research. We shall discuss (1) its scope, (2) the typical procedure in a marketing research investigation, (3) the organizational structures typically used for marketing research, and (4) the current status of the field.

Table 3-3   MARKETING RESEARCH ACTIVITIES AMONG CANADIAN
FIRMS, 1977

This table presents the results of a survey of 152 companies reporting the existence
of a marketing research function. These companies tend to be rather large, as approximately two-thirds have annual sales of more than $100 million.

Research activity	% Engaged in Activity
Sales and Market Research	
Measurement of market potentials	99
Market share analysis	99
Determination of market characteristics	99
Sales analysis	97
Establish sales quotas, territories	90
Distribution channel studies	77
Sales compensation studies	68
Test markets, store audits	60
Promotional studies	56
Consumer panel operations	45
Advertising Research	
Studies of ad effectiveness	73
Copy research	73
Media research	73
Product Research	
Competitive product studies	89
New product acceptance and potential	86
Testing existing products	79
Packaging research: physical design	62
Business Economic and Corporate Research	
Short-range forecasting	97
Long-range forecasting	98
Studies of business trends	93
Pricing studies	92
Product mix studies	85
Acquisition studies	81
Internal company employee studies	79
Plant and warehouse location	77
Export and international studies	62

Source: Kenneth B. Wong and Randell G. Chapman, *Marketing Research in Canada: A Status
Report*, The Conference Board in Canada, Ottawa, 1978, pp. 36–37.

During the past fifty years or so, there has been a steady growth in marketing research activities in Canadian businesses, reflecting management's
recognition of the importance of marketing research (see Table 3-3). However, the scope and status of marketing research in Canada does not appear to be as well developed as is the case in the United States. A Canadian
study conducted by the Conference Board in Canada in 1977 surveyed a
sample of 400 firms with sales of more than $10 million annually.[4] Within

**SCOPE OF
MARKETING
RESEARCH
ACTIVITIES**

[4]Kenneth B. Wong and Randell G. Chapman, *Marketing Research in Canada: A Status Report*,
The Conference Board in Canada, Ottawa, 1978.

this sample, 39 percent had formal marketing research departments. Among large firms (those with $500 million annual sales and more), however, 64 percent had formal marketing research departments. A similar study conducted in 1978 by the American Marketing Association in the United States found that 73 percent of firms in that country acknowledged having a formal marketing research department.[5] This percentage increased to 87 percent for firms with sales over $500 million annually. While these results indicate that the percentage of firms with a formal marketing research function has increased in both Canada and the United States in recent years, the Canadian experience still lags behind the American.

The substantial difference between the Canadian and Amercian experience with respect to the existence of a marketing research department can be attributed in large measure to the differences in market and company size that exist between the two countries. In addition, many Canadian companies that are owned by American parent firms still rely on research conducted in the United States and simply apply it to Canada. While this is a dangerous practice in some cases, nevertheless some new products are introduced into Canada on the basis of research conducted on American markets. Although the Canadian market is much smaller than that of the United States, the costs of conducting research are at least as high in this country. Consequently, budgets are often lower here.

With lower research budgets, projects in Canada are often on a smaller scale and involve less sophisticated techniques than are used in the United States. Also, the percentage of companies participating in the various research activities remains lower in Canada.[6] What is clear, however, is that companies on both sides of the border are continuing to expand their marketing research activities, both geographically and in terms of the types of research functions performed. Moreover, marketing research is being linked — both by organization and by procedure — with planning and decision making.

PROCEDURE IN A MARKETING RESEARCH INVESTIGATION

The general procedure illustrated in Fig. 3-2 is applicable to most marketing research projects. However, some of the steps listed there are not needed in every project. (The numbers in the following section headings correspond to the steps in the research procedure in Fig. 3-2.)

---

[5]Dik Warren Twedt (ed.), *1978 Survey of Marketing Research*, American Marketing Association, Chicago, 1978, p. 11.

[6]A detailed discussion of the types of marketing research activities performed by Canadian firms may be found in Kenneth B. Wong and Randell G. Chapman, *op. cit.*, and in Stephen B. Ash and James W. Hanson, "The Use of Research Techniques by Professional Marketing Researchers," in Robert Wyckham (ed.), *Marketing*, vol. 2, part 3, Proceedings of the Annual Conference of the Administrative Sciences Association of Canada — Marketing Division, Halifax, 1981, pp. 11–20. An excellent discussion of techniques used in advertising research may be found in Hugh F. Dow, "Advertising Research," in Peter T. Zarry and Robert D. Wilson (eds.), *Advertising in Canada: Its Theory and Practice*, McGraw-Hill Ryerson, Toronto, 1981, pp. 297–348.

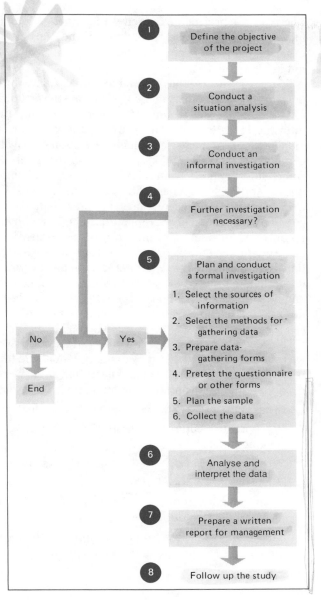

Figure 3-2
PROCEDURE IN
A MARKETING
RESEARCH
INVESTIGATION.

Researchers should have a clear idea of what they are trying to accomplish in a research project — that is, what is the goal of the project. Usually the objective is to solve a problem, but this is not always so. Often the purpose is to *define* the problem, or to determine whether the firm even *has* a problem. To illustrate, a manufacturer of commercial air-conditioning and refrigeration equipment had been enjoying a steady increase in sales volume over a period of years. Management decided to make a sales analysis.

1: Define the Objective

This research project uncovered the fact that although the company's volume had been increasing, its share of the market had declined. In this instance, marketing research uncovered a problem that management did not know existed.

The case history of the Aurora Electronics Company (an actual company but a fictitious name) can be used to illustrate the first three steps in a marketing research project — namely, problem definition, situation analysis, and informal investigation. The Aurora Company was a small electronics manufacturer. Annual sales volume was $6 million, with 90 percent of this coming from contracts with the federal government. The other 10 percent came almost entirely from sales of an electronic component used in automatic garage-door openers. This component was sold directly to a large door manufacturer. Joseph Stacy, the president, was an engineer, and his company had an excellent reputation. The firm had no marketing department, no sales manager, and no sales force. It had a fine engineering department; the entire company was heavily engineering-oriented. At the time of the case, the firm was interested in diversifying its product line and its market, to reduce its heavy dependence on government contracts. The engineering department developed an FM auto radio — a tuner and amplifier unit that could be connected to the regular AM auto radio and could use the AM speaker.

The general problem, as presented to an outside marketing research firm, was to determine whether the company should add this product to its line. A breakdown of the problem into parts that could be handled by research resulted in the following specific questions:

1. What is the market demand for such a product?
2. What product features are desired, such as push-button tuning or signal-seeking tuning?
3. What channels of distribution should be used for such a product?
4. What should its price be?
5. What changes in the company's organizational structure will be required if the product is added?

With this tentative restatement of the problem, the researchers were ready for the next procedural step, the situation analysis.

2: Conduct Situation Analysis

The **situation analysis** involves obtaining information about the company and its business environment by means of library research and extensive interviewing of company officials. The researchers try to get a "feel" for the situation surrounding the problem. They analyse the company, its market, its competition, and the industry in general.

In the situation analysis, the researchers also try to define the problem more clearly and develop hypotheses for further testing. In a research project, a **hypothesis** is a tentative supposition or a possible solution to a problem. It is something that is assumed or conceded merely for purposes of argument or action. In a well-run research project, each hypothesis should be proved or disproved on the way to fulfilling the project's objectives.

In the Aurora Company case, the situation analysis suggested the following hypotheses:

1. The company organization is inadequate to take on a consumer product.
2. The market for FM radios is limited geographically to a radius of 40 kilometres from FM stations. (This distance is the approximate sending or receiving limit for FM broadcasting signals.)
3. Marketing channels should be the same as those used for AM *auto* radios. Distribution patterns for *home* radios are substantially different.

Having gotten a feel for the problem, the researchers are now ready to conduct an informal investigation. To some extent this step overlaps the preceding one, which involves getting background information from *within* the company or from a library. The **informal investigation** consists of talking to people *outside* the company — middlemen, competitors, advertising agencies, and customers.

3 and 4: Conduct Informal Investigation

In the Aurora case, the researchers talked with many people. FM station managers were of considerable help. Wholesalers and retailers of automobile radios were consulted, as were people who repaired auto radios. Long interviews were held with automobile dealers handling German FM auto radios — the Blaupunkt and the Becker. Consumers who had purchased these imports were interviewed. Helpful information was derived from talks with sales representatives of the Motorola Company. (This source was extremely valuable, since there were rumours in the trade that Motorola had already engineered and produced models of an FM auto radio. As it turned out, the rumours were true, and a year later Motorola introduced such a product to the market.)

This important step in a research project will often determine whether further study is necessary. Decisions regarding the problem are frequently made after the informal investigation is completed. As a matter of fact, at this point the Aurora executives decided not to market the FM auto radio.

If the informal investigation has shown that the project is economically feasible, management then determines what additional information is needed. The next step for the researcher is to plan where and how to get the desired data.

5: Plan and Conduct Formal Investigation

Select the Sources of Information

Primary data, secondary data, or both can be used in an investigation. **Primary data** are original data gathered specifically for the project at hand. **Secondary data** have already been gathered for some other purpose. For example, when researchers stand in a supermarket and observe whether people use shopping lists, they are collecting primary data. When they get information from Statistics Canada, they are using a secondary source.

One of the biggest mistakes made in marketing research is to collect primary data before exhausting the information available in secondary sources. Ordinarily, secondary information can be gathered much faster and at far less expense than primary data.

Sources of Secondary Data   Several readily available, excellent sources of secondary information are at the disposal of a marketing researcher.

1. *Internal company records.* Companies regularly maintain orderly records of salespeople's daily reports, call reports, sales orders, and customers' complaints. Companies also usually keep sales records for each territory, product, and class of customer. When a problem must be solved, the first place a company should go for information is to its own files. In many cases, this source may well be the only place where the needed information can be found.

2. *Parent company records.* Foreign parents of Canadian subsidiaries (mainly U.S. parents) are able to provide useful data on activities in the American market. If the parent is involved in multinational operations, experiences and data on worldwide market conditions and consumer reactions to marketing programs can be available. In those cases where the Canadian company has a market posture which is similar to that of the parent and where Canadian strategy and market conditions are viewed as lagging the parent's by a number of years, then access to such data is an invaluable asset. The problem of comparability of data and situations is, however, a constant one.

3. *Government.* The Canadian government regularly furnishes more marketing data than any other single source. These data are available at very low prices, even though there is a tremendous cost involved in collecting them. Also, the government has access under the law to types of information (company sales and profits, personal income, etc.) that it is impossible for a private company to obtain.

   Statistics Canada is the statistical arm of the Government of Canada. Statisics Canada was established in 1918 and regularly collects and publishes information on agriculture, construction and housing, education, fisheries, forestry, health and welfare, international commodity trade, employment, labour income, tourist travel, manufacturing, retail and wholesale trade, service trades, mining, national income and expenditure, prices and public finance, public utilities, and transportation, as well as the Census of Canada. Most government departments also publish both regular and incidental papers independently. The data published are both historical and on a forecast basis. The annual *Canadian Government Publications* lists all federal government publications according to the agency or department that prepared them. In addition, Statistics Canada publishes an annual catalogue.

   Of the numerous reports published by Statistics Canada, one of the most useful to marketers is the *Market Research Handbook*. This publication appears annually (catalogue number 63-224) and contains a considerable amount of data under the following headings: selected economic indicators; merchandising and services; population characteristics; personal income and expenditure; housing, motor vehicles, and household facilities and equipment; Metropolitan Area data; and Census Agglomeration data.

The *Canada Year Book* is an annual publication that contains somewhat less detailed historical data on many aspects of Canada's economy and population. In additon, much information of interest to marketers is contained in the decennial census. Many volumes of data are published following each census, and Statistics Canada publishes a separate catalogue of census publications. The marketer should be aware, however, that despite the availability and detail of census data, these data should be used with caution since they are usually not published until three or four years after the census is taken. For example, most of the reports from the 1981 Census were not published until 1983 or 1984. Consequently, appropriate adjustments must be made in census data before they can be used for marketing purposes.

Statistics Canada also provides CANSIM, its computerized data bank and information retrieval service, and Telichart, an information service that links the CANSIM database with the colour graphics of Telidon. Using Telichart, the marketer can obtain data on more than 5,000 continually updated economic and social indicators.

One department of the Government of Canada that produces reports and studies of particular interest to marketing managers is the Department of Consumer and Corporate Affairs. This department regularly conducts studies on such topics as consumer problems, energy usage, and regulation. The department also publishes a quarterly *Misleading Advertising Bulletin* that contains valuable information to guide advertising decisions, particularly those of small businesses.

A number of provinces also publish many reports and statistical summaries that are of interest. These provincial data are often not as well catalogued or easily located as are Government of Canada and Statistics Canada publications. However, many provinces do publish annual catalogues of their reports and publications, and these are available from provincial government offices.

4. *Trade, professional, and business associations.* Associations are excellent sources of information for their members. They also supply data for outside groups. Through trade journals and periodic reports, members of associations can also keep up-to-date on activities in their given trades.

5. *Private business firms.* Private marketing research firms, advertising agencies, and individual manufacturers and middlemen may be able to provide information needed by a researcher. Companies such as the A. C. Nielsen Company, Canadian Facts, and Market Facts of Canada conduct various kinds of marketing research. In addition, the various management consulting firms such as Woods, Gordon and Company,

Stevenson and Kellogg Limited, and Peat, Marwick and Partners regularly conduct marketing research projects on behalf of their clients. The types of reports prepared by these research companies are many and diverse. The Nielsen Company, for example, prepares a food-drug index giving information on a client's sales and on its competitors' sales for particular products. Data regarding inventories, retail prices, and promotional activity at the retail level are also published. The Daniel Starch Company regularly measures readership of advertisements in various magazines and newspapers. Elliott Research Corporation, through is subsidiary, Media Measurement Limited, collects and supplies national advertising data by media for a large variety of major industries.

Marketing research companies such as Market Facts of Canada, International Surveys Limited (ISL), and Dialogue Canada operate consumer mail panels from which data are collected on a regular basis, dealing with media patterns, purchase, usage, and attitudes toward various products.

6. *Advertising media.* Many magazines, newspapers, radio and television networks and stations, and outdoor advertising companies publish information that marketing researchers may not find available elsewhere. *The Financial Post* publishes its *Canadian Markets* annually. It is a handbook of marketing data and facts gleaned mainly from Statistics Canada sources. It also includes "Buying Power Indices," which are indicators of the relative strength of consumer markets across Canada, and the "Focus on Industrial Development" section, which contains information on industrial parks, transportation, and industrial contacts for more than 500 areas in Canada.

Many media publish circulation data, station reach and coverage maps, and statistics on their trading areas. Researchers should be aware that much of the data published by the media are produced for the purpose of attracting advertising revenue. For this reason, these data may not be appropriate in certain marketing research situations. Accurate data on circulation, reach, and rates for all advertising media in Canada are published monthly in Maclean-Hunter's *Canadian Advertising Rates and Data.*

7. *University research organizations.* Some of our universities operate research units and publish findings that are of value to the business community. Business research units play a leading role in this activity, although marketers may also obtain useful reports from a bureau of agricultural research or social research.

8. *Foundations.* Nonprofit research foundations and related groups carry out many kinds of research projects. Statistical analyses and reports on special topics of interest to Canadian business, or specifically Canadian in content, are published by such groups as the Conference Board of Canada (which produces an excellent overview of the Canadian

market entitled *Handbook of Canadian Consumer Markets*), the Institute for Research in Public Policy, the Fraser Institute, the Hudson Institute, and the C. D. Howe Institute. While national and international foundations, such as Ford, Carnegie, and Killam, are not limited to business research, many of their reports are of interest to marketers.

9. *Royal Commissions and the Economic Council of Canada.* Many federal and provincial royal commissions conduct studies that are of direct interest to business, and often to marketers in particular. Royal Commission reports on Corporate Concentration, Banking and Finance, and Canada's Economic Prospects are examples of such studies. The Economic Council of Canada issues an annual report as well as occasional studies on general economic conditions and on specific topics such as population and labour-force projections, wage trends, and international trade. Very useful information for marketers (although now a little out of date) is found in reports of the Canadian Consumer Council and of the Food Prices Review Board. These reports are usually available in the Government Documents section of most municipal and university libraries.

10. *Libraries.* For the marketing researcher and the student of marketing, a good library is probably the best, single, all-around source of secondary information. It will contain publications from practically all of the sources mentioned here. All researchers and students should be familiar with such resources as the *Business Periodicals Index*, the *Canadian Periodicals Index*, and the *Canadian Business Index*. These indices contain references to articles that have appeared in various business publications. The *ProFile Index* contains references to provincial government publications and reports that are available on microfiche in many libraries. The ability to use bibliographies, card indices, and periodical indices is virtually a prerequisite for anyone hoping to do any kind of research.

There are literally hundreds of databases in existence. Most of them can be searched by computer, which can save hours of torturous labour in the library. The *Canadian Business Index* is just one example of such a computerized database. In order to conduct a literature search of the *Canadian Business Index* a list of terms or keywords that best describe the subject-area of interest is needed. These are then entered into the computer, and the final result will be a list of citations matching the search requirements. The formats of the printouts vary, but all formats include a basic bibliographic citation consisting of author, title, journal, date, and page numbers.

Several databases are of particular value to marketing researchers. Mention should be made of these, despite the fact that they are not Canadian. *ADTRACK* indexes advertisements appearing in 150 U.S. consumer magazines and reflects the promotional emphasis in magazine advertising, covering a wide variety of industries. *FIND/SVP* is a guide to published, commercially available market research reports, studies, and surveys from over 300 U.S. and international publishers, including Canadian publishers. *HARFAX* contains information on bibliographic sources of financial and marketing data for 60 major industries. Both primary and secondary sources of industry data are listed, including market research reports, investment banking studies, special issues of trade journals, economic forecasts, and numeric research databases. All of the major industries in the United States and Canada are included, and entries are indexed by Standard Industrial Classification (SIC) codes. *PTS F & S IND* contains articles relevant to business research from newspapers, journals, government documents, and the like. This index contains information that indexes articles about Canada as well as many other countries outside the United States.

Sources of Primary Data   After exhausting all reasonable secondary sources of information, researchers may still lack sufficient data. Then they will turn to primary sources and gather the information themselves. In a company research project, for instance, a researcher may interview that firm's salespeople, middlemen, or customers to obtain the pertinent market information.

Determine Methods for Gathering Primary Data

There are three widely used methods of gathering primary data: survey, observation, and experimentation. Normally, all three are not used on one project. The choice of method will be influenced by the availability of time, money, personnel, and facilities.

Survey Method   A **survey** consists of gathering data by interviewing a limited number of people (a sample) selected from a larger group. A survey has the advantage of getting to the original source of information. In fact, this may be the *only* way to find out the opinions or buying intentions of a group.

expensive

Personal interviews can be flexible and comprehensive, are usually slow and costly, and may show interviewer bias.

While interviewing is still the most widely used method of collecting primary data, there may be a trend away from it. Other methods have been improved and their value has been more fully realized. The survey method contains certain inherent limitations. There are opportunities for error in the construction of the survey questionnaire and in the interviewing process. Surveys may be very expensive, and they are time-consuming. Another key weakness is that respondents often cannot or will not give true answers.

The interviewing in a survey may be done by the researcher in person, by telephone, or by mail.

Personal interviews are more flexible than the other two types because interviewers can alter the questions to fit the situation as they see it. They are able to probe more deeply if an answer is not satisfactory. Ordinarily, it is possible to obtain more information by personal interview than by telephone or mail. Also, the interviewer can, by observation, obtain data regarding the respondents' socioeconomic status — their home, neighbourhood, and apparent standard of living.

The major limitations of this method of interviewing are (1) its relatively high cost, (2) the length of time needed to conduct the survey, and (3) the chance of introducing errors during the interview.

One of the most important developments in marketing research in recent years involves a movement toward greater use of *qualitative* research studies. The most common application of qualitative techniques is in the *focus group interview*, where a researcher will interview a group of consumers about a particular topic in a session that may last 90 minutes or more. This approach is particularly useful in order to obtain deeply held opinions and explore a new area of study before a major survey-based research project is undertaken.[7]

In a **telephone survey**, the respondent is approached by telephone, and the interview is completed at that time. Telephone surveys can usually be conducted more rapidly and at less cost than either personal or mail surveys. Telephone surveys are less flexible than personal interviews, but more flexible than mail surveys. Since a few interviewers can make any number of calls from a few central points, this method is quite easy to administer. Another significant advantage is that a telephone survey may be timely. For instance, people may be asked whether they are watching television at the moment and, if so, the name of the program and the sponsor. One limitation of the telephone survey is that interviews must be short. Lengthy interviews cannot be conducted satisfactorily over the phone.[8]

Telephone interviews are not so flexible or comprehensive, are usually short (speedy) and inexpensive, but may show bias.

Interviewing by mail involves mailing a questionnaire to potential respondents and having them return the completed form by mail. Since no interviewers are involved, this type of survey is not hampered by interviewer bias or problems connected with the management of interviewers. Mailed questionnaires are more economical than personal interviews and are particularly useful in national surveys. Also, if the respondents remain anonymous, they are more likely to give true answers because they do not feel the need to impress the interviewer.

A major problem with mail questionnaires is the compilation of a good mailing list, especially for a *broad-scale* survey. If the sample can be drawn from a *limited* list, such as property taxpayers in certain counties or subscribers to a certain magazine, the list presents no problem. Another significant limitation concerns the reliability of the questionnaire returns, particularly when the returns are anonymous. If the respondents have characteristics that differentiate them from nonrespondents, the survey results will be invalid. Further, the questionnaire must be reasonably short and the questions very simple; there is no way to explain a puzzling question.

Mail interviews are flexible but not very comprehensive, are slow but inexpensive, show no interviewer bias, but may not be completely reliable.

[7]Colin Wright, "Emphasis on Qualitative," *Marketing*, June 6, 1983, p. 7.

[8]For a report on telephone interviewing — its management, data validity, response rates, sampling, and questionnaire design — along with an excellent bibliography, see Tyzoon T. Tyebjee, "Telephone Survey Methods: The State of the Art," *Journal of Marketing*, Summer 1979, pp. 68–78.

In the observation method, the investigator does not contact respondents, except perhaps in a follow-up interview.

Observational Method

In the **observational method,** the data are collected by observing some action of the respondent. No interviews are involved, although an interview may be used as a follow-up to get additional information. For example, if customers are observed buying beer in cans instead of bottles, they may be asked why they prefer that one form of packaging to the other.

Information may be gathered by personal or mechanical observation. In one form of personal observation, the researcher poses as a customer in a store. This technique is useful in getting information about the calibre of the salespeople or in determining what brands they push. Mechanical observation is illustrated by an electric cord stretched across a highway to count the number of cars that pass during a certain time period. Another example is a study on food prices, conducted on behalf of a provincial government. Observers were sent to a large sample of retail food stores to obtain price data on every brand available in 65 categories of food products.

The observation method has several merits. It can be highly accurate. Often it removes all doubt about what the consumer does in a given situation. The consumers are unaware that they are being observed, so presumably they act in their usual fashion.

The observation technique reduces interviewer bias. However, the possibility of bias is not completely eliminated as long as people are used as observers. Another disadvantage is that the technique is limited in its application. Observation tells *what* happened, but it cannot tell *why.* It cannot delve into motives, attitudes, or opinions.

Experimental Method

The **experimental method** of gathering primary data involves the establishment of a controlled experiment that simulates the real market situation as much as possible. The theory is that the small-scale experiment will furnish valuable information for designing a large-scale marketing program.

In the experimental method, a small sample is used to simulate a real market situation.

The experimental method may be used in several different ways. In one instance, a firm may manufacture a few units of a product and give them to employees or consumers to try out. Probably the major application of the experimental method has been in market testing. This technique consists of establishing (1) a control market, in which all factors remain constant, and (2) one or more test markets, in which one factor is varied. A firm may be trying to determine whether to change the colour of its package. In city A, the product is marketed in its traditional colour. In each of cities B, C, and D, a different colour is used. All other factors are kept constant. By measuring sales in the four markets over a period of time, the manufacturer hopes to determine which colour is most effective.

The outstanding merit of the experimental method is its realism. It is the only one of the three methods of gathering primary data that simulates an actual market situation.

Two big problems are encountered in market testing: selecting the control and test markets, and controlling the variables. It is difficult — though necessary — to select markets that are identical in all significant socio-

---

Some Typical Errors in Questionnaire Design

- The respondent feels the information requested is none of your business: What is your family's income? How old are you? What percentage of your home mortgage remains to be paid?

- Questions lack a standard of reference: Do you like a large kitchen? (What is meant by "large"?) Do you attend church regularly?

- The respondent does not know the answer: What is your spouse's favourite brand of ice cream?

- The respondent cannot remember and, therefore, guesses: How many calls did you (as a sales rep) make on office supply houses during the past year?

- Questions are asked in improper sequence. Save the tough, embarrassing ones for late in the interview. By then, some rapport ordinarily has been established with the respondent. A "none-of-your-business" question asked too early may destroy the entire interview.

---

economic factors. Some variables are really uncontrollable, and these may upset the comparability of results. Competitors may get wind of the test and try to confuse the picture by suddenly increasing their advertising, for example. Furthermore, the experimental method is expensive; it requires long periods of careful planning and administration.[9]

Prepare Data-Gathering Forms

When the interviewing or observation method is used, the researcher must prepare standard forms to record the information. However, the importance of the questionnaire in the survey method and the difficulty of designing it cannot be overemphasized. In fact, most of the problems in data collection, whether it is done by personal, mail, or telephone survey, centre on the preparation of the questionnaire. Extreme care and skill are needed in designing questionnaires to minimize bias, misunderstanding, and respondent anger.

Pretest the Questionnaire or Other Forms

No matter how good a researcher thinks the questionnaire is, it still should be pretested. This process is similar to field-testing a product. In pretesting, a questionnaire is simply tried out on a small number of people similar to those who will be interviewed. Their responses should tell the researcher whether there are any problems with the questionnaire.

---

[9]For a report on the use of laboratory (instead of field) experiments to simulate market situations, see Alan G. Sawyer, Parker M. Worthing, and Paul E. Sendak, "The Role of Laboratory Experiments to Test Marketing Strategies," *Journal of Marketing*, Summer 1979, pp. 60–67.

Plan the Sample

Normally, it is unnecessary to survey every person who could shed light on a given research problem. It is sufficient to survey only some of these people, if their reactions are representative of the entire group. However, before the data can be gathered, the researchers must determine whom they are going to survey. That is, they must plan or establish a sample. Sampling is no stranger to us because we employ it frequently in our everyday activities. We often base our opinion of a person on only one or two conversations with that person. We often take a bite of food before ordering a larger quantity.

The fundamental idea underlying the concept of **sampling** is as follows: If a small number of items (the sample) is selected at random from a larger number of items (called a "universe"), then the sample will have the same characteristics, and in about the same proportion as the universe. In marketing research, sampling is another procedural step whose importance is difficult to overestimate. Improper sampling is a source of errors in many survey results. In one study, an opinion on student government was derived by interviewing a sample of fraternity and sorority members. With no dormitory students, off-campus residents, or commuting students included, this was obviously a biased (nonrepresentative) sample of student opinion.

One of the first questions asked regarding sampling is: How large should the sample be? To be statistically reliable, a sample must be large enough to be truly representative of the universe or population.

To be satistically reliable, a sample must also be proportionate. That is, all types of units found in the universe must be represented in the sample. Also, these units must appear in the sample in approximately the same proportion as they are found in the universe. Assume that a manufacturer of power lawn mowers wants to know what percentage of families in a certain metropolitan area own this product. Further, assume that one-half of the families in the market live in the central city, and the other half in the suburbs. Relatively more families in the suburbs have power mowers than do families in the city. If 80 percent of the sample is made up of suburban dwellers, the percentage of families owning power mowers will be overstated because the sample lacks proportionality.

Several sampling techniques can be used in marketing research. Some of these are quite similar, and some are hardly ever used. For a basic understanding of sampling, we shall consider three types: (1) simple random samples, (2) area samples, and (3) quota samples. The first two are probability (random) samples, and the third is a nonrandom sample. A random sample is one that is selected in such a way that every unit in the predetermined universe has a known and equal chance of being selected.

In a **simple random sample**, each unit in the sample is chosen directly from the universe. Suppose we wished to use a simple random sample to determine department store preferences among people in Calgary. We would

Choosing a random sample is like picking names out of a hat.

need an accurate and complete listing of all people within the city limits. This would be our universe. Then in some random fashion we would select our sample from this universe.

A widely used variation of the simple random sample is the **area sample**. An area sample may be used where it is not economically feasible to obtain a full list of the universe. In the Calgary department store study, for example, one way to conduct an area sample would be first to list all the blocks in the city. Then select a random sample of the blocks. Then every household or every other household in the sample blocks could be interviewed.

A **quota sample** is both nonrandom and stratified (or layered). Randomness is lost because the sample is "forced" to be proportional in some characteristic. Every element in the universe does *not* have an equal chance of being selected. To select a quota sample, the researchers first must decide which characteristic will serve as the basis of the quota. Then they determine in what proportion this characteristic occurs in the universe. The researchers then choose a sample with the same characteristic in the same proportion.

As an example, let us consider a research study of tourists who visited Newfoundland during the summer of 1985. A researcher conducting such a study might decide to use a quota sample based on the tourists' home province. If we assume that the researcher finds from secondary sources— possibly from previous studies — that 30 percent of the tourists who visit Newfoundland are from Nova Scotia, 25 percent come from Ontario, and 10 percent each from New Brunswick and Quebec, the reseacher might then choose a sample of vacationers in which 30 percent of the sample is from Nova Scotia, 25 percent from Ontario, and so on. The sample is forced to the extent that it is constructed on a nonrandom basis according to the home province of the tourist. That is, not every tourist to visit Newfoundland had an equal chance of being included in the sample.

Random sampling has one big advantage: Its accuracy can be measured with mathematical exactness. In quota sampling, much reliance is placed on the judgment of those designing and selecting the samples. There is no mathematical way of measuring the accuracy of the results.

Choosing a nonrandom sample is like peeking before you choose. It may sometimes be necessary.

Collect the Data

The actual collection of primary data in the field—by interviewing, observation, or both — normally is the weakest link in the entire research process. Ordinarily, in all other steps, reasonably well-qualified people are working carefully to ensure the accuracy of the results. The fruits of these labours may be lost if the fieldworkers (data gatherers) are inadequately trained and supervised. The management of fieldworkers is a difficult task because they usually are part-time workers with little job motivation. Also, their work is done where it cannot be observed, often at many widely separated locations.

A myriad of errors may creep into a research project at this point, and poor interviewers only increase this possibility. Bias may be introduced because people in the sample are not at home or refuse to answer. In some instances, fieldworkers are unable to establish rapport with respondents. Or the interviewers revise the wording of a question and thus obtain untrue responses. Finally, some interviewers just plain cheat in one way or another.

6 and 7: Analyse the Data and Prepare a Written Report

The final steps in a marketing research project are to analyse the data, interpret the findings, and submit a written report. Today sophisticated electronic data-processing equipment enables a researcher to tabulate and analyse masses of data quickly and inexpensively. The end product of the investigation is the researcher's conclusions and recommendations, submitted in written form.

8: Follow Up the Study

For their own best interests, researchers should follow up each study to determine whether their recommendations are being followed. Too often, the follow-up is omitted. Actually, an analyst's future relations with an organization can depend on this follow-up, whether the analyst works in the organization or for an outside agency. Unless there is a follow-up, the company may not pay much attention to the report. It may be filed and forgotten.

WHO DOES MARKETING RESEARCH

When a firm wishes to carry out a research project, the job can be done by the company's own personnel or by an outside organization.

Within the Company

Recent studies by the Conference Board of Canada and by the American Marketing Association have indicated a trend toward companies having separate marketing research departments.[10] Such departments exist primarily in larger companies and are usually quite small. The marketing research department may consist of only a single manager or may be as large as four or five professionals in large consumer products companies. In most such situations, the marketing research department rarely conducts research utilizing its own staff, but rather contracts the work out to suppliers outside the company. The primary role of the marketing research department, therefore, is to organize, monitor, and coordinate marketing research, which may be done by a number of different suppliers throughout the country. The manager of the marketing research department reports either to the chief marketing executive or directly to top management. The researchers who staff this department must be well versed in company procedures and know what information is already available within the company. They must also be familiar with the relative strengths and weaknesses of potential marketing research suppliers.

---

[10]Kenneth B. Wong and Randell G. Chapman, *op cit.*, p. 5, and Dik Warren Twedt (ed.), *op. cit.*, pp. 11–13.

A sign of maturity in marketing research is the fact that it has already developed many institutions from which a company may seek help in marketing research problems. There exist in Canada today more than 100 companies that operate in the field of marketing research. When a marketing manager requires information on Canadian marketing research suppliers, a number of sources exist that may be consulted in order to obtain a list of potential suppliers. Two such listings of such suppliers are the *Directory of Survey Organizations*, produced by Statistics Canada, and the *Directory of Canadian Marketing Research Organizations*, produced by the Professional Marketing Research Society. These directories provide detailed information on well over 100 companies that operate in Canada in the marketing research and related fields.

Statistics Canada lists 28 full-service marketing research companies in Canada. These companies include such firms as the Creative Research Group, Canadian Facts, Market Facts of Canada, and Daniel Starch (Canada) Limited. These companies provide a full range of marketing research services, from the design of a research study to the submission of a final report. In addition to the full-service marketing research companies, there are in Canada virtually hundreds of smaller firms that operate in various specialized areas of marketing research. These companies are usually small and may specialize by geographic region, by industry, or by service performed. Some concentrate in either consumer or industrial research or carry out studies that involve the application of specialized techniques. Other companies provide specialized marketing research services, such as the analysis of survey data. Some marketing research is also conducted in Canada by advertising agencies and by management consulting firms such as Woods, Gordon & Company and Stevenson, Kellogg.

Outside the Company

Canadian business is just beginning to realize the full potential of marketing research. Significant advances have been made in both quantitative and qualitative research methodology, to the point where researchers are making effective use of the behavioural sciences and mathematics. At the same time, however, far too many companies are still spending dollars on manufacturing research for their products, but only pennies to determine the market opportunities for these products.

Several factors account for this less-than-universal acceptance of marketing research. Unlike the results of a chemical experiment, the results of marketing research cannot always be measured quantitatively. The research director cannot do a given job and then point to x percent increase in sales. Also, because management is not yet convinced of the value of marketing research, it will not always spend the amount of money necessary to do a good job. Good research costs money. Executives may not realize that they cannot always get half as good a job for half the amount of money.

Marketing research is far from perfect. We have noted several limitations and several areas where errors can occur — in sampling, field interviewing, and so on. Even when marketing research is accurate, it is not a

STATUS OF MARKETING RESEARCH

substitute for judgement. A researcher gathers, analyses, and interprets facts, but the executive must make the decision.

Marketing research cannot predict future market behaviour accurately in many cases, yet often that is what is expected of it. In fact, when dealing with consumer behaviour, the researcher is hard pressed to get the truth regarding *present* attitudes or motives, much less those of next year.

Possibly a more fundamental reason for the modest status of marketing research has been the failure of researchers to communicate adequately with management. Admittedly, there are poor researchers and poor research. Moreover, sometimes the mentality of the quick-acting, pragmatic, decision-making executive may be at odds with the cautious, complex, hedging-all-bets mentality of a marketing researcher. However, researchers, like many manufacturers, are often product-oriented when they should be market-oriented. They concentrate on research methods and techniques, rather than on showing management how these methods can aid in making better marketing decisions. Executives are willing to invest heavily in technical research because they are convinced there is a payoff in this activity. Management is not similarly convinced of a return on investments in marketing research.

Another basic problem is the apparent reluctance of management (1) to treat marketing research as a continuing process and (2) to relate marketing research and decision making in a more systematic fashion. Too often, marketing research is viewed in a fragmented, one-project-at-a-time manner. It is used only when management realizes it has a marketing problem. One way to avoid such a view is to incorporate marketing research as one part of a marketing information system — a system that provides a continuous flow of data concerning the changing marketing environment.[11]

Looking to the future, however, we think the prospects for marketing research are encouraging. As more top marketing executives embrace the concept of strategic marketing planning, we should see a growing respect for marketing research and marketing information systems. The strategic planning process requires the generation and careful analysis of information. Marketing researchers have the particular training, capabilities, and systems techniques that are needed for effective information management.[12]

SUMMARY

For a company to operate successfully today, management must develop an orderly method for gathering and analysing the mass of information that is relevant to the organization. A marketing information system is such a method. It is a structure designed to generate and process an information flow to aid managerial planning and decision making in a company's

---

[11]For some suggestions on how to improve the effectiveness of marketing research departments, see David J. Luck and James R. Krum, *Conditions Conducive to the Effective Use of Marketing Research in the Corporation*, Marketing Science Institute, Cambridge, Mass., 1981. Also see David A. Aaker and George S. Day, "Increasing the Effectiveness of Marketing Research," *California Management Review*, Winter 1980, pp. 59–65.

[12]See Linden A. Davis, Jr., "What's Ahead in Marketing Research?" *Journal of Advertising Research*, June 1981, pp. 49–51.

marketing program. A marketing information system is a future-oriented, continuously operating, computer-based process. It is designed to handle internal and external data and to prevent problems as well as to solve them.

Marketing research is a major component or subsystem within a marketing information system. It is used in a very wide variety of marketing situations. Typically, in a marketing research study, the problem to be solved is first identified. Then a researcher normally conducts a situation analysis and an informal investigation. If a formal investigation is needed, the researcher decides whether to use secondary or primary sources of information. To gather primary data, the researcher may use the survey, observation, or experimental method. Normally, primary data are gathered by sampling. Then the data are analysed, and a written report is prepared.

KEY TERMS AND CONCEPTS

Marketing information system 40

Marketing research 43

Situation analysis 48

Hypothesis 48

Informal investigation 49

Primary data 49

Secondary data 49

Survey method 54

Telephone survey 55

Observational method 56

Experimental method 56

Pretesting 57

Random sample 58

Quota sample 59

QUESTIONS AND PROBLEMS

1. Why does a company need a marketing information system?

2. How does a marketing information system differ from marketing research?

3. "The marketing information executive — rather than an operating, decision-making executive — should be the one to identify marketing problems, delineate the area to be studied, and design the research projects." Do you agree? Explain.

4. A large wholesaler of electrical supplies and equipment located in Western Canada wanted to learn as much as possible about the potential market for an electric milk cooler. This was essentially a chestlike container that could hold ten standard-sized farm milk cans.

   Many small farmers stored their cans of fresh milk in cool well water. Before the cans were collected by a local dairy or shipper, the temperature of the water — and the milk — might fluctuate considerably. Heat tended to raise the bacteria count in milk. In some provinces, milk having more than a certain level of bacteria count could not by law be processed for human consumption.

   The manufacturer of the electric cooler had approached the wholesaler about adding the product to his line. Before making a decision, the wholesaler wanted to do some informal investigating of the product's market possibilities. What should this informal investigation consist of?

5. A group of wealthy business executives regularly spend some time each winter at a popular ski resort — Aspen, Colorado; Sun Valley, Idaho; Banff, Alberta; or Squaw Valley, California. They were intrigued with the possibility

of forming a corporation to develop and operate a large ski resort in the Canadian Rockies. This would be a totally new venture and would be a complete resort with facilities appealing to middle- and upper-income markets. What types of information might they want to have before deciding whether to go ahead with the venture? What sources of information would be used?

6. Acquire the following information for the most recent year available, using secondary sources. In each case, cite your source of information and list alternative sources where the information is also available.
   a. Tons of iron ore mined in Labrador
   b. Wholesale sales in Saskatchewan
   c. Value of vegetables produced in Ontario
   d. Population of Prince Edward Island
   e. Total number of housing starts in each province
   f. Gross-margin percentage of Dominion Stores Limited
   g. Average annual labour force (male and female) in Canada
   h. Number of department stores in Quebec
   i. Operating expense ratio for drugstores
   j. Consumer expenditures for personal services and for durable goods
   k. Consumer price index for any given month for Canada as a whole and for the province in which you live

7. A manufacturer of liquid glass cleaner competitive with Windex and Glass Wax wants to determine the amount of the product that it can expect to sell in various markets throughout the country. To help it in this project, prepare a report that shows the following information for your home province and, if possible, your home city. Carefully identify the source you use for this information, and state other sources that provide this information.
   a. Number of households or families
   b. Income or buying power per family or per household
   c. Total retail sales in the most recent year for which you can find reliable data
   d. Total annual sales of food stores, hardware stores, and drugstores
   e. Total number of food stores

8. Evaluate surveys, observation, and experimentation as methods of gathering primary data in the following projects:
   a. A sporting-goods retailer wants to determine college students' brand preferences for skis, tennis rackets, and golf clubs.
   b. A supermarket chain wants to determine shoppers' preferences for the physical layout of fixtures and traffic patterns, particularly around checkout stands.
   c. A manufacturer of conveyor belts wants to know who makes buying decisions for its product among present and prospective users.

9. Carefully evaluate the relative merits of personal, telephone, and mail surveys on the bases of flexibility, amount of information obtained, accuracy, speed, cost, and ease of administration.

10. What kind of sample would you use in each of the research projects designed to answer the following questions:
    a. What brand of shoes is most popular among the female students on your campus?
    b. Should the department stores in or near your hometown be open all day on Sundays?
    c. What percentage of the business firms in the large city nearest your campus have automatic sprinkler systems?

Case 1
Moosehead Breweries
Limited*

Repositioning an Existing Product

Mr. Stuart Strathdee had recently been appointed marketing manager for Moosehead Breweries Limited in Dartmouth, Nova Scotia. Moosehead Breweries, owned by the Oland family, is Canada's largest independent brewery and operates breweries at Saint John, New Brunswick and at Dartmouth. Its products are distributed throughout the provinces of New Brunswick, Nova Scotia, and Prince Edward Island, and its Moosehead beer is now distributed in all fifty of the United States.

The Oland name has been synonymous with brewing in Atlantic Canada for 120 years. The family company, S. Oland and Sons, was established in Halifax in the 1860s. Following the Halifax explosion of 1917, which destroyed the family brewery, one member of the Oland family, George B. Oland, moved to Saint John, New Brunswick where he bought the Red Ball Brewery. Other family members remained in Halifax to rebuild the Oland operations there. The Saint John operation became New Brunswick Breweries in 1928 and was renamed Moosehead Breweries in 1947. The company gradually assumed a dominant position in the New Brunswick beer market and until the 1960s, the two branches of the Oland family practically shared the brewing business in the Maritime Provinces.

Moosehead Breweries opened a brewery in Dartmouth, Nova Scotia in 1964 and by the early 1970s held more than 50 percent of the New Brunswick and Prince Edward Island market and approximately 30 percent of the market in Nova Scotia. Its brands included Alpine Lager, Moosehead Pale Ale, TenPenny Old Stock Ale, Moosehead Golden Light, and Moosehead Special.

In 1978 Moosehead Breweries began to export its Moosehead Canadian Lager Beer to the United States market. In the highly competitive American import beer market, Moosehead rose rapidly until by 1981 it had climbed to fourth place among imports behind Heineken, Molson, and Labatt. It was widely acknowledged to be a major success story in the American beer industry. The capacity of the Saint John brewery was expanded to meet the demand from the United States.

The Nova Scotia market continued to be important for Moosehead Breweries. The Halifax branch of the Oland family had sold its brewing operations to John Labatt Limited in 1970 and the Oland/Labatt brands of Schooner, Keith's Pale Ale, Oland's Export, and Labatt's Blue dominated the Nova Scotia market.

---

*Case prepared by Professor James G. Barnes, with the permission of Moosehead Breweries Limited. It is intended to stimulate classroom discussion of a management problem and not to illustrate either effective or ineffective management. The author acknowledges the contribution and support of Mr. Stuart Strathdee. Copyright 1982.

Stuart Strathdee had been marketing manager for only six months and had been conducting a brand by brand review of the Moosehead brands in Nova Scotia. He was now ready to turn his attention toward Moosehead Special. This brand had been introduced into the Nova Scotia market in November 1978 and had been positioned in the market to compete with Schooner and Keith's Pale Ale. The Moosehead Special brand had not achieved the success that had been anticipated for it and currently held approximately 2½ percent of the Nova Scotia market. Mr. Strathdee was concerned about the image the brand apparently held in the market and was considering a repositioning strategy.

Mr. Strathdee felt that the recent success enjoyed by Moosehead in the United States would be a definite asset upon which the company could trade to increase its share of the Nova Scotia market. The Moosehead Special brand had the advantage of having already the same distinctive label that was used on the product exported to the United States (see Exhibit 1). The idea Mr. Strathdee was most seriously considering was to change the brand name of the product from Moosehead Special to Moosehead Export Ale and to retain the same basic label with some slight modification. He felt a change to Moosehead Export Ale would position the brand against the Oland's Export and Keith's Pale Ale brands and would capitalize on the success that Moosehead was enjoying in the United States. The advertising that would support the brand repositioning would concentrate on the fact that the product had been overwhelmingly successful in the American market and it therefore must be a good beer.

Mr. Strathdee also viewed a repositioning of the brand as an opportunity to move Moosehead Special out of the fringe position it currently occupied in the Nova Scotia market to a position where it would compete with the "mainstream" brands of Oland's Export, Schooner, and Keith's Pale Ale.

Before making his final decision on the name change, Mr. Strathdee undertook some research that would provide a clearer picture of the existing image of Moosehead Special and would explore consumer reaction to the proposed change. Mr. Strathdee also had developed a modified label design (Exhibit 2), a new packaging design, and supporting advertising materials. A series of three focus-group interviews were conducted in the Halifax area by a local marketing research company. Participants were regular beer drinkers who consumed a minimum of 12 bottles per week, were aged 19 to 35, and were regular consumers of Moosehead Special, Oland's Export, or Keith's Pale Ale.

From the discussions in the focus-group interviews, Mr. Strathdee learned that the typical consumer of Moosehead Special was seen to be younger, somewhat more feminine, and not a serious beer drinker. He was perceived to be more easygoing, more sophisticated and mild mannered, and a person who was likely to try something different. He was not perceived to be a blue collar worker, but more likely an office or business type. He was clearly not seen to be a "typical guy." On the other hand, the typical drinker of Oland's Export was seen to be older, more mature, rugged, hard working, and generally a heavier consumer of beer. The Oland's Export drinker was perceived to be an aggressive person who had been drinking beer for some time, and who enjoyed taverns, bowling, darts, and fishing. He was seen to be an individual who clearly enjoyed his beer.

Exhibit 1   Exhibit 2

During the course of the focus-group interviews Moosehead Special was consistently perceived as a lighter, smoother beer and one that is easy to drink and easy going down. It was seen as a new beer that had not yet built a major reputation and would not appear to be especially popular at taverns or at parties. To the participants in the focus groups the word "Special" implied a lighter, premium beer not meant for serious beer drinkers. The idea of possibly changing the name of Moosehead Special was generally well received, and many participants in the group interviews observed that Moosehead Breweries would have little to lose by changing the Moosehead Special name.

The proposed Moosehead Export brand was generally perceived as a beer that would not be as light as Moosehead Special but would be stronger, heavier, and a working-man's beer.

Some focus-group participants felt that the new Moosehead Export name would give the brand a new image as a more masculine beer. Mr. Strathdee now had to decide whether this new image was sufficient to move Moosehead Special from its fringe position into the mainstream of the Nova Scotia beer market.

Questions

1. Should Mr. Strathdee change the Moosehead Special brand? What other information might he need?
2. If the name of Moosehead Special is changed to Moosehead Export, how would you recommend the change be brought about? What advertising support is needed and what should the advertising say?

Case 2
Bookends, Limited*

Planning a Marketing Research Project

Late one August morning, Katie Martin, co-owner of Bookends, Limited, sat at her desk near the back wall of her cluttered office. With some irritation, she had just concluded that the calculator on her desk could help no more. "What we still need," she thought, "are estimates of demand and market share . . . but at least we have two weeks to get them."

Martin's office was located at the rear of Bookends, a 200-square-metre bookstore specializing in quality paperbacks. The store carried over 10,000 titles and had sold more than $600,000 worth of books in 1984. Titles were stocked in 18 categories ranging from art, biography, and cooking, to religion, sports, and travel.

Bookends was located in a small strip shopping centre, across the street from the main entrance of Prairie University (PU). The university had a student population of approximately 10,000 students, enrolled in arts and science programs and in a number of professional schools (including Business, Engineering, Social Work, and Education). Despite downward trends in enrolment in many Canadian universities, the PU admissions office had predicted that the number of students entering first year would grow at about 1 percent a year until the early 1990s. The city in which PU was located, with a population of approximately 150,000, was expected to grow at about twice that rate.

Bookends carried no textbooks, even though many of its customers were PU students. Both Martin and her partner, Susan Campbell, felt that the PU campus bookstore had too firm a grip on the textbook market in terms of price, location, and reputation to allow Bookends to make any inroads into that market. Bookends also carried no classical records. They had been part of the regular stock of the store until two months earlier, when that area of the store was converted to an expanded fitness and nutrition section. Martin recalled with some discomfort the $15,000 or so they had lost on classical records. "Another mistake like that and the bank will end up running Bookends," she thought. "And, despite what Susan thinks, the photocopy service could just be that final mistake."

The idea for a photocopy service had come from Susan Campbell. She had seen the candy store next door to Bookends go out of business in July. She had immediately asked the owner of the shopping centre, Angus Anderson, about the future of the 80-square-metre space. Upon learning it was available, she had met with Martin to discuss her idea for the photocopy service. She had spoken excitedly about the opportunity: "It can't help but make money. I could work there part-time and the rest of the time we could hire students. We could call it 'Copycats' and even use a sign with the same type of letters as we do in 'Bookends.' I'm sure we could get Angus to knock out the wall between the two stores, if you think it would be a good idea. Probably we could rent most of the copying equipment, so there's not much risk."

Martin was not so sure. A conversation yesterday with Anderson had disclosed his preference for a 5-year lease (with an option to renew) at $1,000 per month. He had promised to hold the offer open for 2 weeks

---

* Case prepared by James G. Barnes, adapted from a case originally developed by James E. Nelson.

before attempting to lease the space to anyone else. Representatives from copying equipment suppliers had estimated that charges would run between $200 and $2,000 per month, depending on equipment, service, and whether the equipment was bought or leased. The photocopy service would also incur other fixed costs in terms of utility expenses, interest, and insurance. Further, Bookends would have to invest a sizable sum in fixtures and inventory (and possibly equipment). Martin concluded that the service would begin to make a profit at about 20,000 copies per month under best-case assumptions, and at about 60,000 copies per month under the worst-case scenario.

Further formal investigation had identified two major competitors. One was the copy centre located in the university library on the west side of the campus, about a kilometre away. The other was a private firm, Goodland's Stationery, located on the northern boundary of the campus, also about a kilometre from Bookends. Both offered service "while you wait," on several copying machines. The library's price was about ½ cent per copy higher than Goodland's. Both offered collating, binding, colour copying, and other services. The library copying centre was open seven days a week and Goodland's closed on Sundays.

Actually, Martin had discovered in talking with a number of students and faculty members that a third major "competitor" consisted of the photocopying machines scattered throughout the university's various departments and faculties. Most faculty and adminstrative copying was done on these machines, but students were also allowed the use of some, at cost. In addition, at least 20 self-service coin-operated copying machines were located on campus in the library, the student centre, and several other buildings.

Moving aside a stack of books on her desk, Katie Martin picked up the telephone and dialled her partner. When Campbell answered, Martin asked, "Susan, do you know how many copies a student might make in a semester? I mean, according to my figures, we would break even somewhere between 20,000 and 60,000 copies per month. I don't know if this is half the market or what."

"You know, I have no idea," Campbell answered. "I suppose when I was going to university I probably made 10 copies a month — for articles, class notes, old exams, and so on."

"Same here," Martin said. "But some of the graduate students I knew made at least that many copies each week. I think we ought to do some marketing research before we go much farther with this. What do you think?

"Sure. But we can't afford to spend much time or money on it. What do you have in mind, Katie?"

"Well, we could easily interview our customers as they leave the store and ask them how many copies they have made in the past week or so. Of course, we would have to make sure they were students."

"What about a telephone survey?" Campbell asked. "That way we can have a random sample. We would still ask about the number of copies, but now we would know for sure that they were students."

"Or, what about interviewing students in the cafeteria in the student centre? There's always a large crowd there at lunchtime, and that would be even quicker."

"I just don't know," Campbell replied. "Why don't I come in this afternoon? We can talk about it some more."

"Good idea," Martin responded. "Between the two of us, we should be able to come up with something."

Questions

1. What sources of information should Martin and Campbell use?
2. How should Martin and Campbell collect the information they need?
3. What questions should they ask?
4. How should they select a sample of people to interview?

Case 3 Bentley Fresh Brew Tea (A) *

Planning a New Brand of Tea for the Consumer Market

Mr. Don Evans, president and owner of The Newfoundland Tea Company, had to make a critical decision regarding the future of his organization. After much deliberation and research, as well as a number of years' experience as a distributor of various food and beverage products to the food service/institutional market in Newfoundland, he had decided to form the Newfoundland Tea Company and introduce his own brand of tea bags to the retail market. As he considered the contents of the many files of research and other pertinent information lying around his desk, he realized that a mammoth task lay ahead. While he had determined that an opportunity did exist and that he would indeed develop and introduce a new brand, he had yet to plan the exact nature of the product as well as how he would market it; specifically, he needed to decide on product, pricing, distribution, and promotion strategies — and he needed to do so in the very near future.

Don Evans first became involved with the food and beverage market during 1977 when he incorporated Devon Foods Limited as the Newfoundland distributor for several brands of tea, coffee, food, and condiments to the food service/institutional market (which includes restaurants, hospitals, and other institutions). Devon Foods prospered and grew in ensuing years, and Mr. Evans gained valuable experience and knowledge of the nature of the local institutional market and its buying habits. In addition, he became very interested in teas, visiting several tea growing regions in Asia, tea packaging plants, and various distributors and auction houses in Canada and Britain; indeed, he became quite adept at tea tasting and somewhat of an expert on tea and its characteristics.

In 1979 he perceived an opportunity to increase gross profits by packaging and marketing his own brands of tea to the food service/institutional market rather than distributing brands packaged by national companies;

---

* This case was written by Professor Noel O'Dea, Faculty of Business Administration, Memorial University of Newfoundland, and is designed to stimulate class discussion concerning management problems rather than to illustrate effective or ineffective handling of these problems. Many facts and situations have been changed or omitted so as to protect confidential information and/or to improve the learning experience.

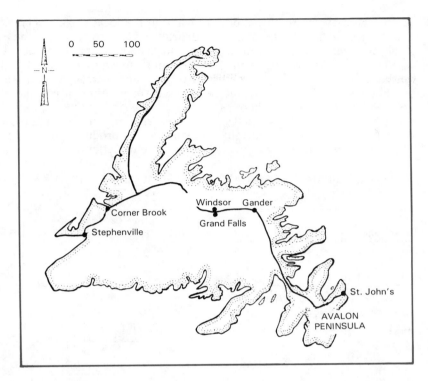

Figure A-1
MAP OF
NEWFOUNDLAND

he felt that such a strategy could be successful given the high price sensitivity and low brand preference of this market. He purchased reconditioned tea packaging machinery, decided on several blends of teas, and started production. The operation proved very successful, though profitability was low due to extreme price competition in this market. Later that year he expanded operations to package a private label brand of tea for a local wholesale/retail operation.

Mr. Evans' increased knowledge of and experience in both the packaging and marketing of teas to the institutional market eventually led him to consider the consumer (retail) market for tea. After obtaining some information on market potential, and upon completion of initial feasibility calculations and requirements, he arranged for a local marketing research firm to conduct formal investigations of the market and its size, as well as a consumer usage and attitude study. After examining the research results (selected portions of which are presented in the tables in this section and the other sections of the case), he decided to act and formed The Newfoundland Tea Company.

Having made the decision to enter the market and the commitment to form another company, Mr. Evans was still a long way from success. His company was dwarfed by the experience and human and financial resources of the market leaders. The main brands, Tetley and Red Rose, were international companies with efficient plants, strong financial resources and backing, established distribution, experienced sales staff, and strong brand franchises.

As indicated by the research, brand loyalty in the local market seemed strong—a condition that could be very difficult and expensive to overcome. While Mr. Evans was very familiar with the local market, and the company had had some experience in the blending and packaging of teas, it had neither a retail sales force nor existing retail channel arrangements. He was also very apprehensive about the high costs of entering the retail market and becoming established, as well as the possibility of competitive retaliation. Indeed, his total first year's advertising production and media budget was less than one-third the estimated cost of producing one of the TV commercials currently running for Red Rose or Tetley.

Table A-1   APPARENT PER CAPITA CONSUMPTION OF BEVERAGES IN CANADA

Beverage	Pounds Per Capita Per Year			
	1965	**1970**	**1975**	**1979**
Tea	2.4	2.2	2.3	2.1
Coffee	8.8	9.2	9.5	9.9
Citrus Fruit Juices	10.8	14.8	22.2	28.5

Source: Statistics Canada, *Bulletins* 32-229 and 32-226.

Table A-2   MARKET-RELATED DATA FOR ATLANTIC PROVINCES, 1980

	Newfoundland	**Nova Scotia**	**New Brunswick**	**P.E.I.**
Total Population	578,600	852,900	706,900	124,000
Total Households	110,476	208,422	158,100	27,898
Current Growth Rate (per decade)	10%	8%	11%	13%
Average Weekly Earnings	$248.36	$223.72	$232.89	$196.72
Total Retail Sales (000)	$1,547,300	$2,839,700	$2,211,600	$386.60
Unemployment Rate	13.5%	9.8%	10.8%	10.8%

Source: Statistics Canada

Table A-3   THE NEWFOUNDLAND MARKETPLACE, 1980

Population of Province	578,600
Population of Largest Cities and Towns:	
St. John's	150,700
Corner Brook	24,100
Grand Falls-Windsor	15,100
Stephenville	11,200
Gander	9,300
Estimated Share of Food Sales in the St. John's Metro Area:	
Dominion	38%
Sobey's	27%
Stop & Shop	10%
All Others	25%

Newfoundlanders are ranked with the Irish as having the highest per capita consumption of tea in the Western world. Newfoundland's per capita consumption of tea is estimated to be approximately three times higher than the Canadian average (see Table A-1). Research shows that more than 90 percent of all households (and 100 percent of households headed by persons aged 50 and over) in the province purchase tea bags at least once per month (see Table A-4). Industry sources estimate that between 2,500,000 and 3,500,000 pounds of tea, valued at $8 million to $15 million, were sold at the retail level in Newfoundland during 1980; such consumption levels were exceptional given the province's relatively small population of 575,000.

Consumer taste and brand preferences have changed significantly in the Newfoundland market over the past 10 to 20 years; sales of loose teas had been reduced to miniscule levels as consumers switched to tea bags. In addition, consumers have shifted from stronger teas (of generally high quality) to weaker blends of tea (of generally lower quality).

Some industry observers suggest that Newfoundlanders are gradually moving toward national trends and, as such, per capita consumption of tea may be falling as consumption increases in coffee and other beverages; however, no statistics are available to substantiate this suggestion.

Research conducted for The Newfoundland Tea Company indicated that females have the greatest influence on choice of tea brand, being the key decision maker in 76 percent of households and a joint decision maker in an additional 14 percent of households. In addition, heavy users of boxed tea bags tended to include a disproportionate number of both blue collar

Table A-4   HOUSEHOLDS PURCHASING BOXED TEA BAGS
IN PAST MONTH

Characteristics	%
I *Household Size**	
1 or 2 persons	81%
3 or 4 persons	92
5 or more persons	98
II *Age**	
Less than 25	68%
25 to 34	89
35 to 49	95
50 and over	100
III *Occupation**	
Professional	82%
White Collar	91
Skilled Labour	93
Unskilled Labour	100
All Others	99
IV *Geographic Location*	
St. John's Metro Area	85%
All Other Areas	96
V *Total Sample*	93%

* Indicates chi-square statistic significant at the 0.05 level.

and larger-size households. There also appeared to be strong brand loyalty among purchasers of boxed tea; 78 percent of respondents reported using the same brand for 4 or 5 years, and 75 percent reported purchasing the same brand in all of the past 10 purchase occasions. Additional information is presented in Tables A-4 and A-5.

In addition to the many competing brands of tea bags, tea itself is in competition (from a generic viewpoint) with all other beverages — particularly with hot beverages such as coffee. As noted in Table A-1, Canadian per capita consumption of coffee is more than four times that of tea, and while coffee consumption is increasing, consumption of tea is decreasing.

There were more than 15 brands of tea bags available in the Newfoundland retail market in 1980. Most were relatively minor brands packaged in poly bags, with the brand name, other information, and graphics printed directly on the poly wrapper; these polybag brands, accounting for approximately 30 percent of retail sales, were marketed primarily on the basis of lower prices. Brands packaged in heavyweight paper-based boxes accounted for an estimated 70 percent of tea sales; these brands, perceived (accurately) by most consumers to be of higher quality than polybag brands, also exhibited much stronger brand loyalty. In addition to national and regional brands, each of the supermarket chains had private-label brands packaged in both polybags and boxes. Indeed, Dominion Stores had three private-brand names of tea bags.

Tetley was the market leader in the Newfoundland market, accounting for approximately 70 percent of retail sales of boxed tea bags during 1980 (see table A-5). Available in four different package sizes (of 36, 72, 144, and 216 bags), it is a milder tea than traditionally preferred. It is blended and packaged in Britain (where it is also a major brand) and distributed in Canada through an Ontario-based branch operation. Marketed in Newfoundland since 1970, Tetley is the most widely available brand in both urban and rural areas of the province; distribution is achieved via a wholesale distributor (located in St. John's), which sells both through independent wholesalers and directly to retail stores. It has exceptionally high brand awareness and good brand loyalty; its package design is very professional, utilizing shaded colours of blue and yellow and illustrating a warm "use-experience" setting via a teapot, cookies, and china teacup.

Tetley's package of 72 bags is the largest seller; its list price of $2.29 is similar to that of Red Rose's package of 60 tea bags. However, partly due to its popularity (and certainly adding to it), Tetley is frequently promoted as a loss leader by supermarkets at prices ranging from $1.49 to $1.89 per 72-bag package. Advertising and promotion for Tetley is the heaviest of all brands, with extensive exposure in television and radio. Television ads, utilizing warm and slightly humorous animated commercials featuring whimsical "wee-folk," position the brand on two key appeals: "better, not bitter" in taste; and "flavour-through tea bags, with thousands of tiny perforations" allow the great flavour to flow out. Radio is used primarily as a sales promotion vehicle for the "Tetley Tea Contest" during the fall and winter months. An annual event for a number of years, this contest requires respondents to send a package end flap and their guess as to "what's in the Tetley tea pot"; entries are selected and announced on-air several times daily, with the cash jackpot (sometimes involving several thousand dollars) increasing daily until won.

Table A-5   CUSTOMER PROFILE OF TETLEY AND RED ROSE
                BOXED TEA BAGS

Characteristics	Tetley	Red Rose	Other	Total
I *Household Size*				
1 or 2 persons	62%	28%	10%	100%
3 or 4 persons	74	18	8	100
5 or more persons	82	16	2	100
II *Age**				
Less than 25	91%	8%	1%	100%
25 to 34	79	14	7	100
35 to 49	78	18	4	100
50 and over	61	27	12	100
III *Occupation*				
Professional	72%	26%	2%	100%
White Collar	75	24	1	100
Skilled Labour	76	14	10	100
Unskilled Labour	64	18	18	100
All Others	40	32	28	100
IV *Household Consumption Per Month**				
Light	54%	32%	14%	100%
Medium	82	14	4	100
Heavy	76	17	7	100
V *Total Sample*	69%	21%	10%	100%

*Indicates chi-square statistic significant at the 0.05 level.

Red Rose, traditionally the market leader in Newfoundland, accounted for approximately 20 percent of retail sales in 1980 (see Table A-5). This drastic decline has been attributed to many factors, including a switch in consumer taste preference to weaker teas such as Tetley and aggressive advertising and promotion by Tetley. Red Rose is packaged in 15, 30, 60, 120, 180, and 250 bag sizes; package design is simple, with red lettering on a plain white background, and a long-stemmed rose lying next to a china cup. Brand awareness is exceptionally high, and distribution throughout the province is excellent. Brooke Bond, the owner of the brand, maintains a branch office and retail sales force in St. John's. Its retail prices are similar to Tetley's, although the brand is rarely promoted with special prices at the retail level. Advertising is concentrated in television, utilizing British actors and settings and a "sophisticated" taste appeal based on an "Only in Canada? Pity!" theme. In the past, Brooke Bond had promoted Red Rose using various free in-pack premiums such as wildlife picture cards and tiny ceramic figurines.

King Cole is a traditional Maritime brand of tea bags packaged in New Brunswick; its package sizes correspond to those of Red Rose. Market share has decreased over the years to its present level of approximately 5 percent, despite the fact that it is a high-quality tea blend. Its package design is somewhat cluttered and old-fashioned in appearance, with copious lettering and lacking professional illustrations and graphics; colours utilized include black lettering on a light orange background. Brand awareness is high, and distribution is adequate. Advertising and promotion is limited in both amount and scope; during 1980 it conducted a "Gold Rush" contest requiring consumers to mail in an end flap to a local radio station.

There were approximately ten other brands of boxed tea bags in distribution within the province during 1980, which in total accounted for approximately 5 percent of total retail sales. In addition to national or regional brands such as Salada, Clipper, McConnells, and Mug-Up, there were numerous private label brands.

On the basis of the market research and other investigations, Mr. Evans had decided to introduce a brand of tea bags to the retail market. A local marketing research agency assisted in generating more than 100 potential brand names; as a result of several focus-group interviews conducted with heavy tea drinkers from the St. John's area, it recommended the brand name "Bentley Fresh Brew." Mr. Evans accepted the recommendation and reaffirmed his earlier opinion to enter the boxed (versus the polybag) tea market. He also scheduled a meeting with his bank manager to discuss possible financing arrangements to assist The Newfoundland Tea Company in underwriting the heavy costs normally associated with developing and marketing a new consumer product.

Questions

1. Do you think this market represented a "good opportunity" for Mr. Evans? Are there better opportunities? Why or why not?

2. What additional information do you feel would be required in assessing this market opportunity? How and where would you obtain it?

3. Which market segment(s) would you say have the greatest potential for Bentley Fresh Brew tea? Why?

4. What types of retaliation by competitors should Mr. Evans expect?

Target Markets

AN ANALYSIS OF THE PEOPLE AND ORGANIZATIONS
WHO BUY, WHY THEY BUY, AND HOW THEY BUY

In Part 1 we stressed the importance of customer orientation in an organization's marketing efforts. We also noted that management creates and implements a marketing mix that is intended to satisfy its customers' wants. These notions suggest that early in the strategic marketing planning process, an organization should determine who its customers are. Once the customers are identified, management is in a position to develop its marketing mix. Therefore, in Part 2, we discuss the selection and definition of an organization's intended customers — that is, its target market.

In Chapter 4 we discuss the concepts of a market and market segmentation, and we analyse the demographic and buying-power dimensions of markets. Chapters 5 and 6 are devoted to the behavioural aspects of consumer markets. In Chapter 5 we consider the *sociocultural* influences on consumer buying behaviour, and in Chapter 6 we discuss the *psychological* influences. Chapter 6 also includes a classification of consumer goods that is based on buying behaviour. Chapter 7 covers various aspects of the industrial market.

Chapter 4

Selecting a Target Market: Demographics and Buying Power

CHAPTER GOALS

This is the first of four chapters on the consumer—the target of most marketing programs. After studying this chapter, you should understand:

1. *The meaning of the term* market
2. *Some fundamentals regarding the selection of target markets*
3. *The idea of market segmentation—the benefits of and the bases for segmenting markets*
4. *The difference between ultimate-consumer markets and industrial-user markets*
5. *The marketing implications of the distribution and composition of population*
6. *The influences of consumer-income distribution on marketing*
7. *Consumer spending patterns and the way they affect marketing*

Strategic planning was defined in Chapter 2 as the matching of an organization's resources with its marketing opportunities. In this chapter we look at a company's marketing opportunities, focusing on the selection of the target market and an analysis of the demographic and buying-power dimensions of that market.

WHAT IS A MARKET?

The word *market* is used in a number of ways. There is a stock *market* and an automobile *market*, a retail *market* for furniture and a wholesale *market* for furniture. One person may be going to the market; another may plan to *market* a product. *What, then, is a market?* Clearly, there are many usages of the term in economic theory, in business in general, and in marketing in particular. A *market* may be defined as a place where buyers and sellers meet, goods or services are offered for sale, and transfers of ownership occur. A *market* may also be defined as the demand made by a certain group of potential buyers for a product or service. For example, there is a farm market for petroleum products. The terms *market* and *demand* are often used interchangeably, and they may also be used jointly as *market demand*.

These definitions of a market may not be sufficiently precise to be useful to us here. Consequently, in this book a **market** is defined as people with needs to satisfy, money to spend, and willingness to spend it. Thus, in the market demand for any given product or service, there are three factors to consider — people with needs, their purchasing power, and their buying behaviour.

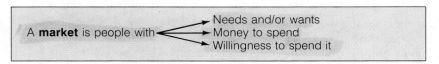

A **market** is people with → Needs and/or wants
→ Money to spend
→ Willingness to spend it

We shall employ the dictionary definition of *needs*: A need is the lack of anything that is required, desired, or useful. As noted in Chapter 1, we do not limit needs to the narrow physiological requirements of food, clothing, and shelter essential for survival. In effect, in our discussion, the words *needs* and *wants* may be used synonymously and interchangeably.

SELECTING A TARGET MARKET

An organization's marketing planning begins with a decision on its marketing goals. Once the goals are established, the next step in the process of strategic marketing planning is to select and analyse the organization's target market(s). A **target market** is a group of customers at whom the organization specifically intends to aim its marketing effort. Careful selection and accurate definition (identification) of the target market are essential to the development of an effective marketing mix. By the same token, the target-market selection is influenced by the type of marketing mix that the organization is capable of developing.

Guidelines Regarding Market Selection

There are some general guidelines that management should follow in the course of selecting an organization's target markets. The first is that the target markets should be compatible with the organization's goals and image. A firm that is marketing high-priced personal computers should not sell through discount chain stores in an effort to reach a mass market.

A second guideline — consistent with our definition of strategic planning — is to match the marketing opportunity with the company's resources. Coca-Cola followed this guideline when it decided to introduce caffeine-free Diet Coke. By so doing, the company was able to address a growing segment of the market that is concerned with nutrition and the potential effects of caffeine and sugar, while at the same time trading on the established reputation of Diet Coke. In this way, Coca-Cola matched its marketing-mix resources with its intended target market.

Over the long run, a business must generate a profit if it is to continue in existence. This rather obvious point translates into what is perhaps an

The target market and marketing mix are developed in relation to the marketing goal.

obvious market-selection guideline. That is, an organization should consciously seek markets that will generate a sufficient sales volume at a low enough cost to result in a profit. Unfortunately, through the years, companies often overlooked the profit factor in their quest for high-volume markets. The goal often was sales volume alone, not *profitable* sales volume.

Finally, a company ordinarily should seek a market wherein the number of competitors and their size are minimal. An organization should not enter a market that is already saturated with competition unless it has some overriding competitive advantage that will enable it to take customers away from existing firms.

Target-Market Strategy: Market Aggregation or Market Segmentation?

In defining the market or markets it will sell to, an organization has its choice of two general approaches. In one, the total market is viewed as a single unit — as one mass, aggregate market. This approach leads to the strategy of *market aggregation*. In the other approach, the total market is seen as being composed of many smaller, homogeneous segments. This approach leads to the strategy of *market segmentation*, in which one or more of these segments are selected as target markets.

Deciding which of these approaches (and strategies) is appropriate is a very important step in selecting a target market. The decision regarding the aggregation-segmentation strategy question is discussed in more detail in the next major section of this chapter.

Market Factors to Analyse

We defined a market as people with (1) wants to satisfy, (2) the money to spend, and (3) the willingness to spend it. Therefore, in the course of selecting its target markets, management should analyse these three components in detail. The first component may be studied by analysing the geographic distribution and demographic composition of the population. The second component is analysed through the distribution of customer income and customer expenditure patterns. These first two components are discussed more fully later in this chapter. Finally, to determine customers' "willingness to spend," management must study their buying behaviour. This involves the sociological and psychological factors that influence buyer behaviour — the topics covered in Chapters 5 and 6.

Measuring the Selected Markets

In the course of selecting its target market, a company should make quantitative estimates of the sales-volume size of the market for the seller's product or service. This step involves estimating the total-industry potential for the company's product in the target market. (This industry figure is called the *market potential* for the product.) Then the seller should estimate its share of this total market. (This company figure is called the *sales potential*.)

It is essential that management prepare a sales forecast, usually for a one-year period. A sales forecast is the foundation of all budgeting and short-term operational planning in all company departments — marketing, production, and finance. Sales forecasting will be discussed in more detail in Chapter 24, after we build a foundation in the fundamentals of marketing.

As noted above, the decision between market aggregation (a total mass market) and market segmentation (smaller, homogeneous market segments) is an important one. The company's view of its market greatly affects its marketing mix and possibly its production, research and development, and other operating departments.

By adopting the strategy of **market aggregation**, an organization treats its total market as a unit—as one mass, aggregate market whose parts are considered to be alike in all major respects. Management then develops a single marketing mix to reach as many customers as possible in this aggregate market. That is, the company develops a single product for this mass audience; it develops one pricing structure and one distribution system for its product; and it uses a single promotional program that is aimed at the entire market.

When is an organization likely to adopt the strategy of market aggregation? Generally, when a large group of customers in the total market tends to have the same perception of the product's want-satisfying benefits. Therefore, this strategy often is adopted by firms that are marketing a nondifferentiated, staple product such as gasoline, salt, or sugar. In the eyes of many people, cane sugar is cane sugar, regardless of the brand. All brands of table salt are pretty much alike, and one unleaded gasoline is about the same as another.

Basically, market aggregation is a production-oriented strategy. It enables a company to maximize its economies of scale in production, physical distribution, and promotion. Producing and marketing one product for one market means longer production runs at lower unit costs. Inventory costs are minimized when there is no (or a very limited) variety of colours and sizes of products. Warehousing and transportation efforts are most efficient when one product is going to one market.

The total market for most types of products is too varied — too heterogeneous—for management to consider it as a single, uniform entity. To speak of the market for vitamin pills, or electric razors, or tractors is to ignore the fact that the total market for each product consists of submarkets that differ significantly from one another. This lack of uniformity may be traced to differences in buying habits, in ways in which the product is used, in motives for buying, or in other factors. Market segmentation takes these differences into account.

What Is Market Segmentation?

In **market segmentation**, the total, heterogeneous market for a product is divided into several segments, each of which tends to be homogeneous in all significant aspects. Management then selects one or more of these segments as the organization's target market. Finally, a separate marketing mix is developed for each segment in this target market.

MARKET AGGREGATION OR MARKET SEGMENTATION

Market Aggregation

An aggregate market is assumed to be a single uniform mass of potential customers.

Market Segmentation

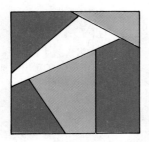

A segmented market consists of distinguishable segments, or parts, each of which is assumed to be uniform.

In terms familiar to an economist, market segmentation means determining several demand schedules—a separate one for each market segment. Thus, instead of speaking of *the* market for portable electric typewriters, we can segment this market into several submarkets—perhaps those for college students, high-school students, homemakers, travelling salespeople, and small businesses where there is the need for occasional typing.

Market segmentation is a customer-oriented philosophy. We first identify the needs of the customers within a submarket (segment) and then satisfy those needs. Stated another way, in market segmentation we employ a "rifle" approach (separate programs, pinpointed targets) in our marketing activities. In contrast, market aggregation is a "shotgun" approach (one program, broad target).

Single and Multiple Segmentation

In adopting the target-market strategy of market segmentation, management can further choose either *single segmentation* or *multiple segmentation*.

Single Segmentation
A **single-segmentation** strategy involves selecting as the target market one homogeneous group from within the total market. One marketing mix is then developed to reach this single segment. A small company may want to concentrate on a single market segment, rather than to take on many competitors in a broad market. For example, a Toronto restaurant started in business as a place where customers could obtain gourmet-quality dining at reasonable prices — a no-frills gourmet restaurant. A number of travel agents and tour companies target their marketing effort at one major market segment — the older, financially well-off people who also have time to travel.

This strategy enables a company to penetrate one small market in depth and to acquire a reputation as a specialist or an expert in this limited market. A company can enter such a market with limited resources. But the big risk is that the seller has all its eggs in one basket. If that single segment declines in market potential, the seller can suffer considerably.

Multiple Segmentation
In the strategy of **multiple segmentation**, two or more different groups of potential customers are identified as target-market segments. Then a separate marketing mix is developed to reach each segment. A marketer of personal computers, for example, might identify three separate market segments — college students, small businesses, and homemakers — and then design a different marketing mix to reach each segment. In segmenting the passenger automobile market, General Motors develops separate marketing programs built around its five brands — Chevrolet, Pontiac, Buick, Oldsmobile, and Cadillac. General Motors, in effect, tries to reach the total mass market for autos, but does so on a segmented basis.

As part of the strategy of multiple segmentation, a company frequently will develop a different variety of the basic product for each segment.

However, market segmentation can also be accomplished with no change in the product, but rather with separate marketing programs, each tailored to a given market segment. A producer of vitamin pills, for instance, can market the identical product to the youth market and to the over-65 market. But the promotional programs (and probably the channels of distribution) for the two markets will be different. A multiple-segment strategy normally results in a greater sales volume than a single-segment approach. However, the unit costs of production and marketing also increase when multiple segments are targeted.

By tailoring marketing programs to individual market segments, management can do a better marketing job and make more efficient use of marketing resources. A small firm with limited resources might compete very effectively in one or two market segments, whereas the same firm would be buried if it aimed for the total market. By employing the strategy of market segmentation, a company can design products that really match the market demands. Advertising media can be used more effectively because promotional messages — and the media chosen to present them — can be more specifically aimed toward each segment of the market.[1]

Benefits of Market Segmentation

Ideally, management's goal should be to segment its markets in such a way that each segment responds in a homogeneous fashion to a given marketing program. These conditions will help management move toward this goal.

Conditions for Effective Segmentation

1. The basis for segmenting — that is, the characteristics used to categorize customers — must be *measurable*, and the data must be *accessible*. The "desire for ecologically compatible products" may be a characteristic that is useful in segmenting the market for a given product. But data on this characteristic are neither readily accessible nor easily quantified.

2. The market segment itself should be *accessible* through existing marketing institutions — channels of distribution, advertising media, company sales force, and so on — with a minimum of cost and waste. To aid marketers in this regard, some national magazines, such as *Maclean's* and *Chatelaine*, publish separate geographical editions. This allows an advertiser to run an ad aimed at, say, a Western Canada segment of the market, without having to pay for exposure in other, nonmarket areas.

3. Each segment should be *large enough* to be profitable. In concept, management could treat each single customer as a separate segment.

---

[1]For the idea that rising prices and conservative life-styles can support a strategy of combining or clustering formerly segmented markets, see Alan J. Resnik, Peter B. B. Turney, and J. Barry Mason, "Markets Turn to 'Countersegmentation'," *Harvard Business Review*, September-October 1979, pp. 100-106. In return for a lower price, people seem more willing to "accept a little less" — that is, to use a product or service not as precisely tailored to their wants as in times of more stable prices.

(Actually, this situation may be normal in industrial markets, as when Westinghouse markets turbines to provincial hydroelectric utilities.) But in segmenting a consumer market, a firm must not develop too wide a variety of styles, colours, sizes, and prices. Usually, the diseconomies of scale in production and inventory will put reasonable limits on this type of oversegmentation.

Bases for Market Segmentation

A company can segment its market in many different ways. And the bases for segmentation vary from one product to another.

Ultimate Consumers and Industrial Users

An obvious (but important) market division is by reason for buying.

One very important way of segmenting the entire Canadian market is to divide it into ultimate consumers and industrial users. The sole criterion for this segmentation is the *reason for buying*. **Ultimate consumers** buy and/or use products or services for their own personal or household use. They are satisfying strictly nonbusiness wants, and they constitute what is called the "consumer market." A homemaker who buys food and clothing and the family members who eat the food and wear the clothing are all ultimate consumers.

Industrial users are business, industrial, or institutional organizations that buy products or services to use in their own businesses or to make other products. A manufacturer that buys chemicals with which to make fertilizer is an industrial user of these chemicals. Farmers who buy the fertilizer to use in commercial farming are industrial users of the fertilizer. (If homeowners buy fertilizer to use on their yards, they are ultimate consumers because they buy it for household use.) Supermarkets, hospitals, or paper manufacturers that buy floor wax are industrial users of this product because they use it in a business or institution. Industrial users in total constitute the "industrial market."

The segmentation of all markets into two groups—consumer and industrial—is extremely significant from a marketing point of view because the two markets buy differently. Consequently, the composition of a seller's marketing mix—the products, distribution, pricing, and promotion—will depend upon whether it is directed toward the consumer market or the industrial market.

Bases for Segmenting Consumer Markets

Simply dividing the total market into consumer and industrial segments is a worthwhile start. But it still leaves too broad and heterogeneous a grouping for most products. Consequently, we shall next identify some of the widely used bases for further segmenting the consumer market. The model we shall use is related to the three components of a market as defined early in this chapter. It also is a topical outline of Chapters 4 through 6.

MORE WAYS TO SEGMENT A MARKET

- ''Big can be beautiful'' in women's clothing fashions. Leading designers are creating attractive clothes for larger women. Several stores are aiming at the market segment that wear sizes 14 to 26 and even up to size 50. Not long ago this market segment was virtually ignored by manufacturers and retailers.

- Support bras are designed especially for active sportswomen.

- For people who like to drink beer but who are also concerned about calories, the Canadian market now has available a variety of different brands of ''light beers.'' Brands such as Labatt's Lite, Molson Light, Carlsberg Light, and Moosehead Golden Light are variations on their parent brands and contain far fewer calories per serving than regular beers.

- Products available for the physically impaired include:
  — telegrams and menus written in Braille.
  — telephones that are activated by voice and do not have to be lifted by hand.
  — directional ''beeping crickets'' that are mounted on the tricycle of a seeing child, so that a blind child can hear and follow on his or her own tricycle.

- In cigarettes, we have regular lengths, long (100 millimetres), and longer (120 millimetres). We have cigarettes with or without filters, and with or without menthol. We have low tar, low nicotine, light, and ''full flavour'' brands. We even have brands that are particularly directed toward the female market segment.

- And now we have chequebooks for left-handed people. The binding and the cheque stubs are on the right side.

Markets, we noted, are:

- **People with wants** (Chapter 4). Thus, we can segment markets on demographic bases such as:

  1. Regional population distribution
  2. Urban-suburban-rural population
  3. Age
  4. Sex
  5. Family life-cycle stage
  6. Others: race, religion, nationality, education, occupation

- **with money to spend** (Chapter 4). Thus, segmentation can also be based on the distribution of disposable income.

- **and the willingness to spend it** (Chapters 5 and 6). This gets us into segmentation via consumer buying behaviour, where the prime determinants are:

  1. Sociological factors such as:
     a. Cultural groups
     b. Large social classes
     c. Small groups, including the family

Figure 4-1   POPULATION GROWTH IN CANADA, 1871–1981.

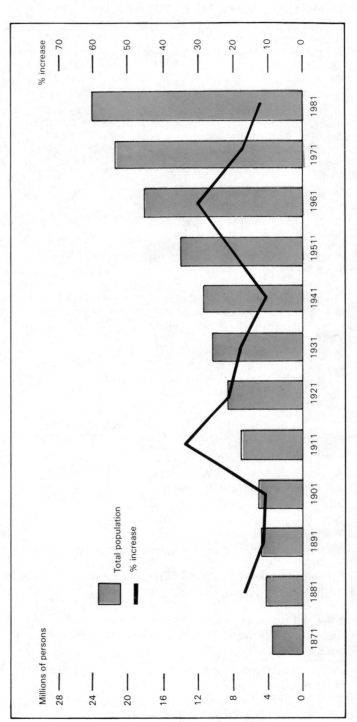

[1]Includes Newfoundland for the first time.
Source: Statistics Canada, *Canada's Changing Population Distribution*, cat. no. 99–931, July 1984.

2. Psychological (psychographic) factors such as:
   a. Personality
   b. Attitudes
   c. Product benefits desired

In using these bases to segment markets, we should note two points. First, buying behaviour is rarely traceable to only one segmentation factor. Useful segmentation typically is developed by including variables from several of the above bases. To illustrate, the market for a product rarely consists of all the people living in the Atlantic Provinces, or all people over 65. Instead, the segment is more likely to be described with several of these variables. Thus a market segment might be women living in Atlantic Canada, married, with young children, and earning above a certain income level.

The other point to observe is the interrelationships among these factors, especially among the demographic factors. For instance, age and life-cycle stage typically are related. Income depends to some degree on age, life-cycle stage, education, and occupation.

Bases for Segmenting Industrial Markets

Like consumer markets, the broad, diverse industrial market usually must be further segmented in order to develop effective marketing programs that reach industrial users. The industrial market is discussed (and segmented) in Chapter 7; here we deal only with the consumer market.

POPULATION — ITS DISTRIBUTION AND COMPOSITION

According to our definition, people are the main component of a market. Therefore, marketers should analyse the geographic distribution and demographic composition of the population as a first step toward understanding the consumer market. There are several general references that provide information on the Canadian population.[2]

Total Population

A logical place to start is with an analysis of total population. The total population of Canada rose from 7 million in 1911 to just over 10 million in 1931, and by 1984 had increased to approximately 25 million. Projections indicate, based on certain assumptions regarding immigration and fertility rates, an increase to 30 million or more by the end of this century. These projections indicate also a downturn in the expected increase in population, as compared with predictions of a few years ago. This reflects a decrease in the birthrate in recent years, an expectation that it will remain at its present low level, and a reduction in the level of immigration into Canada. The rate of growth in the Canadian population is shown in Fig. 4-1.

---

[2]See, for example, Roderic P. Beaujot, "Canada's Population: Growth and Dualism," *Population Bulletin*, vol. 33, no. 2 (Population Reference Bureau, Inc., Washington, D.C., 1978); Leroy O. Stone and Claude Marceau, *Canadian Population Trends and Public Policy Through the 1980s*, The Institute for Research on Public Policy, McGill-Queen's University Press, Montreal, 1977; Lawrence R. Small, *Handbook of Canadian Consumer Markets, 1979*, The Conference Board in Canada, Ottawa, 1979; and Warren E. Kalbach and Wayne W. McVey, *The Demographic Bases of Canadian Society*, McGraw-Hill Ryerson Limited, Toronto, 1979.

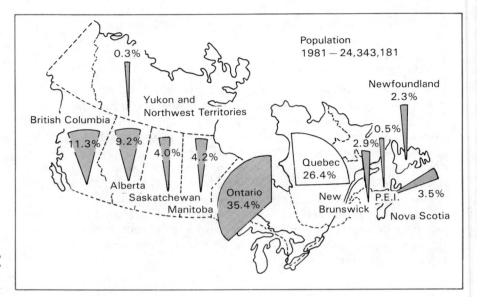

Figure 4-2
REGIONAL
DISTRIBUTION OF
POPULATION, 1981.

Source: Statistics Canada, *1981 Census of Canada*, cat. no. 92–901.

Increases in total population have implications for marketing. Total consumer expenditures for food, clothing, recreational and sporting goods, services, houses and home furnishings, automobiles, snowmobiles, appliances, and all of the other products and services demanded by the population will increase by several billion dollars. The size and heterogeneity of the Canadian market make it necessary to analyse it in segments. Significant shifts are occurring in regional and urban-rural population distribution patterns. Market differences traceable to differences in age, sex, household arrangements, life-styles, and ethnic backgrounds pose real challenges for marketing executives.

Regional
Distribution

Figure 4-2 shows the distribution of population in 1981, and the projected growth by province or region from 1976 to 2001 is illustrated in Table 4-1.

The regional distribution of population is important to marketers because sectional differences lead to differences in the demand for many products. These differences can be traced to climate, social customs, and other factors. Thus, bright warm colours are preferred in British Columbia, while greys and cooler colours predominate in the Atlantic Provinces. People in the West are less formal than Easterners, and they spend more time outdoors. Consequently, as the Western population increases, there will be a larger market for such products as patio furniture, sports clothes, and barbecue equipment.

Table 4-1   DISTRIBUTION OF POPULATION BY PROVINCE, 1976, 1983, WITH PROJECTIONS
TO 2001

Province/territory	1976 population (000)	% of Canada	estimated 1983 population (000)	% of Canada	Projection 1[1] 2001 Population (000)	% of Canada	Projection 4[2] 2001 Population (000)	% of Canada
Newfoundland	557.7	2.43	577.0	2.32	620.0	2.00	671.1	2.39
Prince Edward Island	118.3	0.51	124.0	0.50	132.8	0.43	161.9	0.58
Nova Scotia	828.6	3.60	859.0	3.45	931.8	3.01	1,008.5	3.59
New Brunswick	677.2	2.95	706.0	2.84	781.3	2.52	888.7	3.17
Quebec	6,234.5	27.12	6,524.0	26.21	7,614.5	24.58	6,508.9	23.20
Ontario	8,264.5	35.94	8,816.0	35.42	11,917.1	38.47	10,133.5	36.12
Manitoba	1,021.4	4.44	1,047.0	4.21	1,185.3	3.82	1,169.0	4.17
Saskatchewan	921.4	4.01	992.0	3.99	968.0	3.12	1,211.3	4.32
Alberta	1,838.0	7.99	2,348.0	9.44	2,835.0	9.15	3,080.3	10.98
British Columbia	2,466.6	10.73	2,823.0	11.34	3,861.8	12.47	3,122.5	11.13
Yukon	21.8	0.09⎰	70.0	0.28	44.6	0.14	32.9	.12
Northwest Territories	42.6	0.29⎱			88.6	0.29	64.8	.23
Canada	22,992.6	100.	100.	100.	30,980.7	100.	28,053.5	100.

[1]Projection 1 assumes a fertility rate of 2.1 and a net immigration to Canada of 100,000 persons per year.
[2]Projection 4 assumes a fertility rate of 1.7 and a net immigration to Canada of 50,000 persons per year.

Source: Statistics Canada, *Population Projections for Canada and the Provinces, 1976-2001*, cat. no. 91-520, Ottawa, June 1980, pp. 29, 36-40; and The Financial Post, *Canadian Markets, 1984*, Maclean-Hunter Ltd., Toronto, 1984, p. 86.

For a number of years in Canada there has been a relative and an absolute decline in the farm population, and this decline is expected to continue. The declining farm population has led some marketing people to under-rate the rural market. However, both as an industrial market for farm equipment and supplies and as a consumer market with increased buying power and a more urbanlike sophistication, the farm market is still a big one. Sociological patterns (like average family size and local customs) among rural people differ significantly from those of city dwellers. These patterns have considerable influence on buying behaviour. Per capita consumption of cosmetics and other beauty aids, for example, is much lower in farm markets than in city markets. Canada is by no means the most urbanized nation on earth. It ranks 16th, behind such countries as Belgium, Australia, Israel, Sweden, Britain, and Japan.[3]

Urban, Rural, Suburban, and Interurban Distribution

As the farm population has shrunk, the urban and suburban population has expanded. In recognition of the growing urbanization of the Canadian market, some years ago the federal government established the concept of a Census Metropolitan Area (CMA) as a geographic market-data-measurement unit. A CMA is defined by Statistics Canada as the main labour

Census Metropolitan Areas

[3]Statistics Canada, *Canada's Cities*, Update from the 1981 Census, vol. 2. no. 4, March 1984.

market of a continuous built-up area having a population of 100,000 or more. Table 4-2 indicates the growth in the population of the 24 CMAs in Canada from 1976 to 1981. By 1981, these 24 population centres accounted for over 75 percent of the total population of Canada. This figure is expected to increase to 85 percent by 1991. Obviously these areas present attractive, geographically concentrated market targets with considerable sales potential.

In several places in Canada the metropolitan areas have expanded to the point where there is no rural space between them. This joining of metropolitan areas has been called "interurbia." Where two or more city markets once existed, today there is a single market. For example, there is virtually no space between Quebec City and Niagara Falls that is not part of a major urban area.

Table 4-2   GROWTH IN CANADA'S MAJOR METROPOLITAN AREAS, 1976–1981

Rank 1981	Rank 1976	Metropolitan Area	Population 1976[1]	1981	Percentage Change
1	1	Toronto	2,803,101	2,998,947	7.0
2	2	Montréal	2,802,547A	2,828,349	0.9
3	3	Vancouver	1,166,348	1,268,183	8.7
4	4	Ottawa-Hull	693,288	717,978	3.6
5	6	Edmonton	556,270A	657,057	18.1
6	9	Calgary	471,397A	592,743	25.7
7	5	Winnipeg	578,217	584,842	1.2
8	7	Québec	542,158	576,075	6.3
9	8	Hamilton	529,371	542,095	2.4
10	10	St. Catharines-Niagara	301,921	304,353	0.8
11	11	Kitchener	272,158	287,801	5.8
12	12	London	270,383	283,668	4.9
13	13	Halifax	267,991	277,727	3.6
14	14	Windsor	247,582	246,110	−0.6
15	15	Victoria	218,250	233,481	7.0
16	17	Regina	151,191	164,313	8.7
17	18	St. John's	145,400A	154,820	6.5
18	19	Oshawa	135,196	154,217	14.1
19	20	Saskatoon	133,793A	154,210	15.3
20	16	Sudbury	157,030	149,923	−4.3
21	21	Chicoutimi-Jonquière	128,643	135,172	5.1
22	22	Thunder Bay	119,253	121,379	1.8
23	23	Saint John	112,974	114,048	1.0
24	24	Trois-Rivières	106,031A	111,453	5.1

[1]Based on 1981 area.
A — Adjusted figures due to boundary changes.

Source: Statistics Canada, *Canada's Cities*, Update from the 1981 Census, Vol. 2, No. 4, March 1984.

As the metropolitan areas have been growing, something else has been going on *within* them. The central cities are growing very slowly, and in some cases the older established parts of the cities are actually losing population. The real growth is occurring in the fringe areas of the central cities or in the suburbs outside these cities. For the past 35 years, one of the most significant social and economic trends in Canada has been the shift of population to the suburbs. As middle-income families have moved to the suburbs, the economic, racial, and ethnic composition of many central cities (especially core areas) has changed considerably, thus changing the nature of the markets in these areas.

Suburban Growth

The growth of the suburban population has some striking marketing implications. Since a great percentage of suburban people live in single-family residences, there is a vastly expanded market for lawn mowers, lawn furniture, home furnishings, and home repair supplies and equipment. Suburbanites are more likely to want two cars than are city dwellers. They are inclined to spend more leisure time at home, so there is a bigger market for home entertainment and recreation items.

In the mid-1980s, marketing people are watching two possible counter-trends. One is the movement from the suburbs back to the central cities by older people whose children are grown. Rather than contend with commuting, home maintenance, and other suburban challenges, older people are moving to new apartments located nearer to downtown facilities.

The other reversal is that there has been an increase in rural population near the major Census Metropolitan Areas. The rural population of Canada increased by 481,000 between 1976 and 1981. Almost half of this increase occurred within the Census Metropolitan Areas and Census Agglomerations (the main labour market area of a continuously built-up area having a population of between 10,000 and 99,999). If this increase had been distributed in the same proportion as the 1976 rural population, an increase of 107,000 would have been expected in these areas. In other words, there has been an increase in the number of Canadians choosing to live in rural areas in close proximity to major urban centres. This change in rural population is reflected in Table 4-3.

Age Groups

Segmenting the consumer market by age groups is a useful approach in the marketing of many products. But a marketing executive must be aware of the changing nature of the age mix. Looking ahead to the year 2001, we anticipate both a slower growth in population and an aging population. (See Table 4-4.)

The *youth* market (roughly grade-school ages 5 to 13) carries a three-way marketing impact. First, these children can influence parental purchases. Second, billions of dollars are spent on this group by their parents. Third, these children themselves make purchases of goods and services for their own personal use and satisfaction. Promotional programs are often geared to this market segment. Children's television shows, for instance, are sponsored by cereal, toy, and video-game manufacturers and other advertisers in an effort to develop brand preferences at an early age.

Table 4-3   CHANGE IN RURAL POPULATION, CANADA
AND PROVINCES, 1976–1981

	Population change			Percentage change		
	Total	Outside CMAs[1] CAs[2]	Within CMAs[1] CAs[2]	Total	Outside CMAs[1] CAs[2]	Within CMAs[1] CAs[2]
Canada[3]	480,846	264,021	216,825	8.9	6.3	18.0
Newfoundland	8,562	3,737	4,825	3.8	1.9	16.5
Prince Edward Island	6,108	1,201	4,907	8.5	2.2	28.8
Nova Scotia	20,184	11,288	8,896	5.6	4.6	7.6
New Brunswick	28,412	14,875	13,537	9.0	6.1	19.5
Quebec	176,435	94,039	82,396	13.9	9.2	33.8
Ontario	84,919	34,746	50,173	5.7	3.5	10.2
Manitoba	329	− 2,795	3,124	0.1	− 1.0	12.2
Saskatchewan	− 1,549	− 2,076	527	− 0.4	− 0.5	4.4
Alberta	65,628	52,888	12,740	14.8	12.9	38.3
British Columbia	89,694	53,994	35,700	17.4	15.7	20.9

[1]Census Metropolitan Area—Main labour market area of a continuously built-up area having 100,000 or more population.
[2]Census Agglomeration—Main labour market area of a continuously built-up area having between 10,000 and 99,999 population.
[3]Includes Yukon and Northwest Territories, which contain no CMAs or CAs.
Source: 1981 Census of Canada, cat. nos. 93-901 to 93-912, Tables 2 and 5.

The *teenage* market is recognized as an important one, and yet it has proved to be difficult to reach. The mistake might be in attempting to lump all teenagers into one group, thus ignoring the many subgroups segmented by income, race, geographic location, and so on. Moreover, all teenagers are not alike; certainly the 13-to-16 age group is very different from the 17-to-20 age bracket.

Yet marketers must understand teenage consumers because of the size of this market and because its members have an increasing amount of money to spend. They are good customers for tape cassettes, automobiles, cosmetics, clothes, jewellery, and other products. To tap this market, many manufacturers are adopting new product and distribution policies. For instance, some clothing manufacturers are now designing junior ready-to-wear dresses that reflect the age and not merely the size of the teenager.

The huge youth market of the 1960s and 1970s has become the booming *young adult* (20-to-39 age group) market of the 1980s. This group is especially important to marketers because it is in this age bracket that people usually begin their careers, get married, start families, and spend money in a big way. Equally important is the fact that today's young adults — the rebels of the 1960s — typically have far different personal values and lifestyles from those of their counterparts in preceding generations.[4]

---

[4]See, for example, Philip Marchand, "Life Inside the Population Bulge," *Saturday Night*, October 1979, p. 17, and Robert L. Brown, "The Revenge of the Empty Cradle," *Quest*, October 1979, p. 10.

Table 4-4   POPULATION PROJECTIONS TO 2001 BY AGE GROUPS
(PERCENTAGE OF TOTAL POPULATION)

Age Group	Population 1976	Population 1981	Population 2001	
			Proj. 1	Proj. 4
0–19	35.9	32.0	29.7	26.3
20–44	36.3	39.1	36.7	37.8
45–64	19.1	19.1	22.4	23.8
65 +	8.7	9.7	11.2	12.1

Source: Statistics Canada, *Population Projections for Canada and the Provinces, 1976–2001,* cat. no. 91-520, Ottawa, June 1980, p. 41; and *1981 Census of Canada.*

At the older end of the age spectrum are two market segments that should not be overlooked. One is the group of people in their 50s and early 60s. This *mature* market is large and financially well off. Its members are at the peak of their earning power and typically no longer have financial responsibility for their children. Thus, this segment is a good target for marketers of high-priced, high-quality products and services.[5]

The other older age group comprises people over 65 — a segment that is growing both absolutely and as a percentage of the total population. Manufacturers and middlemen alike are beginning to recognize that people in this age group are logical prospects for small, low-cost housing units, cruises, and foreign tours, health products, and cosmetics developed especially for older people. Many firms are also developing promotional programs to appeal to the buying motives of this group and to cater to its buying habits.[6]

The overall birth rate in Canada continues to decline and currently stands at 14.9 per 100 Canadians, down from 16.8 per 100 in 1971. There are a number of sociocultural factors contributing to the continuing decline in the birth rate, including increased education and labour-force participation of women, widespread use of birth-control methods, and a decrease in peer pressure to have children. However, the number of women in the child-bearing age group is so large at present that there will in fact be more babies born in Canada during the 1980s than were born in the 1970s, although the actual birth rate per 100 population is down.

---

[5]See, for example, John Masters, "The Golden Youth Market Shows its Grey Hairs," *Maclean's,* December 8, 1980, p. 46; Paul Moroz, "Do Consumers Kick the Bucket When They Pass the Age of 49?" *Marketing,* March 2, 1981, p. 8; Andrew Weiner, "The Maturing of the Marketplace," *The Financial Post Magazine,* April 30, 1981, p. 21; Rena Bartos, "Over 49: the Invisible Consumer Market," *Harvard Business Review,* vol. 58, no. 1, January-February 1980, pp. 140–148; and Betsy D. Gelb, "Gray Power: Next Challenge to Business?" *Business Horizons,* April 1977, pp. 38–45.

[6]See Betsy D. Gelb, "Discovering the 65 + Consumer," *Business Horizons,* May-June 1982, pp. 42–46.

The major developments in terms of age distribution of the population are as follows:

- The Baby Boom generation has grown up and is now between 19 and 34 years of age. This group is having a significant effect on Canada's employment picture and is beginning to make its impact in terms of buying power.
- The 35-to-49 age group will grow four times faster than average population growth over the next 10 years (see Fig. 4-3).
- More than 25 percent of Canadians are already over 50 years of age.
- The structure of the Canadian family is changing and an increasing percentage of Canadians is living in nontypical household units.
- The number of women over the age of 30 and beginning a family is rising. In 1973, only 8 percent of first-time mothers were over 30, while by 1983 this figure had risen to 14 percent.[7]

THE AVERAGE AGE OF OUR POPULATION IS RISING, SO —

- Johnson & Johnson is persuading adults to use its baby oil and baby shampoo.
- Gerber, the baby food company, now sells life insurance to older people, using the theme "Gerber now babies the over-50s."
- Levi Strauss markets a three-piece suit and "Levi's for Men" that are more fully cut "to accommodate the guy who has stopped playing football and is now watching it." The clothing is cut "to fit a man's build with a little more room in the seat and thighs."
- Wrigley's, the chewing gum company, now markets stick-proof Freedent gum for people who have dentures.
- In cosmetics, Helena Rubenstein offers a line of skin-care products for women over 50. Noxell's makeup products for older women include a "Moisturizing Wrinkle Stick."

Sex

Sex is an obvious basis for consumer market segmentation. Many products are made for use by members of one sex, not both. In many product categories — autos, for example — women and men typically look for different product benefits. Market segmentaton by sex is also useful because many products have traditionally been purchased by either men only or women only.

However, some of these traditional buying patterns are breaking down, and marketers certainly should be alert to changes involving their products. Not too many years ago, for example, the wife did practically all the grocery shopping for her family, and the husband bought the products and services needed for the automobile. Today, men are frequent food shoppers, and women buy the gas and arrange for repair and maintenance. Many products and activities once considered limited to the male market are now readily accepted by women.

[7]Clarkson, Gordon, *Tomorrow's Customers in Canada*, 18th ed., 1984, p. 16.

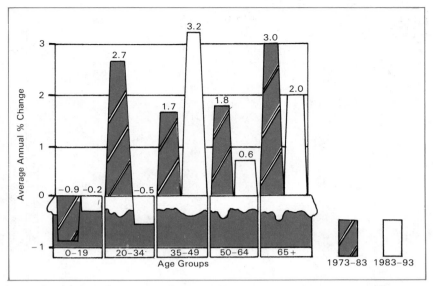

Figure 4-3
CHANGING AGE
DISTRIBUTION OF
THE CANADIAN
POPULATION.

Source: Clarkson, Gordon, *Tomorrow's Customers in Canada,* 18th ed., 1984, p. 16.

The changing role of women also has tremendous marketing implications. The number of working women (married or single) is increasing dramatically. By 1984, more than 52 percent of all Canadian women were employed, and women made up more than 44 percent of the Canadian labour force. These facts are significant to marketers, because the life-style and buying behaviour of working women are quite different from those of nonworking women.[8]

The fact that increasing numbers of women are employed in managerial and professional positions offers many opportunities for marketers. For example, there is an obvious need among families where both spouses are working for franchised housekeeping services, take-out food, after-school entertainment for children, day-care services, and at-home shopping services. Such families are typically quite busy with their dual careers and find themselves with little extra time. Consequently any products and services that ease time pressures are likely to find a ready market among this segment of the Canadian population.

The demographic factors of sex and age alone often do not adequately explain consumer buying behaviour. Frequently, the factor accounting for differences in consumption patterns between two people of the same age

Family Life Cycle

---

[8]For some marketing considerations related to the increase in the number of working women, see Mary Joyce and Joseph Guiltinan, "The Professional Woman: A Potential Market Segment for Retailers," *Journal of Retailing,* Summer 1978, pp. 59–70; Rena Bartos, "What Every Marketer Should Know about Women," *Harvard Business Review,* May-June 1978, pp. 73–85; and in *Journal of Marketing,* July 1977, see Suzanne H. McCall, "Meet the 'Workwife'," pp. 55–65, and Fred D. Reynolds, Melvin R. Crask, and William D. Wells, "The Modern Feminine Life Style," pp. 38–45.

Figure 4-4   FAMILY LIFE-CYCLE FLOWS.

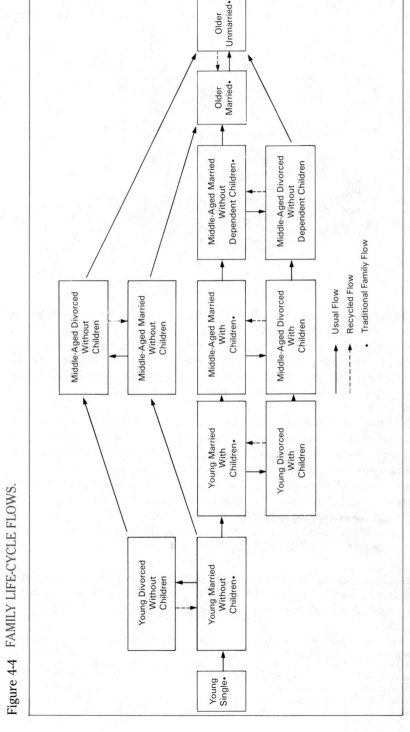

Source: Patrick E. Murphy and William A. Staples, "A Modernized Family Life Cycle," *Journal of Consumer Research,* vol. 6, June 1979, p. 17.

and sex is that they are in different life-cycle situations. The concept of a family life cycle refers to the important stages in the life of an ordinary family. In the past, the family life cycle has generally been broken down into six stages: (1) bachelor stage; (2) young married couples with no children; (3) full nest I — young married couples with children; (4) full nest II — older married couples still with dependent children; (5) empty nest — older married couples with no children living with them; and (6) older single people, still working or retired. Recent changes in the structure of the North American family, occasioned by increases in divorce rates, single-parent families, and decisions not to have children, have led to a considerable fragmentation of the family life cycle.[9] We now have far more than the six stages originally conceived. A depiction of the numerous stages which might now be identified in the life cycle of the North American family is presented in Figure 4-4.

This figure depicts the flow of families through the different possible stages of the family life cycle. Inclusion of the divorced and middle-aged, married without children stages accounts for a fairly large percentage of people who were not previously taken into consideration in the older six-stage life cycle and allows for potential changes in the future.

A segmentation factor related to the life cycle is the *rate* of household and family formation. (A **household** is defined as one or more persons living in the same dwelling unit; a **family** is a group of two or more related persons living together.) Every new household or family is potentially a market for a dwelling place, furniture, and other home furnishings. For manufacturers of appliances and furniture, the *number* of families is often more important than the *size* of the family. A refrigerator manufacturer, for example, may hope to sell three refrigerators to three couples but would probably sell only one to a family with six people in it.

Throughout the 1970s, there was a marked increase in the number of households consisting of only one person. These *singles* households were increasing in number because of:

- the growing number of working women;
- people marrying at a later age;
- increasing affluence of the Baby Boom children of the 1950s, now in their 20s;
- a reduced tendency for children to live with their parents;
- a rising divorce rate.

But the early 1980s brought a reversal of this trend. Because of economic difficulties brought about by the recession of the late 1970s and early 1980s, many Canadians who had been living alone were forced for economic reasons to consolidate households by moving back with parents or by moving

---

[9]Discussion of the changing nature of the North American family may be found in: George Clements, "Marketers: Why Pay Lip Service to the 'Ideal' or 'Normal' Family and Ignore What's Real?" *Marketing*, January 31, 1978; and Patrick E. Murphy and William A. Staples, "A Modernized Family Life Cycle," *Journal of Consumer Research*, vol. 6, June 1979, pp. 12–22.

Figure 4-5   MOBILITY PATTERNS OF THE CANADIAN POPULATION, 1976–1981.

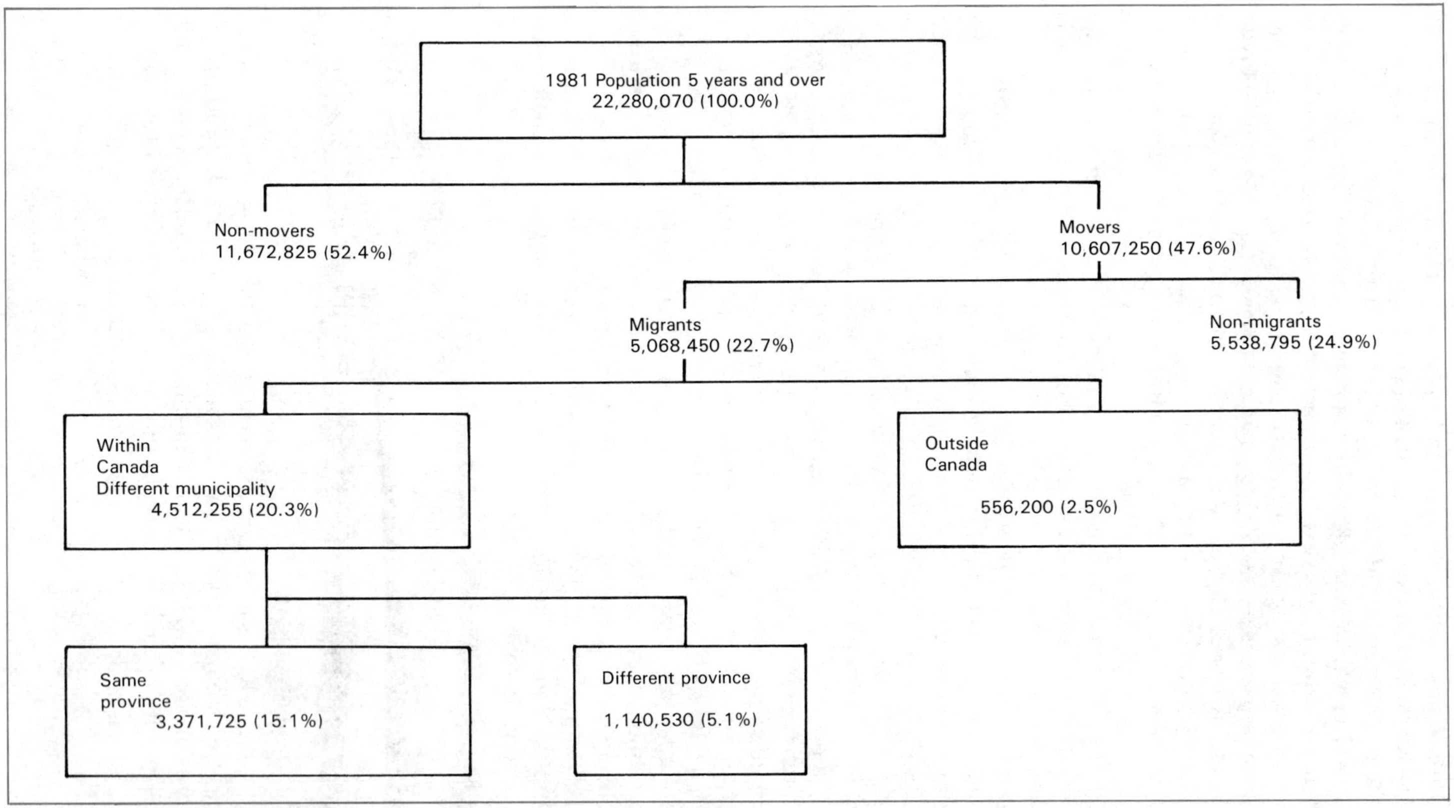

1981 Population 5 years and over 22,280,070 (100.0%)	
Non-movers 11,672,825 (52.4%)	
Movers 10,607,250 (47.6%)	
Non-migrants 5,538,795 (24.9%)	
Migrants 5,068,450 (22.7%)	
Within Canada Different municipality 4,512,255 (20.3%)	
Same province 3,371,725 (15.1%)	
Different province 1,140,530 (5.1%)	
Outside Canada 556,200 (2.5%)	

Source: Statistics Canada, 1981 Census of Canada, *Mobility Status*, cat. no. 92–907.

in with other, unrelated adults. In some parts of Canada, telephone companies experienced an actual decrease in the number of residential telephone lines during this period.

The number of unmarried couples of opposite sex living together (often called the *mingles* segment) has been increasing rapidly during the 1970s and 1980s, especially for people under the age of 25. Even though the actual percentage of households that fall into this segment is still relatively small, the marketing implications of this trend are far-reaching.

Compared with the population as a whole, the 18-to-34 singles segment is:

* More affluent
* More mobile
* More experimental and less conventional
* More fashion- and appearance-conscious
* More active in leisure pursuits
* More sensitive to social status

The impact that single people of both sexes have on the market is demonstrated by such things as apartments for singles, social clubs for singles, and special tours, cruises, and eating places seeking the patronage of singles.

The market for some consumer products is influenced by such factors as education, occupation, race, national origin, and religion. With an increasing number of people attaining higher levels of **education**, for example, we can expect to see (1) changes in product preferences and (2) buyers with more discriminating taste and higher incomes. **Occupation** may be a more meaningful criterion than income in segmenting some markets. Truck drivers or auto mechanics may earn as much as young retailing executives or college professors. But the buying patterns of the first two are different from those of the second two because of attitudes, interests, and other lifestyle factors.

Geographically mobile consumers constitute a sizable and perhaps unique market segment that is just beginning to receive attention. In Canada, during the period from 1976 to 1981, almost 50 percent of the population moved household (see Figure 4-5). More than 20 percent moved to a different municipality within Canada, and more than 5 percent moved to a different province. There is evidence to suggest that the mobility of Canadians has slowed somewhat in recent years. For example, 48.5 percent of Canadians moved household between 1971 and 1976, while 47.6 percent moved in the 5-year period between 1976 and 1981. This, too, is likely a result of the slowdown in the Canadian economy experienced during that period, as Canadians were slightly less inclined to seek new employment opportunities in different parts of the country.

The mobile segment of the population presents a rather attractive market. Many such consumers have high incomes, and their moves force them to

Other Demographic Bases for Segmentation

develop new shopping habits, seek new sources of products and services, and possibly develop new brand preferences.[10]

For some products, it is quite useful to analyse the population on the basis of *race, religion, and national origin*. One group that merits considerable attention is the French-Canadian market, which represents approximately 27 percent of Canada's population. Although this important cultural subgroup is dealt with in considerable detail in Chapter 5, it should be noted here that there are distinct differences between French Canada and the rest of the Canadian population in terms of income, consumption patterns, leisure-time behaviour, and, of course, language. To market successfully to French-Canadian consumers, a company must understand something of the distinct consumption behaviour of this segment and of the culture that motivates such behaviour. Furthermore, the marketer must realize that French Canada is not limited to the Province of Quebec, as Canadians who have French as their mother tongue also reside in considerable numbers in parts of British Columbia, eastern Ontario, Manitoba, and northern New Brunswick.

For certain products and services, other ethnic groups in Canada may constitute important markets. These include Canadians of German, Italian, Ukrainian, Portuguese, and Chinese descent who reside in large numbers in certain parts of Canada. Large cities such as Toronto, Montreal, Vancouver, and Winnipeg have considerable proportions of their populations made up of such ethnic groups. This concentration of consumers with a particular cultural background often represents a viable market segment for products that may not be purchased by the vast majority of Canadians.

It is important to note not only that net immigration to Canada has slowed somewhat in recent years, but more importantly, that the origin of immigrants has changed dramatically. Immigrants from Asian countries now exceed those from Europe and the United States. The number of people speaking an Asian language at home increased by 4.1 times between 1971 and 1981 and now totals more than one-half million. Of these, 35 percent speak Chinese and 18 percent speak Indian and Pakistani languages.

For marketers, it is important to recognize that recent immigrants differ from the general population in many ways. They are younger and generally have:

- higher birth rates
- a higher level of education
- a narrower income distribution (they tend to be in the middle- to low-income groups, largely due to the age factor)
- widely differing life-styles and buying habits
- a strong preference to preserve their ethnic traditions and customs.

---

[10]See William R. Darden, Warren A. French, and Roy D. Howell, "Mapping Market Mobility: Psychographic Profiles and Media Exposure," *Journal of Business Research*, vol. 7, no. 1, 1979, pp. 51–74.

As ethnic groups continue to grow faster than the general population, each one is becoming a lucrative, individual market.[11]

People alone do not make a market; they must have money to spend. Consequently, income, its distribution, and how it is spent are essential factors in any quantitative market analysis.

What is income? There are so many different concepts of income that it is good to review some definitions. The following outline is actually a "word equation" that shows how the several concepts are related.

CONSUMER INCOME AND ITS DISTRIBUTION

Nature and Scope of Income

National Income:

Total income from all sources, including employee compensation, corporate profits, and other income.
Less: Corporate profits and social security contributions
Plus: Dividends, government transfer payments to persons, and net interest paid by government
Equals:

Personal Income:

Income from wages, salaries, dividends, rent, interest, business and professions, social security, and farming.
Less: All personal federal, provincial, and local taxe and nontax payments
Equals:

Disposable Personal Income:

The amount available for personal consumption expenditures and savings.
Less: (1) Essential expenditures for food, clothing, household utilities, and local transportation and (2) fixed expenditures for rent, house mortgage payments, insurance, and instalment debt payments
Equals:

Discretionary Purchasing Power:

The amount of disposable personal income available after fixed commitments (debt repayments, rent) and essential household needs are taken care of. Consequently, as compared with disposable personal income, discretionary purchasing power is a better (more sensitive) indicator of consumers' ability to spend for nonessentials.

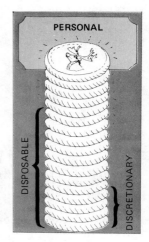

[11]Clarkson, Gordon, *Tomorrow's Customers in Canada*, 18th ed., 1984, p.18.

Table 4-5   PERSONAL INCOME AND PERSONAL DISPOSABLE
INCOME, 1950–1982 (in millions of dollars)

	1950	1960	1970	1976	1979	1982
Total Personal Income	14,262	29,595	66,633	155,343	210,728	316,284
Total Personal Disposable Income	13,285	26,567	54,009	125,510	172,478	255,296

Source: Statistics Canada, *National Income and Expenditure Accounts*, cat. no. 13-201.

Table 4-6   PER CAPITA PERSONAL INCOME, 1964–1982
(in current dollars)

Year	Per Capita Personal Income	Year	Per Capita Personal Income	Year	Per Capita Personal Income
1964	1,933	1970	3,129	1976	6,756
1965	2,091	1971	3,435	1977	7,352
1966	2,303	1972	3,839	1978	8,032
1967	2,482	1973	4,405	1979	8,902
1968	2,690	1974	5,116	1980	10,163
1969	2,943	1975	5,838	1981	11,810
				1982	12,839

Source: Statistics Canada, *National Income and Expenditure Accounts*, cat. no. 13-201.

In addition, we hear the terms "money income," "real income," and "psychic income." **Money income** is the amount a person receives in actual cash or cheques for wages, salaries, rents, interest, and dividends. **Real income** is what the money income will buy in goods and services; it is purchasing power. If a person's money income rises 5 percent in one year but the cost of purchases increases 8 percent on the average, then real income decreases about 3 percent. **Psychic income** is an intangible but highly important income factor related to comfortable climate, a satisfying neighbourhood, enjoyment of one's job, and so on. Some people prefer to take less real income so they can live in a part of the country that features a fine climate and recreation opportunities — greater psychic income.

On the basis of income, the Canadian market has grown considerably since the end of World War II. Total personal disposable income increased from $13,285 million in 1950 to $255,296 million in 1982, an increase of almost 2,000 percent in 32 years (see Table 4-5). From 1964 to 1982, per capita personal income increased from $1,933 to $12,839 (Table 4-6).

Income Distribution   To get full value from an analysis of income, marketing executives should carefully study the variations and trends in the distribution of income among regions and among population groups. Regional income data are particularly helpful in pinpointing the particular market to which a firm wishes to appeal. Income data on cities and even sections within cities may indicate the best locations for shopping centres and suburban branches of downtown stores.

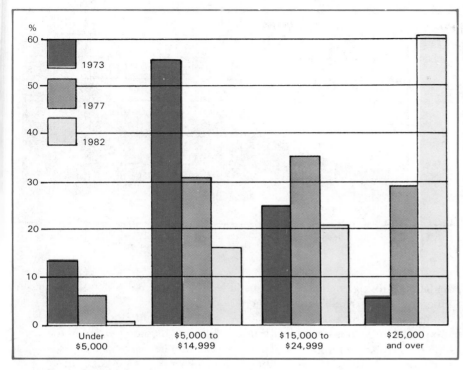

Figure 4-6
DISTRIBUTION OF
FAMILY INCOME,
1973–1982.

Source: Statistics Canada.

The income revolution that has been going on in Canada in recent decades has dramatically changed the profile of family income distribution.
Figure 4-6 shows the change that has taken place in the distribution of
family incomes in Canada since 1973. As recently as 1973, 14 percent of
Canadian families had annual incomes of less than $5,000. By 1982, that
percentage had dropped to below 2 percent. Even more dramatic is the
increase in the number of families in the higher income categories. The
percentage of Canadian families with annual incomes of $25,000 and more
has increased from about 6 percent in 1973 to more than 60 percent in
1982. The figures are, of course, expressed in current dollars. Adjustment
for inflation (as shown in Fig. 4-7) reveals that much of the increase in
family income has been illusory in that it has resulted from incomes keeping pace with or slightly ahead of inflation rates. In fact, there has been no
real growth in average family income in recent years (1980–1984) owing
to inflation.

Only the top 20 percent of Canadian household income groups were better off in 1984 than in 1980. The lower 80 percent experienced no growth
or a slight decline in real income during this period. The higher income
group is expected to continue to be the growth market for the next 10
years or so because of the increasing number of dual-income families, growth
in the professional occupations, the movement of older members of the

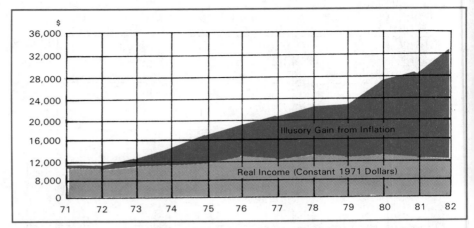

Source: Tomorrow's Customers 1981, Woods, Gordon, Toronto, April 1981, p. 11; and Statistics Canada.

Figure 4-7
AVERAGE FAMILY
INCOME ADJUSTED
FOR INFLATION,
1971–1982.

population into higher income groups (a legacy of the Baby Boom), and an increase in inherited income from parents.[12]

Annual incomes in excess of $50,000 are not uncommon today and are quite prevalent in households with more than one income earner. Much of the growth in the number of higher-income families in recent years is a result of the increase in the number of families with two incomes and of the fact that many professional wives are entering the labour force. The dual-income family constitutes an extremely lucrative new target market that marketers should cultivate.[13]

Marketing Significance of Income Data

The declining percentage of families in the poverty bracket, coupled with the sharp increases in the upper-income groups, presages an explosive growth in discretionary purchasing power. The level of discretionary income is of particular importance because as this type of income increases, so too does the demand for items that once were considered luxuries.

The middle-income market is a big and growing market, and it has forced many changes in marketing strategy. Many stores that once appealed to low-income groups are now "trading up" to the huge middle-income market by upgrading the quality of the products they carry and by offering additional services.

In spite of the considerable increase in disposable income and purchasing power in the past 25 years, many households are still in the low-income bracket or find their higher incomes inadequate to fulfil all their wants.

[12]Clarkson, Gordon, *Tomorrow's Customers in Canada*, 18th ed., 1984, pp. 18, 19.
[13]See Ronald D. Michman, "The Double Income Family: A New Target Market," *Business Horizons*, August 1980, pp. 31–37; and Walter Kiechel III, "Two-Income Families Will Reshape the Consumer Markets," *Fortune*, March 10, 1980, p. 110.

Furthermore, many customers are willing to forego services in order to get lower prices. One consequence of this market feature has been the development of self-service retail outlets, discount houses, and no-frills food stores.

We have noted above the dramatic increase during the 1970s in the number of working women. This demographic factor has had a tremendous impact on family income levels. This increase in two-income families has significant marketing and sociological implications. Dual incomes enable a family to offset the ravages of inflation. But, more than that, two incomes enable a family to buy within a short time the things that their parents worked years to acquire.

In recent years, a very large percentage of Canadian families have had to adapt to a new environment characterized by extreme economic hardship. Inflation, recession, and unemployment have had a profound effect and have caused consumers to modify their approach to the marketplace dramatically. Consumers cut back on discretionary purchases, became more self-reliant, bought used items, borrowed and shared with neighbours, and delayed replacing assets, in order to try to get by on reduced real income. The long-term effects of such modifications in consumer behaviour should not be ignored by marketers.[14]

How consumers' income is spent is a major market determinant for most products and services. Consequently, marketers need to study consumer spending patterns, as well as the distribution of consumer income. Table 4-7 shows personal expenditure on consumer goods and services for the period 1965–1982, in current dollars.

Expenditure Patterns

Relation to Population Distribution

In Table 4-8 the expenditure patterns for families and unattached individuals are presented in actual dollars and in percentages for the five regions of Canada. In all of the regions the average percentage expenditure on shelter was relatively consistent, ranging from 15.4 percent to 19.1 percent. On clothing, residents of British Columbia spend on average a smaller percentage of family income. Expenditures on household operation are marginally higher in Atlantic Canada, and transportation expenditure is least in Ontario. Food expenditure is highest in the Atlantic Provinces, accounting for 17.8 percent of total family expenditure, which may be contrasted with 14.0 percent in the Prairie Provinces and 14.3 percent in British Columbia.

The key question at this point is: Why should a marketing person study the population in such detail if (at least at first glance) there is considerable homogeneity among the various segments? The reasons are several. In the first place, homogeneity is not complete. Even among the five regions

---

[14]James G. Barnes and Lessey Sooklal, "The Changing Nature of Consumer Behavior: Monitoring the Impact of Inflation and Recession," *Business Quarterly*, Summer 1983, pp. 58–64.

Table 4-7   PERSONAL EXPENDITURE ON CONSUMER GOODS AND SERVICES IN CURRENT DOLLARS (millions of dollars)

	1965	1969	1974	1979	1982
Food, beverages and tobacco	8,097	10,471	17,762	30,864	42,282
Food and nonalcoholic beverages, (N-D)	5,885	7,445	12,936	22,966	30,618
Alcoholic beverages, (N-D)	1,252	1,742	3,027	4,816	7,241
Tobacco products, (N-D)	960	1,284	1,799	3,082	4,423
Clothing and footwear	2,855	3,908	6,412	10,667	13,227
Men's and boys' clothing, (S-D)	857	1,143	2,009	3,153	3,746
Women's and children's clothing, (S-D)	1,518	2,116	3,465	5,830	7,398
Footwear and repair, (S-D)	480	649	938	1,684	2,083
Gross rent, fuel and power	6,064	8,742	14,271	27,190	44,824
Gross imputed rent, (S)	3,211	4,699	7,536	14,590	25,064
Gross rent paid, (S)	1,472	2,289	3,727	6,684	10,437
Other lodgings, (S)	77	114	180	332	436
Electricity, (N-D)	459	668	1,160	2,802	4,077
Gas, (N-D)	194	248	334	900	2,067
Other fuels, (N-D)	651	724	1,334	1,882	2,743
Furniture, furnishings, household equipment and operation	3,426	4,658	8,652	14,306	17,247
Furniture, carpets and other floor coverings, (D)	719	1,002	1,930	3,020	3,267
Household appliances, (D)	582	833	1,474	2,399	2,820
Semi-durable household furnishings, (S-D)	1,126	1,535	3,278	5,307	6,320
Nondurable household supplies, (N-D)	466	646	1,124	2,097	2,883
Laundry and dry cleaning, (S)	227	283	311	490	667
Domestic services, (S)	220	267	369	938	864
Other household services, (S)	86	92	166	355	426
Medical care and health services	1,516	1,912	2,466	4,555	7,192
Medical care, (S)	790	903	731	1,485	2,381
Hospital care and the like, (S)	225	310	396	735	1,261
Other medical care expenses, (S)	40	41	209	296	413
Drugs and sundries, (N-D)	416	658	1,130	2,039	3,137
Transportation and communication	5,114	6,863	12,161	22,380	30,113
New and used (net) automobiles, (D)	2,223	2,727	4,223	7,551	7,494
Repairs and parts, (D)	618	920	1,692	3,122	3,881
Gasoline, oil and grease (N-D)	934	1,262	2,627	4,605	8,136
Other auto related services, (S)	310	432	794	1,497	2,385
Purchased transportation, (S)	567	830	1,593	3,073	4,490
Communications, (S)	462	692	1,232	2,532	3,727
Recreation, entertainment, education and cultural services	2,400	4,104	8,655	15,349	21,012
Recreation, sporting and camping equipment, (D)	943	1,493	3,820	6,509	8,335
Books, newspapers and magazines, (S-D)	470	674	918	1,680	2,214
Recreational services, (S)	445	721	1,615	3,025	4,574
Educational and cultural services (S)	542	1,216	2,302	4,135	5,889

Table 4-7 — Continued

	1965	1969	1974	1979	1982
Personal goods and services (S)	4,460	6,683	12,870	24,403	33,007
Jewellery, watches and repairs, (S-D)	200	309	576	1,177	1,327
Toilet articles, cosmetics, (N-D)	264	396	747	1,324	1,906
Personal care, (S)	333	499	681	1,123	1,537
Expenditure on restaurants and					
hotels, (S)	1,854	2,582	5,354	10,341	13,096
Financial, legal and other services, (S)	1,396	2,293	3,899	7,285	10,546
Operating expenses of nonprofit					
organizations, (S)	393	604	1,613	3,153	4,595
Net expenditure abroad, (S)	15	151	139	775	897
Total	33,947	47,492	83,388	150,489	209,801
Durable goods	5,085	6,975	13,139	22,601	25,797
Semidurable goods	4,671	6,426	11,184	18,831	23,088
Nondurable goods	11,526	15,073	26,218	46,513	67,231
Services	12,665	19,018	32,847	62,544	93,685

Note: D = durable goods   S-D = semidurable goods   N-D = nondurable goods   S = service
Source: Statistics Canada, *National Income and Expenditure Accounts*, cat. no. 13-201.

examined in Table 4-8, there are substantial differences in the food and clothing categories. Second, the simple percentages shown in Table 4-8 can be misleading. A variance range of 1 or 2 percent may be quite substantial when the absolute percentage across cities for the expenditure category being examined is 5 or 6 percent. Based upon the absolute percentages, the variation becomes 20 or 40 percent. Thus, for each product or service grouping, the variation is considerable if the variation in percentage terms between the cities with the highest and lowest figures is expressed as a percentage of the lowest city's figure. Thirdly, similarity exists only when we aggregate broad product categories. A detailed breakdown of each individual category shows large internal variations. Finally, differences exist among population segments with respect to buying motives and habits. Though families in the Atlantic Provinces and Quebec may spend approximately the same share of their annual income on clothing, the type of clothes they buy and the appeals to which they respond may be polar opposites. Also, the differences in average family income between the regions may mean that the *actual amounts* spent are quite different. For example, although percentages are similar, the average family expenditure on clothing in Quebec in 1982 was $1,694, while in the Atlantic Provinces the figure was $1,523. Hence a much deeper probing of various characteristics is demanded of the marketer.

Relation to Stage of Family Life Cycle

Consumer expenditure patterns are influenced considerably by the life-cycle stage a family is in. Marketing people surely need to be aware of the striking contrasts in spending patterns between, say, people who are married with very young children and older people whose children have grown

Table 4-8 SUMMARY OF FAMILY EXPENDITURE BY REGION, CANADA, 1982, FOR ALL FAMILIES AND UNATTACHED INDIVIDUALS

	Canada	Atlantic Provinces	Quebec	Ontario	Prairie Provinces	British Columbia
Family Characteristics						
Number of Families in Sample	10,952	2,159	2,148	2,583	2,702	1,360
Estimated Number of Families	8,421,130	690,590	2,209,480	3,000,610	1,479,260	1,041,190
Average						
Family size	2.72	3.10	2.77	2.71	2.66	2.51
Number of children under 5 years	.19	.23	.21	.18	.19	.17
Number of children 5 to 15 years	.47	.64	.44	.46	.50	.44
Number of adults 16 and 17 years	.09	.13	.10	.09	.08	.06
Number of adults 18 to 64 years	1.71	1.79	1.80	1.72	1.63	1.55
Number of adults 65 years and over	.26	.31	.23	.26	.25	.29
Number of full-time earners	.76	.63	.71	.83	.82	.63
Age of head	45.9	47.3	45.4	46.3	44.9	46.3
Income before tax	29,087.8	23,964.5	26,801.2	30,498.2	31,120.1	30,386.0
Other money receipts	536.8	399.9	407.9	537.9	618.5	781.6
Net change in assets & liabilities	2,415.8	1,945.0	1,436.5	2,773.8	3,131.2	2,758.6
Percentage						
Homeowners	61.7	73.8	51.9	63.7	65.2	63.5
Automobile or truck owners	79.2	78.0	73.0	80.0	84.4	83.3
Married couple family	66.2	70.1	66.7	66.4	65.2	63.2
With wife employed full-time	16.7	13.6	14.0	19.6	18.7	13.7
Average Dollar Expenditure						
Food	4,131.1	3,988.9	4,211.6	4,201.6	3,987.2	4,055.9
Shelter	4,742.0	3,458.1	4,206.4	5,011.6	5,126.6	5,406.6
Principal accommodation	4,473.6	3,234.7	3,958.5	4,710.1	4,861.5	5,155.5
rented	1,383.1	717.4	1,355.0	1,279.7	1,386.2	1,546.7
owned	2,228.0	1,373.0	1,730.1	2,477.8	2,492.1	2,756.6
water, fuel and electricity	940.5	1,144.3	873.3	952.6	983.2	852.2
Other accommodation	268.4	223.3	247.9	301.5	265.1	251.1
Household Operation	1,177.1	1,138.4	1,051.6	1,266.6	1,183.4	1,202.2
Household Furnishings and Equipment	972.0	817.1	855.7	1,004.0	1,086.7	1,066.4
Household furnishings	487.4	383.6	409.9	514.8	551.4	550.8
Household equipment	428.4	395.5	389.9	426.2	483.8	459.5
Services	56.2	37.9	55.9	63.0	51.6	56.1
Clothing	1,650.6	1,523.1	1,694.4	1,655.1	1,750.4	1,487.3
Transportation	3,270.6	2,982.8	3,071.2	3,290.7	3,563.0	3,411.5
Private transportation	2,941.8	2,767.3	2,808.6	2,915.5	3,223.5	3,015.6
Public transportation	328.8	215.5	262.7	375.1	339.6	395.8

Health Care	552.8	522.8	583.2	465.1	392.5	522.2
Personal Care	455.2	492.9	514.0	484.6	459.5	490.8
Recreation	1,775.7	1,468.7	1,232.5	1,011.4	967.7	1,261.4
Reading Materials & Other Printed Matter	154.9	149.2	156.9	177.2	124.0	157.9
Education	192.7	189.9	209.7	168.0	150.6	188.3
Tobacco Products and Alcoholic Beverages	828.8	824.5	950.1	905.4	838.9	892.2
Miscellaneous	888.9	810.4	836.6	726.7	676.5	796.5
Total Current Consumption	21,478.9	21,155.7	20,912.7	19,029.2	17,518.1	20,252.8
Personal Taxes	4,917.9	5,072.4	5,039.2	4,866.0	3,235.1	4,836.6
Security	1,070.6	1,178.7	1,161.6	1,253.3	996.1	1,163.8
Gifts and Contributions	908.0	974.4	973.7	467.0	684.5	809.0
TOTAL EXPENDITURE	28,375.3	28,381.1	28,087.1	25,615.5	22,433.8	27,062.3

Percentage Distribution

Food	14.3	14.0	15.0	16.4	17.8	15.3
Shelter	19.1	18.1	17.8	16.4	15.4	17.5
Principal Accommodation	18.2	17.1	16.8	15.5	14.4	16.5
rented	5.5	4.9	4.6	5.3	3.2	4.8
owned	9.7	8.8	8.8	6.8	6.1	8.2
water, fuel and electricity	3.0	3.5	3.4	3.4	5.1	3.5
Other accommodation	.9	.9	1.1	1.0	1.0	1.0
Household Operation	4.2	4.2	4.5	4.1	5.1	4.3
Household Furnishings and Equipment	3.8	3.8	3.6	3.3	3.6	3.6
Household Furnishings	1.9	1.9	1.8	1.6	1.7	1.8
Household Equipment	1.6	1.7	1.5	1.5	1.8	1.6
Services	.2	.2	.2	.2	.2	.2
Clothing	5.2	6.2	5.9	6.6	6.8	6.1
Transportation	12.0	12.6	11.7	12.0	13.3	12.1
Private Transportation	10.6	11.4	10.4	11.0	12.3	10.9
Public Transportation	1.4	1.2	1.3	1.0	1.0	1.2
Health Care	1.9	1.8	2.1	1.8	1.7	1.9
Personal Care	1.6	1.7	1.8	1.9	2.0	1.8
Recreation	6.3	5.2	4.4	3.9	4.3	4.7
Reading Materials & Other Printed Matter	.5	.5	.6	.7	.6	.6
Education	.7	.7	.7	.7	.7	.7
Tobacco Products and Alcoholic Beverages	2.9	2.9	3.4	3.5	3.7	3.3
Miscellaneous	3.1	2.9	3.0	2.8	3.0	2.9
Total Current Consumption	75.7	74.5	74.5	74.3	78.1	74.8
Personal Taxes	17.3	17.9	17.9	19.0	14.4	17.9
Security	3.8	4.2	4.1	4.9	4.4	4.3
Gifts and Contributions	3.2	3.4	3.5	1.8	3.1	3.0
TOTAL	100.0	100.0	100.0	100.0	100.0	100.0

and left home. Table 4-9 summarizes spending patterns for families at various stages of the family life cycle. Young married couples with no children typically devote large shares of their income to clothing, autos, and recreation. When children start arriving, expenditure patterns shift as many young families buy and furnish a home. Families with teenagers find larger portions of the budget going for food, clothing, and educational needs. Families in the empty-nest stage, especially when the head is still in the labour force, are attractive to marketers because typically these families have more discretionary buying power.

Table 4-9   BEHAVIOURAL INFLUENCES AND BUYING PATTERNS, BY FAMILY LIFE-CYCLE STAGE

Bachelor Stage; Young Single People Not Living at Home	Newly Married Couples; Young, No Children	Full Nest 1; Youngest Child under 6
Few financial burdens. Fashion opinion leaders. Recreation-oriented. Buy: Basic kitchen equipment, basic furniture, cars, equipment for the mating game, vacations.	Better off financially than they will be in near future. Highest purchase rate and highest average purchase of durables. Buy: Cars, refrigerators, stoves, sensible and durable furniture, vacations.	Home purchasing at peak. Liquid assets low. Some wives work. Dissatisfied with financial position and amount of money saved. Interested in new products. Like advertised products. Buy: Washers, dryers, TV sets, baby food, chest rubs and cough medicine, vitamins, dolls, wagons, sleds, skates.

Full Nest II; Youngest Child 6 or Over	Full Nest III; Older Married Couples with Dependent Children	Empty Nest I; Older Married Couples, No Children Living with Them, Head in Labour Force
Financial position better. Many wives work. Less influenced by advertising. Buy larger-sized packages, multiple-unit deals. Buy: Many foods, cleaning materials, bicycles, music lessons, pianos.	Financial position still better. Many wives work. Some children get jobs. Hard to influence with advertising. High average purchase of durables. Buy: New, more tasteful furniture, auto travel, nonnecessary appliances, boats, dental services, magazines.	Home ownership at peak. Most satisfied with financial position and money saved. Interested in travel, recreation, self-education. Make gifts and contributions. Not interested in new products. Buy: Vacations, luxuries, home improvements.

Empty Nest II; Older Married Couples, No Children Living at Home, Head Retired	Solitary Survivor, in Labour Force	Solitary Survivor, Retired
Drastic cut in income. Keep home. Buy: Medical appliances, medical care, products that aid health, sleep, and digestion.	Income still good, but likely to sell home.	Same medical and product needs as other retired group; drastic cut in income. Special need for attention, affection, and security.

Source: William D. Wells and George Gubar, "Life Cycle Concept in Marketing Research," *Journal of Marketing Research*, November 1966, p. 362.

Relation to Income Distribution

The size of a family income is probably an obvious determinant of how that family spends its income. Consequently, marketers should analyse the expenditure patterns of the various income classes (under $10,000, $10,000 to $14,999, and so on). For each income group, Table 4-10 shows average amounts and percentages of total income spent on each of the major categories of products and services. Despite some general similarity of expenditure patterns, significant differences are observable in certain categories of goods and services and we can safely conclude that income distribution is a major determinant of these differences.

Some of the differences that might be observed from studies on consumer expenditure and from the data presented in Table 4-10 are summarized below. These findings suggest the type of information that marketers might get from analyses of spending patterns by income groups.

1. There is a high degree of uniformity in expenditure patterns of *middle-income* spending units. As we shall note in Chapter 5, however, social-class structure is a much more meaningful criterion for determining expenditure patterns.

2. For each product category, there is a considerable *absolute* increase in dollars spent as income rises (or, more correctly, as we compare one income group with a higher income group). In other words, people in a given income bracket spend significantly more *dollars* in each product category than their less well-off neighbours, even though the lower-income households devote a larger *percentage* of their total expenditures to the given product class. Marketers are probably more concerned with the total *dollars* available from each income group than with the *percentage* share of total expenditures.

3. In each successively higher income group, the amount spent for food declines as a percentage of total expenditures.

4. The percentage of expenditures devoted to the total of housing (shelter) and household operation declines rapidly as incomes increase in the lower- and middle-income brackets.

5. Amounts spent for personal, medical, and health care very gradually decrease as a percentage of total expenditures as incomes increase.

6. The share of expenditures going for transportation (primarily automobile purchase and operation) tends to increase as incomes increase in the low- and middle-income groups. The proportion levels off and drops a bit in the higher-income brackets.

7. The percentage of total expenditures going to clothing tends to be fairly stable beyond the $10,000 annual income level, until a slight increase is noted among the very highest income earners.

Average total family expenditure in Canada rose from $18,700 in 1978 to more than $27,000 in 1982; an average increase of 9.6 percent annually. Over this period, Canadians spent a larger proportion of their income on housing and less on food and clothing.

Table 4-10   SUMMARY OF FAMILY EXPENDITURE, BY FAMILY INCOME GROUP, CANADA, 1982,

	Canada	Under $10,000	$10,000– $14,999	$15,000– $19,999
Family Characteristics				
Number of Families in Sample	10,952	1,457	1,300	1,195
Estimated Number of Families	8,421,130	1,182,190	978,040	935,850
Average				
Family size	2.72	1.49	2.15	2.47
Number of children under 5 years	.19	.07	.13	.20
Number of children 5 to 15 years	.47	.12	.28	.39
Number of adults 16 and 17 years	.09	.02	.04	.10
Number of adults 18 to 64 years	1.71	.72	1.05	1.54
Number of adults 65 years and over	.26	.55	.64	.25
Number of full-time earners	.76	.06	.21	.52
Age of head	45.9	57.8	52.6	44.4
Income before tax	29,087.8	6,777.4	12,461.8	17,497.6
Other money receipts	536.8	409.9	406.6	444.9
Net change in assets & liabilities	2,415.8	596.5-	47.3-	86.0
Percentage				
Homeowners	61.7	35.6	50.4	48.7
Automobile or truck owners	79.2	33.3	62.7	78.8
Married couple family	66.2	19.7	52.0	58.2
With wife employed full-time	16.7	.7	.7	6.4
Average Dollar Expenditure				
Food	4,131.1	1,891.6	2,733.5	3,321.3
Shelter	4,742.0	2,325.1	3,095.3	3,686.6
Principal accommodation	4,473.6	301.4	3,019.6	3,552.8
rented	1,305.1	1,335.4	1,390.0	1,714.0
owned	2,228.0	439.3	854.9	1,096.1
water, fuel and electricity	940.5	526.7	774.8	742.7
Other accommodation	268.4	23.7	75.7	133.8
Household Operation	1,177.1	496.3	744.9	917.4
Household Furnishings and Equipment	972.0	249.3	487.9	651.2
Household furnishings	487.4	123.0	223.7	315.6
Household equipment	428.4	109.9	228.3	299.0
Services	56.2	16.4	35.8	36.6
Clothing	1,650.6	438.6	795.6	1,149.0
Transportation	3,270.6	745.2	1,606.7	2,473.1
Private transportation	2,941.8	593.1	1,380.5	2,232.4
Public transportation	328.8	152.2	226.2	240.2
Health Care	522.2	187.6	308.1	428.8
Personal Care	490.8	193.8	286.8	400.7
Recreation	1,261.4	244.0	525.7	750.9
Reading Materials & Other Printed Matter	157.9	64.6	101.6	119.0
Education	188.3	53.3	78.2	86.2
Tobacco Products and Alcoholic Beverages	892.2	341.1	559.8	756.3
Miscellaneous	796.5	220.9	352.4	516.6
Total Current Consumption	20,252.8	7,451.6	11,676.5	15,257.1
Personal Taxes	4,836.6	22.0	579.2	1,590.3
Security	1,163.8	69.3	240.9	591.1
Gifts and Contributions	809.0	253.7	496.9	537.1
TOTAL EXPENDITURE	27,062.3	7,796.5	12,993.5	17,975.6

FOR ALL FAMILIES AND UNATTACHED INDIVIDUALS

$20,000–$24,999	$25,000–$29,999	$30,000–$34,999	$35,000–$39,999	$40,000–$49,999	$50,000 and over
1,237	1,205	1,111	861	1,233	1,353
981,330	921,250	831,350	654,400	927,890	1,008,850
2.69	2.93	3.17	3.26	3.42	3.44
.23	.25	.28	.25	.22	.15
.48	.53	.67	.64	.71	.60
.07	.11	.12	.12	.13	.14
1.70	1.92	1.99	2.15	2.29	2.44
.21	.12	.12	.10	.07	.12
.66	.88	.96	1.09	1.21	1.52
43.0	41.0	40.5	42.6	41.6	44.7
22,498.1	27,424.4	32,351.1	37,397.2	44,510.3	67,765.8
399.4	419.5	670.7	654.9	621.5	872.6
703.5	1,457.4	2,237.9	3,532.1	4,259.8	10,762.3
54.9	63.2	68.4	74.4	82.7	87.1
86.7	89.8	92.6	95.2	96.1	95.3
67.3	76.3	78.0	86.3	88.0	88.7
9.8	16.7	20.3	26.0	32.2	44.2
3,797.3	4,311.5	4,760.4	5,043.0	5,598.4	6,561.9
4,147.3	4,830.8	5,324.8	5,668.8	6,440.9	8,002.7
3,995.1	4,603.2	5,046.0	5,309.6	6,053.6	7,162.3
1,587.5	1,423.3	1,379.0	1,141.0	938.0	808.2
1,564.1	2,236.8	2,660.2	3,068.8	3,881.6	4,920.7
843.5	943.2	1,006.8	1,099.7	1,234.0	1,433.4
152.2	227.6	278.8	359.2	387.3	840.4
1,006.1	1,156.7	1,334.8	1,442.8	1,586.0	2,141.2
728.2	961.8	1,105.8	1,289.8	1,597.9	1,940.1
349.6	468.2	524.0	640.1	824.8	1,041.6
330.7	452.6	521.4	585.1	672.5	785.5
48.0	41.0	60.4	64.7	100.6	113.0
1,276.7	1,556.8	1,917.0	2,175.0	2,583.2	3,397.0
3,147.6	3,377.5	3,571.4	4,468.2	4,710.0	6,256.4
2,896.1	3,036.8	3,234.4	4,131.7	4,291.3	5,569.2
251.5	340.7	337.0	336.4	418.7	687.2
477.2	541.9	582.4	616.9	718.8	942.3
434.4	498.7	556.4	614.6	698.9	842.5
955.7	1,176.5	1,487.9	1,519.6	1,887.8	3,085.1
128.4	156.9	173.7	184.2	216.5	303.8
143.8	134.2	196.1	216.0	307.9	506.6
873.6	993.9	1,079.5	1,046.5	1,233.7	1,343.0
690.6	778.1	1,050.4	1,087.8	1,174.6	1,535.3
17,806.8	20,475.3	23,140.6	25,373.2	28,754.6	36,857.8
2,824.0	4,081.0	5,317.7	6,554.2	8,323.5	15,547.5
888.8	1,174.8	1,397.4	1,659.4	2,009.5	2,838.3
619.3	668.4	858.9	859.9	1,223.6	1,872.2
22,138.9	26,399.4	30,714.6	34,446.7	40,311.1	57,115.7

Table 4-10   SUMMARY OF FAMILY EXPENDITURE, BY FAMILY INCOME GROUP, CANADA, 1982,

	Canada	Under $10,000	$10,000–$14,999	$15,000–$19,999
Percentage Distribution				
Food	15.3	24.3	21.0	18.5
Shelter	17.5	29.8	23.8	20.5
Principal Accommodation	16.5	29.5	23.2	19.8
rented	4.8	17.1	10.7	9.5
owned	8.2	5.6	6.6	6.1
water, fuel and electricity	3.5	6.8	6.0	4.1
Other accommodation	1.0	.3	.6	.7
Household Operation	4.3	6.4	5.7	5.1
Household Furnishings and Equipment	3.6	3.2	3.8	3.6
Household Furnishings	1.8	1.6	1.7	1.8
Household Equipment	1.6	1.4	1.8	1.7
Services	.2	.2	.3	.2
Clothing	6.1	5.6	6.1	6.4
Transportation	12.1	9.6	12.4	13.8
Private Transportation	10.9	7.6	10.6	12.4
Public Transportation	1.2	2.0	1.7	1.3
Health Care	1.9	2.4	2.4	2.4
Personal Care	1.8	2.5	2.2	2.2
Recreation	4.7	3.1	4.0	4.2
Reading Materials & Other Printed Matter	.6	.8	.8	.7
Education	.7	.7	.6	.5
Tobacco Products and Alcoholic Beverages	3.3	4.4	4.3	4.2
Miscellaneous	2.9	2.8	2.7	2.9
Total Current Consumption	74.8	95.6	89.9	84.9
Personal Taxes	17.9	.3	4.5	8.8
Security	4.3	.9	1.9	3.3
Gifts and Contributions	3.0	3.3	3.8	3.0
TOTAL	100.0	100.0	100.0	100.0

In the future, changing expenditure patterns will likely see an increasing percentage of total income being spent on nonessential items in the following growth areas:

- luxury items, such as jewellery and recreational equipment
- home entertainment products, swimming pools, home computers
- higher-priced food items, such as delicatessen poducts
- high-fashion clothing
- vacations to exotic destinations
- investment services and counselling
- home-based fitness products[15]

[15]Clarkson, Gordon, *Tomorrow's Customers in Canada*, 18th ed., 1984, p. 19.

FOR ALL FAMILIES AND UNATTACHED INDIVIDUALS — Continued

$20,000– $24,999	$25,000– $29,999	$30,000– $34,999	$35,000– $39,999	$40,000– $49,999	$50,000 and over
17.2	16.3	15.5	14.6	13.9	11.5
18.7	18.3	17.3	16.5	16.0	14.0
18.0	17.4	16.4	15.4	15.0	12.5
7.2	5.4	4.5	3.3	2.3	1.4
7.1	8.5	8.7	8.9	9.6	8.6
3.8	3.6	3.3	3.2	3.1	2.5
.7	.9	.9	1.0	1.0	1.5
4.5	4.4	4.3	4.2	3.9	3.7
3.3	3.6	3.6	3.7	4.0	3.4
1.6	1.8	1.7	1.9	2.0	1.8
1.5	1.7	1.7	1.7	1.7	1.4
.2	.2	.2	.2	.2	.2
5.8	5.9	6.2	6.3	6.4	5.9
14.2	12.8	11.6	13.0	11.7	11.0
13.1	11.5	10.5	12.0	10.6	9.8
1.1	1.3	1.1	1.0	1.0	1.2
2.2	2.1	1.9	1.8	1.8	1.6
2.0	1.9	1.8	1.8	1.7	1.5
4.3	4.5	4.8	4.4	4.7	5.4
.6	.6	.6	.5	.5	.5
.6	.5	.6	.6	.8	.9
3.9	3.8	3.5	3.0	3.1	2.4
3.1	2.9	3.4	3.2	2.9	2.7
80.4	77.6	75.3	73.7	71.3	64.5
12.8	15.5	17.3	19.0	20.6	27.2
4.0	4.4	4.5	4.8	5.0	5.0
2.8	2.5	2.8	2.5	3.0	3.3
100.0	100.0	100.0	100.0	100.0	100.0

Generalizations such as these provide a broad background against which marketing executives can analyse the market for their particular product or service. People with needs to satisfy and money to spend, however, must be *willing* to spend before we can say a market exists. Consequently, in the next two chapters we shall look into consumer motivation and buying behaviour — the "willingness to buy" factor in our definition of a market.

SUMMARY

A sound marketing program starts with the identification and analysis of the market for a product or service. A market is people with money to spend and the willingness to spend it. For most products, the total market is too broad and heterogeneous for a strategy of market aggregation — that is, developing one product and one marketing program to reach the entire market. A more effective strategy is market segmentation, in which the total market is viewed as several smaller but more uniform submarkets.

As a first step, the market is divided into the ultimate-consumer and industrial-user submarkets. There are then several bases for further segmenting the consumer submarket.

The makeup of the population — its distribution and composition — has a major effect on marketing and market segmentation. For some products it is useful to segment population on a regional basis. Another useful division is by urban, suburban, and rural segments. In this context, the bulk of the population is concentrated in Census Metropolitan Areas. Moreover, these areas are expanding and joining together in several parts of the country.

The major age groups of the population make up another significant basis for market segmentation — young adults, teenagers, the over-65 group, and so on. The stage of the family life cycle influences the market for many products. Other demographic bases for segmentation include occupation, race, religion, and national origin.

Consumer income — especially disposable income and discretionary income — are meaningul measures of buying power and market potential. The distribution of income affects the market for many products. Income distribution has shifted considerably during the past 20 years. Today a much greater percentage of families are in the over $25,000 bracket and a much smaller percentage are in the under $15,000 category. A family's income level and life-cycle stage are partial determinants of its spending patterns.

KEY TERMS AND CONCEPTS

QUESTIONS AND PROBLEMS

1. What benefits can a company expect from segmenting its market?

2. Give several examples of products whose market demand would be particularly affected by each of the following population factors:
   a. Regional distribution
   b. Marital status
   c. Sex
   d. Age
   e. Urban, rural distribution

3. Cite some regional differences in product preferences caused by factors other than climate.

4. Suppose you are marketing automobiles. How is your marketing mix likely to differ when marketing to each of the following market segments?
   a. High-school students
   b. Husbands
   c. Blue-collar workers
   d. Homemakers
   e. Young single adults

5. What users' benefits would you stress in advertising each of the following three products to each of the three markets?

   Product
   a. Stereo record player
   b. Toothpaste
   c. 10-day Caribbean cruise

   Market
   a. School teachers
   b. Retired people
   c. Working women

6. Using the demographic and income segmentation bases discussed in this chapter, describe the segment likely to be the best market for:
   a. Skis
   b. Good French wines
   c. Power hand tools
   d. Birthday cards
   e. Outdoor barbecue grills

7. List three of the major population trends noted in this chapter (for instance, a growing segment of the population is over 65 years of age). Then carefully explain how *each* of the following types of retail stores might be affected by *each* of the trends:
   a. Supermarket
   b. Sporting-goods store
   c. Drugstore
   d. Restaurant

8. In what ways has the rise in disposable personal income since 1950 influenced the marketing programs of a typical department store? A supermarket?

9. Is psychic income a concept applicable to groups or only to an individual? Can psychic income be measured in a quantitative manner?

10. Give examples of products whose demand is substantially influenced by changes in discretionary purchasing power.

11. Describe some of the effects that (*a*) inflation and (*b*) a recession have on consumers' spending patterns. What can marketers do to adjust to these situations?

Chapter
5

Cultural and Social-Group Influences on Buyer Behaviour

CHAPTER GOALS

In Chapter 4 we discussed the population and buying-power (income) components of a market. In this chapter we consider consumers' willingness to buy, as influenced by their motivation, perception, and social environment. After studying the chapter, you should understand:

1. *The importance (and difficulty) of understanding consumer behaviour*
2. *The roles of motivation and perception in consumer behaviour*
3. *Culture as an influence on perceptions*
4. *The influence of social classes on buyer behaviour*
5. *The effects of small reference groups on buyer behaviour*
6. *Family buying behaviour*
7. *The diffusion of innovation*

In the course of doing the family's weekly grocery shopping at a local supermarket on a Friday afternoon, a homemaker selects a 450-gram loaf of whole wheat Wonder Bread. To the casual observer—and perhaps even to the homemaker—this may be a simple, routine purchase. Yet this seemingly simple buying action is the result of decisions made on several issues. Why purchase Wonder Bread instead of another brand? Why whole wheat bread instead of rye or white? Why shop at that particular store, and why on a Friday instead of some other day? In this and the next chapter, we'll try to shed some light on consumer behaviour to help explain buying decisions.

An understanding of customer buying behaviour is critically important to the success of the marketing system in any organization — business or nonbusiness. In Chapter 2 we saw that a major stage in the strategic marketing planning process is to develop a marketing mix that will reach and satisfy our target markets. Now, before designing that marketing mix, we need to know as much as possible about the buying behaviour of the customers in these markets.

We have reasonably good quantitative data on the number of people living in each geographic region: how many are high-school graduates, what their incomes are, and so on. For some products (snow shovels, oil filters), demographic and economic factors alone may explain why a consumer bought the product. Most consumer purchases, however, are also likely to be influenced by psychological or sociological factors. That is, demographic and economic factors alone do not satisfactorily explain some variations in personal buying behaviour. These factors alone cannot account for the difference between the person who loves to cook and the one who does not, or for brand preferences for soft drinks, when in blindfold tests consumers cannot tell one brand from another.

IMPORTANCE AND DIFFICULTY OF UNDER-STANDING CONSUMER BEHAVIOUR

We know very little about what goes on in a buyer's mind before, during, and after a purchase. Sometimes the explanation for buyers' behaviour is not even discernible to the buyers themselves. To illustrate, buying motives may be grouped on three different levels depending upon the consumers' awareness of them and their willingness to divulge them. At one level, buyers recognize, and are quite willing to talk about, their motives for buying certain products. At a second level, they are aware of their reasons for buying but will not admit them to others. (A family may buy a backyard swimming pool because they feel it adds to their social position in the neighbourhood, or a person may buy an expensive coat to keep up with his or her peer group. But when questioned about their motives, they offer other reasons that they think will be more socially acceptable.) The most difficult motives to uncover are those at the *third* level, where even the buyers themselves do not know the real factors motivating their buying actions.

A purchase is rarely the result of a single motive. Furthermore, various motives may conflict with one another. In buying new clothes, a consumer may want to (1) please his or her spouse, (2) be admired (or possibly envied) as a fashion leader by other people in his or her social circle, and (3) strive for economy. To do all these things in one purchase is truly a difficult assignment. And the behaviour of a particular buyer may change as individual motives become relatively more or less important. Buyer behaviour also changes over a period of time because of changes in income, changes in life-cycle stage, and other factors.

If we add to this complexity the countless variations occurring because each consumer has a unique personality, our task of understanding consumer behaviour may seem an impossible dream. Yet try we must, because an understanding of buyer behaviour is critical to the success of a marketing program. In the face of all the individuality and complexity, marketers must search for the behavioural threads that are common to each market segment. Then they can appeal to a wide group with one marketing program. Fortunately, marketing people, working with behavioural scientists, have been able to develop some generalizations about what influences consumer buying behaviour.

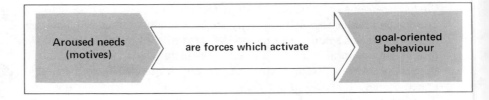

Motivation

To understand why consumers behave as they do, we must first ask why a person acts at all. The answer is, "Because he or she is motivated." That is, all behaviour starts with motivation. A **motive** (or drive) is a stimulated need that an individual seeks to satisfy. Thus hunger, a need for security, and a desire for prestige are examples of motives.

In discussing the behavioural forces that influence consumer buying activity, our model will be as follows: One or more motives within a person trigger behaviour toward a goal that is expected to bring satisfaction.

It is important to note that need must be *aroused* or *stimulated* before it becomes a motive. People sometimes have needs that are latent and therefore do not activate behaviour because these needs are not sufficiently intense. That is, they have not been aroused. The source of this arousal may be internal (we get hungry) or environmental (we see an ad for food). Or just thinking about a need (food) may cause arousal of that need (hunger).

No single classification of motives is generally accepted by psychologists, simply because we do not know enough about human motivation. However, psychologists generally do agree that motives can be grouped into two broad categories. They are (1) aroused **biogenic needs** (such as the needs for food and bodily comfort), which arise from *physiological* states of tension, and (2) aroused **psychogenic needs**, which arise from *psychological* states of tension. Through the years, marketers have used such dual classifications of motives as instinctive versus learned, emotional versus rational, and primary versus selective (reasons for buying a *type* of product versus reasons for buying a certain *brand* of that product).

A. H. Maslow has formulated a useful theory of motivation. He calls it a "holistic-dynamic" theory because it fuses the points of view of different schools of psychological thought. It also comforms to known clinical, observational, and experimental facts.[1] Maslow identified a hierarchy of five levels of needs, arrayed in the order in which a person seeks to gratify them. This hierarchy is shown in Fig. 5-1.

Maslow contended that people remain at one level until all their needs at that level are satisfied. Then new needs emerge on the next higher level. To illustrate, as long as a person is hungry or thirsty, the physiological (biogenic) needs dominate. Once they have been satisfied, the needs in the safety category become important. When safety needs have been largely gratified, new (and higher-level) needs arise, and so on.

---

[1] A. H. Maslow, *Motivation and Personality*, Harper & Row, Publishers, Inc., New York, 1954, pp. 80–106.

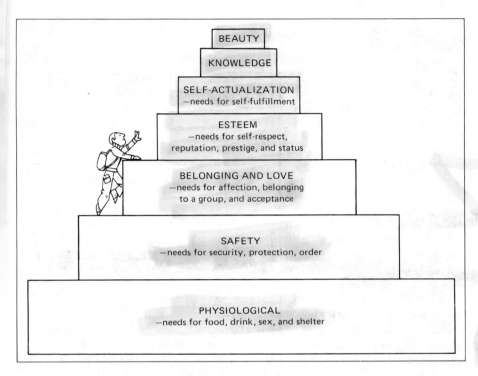

Figure 5-1
MASLOW'S
HIERARCHY
OF NEEDS.

For the relatively few people who move through all five levels, even to fulfilling a need for self-actualization, Maslow identified two additional classes of cognitive needs:

- The need to know and understand
- The need for aesthetic satisfaction (beauty)

Maslow recognized that in real life there is more flexibility than his model seems to imply. Actually, a normal person is most likely to be working toward need satisfaction on several levels at the same time. And rarely are all needs on a given level ever fully satisfied.

While the Maslow construct has much to offer us, it still leaves some unanswered questions and disagreements. For one thing, there is no consideration of multiple motives for the same behaviour. Thus, a teacher may go on a ship's cruise to better his or her knowledge of foreign countries, to meet new people, and to rest his or her frazzled nerves. Other problems not fitting our model are (1) identical behaviour by several people resulting from quite different motives, and (2) quite different behaviour resulting from identical motives.

A motive is an aroused need. It, in turn, acts as a force that *activates* behaviour intended to satisfy that aroused need. But what *influences* or *shapes* this behaviour? What determines the direction or path this behaviour takes? The answer is our *perceptions* (see Fig. 5-2). We may define

Perception

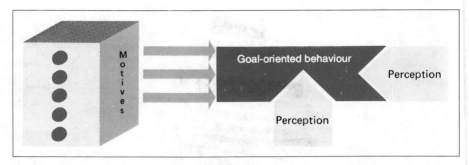

Figure 5-2
AROUSED
NEEDS (MOTIVES)
ACTIVATE
BEHAVIOUR,
WHICH IS SHAPED
BY PERCEPTIONS.

perception as the meaning we attribute, on the basis of past experiences, to stimuli as received through our five senses. Our perceptions, in turn, are shaped by three sets of influences: (1) the physical characteristics of the stimuli, (2) the relation of the stimuli to their surroundings, and (3) conditions within ourselves.

We perceive (that is, we attribute meaning to) the shape, colour, sound, feel, smell, and taste of stimuli. Our behaviour is then influenced by these physical perceptions. Marketers must recognize, however, that people are exposed to a tremendously large number of stimuli. Thus, to gain a consumer's attention, a marketer must provide something special as stimuli. This is the principle behind the use of large ads or the use of colour in a sea of black-and-white ads (or just the opposite — the use of a black-and-white ad in the midst of colourful ads).

A continuous process of selectivity limits our perceptions. Consider that:

- We are exposed to only a small portion of all marketing stimuli (products, ads, stores). We cannot read every magazine or visit every store.
- We perceive only part of what we are exposed to. We can read a newspaper and not notice an ad, or we can watch a television program and ignore the commercials.
- We retain only part of what we selectively perceive. We may read an ad but later forget it.
- We act upon only part of what we retain.

There are many marketing implications in this selectivity. From a marketing point of view, a product or service does not exist by itself, nor does it have any meaning of its own. A product exists in marketing only if consumers perceive that it will satisfy their wants. Moreover, a given product is perceived quite differently by different consumers. Older children in a household may view a video cassette recorder as a welcome device that will allow them to watch their favourite movies or rock videos. One parent may see the same machine as a valuable addition to the household because of its ability to record programs for later viewing (time-shifting). The other parent may see the VCR as an overpriced luxury that prevents the purchase of a new outboard motor or a microwave oven. After all, the ability to receive a number of channels on cable TV was sufficient, without adding the VCR. For other consumers, the VCR may not even exist. That is, it has never entered their field of selective perception.

Marketers cannot afford unlimited advertising exposure, so they strive for the selective exposure that will fall within the perception range of the target market. Then the message must be sufficiently meaningful and strong to survive the consumers' selective retention processes.

To summarize, motives activate people's behaviour, and their perceptions determine the course of that behaviour. We must therefore look to the elements that influence or shape those perceptions. These elements are the many cultural, social-group, and psychological forces that form a person's frame of reference. That is, each individual perceives things within his or her own frame of reference.

The structure for the remainder of our discussion of consumer buying behaviour in this and the next chapter is illustrated in Fig. 5-3. Let's look at that illustration for a preview and a better understanding of the discussion that follows. We start with the *cultural and social-group* forces at the upper left of the figure. Each of these forces influences both our perceptions and the next smaller group. That is, our culture influences our social-class structure, social classes influence small reference groups, and so on. In addition, these sociocultural factors have some influence on the elements in an individual's psychological makeup. That is, a person's culture or family can play some part in shaping that individual's attitudes, personality, and learning experiences. The remainder of this chapter is devoted to these sociocultural forces.

The consumer's psychological field is shown at the upper right in Fig. 5-3. There, note that a person's learning experiences, personality, attitudes, and self-concept all contribute to shaping that person's perceptions. And each of these factors affects the others.

The consumer's perceptions, in turn, influence that person's buying behaviour and buying-decision process. The decision process consists of the five stages identified at the bottom of Fig. 5-3. The psychological field and the buying-decision process are the subjects of Chapter 6.

Structure for Chapters 5 and 6

How we perceive things — and how we think, believe, and act — are determined to a great extent by our cultural surroundings and by the various groups of people with whom we interrelate. All the social-group influences on consumer buying behaviour start with the *culture* in which the consumer lives.

CULTURAL INFLUENCES

A **culture** may be defined as the complex of symbols and artifacts created by a given society and handed down from generation to generation as determinants and regulators of human behaviour. The symbols may be intangible (attitudes, beliefs, values, languages, religions) or tangible (tools, housing, products, works of art). A culture implies a totally learned and

Definition of Culture and Cultural Influence

"handed-down" way of life. It does *not* include instinctive acts. However, standards for performing instinctive biological acts (eating, eliminating body wastes, and sexual relationships) can be culturally established. Thus everybody gets hungry, but what people eat and how they act to satisfy the hunger drive will vary among cultures.

Figure 5-3
SOCIOCULTURAL
AND
PSYCHOLOGICAL
FORCES THAT
INFLUENCE
CONSUMERS'
BUYING
BEHAVIOUR.

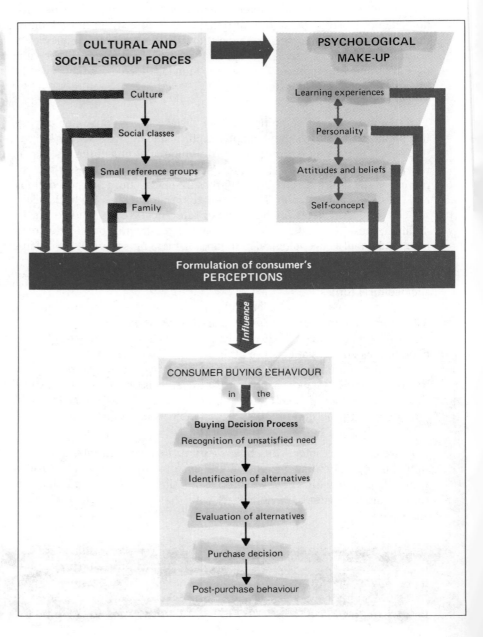

Actually, much of our behaviour is culturally determined. Our sociocultural institutions (family, schools, churches, and languages) provide behavioural guidelines. Kluckhohn observed: "Culture . . . regulates our lives at every turn. From the moment we are born until we die there is constant conscious and unconscious pressure upon us to follow certain types of behaviour that other men have created for us."[2]

Canadian culture is, as are the cultures of all "new" societies, an amalgam of the "old world." We have the two founding cultures or what have been termed charter groups — the French and the British. These charter groups have throughout Canadian history been contending over who should enter the country. The British charter group has usually been dominant and perhaps of more importance, widely distributed throughout the country while the French have been concentrated. Thus outside the Province of Quebec but in an important part of Montreal, the pervasive ethic, established at an early period in terms of growth of the country, has been established by immigrants from the British Isles. It is the value system of this charter group that most immigrants coming to this country have encountered and that has shaped their adaptation and domestication. It was the behaviour flowing from this ethic that was seen as appropriate for successful assimilation.

One component of Canadian culture, as well as of other modern Western societies, is a commitment to active mastery of the world to enhance standards of life.[3] There is a Canadian consensus for this and the means to this control are captured in such dictums as work harder to better yourself; idle hands are the devil's helpers; leisure is akin to laziness; be frugal. Hard work was rewarded with the obvious but not exclusive means to mastery — material well-being and wealth. The result for us has been a relatively high level of political, economic, and social freedom. Immigrants of all types who have embraced and supported the standards of the dominant charter group have been rewarded with material and wealth.

There is a third charter group which we must consider, not because it founded the country and imposed its standards of culture but because we are importers of its culture by virtue of its proximity. American culture is as pervasive as that of the Canadian charter groups — perhaps more so over time. While Canadians value work, Americans prize activity in all spheres. Whereas Canadians believe in orderly change to achieve mastery, Americans value and encourage pragmatic change to the point where change becomes an end rather than a means to one. Within American society there is the espousal of equality and a facing of the problems such an espousal calls forth. In Canada we prize all these values as well, but in a

---

[2]Clyde Kluckhohn, "The Concept of Culture," in Richard Kluckhohn (ed.), *Culture and Behavior*, The Free Press, New York, 1962, p. 26

[3]Kaspar Naegele, "Canadian Society: Some Reflections," in Bernard R. Blishen *et al.* (eds.), *Canadian Society*, The Macmillan Company of Canada Limited, Toronto, 1961, pp. 7–8.

characteristically Canadian muted manner. "The same values are valued but with much more hesitancy. This makes of excess itself a disvalue."[4] Yet while American values are reflected here but to a lesser degree, the American style of living provides a highly visible model for us—often at commuting distance or at least through the media. There are no great animosities that divide Americans and Canadians, and the American style is easier, livelier, more daring, more outspoken, and more varied than distant models from which our charter and other groups sprang. At the same time, the American model seems "unduly risky, precarious and unplanned."[5]

Canadian and American national character have often been compared and in a recent study were compared as a basis for market segmentation.[6] Generally it was found that Americans were more individualistic, whereas Canadians were more collectively oriented. Americans were also found to be more self-confident, greater opinion leaders, and stronger interpersonal communicators. Americans were also found to be much more receptive to such things as trading stamps, advertising, credit, and the print and television media. Studies of this nature are at least indicative of the differences between the two cultures, and marketers in North America should certainly be aware of such differences.

Students and observers of Canadian culture have expressed concern over the years regarding our ability to preserve a uniquely Canadian culture in the face of the influence exerted by living so close to the United States. Of principal concern has been the fact that American media literally dominate the lives of Canadians, especially with regard to television, generally considered to be the most pervasive of all the mass media. The availability of cable television, and its potential to bring greater amounts of American content into the homes of Canadians, has rekindled a concern that Canadian culture may be in danger of disappearing.[7]

Marketing responds within the constraints of this cultural amalgam. Promotional appeals are geared to improving a person's material standard of living. When labour-saving devices are marketed, appeals stress getting hard work done, but mechanically, and thus freeing human energies for, say, the family. But some promotional appeals are too American — and they jangle us. Others are too muted, and although more congenial, they have no impact in our mixed cultural world. Still others are irrelevant in Quebec — be they too American or too Anglo-Canadian.

---

[4]*Ibid.*, pp. 26–27.

[5]*Ibid.*, p. 36.

[6]Stephen J. Arnold and James G. Barnes, "Canadian and American National Character as a Basis for Market Segmentation," in Jagdish N. Sheth (ed.), *Research in Marketing*, vol. 2, JAI Press Inc., Greenwich, Connecticut, 1979, pp. 1–35.

[7]James G. Barnes, *Cable and Canadians: A Sociocultural Study of the Impact of Cable Television on a Canadian Community*, a report prepared for Communications Canada, 1983.

Cultural influences do change over time, as old patterns gradually give way to the new. During the past 10 to 25 years in Canada, cultural changes of far-reaching magnitude have been occurring at an accelerated rate. Marketing executives must be alert to these changing patterns so that they can adjust their planning to be in step with, or even a little ahead of, the times. We shall note a few of the changes that have significant marketing implications.

Cultural Change

Emphasis on Quality of Life

Our emphasis today is on the *quality* of life rather than the *quantity* of goods. The theme is, "Not more — but better." We seek value, durability, and safety in the products we buy. Looking ahead, we will worry more about inflation, crime, and energy shortages, and less about keeping up with the neighbours in autos, dress, and homes. Our growing concern for the environment and our discontent with pollution and resource waste are leading to significant changes in our life-styles. And when our life-styles change, of course marketing is affected.

One of the most important influences on the life-styles of Canadians in recent years has been the economic situation faced by consumers. The combined effects of inflation and recession have forced consumers to make major modifications in their purchase and consumption behaviour. As a result of growing pressures on their incomes, many consumers have turned to more bargain hunting, are sharing with their neighbours, are buying used clothing, and are growing their own vegetables. Some observers feel that many of the changes that consumers have made in their consumption behaviour may be more permanent than many marketers believe, and that the Canadian marketplace will not return to the "normal" situation typical of the early 1970s.[8]

Increasing Evidence of Polarity

At the same time as a large percentage of Canadians have been very worried about not being able to keep their jobs and about earning enough to feed their families, we have seen a dramatic growth in the number of consumers at the high-income end of the social scale. Therefore, at the same time as some consumers are desperately trying to make ends meet, there is a growth in demand for exotic vacations, gourmet foods, wines, and luxury cars. This demand is brought about largely by the number of relatively young, dual-career professional families in Canada today. Products of the postwar Baby Boom and generally armed with a university education, many Canadians under 40 now live in households where both spouses are employed in well-paying professional jobs and where the number of children is small.

[8]James G. Barnes and Lessey Sooklal, "The Changing Nature of Consumer Behaviour: Monitoring the Impact of Inflation and Recession," *Business Quarterly*, vol. 48, no. 2, Summer 1983, p. 58–64.

The buying power of this group is impressive and is characterized by a demand for high-priced, tasteful, and exotic products. Growth in demand for products and services to satisfy this demand is anticipated at the same time as large numbers of Canadian families struggle to get by on a single income that is often threatened by unemployment. The differences between the two ends of the income scale may well be increasing, prompting the observation that a polarity is developing.[9]

Simplification

Another change that has taken place within Canadian culture in recent years has been a definite attempt on the part of some consumers to simplify their life-styles. This, too, is related to the problems brought about by inflation and recession, which have caused many consumers to question the consumption-oriented North American life-styles of the 1960s and 1970s. As a result, many have begun to adopt consumption behaviour that would have been more common among our grandparents. Doing things for ourselves, helping neighbours, growing vegetables, knitting, and sewing are all examples of a simpler life-style. Many consumers seem almost to want to turn back the clock to a less complicated time. This attitude is also related to a desire to conserve and to preserve certain skills and resources so that they may be used by future generations.[10]

Changing Role of Women

One of the most dramatic occurrences in our society in recent years has been the changing role of women. The marketing impact of the growing number of working women was noted in Chapter 4. What is even more significant, however, is how women have succeeded in breaking from the traditional and sometimes discriminatory patterns that have stereotyped the male-female roles in families, jobs, recreation, product use, and many other areas. Today, women's growing political power, economic power, and new job opportunities have considerably changed their perspectives and those of men as well. The changing male-female roles have considerable implications for marketers, as the targeting of a product toward an exclusively male or female market may no longer be appropriate. Certainly, the assumption that all food-marketing efforts should be directed at women is no longer valid.[11]

---

[9]See, for example, "Baby Boomers Push for Power," *Business Week*, July 2, 1984, pp. 52-60; and Woods, Gordon, *Tomorrow's Customers in Canada*, 18th ed., 1984, p. 18.

[10] See, for example, Alan J. Mayer, "Nostalgia," *The Financial Post Magazine*, March 1982, pp. 22–33; and T. L. Leonard, T. K. Clarke, and D. A. Schellinck, "Finding the Ecologically Minded Consumer," in the *Proceedings* of the Marketing Division, Administrative Sciences Association of Canada, 1981, pp. 176–185.

[11]R. Neil Maddox, "The Importance of Males in Supermarket Traffic and Sales," in the *Proceedings* of the Marketing Division, Administrative Sciences Association of Canada, 1982, pp. 137–143.

Changes in Home and Family Life

Other changes are occurring in the nature of the Canadian home and family that have implications for marketers. We see evidence of increased mobility, especially among better-educated and professional consumers who are prepared to move to other cities to take higher-paying jobs. Interestingly, the geographic mobility of blue-collar workers has decreased in recent years as unemployment rates across the country have made blue-collar jobs difficult to find. A new morality has developed as people's attitudes toward sex have become more liberal over the past couple of decades. Today, sex-related products are more openly advertised and marketed, and attitudes toward sex are more liberal, in contrast to the situation that existed not too long ago. Young people seem to be approaching relationships in a more mature manner, generally not marrying until they are older and more able to cope with marriage's emotional and financial demands.

The changes that have occurred in terms of relationships — increased sexual freedom, an increased divorce rate, a reduced birth rate, the changing role of women, dual-career families — have caused many to comment on the future of the institution of the family. Despite these changes, there can be little doubt that the family will survive, but that it will be different from the Canadian family of the 1950s and 1960s. It will be smaller, more mobile, and more subject to change. It will be more likely to involve both spouses working, thereby requiring marketing specialists to modify current approaches to marketing to the family.[12]

Changing Attitudes Toward Work and Pleasure

The Puritan ethic regarding work and pleasure is changing. Today people, especially young people, do *not* view work as the be-all and end-all of their existence. The business rat race, even with its large rewards, has lost its appeal for many people. Both the young and the old are searching for jobs that bring rewards other than good pay and prestigious position.

Of course, in the economic situation that has characterized Canada in the first half of the 1980s, many people have been happy to have any job. A large percentage of Canadians have had to modify their expectations concerning employment and have been forced to accept jobs they may not have considered earlier. The level of unemployment we have experienced has contributed to major social and psychological problems for consumers. In fact, many homemakers have found it necessary to find paying jobs outside the home in order to be able to provide for their families, although doing so creates disruption and anxiety at home.

At the same time, however, Canadians have adopted an attitude that one should enjoy life. It is no longer unacceptable to have a good time or to

---

[12]James W. Hanson and Rosemary Polegato, "Identifying Dual Career, Dual Income and Traditional Family Segments: Some Preliminary Findings," in the *Proceedings* of the Marketing Division, Administrative Sciences Association of Canada, 1983, pp. 133–141.

pamper yourself. In effect, marketers have to deal with a "me" generation that is self-centred and hedonistic. People are more interested in pleasing themselves than in satisfying society. Their attitude is, "What's in it for Number One (me)?" or "What have you done for me lately?" There is a growing interest in self-improvement and self-fulfilment activities. For example, many people are involved in physical fitness and health pursuits. As a result, we see expanding markets for food, clothing, and equipment related to those activities.[13]

Time Polarity

It has become generally accepted in recent years to comment that Canadians have experienced an increase in leisure time. But this is not necessarily the case. In fact, what we now see is a time polarity as well as the income polarity we observed earlier.

Many consumers do indeed have a larger amount of free time available to them as a result of shorter work weeks, longer vacations, and more time-saving household appliances. In fact, because of unemployment, many Canadians have more free time than they would like to have.

The availability of more leisure time, coupled with changing life-styles, has led to an expanding market for sports, recreation activities, physical fitness programs, and all the products and equipment needed to participate in these activities. Spectator sports are booming. Women are increasingly participating in individual and team-sports activities. The market for jogging shoes, keep-fit programs, cross-country skiing equipment, and tennis racquets has been quite healthy, and organizations such as the YM-YWCA are undergoing a resurgence of interest as Canadians use their leisure time to get fit.[14]

At the other end of the scale, however, there are more and more Canadians who, as part of a dual-career family, find that they do not have much free time, as both spouses are busily engaged in furthering their respective careers. Rather than having a surplus of free time, this group has a deficiency of free time. It is interested in conserving time and is prepared to pay for it. It represents a ready market for child-care centres, home-cleaning services, and "get-away-from-it-all" vacations.

Impulse Buying

In the past three decades or so, marketers have noted a tendency among consumers to engage in impulse buying — that is, to purchase products without much advance planning. A shopper may go to the grocery store

---

[13]For some possibly negative repercussions of "me" advertising, see James U. McNeal, "Advertising in the 'Age of Me'," *Business Horizons*, August 1979, pp. 34–38. Also see Bruce Crawford, " 'Age of Me' Poses New Problems for Marketing," *Marketing News*, June 30, 1978, p. 1.

[14]Martin Jones, "Shaping Up at the Y," *Business Journal*, April 1984, pp. 24–27, 38.

with a mental note to buy meat and bread. In the store, he or she may also select some fresh peaches because they look appealing or are priced attractively. Another shopper, seeing some cleansing tissues on the shelf, may be reminded that the supply at home is running low and so may buy two boxes. These are impulse purchases.

A key point to understand is that some impulse buying is done on a very rational basis. Self-service, open-display selling has brought about a marketing situation wherein planning may be postponed until the buyer reaches the retail outlet. Because of the trend toward impulse buying, greater emphasis must be placed on promotional programs to get people into a store. Displays must be more appealing because the manufacturer's package must serve as a silent salesperson.

More recently, however, there has been evidence that some consumers are not buying as much on impulse as they may have done in the past. Because of the pressures on their incomes brought about by inflation, many consumers are now engaging in more planning of their shopping trips. They also may have more time available and are almost certainly prepared to spend more time shopping around for better prices and quality. This willingness to plan and shop around has led some authors to question whether consumers will be as likely to develop loyalties to certain stores and brands as they have in the past.[15]

Desire for Convenience

As an outgrowth of the increase in discretionary purchasing power and the importance of time, there has been a substantial increase in the consumer's desire for convenience. We want products ready and easy to use, and convenient credit plans to pay for them. We want these products packaged in a variety of sizes, quantities, and forms. We want stores located close by, and open at virtually all hours.

Every major phase of a company's marketing program is affected by this craving for convenience. Product planning is influenced by the need for customer convenience in packaging, quantity, and selection. Pricing policies must be established in conformity with the demand for credit and with the costs of providing the various kinds of convenience. Distribution policies must provide for convenient locations and store hours.

One particular outgrowth of the desire for convenience has been a resurgence of "in-home" shopping. In the old days, wagon peddlers and others sold on a door-to-door basis and consumers bought from mail-order catalogues. In-home shopping in the 1980s, however, features television, computerized communication systems, and payment of bills by the electronic transfer of money. While the technology certainly exists to allow consumers to shop and access various services from the home, trials of various interactive systems have not shown an acceptance on the part of consumers.

---

[15]Barnes and Sooklal, *op. cit.*, p. 63.

The growth of such systems will, therefore, likely be quite gradual, depending on the nature of the services being offered and the group of consumers to whom the service is directed. The younger, dual-career families described above who suffer from a time deficiency will be the most likely target for this service. Lack of personal contact with sales personnel and with merchandise is inherent in such in-home services. This will inhibit consumer acceptance in some areas, such as shopping for clothing, but has not prevented early success in other applications, such as the automated-teller machines now used by the major banks.

Subcultures

Given the nature of Canadian culture, marketers should understand the concept of subcultures and analyse them as potentially profitable market segments. Any time there is a culture as heterogeneous as ours, there are bound to be significant subcultures based upon factors such as race, nationality, religion, geographic location, age, and urban-rural distribution. Some of these were recognized in Chapter 4, when we analysed the demographic market factors. Religion, for example, is a cultural factor that has significant marketing implications. Concentrations of Middle or Eastern Europeans in the Prairies provide a market for some products that would go unnoticed in Italian or Portuguese sections of Toronto.

The cultural diversity of the Canadian market has taken on increased importance for some companies in recent years. A decade ago, most advertisers ignored the ethnic market, but the 1981 Census showed that about one-third of Canada's population had origins other than English, French, or native. Six million Canadians claimed a mother tongue other than English or French. The availability of ethnic media and the growth in the number of Italian, Portuguese, Greek, Chinese, Asian, and West Indian Canadians has prompted many companies to advertise directly to these cultural segments. The Royal Bank of Canada spent 30 percent of its 1983 Ontario advertising budget on the ethnic market. Labatt Breweries have developed television commercials for broadcast on ethnic television programs in southern Ontario.[16]

The sharpest subcultural differences are portrayed in behavioural differences between English- and French-Canadian communities on a country-wide basis, although to the urban dweller in Toronto or Montreal the acceptance (or ritual avoidance) of the obvious differences between a diversity of ethnic minorities is now a matter of course. As indicated in Chapter 4, marketing to French Canada involves considerably more than cursory acknowledgement of ethnic differences.

The Changing Nature of the French-Canadian Market

French Canada, as a subculture, has undergone a revolution since the death of Maurice Duplessis in 1959. This cultural revolution—sometimes termed the Quiet Revolution—has had a profound effect on the nature of the French-Canadian market. Prior to the political and social changes of the Quiet Revolution, Quebec had been

---

[16]Sandy Fife, "Piercing the Ethnic Barrier," *Financial Times*, August 8, 1983, p. 8.

a predominantly rural province with strong, nominally patriarchal, family units. The dominant overall institution was the Roman Catholic Church, which guided not only the educational system but, thanks to the power of its parish priests, much of the day-to-day life of the people. French Canada maintained and developed its traditional culture — of which the cornerstones were the Catholic religion and the French language — in relative isolation from the industrial and economic developments taking place in the United States, England, and English Canada. Ideologically it glorified its past, and spokesmen concerned themselves with the retour à la terre *and* la revanche des berceaux — *the return to the land and the revenge of the cradle.*

English-French relationships, which have always been a basic dimension in French Canada, took a distinctive turn in the latter part of the nineteenth and twentieth centuries with the introduction of industry into Quebec by English-speaking outsiders. The symbiotic type relationship which developed did not displease the leaders of French Canada — the English needed workers and the French Canadians, with their high fertility rate and dwindling access to good farmland, welcomed the opportunities for more jobs. The French Canadians became the drawers of water and hewers of wood while the English controlled and managed industry and commerce. The language of communication between the two groups was English, with the bilingual French-Canadians serving as intermediaries.[17]

Since the beginnings of the Quiet Revolution, however, French-Canadians have taken major steps to preserve their cultural identity in the English-dominated North American society and to prevent the assimilation of French Canada into this society. The Quiet Revolution has been a modern, progressive movement that has been manifest in programs to preserve the French language, improved health and education programs, renewed interest in French-Canadian crafts and culture, and the confidence shown in Quebec's hosting of Expo 67 and the 1976 Summer Olympics. As a movement, it has been exemplified in the slogan *Maîtres Chez Nous* — masters in our own house.

At the same time, there is evidence of other social change in French Canada, which is of considerable interest to marketers. There is a suggestion of a diminishing role of the Church in French-Canadian life; a lesser role is being assigned to the family unit and women are playing a much larger role in the labour force; and there is a shift in the prestige attached to certain occupations. No longer do the traditional professions of the priesthood, law, and medicine dominate the cultural hierarchy. A new middle

---

[17]Frederick Elkin, *Rebels and Colleagues: Advertising and Social Change in French Canada*, McGill-Queen's University Press, Montreal, 1973, p. 3. Elkin's book is highly recommended as an excellent study of advertising as a vehicle for social change in French Canada before and during the Quiet Revolution.

class has developed in French Canada that is less tradition-oriented and more attuned to youth and business.[18]

One noticeable effect of the cultural change in French Canada has been a marked decline in the birthrate among French-Canadian women. The changing role of women in French-Canadian society, increased education levels, reduced influence of the church, and greater labour-force participation among women have all contributed to a decline in the birthrate in Quebec from 4.31 births per woman in 1926 to well below 2 births per woman (the lowest in Canada) in the early 1980s.

Differences in Consumption Behaviour

The differences in consumption behaviour between English- and French-Canadians have been well documented.[19] Certain products sell in much larger quantities in Quebec than in other provinces, while other products that sell well in English Canada are rarely purchased by French-Canadians. Some examples of differences in product preferences and buying behaviour are:[20]

— there is a better acceptance in Quebec of premium-priced products such as premium-grade gasoline and expensive liquors;

— French-Canadians spend more per capita on clothing, personal care items, tobacco, and alcoholic beverages;

— the French-Canadian consumes more soft drinks, maple sugar, molasses, and candy per capita than does the English-Canadian;

— French-Canadians have much higher consumption rates for instant and decaffeinated coffee;

— French-Canadians watch more television and listen to radio more than do English-Canadians;

— premiums and coupons are more popular in Quebec;

— French-Canadians buy more headache and cold remedies than do English-Canadians;

— in Quebec homes a full meal is generally served both at noon and in the evening;

---

[18]Bruce Mallen, "The French-Canadian Retail Customer: Changing? To What? So What?" *The Canadian Marketer*, Winter, 1975, p. 33.

[19]For a review of research directed toward the identification of such differences, see Michael J. Bergier and Jerry Rosenblatt, "A Critical Review of Past and Current Methodologies Used for Classifying English and French Consumers," in *Proceedings* of the Marketing Division, Administrative Sciences Association of Canada, 1982, pp. 11–20.

[20]See Nariman K. Dhalla, *These Canadians: A Sourcebook of Marketing and Socioeconomic Facts*, McGraw-Hill, Toronto, 1966, pp. 287–300; Frederick Elkin and Mary B. Hill, "Bicultural and Bilingual Adaptations in French Canada: The Example of Retail Advertising," *Canadian Review of Sociology and Anthropology*, August 1965, pp. 132–148; M. Brisebois, "Marketing in Quebec," in W. H. Mahatoo (ed.), *Marketing Research in Canada*, Thomas Nelson and Sons, Toronto, 1968, pp. 88–90; Bruce Mallen, "The Present State of Knowledge and Research in Marketing to the French-Canadian Market," in Donald N. Thompson and David S. R. Leighton (eds.), *Canadian Marketing: Problems and Prospects*, Wiley, Toronto, 1973, pp. 100–101; and Jean-Charles Chebat and Georges Hénault, "The Cultural Behavior of Canadian Consumers," in Vishnu H. Kirpalani and Ronald H. Rotenberg (eds.), *Cases and Readings in Marketing*, Holt, Rinehart & Winston of Canada Limited, Toronto, 1974, pp. 178–180.

— French-Canadians appear to be less concerned about ecological matters and would prefer rationing to increased energy prices;[21]

— French-Canadian consumers may be experiencing higher levels of dissatisfaction with repairs and general consumer services and with professional and personal services than is the case for English-speaking Canadians.[22]

In addition to examining these examples of specific product-related differences between English-Canadian and French-Canadian buying behaviour, it might also be important for the marketer to get a more general overview of the differences in life-style exhibited within the two cultures. An interesting study of life-style differences between the two markets concluded that (at least in the mid-1970s) the French-Canadian female was:

— more oriented toward the home, the family, the children, and the kitchen;

— more interested in baking and cooking and more negative toward convenience foods;

— more concerned about personal and home cleanliness, and more fashion and personal appearance conscious than her English counterpart;

— more price conscious;

— much more concerned about a number of social, political, and consumer issues, including youth, liquor, drugs, big government, big business, and the value of advertising;

— more religious, especially in feelings about the life hereafter;

— more security conscious and less prone to take risks;

— more positive toward television and less positive toward newspapers;

— more negative toward the use of credit in terms of bank borrowing and in terms of credit cards;

— able to be characterized by a set of values described as steady and consistent.[23]

While it is relatively easy to determine where actual differences in consumption behaviour exist between French- and English-Canadians, it is somewhat more difficult to identify reasons for the existence of such differences. And yet, it is important for marketers to have some understanding of the factors that contribute to these differences if they are to market effectively to both market segments.

Factors Influencing French–English Consumption Differences

---

[21]S. A. Ahmed, Renaud DeCamprieu and Paul Hope, "A Comparison of English and French Canadian Attitudes Toward Energy and the Environment," in Robert Wyckham (ed.), *Marketing*, vol. 2, part 3, *Proceedings* of the Administrative Sciences Association of Canada, Marketing Division, Halifax, 1981, pp. 1–10.

[22]S. B. Ash, Carole P. Duhaime, and John A. Quelch, "Consumer Satisfaction: A Comparison of English and French-Speaking Canadians," in Vernon J. Jones (ed.), *Marketing*, vol. 1, part 3, *Proceedings* of the Administrative Sciences Association of Canada, Marketing Division, Montreal, 1980, pp. 11–20.

[23]Douglas J. Tigert, "Can a Separate Marketing Strategy for French Canada be Justified: Profiling English-French Markets Through Life Style Analysis," in Donald N. Thompson and David S. R. Leighton (eds.), *Canadian Marketing: Problems and Prospects*, Wiley Publishers of Canada Limited, Toronto, 1973, pp. 113–142.

A number of authors have pointed out that French-Canadians have a lower per capita income than do English-Canadians, that they have lower average education levels, and that they are a much more rural population. These differences along income and other demographic lines might suggest that the differences in product purchase rates and shopping behaviour between French-Canadians and English-Canadians may be attributable simply to demographic differences and that the consumption behaviour of French-Canadians is really no different from that of English-Canadians of similar demographic characteristics. At least two studies have refuted this argument.

The first study indicated that consumption behaviour was significantly different between Quebec and Ontario households when households of *similar size and income levels were compared.*[24] A second study found significant differences in household expenditure levels between English-Canadian and French-Canadian households for eight consumption expenditure categories after certain noncultural differences (such as the rural-urban breakdown of the groups and stage of the family life cycle) between the two groups were controlled.[25] Such findings suggest that the consumption behaviour differences between French- and English-Canadians are not attributable solely to demographic differences but, rather, are more likely explained by cultural differences.

Certain characteristics of the French-Canadian culture and directions in which that culture appears to have changed were discussed earlier. The important message for the marketer is that French Canada is culturally distinctive from English Canada and that certain products and other elements of the marketing mix are perceived quite differently by the French-Canadian than they are by the English-Canadian. As has been suggested, the *function* and *meaning* of products sold to French Canada must be perceived by the French-Canadian culture as consistent with that culture.

The Impact of Cultural Differences on Marketing

The fact that French Canada represents a distinctively different culture from that found in English Canada requires that marketers who wish to be successful in the French-Canadian market develop unique marketing programs for this segment. There must be an appreciation of the fact that certain products will not be successful in French Canada simply because they are not appropriate to the French-Canadian life-style and culture. In other cases, products that are successful in English Canada must be marketed differently in French Canada because the French-Canadian has a different perception of these products and the way in which they are used. It may be necessary for companies to develop new products or appropriate

---

[24]Kristian S. Palda, "A Comparison of Consumer Expenditures in Quebec and Ontario," *Canadian Journal of Economics and Political Science*, February 1967, p. 26.

[25]Dwight R. Thomas, "Culture and Consumption Behavior in English and French Canada," in Bent Stidsen (ed.), *Marketing in the 1970s and Beyond*, Canadian Association of Administrative Sciences, Marketing Division, Edmonton, 1975, pp. 255–261.

variations of existing products specifically for the French-Canadian market. Similarly, the retail buying behaviour of French-Canadians may necessitate the use of different channels of distribution in Quebec.

In the area of advertising, many national companies have encountered problems in reaching the French-Canadian market. Until the 1960s, the great majority of advertisements used by such companies in Quebec were first prepared in English and then translated into French, often with devastating results. Examples are numerous of advertisements containing English expressions and phrases that were translated literally into French only to find that the translated expression was meaningless or offensive to French-Canadians. Before the late 1960s, much of the national advertising in Canada was prepared by English-Canadian advertising agencies (usually based in Toronto) that developed advertisements for use in both English and French Canada. These agencies generally employed translators whose responsibility it was to translate the advertisements, which had been developed by English-Canadians for the English culture, so that they might be used in the Quebec market. In many cases, literal translations were demanded and the end results were inappropriate for the French market.

The challenges of advertising in French Canada go far beyond those of translating English to French. Even where the translation is a good one and English expressions and slang are converted into expressions that are meaningful to French-Canadians, the problem still remains that the basic approach to the advertisement is based in English-Canadian or even American culture. Many advertisements contain illustrations, themes, and representations of life-styles that are quite appropriate in English Canada but quite inappropriate in Quebec. What is needed is that advertising which is to be directed to the French-Canadian market be planned from "scratch" with that market in mind. The advertising content must be consistent with the culture of the market, and this requires that it be developed and written by French-Canadians.

Recent years have seen a greater appreciation of this fact on the part of Canadian advertisers. During the 1960s, many large English-language advertising agencies in Canada established French departments that contained complete advertising staffs, rather than simply translators, and that developed advertising for French Canada. More importantly, since the early 1960s, there have been established in Quebec a number of highly successful French-language agencies. Many national advertisers now place their English-language advertising with an English-Canadian agency, but use a Montreal-based French-language agency to develop advertising for the French market.[26]

---

[26]For a discussion of the evolution of advertising agencies in Quebec, see Madeleine Saint-Jacques and Bruce Mallen, "The French-Canadian Market," in Peter T. Zarry and Robert D. Wilson (eds.), *Advertising in Canada: Its Theory and Practice*, McGraw-Hill Ryerson Limited, Toronto, 1981, pp. 349–368; and Robert MacGregor, "The Impact of the Neo-Nationalist Movement on the Changing Structure and Composition of the Quebec Advertising Industry," in the *Proceedings* of the Marketing Division, Administrative Sciences Association of Canada, 1980, p. 237.

In the packaging and labelling of consumer products there have also been recent developments that are important for marketing in French Canada. For many years, Canadian companies made no special effort to prepare product labels for use in French Canada, with the result that most of the products on the shelves of Quebec retail stores bore English labels. Since 1967, however, it has been a requirement of the Quebec government that all labels on food products sold in that province give at least equal prominence to the French language. Similarly, the federal government's Consumer Packaging and Labelling Act and its regulations require that all label information on consumer products produced in Canada or imported into this country be conveyed in both English and French.

INFLUENCE OF SOCIAL CLASS

Another sociocultural determinant of consumers' perceptions and buying behaviour is the social class to which they belong. Social classes do exist in Canada, and people's buying behaviour is often more strongly influenced by the class to which they belong, or to which they aspire, than by their income alone. The idea of a social-class structure and the terms *upper,* *middle*, and *lower* class may be repugnant to many Canadians. However, the sociologists who identify the class structure and the marketers who use it do not impute value judgements to it. We do not claim that the so-called upper class is superior to, or happier than, the middle class — only that both do exist.

While the concept of a class structure may be abhorrent to some, it does represent a useful way to look at a market. We can consider social class as another useful basis for segmenting consumer markets.[27]

More than 40 years ago, Warner and Lunt conducted a study that identified a six-class system within the social structure of a small American town.[28] The placement of people in the structure was based on their *type*, not amount, of income, and on their occupation, type of house, and area of residence within the community. Through the years, other researchers have made similar social-class studies in other locations, sometimes using different bases of measurement.

Descriptions of the six classes identified by Warner and Lunt are presented below. The percentages are those they used as their estimate of the percentage of population in each group. These *figures* should be viewed as arbitrary, as they will vary over time and across cities and regions studied. In fact, there is reason to believe that the relative size of the groups and indeed the number of classes may have changed considerably in recent years as income and education levels have increased. Certainly, there are now more professionals and white-collar workers and fewer blue-collar

[27]D. W. Greeno and W. F. Bennett, "Social Class and Income as Complementary Segmentation Bases: A Canadian Perspective," in *Proceedings* of the Marketing Division, Administrative Sciences Association of Canada, 1983, p. 113–122.

[28]W. Lloyd Warner and Paul Lunt, *The Social Life of a Modern Community*, Yale University Press, New Haven, Conn., 1941; and W. Lloyd Warner, Marchia Meeker, and Kenneth Eells, *Social Class in America*, Science Research Associates, Inc., Chicago, 1949.

workers than was the case in the 1940s and 1950s. Nevertheless, the concept of social class remains a useful one for examining a market as long as we realize that it is just that, and not a rigid categorization of consumers.

The six social classes identified by the Warner and Lunt study, and the percentage of the population estimated in each, were:

1. The *upper-upper class*, about 0.5 percent, includes the "old families" in the community—the aristocracy of birth and inherited wealth. Usually they are second- or third-generation families, living graciously in large old homes in the best neighbourhoods and displaying a sense of social responsibility.

2. The *lower-upper class*, about 1.5 percent, includes the "new rich," who are wealthy but who have not been accepted socially by the upper-upper families. This class includes the top executives, well-to-do doctors and lawyers, and owners of large businesses. This group now includes the young, dual-career professional families.

3. The *upper-middle class*, about 10 percent, is composed of moderately successful business and professional people, and owners of medium-sized companies. They are well educated, live well, and have a strong drive for success.

4. The *lower-middle class*, about 33 percent, is made up of the white-collar class of office workers, most salespeople, and owners of small businesses. This is the group striving for "respectability" — holding good jobs, living in modest but well-cared-for homes, and saving for the children's college education. This class is the source of America's moral code and aspirational system and is the most conforming, church-going part of the society.

5. The *upper-lower class*, about 40 percent, consists of the blue-collar class of factory workers and semi-skilled workers. This class also includes the politicians and union leaders who would lose their power if they moved out of this class. Many earn good incomes, but they are usually oriented toward enjoying life on a day-to-day basis.

6. The *lower-lower class*, about 15 percent, includes unskilled workers, the chronically unemployed, unassimilated racial immigrants from other parts of the country, those frequently on welfare, and many inhabitants of slums. Classes above this one consider this group to be lazy, when often their only sin is being poor and uneducated.

The *Chicago Tribune* later made a study, under Professor Warner's guidance, to determine whether his own analysis of social-class structure —developed from studies of small towns—also applied to a large metropolitan centre.[29] Three basic conclusions, highly significant for marketing, came out of the *Chicago Tribune* study:

---

[29]See Pierre D. Martineau, "Social Classes and Spending Behavior," *Journal of Marketing*, October 1958, pp. 121–130.

- There is a social-class system in large metropolitan markets. And substantial differences exist between classes with respect to their buying habits.

- There are far-reaching psychological differences between classes (see Table 5-1). The classes do *not* think in the same way. Thus they respond differently to a seller's marketing program, particularly the advertising.

- Class membership is a more significant determinant of buyer behaviour than is the amount of income. Traditionally, marketing people have relied on income as an index to buying behaviour. With what we now know about social class, however, we question the accuracy of this index. There is an old saying that a rich person is just a poor person with money — and that, given the same amount of money, a poor person would behave exactly like a rich person. Studies of social-class structure have proved that this statement is just not true.[30]

A word of caution, however: Buying behaviour may very well be different at the various income levels *within* each social class or occupational group. For example, a carpenter's family with an income of $15,000 a year has consumption patterns that are different from those of another carpenter's family whose annual income is $25,000. Thus a more useful basis for market segmentation might be some index that combines both occupation and income.[31]

Some of the points in the preceding paragraphs may be illustrated with Coleman's example of typical behaviour for three families. They each earn about the same amount of money, but each comes from a different social class.[32] There are quite significant marketing implications in their differential behavior. An *upper-middle-class* family in this income bracket — where the head of the household is possibly a lawyer, or where both spouses work because they both want a career — is likely to spend a relatively large share of its resources on a home in a prestige neighbourhood, expensive furniture, clothing from quality stores, travel, and club memberships or cultural amusements. In comparison, a *lower-middle-class* family — that of a salesperson or diesel engineer, for example — probably has a better house, but not in so fancy a neighbourhood; more furniture and clothes, but not from name stores or by top designers; and a much bigger savings account.

---

[30]More recent research suggests that for *some products*, income may be stronger than social class as a determinant of buyer behaviour. See Charles M. Schaninger, "Social Class versus Income Revisited: An Empirical Investigation," *Journal of Marketing Research*, May 1981, pp. 192–208. Also see Luis V. Dominguez and Albert L. Page, "Use and Misuse of Social Stratification in Consumer Behavior Research," *Journal of Business Research*, June 1981, pp. 151–173.

[31]See William H. Peters, "Income and Occupation as Explanatory Variables: Their Power Combined vs. Separate," *Journal of Business Research*, Summer 1973, pp. 81–89.

[32]Richard P. Coleman, "The Significance of Social Stratification in Selling," in Martin L. Bell (ed.), *Marketing: A Maturing Discipline*, American Marketing Association, Chicago, 1961, pp. 171–184.

Table 5-1   PSYCHOLOGICAL DIFFERENCES BETWEEN TWO
SOCIAL CLASSES

There are many exceptions to this picture of class attitudes. For instance, can you think of a lower-class person (in terms of income and social status) who has middle-class attitudes? Are there enough exceptions to these patterns to render them invalid in planning marketing campaigns?

Middle Class	Lower Class
1. Is pointed to the future	1. Is pointed to the present and past
2. Lives and thinks in a long expanse of time	2. Lives and thinks in a short expanse of time
3. Is more urban in identification	3. Is more rural in identification
4. Stresses rationality	4. Is essentially nonrational
5. Has a well-structured sense of the universe	5. Has a vague and unstructured sense of the world
6. Has horizons that are vastly extended	6. Has horizons that are sharply defined and limited
7. Feels a greater sense of choice-making	7. Feels a limited sense of choice-making
8. Is self-confident, willing to take risks	8. Is very much concerned with security
9. Thinks in an immaterial and abstract way	9. Thinks in a concrete and perceptive way
10. Sees self as tied to national happenings	10. Sees the world as revolving around self and family

Source: Adapted from Pierre D. Martineau, "Social Classes and Spending Behavior," *Journal of Marketing*, October 1958, p. 129.

Finally, the *upper-lower-class* family of a welder or truck driver has a smaller house in a less desirable neighbourhood. In this family, both spouses may also work, but it is because they need two incomes to make ends meet. However, this family will have a later-model car, more kitchen appliances, and a bigger television set. This family also spends more on sports (ball games, hunting, bowling, fishing).

Small-group influence on buyer behaviour introduces to marketing the concept of reference-group theory, which we borrow from sociology. A **reference group** may be defined as a group of people who influence a person's attitudes, values, and behaviour. A reference group's standards of behaviour serve as guides or "frames of reference" for the individual. The reference-group concept may be applied to the full range of social influences from a total culture down to the family. However, the concept was originally developed in connection with small groups.

Consumer behaviour is influenced by the small groups to which consumers belong or aspire to belong. These groups may include family, fraternal organizations, labour unions, church groups, athletic teams, or a circle of close friends or neighbours. Each group develops its own set of attitudes and beliefs that serve as norms for members' behaviour. The members

INFLUENCE OF SMALL REFERENCE GROUPS

share these values and are expected to conform to the group's normative behavioural patterns (see Fig. 5-4).

A person may agree with all the standards set by the group or only part of them. Moderate Liberals or Conservatives may not agree with *all* the political views of their provincial party executive. Also, a person does not have to belong to a group to be influenced by it. Young people frequently pattern their dress and other behaviour after that of an older group that the younger ones aspire to join. Another point is that some reference groups serve as negative influences on individuals, who relate to these groups by doing the opposite of what they recommend. Banning a book or X-rating a movie will often increase the sales of the book or attendance at the movie.

The type of social group with the most direct influence on a consumer's behaviour is the small group in which the members normally can interact on a face-to-face basis. Such a group might be a family, a circle of friends, a local sorority chapter, or an athletic team, for example. Studies have shown

Figure 5-4
SOME REFERENCE
GROUPS.
Your buying behaviour is
influenced by the various
reference groups to which
you belong.

that personal advice in face-to-face groups is much more effective as a behavioural determinant than advertising in newspapers, television, or other mass media. That is, in selecting products or changing brands, a prospective buyer is more likely to be influenced by word-of-mouth advertising from satisfied customers in his or her reference group. This is true especially when the speaker is considered to be knowledgeable regarding the particular product.

Another useful finding pertains to the flow of information between and within groups. For years marketers operated in conformity with the "snob appeal" theory. This is the idea that if you can get social leaders and high-income groups to use your products, the mass market will also buy them. The assumption has been that influence follows a *vertical* path, starting at levels of high status and moving downward through successive levels of groups. Contrary to this popular assumption, studies by Katz and Lazarsfeld and by others have emphasized the *horizontal* nature of opinion leadership. Influence emerges on each *level* of the socioeconomic scale, moving from the opinion leaders to their peers.[33]

The proven role of face-to-face groups as behaviour determinants for some products, plus the concept of horizontal information flow, suggests that a marketing person is faced with two key problems. These are (1) identifying the relevant reference group likely to be used by consumers in a given buying situation, and (2) measuring the extent of the group's influence on these consumers. Then the marketing strategy should focus on identifying and communicating with two key people in the group — the innovator (early buyer) and influential person (opinion leader). Every group has a leader—a tastemaker, or **opinion leader**—who influences the decision making of others in the group. The key is for marketers to convince that person of the value of their products or services. The opinion leader in one group may be an opinion follower in another. Married women with children may be influential in matters concerning food, whereas unmarried women are more likely to influence fashions in clothing and makeup. The innovator is discussed later in this chapter.

The effectiveness of small reference groups as behavioural influences will vary, depending upon the product and the availability of information for the consumer. The less information or experience a person has concerning a given product, the stronger the reference-group influence will be for this product and this person.

Of all the small groups a person belongs to through the years, one group normally exerts the strongest and most enduring influence on that person's perceptions and behaviour. That group is his or her family.

FAMILY BUYING BEHAVIOUR

---

[33]See Elihu Katz and Paul Lazarsfeld, *Personal Influence*, Free Press, New York, 1955, especially p. 325; see also Elihu Katz, "The Two-Step Flow of Communications: An Up-to-Date Report on an Hypothesis," *Public Opinion Quarterly*, Spring 1957, pp. 61–78.

Who Does the Family Buying?

Marketers should treat this question as four separate ones, because each may call for different marketing strategies and tactics. The four questions are:

1. Who influences the buying decision? (This may be a member of the family, or the influence may come from an outside reference group.)
2. Who makes the buying decision?
3. Who makes the actual purchase?
4. Who uses the product?

Four different people may be involved, or only one member may do all four, or there may be some other combination of influences.

For many years, women have done most of the family buying. They still exert substantial influence in buying decisions and do a considerable amount of the actual purchasing. However, men have increasingly entered the family buying picture. Self-service stores are especially appealing to men. Night and Sunday openings in suburban shopping centres also encourage men to play a bigger role in family purchasing.[34]

In recent years, teenagers and young children have become decision makers in family buying as well as actual purchasers. The amount of money teenagers spend now is substantial enough to be considered in the marketing plans of many manufacturers and middlemen. Even very young children are an influence in buying decisions today because they watch television programs or shop with their parents.

Purchasing decisions are often made jointly by husband and wife (sometimes even the children are included). Young married people are much more likely to make buying decisions on a joint basis than are older couples. Apparently the longer a husband and wife live together, the more they feel they can trust each other to act unilaterally.

Who buys a product will influence a firm's marketing policies regarding its product, channels of distribution, and promotion. If children are the key decision makers, as is often the case in purchasing breakfast cereals, for instance, then a manufacturer may include some type of premium with the product. In a department store, the men's furnishings department is often located on the street floor near a door. This permits men to enter, shop, and leave the store without having to wade through crowds of shoppers. The entire advertising campaign — media appeals, copy, radio, and televison programming and so forth — is affected by whether the target consists of men, women, or children.

---

[34]See, for example, "More Food Advertisers Woo the Male Shopper as He Shares the Load," *The Wall Street Journal*, Aug. 26, 1980, p. 1; "Large Numbers of Husbands Buy Household Products, Do Housework," *Marketing News*, Oct. 3, 1980, p. 1; and R. Neil Maddox, "The Importance of Males in Supermarket Traffic and Sales," in *Proceedings* of the Marketing Division, Administrative Sciences Association of Canada, 1982, pp. 137–143.

In Chapter 4 we observed that consumer expenditure patterns are influenced considerably by the stage of the life cycle the family is in at any given time. The life-cycle concept can also serve as (1) an explanation for family buying behaviour and (2) a guide to marketers in planning marketing programs consistent with that behaviour. (Refer to Table 4-9, where we summarized the buying patterns for families in each stage of the cycle.)

Influence of Family Life Cycle

In addition to understanding *why* consumers buy, marketers also need to know *when*, *where*, and *how* they buy. We are talking now about consumers' buying *habits*, or overt buying *patterns*, in contrast to their buying *motives* (*why* they buy). This section on buying habits applies to consumers living alone as well as to families.

Buying Habits (Overt Buying Patterns)

When Consumers Buy

Marketing executives should be able to answer at least three questions about *when* people buy their products or services: During what season do they buy? On what day of the week do they buy? At what time of the day do they buy? If seasonal buying patterns exist, marketing executives should try to extend the buying season. There is obviously little opportunity for extending the buying season for Easter bunnies or Christmas-tree ornaments. But the season for vacations has been shifted to such an extent that winter and other "off-season" vacations are now quite popular.

When people buy may influence the product-planning, pricing, or promotional phase of a firm's marketing program. After-shave lotion and alcoholic beverages often are distinctively packaged at Christmastime because they are purchased for gifts. To smooth the seasonal peaks and valleys in the production schedule, a fishing tackle manufacturer may want retailers to buy well in advance of the summer season. To get retailers to do this, the manufacturer may offer them "seasonal datings." This is a pricing strategy whereby retailers take delivery in April but do not have to pay for the merchandise until July.

Where Consumers Buy

A firm should consider two factors with respect to *where* people buy — where the buying decision is made and where the actual purchase occurs. For many products and services the decision to buy is made at home. For others, the decision is often made in whole or in part at the point of purchase. A man shopping in a sporting-goods store for golf clubs may see some tennis balls on sale. Knowing he needs some, he decides on the spot to buy them. A woman may decide at home to buy a birthday gift for her husband, but she will wait until she gets to the store before deciding whether it will be a shirt or a book.

A company's promotional program, and in many cases its product planning, must be geared to carry the greatest impact at the place where the buying decision is made. If the decision to buy is made in the store, then attention must be devoted to packaging and other point-of-purchase display materials, particularly in self-service stores. A shopper may decide at home to buy some cold cereal, but the key decision regarding which type and which brand may be made at the store.

How Consumers Buy

The *how* part of consumers' buying habits encompasses several areas of behaviour and, consequently, many marketing decisions. Long ago, for example, many firms found that consumers prefer to buy such products as pickles, cookies, and butter already packaged. The advantages of cleanliness and ease of handling offset the higher unit price.

The trend toward one-stop shopping has encouraged retailers to add related and even unrelated lines of merchandise to their basic groups of products. The increase of credit-card buying has led several department stores to accept Visa or MasterCard credit cards. In the past, these retailers would accept only their own charge-account cards.

NEW-PRODUCT ADOPTION AND DIFFUSION

The process by which a new product is adopted, and the diffusion of that innovation through a group of people, are a logical extension of reference-group theory. By definition, an **innovation** is anything—product, service, idea—that is perceived by a person as being new. The **adoption process** is the decision-making activity of an *individual* through which the innovation is accepted. The **diffusion** of innovation is the process by which the innovation is communicated within social systems over time.[35]

Stages in Adoption Process

A prospective user goes through the following six stages in the process of deciding whether to adopt something new:

STAGE	ACTIVITY IN THAT STAGE
Awareness	Individual is exposed to the innovation; becomes a prospect.
Information	Prospect is interested enough to seek information.
Evaluation	Prospect mentally measures relative merits.
Trial	Prospect adopts the innovation on a limited basis. A consumer buys a small sample, for example. If for some reason (cost or size) an innovation cannot be sampled, the chances of its being adopted will decrease.
Adoption	Prospect decides whether to use the innovation on a full-scale basis.
Postadoption confirmation	The innovation is adopted; then the user continues to seek assurance that the right decision was made.

---

[35]For some foundations of diffusion theory, a review of landmark studies on diffusion of innovation, and extensive bibliographical references, see Everett M. Rogers, *Diffusion of Innovations*, 3d ed., The Free Press, New York, 1983; and Everett M. Rogers, "New Product Adoption and Diffusion," *Journal of Consumer Research*, March 1976, pp. 290–301.

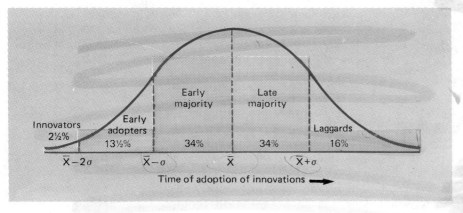

Figure 5-5
DISTRIBUTION
OF INNOVATION
ADOPTERS.

The distribution of adopters (based on when they adopted the innovation) generally follows the normal (black) curve. Thus, the area lying *more than* one standard deviation (σ) to the left of the mean time of adoption (X) represents the first 16 percent of the adopters — the innovators and early adopters. (*Source*: Everett M. Rogers, *Diffusion of Innovations*, 3d ed., The Free Press, New York, 1983.

Adopter Categories

Some people will adopt an innovation quickly after it is introduced. Others will delay for some time before accepting the new product. Still others may never adopt it. Researchers have identified five categories of individuals, based on the relative time when they adopted a given innovation. Figure 5-5 illustrates the proportion of adopters in each category. The categories are rather arbitrarily partitioned on a time scale to represent unit standard deviations from the average time of adoption. For example, innovators are those who are more than two standard deviations away (to the left) of the mean time of adoption — less than 3 percent of all adopters. Also, *non-adopters are excluded.*

Innovators

Innovators, a *venturesome* group, constitute about 3 percent of the market and are the first to adopt an innovation. In relation to later adopters, the innovators are likely to be younger, have a higher social status, and be in a better financial position. Innovators also tend to have broader, more cosmopolitan social relationships. They are likely to rely more on impersonal sources of information, including those external to their own social system, than on salespeople or other word-of-mouth sources.

Early Adopters

Early adopters — about 13 percent of the market — tend to be a more integrated part of a local social system. That is, whereas innovators are cosmopolites, early adopters are localites. Thus the early-adopter category includes more opinion leaders than any other adopter group. Early adopters are greatly *respected* in their social system. An "agent of change" is a person who is seeking to speed up the diffusion of a given innovation. This change agent will often try to work through the early adopters because they are not too far ahead of others in their peer group. Salespeople are probably used more by the early adopters than by any other category.

Early Majority

The more *deliberate* group, the early majority, represents about 34 percent of the market. This group tends to accept an innovation just before the "average" adopter in a social system. This group is a bit above average in social and economic measures. Its members rely quite a bit on advertisements, salespeople, and contact with early adopters. Business firms in this category are average-sized operations.

Late Majority

Representing about another 34 percent of the market, the late majority is a *sceptical* group. Usually its members adopt an innovation in response to an economic necessity or to social pressure from their peers. They rely on their peers — late or early majority — as sources of information. Advertising and personal selling are less effective with this group than is word-of-mouth.

Laggards

This *tradition-bound* group — 16 percent of the market — includes those who are the last to adopt an innovation. Their point of reference is what was done in the past. Laggards are suspicious of innovations and innovators. By the time laggards adopt something new, it may already have been discarded by the innovator group in favour of a newer idea. Laggards are older and are at the low end of the social and economic scales.

At this point we might recall that we are discussing only *adopters* (early or late) of an innovation. For most innovations, there still are many people who are *not* included in our percentages. These are the people who *never* do adopt the innovation — the nonadopters.

Some key differences between earlier and later adopters are summarized in Table 5-2. It should be pointed out that these characteristics should be interpreted cautiously, as the nature of the adopter may be different from innovation to innovation. For example, the early adopter of cable television in one Canadian city was found to be younger and to have a higher income, but to be less well-educated and more likely to be employed in a blue-collar job.[36]

---

[36] James G. Barnes, *Cable and Canadians: An Examination of the Sociocultural Impact of Cable Television on a Canadian Community*, a report prepared for Communications Canada, 1983.

Table 5-2   DIFFERENCES IN CHARACTERISTICS OF EARLY- AND
LATE-ADOPTER CATEGORIES

	Adopters	
	Early	**Late**
Key Characteristics	Innovators: venturesome Early adopters: respected Early majority: deliberate	Late majority: sceptical Laggards: tradition-bound
Other Characteristics		
Age	Younger	Older
Education	Well Educated	Less Educated
Income	Higher	Lower
Social relationships: within or outside community	Innovators: cosmopolites Others: more localites	Totally local
Social status	Higher	Lower
Information sources	Wider variety; many media	Limited media exposure; limited reliance on outside media; rely on local peer groups

The time required for a given innovation to be adopted may range from a few weeks to several decades. Five characteristics of an innovation, as perceived by individuals, seem to influence the adoption rate.[37] One is **relative advantage** — the degree to which an innovation is superior to preceding ideas. Relative advantage may be reflected in lower cost, higher profitability or some other measure. Another characteristic is **compatibility** — the degree to which an innovation is consistent with the cultural values and experiences of the adopters.

The degree of complexity of an innovation will affect its adoption rate. The more complex an innovation is, the less quickly it will be adopted. The fourth characteristic — **trialability** — is the degree to which the new idea may be sampled on some limited basis. On this point, a central home air-conditioning system is likely to have a slower adoption rate than some new seed or fertilizer, which may be tried on a small plot of ground. Finally, the **observability** of the innovation affects its adoption rate. A weed killer that works on existing weeds will be accepted sooner than a pre-emergent weed killer. The reason is that the latter — even though it may be a superior product — produces no dead weeds to show to prospective adopters.

Characteristics of Innovations Affecting Adoption Rate

In Chapter 4, markets were defined as people with money to spend and the willingness to spend it. This chapter and the next are devoted to the "willingness-to-buy" factor — that is, consumer buying behaviour. It is

SUMMARY

---

[37]Rogers.

| Aroused needs (motives) | are forces which activate | goal-oriented behaviour to bring want satisfaction |

extremely important that marketers understand buying behaviour. At the same time, it is also very difficult, because we do not know what goes on in a person's mind.

The simplified behavioural model we follow is shown above. Maslow's hierarchy of needs is used as our model for motivation. Motivation triggers goal-oriented behaviour, and perceptions shape behaviour. The factor of selectivity also modifies perceptions.

Perceptions are shaped by the cultural, social-group, and psychological forces that constitute a person's frame of reference. Marketers must be aware of cultural change and of the importance of segmenting the market into subcultures. A social-class structure exists in Canadian society; our society may be categorized into six social classes. And there are significant differences in buying behaviour among those classes.

Small reference groups to which we belong, or aspire to belong, also influence our perceptions. Reference groups stress conformity to the behavioural standards set for the groups' members and often enforce these standards. Most groups have opinion leaders. A company's marketing effort should be directed toward identifying and communicating with these leaders. An application of reference-group theory is the adoption process for new products and the diffusion of an innovation among social groups.

The family is the smallest social group to influence our perceptions, and in many cases it is the most powerful social force affecting buyer behaviour. The stage of the family life cycle influences buyer behaviour. Marketers need to know **who** does the family buying and *when*, *where*, and *how* people buy — that is, the buying habits of consumers.

KEY TERMS AND CONCEPTS

1. Which needs in Maslow's hierarchy might be satisfied by each of the following products or services?
   a. Marlboro cigarettes
   b. A travel agency located in your bank building
   c. *Webster's Collegiate Dictionary*
   d. Suntan lotion
   e. The services of a securities broker

2. The following statements were taken from ads in magazines. Which, if any, of Maslow's needs is each of the products or services (as advertised) trying to satisfy?
   a. "That Maytag washer came to live with us over 14 years ago and it's only seen the repairman four times." (Clothes-washing machine.)
   b. "Come to where the flavor is. Come to Marlboro country." (Cigarettes and cowboy country.)
   c. "Guaranteed to take from 1 to 3 inches off your waistline in just 3 days or your money refunded." (Sauna belt waistline reducer.)
   d. "How sweet it isn't." (Squirt, the semi-soft drink.)
   e. "Explore the marvelous mechanism that is THE BODY." (*Life* magazine's science library; book entitled *The Body*.)
   f. "A diamond is forever." (DeBeers diamond mines; the company name is very obscure in this ad.)

3. Explain what is meant by the selectivity factors in perception.

4. What are some of the marketing implications in the cultural trend toward an "age of me"?

5. What were the major conclusions drawn from the *Chicago Tribune's* study of social-class structure in a large industrial city?

6. Which of the six social classes do you associate with each of the following products or activities? In some cases more than one class should be listed, but try to associate each item with only one class.
   a. Debutante parties
   b. A cocktail before dinner
   c. Wine and liqueurs with dinner
   d. Beer with dinner
   e. A Cadillac
   f. *The New Yorker* magazine
   g. Boats
   h. Sitting on the front porch in warm weather in an undershirt
   i. Shopping at a credit jeweller
   j. Borrowing from a bank
   k. Borrowing from a pawnbroker

7. Discuss the concept of a reference group, explaining:
   a. The meaning of the concept
   b. Its use in marketing

8. "Reference groups stifle initiative, foster robot-like conformity among the members, and inflict severe penalties for failure to meet the group's standards of behaviour." Discuss.

9. Cite a few examples of products for which the same person normally makes the buying decisions and the physical purchase and also uses the product. Then give some examples in which two or three different people are involved in these processes. Explain how a firm's marketing program may be affected by the number of people involved in each case.

10. In which stage of the life cycle are families likely to be the best prospects for each of the following products or services?
    a. Braces on teeth
    b. Suntan lotion
    c. Second car in the family
    d. Vitamin pills
    e. Refrigerators
    f. Life insurance
    g. Jogging suits
    h. 46-day Mediterranean cruise

11. Explain how the factors of *when* and *where* people might buy affect the marketing program for each of the following products:
    a. House paint
    b. High-quality sunglasses
    c. Outboard motors
    d. Room air conditioners

12. In the "trial" stage of deciding whether to adopt some innovation, the likelihood of adoption is reduced if the product cannot be sampled because of its cost or size. What are some products that might have these drawbacks? How might these drawbacks be overcome?

13. Describe the people likely to be found in (*a*) the innovator category of adopters and (*b*) the late-majority category.

Psychological Influences on Buyer Behaviour, and the Classification of Consumer Goods

Chapter 6

CHAPTER GOALS

This is the last of the three chapters on consumer buying behaviour. Its title is quite descriptive. After studying the chapter, you should understand:

1. *The psychological forces that influence buyer behaviour, especially the consumer's learning experiences, personality, attitudes and beliefs, and self-concept*
2. *The decision-making process in buying, especially patronage buying motives and postpurchase behaviour (cognitive dissonance)*
3. *The distinction between consumer goods and industrial goods*
4. *The classification of consumer products as convenience, shopping, and specialty goods — and the marketing implications of these classes or goods*

In the preceding chapter we saw how individuals' perceptions are determined to a great extent by their cultural surroundings and by the various groups of people with whom they associate. In this chapter, our focus shifts to the *psychological* forces that influence an individual's perceptions. Then we tie together our psychological and sociocultural discussions as we examine the process that consumers go through when they make a buying decision. In the final section, we discuss a behavioural classification of consumer products.

PSYCHOLOGICAL DETERMINANTS OF BUYER BEHAVIOUR

In discussing the psychological forces in consumer behaviour, we shall continue to use the model we set up in Chapter 5. That is, one or more motives within a person trigger behaviour toward a goal that is expected to bring satisfaction. This goal-oriented behaviour is influenced by the person's perceptions. In this chapter, we discuss the effects that learning experiences, personality, attitudes and beliefs, and self-concept have on perceptions. (See Fig. 6-1, which is essentially the same as Fig. 5-3.)

These psychological variables are reflected in various ways in a person's life-style. The term **psychographics** is being used by many researchers as a collective synonym for the combination of psychological variables and life-style preferences.[1]

Learning Experiences

As a factor influencing a person's perceptions, **learning** may be defined as changes in behaviour resulting from previous experiences. However, also by definition, learning does *not* include behaviour changes attributable to instinctive responses, growth, or temporary states of the organism, such as hunger, fatigue, or sleep.[2]

The ability to understand and predict the results of the consumer's learning process is a real key to understanding buying behaviour. Therefore, it is unfortunate that no simple learning theory has emerged as universally workable and acceptable. The principle learning theories described here are (1) stimulus-response theories, (2) cognitive theories, and (3) gestalt and field theories.[3]

Stimulus-Response Theories

These theories were first formulated by psychologists such as Pavlov, Skinner, and Hull on the basis of their laboratory experiments with animals. This school of theorists holds that learning occurs as a person (or animal) (1) responds to some stimulus and (2) is reinforced with need satisfaction for a correct response or penalized for an incorrect one. When the same correct response is repeated in reaction to a given stimulus, behavioural patterns are established.

An application of the stimulus-response (S-R) model is the **behaviourism** approach, expounded by Watson and still applied in advertising today.[4] He suggested that the same stimulus be repeated to strengthen the response pattern. From this came the idea of constantly repeating an advertisement to firmly reinforce a given purchasing response. An application of this idea is the advertising for the Prudential Insurance Company, which for many

According to S-R theory, this:

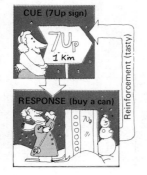

eventually becomes this:

---

[1]No universally accepted definition for the term *psychographics* has as yet been developed. See William D. Wells, "Psychographics: A Critical Review," *Journal of Marketing Research*, May 1975, pp. 196–213. Also see William Lazer, "Analyze Lifestyle Trends to Predict Future Product/Market Opportunities," *Marketing News*, July 10, 1981, p. 8; and Niles Howard, "A New Way to View Consumers," *Dun's Review*, August 1981, p. 42.

[2]For a discussion of other definitions of learning, see John F. Hall, *Psychology of Learning*, J. B. Lippincott Company, Philadelphia, 1966, pp. 3–6.

[3]See Earnest R. Hilgard and George H. Bower, *Theories of Learning*, Appleton-Century-Crofts, Inc., New York, 1966.

[4]See John B. Watson, *Behaviorism*, The People's Institute Publishing Co., New York, 1925.

years has featured the Rock of Gibraltar. The advertising stresses the theme of security, dependability, and stability as people are urged to "buy a piece of the Rock." The concept of behaviourism is probably too simplistic, however. Today we realize that attitudes and other factors (not just the mechanical stimulus-response) also play a role in explaining a consumer's response to repetitive advertising.

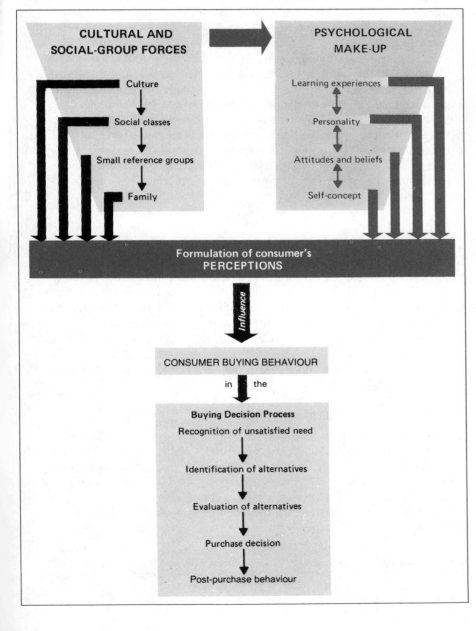

Figure 6-1
SOCIOCULTURAL AND PSYCHOLOGICAL FORCES THAT INFLUENCE CONSUMERS' BUYING BEHAVIOUR.

Nevertheless, the stimulus-response model, with reinforcement as an essential element, is a useful explanation of the learning process. Four factors—drive, cue, response, and reinforcement—are fundamental to the process. A **drive** (or motive) is a strong stimulus that requires satisfaction —a response of some sort. The **cues** are weaker stimuli that determine the pattern of this response—the "when," "where," and "how" of the response behaviour. For instance, a TV commercial or a change in price is a cue that might shape a consumer's behaviour in seeking to satisfy an aroused hunger drive. The **response** is simply the behavioural reaction to the cues and drive. **Reinforcement** results when the response is rewarding (satisfying).

If the response is gratifying, a connection between cue and response will be established; that is, a behavioural pattern will be learned. Learning, then, emerges from reinforcement. Continual reinforcement leads to habit. Once a habitual pattern of behaviour is established, it replaces conscious, wilful behaviour. The stronger the habit, the more difficult it is for a competitive product to break the habit, and enter a consumer's learning field. On the other hand, if the original response action is not rewarding, the consumer's mind is open to another set of cues leading to another response. For example, the consumer will buy a substitute product or switch to another brand.

Cognitive Theories

Cognitive learning theories reject the S-R model as being too mechanistic. In S-R theory, behaviour is the result of *only* the degree of reinforcement stemming from a response to some stimulus. No other influences are recognized as intervening in the S-R channel. Proponents of cognitive theory insist that learning is influenced by factors such as attitudes and beliefs, past experience, and an insightful understanding of how to achieve a goal. Cognitive theorists believe that a person can use thinking ability to solve a current problem, even if there are no historical precedents in the person's experience. Habitual behavioural patterns, then, are the result of perceptive thinking and goal orientation.

Gestalt and Field Theories

Gestalt is a German word that roughly means "configuration," "pattern," or "form." Gestalt psychologists are concerned with the "whole" of a thing — the total scene — rather than its component parts. They maintain that learning and behaviour should be viewed as a total process, in contrast to the individual-element approach in the S-R model.[5]

Field theory, as formulated by Kurt Lewin, is a useful refinement of gestalt psychology.[6] This theory holds that the only determining force ac-

---

[5]See K. Koffka, *Principles of Gestalt Psychology*, Harcourt, Brace, & World, Inc., New York, 1935; Wolfgang Kohler, *Gestalt Psychology*, Liveright Publishing Corporation, New York, 1947.

[6]See Kurt Lewin, *A Dynamic Theory of Personality* (1935) and *Principles of Topological Psychology* (1936), McGraw-Hill Book Company, New York.

counting for a person's behaviour at any given time is that person's psychological "field" at that time. A person's *field* or *life space* may be defined as the totality of existing facts pertaining to the individual and his or her environment at the time of the behaviour. Thus, to understand consumers' behaviour, we must understand their perceptions of their environment. That is, we must understand all the complex forces that influence consumers as they strive to satisfy the drive that initiated the goal-seeking process.

Gestalt psychologists are concerned with individuals' perception and understanding of their total environment. They believe that a person perceives the whole rather than its parts. They further postulate that a person's perception of the whole is quite different from what we might expect if each part were considered separately. Thus, looking at the following configuration,

most people will perceive four sets of tracks, four pairs of lines, or four columns, but rarely do they perceive eight vertical lines.

Moreover, rather than perceive separate parts, people will organize them (in their perception) into a whole that is meaningful in light of their past experience. Thus, the properties of the *total field* influence people's perceptions of the stimuli in that field. To illustrate, a distinguished-looking man in a white coat can speak in a serious tone in a TV commercial advertising a pain reliever. Many viewers will perceive him as a doctor because that is how they interpret the total scene in light of their past experience.

Several "field" principles, which have applications in marketing, deal with the ways in which properties of stimuli affect our perception of them.[7] The principle of **closure** postulates that we tend to complete (close) figures to make them meaningful. Thus, "13 0" will be "closed" by the viewer to get "B O." A change in spacing (illustrating the principle of **proximity**) can give different results — "1 3 0" will be viewed as the number "130" rather than as two letters.

According to another "field" principle, marketing messages must be placed in a reasonable **context** — a smartly dressed woman should not be shown painting her house. Ads should also be **simple** in both structure and content. Because of **locational properties**, some items will stand out in a sea of similar-looking products. This principle places a premium on eye-level shelf position in a supermarket, for example. And all parts of a marketing program — price, type of ads, product quality, and the like — must be in **harmony**, that is, consistent with consumers' expectations.

Personality

The study of human personality has given rise to many, sometimes widely divergent, schools of psychological thought. Yet, perhaps because of this multifaceted attention, we still lack even a consensus definition of the term.

---

[7] Adapted from James H. Myers and William H. Reynolds, *Consumer Behavior and Marketing Management*, Houghton Mifflin Company, Boston, 1967, pp. 21–34.

Attempts to inventory and classify personality traits have understandably produced many different structures. In this discussion, **personality** is defined as an individual's pattern of traits that are a determinant of behavioural responses.

It is generally agreed that consumers' personality traits influence their perceptions and buying behaviour. Unfortunately, however, there is no agreement as to the nature of this relationship, that is, *how* personality influences behaviour. Two points of view prevail. One holds that personality traits are the dominant force in determining behaviour, overpowering any external influences. The opposite contention, advocated by many sociologists and social psychologists, is that the situational environment is the key determining factor. Perhaps the answer lies in an approach that represents the *interaction* of the two—that is, a blend of (1) the past-experience, individual-difference factor and (2) the external situation (as in Fig. 6-1).

Psychoanalytic Theories of Personality

The psychoanalytic school of thought, founded by Sigmund Freud and later modified by his followers and critics, has had a tremendous impact on the study of human personality and behaviour. Freud contended that there are three parts to the mind — the id, the ego, and the superego. The **id** houses the basic instinctive drives, many of which are antisocial. The **superego** is the conscience, accepting moral standards and directing the instinctive drives into acceptable channels. The id and the superego are sometimes in conflict. The **ego** is the conscious, rational control centre that maintains a balance between the uninhibited instincts of the id and the socially oriented, constraining superego.

Freud's behavioural thesis was that we enter the world with certain instinctive biological drives that cannot be satisfied in a socially acceptable fashion. As we learn that we cannot gratify these needs in a direct manner, we develop other, more subtle means of seeking satisfaction. These other means require that the basic drives be repressed, and consequently, inner tensions and frustrations develop. Also, feelings of guilt or shame about these drives cause us to suppress and even sublimate them to the point where they become subconscious. For satisfactions of these drives, we substitute rationalizations and socially acceptable behaviour. Yet the basic urges are always there. The net result is very complex behaviour. Sometimes even we ourselves do not understand why we feel or act as we do.

One significant marketing implication of psychoanalytic theory is that a person's real motive for buying a given product or shopping at a certain store may well be hidden. The usual research techniques that are adequate for determining demographic and economic data normally prove fruitless in uncovering the real reasons for a person's behaviour.

Psychoanalytic theory has caused marketers to realize that they must provide buyers with socially acceptable rationalizations for their purchasing. Yet we also can appeal subconsciously to buyers' dreams, hopes, and fears.

The Freudians suggest that there are conflicts between our instinct (id) and conscience (superego). Our rational side (ego) attempts to resolve these conflicts, and the effort leads to tensions, frustrations, and guilt that we unconsciously tend to hide from ourselves and others. This makes motivation very difficult to understand.

Attitudes and Beliefs

An **attitude** may be defined as a person's enduring cognitive evaluation, emotional feeling, or action tendency toward some object or idea. Attitudes involve thought processes as well as emotional feelings, and they vary in intensity. Attitudes influence beliefs, and beliefs infuence attitudes. In fact, for the purpose of our generalized, introductory-level discussion of buying behaviour, we shall use the two concepts interchangeably. They both reflect value judgments and positive or negative feelings toward a product, service, or brand.

Attitudes and beliefs are strong and direct forces affecting consumers' perceptions and buying behaviour. Attitudes significantly influence people's perceptions by selectively screening out any stimuli that conflict with those attitudes. They also can distort the perception of messages and affect the degree of their retention.

Various studies report a relationship between consumers' attitudes and their buying decisions in regard to both the type of product and the brand selection. Surely, then, it is in a marketer's best interest to understand how attitudes are formed, measured, and changed. Attitudes are **formed**, generally speaking, by the information individuals acquire (1) through their past learning experiences with the product or idea, or (2) through their relations with their reference groups (family, social and work groups, etc.). The perception of this information is influenced by personality traits.

Attitude **measurement** is far from easy. In limited instances a researcher may simply employ the direct-question, survey technique. The most widely used techniques, however, have been some form of attitude scaling. Respondents may be asked, for instance, to rank several models or products by order of preference. Or, they may be asked to rate some item according to a verbal scale ranging from one extreme to another (from ultramodern to very old-fashioned, for example).

Attitude **change**, as it affects marketing, means this: How can a company create a situation in which consumers perceive their needs to be best satisfied by that company's product or brand? A marketer has two choices —either (1) to change consumers' attitudes to be consonant with the product, or (2) to determine what consumers' attitudes are and then change the product to match those attitudes. In general, it is easier to change the product than to change consumers' attitudes.

Marketers should face the fact that it is *extremely* difficult to change consumers' attitudes, regardless of marketing critics' opinions to the contrary. Highly persuasive communication is ordinarily needed to change buyers' attitudes. The communication (advertisement, personal sales talk, or other message) should attempt to change one or more of the three factors in our definition of attitude — evaluation, feeling, and action tendency.

By providing effective information about its brand, for example, a marketer might change consumers' **cognitive evaluation** of that brand. With a strong, emotionally appealing ad, the seller might change buyers' **emotional feelings**. Buyers' **action tendencies** toward a brand might be changed by getting buyers to do something that contradicts their current preferences. For instance, "cents-off" coupons or free samples might induce buyers to change their action patterns—at least long enough to try a new brand. Even then, the buyers must be convinced before they will let their present brand preferences be challenged—no easy task for the seller.

The Self-Concept

Another behaviour determinant is the self-concept, or self-image. Your **self-image** is the way you see yourself. At the same time, it is the picture you think others have of you. Some psychologists distinguish between the *actual* self-concept (the way you really see yourself) and the *ideal* self-concept (the way you want to be seen or would like to see yourself). To some extent, the self-image theory is a reflection of other psychological and sociological concepts already discussed. A person's self-image is influenced, for instance, by innate and learned physiological and psychological needs. It is conditioned also by economic factors, demographic factors, and social-group influences.

Studies of actual purchases show that people generally prefer brands and products that are compatible with their own self-concept. There are mixed reports concerning the degree of influence of the actual and ideal self-concepts on brand and product preferences. Some psychologists contend that consumption preferences correspond to a person's *actual* self-image. Others hold that the *ideal* self-image is dominant in consumers' choices.

As marketing people, we want to be able to identify consumers' goals because they influence buying behaviour. In many situations, we can determine those goals if we know what individuals' self-images are. Note, however, that individuals' self-images tell us only *what* their goals are. We cannot determine *why* their self-images are as they are, nor *why* different people have *different* self-images. However, it is helpful just to understand that people do have different pictures of themselves. Our job is to determine what these self-images are. Then we can predict what the consumers' goals are and what their behaviour is apt to be in the marketplace.

It is time now to tie together some of the points we have discussed regarding consumer behaviour, and to describe the process consumers go through when making purchasing decisions. The process is a problem-solving approach consisting of the following five stages, also shown in the lower half of Fig. 6-1:

DECISION-MAKING PROCESS IN BUYING

1. Recognition of an unsatisfied need
2. Identification of alternative ways of achieving satisfaction
3. Evaluation of alternatives
4. Purchase decisions
5. Postpurchase behaviour

Once the process has been started, potential buyers can withdraw at any stage prior to the actual purchase, and some stages can be skipped. A total-stage approach is likely to be used only in certain buying situations — a first-time purchase of a product, for instance, or in buying high-priced infrequently purchased articles. For many products the purchasing behaviour is a routine affair in which the aroused need is satisfied in the usual manner by repurchasing the same brand. That is, past reinforcement in learning experiences leads directly to the buying response-act, and thus the second and third stages are bypassed. However, if something changes appreciably (price, product, services), buyers may reopen the full decision process and consider alternative brands or products.

The process starts when an unsatisfied need (motive) creates inner tension. This may be a biogenic need, aroused internally (the person feels hungry). Or the need may have been dormant until it was aroused by an external stimulus, such as an ad or the sight of the product. Or perhaps dissatisfaction with the present product created the tension.

Recognition of Unsatisfied Need

Once the need has been recognized, often consumers become aware of conflicting or competing uses for their scarce resources of time or money. Let us say that a husband has a desire to install a swimming pool in the backyard at a cost of $6,000. His wife may remind him that they need new furniture for the living room. Or the man may fear that one of his key reference groups would not approve. A person must resolve these conflicts before proceeding. Otherwise, the buying process stops at this point.

Identification of Alternatives

Once a need has been recognized, both product and brand alternatives must be identified. Suppose a woman wants to make her hands feel softer. Some alternative solutions include buying a new dishwasher, using rubber gloves, or trying a different detergent or a new hand cream. Or she can get her husband and her kids to wash the dishes and scrub the floors. If one of the product alternatives is selected, then there still are several brand alternatives to choose from.

The search for alternatives is influenced by such factors as (1) what the time and money costs are (not much time is spent buying a hamburger, in comparison with the time spent buying a new winter coat); (2) how much information the consumer already has from past experience and other sources; and (3) the amount of the perceived risk if a wrong selection is made.

Evaluation of Alternatives

Once all the reasonable alternatives have been identified, the consumer must evaluate each one preparatory to making a purchase decision. The criteria that consumers use in their evaluations should be familiar by now. They include past experience and attitudes toward various brands. Consumers also use the opinion of members of their families and other reference groups as guidelines in these evaluations.

Purchase Decisions

After searching and evaluating, the consumer at some point must decide whether or not to buy. If the decision is to buy, the buyer must make a series of decisions regarding brand, price, store, colour, and so on.

Anything marketers can do to simplify decision making will be attractive to buyers, because most people find it very hard to make a decision. Sometimes several decision situations can be combined and marketed as one package. A travel agency simplifies travellers' decisions concerning transportation, hotels, and which tours to take, by selling a packaged tour.

At this point in the buying process, marketers are trying to determine the consumers' **patronage buying motives**. These are the reasons that a consumer patronizes (shops at) a certain store. These are different from *product buying motives*, which are reasons for buying a certain product. Some of the more important patronage buying motives are:

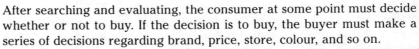

1. Convenience of location
2. Level of service
3. Ease of locating merchandise
4. Transaction ease
5. Price/value
6. Assortment of merchandise
7. Store ambience
8. Store appearance
9. Calibre of sales personnel

The patterns of store choice that result from satisfying patronage motives are related to the concept of social-class structure described in Chapter 5. Patronage studies show that shoppers often match their own values and expectations with those of a store and that these are social-class related in many cases. Not all people want to shop at glamorous, high-status stores. For them, such stores have the wrong ambience. They believe they will be punished in subtle ways by the clerks and other customers if they go into an exclusive department store. "The clerk treats you like a crumb," was one response.

Because social-class awareness or identification and choice of store are related, an important function of retail advertising today is to help shoppers make the necessary social identification. Shoppers do not want to go to a store where they do not fit. If they have any doubts, they are apt to stay away from a store whose social advertising appeal is not clear-cut. Usually, retailers must select a desired niche in the social structure and then set up their marketing and advertising accordingly. Normally, no one —not even a large department store with a bargain basement as well as exclusive boutique departments—can appeal strongly to all social groups.

All the steps in the buying process up to this point occur *before* or *during* the time a purchase is made. However, a buyer's feelings *after* the sale are also significant for the marketer. They can influence repeat sales and what the buyer tells others about the product.

Postpurchase Behaviour

Typically, buyers experience some postpurchase anxieties in all but routine purchases. Leon Festinger refers to this state of anxiety as **cognitive dissonance**.[8] Festinger theorizes that people strive for internal harmony and consistency among their "cognitions" (knowledge, attitudes, beliefs, values). Any inconsistency in the cognitions is called "dissonance."

Postpurchase cognitive dissonance occurs because each of the alternatives considered by the consumer usually has both advantages and limitations. Thus, when the purchase decision is finally made, the selected alternative has some drawbacks, while the rejected alternatives each possess some attractive features. That is, *negative* aspects of the item *selected*, and the *positive* qualities of the *rejected* products, create cognitive dissonance in the consumer.

Festinger developed some hypotheses about the intensity of cognitive dissonance. Dissonance increases as (1) the dollar value of the purchase increases, (2) the relative attractiveness of the unselected alternatives increases, and (3) the relative importance of the decision increases (buying a house or car creates more dissonance than buying a candy bar).

The beginning of an acute case of cognitive dissonance.

To restore internal harmony and minimize discomfort, people will try to reduce their postpurchase anxieties. Thus they are likely to avoid information (such as ads for the rejected products) that is likely to increase dissonance. Prior to making the purchase, they may shop around quite a bit, especially for high-priced, infrequently purchased articles. In this way they seek to minimize postdecision dissonance by spending more time in predecision evaluations.

---

[8]Leon Festinger, *A Theory of Cognitive Dissonance*, Stanford University Press, Stanford, Calif., 1957; see also Jack W. Brehm and Arthur R. Cohen, *Explorations in Cognitive Dissonance*, John Wiley & Sons, Inc. New York, 1962.

Some useful generalizations can be developed from the theory. For example, anything sellers can do in their advertising or personal selling to reassure buyers — say, by stressing desirable features of a product — will reduce dissonance. This reduction will reinforce consumers and increase the likelihood of repeat purchases. When the product in question is expensive and infrequently purchased, the sellers' postsale service program can be a significant factor in reducing dissonance.

TOWARD A COMPREHENSIVE THEORY OF BUYER BEHAVIOUR

The traditional approach to the study of buyer behaviour has typically been a fragmented one. That is, research is done on attitudes or personality or social-group influence. Certainly, many of the theories and research findings on separate parts of buyer behaviour have shed some light on the mental processes involved. Also, many of the findings have been profitably applied by marketing practitioners.

In recent years, however, some notable attempts have been made to formulate a comprehensive theory of buyer behaviour. Two models are described here *very* briefly. Typically, any comprehensive model poses some problems. First, the models are complicated and very difficult to explain. (But then, consumer behaviour is a complex activity.) Second, the validity of the models needs further support. Third, it is difficult for a business to translate the theoretical abstractions into practical company activities.

The Howard-Sheth Theory

One broad theory developed by Howard and Sheth over a period of time included a 3-year validation test.[9] The model is based on the assumptions that (1) buying is a rational exercise in problem solving and (2) buyer behaviour is systematic (not random). Thus buyer behaviour is caused by inputs (stimuli) and results in outputs (buying behaviour). The theory is an attempt to describe what occurs between the inputs and outputs. This is reminiscent of the learning theories discussed earlier in this chapter.

The Howard-Sheth (H-S) theoretical model is based on the idea that four sets of variables determine buyer behaviour:

1. Stimulus-input variables from the marketing program and social environment

2. Internal variables that together show the state of the buyer (his or her motives, attitudes, experiences, perceptions)

3. Seven variables that affect the internal state of the buyer (these are called "exogenous" variables and include social class, culture, time pressure and financial status)

4. Response-output variables (the buyer's behaviour based on interactions of the first three sets of variables)

[9]Adapted from John A. Howard and Jagdish N. Sheth, "A Theory of Buyer Behavior," in Harold H. Kassarjian and Thomas S. Robertson (eds.), *Perspectives in Consumer Behavior*, rev. ed., Scott, Foresman and Company, Glenview, Ill., 1973, pp. 519–540. For a revision of the Howard-Sheth model, see John U. Farley, John A. Howard, and L. Winston Ring, *Consumer Behavior Theory and Application*, Allyn & Bacon, Inc., Boston, 1974.

Summary of the Theory

Much buying behaviour is repetitive. When confronted with a repetitive brand-choice decision, consumers tend to simplify their task by storing relevant information and establishing a routine in their decision process. The elements in this brand-choice decision are (1) a set of motives, (2) alternative choices of products and brands (called the **evoked set**), and (3) decision mediators.

Decision mediators are a set of rules that buyers use to match their motives and the alternatives for satisfying these motives. These mediators are assumed to rank-order the motives and then rank-order the brands on the basis of their potential for satisfying these motives. The rank-ordering of the brands is based on learning experiences or outside information (ads, reference-group advice, and so on). From these influences, buyers develop their attitudes (H-S theory calls them "predispositions"). **Inhibitors** (price, availability, buyer's financial status) may interfere in the buying process.

A buyer who is considering new types of products has no readily available set of decision mediators. The buyer actively seeks information from his or her environment and tries to draw from experiences with similar types of products.

If a buyer's brand choices prove to be satisfactory, those choices are repeated in future purchases. The buyer thus strives to develop a routine, to reduce the complexity of buying. This is called the **psychology of simplification**. On the other hand, sometimes the same routines and the same brands become boring. A buyer who is tired of his or her preferred brands will complicate the situation by starting the product-search process all over again. This is called the **psychology of complication**.

The theory also explains how a given stimulus may result in different responses among buyers, depending on each person's "level of motivation." In response to the stimulus of an advertisement, for example, one person may buy the brand, and another may simply read the ad and store the information. A third may ignore the ad. The concept of "predisposition toward a brand" is used to explain how two buyers may both need the same product but buy two different brands.

Engel, Kollat, and Blackwell developed a comprehensive theoretical model that conceives of a person as being a system of *outputs* (behaviour) that respond to *inputs*.[10] The model recognizes the existence of "intervening variables" between the inputs and the outputs. Marketers must try to understand how these variables affect the processes going on in the consumer's mind. This theory holds that a person's psychological makeup (personality, attitudes, learning experiences) affects the person's mental processes.

The Engel-Kollat-Blackwell Theory

---

[10]James F. Engel and Roger D. Blackwell, *Consumer Behavior*, 4th ed., Dryden Press, Hinsdale, Ill., 1982. The model serves as the conceptual framework for the entire book. But see especially pp. 25–38 for a brief description of the model, including two examples of its use.

According to the theory, inputs in the form of physical and social stimuli hit a person's sensory receptors and arouse needs. How these stimuli are received and interpreted depends on the person's selective perceptions. These perceptions determine whether action will result. If it does, problem recognition occurs and the decision process goes into operation. This process involves the search for, and evaluation of, alternatives. The process also involves the purchase and then the postpurchase evaluations.

CLASSIFICATION OF PRODUCTS

In this final part of the chapter we discuss the classification of products, especially *consumer* products. The classification of consumer goods is based on consumer behaviour as related to the purchase of other goods.

Just as it is necessary to segment markets to improve the marketing programs in many firms, so also it is helpful to separate *products* into homogeneous classifications. First we shall divide all products into two groups — consumer goods and industrial goods — in a classification that parallels our segmentation of the market. Then we shall divide each of these two product categories still further.

Consumer Goods and Industrial Goods

Consumer goods are products intended for use by ultimate household consumers for nonbusiness purposes. **Industrial goods** are products intended to be sold primarily for use in producing other goods or for rendering services in a business.

The fundamental basis for distinguishing between the two groups is the *ultimate* use for which the product is intended in its present form. A cash register purchased for use in a retail store (the product renders a service in a business) and materials bought by a manufacturer for use in making a product are industrial goods.

Particular stages in a product's distribution have no effect upon its classification. Cornflakes and children's shoes are classed as consumer products, whether they are in the manufacturer's warehouse or on retailers' shelves, if ultimately they will be used in their present form by household consumers. Cornflakes sold to restaurants and other institutions, however, are classed as industrial goods.

Often it is not possible to place a product definitely in one class or the other. A microcomputer may be considered a consumer good if it is purchased by a student or a homemaker for nonbusiness use. But if it is bought by a travelling sales representative for business use, it is classed with industrial goods. The manufacturer of such a product recognizes that the product falls in both categories and therefore develops separate marketing programs for the two markets.

The two-way product classification is a useful framework for the strategic planning of marketing operations. Each major class of products ultimately goes to a different type of market and thus requires different marketing methods. In the field of product planning, for example, branding, packaging, and fashion are generally far more significant for a consumer product than for an industrial good.

The marketing differences between consumer and industrial goods make this two-part classification of products a valuable one. However, the range of consumer goods is still too broad for a single class. Consequently, consumer products are further classified as convenience goods, shopping goods, and specialty goods (see Table 6-1). This is the traditional classification. While it raises objections in some quarters, it is still better understood and more generally followed by businesspeople than any of the alternatives yet suggested. It is important to note that this three-way subdivision is based on consumer *buying habits* rather than on *types of products*. Specifically, the two criteria used as bases for classifying consumer products are (1) the degree to which consumers are aware of the exact nature of the product *before* they start on their shopping trips, and (2) the satisfaction received from comparing products, weighed against the time and effort required for this task.

Classification of Consumer Products

Convenience Goods

The significant characteristics of convenience goods are (1) that the consumer has complete knowledge of the particular product wanted *before* going out to buy it, and (2) that the product is purchased with a minimum of effort. Normally, the gain resulting from shopping around to compare price and quality is not considered worth the extra time and effort required. A consumer is required to accept any of several substitutes and thus will buy the one that is most accessible. For most buyers, this subclass of goods includes groceries, tobacco products, inexpensive candy, drug sundries such as toothpaste, and staple hardware items such as light bulbs and batteries. When the need for this type of good arises, a consumer wants to make the purchase as rapidly and as easily as possible. Consequently, convenience products must be readily accessible in any shopping area.

Convenience goods typically have a low unit price, are not bulky, and are not greatly affected by fad and fashion. Among well-known brands, one is not usually *strongly* preferred over another. Convenience goods usually are purchased frequently, although this is not a necessary characteristic. Items such as Christmas-tree lights or Mother's Day cards are convenience goods for most people, even though they may be bought only once a year.

Marketing Considerations   A convenience good must be readily accessible when the consumer demand arises, so the manufacturer must secure wide distribution. But, since most retail stores sell only a small volume of the manufacturer's output, it is not economical to sell directly to all retail outlets. Instead, the producer relies on wholesalers to reach part of the retail market.

The promotional strategies of both the manufacturer and the retailer are involved here. Retailers typically carry several brands of a convenience item, so they are not able to promote any single brand. They are not interested in doing much advertising of these articles because many other stores

Table 6-1   CHARACTERISTICS OF CLASSES OF CONSUMER GOODS
AND SOME MARKETING CONSIDERATIONS

Characteristics and Marketing Considerations	Type of Good		
	Convenience	Shopping	Specialty
Characteristics			
1. Time and effort devoted by consumer to shopping	Very little	Considerable	Cannot generalize. Consumer may go to nearby store and buy with minimum effort or may have to go to distant store and spend much time and effort
2. Time spent planning the purchase	Very little	Considerable	Considerable
3. How soon want is satisfied after it arises	Immediately	Relatively long time	Relatively long time
4. Are price and quality compared?	No	Yes	No
5. Price	Low	High	High
6. Frequency of purchase	Usually frequent	Infrequent	Infrequent
7. Importance	Unimportant	Often very important	Cannot generalize
Marketing Considerations			
1. Length of channel	Long	Short	Short to very short
2. Importance of retailer	Any single store is relatively unimportant	Important	Very important
3. Number of outlets	As many as possible	Few	Few; often only one in a market
4. Stock turnover	High	Lower	Lower
5. Gross margin	Low	High	High
6. Responsibility for advertising	Manufacturer's	Retailer's	Joint responsibility
7. Importance of point-of-purchase display	Very important	Less important	Less important
8. Advertising used	Manufacturer's	Retailer's	Both
9. Brand or store name important	Brand name	Store name	Both
10. Importance of packaging	Very important	Less important	Less important

carry them, and any advertising by one retailer may help its competitors. As a result, virtually the entire advertising burden is shifted to the manufacturer.

Shopping Goods

Shopping goods are products for which customers usually wish to compare quality, price, and style in several stores before purchasing. A key identifying characteristic is that consumers lack full knowledge about shopping goods before embarking upon the shopping trip. Thus, on the trip, they must assess the relative suitability of alternative products before they make the purchase. This search continues only as long as the customer believes that the gain from comparing products offsets the additional time and effort required. Examples of shopping goods include women's apparel, furniture and other durable goods, jewellery, and, to some extent, men's ready-to-wear and shoes. In general, shopping goods cost more and are purchased less frequently than convenience goods.

Marketing Considerations   The buying habits with shopping goods affect the distribution and promotional strategy of both manufacturers and middlemen. Manufacturers of shopping goods require fewer retail outlets because consumers are willing to look around a bit for what they want. To increase the convenience of comparison shopping, manufacturers try to place their products in stores located near other stores carrying competing items. Similarly, department stores and other retailers who carry primarily shopping goods like to be bunched together.

Manufacturers usually work closely with retailers in the marketing of shopping goods. Since manufacturers use fewer retail outlets, they are more dependent upon those they select. Retail stores typically buy shopping goods in large quantities. Thus, distribution direct from manufacturer to retailer is common. Finally, store names are often more important to buyers of shopping goods than manufacturers' names. This is true particularly for items such as wearing apparel, where the average customer does not know or care who made the product.

Specialty Goods

Specialty goods are those products for which consumers have a *strong* brand preference, and are willing to expend special time and effort in purchasing them. In the case of specialty goods, as with convenience goods but unlike shopping goods, the buyer has complete knowledge of the particular product wanted before going on the buying trip. The distinctive feature of specialty goods is that the buyer will accept only a specific brand. The consumer is willing to forgo more accessible substitutes in order to procure the wanted brand, even though this may require a significant expenditure of time and effort. Examples of products usually classified as specialty goods include expensive men's ready-to-wear, fancy groceries, health foods, hi-fi components, photographic equipment, and, for many people, automobiles and certain home appliances.

Ordinarily, only certain *brands* of these products fall into the specialty goods classification. For many men, a Shiffer-Hillman suit would be considered a specialty good — they insist on that brand and will accept no other — but men's suits in general would not be so classified.

Marketing Considerations   Since consumers *insist* on a particular brand and are willing to expend considerable effort to find it, manufacturers can afford to use fewer outlets. Ordinarily, the manufacturer deals directly with these retailers. The retailers are extremely important, particularly if the manufacturer uses only one in each area. And, where the franchise to handle the product is a valuable one, the retailer may become quite dependent upon the producer. Thus, they are interdependent; the success of one is closely tied to the success of the other.

Because brand is important and because only a few outlets are used, both the manufacturer and the retailer advertise the product extensively. Often, the manufacturer pays some portion of the retailer's advertising costs, and the retailer's name frequently appears in the manufacturer's advertisements.

Classification Extended to Retail Stores[11]

Bucklin proposes that the system for classifying consumer goods can be extended to retailing. That is, we can speak of convenience stores, shopping stores, and specialty stores. The category in which a given store is placed depends upon whether customers shop there because it is accessible or because they prefer that store regardless of its accessibility.

By cross-classifying product and patronage motives, we get a nine-cell matrix, as in Table 6-2. This matrix is a realistic representation of how people buy. Supermarkets (convenience stores) do carry some exotic specialty foods, and we can buy common brands of after-shave lotion (convenience goods) in exclusive men's shops. Normally, however, consumer behaviour toward a given product can be represented by only three or four of the cells in Table 6-2. With this cross-classification system to guide them, retailers can first select their target markets and then develop appropriate strategies to reach those market segments. For example, to appeal to consumers interested in the convenience-store/specialty-good segment, the retailer would need (1) a highly accessible location and (2) a good selection of widely accepted brands.

SUMMARY   This concludes our two-chapter discussion of consumer buying behaviour. Recall our basic model from Chapter 5: Buying behaviour is initiated when aroused needs (motives) create inner tensions that lead to behaviour designed to satisfy the needs and thus reduce the tensions. The direction taken by this goal-oriented behaviour is influenced by our perceptions.

---

[11]This section is adapted from Louis P. Bucklin, "Retail Strategy and the Classification of Consumer Goods," *Journal of Marketing*, January 1963, pp. 50–55.

Table 6-2   CONSUMER BUYING BEHAVIOUR COMBINING TYPES
OF PRODUCTS AND STORES

Type of Product \ Type of Store	Convenience	Shopping	Specialty
Convenience	Prefers most available brand at most accessible store	Buys any brand but shops around to get better service and lower price	Prefers store but is indifferent as to brand
Shopping	Selects from assortment at most accessible store	Shops around; wants to compare store factors and products	Prefers one store but wants to shop the assortment at that store
Specialty	Buys favourite brand at most accessible store that has that brand	Has strong brand preference but shops for best deal at stores carrying that brand	Prefers specific brand and specific store

Perceptions are shaped by sociocultural forces and by the forces that constitute a person's psychological makeup. One of these psychological forces is a person's learning experience. Three sets of learning theories — the stimulus-response model, cognitive theory, and the gestalt and field theory — describe learning and its effect on behaviour. Another psychological influence on perceptions is personality, although there is no agreement as to how personality influences behaviour. We also recognize that the Freudian psychoanalytic theory of personality has significant marketing implications. Finally, perceptions are also influenced by attitudes and beliefs and by self-image.

Consumers are assumed to go through a logical, five-stage process in the course of making a buying decision. First, the unsatisfied need is recognized. Next, the reasonable alternatives are first identified and then evaluated. The actual decision to purchase is then made. (This stage involves patronage buying motives and retail-store image.) In the final stage, postpurchase behaviour may involve some cognitive dissonance on the part of the buyer — something to be kept in mind by sellers. Tying our discussion of behaviour together are two comprehensive theories (or models) of consumer behaviour.

An aid in building effective marketing programs is the classification of consumer products, based on consumer buying habits. The three classes — convenience goods, shopping goods, and specialty goods — each generally require different distribution, promotion, and other marketing considerations. This classification scheme may be extended to retail stores.

KEY TERMS AND CONCEPTS

QUESTIONS AND PROBLEMS

1. Distinguish between *drives* and *cues* in the learning process.

2. Does the Freudian psychoanalytic theory of personality have any practical application in the marketing of:
   a. Eye shadow
   b. Electric dishwashers
   c. Outboard motor boats

3. Explain the relationship between consumers' attitudes and the brands they purchase.

4. Select two or three products or brands you are familiar with, and explain what marketing action might be employed to change consumers' attitudes toward these products or brands.

5. Describe the differences you would expect to find in the self-concepts of an insurance salesperson and an assembly-line worker in an automobile plant. Give some examples of resultant buying behaviour. (Assume that both have the same income.)

6. Explain some practical marketing applications of the self-concept theory.

7. What patronage motives influence your choice of the following?
   a. Restaurant
   b. Movie theatre
   c. Department store
   d. Sporting-goods store
   e. Shoe store

8. Following is a series of headlines or slogans taken from advertisements of various retailers. To what patronage motive does each appeal?
   a. "Factory-trained mechanics at your service."
   b. "We never close."
   c. "Nobody but nobody undersells Grant's."
   d. "Where Calgary shops with confidence."
   e. "One dollar down, no payments until the forestry strike is over."

9. Explain the concept of cognitive dissonance as it operates in the buying-decision process.

10. What causes cognitive dissonance to increase in a buying situation? What can a seller do to decrease the level of dissonance in a given purchase of the seller's product?

11. "As brand preferences are established with regard to women's ready-to-wear, these items, which traditionally have been considered shopping goods, will move into the specialty goods category. At the same time, women's clothing is moving into supermarkets and variety stores, thus indicating that some articles are convenience goods." Explain the reasoning involved in these statements. Do you agree that women's clothing is shifting away from the shopping goods classification? Explain.

12. In what way is the responsibility for advertising a convenience good distributed between the manufacturer and the retailers? A shopping good? A specialty good?

13. Compare the elements of a manufacturer's marketing mix for a convenience good with those of the mix for a specialty good.

Chapter

7

The Industrial Market

CHAPTER GOALS

This chapter is a discussion of the huge market for industrial goods. As you read, try to form a comparison between the industrial market and the consumer market. After studying this chapter, you should understand:

1. *The nature and importance of the industrial market*
2. *The classes of industrial products and the marketing implications of each class*
3. *The major characteristics of industrial market demand*
4. *The demographic makeup of the industrial market*
5. *Industrial buying motives, the industrial buying process, and buying patterns of industrial users*

The industrial market is big, rich, and widely diversified. It requires the efforts of thousands of workers in thousands of different jobs. Firms producing for this market are not criticized for extreme claims in selling or advertising. They are not accused of offering duplicate brands or of paying middlemen exorbitant profits. The market is not a target for widespread complaint because it is largely unknown to the public.

NATURE AND IMPORTANCE OF THE INDUSTRIAL MARKET

In Chapter 4, **industrial users** were defined as businesses or institutions that buy products or services to use either (1) in making other goods and services or (2) in conducting their own operations. **Industrial goods** are differentiated from consumer goods on the basis of their ultimate use. That is, industrial goods are those intended for use in making other products or operating a business or institution. **Industrial marketing**, then, is the marketing of industrial goods and services to industrial users.

Because the industrial market is largely unknown to the average consumer, we are apt to underrate its significance. Actually, this market is a huge one in terms of its total sales volume and the number of firms involved in it. About 50 percent of all manufactured goods are sold to the industrial market. In addition, about 80 percent of all farm products and virtually all minerals and forest and sea products are industrial goods. These are sold to firms for further processing.

The magnitude and complexity of the industrial market are also shown by the many transactions required to produce and market a product. Consider, for example, the industrial marketing transactions and the total sales volume involved in getting a pair of cowhide work shoes to their actual user. First, the cattle are sold through one or two middlemen before reaching a meat packer. Then the hides are sold to a tanner, who in turn sells the leather to a shoe manufacturer. The shoe manufacturer may sell finished shoes to a shoe wholesaler, who markets the products to retail stores or to factories that supply shoes to their workers. Each sale of the cow, leather, or shoe is another industrial marketing transaction.

In addition, the shoe manufacturer buys metal eyelets, laces, thread, steel safety-toe plates, heels and soles, and shoe polish. Consider something as simple as the shoelaces. Other industrial firms must first buy the raw cotton and then spin, weave, dye, and cut it so that it becomes shoestring material. All the manufacturers involved have factories and offices with furniture, machinery, and other equipment — and these also are industrial goods that have to be produced and marketed. Factories also are industrial products, as are the heating and maintenance equipment and supplies required to run them. In short, a myriad of industrial products and industrial marketing activities come into play before almost any product — consumer good or industrial good — reaches its final destination.

Another indication of the scope and importance of the industrial market is the following range of industries that make up this market. This classification also provides a very useful basis for segmenting the industrial market.

1. Agriculture, forestry, and fishing
2. Mining and quarrying
3. Contract construction
4. Manufacturing
5. Transportation, communication, and other public utilities
6. Wholesale trade
7. Retail trade
8. Finance, insurance, and real estate
9. Services
10. Government — federal, provincial, and municipal

Every retail store and wholesaling establishment is an industrial user. Every bus company, airline, and railroad is part of this market. So is every hotel, restaurant, bank, insurance company, hospital, theatre, and school. While there are fewer industrial users than there are consumers (approximately half a million compared with 25 million), the total sales volume in the industrial market far surpasses total sales to consumers. This difference is due to the very many industrial marketing transactions that take place before a product is sold to its ultimate user.

The Farm Market
and the Government
Market

Two large segments of the industrial market—the agricultural market and the government market — deserve an expanded discussion at this point. They often are underrated and overlooked, because most attention typically is devoted to the manufacturing segment.

The Farm Market

The absolute level of cash income from the sale of farm products gives farmers, as a group, the purchasing power that makes them a highly attractive market. Moreover, world population forecasts and food shortages in many countries undoubtedly will keep pressure on farmers to increase their output. Companies hoping to sell to this farm market must analyse it carefully and be aware of significant trends. For example, both (1) the proportion of farmers in the total population and (2) the number of farms have been decreasing and probably will continue to decline. Counterbalancing this has been an increase in corporate and business-managed farms. Even the surviving "family farms" are tending to expand in size. Farming continues to become more automated and mechanized. This means, of course, that capital investment in farming is increasing. Truly, **agribusiness** is becoming big business in every sense of the word.

As industrial buyers, most farmers—especially the owners of large farms—are quite discerning and well informed. Like business executives, farmers are looking for better ways to increase their crop yields, to cut their expenses, and to manage their cash flow. And, as farms become more sophisticated, manufacturers must change their distribution and promotion strategies to reach the farm market effectively.

In distribution, for example, producers must recognize the key role played by farm cooperatives, equipment dealers, and feed-seed suppliers located in farm communities. Farmers tend to buy locally, where they can get repair service, parts, and supplies from people they know. Even a major capital expenditure for large equipment usually is made through a local dealer. This is unlike the buying behaviour of most industrial users, who typically buy large equipment directly from the manufacturer.

When promoting their products, manufacturers should be aware of the high degree of specialization in the farm market. Some producers of fertilizer, for example, will send a salesperson directly to a large farm. There, working with the farmer, the sales rep will analyse the soil and determine exactly what fertilizer mix is best for that farm. From that analysis, the manufacturer will prepare, as a special order, the appropriate blend of fertilizers for that particular farm.

On the other side of a farm market exchange transaction, *buying from* farmers sometimes is done on a contract basis. This is particularly the case where marketing boards do not exist to handle the crop or commodity. In fact, **contract farming**, while it has existed for a long time, seems to be on the increase in recent years. Under one type of contract-farming arrangement, one firm (a middleman or a manufacturer) agrees to furnish the farmer with supplies and possibly with equipment and working capital to grow a crop. The farmer, in turn, agrees to sell the entire crop to this supplier at some predetermined price. In effect, the farmer is an employee of this supplier. In another type of contract-farming arrangement, the farmer furnishes the supplies and equipment. But a processor (perhaps a canner or freezer of fruits or vegetables) agrees in advance to buy that farmer's entire crop. The price may be set before the growing season, or it may be negotiated at some time during the season. Contract farming also affects the marketing of farm supplies and equipment. Often, it is difficult for the seller to determine who makes a buying decision. Is it the farmer, the contract buyer, or both?

The Government Market

The large government market includes hundreds of federal, provincial, and local units buying for government institutions such as schools, offices, hospitals, and (depending on which sectors they operate in) a large number of crown corporations. Spending by the federal government alone accounts for about 20 percent of our gross national product. Spending at the provincial and municipal levels accounts for another 20 percent. The government as a buyer is so big and complex, however, that it is difficult to comprehend and deal with. Government procurement processes are different from those in the private sector of the industrial market.

A unique feature of government buying is the bidding system. Much government procurement, by law, must be done on a bid basis. That is, the government advertises for bids, stating the product specifications. Then it must accept the lowest bid that meets these specifications. In other buying situations, the government may negotiate a purchase contract with an individual supplier. This marketing practice might be used, for example, when the Department of National Defence wants someone to develop and build a new surveillance system for Arctic patrol aircraft and there are no comparable products on which to base bidding specifications.[1]

Many companies make no real effort to sell to the government, preferring not to contend with the red tape. Yet government business can be quite profitable. Dealing with the government to any significant extent, however, usually requires specialized marketing techniques and information.

CLASSIFICATION OF INDUSTRIAL PRODUCTS

The general category "industrial products" is too broad to use in developing a marketing program. The practices used in marketing the various industrial goods are just too different. Consequently, some subdivision is necessary. The usual classification scheme separates industrial goods into five categories: raw materials, fabricating materials and parts, installations, accessory equipment, and operating supplies (see Table 7-1). This classification is based on the *uses* of the product, in contrast to the classification of consumer products on the basis of buying habits.

---

[1]For some ideas on bidding strategy that are applicable to both the government market and to other industrial markets, see Stephen Paranka, "Question: To Bid or Not to Bid? Answer: Strategic Prebid Analysis," *Marketing News*, April 4, 1980, p. 16.

Table 7-1   CLASSES OF INDUSTRIAL PRODUCTS: SOME CHARACTERISTICS AND MARKETING CONSIDERATIONS

Characteristics and Marketing Considerations	Type of Product				
	Raw Materials	Fabricating Parts and Materials	Installations	Accessory Equipment	Operating Supplies
Example:	Iron ore	Engine blocks	Blast furnaces	Storage racks	Paper clips
Characteristics:					
1. Unit price	Very low	Low	Very high	Medium	Low
2. Length of life	Very short	Depends on final product	Very long	Long	Short
3. Quantities purchased	Large	Large	Very small	Small	Small
4. Frequency of purchase	Frequent delivery; long-term purchase contract	Infrequent purchase, but frequent delivery	Very infrequent	Medium frequency	Frequent
5. Standardization of competitive products	Very much; grading is important	Very much	Very little; custom-made	Little	Much
6. Limits on supply	Limited; supply can be increased slowly or not at all	Usually no problem	No problem	Usually no problem	Usually no problem
Marketing Considerations:					
1. Nature of channel	Short; no middlemen	Short; middlemen only for small buyers	Short; no middlemen	Middlemen used	Middlemen used
2. Negotiation period	Hard to generalize	Medium	Long	Medium	Short
3. Price competition	Important	Important	Not important	Not main factor	Important
4. Presale/postsale service	Not important	Important	Very important	Important	Very little
5. Demand stimulation	Very little	Moderate	Sales people very important	Important	Not too important
6. Brand preference	None	Generally low	High	High	Low
7. Advance buying contract	Important; long-term contracts used	Important; long-term contracts used	Not usually used	Not usually used	Not usually used

Raw materials are industrial goods that will become part of another physical product. They have not been processed in any way, except as necessary for economy or protection during physical handling. Raw materials include (1) goods found in their natural state, such as minerals, land, and products of the forests and the seas; and (2) agricultural products, such as wheat, corn, tobacco, fruits, vegetables, livestock, and animal products — eggs and raw milk. These two groups of raw materials are marketed quite differently.

Raw Materials

Marketing Considerations

The marketing of raw materials in their natural state is influenced by several factors. The supply of these products is limited and cannot be substantially increased. Usually only a few large producers are involved. The products must be carefully graded and, consequently, are highly standardized. Because of their great bulk, their low unit value, and the long distance between producer and industrial user, transportation is an important consideration.

These factors necessitate short channels of distribution and a minimum of physical handling. Frequently, raw materials are marketed directly from producer to industrial user. At most, one intermediary may be used. The limited supply forces users to assure themselves of adequate quantities. Often this is done either (1) by contracting in advance to buy a season's supply of the product (as we discussed in relation to farm marketing) or (2) by owning the source of supply. Advertising and other forms of demand stimulation are rarely used. There is little branding or other product differentiation. Competition is built around price and the assurance that a producer can deliver the product as specified.

Agricultural products used as industrial raw materials are supplied by many small producers located some distance from the markets. The supply is largely controllable by producers, but it cannot be increased or decreased rapidly. The product is perishable and is not produced at a uniform rate throughout the year.

Close attention must be given to transportation and warehousing. Transportation costs are high relative to unit value, and standardization and grading are very important. Because producers are small and numerous, marketing boards have been developed to replace the many middlemen and deal with the long channels of distribution often needed. While very little promotional or demand-creation activity would exist as a result of the support of an individual producer, through the strength of marketing boards a great deal of promotion and demand-creation activity is producer-group sponsored. Milk, turkey, and beef marketing boards, for example, sponsor highly visible advertising campaigns.

Fabricating Materials and Parts

Fabricating materials and parts are industrial goods that become an actual part of the finished product. They have already been processed to some extent (in contrast to raw materials). Fabricating **materials** will undergo further processing. Examples include pig iron going to steel, yarn being woven into cloth, and flour becoming part of bread. Fabricating **parts** will be assembled with no further change in form. They include such products as zippers on clothing and semiconductor chips in computers.

Marketing Considerations

Fabricating materials and parts are usually purchased in large quantities. To ensure an adequate, timely supply, a buyer may place an order a year or more in advance. Because of such buying habits, most fabricating products are marketed on a direct-sale basis from producer to user. Individual industries may provide exceptions to this rule, as does the textile industry.

Middlemen are used most often where the buyers are small or where they place small fill-in orders for a rapid delivery. Normally, buying decisions are based on the price and the service provided by the seller. Branding is generally unimportant. However, some firms have made successful attempts to pull their products out of obscurity by identifying them with a brand. Talon zippers and Tex-Made fabrics are notable examples.

Installations

Installations are manufactured industrial products — the long-lived, expensive, major equipment of an industrial user. Examples include large generators in a dam, a factory building, diesel engines for a railroad, blast furnaces for a steel mill, and jet airplanes for an airline. *The differentiating characteristic of installations is that they directly affect the scale of operation in a firm.* Adding 12 new typewriters will not affect the scale of operation at Eastern Provincial Airlines, but adding 12 new jet airplanes certainly will. Therefore, the airplanes are classed as installations, but the typewriters are not.

Marketing Considerations

The marketing of installations presents a real challenge to management because every single sale is important. Usually no middlemen are involved; sales are made directly from producer to industrial user. Typically, the unit sale is large, and often the product is made to the buyer's detailed specifications. Much presale and postsale servicing is required. A high-calibre sales force is needed to market installations, and often sales engineers are used. Promotional emphasis is on personal selling rather than advertising, although some advertising is used.

Accessory Equipment

Accessory equipment is used in the production operations of an industrial firm, but it does not have a significant influence on the scale of operations in the firm. Accessory equipment does not become an actual part of the finished product. The life of accessory equipment is shorter than that of installations and longer than that of operating supplies. Examples include cash registers in a retail store, small power tools, forklift trucks, and the typewriters mentioned above.

Marketing Considerations

It is difficult to generalize about the distribution policies of firms marketing accessory equipment. In some cases, direct sale is used. This is true particularly where the order is for several units of the product or where the product is of relatively high unit value. A firm like Hyster Canada, which manufactures forklift trucks, may sell directly because the price of a single unit is large enough to make this distribution policy profitable. In the main, however, manufacturers of accessory equipment use middlemen. They do so because (1) the market is geographically dispersed, (2) there are many different types of potential users, and (3) individual orders may be relatively small.

Operating supplies are the "convenience goods" of the industrial field. They are short-lived, low-priced items usually purchased with a minimum of effort. They aid in a firm's operations but do not become a part of the finished product. Examples are lubricating oils, pencils and stationery, registration supplies in a university, heating fuel, and washroom supplies.

Operating Supplies

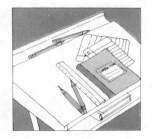

Marketing Considerations

Like consumer convenience products, industrial operating supplies must be distributed widely. The producing firm makes extensive use of wholesaling middlemen. This is done because the product is low in unit value, is bought in small quantities, and goes to many users. Price competition is heavy because competitive products are quite standardized and there is little brand insistence.

Four general demand characteristics help to differentiate the industrial market from the consumer market: (1) demand is derived, (2) demand is inelastic, (3) demand is widely fluctuating, and (4) the market is knowledgeable.

CHARACTERISTICS OF INDUSTRIAL MARKET DEMAND

Demand Is Derived

The demand for each industrial good is derived from the demand for the consumer products in which the industrial item is used. The demand for steel depends partially upon the consumer demand for automobiles and refrigerators, for example. The demand for steel also depends upon the demand for butter, baseball gloves, and bongo drums, because the tools, machines, and other equipment involved in making these items are made of steel. Thus, as the demand for baseball gloves increases, glove manufacturers may buy more steel sewing machines or filing cabinets.

There are several marketing implications in the fact that industrial market demand is a derived demand. For example, the producers of industrial products may direct a considerable share of their promotion toward the ultimate consumer. Thus steel manufacturers, through TV and magazines, have urged consumers to have a "white Christmas" by buying new refrigerators and stoves. At one time, the Du Pont Company advertised to the consumer the advantages of shoes made of its Corfam.

Demand Is Inelastic

Another significant characteristic of the industrial market is related to the derived-demand feature: The demand for many industrial products is relatively inelastic. That is, the demand for a product responds very little to changes in its price. If the price of buttons for men's jackets should suddenly rise or fall considerably, there would probably be no appreciable change in the demand for buttons.

This demand is inelastic because the cost of a single part or material is ordinarily a small portion of the total cost of the finished product. The cost of the chemicals in paint is a small part of the price that a consumer pays for paint. The cost of the enamel on a refrigerator is a small part of its retail price. Even the cost of expensive capital equipment (installations), when distributed over thousands of units of a product, becomes a very small part of the unit cost. As a result, when the price of the industrial product changes, there is very little shift in the demand for the related consumer products. If there is no appreciable shift in the demand for the consumer goods, then (by virtue of the derived-demand feature) there is no change in the demand for the industrial product.

From a marketing point of view, there are three factors to consider regarding this inelasticity of industrial demand. The first is the position of an entire industry as contrasted with that of an individual firm. An industry-wide cut in the price of steel belts used in tires will have little effect on the demand for automobile tires. Consequently, it will cause little change in the total demand for steel belts.

The pricing policy of an individual firm, however, can substantially alter the demand for that firm's products. If one supplier significantly cuts the price of steel belts, the drop in price may draw a great deal of business away from competitors. The advantage will, of course, be temporary, because competitors will undoubtedly retaliate in some way to recapture their lost business. Nevertheless, in the short run, the demand curve faced by a single firm is much more elastic than the industry's curve.

Another marketing factor involved here is time. Much of our discussion refers to short-run situations. Over the long run, the demand for a given industrial product is more elastic. If the price of cloth for women's suits is raised, there probably will be no immediate change in the price of the finished garment. However, the increase in the cost of materials could very well be reflected in a $25 rise in suit prices for next year. This rise could then influence the demand for suits, and thus for cloth, a year or more hence.

One modifying aspect is the relative importance of a specific industrial product in the cost of the finished good. We may generalize to this extent: The greater the cost of an industrial product as a percentage of the total price of the finished good, the greater the elasticity of demand for this industrial product.

Although the demand for industrial goods does not change much in response to price changes, it is far from steady. In fact, the market demand for most classes of industrial goods fluctuates considerably more than the demand for consumer products. The demand for installations — major plant equipment, factories, etc. — is especially subject to change. Substantial fluctuations also exist in the market for accessory equipment — office furniture and machinery, delivery trucks, and similar products. These tend to accentuate the swings in the demand for industrial raw materials and fabricating parts. This was exemplified by the recent downturn in the construction and auto industries, which affected the suppliers of lumber, steel, and other materials and parts. One exception to this generalization is found in agricultural products intended for processing. There is a reasonably consistent demand for animals intended for meat products, for fruits and vegetables that will be canned or frozen, and for grains and dairy products.

Fluctuations in the demand for industrial products can influence all aspects of a firm's marketing program. In product planning, they may stimulate a firm to diversify into other products to ease production and marketing problems. Distribution strategies may be affected. Consider a firm's sales force; when demand declines, the sales force must be either trimmed back or maintained at full strength (but at a loss). Rather than try to cope with this problem, a seller may decide to make greater use of wholesalers to reach its market. In its pricing, management may attempt to stem a decline in sales by cutting prices, hoping to attract customers away from competing firms.

Demand Is Widely Fluctuating

Unlike ultimate consumers, typical industrial buyers are usually well informed about what they are buying. They know the relative merits of alternative sources of supply and competitive products. The position of purchasing agent is being upgraded in many firms, and purchasing executives are using sophisticated tools to improve their performance.[2]

Market Is Knowledgeable

[2]See Richard M. Hill, "Industrial Marketers Should Heed Shift in Purchasing Emphasis with 5 New 'Tools'," *Marketing News*, June 12, 1981, p. 18. Also see Gregory D. Upah and Monroe M. Bird, "Changes in Industrial Buying: Implications for Industrial Marketers," *Industrial Marketing Management*, April 1980, pp. 117–121.

These improvements in purchasing skills carry significant marketing implications, then, for the sellers of industrial products. For example, producers of industrial goods place greater emphasis on personal contact than do firms marketing consumer products. Industrial representatives must be carefully selected, properly trained, and adequately compensated. They must give effective presentations and furnish satisfactory service both before and after each sale is made. Sales executives are devoting increased effort to the assignment of salespeople to key accounts to ensure that these reps are compatible with industrial buyers.

DETERMINANTS OF INDUSTRIAL MARKET DEMAND

To analyse a consumer market, a marketer would study in detail the distribution of population and income and then try to determine the consumers' buying motives and habits. Essentially the same type of analysis can be used by a firm selling to the *industrial* market. The factors affecting the market for industrial products are the number of potential industrial users and their purchasing power, buying motives, and buying habits. In the following discussion we identify several basic *differences* between consumer markets and industrial markets.

Number and Types of Industrial Users

Total Market

Analysis of the industrial market shows that it contains relatively few buying units when compared with the consumer market. There are approximately one-half million industrial users, in contrast to 25 million consumers divided into more than 6 million households. The industrial market will seem particularly limited to most companies, because they sell to only a segment of the total. A firm that sold to meat processing plants in 1978, for example, would find only 49 potential customers in Canada. Similarly, there were only 199 plants engaged in metal stamping and pressing, which employed more than 20 employees in 1978, and only 30 companies manufacturing batteries in Canada in that year.[3] Consequently, marketing executives should try to pinpoint their market carefully by type of industry and geographic location. A firm marketing mining equipment is not interested in the total industrial market or even in all of the many companies engaged in mining in this country. This seller is interested in information that will help it identify the market for its particular products.

One very useful source of information is the Standard Industrial Classification system (SIC), which enables a company to identify relatively small segments of its industrial market.[4] All types of businesses in Canada are divided into twelve groups, as follows:

---

[3]Statistics Canada, *Slaughtering and Meat Processing, 1978*, cat. no. 32-221, President of the Treasury Board, Ottawa, 1980, p. 6; *Metal Stamping, Pressing and Coating Industry, 1978*, cat. no. 41-227, President of the Treasury Board, Ottawa, 1980; *Battery Manufacturers, 1978*, cat. no. 43-208, President of the Treasury Board, Ottawa, 1980.

[4]Statistics Canada, *Standard Industrial Classification Manual*, cat. no. 12-501, Information Canada, Ottawa, 1970.

1. Agriculture
2. Forestry
3. Fishing and trapping
4. Mines, quarries, and oil wells
5. Manufacturing industries (20 major groups)
6. Construction industry
7. Transportation, communication, and other utilities
8. Trade
9. Finance, insurance, and real estate
10. Community, business, and personal service industries (8 major groups)
11. Public administration and defence
12. Industry unspecified or undefined

A separate number is assigned to each major industry within each of the above groups; then, three- and four-digit classification numbers are used to subdivide each major category into finer segments. To illustrate, in division 5 (manufacturing), major group 4 (leather) contains:

SIC code	Industrial group
172	Leather tanneries
174	Shoe factories
175	Leather-glove factories
179	Luggage, handbag, and small-leather goods manufacturers

Size of Industrial Users

While the market may be limited in the total number of buyers, it is large in purchasing power. As one might expect, industrial users range in size from very small companies with fewer than 5 employees to firms with over 1,000 workers. A relatively small percentage of firms account for the greatest share of the value added by a given industry. As an example from a recent Statistics Canada report (Table 7-2), 1.4 percent of the firms — those with 500 or more employees — accounted for about 38 percent of the total dollar value added by manufacturing and for 32 percent of the total employment in manufacturing. The firms with fewer than 50 employees accounted for 81 percent of all manufacturing establishments, but produced only 14 percent of the value added by manufacturing.

The marketing significance in these facts is that the buying power in the industrial market is highly concentrated in relatively few firms. This market concentration has considerable influence on a seller's policies regarding its channels of distribution. It has greater opportunity to deal directly with the industrial users. Middlemen are not so essential as in the consumer market.

Table 7-2   SIZE DISTRIBUTION OF MANUFACTURING ESTABLISHMENTS IN CANADA, 1981,
                 BY NUMBER OF EMPLOYEES

This table shows that buying power in the industrial market is highly concentrated in relatively few firms.
4.8 percent of the companies, those with 200 or more employees, accounted for 60 percent of the value added
by manufacturing. How might this concentration affect a seller's marketing program?

Number of Employees	Number of Establishments	Total Number of Employees	Value Added	Percentage of Firms	Percentage of Employees	Percentage of Value Added
1–4	10,478	20,193	568,086	29.3	1.1	0.7
5–9	6,366	41,505	1,109,453	17.8	2.2	1.4
10–19	5,925	81,109	2,454,545	16.6	4.4	3.1
20–49	6,273	196,645	6,992,636	17.5	10.6	9.0
50–99	2,997	208,017	8,148,648	8.4	11.2	10.4
100–199	1,999	280,379	11,356,883	5.6	15.1	14.5
200–499	1,268	382,350	17,931,387	3.5	20.0	22.9
500–999	318	216,473	11,691,394	0.9	11.7	15.0
1000 +	156	322,704	16,819,177	0.4	17.4	21.5
Head offices, sales offices, etc.	—	104,351	1,188,369	—	5.6	1.5
TOTAL	35,780	1,853,726	78,260,578	100.0	100.0	100.0

Source: Statistics Canada, *Manufacturing Industries of Canada: National and Provincial Areas, 1981*, cat. no. 31–203, Ottawa,
1983, pp. 190–191.

Regional Concentration of Industrial Users

There is a substantial regional concentration in many of the major industries and among industrial users as a whole. A firm selling products usable
in oil fields will find the bulk of its market in Alberta, the Northwest
Territories, and the U.S. and abroad. Rubber products manufacturers are
located mostly in Ontario, shoes are produced chiefly in Quebec, and most
of the nation's garment manufacturers are located in southern Ontario and
Quebec. There is a similar regional concentration in the farm market.

Four-fifths of all manufacturing plants are located in Ontario and Quebec.
As shown in Fig. 7-1, five Census Metropolitan Areas—Toronto, Montreal,
Hamilton, Vancouver, and Windsor—accounted for about 45 percent of all
Canadian manufacturing industries. If Winnipeg, Kitchener, St. Catharines,
and Edmonton are added, these nine centres account for over 35 percent
of all goods produced by manufacturers in Canada.

While a large part of a firm's market may be concentrated in limited
geographic areas, a good portion may lie outside these areas. Consequently,
a distribution policy must be developed that will enable a firm to deal directly with the concentrated market and also to employ middlemen (or a
company sales force at great expense) to reach the outlying markets.

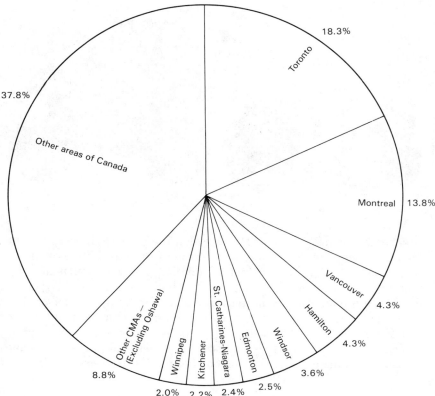

Source: Statistics Canada, *Manufacturing Industries of Canada: Sub-Provincial Areas, 1977,* Ministry of Supply and Services, Canada, Ottawa, August 1980.

Vertical and Horizontal Industrial Markets

For effective marketing planning, a company should know whether the market for its products is vertical or horizontal. If an industrial product is usable by virtually all firms in only one or two industries, it has a **vertical** market. For example, some precision instruments are intended only for the marine market, but every boatbuilder or shipbuilder is a potential customer. If the product is usable by many industries, its market is said to be broad, or **horizontal**. Industrial supplies, such as lubricating oils and greases, small motors, and some paper products, may be sold to a wide variety of industries.

A company's marketing program ordinarily is influenced by whether that firm's markets are vertical or horizontal. For example, in a vertical market a product can be tailor-made to meet the specific needs of one industry. In a horizontal market the product must be developed as an all-purpose item. Moreover, advertising and personal selling efforts can be directed more effectively in vertical markets.

The industrial market for tire-making machinery is vertical.

The industrial market for
tires is horizontal.

Buying Power of Industrial Users

Another determinant of industrial market demand is the purchasing power of industrial users. This can be measured either by the expenditures of industrial users or by their sales volume. Many times, however, such information is not available or is very difficult to estimate. In such cases it is more feasible to use an **activity indicator** — that is, some market factor that is related to income generation and expenditures. Sometimes an activity indicator is a combined indicator of purchasing power and the number of industrial users. Following are examples of activity indicators that might be used to estimate the purchasing power of industrial users.

Measures of Manufacturing Activity

Firms selling to manufacturers might use as market indicators such factors as the number of employees, the number of plants, or the dollar value added by manufacturing. One firm selling work gloves used the number of employees in manufacturing establishments to determine the relative values of various geographic markets. Another company that sold a product that controls stream pollution used two indicators — (1) the number of firms processing wood products (paper mills, plywood mills, and so forth) and (2) the manufacturing value added by these firms.

Measures of Mining Activity

The number of mines operating, the volume of their output, and the dollar value of the product as it leaves the mine all may indicate the purchasing power of mines. This information can be used by any firm marketing industrial products to mine operators.

Measures of Agricultural Activity

A company marketing fertilizer or agricultural equipment can estimate the buying power of its farm market by studying such indicators as cash farm income, acreage planted, or crop yields. The chemical producer that sells to a fertilizer manufacturer might study the same indices because the demand for chemicals in this case is derived from the demand for fertilizer.

Measures of Construction Activity

If an enterprise is marketing building materials, such as lumber, brick, gypsum products, or builders' hardware, its market is dependent upon construction activity. This may be indicated by the number and value of building permits issued, or by the number of construction starts by type of housing (single-family residence, apartment, or commercial).

Buying Motives of Industrial Users

Industrial buying behaviour, like consumer buying behaviour, is initiated when an aroused need (a motive) is recognized. This leads to goal-oriented activity designed to satisfy the need. Once again, marketing practitioners must try to determine what motivates the buyer.

Industrial buying motives, for the most part, are presumed to be rational, and an industrial purchase normally is a methodical, objective undertaking. Industrial buyers are motivated primarily by a desire to maximize their firms' profits. More specifically, their buying goal is to achieve the optimal combination of price, quality, and service in the products they buy. On the other hand, salespeople would maintain that some industrial buyers seem to be motivated more toward personal goals that are in conflict with their employers' goals.

Actually, industrial buyers do have two goals — to improve their positions in their firms (self-interest) and to further their company's position (in profits, in acceptance by society). Sometimes these goals are mutually consistent, and sometimes they are in conflict. Obviously, the greater the degree of consistency, the better for both the organization and the individual. When very little mutuality of goals exists, the situation is poor. Probably the more usual situation is to find some overlap of interests, but also a significant area where the buyer's goals do not coincide with those of the firm. In these cases, a seller might appeal to the buyer both on a rational, "what's-good-for-the-firm" basis and on an ego-building basis. Promotional efforts attuned to the buyer's ego are particularly useful when two or more competing sellers are offering essentially the same products, prices, and services.

The Industrial Buying Process

Competition and the complexity of industrial marketing have encouraged companies to focus attention on the *total* buying process. Buying is treated as an ongoing relationship of mutual interest to both buyer and seller. As one example of this approach, researchers in a Marketing Science Institute study developed a framework to explain different types of industrial buying situations.[5] The model for this framework — called a **buy-grid** — is illustrated in Fig. 7-2. The model reflects two major aspects of the industrial buying process: (1) the classes of typical buying situations and (2) the sequential steps in the buying process.

Three typical buying situations (called **buy classes**) were identified as follows: new tasks, modified rebuys, and straight rebuys. The **new task** is the most difficult and complex of the three. More people influence the new-task buying-decision process than influence the other two types. The problem is that new-information needs are high, and the evaluation of alternatives is critical. Sellers are given their best opportunity to be heard and to display their creative selling ability in satisfying the buyer's needs.

Straight rebuys — routine purchases with minimal information needs and no real consideration of alternatives — are at the other extreme. Buying decisions are made in the purchasing department, usually from a list of acceptable suppliers. Suppliers, especially those from new firms not on the list, have difficulty getting an audience with the buyer. **Modified rebuys** are somewhere between the other two in terms of time required, information needed, alternatives considered, and other characteristics.

The other major element in the buy-grid reflects the idea that the industrial buying process is a sequence of eight stages, called **buy phases**. The process starts with the recognition of a problem. It ranges through the determination and description of product specifications, the search for an evaluation of alternatives, and the buying act. It ends with postpurchase feedback and evaluation. (This surely is reminiscent of the consumer's buying-decision process outlined in Chapter 6.)

Buying Patterns of Industrial Users

Overt buying behaviour in the *industrial* market differs significantly from *consumer* behaviour in several ways. These differences obviously stem from the differences in buying motives and buyer-seller relationships.

Length of Negotiation Period

The period of negotiation in an industrial sale is usually much longer than that in a consumer market sale. Some of reasons for the extended negotiations are: (1) several executives are involved in the buying decision, (2) the sale often involves a large amount of money, (3) the industrial product is often made to order, and considerable discussion is involved in establishing the exact specifications, and (4) bids are often involved (as in construction work), and the seller needs time to prepare careful estimates.

---

[5]Patrick J. Robinson, Charles W. Faris, and Yoram Wind, *Industrial Buying and Creative Marketing*, Allyn and Bacon, Inc., Boston, 1967. For a literature review and updating of the subject, see Rowland T. Moriarity and Morton Galper, *Organizational Buying Behavior: A State-of-the-Art Review and Conceptualization*, report no. 78-101, Marketing Science Institute, Cambridge, Mass., 1978. Also see Wade Ferguson, "An Evaluation of the BUYGRID Analytic Framework," *Industrial Marketing Management*, January 1979, pp. 40–44.

	BUY CLASSES		
BUY PHASES	New task	Modified rebuy	Straight rebuy
1. Anticipation or recognition of a problem (need) and a general solution	Yes	Maybe	No
2. Determination of characteristics and quantity of needed item	Yes	Maybe	No
3. Description of characteristics and quantity of needed item	Yes	Yes	Yes
4. Search for and qualification of potential sources	Yes	Maybe	No
5. Acquisition and analysis of proposals	Yes	Maybe	No
6. Evaluation of proposals and selection of supplier(s)	Yes	Maybe	No
7. Selection of an order routine	Yes	Maybe	No
8. Performance of feedback and evaluation	Yes	Yes	Yes

Figure 7-2
THE BUY GRID
FRAMEWORK.

The most complex buying situations occur in the upper-left portion of the "buy grid" framework, where the largest number of decision makers and buying influences are involved. The initial phases of a new task generally represent the greatest difficulty for management. (Adapted from Patrick J. Robinson, Charles W. Faris, and Yoram Wind, *Industrial Buying and Creative Marketing*, Allyn and Bacon, Inc., Boston, 1967, p. 14.)

Frequency of Purchase

In the industrial market, firms buy certain products very infrequently. Large installations are purchased only once in many years. Smaller parts and materials to be used in the manufacture of a product may be ordered on long-term contracts, so that an actual selling opportunity exists only once every year. Even standardized operating supplies, such as office supplies or cleaning products, may be bought only once a month.

Because of this buying pattern, a great burden is placed on the advertising and personal selling programs of industrial sellers. Their advertising must keep the company's name constantly before the market. Then, when buyers are in the market, they will already be acquainted with the selling firm. The sales force must call on potential customers often enough to know when a customer is considering a purchase.

Size of Order

The average industrial order is considerably larger than its counterpart in the consumer market. This fact, coupled with the infrequency of purchase, means that an industrial seller cannot afford to lose sales because of weaknesses such as poor selling techniques, noncompetitive pricing, uncertain delivery, or imperfect products.

Direct Purchase

Direct sale from the producer to the ultimate consumer is rare. In the industrial market, however, direct marketing from the producer to the industrial user is quite common. This is true especially when the order is large and the buyer needs much technical assistance. From a seller's point of view, direct marketing is reasonable, especially when there are relatively few potential buyers, they are big, and they are geographically concentrated. Nevertheless, some products, such as office supplies and many manufacturing supplies, are marketed through middlemen, as are most industrial agricultural products.

Multiple Influences on Purchases

In the industrial market, the purchasing decision is frequently influenced by more than one person, particularly in medium-sized and large firms. Even in small firms where owner-managers make all major decisions, they usually consult with knowledgeable employees before making certain purchases.

In firms large enough to have a separate purchasing department, a seller may be misled into thinking that the real purchasing power lies in one person or one department. Here, we must distinguish among (1) initiating a purchasing project, (2) determining product specifications, and (3) selecting a supplier. Frequently, the first two of these activities are initiated and/or strongly influenced by workers or managers in departments other than the purchasing department. Typically, the purchasing department places the orders. In many instances, purchasing agents also select the individual suppliers. But they must select those who carry the items or brands agreed upon by others in the firm.[6]

This buying pattern requires that salespeople be capable of determining who influences the buying decisions. Very often, salespeople will call on the wrong executives. Even knowing who the decision makers are sometimes is not enough—these people may be very difficult to reach. Moreover,

---

[6]For additional insights into who makes industrial buying decisions, see Joseph A. Bellizzi and C. K. Walter, "Purchasing Agent's Influence in the Buying Process," *Industrial Marketing Management*, April 1980, pp. 137–141; Joseph A. Bellizzi, "Organizational Size and Buying Influence," *Industrial Marketing Management*, February 1981, pp. 17–21; and Thomas Bonoma, "Major Sales: Who *Really* Does the Buying?" *Harvard Business Review*, May–June 1982, pp. 111–119.

different types of sales presentations may be needed, depending upon what level of industrial executive the sales rep is approaching.[7]

Reciprocity Arrangements

A highly controversial industrial buying habit is the practice of reciprocity — the policy of "I'll buy from you if you'll buy from me." Traditionally, reciprocity was common among firms marketing homogeneous basic industrial products such as oil, steel, rubber, paper products, and chemicals. In these industries, price competition generally did not exist, and a firm in one industry was a major supplier to a firm in another industry (and vice versa). Then, through the years, reciprocal selling expanded to a wide variety of industries. Many companies established "trade relations" departments to make effective use of this powerful selling tool.

Today, however, most of these departments have vanished. There has been a significant decline in the practice of reciprocity on a systematic basis. From an economic point of view, reciprocity may not make sense because the morale of both the sales force and the purchasing department may suffer. Under any circumstances, it is difficult to justify purchasing from customers unless the buyer is getting competitive price, quality, and service from the seller.

Reciprocity undoubtedly still exists in many buyer-seller relationships. However, it is done largely in an informal, low-key manner. At the same time, however, a company's marketing information system (involving sales records and purchasing data) provides the potential for practising reciprocity on a systematic basis.[8]

Demand for Product Servicing

The user's desire for excellent service is a strong industrial buying motive that may determine buying patterns. Consequently, many sellers emphasize their service as much as their products. Frequently a firm's only attraction is its service, because the product itself is so standardized that it can be purchased from any number of companies.

Sellers must stand ready to furnish services both before and after the sale. A manufacturer of office computers may study a customer firm's accounting operations and suggest more effective systems that involve using the seller's products. They will also arrange to retrain the present office staffs. After the machines have been installed, other services, such as repairs, may be furnished.

---

[7]See William A. Staples and John I. Coppett, "Sales Presentations at Three Company Levels," *Industrial Marketing Management*, April 1981, pp. 125–128.

[8]For a report on reciprocity — its history (in brief), present-day situation, and future prospects — see F. Robert Finney, "Reciprocity: Gone but Not Forgotten," *Journal of Marketing*, January 1978, pp. 54–59.

Quality and Supply Requirements

Another industrial buying pattern is the user's insistence upon an adequate quantity of uniform-quality products. Variations in the quality of materials going into finished products can cause considerable trouble for manufacturers. They may be faced with costly disruptions in their production processes if the imperfections exceed quality-control limits. Adequate quantities are as important as good quality. A work stoppage that is caused by an insufficient supply of material is just as costly as one that is caused by inferior quality of material. In one study of problems faced by purchasing agents for smaller manufacturers, the problem most often reported was sellers failing to deliver on schedule.[9]

Adequacy of supply is important for sellers and users of industrial raw materials such as agricultural products, metal ores, or forest products. Climatic conditions may disrupt the normal flow of goods—for example, when logging camps or mining operations become snowbound. Agricultural products fluctuate in quality and quantity from one growing season to another. These "acts of God" create additional managerial problems for both buyers and sellers with respect to warehousing, standardization, and grading.

(Courtesy of Jordan-Milton Machinery, Inc.)

Leasing Instead of Buying

A growing behavioural pattern among firms in the industrial market is that of **leasing** industrial products instead of buying them outright. In the past, this practice was limited to large equipment, such as data processing machines (IBM), packaging equipment, and heavy-construction equipment. Today, industrial firms are expanding leasing arrangements to include delivery trucks, sales-force automobiles, machine tools, storage bins, and other items generally less expensive than major installations.

Leasing has several merits for the firm leasing out its equipment. Total net income—after charging off pertinent repair and maintenance expenses—is often higher than it would be if the unit were sold outright. Also, the market may be expanded to include users who could not afford to buy the product, especially large-installation equipment. Leasing offers an effective method of getting distribution for a new product. Potential users may be more willing to rent a product than to buy it. If they are not satisfied, their expenditure is limited to a few monthly payments.

From the user's point of view, the benefits of leasing may be summarized as follows:

1. Leasing allows users to retain their investment capital for other purposes.

2. There may be significant tax advantages. Rental payments are totally tax-deductible, and they are usually larger than corresponding depreciation charges on owned products.

---

[9]Monroe M. Bird, "Small Industrial Buyers Call Late Delivery Worst Problem," *Marketing News*, April 4, 1980, p. 24.

3. New firms can enter a business with less capital outlay than would be necessary if they had to buy the equipment outright. This may not be an unmixed blessing, however. While ease of entry increases competition, it can also lead to an overcrowding of the field.

4. Leasing makes available the newest products developed by the lessors.

5. Leased products are usually serviced by lessors; this eliminates one headache associated with ownership.

6. Leasing is particularly attractive to users who need the equipment seasonally or sporadically, as in food canning or construction.[10]

This ends our discussion of the consumer and industrial markets. Once a company's executives know their market or markets, they are in a position to capture their desired share of those markets. They have the four components of the marketing mix — product, price, distribution system, and promotion — with which to attain that goal. Each of Parts 3 to 6 is devoted to one of these components.

SUMMARY

The industrial market consists of organizations that buy goods and services to use in their businesses. It is an extremely large, complex, and important market. It includes a wide variety of industrial users who buy a wide variety of industrial products and services. These products are divided into five groups, mainly because each group requires its own mix of marketing practices. The five groups are raw materials, fabricating materials and parts, installations, accessory equipment, and operating supplies.

Industrial market demand may be characterized generally as being derived, inelastic, and widely fluctuating. Industrial buyers usually are quite well-informed about what they are buying. Industrial market demand is analysed by evaluating the same three basic factors as those in the consumer market: (1) the number and kinds of industrial users, (2) their buying power, and (3) their motivation and buying behaviour. Industrial buying motives generally are rational, but the purchasing agent's self-interest must also be considered.

Buying patterns (habits) of industrial users often are quite different from patterns in the consumer market. In the industrial market, the negotiation period usually is longer, and purchases are made less frequently. Orders are larger, and direct purchases (no middlemen) are more common. Purchasing decisions often are influenced by more than one person. Reciprocity arrangements and leasing (rather than product ownership) are quite common in industrial marketing.

---

[10]For an in-depth report on leasing, see Paul F. Anderson, *Financial Aspects of Industrial Leasing Decisions: Implications for Marketing*, MSU Business Studies, Michigan State University, East Lansing, 1977. Also see Paul F. Anderson, "Industrial Equipment Leasing Offers Economic and Competitive Edge," *Marketing News*, April 4, 1980, p. 20.

KEY TERMS AND CONCEPTS

QUESTIONS AND PROBLEMS

1. "About 80 percent of all farm products are industrial goods." Give some examples of farm products that are *consumer* goods.

2. In which of the five subclassifications of industrial goods should each of the following be included? Which products may belong in more than one category?
   a. Typewriters
   b. Nuts and bolts
   c. Dental chairs
   d. Automobile wax
   e. Land
   f. Printing presses
   g. Copper wires
   h. Trucks

3. If the demand for most industrial goods is inelastic, why is it that sellers do not raise their prices to maximize their revenues?

4. Why does the demand for industrial goods usually fluctuate more widely than that for consumer goods?

5. What are some marketing implications of the fact that the demand for industrial goods:
   a. fluctuates widely?
   b. is inelastic?
   c. is derived?

6. What are the marketing implications for a seller of the fact that customers are geographically concentrated and limited in number?

7. What differences would you expect to find between the marketing strategies of a company selling to horizontal industrial markets and those of a company selling to vertical industrial markets?

8. Select four of the "buy phases" in the industrial buying process and explain how the relative importance of each one changes, depending upon whether the buying situation is a new task or a straight rebuy.

9. Select three advertisements for industrial products and identify the buying motives stressed in the ads.

10. NCR, IBM, Burroughs, and other manufacturers of office machines make a substantial proportion of their sales directly to industrial users. At the same time, wholesalers of office equipment are thriving. Are these two market situations inconsistent? Explain.

11. What suggestions do you have for industrial sellers to help them determine who influences the buying decision among industrial users?

12. What are the marketing implications, for both buyers and sellers, of the fact that often there are multiple influences in the purchasing of industrial goods?

Case 4   Kleen-A-Kar, Inc.*

Identifying a Market

Mary Napko had just received notice of acceptance of her application to become an "independent operator" of a Kleen-A-Kar franchise in a small eastern Canadian university town. Although she was a recent graduate of that university, Mary had not taken any business-related courses, nor had her past work experience involved her in the business world. She had worked every summer on her family's farm.

After reading in a business magazine an article about Kleen-A-Kar's rapid growth, Mary decided that this was an opportunity to realize her long-held dream of going into business for herself. While awaiting a response to her application, she had gone over in her mind the various elements of this business.

One aspect of the business that Mary had not been able to identify was what type of person or company would be most likely to want Kleen-A-Kar's services. That is, she needed detailed information about the quantitative and qualitative nature of her market.

Kleen-A-Kar was started about three years ago by Eric Berner and already had over 1,000 independent operators (franchise holders) in Canada and the United States. The company was marketing an "automotive appearance maintenance" service for virtually any type of automotive vehicle as well as for boats and airplanes.

The company assigned dealerships on a population basis, with a goal of having one operator per 25,000 population: Kleen-A-Kar furnished the materials and supplies for the vehicle servicing. The company also provided an operator's manual, advertising aids, and a monthly advisory newsletter. Each independent operator paid a start-up fee of $1,000 to cover a polishing machine and an initial stock of supplies. Each operator also paid Kleen-A-Kar a royalty fee of $3 per vehicle serviced, regardless of the amount of servicing performed.

Kleen-A-Kar's services were designed to maintain a vehicle's appearance by cleaning and polishing the exterior and interior of the vehicle. These maintenance services could be performed by the Kleen-A-Kar people at any time and wherever the customer's vehicle was parked — at the home or office and during days, evenings, or weekends.

The key to the effective performance of Kleen-A-Kar's service was a special machine called the Wonder Tool. Mr. Berner believed that the conven-

*Adapted from case prepared by Michele Zeleny.

tional rotary buffers, especially when used improperly, had the potential for gouging or otherwise marring the paint on a vehicle. Consequently, he searched extensively for a machine that could buff the various Kleen-A-Kar treatments into a car's finish without harm. He finally found the kind of machine he wanted. Called the Wonder Tool, it originally was developed to polish airplanes.

Mr. Berner also had a chemical company develop a group of specially formulated products for Kleen-A-Kar. These products were used to clean and protect the paint on a vehicle, to revitalize and dress vinyl roofs, to shampoo interiors, and to protect carpeting against water and other stains. The Wonder Tool was used to apply these various treatments, using either wool polishing pads or brush attachments.

One particularly effective and innovative treatment offered by Kleen-A-Kar was called Perma-Shine. This treatment was not a wax but an exclusive formula that was actually buffed in and bonded to the surface by the slight amount of heat generated by the Wonder Tool. Perma-Shine provided a protective, glasslike shine that sealed out the harmful effects of oxidation, road salt, salt-water air, snow, and sun. This treatment was accompanied with a written guarantee good for as long as the customer owned the car.

Kleen-A-Kar provided its operators with a "suggested job pricing schedule," parts of which are shown in Exhibit 1. In addition, the company suggested a package discount of 15 percent if several services were performed on the same vehicle. These prices were not mandatory but were intended only as guidelines. By charging these prices, the operator would earn a gross income of $30 to $50 per hour, depending upon the treatment being performed. The prices varied, depending upon the condition of the vehicle. For example, badly oxidized paint, filthy carpets, or very stained upholstery would require an additional charge.

Mary Napko estimated that she would have very few overhead (fixed) costs. Most of the Kleen-A-Kar operators worked out of their own homes and used their own vehicles. The three main cost items were advertising, the materials used to perform the job, and the $3 per car royalty fee paid to Kleen-A-Kar, Inc. Advertising usually ran about 10 percent of sales — that is, about $7.50 per job. Overall, the cost of materials averaged about 8 percent of the price of the job. However, the cost percentage varied considerably, depending upon the particular services performed.

Kleen-A-Kar operators faced competition from several other companies. Most of the competitors offered long-term protective processes similar to Kleen-A-Kar's Perma-Shine treatment. These companies generally charged anywhere from $80 to $200, their work often required some kind of periodic follow-up, and they gave oral warranties ranging from one to three years. They did very little advertising other than in the Yellow Pages in the telephone directory. A major source of business was referrals from satisfied customers and local auto dealers.

Although not offering completely comparable services, two other types of competitors were automatic car washes and the do-it-yourself market. The car washes usually also offered liquid or paste-wax treatments. Prices ranged from $4 to $25, depending upon the equipment used and services provided.

Ms. Napko was impressed with the overall market potential for car-cleaning services. She understood that the washing and waxing of cars had become the fourth-largest revenue producer in the automotive after-market, surpassed only by the sales of tires, batteries, and oil. She believed that people were keeping their cars longer because of the high price of new cars. Consequently, she reasoned, people would be spending more on the appearance of their cars. According to one marketing information

Exhibit 1   EXCERPTS FROM "SUGGESTED JOB PRICING SCHEDULE"

Service Performed	Vehicle or Part	Newer Vehicle	Older Vehicle
		Autos	
Perma-Shine	Subcompact	$ 55-60	$ 60-75
	Compact	60-65	65-80
	Mid-size	65-70	70-85
	Full-size	75-85	85-100
	Luxury	90-135	105-150
		Station Wagons and Vans	
	Compact	65-70	70-85
	Mid-size	70-85	85-100
	Full-size	85-100	100-115
	Luxury	100-150	115-165
		Pick-up Trucks	
	Smaller	60-85	65-100
	Larger	85-115	100-130
		Recreation Vehicles	
		200-300	250-375
		Small Planes	
		200-325	250-400
		Boats	
		1-4/m	1-4/m
Standard cleaning-polishing		2/3 above	2/3 above
Vinyl roof shampoo and dressing	with above:		
	Half roof	$ 25	
	Full roof	16	
	without above:		
	Half roof	40	
	Full roof	32	
Interior shampoo	Vinyl/leather	$ 32-55	
	Fabric	40-65	
Upholstery protector	Carpets	$ 16-20	
	Upholstery	25	

service, about 40 percent of the adults in North America wax their car at least once a year. Since hand-waxing is a time-consuming, physically exhausting job, Ms. Napko thought that these people would be receptive to a professional car-cleaning service.

Mary Napko realized that, up to this point, her market analysis had dealt only with the "big picture." That is, she had been considering the total market potential for car appearance services in the entire country. Now she was more concerned about the market opportunities in the immediate geographic area close to her home.

To promote her new business more effectively, Mary realized she needed to identify and analyse her local market in some detail. That is, she needed some quantitative measures of this market. For example, she was wondering what type of ultimate consumers or industrial users might be potential customers. She wondered what significant demographic features would characterize her market. She wanted to determine whether there were identifiable psychological or sociological characteristics in this market.

Question

What is the market for Mary Napko's Kleen-A-Kar services? Describe this market in detail. (Assume the franchise is located in your college town. If your school is in a large metropolitan area, then analyse the market in that part of the metropolitan area where your school is located.)

Analysis of a Market

A little over two years ago, Grant Hubbard and his son David were considering purchasing riding lawn mowers for their suburban homes. (A riding mower is the kind you sit on and drive like a small tractor, rather than the kind that you walk behind.) After comparing several competitive models, both men bought the same brand of mower from a local hardware and small-equipment dealer. After using their mowers a few times, they were completely dissatisfied.

The men were confident that they could build a better lawn mower than the ones they had purchased. Since they were the owners and operators of an equipment-manufacturing firm, they had both the experience and the facilities to do so. After two years of engineering development and manufacturing effort, the Hubbards recently unveiled their new Hubbard riding lawn mower. The men believed they had produced a high-quality, compact mower that would be easy to operate and maintain, and that provided for easy bagging of cut grass.

Now that their new mower was available, Grant and David realized that they faced a number of questions concerning the marketing of the product. They especially wanted to determine just what constituted the market for the mower.

Hubbard Manufacturing Co. Ltd. originally began operations about thirty-five years ago as a producer of gasoline-powered utility and golf carts. The

Case 5
Hubbard
Manufac-
turing Co.
Ltd. *

*Adapted from case prepared by Daniel Rye, University of Colorado student.

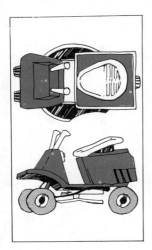

seasonality of golf-cart sales was balanced by a small, multipurpose vehicle that could serve as a flatbed truck, a pickup truck, a tractor, a small bulldozer, or a forklift truck.

In the 1960s, Grant Hubbard sold his rights to these products and the company ceased operations. Then, several years later, he started up again —this time to produce a line of evaporative air coolers that could be used in farm tractor cabs, trucks, vans, and recreation vehicles. The sale and distribution of these coolers were handled by another company; Hubbard had no marketing organization. The coolers were the mainstay of the Hubbard Manufacturing Company at the time the riding lawn mower was developed.

The Hubbard lawn mower was a rotary-type, powered by an 8-hp motor with an electric starter. The shipping weight was either 280 or 310 kilograms, depending upon whether an optional grass-handling attachment was included. The mower had three wheels—two in front and one in the back. The front wheels provided the drive power and the steering through the use of two independent Eaton hydrostatic transmissions. Two hand-operated levers allowed the driver to control the direction (forward/reverse/turning) and the speed. No shifting was required. The mower had a 92-millimetre-wide cutting deck that discharged grass clippings to the side.

The Hubbards believed that their unit had several advantages over conventional riding lawn mowers. Compared with competitive models, the Hubbard machine was much more manoeuvrable, compact, and easy to handle. The controls were easily reached, and the operator did not have to raise or lower the cutting deck. The machine was easy to mount, comfortable to sit on, and safe to ride. A tilt-up body and removable cutting deck made the machine easy to service. Both Grant and David felt that one of the outstanding features was the optional grass-handling system. This is a partially mechanized system for catching and bagging grass clippings and then emptying the clippings into a standard plastic trash bag.

Grant Hubbard expected to sell direct to consumers. The mower would be priced to consumers at $1,895 for the standard model and at $2,245 for the mower with the grass-handling system included. Freight charges from the factory in Milton, Ontario would be additional.

The Hubbards planned to utilize their existing plant and equipment to manufacture the riding lawn mowers. During the first year, production would be limited to 50 to 100 units. If the mower proved to be successful, production, with the existing manufacturing facilities, could go as high as 1,000 to 1,500 per year.

According to Dave Hubbard, the riding lawn mower industry was very competitive, with a large number of producers. However, a few large manufacturers, such as Toro, Jacobsen, John Deere, and Bolens-FMC produced most of the riding lawn mowers. These companies marketed a wide assortment of mowers, distributed them nationwide, and spent considerable funds on promotion and on product research and development. Their products generally were of high quality, selling for $1,000 to $2,500 per mower.

In addition, a substantial number of riding lawn mowers were sold by the large general-merchandise chains, such as Canadian Tire, Sears Canada, and K-Mart. These firms sold their mowers under their own private brands, generally at a much lower price than the national (manufacturers') brands.

Many of these competitive models were also priced lower than the Hubbard mower. And the higher-priced mowers typically offered a large assortment of accessories that increased their versatility. Also, the large competitors offered several different models to more closely meet the needs of different market segments.

Grant and Dave Hubbard realized that before they could develop an effective marketing program, they needed an accurate, detailed description of the market for their lawn mower. At first, they believed that their market consisted of (1) the homeowner with a large lawn and (2) the light commercial user. In fact, they intentionally decided *not* to produce a mower with a 64mm cutting deck, so as to avoid competing with large manufacturers that were targeting on homeowners with small and medium-sized yards.

The Hubbards got some consumer feedback that supported their market contentions. Their new mowers were exhibited recently at a number of fall agricultural falls in southern Ontario. Most people who showed an interest in the mower had anywhere from .2 to 2 hectares of grass to cut. But Dave wondered whether these responses reflected only a local market condition rather than a broader geographical situation.

Executives from Devonian Co. Ltd. — the firm that marketed Hubbard's evaporative coolers — wanted to obtain the marketing rights to the new mower. These executives believed that the Hubbard mower would appeal to homeowners with almost any size of yard. Even with the Hubbards' relatively high price, the Devonian people believed that the mower's competitive advantages would appeal to the wide variety of consumers.

Lee Remington, a local hardware and small-equipment dealer and a friend of the Hubbards, suggested that the mower be sold only to the industrial market. He felt that users such as golf courses, city parks departments, forest services, and professional lawn-mowing services were good target markets. This type of customer would be willing to pay more for the high-quality Hubbard product. Remington also suggested that marketing to homeowner-consumers would be very difficult and expensive.

Dave Hubbard also wondered whether there were any distinctive qualitative factors or behavioural traits that might characterize his potential market.

Question

What is the market for the Hubbard riding lawn mower in your province? Identify this market in some detail, considering quantitative measures as well as any possible qualitative or behavioural dimensions.

Behavioural Considerations in Market Analysis

*Case 6
Bayshore
Co. Ltd. ***

Bayshore Co. Ltd. was a medium-sized manufacturer of electronic components, tools, and repair kits. Bayshore's products were sold to both the professional and the amateur (do-it-yourself) markets for repairing television, stereo, and hi-fi sets. Sales last year totalled $4.7 million.

*Case prepared by Prof. A. H. Kizilbash, Northern Illinois University. Used with permission.

The amateur market currently represented less than 10 percent of company sales. This market was reached through retail-chain outlets. Bayshore sold tools, kits, and chemicals to these stores under its own brand and also under the stores' private brands. Products sold under the two labels generally were identical. The professional repair market was reached through electronic wholesalers, who called on the local electrical supply houses from which most repair people and technicians procured their supplies.

Because of advances in the design and construction of television sets and stereo record and tape players, the need for frequent repairs had declined. When a repair was needed, it could be quickly performed by replacing the defective part with a new one, thus eliminating the need for the usual tools, kits, and chemicals. As a result of these and related developments, Bayshore's sales to the professional repair market had dropped from a high of $5.9 million only six years ago to a low of $4.7 million last year.

Recognizing that its professional repair market was shrinking, two years ago Bayshore's management decided to search for a new product line. After a careful study by the new-products development department, a line of furniture-style stereo speakers was unveiled. The proposed product line consisted of stereo speakers with cabinets made in various furniture styles, such as contemporary, Canadian Knotty Pine, and Mediterranean. The developers believed that a majority of stereo speakers sold were of the "black box" variety and did not blend in well with the décor of a home. It was reasoned that furniture-style speakers would therefore appeal to a vast majority of consumers.

Three months prior to the full-scale production of the new line, management decided to undertake a marketing study to see if there really was a demand for this product. David Tanner, a recent M.B.A. graduate who had been serving as an assistant to the sales manager, was asked to conduct the study. Tanner completed the study in the assigned two months. The following are excerpts from his report to management.

Research Method

In order to gain insights into consumer motivation, perceptions, and preferences for stereo speakers, the investigation was conducted in two phases. The first phase consisted of a focus-group session conducted by a trained psychologist who met with nine middle-aged, married women in London, Ontario.

In the second phase, 106 personal in-store interviews were conducted with shoppers after demonstrating the product in use—also in the London area. One Sears Canada store and two small stores were selected for this purpose. Three *identical* speakers, each encased in a different style of cabinet, were used. The three cabinet styles selected were (1) Knotty Pine, (2) Mediterranean, and (3) black box. Interviewers asked each respondent to listen to a record (chosen by the respondent) on the three speakers. A switching system gave the respondent the opportunity to hear the same record on all three speakers. Respondents were *not* told anything about the similarities and dissimilarities of the three speakers. They were asked to rate each speaker on cabinet style, sound quality, and overall preference. They were also asked to state the reasons for their choice.

Focus-Group Findings

The following represents generalizations developed from one exploratory group discussion with the nine women, approximately half of whom owned console stereo units, while the rest had component units.

- It would appear that when a family decides to purchase its first stereo set, they (1) are young marrieds possibly beginning a family, (2) do not have a great deal of discretionary income, and (3) live in smaller quarters than they expect to occupy once they earn greater income. Therefore, the first stereo purchase is usually a console unit. This unit is compact, fits in a small living room, and becomes a piece of furniture.

- The comparison between console and component stereo systems seems to be that for consoles, you sacrifice sound for style and pay for furniture. In contrast, components offer much better sound, but not much style.

- Two major problems surfaced regarding components. One is the difficulty in hiding the wires that run from the turntable to the amplifier to the speakers. The second problem is that the appearance of stereo component speakers is not attractive.

- The women perceived the furniture-style speakers as being highly decorative and much preferred over the plain box speaker. However, there will be consumer resistance to purchasing these more decorative speakers if they are priced much higher than the box speaker. This is so simply because any speaker is viewed as a necessity, rather than an addition to a room that a woman makes voluntarily. That is, speakers are more or less forced on her, and she must arrange them in her room to accommodate the sound from a stereo. She apparently does this reluctantly, especially if she feels it interferes with her planned décor.

- None of the three speakers shown to this group of women was rejected. However, the women would like to have a choice of colours in the cloth behind the speaker grille. Thus the speakers could be better integrated with the colour scheme in a room.

- In summary, these women ideally wanted the speakers to be invisible. Since this obviously is not possible, the women wanted the speakers (1) to blend in as much as possible with a room's décor and (2) to be multifunctional in use.

Survey Findings

Tables 1 through 4 are a summary of findings based on a survey of consumers after an in-store demonstration of three *identical* speakers encased in three *different* cabinet styles. Some of the columns in the tables do not total 106 (the number of people interviewed) because a few respondents did not express a second or third choice.

Table 1 CABINET STYLES RATED FOR SPEAKER SOUND QUALITY

Cabinet	First		Second		Third	
	No.	%	No.	%	No.	%
Knotty Pine	44	42%	31	30%	29	28%
Mediterranean	32	30	39	38	33	32
Black box	30	28	33	32	41	40
Totals	106	100%	103	100%	103	100%

Table 2 CABINET STYLES RATED FOR APPEARANCE

Cabinet	First		Second		Third	
	No.	%	No.	%	No.	%
Knotty Pine	47	44%	35	34%	22	21%
Mediterranean	13	12	42	41	49	48
Black box	46	44	26	25	32	31
Totals	106	100%	103	100%	103	100%

Table 3 RESPONDENTS' OVERALL PREFERENCE

Cabinet	First		Second		Third	
	No.	%	No.	%	No.	%
Knotty Pine	51	48%	23	22%	29	28%
Mediterranean	20	19	42	40	43	41
Black box	35	33	39	38	32	31
Totals	106	100%	104	100%	104	100%

Table 4 REASON FOR FIRST CHOICE

Reason	No.	%
Sound quality	63	59%
Cabinet style	26	25
Both sound and appearance	17	16
	106	100%

Questions

1. Evaluate the research method employed in this study.
2. On the basis of this study, what conclusion can you draw regarding the behaviour of adult women consumers toward stereo speakers?

Analysis of Consumer Behaviour Aspects of a Market

Case 7
Harper
*Bank**

Mr. Peter Forest had been installed as the new manager of the new Public Relations and Advertising Department. He had taken over a group that had been led by Mr. John Morgan since early 1978. Mr. Morgan had brought along the habit of thought he had learned in mass consumer marketing. He had wanted Harper Bank to increase its advertising expenditures and to radically alter the nature of the content of its advertising messages. He had advocated "slice-of-life" consumer interviews for both radio and television commercials with real consumers telling why they were loyal Harper Bank customers. Mr. Morgan had also advocated higher promotion expenditures and a policy of, as he put it, "selling money" to consumers. Some of these ideas were considered unorthodox by both his superiors and subordinates. After a clash with Mr. Fred McKenzie, the General Manager to whom he reported, Mr. Morgan left to seek employment elsewhere.

The first few years of Mr. Forest's tenure were spent repairing relationships with his staff and superiors. The approach to marketing during these years had been very conservative and cautious. There was a general desire on the part of everyone concerned not to repeat past mistakes. But after Mr. McKenzie's retirement, the new General Manager, Mr. Walter Howson, indicated to Mr. Forest that he thought the time had come for another review of the bank's marketing posture and policies. "Let's just be sure we do it in an orderly and sensible fashion, Peter," he said. "We do not want the ghosts of the past to pop up and haunt us."

Mr. Forest thought of marketing primarily as a discipline. He believed marketing knowledge should be used to analyse the needs of buyers. This analysis should lead to the creation of products and services that would satisfy the consumer, and to methods for communicating effectively what Harper Bank had to offer to present and potential customers. Therefore, he believed the most important thing to do was to research the needs and behaviour of bank customers. This research could then be used to develop a marketing program appropriate to the banking industry, rather than simply trying to use a canned marketing program that was believed to have worked well in another industry.

Mr. Forest, in the course of his deliberations, began to think about the various theories of consumer behaviour and their implications for bank marketing in the unique Canadian banking environment. He jotted down the major components of each theory, the resultant hypotheses relevant to bank marketing, and then some questions he felt he would put to his staff. His objective, of course, was to home in on those elements in the marketing mix that could be manipulated in the banking environment to provide a unique, identifiable, market position for Harper Bank with the end result of an increase in market share and profitability. Mr. Forest also felt he and his department should provide some direction for future marketing strategy at both the corporate and branch level. The summary of Mr. Forest's notes may be found in Exhibit 1.

*Case prepared by Douglas J. Tigert and George H. Haines, Jr. Case material prepared by the University of Toronto Canadian Case Preparation Project is solely for use as a basis for class discussion and is not intended to necessarily illustrate either good or bad aspects of management of business.

This case is based on the original Harper Bank case prepared by Professor Lionel A. Mitchell, Acadia University.

Exhibit 1   A SUMMARY OF MR. PETER FOREST'S NOTES ABOUT
CONSUMER BEHAVIOUR THEORIES

I.   *Marshallian Economic Model: Modern Utility Theory*

   Major Theme: Consumers act in a rational manner to maximize their total utility.

   Hypotheses for Banking Environment:
   i)   lower prices lead to higher sales (loans)
   ii)   trust companies, with higher interest rates on savings accounts, will attract a higher than average amount of savings dollars
   iii)   higher promotional dollars will lead to higher awareness (effective communication) and a higher market share.

   Questions for Marketing Staff:
   i)   what is the role of *price* in the financial markets in general and in the banking environment in particular?
   ii)   what is it that we want to tell consumers; how much should we be spending; what should our media mix be?

II.   *The Pavlovian Learning Model*

   Model Components: Consumers have a set of drives (needs and motives). They react to a set of cues in the environment. They react to those cues by taking some sort of action. They experience either positive or negative reinforcement, and they react again in a similar or different fashion (brand loyalty or brand rejection result).

   Hypotheses for Banking Environment:
   i)   a strong cue about our bank (e.g. a free sample) might generate high trial of our bank
   ii)   high positive reinforcement inside the branch should lead to customer loyalty
   iii)   cues about our bank that differentiate us from other banks should lead to high trial

   Questions for Marketing Staff:

   i)   what does it take to make a customer aware of and interested in our bank?
   ii)   what sort of cues can you provide? Does the concept of free sampling have any relevance in bank marketing?
   iii)   what are the needs and motives of consumers in the area of financial services?
   iv)   if reinforcement inside or outside the branch is negative, what are the consequences? More important, how much negative reinforcement has to occur inside the branch before we lose the customer?

III.   *Freudian Psychoanalytic Model*

   Model Components: The Id (drives and urges), the Ego (planning centre), and the Superego (channels drives into socially approved outlets). Buyers are motivated by *symbolic*, as well as economic/functional, product characteristics.

   Hypotheses for Banking Environment:
   i)   some consumers may go to a finance company for a loan because they fear rejection at a bank, i.e. they fear they do not belong in a bank environment
   ii)   a bank with distinguishing positive symbolic characteristics (i.e. a unique market position), will attract a disproportionately high share of customers whose drives and needs are compatible with those characteristics

Questions for Marketing Staff:
i) what are the symbolic characteristics of our bank at the corporate and branch level? Should we be doing more in this area?
ii) how many potential customers are we losing to other financial institutions because our characteristics are not compatible with their needs and drives?

IV. *Veblen's Social-Psychological Model:*

Major Theme: Man is a social animal in a social environment. He interacts in a personal interaction environment with individuals and groups in a social hierarchy.

Hypotheses for Banking Environment:
i) different social classes have different financial needs
ii) the various trading areas of our branches ought to have some autonomy in identifying and satisfying those differentiated needs

Questions for Marketing Staff:
i) do we need to think seriously about market segmentation? Does the concept of full service banking apply equally across all our branches?
ii) what is there about our bank that attracts different consumer segments to our door? Are we doing a better job with some segments than with others?
iii) should we be thinking about market segments in terms of financial needs or in terms of social characteristics, or both? Is there any overlap? Should we try to appeal to a certain life-style?

Mr. Forest was not sure whether he had made any progress as he looked at these notes. True, he had examined four theories of consumer behaviour. There was some obvious overlap in these theories because he had asked some of the same questions more than once. More important, however, he was concerned about translating the academic jargon into pragmatic bank marketing strategy. After re-examining his notes, he wrote down some additional questions. These are reproduced in Exhibit 2.

Exhibit 2 QUESTIONS TO CONSIDER FOR REVIEW OF HARPER BANK'S MARKETING POSTURE AND POLICIES

---

1) What business are we in?
2) What is the nature of our product line?
3) Who is in the market for our product line? Is there more than one market segment?
4) What is the structure of the market?
   i) Who are the major competitors?
   ii) What are the major trends in the industry?
   iii) What do I know about the strategy of my major competitors:
      a) product line,   c) pricing policies, and
      b) advertising and promotion, d) location?
5) What marketing research data is available to help me understand the structure of the market and the potential alternatives for marketing strategy (i.e. what items in the marketing mix can be manipulated)?
6) What are the distinguishing characteristics of our major competitors?
7) What are the determinants of bank patronage, especially at the branch level? How do we rate on those variables?

Satisfied that he had at least asked the relevant questions, and knowing he did not have all the answers, Mr. Forest turned the assignment over to his marketing staff and asked for a group meeting several weeks hence.

At that meeting, the marketing group began to synthesize their findings. What evolved were some pretty fast conclusions. Peter tried to summarize the major findings of that meeting:

1) The Canadian banking industry can be characterized as a semi-monopoly wielding economic power that in magnitude and extent rivals any economic power bloc in the world. Between them, the five major Canadian banks control over $70 billion in assets and they are the single most potent force in the Canadian economy.

2) Unlike the situation in the United States, with over 14,000 banks, the Canadian scene is represented by "national banks" with approximately twice as many branches per capita as in the U.S. The average bank customer can choose between two or three branches about equally convenient to his/her home or work. Thus, while it is important for corporate strategy to consider location in positioning new branches, location is probably not an important determinant of patronage of one bank or another on the part of the customer.

3) Unlike the packaged-goods industry, there is very little unmatched product differentiation across the major banks. Innovations have been coming more rapidly — charge cards, automated bank tellers (cash dispensers), and new pricing concepts for services.

4) The Continental Bank and the Bank of British Columbia represent new competition, but their national impact is relatively minor at present.

5) While the trust companies and the finance companies play a role in the financial services market and while they are playing an increasing role in consumer loans, the potential move by the banks into the trust business represents a serious threat to the trust companies.

6) There is some price competition within the banking industry; branch managers do have a little discretion on rates for personal loans. Thus the role of price is still minor compared to other industries, such as merchandise retailing (e.g. discount department stores).

7) Most banking executives define our business as "full-service banking."

8) Examination of the major copy themes of corporate bank advertising does not provide much insight into the marketing or advertising objectives that might have led to those copy themes.

9) There appears to be little evidence that the five major banks have a differentiated marketing program or a differentiated image in the consumer environment.

"In short," said Peter," when you think about the variables that we traditionally manipulate in the marketing mix (price, product, physical distribution, and promotion), the banking industry does not appear to be working that much with any of them. I wonder how a customer chooses a bank in Canada? Let's see what we have to work with."

The marketing group was looking at two pieces of U.S. consumer research in an effort to come to grips with this problem. One study, done by the Gallup Organization, involved a straightforward survey that asked consumers how they chose a bank in their community. The results, replicated in a number of markets, always came out the same, with *convenience to home* or *convenience to work* as the key patronage determinant. There was also some evidence that drive-in windows, variations in interest on saving accounts, bank hours, and customer service played a role.

A second study, done by a Chicago bank, used a different research technique, with some rather interesting results. In this study consumers were given a list of bank characteristics, two at a time, and asked which characteristic was more important in choosing a bank. A section of the questionnaire is illustrated in Exhibit 3, with the resultant ranking of the important bank characteristics depicted in Exhibit 4. This paired comparison technique indicated that "high interest on savings" was the most important reason for choosing a bank, followed by "full range of bank services," "friendly, courteous staff," and "convenince to home." The three highest-ranking variables fall into the price/quality/product sphere, with location ranking only fourth.

Exhibit 3   CHICAGO BANKING STUDY: PAIRED COMPARISON
             QUESTIONNAIRE

If you were choosing a new bank for all your banking needs, would it be more important to you that the bank have . . . . . or . . . . .

CH	Highest interest on savings	1	2	Is easy to get a loan at
GH	Offers full range banking services	1	2	Is easy to get a loan at
DF	Has good parking	1	2	Has friendly, courteous staff
DE	Be convenient to work	1	2	Stays open at night
AG	Be convenient to home	1	2	Offers full range banking services
FG	Has friendly, courteous staff	1	2	Offers full range banking services
BD	Be convenient to work	1	2	Has good parking
CD	Highest interest on savings	1	2	Has good parking
BG	Be convenient to work	1	2	Offers full range banking services
CF	Highest interest on savings	1	2	Has friendly, courteous staff
AB	Be convenient to home	1	2	Has good parking
BF	Be convenient to work	1	2	Has friendly, courteous staff
BG	Has good parking	1	2	Offers full range banking services
EH	Stays open at night	1	2	Is easy to get a loan at
EF	Stays open at night	1	2	Has friendly, courteous staff
BC	Be convenient to work	1	2	Highest interest rate on savings
AB	Be convenient to home	1	2	Be convenient to work
CE	Highest interest on savings	1	2	Stays open at night
EG	Stays open at night	1	2	Offers full range banking services
AE	Be convenient to home	1	2	Stays open at night
AC	Be convenient to home	1	2	Has the highest interest rate on savings
DH	Has good parking	1	2	Is easy to get a loan at

"Of course," said Peter, "if the major banks in Canada are really indistinguishable one from the other in terms of price, product line, and quality of service, then the fact that these variables are important determinants of patronage is of little consequence. I wonder how consumers feel about these issues?

"However," concluded Peter, "I think we can summarize our conclusions and get to work. If the Canadian banks do not compete much on the basis of price, product line or location, what we are left with, it seems to me, is *competition based on what happens inside the branch, namely Customer*

Exhibit 4   CHICAGO BANKING STUDY: RANKING OF IMPORTANCE OF ATTRIBUTES IN CHOOSING A BANK (0–1) SCALE)

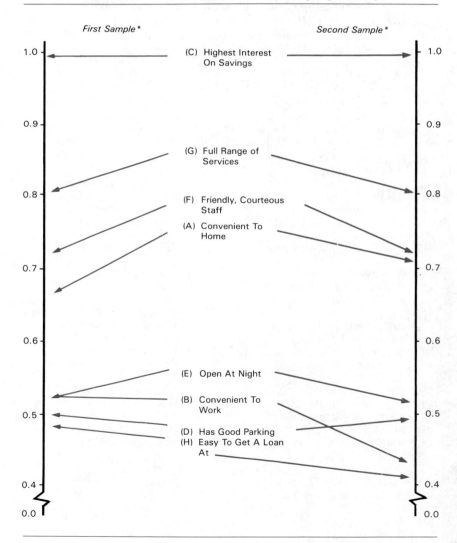

First Sample *   *Second Sample* *

(C) Highest Interest On Savings
(G) Full Range of Services
(F) Friendly, Courteous Staff
(A) Convenient To Home
(E) Open At Night
(B) Convenient To Work
(D) Has Good Parking
(H) Easy To Get A Loan At

Service. Therefore a marketing strategy for our bank should really revolve around a maximization of customer satisfaction at the branch level and an advertising strategy that effectively communicates that concept to current and potential customers. Of course, if one of the banks comes along with a unique idea, i.e. a new product or service with higher consumer appeal, we can throw this strategy out the window."

Peter had one additional piece of research to get him started on evaluating the current status of in-branch service and to give some ideas for improving customer service at the bank. This research was initiated by a group of undergraduate commerce students at the University of Toronto. The research objective was to examine the extent to which the banking industry at the branch level understood the marketing concept expressed as profits through customer satisfaction rather than profits through sales volume. The students acted as seekers of information, making contacts with some 280 branches in the Toronto area and monitoring the methodology by which bank personnel interacted with prospective customers. Following is a summary of the study conclusions:

1) Branch personnel had trouble as problem solvers in inquiring into the needs of prospective customers. They answered questions adequately but they could not initiate.

2) There was very little cross-selling of services inside the branch.

3) In only two of the 280 contacts made did anyone attempt to acquire the interviewer's name, address, or telephone number for a later follow-up.

4) While letters of inquiry (one of the three contact methodologies used) were answered quickly, they tended to be cold, impersonal, and factual. The responder almost never tried to *sell* that specific branch or bank as the "right one for the customer."

5) When asked why that particular bank should be picked for a new account, most bank personnel gave a standard answer: "All banks are the same, so might as well bank here." To quote one respondent in the study: "We're like Eaton's or Simpsons. . . . We try to appear different, but we're really all the same."

6) There was no standard procedure for answering inquiries.

7) Promotional literature was seldom handed out and was often not available when requested.

The students also spent some time talking with head-office marketing personnel (who were sometimes hard to find) and reached several additional conclusions:

1) In general, banks know very little about their customers or how their customers differ from those of the other banks.

2) There were no well-defined criteria for closing a branch.

3) Marketing personnel believe that banks are generally perceived by consumers to be the same and that banks in Canada are not a very salient issue with consumers. They are perceived as big, secure, traditional, conservative institutions.

4) No one seemed to know how much it was worth to attract a new customer, but the notion of paying a bonus to branch employees of $15–20 for a new customer seemed out of the question.

5) Not much research was going on to measure retention rates of customers or to combine this research with analysis of the growth of average balances to measure the long-term profitability of new customers.

6) The banks had expermiented with drive-ins and longer hours, but customers seemed to want to bank in the traditional manner, so the experiments were abandoned.

7) In general the bank marketing personnel confirmed that some of the problems uncovered by the students existed but that no one seemed to be too worried about them.

"You know, it's curious," said Peter, after reviewing this research. "The weakest link in our operation, *bank service*, seems to be the only marketing variable around which our marketing strategy can evolve. Furthermore there are some additional conflicts in the bank's operations. We pay extremely low wages for branch personnel with a resultant high personnel turnover. And we rotate our branch managers just when they are getting to know their customers and their trading area. Yet when you consider what should be the appropriate marketing strategy and tactics to accomplish our basic strategy of maximizing customer satisfaction, we should be doing just the opposite. That is, we should be minimizing personnel turnover and we should be developing branch managers who will build a business at a particular branch, i.e. who will develop a high rapport with the community. In short, our manager should be our entrepreneur in that location and he should run that branch like it was his own business. And he should be compensated appropriately for his performance at that branch, with profit sharing or some other mechanism. If we move that manager just when he is starting to generate that performance, then we have to start all over again in that location. Good in-branch service is synonymous with 'know the customer!' "

The Tactics of Good Branch Management

Peter and his subordinates went to work on developing a strategy for the branch level, leaving the development of corporate advertising for later interaction with the bank's advetising agency. After spending several weeks in the field observing various branches in action and after discussing the branch manager's needs with several managers, a proposed marketing program evolved.

The strategy of retail bank marketing at the branch level became synonymous with the concept of maximization of in-branch service in this proposed marketing program. Given the constraints of corporate philosophy concerning personnel, Peter and his subordinates identified ten tactics for the implementation of the proposed marketing strategy. These ten are given in Exhibit 5.

Exhibit 5 TEN TINY TIDBITS FOR THE BRANCH MANAGER

1. No customer with an unusual inquiry/problem should be left standing, especially a new customer. *Find him/her a chair!!*

2. Anyone who answers a phone should have the basic knowledge to answer *any* inquiry . . . without having to transfer the caller to someone else . . . unless it is a problem that only the branch manager can handle.

3. Tellers and other personnel must be trained to *initiate* . . . to ask relevant questions . . . to indicate that he/she wants to understand the customer's needs. The teller must be a *problem solver*.

4. It is not enough to rhyme off the services the bank offers . . . *define the need* first . . . then suggest an *action program*.

5. Never let a potential customer leave without at least trying to obtain name, address, and phone number . . . for later follow-up.

6. a) Constantly rotate your point-of-purchase materials on display.
   b) Don't expect customers to pick up display material . . . *find* a way to give it to them.

7. Set aside one day a week for *after hours role-playing* exercises with your tellers. The high teller turnover means this is a never-ending task. The same problems will occur and recur, but with new tellers.

8. All phone inquiries should be handled by *articulate English-speaking personnel*. Foreign-speaking customers tend to handle their problems by a personal visit to the bank.

9. Don't be afraid to have a new teller tell a customer she's a "trainee" if she can't handle a customer problem . . . but make sure she directs the customer to a problem solver.

10. *Your needs come second* . . . the customer's needs are paramount . . . *even if it inconveniences your operation.*

Peter felt that by implementing this ten-point action plan, Harper Bank would develop a different marketing image from all other Canadian banks. Customers would start to beat a path to their door. He felt sure no other Canadian bank would attempt to implement this strategy. He realized that this next step was to develop an implementation strategy and to sell the idea inside Harper Bank. He and his staff began work on a formal presentation for Mr. Howson although, of course, Mr. Howson already knew the results that they had come to on an informal basis.

At this time his wife's uncle, Charles Peters, approached him to take up pig farming on a partnership basis. Mr. Peters had been a farmer for about twenty years, starting with a joint operation with his father but now on his own. Over the years Mr. Peters' farm had gradually changed from a general family farm to a highly specialized pig farm. "The Ontario Pork Marketing Board," Mr. Peters said, "is doing a terrific job." Since they had no quotas, he felt sure the pork market was going to expand enormously in the decade ahead. "Come in with me, Peter," Charles said, "and stop tilting at windmills in the bank. But you have to act now, while the farm next to mine is for sale. You know, when we sell the business off in twenty years we will both retire wealthy. You'll never get rich as a bank marketing manager. The future's in pigs."

Questions

1. Can the bank's competitiveness be improved by using price, product line, or location?

2. What kind of marketing strategy focusing on customer service would be appropriate?

The Product

THE PLANNING, DEVELOPMENT, AND MANAGEMENT OF
THE WANT-SATISFYING GOODS AND SERVICES THAT ARE
A COMPANY'S PRODUCTS

Part 2 was concerned with the selection and identification of target markets in accordance with the firm's marketing goals. The next step in the strategic marketing planning process is to develop a marketing mix that will achieve these goals in the selected target markets. The marketing mix is a strategic combination of four variables — the organization's product, pricing structure, distribution system, and promotional program. Each of these is closely interrelated with the other three variables in the mix.

Part 3, consisting of three chapters, is devoted to the product phase of the marketing mix. In Chapter 8 we define the term *product*, consider the importance of product planning and innovation, and discuss the new-product development process. Chapter 9 deals mainly with product-mix strategies, the management of the product life cycle, and a consideration of style and fashion. Chapter 10 is concerned with branding, packaging, labelling, and other product features.

Chapter 8

Product Planning and Development

CHAPTER GOALS

This chapter will show you why "building a better mousetrap" is not enough to ensure success. After studying the chapter, you should understand:

1. *The meaning of the word* product *in its fullest sense*
2. *What a "new" product is*
3. Merchandising *as it relates to the marketing mix*
4. *The importance of product innovation*
5. *The steps in the product-development process*
6. *The criteria for adding a product to a company's line*
7. *Organizational structures for new-product planning and development*

In developing a program to reach its intended market, a company starts with the product or service designed to satisfy the wants of that market. Executives must plan, develop, and manage both the individual product and the company's product assortment. This is no easy task, as is shown by the large number of product failures in our economy.

THE MEANING OF "PRODUCT"

In a very *narrow* sense, a product is a set of tangible physical attributes assembled in an identifiable form. Each product carries a commonly understood descriptive (or generic) name, such as apples, steel, or baseball bats. Product attributes appealing to consumer motivation or buying patterns play no part in this narrow definition. A Sunbeam Shavemaster and a Braun shaver are one and the same product — an electric shaver.

A *broader* interpretation recognizes each *brand* as a separate product. In this sense an Eaton's man's suit and a Tip Top man's suit are two different products. Lantic Sugar and St. Lawrence Sugar are also separate products, even though their only tangible difference may be the brand name on the package. But the brand name suggests a product difference to the consumer, and this brings the concept of consumer want-satisfaction into the definition.

Any change in a physical feature (design, colour, size, packaging), however minor it may be, creates another product. Each such change provides

PRODUCT

the seller with an opportunity to use a new set of appeals to reach what essentially may be a new market. Cold remedies (Contac-C, Dristan) in capsule form are a different product from the same brand in tablet form, even though the chemical contents of the tablet and the capsule are identical.

We can broaden this interpretation still further. A Zenith television set bought in a discount store on a cash-and-carry basis is a different product from the identical model purchased in a department store. In the department store, the customer may pay a higher price for the TV set but buys it on credit, has it delivered free of extra charge, and receives other store services. Our concept of a "product" now includes services accompanying the sale, and we are close to a definition that is valuable to marketing people.

Our definition is as follows: A **product** is a set of tangible and intangible attributes, including packaging, colour, price, manufacturer's prestige, retailer's prestige, and manufacturer's and retailer's services, which the buyer may accept as offering want-satisfaction.

The key idea in this definition is that the consumers are buying more than a set of physical attributes. Fundamentally, they are buying want-satisfaction. Thus, a wise firm sells product *benefits* rather than just products. As Elmer Wheeler, an author and sales training consultant, said, "Don't sell the steak, sell the sizzle." A travel agency should not sell a two-week Caribbean cruise. Rather, it should sell romance, glamour, rest, a chance to meet people, and the opportunity for education.

Manufacturers sell symbols as well as products. "People buy things not only for what they can do, but also for what they mean."[1] Goods are psychological symbols of personal attributes, goals, and social patterns. As was suggested in Chapter 6, we buy products that reinforce our self-image, and people are shrewd judges of symbols.

What Is a "New" Product?

Just what is a "new" product? Are the new models that auto manufacturers introduce each autumn new products? If a firm adds a wrinkle-remover cream to its assortment of women's cosmetics, is this a new product? Or

[1]Sidney J. Levy, "Symbols for Sale," *Harvard Business Review*, July–August 1959, p. 118.

A PRODUCT IS ITS BENEFITS

We don't want sandpaper: we want a smooth surface. We don't want a ¼-inch drill; we want a ¼-inch hole. So tell us what your product can do for us — the end benefits. The product itself is only a means to that end.

- André Michel or Jordache blue jeans are not blue jeans. They are a sex symbol and a fashion status symbol.
- Labatt's Blue isn't a beer. It's a blue-collar macho symbol.
- Visa and American Express cards are not credit cards that let you charge what you buy. They are a security blanket.
- Canada's Wonderland and Marineland are not simply amusement parks with rides and shows. They are an escape from reality.
- Peoples Jewellers is not a chain of jewellery stores. It's a place that takes the risk out of buying diamonds and lets you buy with confidence.

Source: Adapted from Robert H. Bloom, "Product Redefinition Begins with Consumer," *Advertising Age*, Oct. 26, 1981, p. 51.

---

must an item be totally new in concept before we can class it as a *new* product?

Here, we need not seek a very limited definition. Instead, we can recognize several possible categories of new products. What is important, however, is that each separate category may require a quite different marketing program to ensure a reasonable probability of market success.

Three recognizable categories of *new products* are as follows:

1. Products that are *really* innovative—truly unique. Examples would be hair restorer or a cancer cure—products for which there is a real need but for which no existing substitutes are considered satisfactory. In this category we can also include products that are quite different from existing products but satisfy the same needs. Thus, television to a great extent replaced radio and movies, plastics compete with wood and metals, and solar power competes with other energy sources.

2. Replacements for existing products that are *significantly* different from the existing goods. Instant coffee replaced ground coffee and coffee beans in many markets; then freeze-dried instant replaced instant coffee. Dry cereal manufacturers introduce new cereals and often discontinue existing ones that no longer fulfil sales and profit expectations. Annual model changes in autos and new fashions in clothing belong in this category.

3. Imitative products that are new to a particular company but not new to the market. The company simply wants to capture part of an existing market with a "me-too" product.

Perhaps the key criterion as to whether a given product is new is how the intended market perceives it. If buyers perceive that a given item is significantly different (from competitive goods being replaced) in some characteristic (appearance, performance), then it is a new product.

Many new products are introduced into the Canadian market each year and meet with varying degrees of success. Most represent relatively minor variations on existing products but are, nevertheless, seen by consumers to be *new* products. Carlton Cards introduced a line of greeting cards that produce sound effects and talk. Rothmans is testing Passport, a cigarette that produces less smoke than conventional cigarettes. Labatt's repackages Blue and Labatt's Lite in tall bottles with twist caps. These represent relatively minor changes in the physical product, but create interest among consumers and serve to differentiate the brand from the competition.

More important variations on existing products would include the new system introduced by Polaroid that allows photographers to develop and mount 35mm slide films in minutes. Similarly, the Bic disposable lighter, Cabbage Patch Kids, and the Kodak disc camera represented major changes from existing products in these product categories.

Rarely are new products introduced that constitute a radically new entry into the market. The Ski-Doo recreational snowmobile developed by Bombardier, the videocassette recorder, and the personal computer are clearly new products that represent a departure from existing products — they either perform totally new functions or perform tasks far better or more efficiently than do any existing products.

Related Terms

In discussions of products and product policies, you will hear such terms as *product planning*, *product development*, and *merchandising*. These terms, while related, do have different meanings.

Product Planning and Product Development

Product planning embraces all activities that enable a company to determine what products it will market. **Product development**, a more limited term, encompasses the technical activities of product research, engineering, and design. More specifically, the combined scope of product planning and product development includes activities related to the following strategy decisions:

1. Which products should the firm make and which should it buy?

2. Should the company market more or fewer products?

3. What new uses are there for each product?

4. What brand, package, and label should be used for each product?

5. How should the product be styled and designed, and in what sizes, colours, and materials should it be produced?

6. In what quantities should each item be produced?

7. How should the product be priced?

Merchandising

Merchandising is probably one of the two most loosely used terms in the marketing vocabulary. (The other, *sales promotion*, is discussed in Part 6.)

To some people, merchandising is synonymous with marketing. Retailers make particularly heavy use of the word as a verb, noun, or adjective. A clothing buyer may be complimented for having "merchandised" a new sports shirt very well this season. Another executive may claim that sound "merchandising" is the foundation of a store's success. A third may note that the "merchandising" plans for next season are completed. One high-level executive in a department store is usually called the merchandising manager, and retail stores normally have no one with the title "marketing manager" or "sales manager."

In this book, **merchandising** is synonymous with product planning. That is, merchandising includes all company planning activities designed to prepare an assortment of products to meet a market demand.

IMPORTANCE OF PRODUCT INNOVATION

The social and economic justification for the existence of a business is its ability to satisfy its customers. A company meets its basic responsibility to society through its products. (We use the term broadly here to include nontangible goods, usually called services.) Unless it fulfils this mission, a firm should not exist. And normally the competitive forces in our socio-economic system do not permit it to exist, at least not for long.

In this section we point out some of the reasons why effective new-product planning and development are so important to a company today. Good executive judgement elsewhere cannot offset weaknesses in product planning. A company cannot successfully sell a poor product over the long run.

Products Have Life Cycles

Like people, products go through a life cycle. They grow (in sales), then decline, and eventually are replaced. From birth to death, a product's life cycle can generally be divided into five stages — introduction, growth, maturity, decline, and abandonment. The sales-volume curve in Fig. 8-1 illustrates the typical pattern of sales growth and decline for products as they go through their life cycle.

Two points related to the life-cycle concept help to explain why product innovation is so important. First, every company's present products will eventually become obsolete as their sales volume and market share are reduced by competitive products. Second, as a product ages, its profit generally declines (as shown in Fig. 8-1). If those products are not changed or replaced, the company's sales volume, market share, and profit will be reduced. And, eventually, the company itself will fail.

Product Is a Basic Profit Determinant

New products are essential for sustaining a company's expected rate of profit. Figure 8-1 illustrates a typical relationship between the sales-volume curve and the profit curve through the life cycle of a product. While similar in shape, the two curves have different timing. Note that the profit curve for most new products is negative through most of the introductory stage. Also, the profit curve starts to decline while the sales volume is still ascending. This occurs because a company usually must increase its advertising and selling effort or cut its prices (or do both) to continue its sales growth during the maturity stage in the face of intensifying competition. These

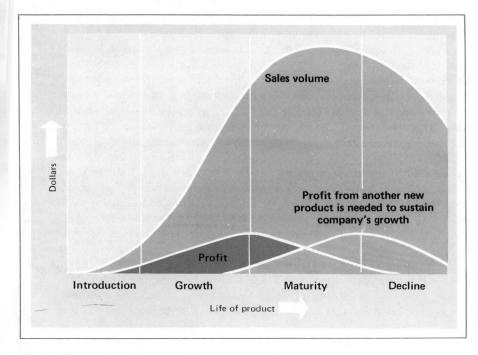

Figure 8-1
SALES VOLUME CURVE AND PROFIT MARGIN CURVE IN RELATION-SHIP TO THE LIFE OF A PRODUCT.

Profit margin usually starts to decline while a product's sales volume is still increasing. How does the relationship between these curves influence the time at which additional new products should be introduced?

additional promotional efforts or price reductions result in lower profit margins.

Often the sales-volume curve is used as the basis for marketing planning. The action of the profit curve, however, suggests that management should gear its product strategy to this curve rather than to the sales curve. *The introduction of a new product at the proper time will help to maintain the company's desired level of profits, as shown in Fig. 8-1.*

New Products Are Essential to Growth and Competition

The watchword for management must often be "innovate or die," and this innovating attitude can become a philosophy almost paralleling that of the marketing concept. Peter Drucker recognized the importance of the two concepts when he said, "Because it is its purpose to create a customer, any business enterprise has two — and only these two — basic functions: marketing and innovation."[2]

Many companies will get a substantial portion of their sales volume and net profit this year from products that did not exist five to ten years ago. Moreover, various studies have shown that the growth industries are those that are oriented to new products.[3]

[2]Peter Drucker, *The Practice of Management*, Harper & Row, Publishers, Incorporated, New York, 1954, p. 37.

[3]See Robert G. Cooper, "The Myth of the Better Mousetrap: What Makes a New Product a Success?" *Business Quarterly*, Spring 1981, pp. 69–81.

Also, companies in very competitive industries must maintain a constant flow of new or modified products in order to keep up with the competition. An excellent current example of this situation is the Canadian brewing industry, which has been facing a "no growth" market since the early 1980s. Faced with no increase in total demand, the major brewing companies have rushed to make modifications and improvements in existing products and to introduce new brands. Through the latter half of the 1970s, all companies introduced light beers. Then, Labatt's brought Budweiser to Canada and Carling O'Keefe followed with the introduction of Miller High Life. More recently, Molson has entered the "import" beer field with Lowenbrau. Labatt's has brought out a premium beer under the John Labatt Classic brand and has added a Blue Light brand extension to its best-selling Labatt's Blue brand. Further brand differentiation was accomplished in 1983 and 1984 with the relaunching of many of the major brands in new tall bottles and the introduction by the Labatt's Brewing Company of a twist-off cap.[4]

Factors Supporting and Impeding New-Product Development[5]

Several factors external to the individual firm will spur the development and introduction of new products, at least throughout the remainder of the 1980s. These forces include advances in technology, changing consumer needs, shortened product life cycles, and increasing international market competition.

At the same time, forces external to and within the firm could *impede* new-product development in the foreseeable future. The external obstacles include the high cost of capital, government regulations, and the high cost of labour. Internally, perhaps the primary deterrents to new-product development are the emphasis on *short-run* profitability and the lack of managerial attention to new products. This lack of a new-product orientation is reflected in inadequate marketing research, delays in new-product decision making, and the lack of a new-product strategy. Another deterrent is the fear that a new product will gain a market position largely at the expense of the innovator's existing products. That is, the company's new product will steal sales from present products in that company.[6]

Increased Consumer Selectivity

In recent years consumers have become more selective in their choice of products. As consumers' disposable income has increased, and as an abundance of products has become available, consumers have fulfilled many of their wants. The big middle-income group is reasonably well-fed, clothed,

---

[4]For recent information on the changes taking place in the Canadian brewing industry, see: "Carling and Labatt's Bring Out Two New Challengers," *Marketing*, May 23, 1983, p. 1; Randy Scotland, "Beer Bottles are Shaping Up," *Marketing*, March 19, 1984, p. 1: "Twist-off Time is Here," *Marketing*, April 2, 1984, p. 1, and a summary article: Randy Scotland and Mark Smyka, "Flat Sales Call for Heads-Up Marketing," *Marketing*, August 27, 1984, pp. 13–21.

[5]This section is adapted from *New Products Management for the 1980s*, Booz, Allen & Hamilton, New York, 1982, p. 5.

[6]See Roger A. Kerin, Michael G. Harvey, and James T. Rothe, "Cannibalism and New Product Development," *Business Horizons*, October 1978, pp. 25–31.

The cure for "product indigestion" may be *innovative* rather than *imitative* product planning.

housed, transported, and equipped. Thorstein Veblen theorized that as members of a social class attain the means to accumulate wealth, they pass through a period of *conspicuous consumption*, during which they acquire products to impress their neighbours. When they have proved that they can pay for a large house or a second car, these people then switch to a practice of conspicuous *underconsumption*.

If market satiation — in terms of quantity — does exist to some extent, it follows that consumers may be more critical in their appraisal of new products. While the consumer is being increasingly selective, the market is being deluged with products that are imitations or that offer only marginal competitive advantages. This situation may be leading to "product indigestion." The cure is to develop *really* new products—to *innovate*, and not just *imitate*.

One author has concluded that there exist a number of factors that are unique to the Canadian situation and influence the development of new products in this country.[7] These factors that should be considered in choosing new products in Canada may be summarized in the following guidelines for marketers:

1. *Avoid* highly scale-sensitive manufactured products and ancillary products; avoid products applicable to human beings in quantity. The big market blocs have basic advantages in mass consumer products, pharmaceuticals, mass transit vehicles, automobiles, large fleet aircraft, large computers, etc. Canada might have a share of some of these manufactures, but we cannot get as big a return from innovation in these fields as others can.

Uniquely Canadian Factors

---

[7]S. S. Grimley, "Canadian Factors in the Generation and Evaluation of New Product Ideas," *Business Quarterly*, Summer 1974, pp. 32–39.

Exceptions: products linked to industries that are very large in Canada by world standards, e.g. mining, pulp and paper; also products for which special export arrangements have been made; also specialized components for scale-sensitive products if made for world use by special arrangement in Canada, e.g. by participation in multi-government consortia.

2. *Avoid* products that rely excessively on export sales for viability and success.

Exceptions: products linked to existing large and successful exports from Canada — export packages for food would be an example; products for which special export arrangements have been made, e.g. via foreign parents, partners, or governments, or via allocation by parent company of a world business to the Canadian subsidiary company.

3. *Choose* products less sensitive to scale, e.g. for which total world need is not large, preferably with a greater than average need in Canada, e.g. airport "carousels," flight training devices, navigation aids, etc.; products for which the need is not large and is variable due to custom requirements, seasonality, fashion, etc., e.g. custom machine shop work, engineering design and consultancy, contract test laboratory work.

Exceptions: note that clothing fashions tend to be tied to the world tourist trade, which establishes the buying circuit.

4. *Choose* products based on special Canadian needs and strengths and exploit them on a world scale, e.g. geophysics instruments for mineral and engineering surveys, resources surveillance (forests, pests, pollution, resources satellites), navigation aids, search and rescue devices for remote places including under the sea, underground tunnelling techniques for mines, expressways, etc., ground gear for aircraft, off-terrain vehicles, ground gear and track for high-speed bulk freight trains, snow and ice controls, etc.

Avoid mainstream pollution control technologies for standard industries, urban centres (except for Arctic and low-temperature problems); mainstream transportation technologies for mass transit of people (large fleet aircraft, high-speed passenger trains, linear electric motors, monorails, ferries, etc.).

5. *Campaign* for a wider association of Canada with other likeminded nations. It will do more to enlarge new product opportunities than anything else.

DEVELOPMENT OF NEW PRODUCTS

It has been said that nothing happens until somebody sells something. This is not entirely true. First, there must be something to sell — a product, a service, or an idea — and that "something" must be developed.

The development process for new products should begin with the selection of an explicit new-product strategy. This strategy then can serve as a meaningful guideline throughout the step-by-step development process used for each individual new product.

Management needs to select an effective overall new-product strategy to guide the firm's new-product development process. The purpose of this selection is to identify the strategic role that new products are to play in helping the company achieve its corporate and marketing goals. For example, a new product might be designed to defend a market-share position, or to maintain the company's position as a product innovator. In other situations, the product's role might be to meet a specific return-on-investment goal or to establish a position in a new market.

A new product's intended role also will influence the *type* of product to be developed. To illustrate:

Selection of New-Product Strategy[8]

Company Goal	Product Strategy
1. To defend a market-share position.	1. Introduce an addition to an existing product line, or revise an existing product.
2. To further the company's position as an innovator.	2. Introduce a *really* new product — not just an extension of an existing one.

Only in recent years have many companies consciously identified new-product strategies as a separate and explicit activity in the development process. Since then, however, there has been a dramatic increase in the efficiency of the development process. To illustrate, a survey by Booz, Allen & Hamilton reported that in 1968 there were fifty-eight new-product ideas considered for every successful new product introduced. In 1981, only seven new-product ideas were required to generate one successful new product.

With the company's new-product strategy acting as a guide, the development of a new product can proceed through the series of six steps (or stages) that are listed below. During each stage, management must decide whether to move on to the next stage, abandon the product, or seek additional information (see Fig. 8-2).

Steps in the Development Process

The first two steps — generating new-product ideas and evaluating them — are tied especially to the overall new-product strategy. This strategy can provide (1) a focus for generating new-product ideas and (2) a criterion for screening and evaluating these ideas.

1. *Generation of new product ideas.* New-product development starts with an idea. The particular source of ideas is not nearly so important as the company's system for stimulating new ideas and then acknowledging and reviewing them promptly.

2. *Screening and evaluation of ideas* to determine which ones warrant further study.

[8]See *New Products Management for the 1980s, op. cit.*, pp. 10–11. Also see Earl L. Bailey (ed.), *Product-Line Strategies*, The Conference Board, New York, report no. 816, 1982, pp. 6–23; and Graham Denton, "How to Develop Successful New Products," *Business Quarterly*, Winter 1983, pp. 62–65.

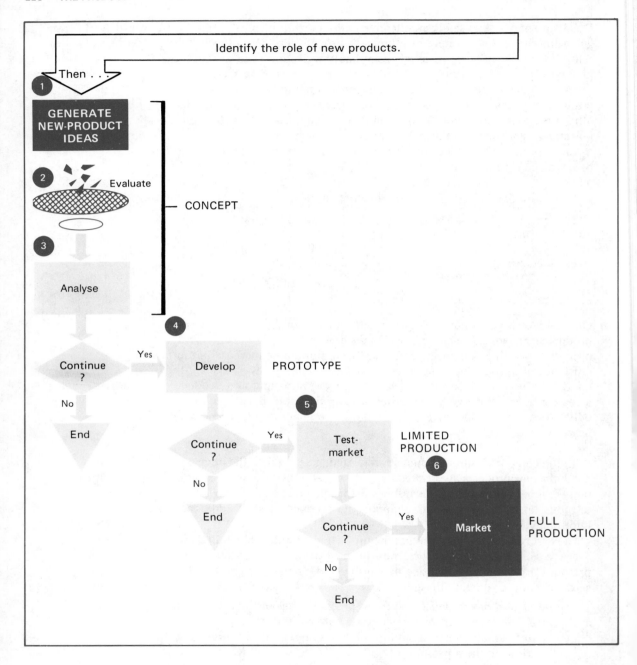

Figure 8-2
THE NEW-PRODUCT
DEVELOPMENT
PROCESS.

A product is more than a thing. It is a set of tangible and intangible attributes that leads to customer satisfaction.

3. *Business analysis.* A new-product idea that survives to this stage is expanded into a concrete business proposal. Management (*a*) identifies product features, (*b*) estimates market demand and the product's profitability, (*c*) establishes a program to develop the product, and (*d*) assigns responsibility for further study of the product's feasibility.

These first three steps are together referred to as "concept testing." This is pretesting the product idea, as contrasted to later pretesting of the product itself and its market.[9]

4. *Product development.* The idea-on-paper is converted into a physical product. Pilot models or small quantities are manufactured to designated specifications. Laboratory tests and other necessary technical evaluations are made to determine the production feasibility of the article.

5. *Test marketing.* Market tests, in-use tests, and other commercial experiments in limited geographic areas are conducted to ascertain the feasibility of a full-scale marketing program. In this stage, design and production variables may have to be adjusted as a result of test findings. At this point, management must make a final decision regarding whether or not to market the product commercially.[10]

6. *Commercialization.* Full-scale production and marketing programs are planned, and then the product is launched. Up to this point in the development process, management has virtually complete control over the product. Once the product is "born" and enters its life cycle, however, the external competitive environment becomes a major determinant of its destiny.

In this six-step evolution, the first three — the idea or concept stages — are the critical ones. Not only are they least expensive — each stage becomes progressively more costly in dollars and scarce human resources. But more important, many products fail because either the idea or the timing is wrong—and those three stages are designed to identify such situations.

Companies increasingly are using mathematical models and other quantitative techniques, both during the stages of new-product development and for evaluation once the product has been marketed commercially. For example, many of Canada's leading manufacturers of food and grocery products are turning away from conducting expensive market tests and are making greater use of computer-based simulations of new-product

---

[9]To avoid overestimating a new product's potential during concept testing, management should recognize that consumers may be favourably disposed toward the new product, yet have no need for it, according to Edward M. Tauber, "Reduce New Product Failures: Measure Needs as Well as Purchase Interest," *Journal of Marketing*, July 1973, pp. 61–64; see also Edward M. Tauber, "Why Concept and Product Tests Fail to Predict New-Product Results," *Journal of Marketing*, October 1975, pp. 69–71. For a further discussion of concept testing, with an excellent bibliography, see William L. Moore, "Concept Testing," *Journal of Business Research*, September 1982, pp. 279–294.

[10]See Jay E. Klompmaker, G. David Hughes, and Russell I. Haley, "Test Marketing in New-Product Development," *Harvard Business Review*, May–June 1976, pp. 128–138.

introductions. Based upon consumer evaluations of new products and estimates of their likelihood of purchasing, the simulation model is able to predict the success of the new-brand entry.[11]

Manufacturer's Criteria for New Products

When should a proposed new product be added to a company's existing product assortment? Here are some guidelines that some manufacturers use in answering that question.

1. There should be an *adequate market demand*. This is by far the most important criterion to apply to a proposed product. Too often, management begins with a question such as, "Can we use our present sales force?" or "Will the new item fit into our production system?" The basic question is, "Do enough people really want our product?" Administrators should try to get quantitative measures of the size and composition of the potential market.

2. The product must be compatible with current *environmental and social standards*. Do the manufacturing processes heavily pollute air or water (as steel or paper mills do)? Will the use of the finished product be harmful to the environment (as automobiles are)? After being used, is the product harmful to the environment (as DDT and some detergents are)? Does the product have recycling potential?

3. The product should fit into the company's present *marketing* structure. The general marketing experience of the company is important here. McCain Foods would probably find it easy to add another variety of frozen french fries to its line, whereas paint manufacturers would find it quite difficult to add margarine to theirs. More specific questions may also be asked regarding the marketing fit of new products: Can the existing sales force be used? Can the present channels of distribution be used?

4. A new-product idea will be more favourably received by management if the item fits in with existing *production* facilities, labour power, and management capabilities.

5. The product should fit from a *financial* standpoint. At least three questions should be asked: Is adequate financing available? Will the new item increase seasonal and cyclical stability in the firm? Are the profit possibilities worthwhile?

6. There must be no *legal* objections. Patents must be applied for, labelling and packaging must meet existing regulations, and so on.

7. *Management* in the company must have the time and the ability to deal with the new product. *Deal with product*

8. The product should be in keeping with the *company's image* and objectives. A firm stressing low-priced, high-turnover products normally should not add an item that suggests prestige or status.

Do Chicken McNuggets satisfy the new-product criteria listed here?

(© Van Bucher 1983)

[11]A widely-used new-product simulation is described in Glen L. Urban, Gerald M. Katz, Thomas E. Hatch, and Alvin J. Silk, "The ASSESSOR Pre-Test Market Evaluation System," *Interfaces*, vol. 13, December 6, 1983, pp. 38–59.

When retailers or wholesalers are considering whether to take on a new product, they should use all the above criteria except those related to production. In addition, a middleman should consider:

1. The relationship with the manufacturer: the manufacturer's reputation, the possibility of getting exclusive sales rights in a given geographic territory, the type of promotional help given by the manufacturer, and so on.

2. In-store policies and practices: What type of selling effort is required for the new product? How does the proposed product fit with store policies regarding repair service, alterations (for clothing), credit, and delivery?

For new-product programs to be successful, they *must* be supported by a strong and continuing commitment from top management over the long term. Furthermore, this commitment must be maintained even in the face of the failures that are sure to occur in some individual new-product efforts. To effectively implement this commitment to innovation, the new-product programs must be effectively organized.

ORGANIZING FOR PRODUCT INNOVATION

There is no "one best" organizational structure for new-product planning and development. In fact, many companies use more than one type of such structures to manage these activities. Four of the most widely used organizational structures for planning and developing new products are briefly explained in the following sections.

Types of Organization

Some authorities on product innovation strongly recommend that the organization responsible for new products be separated from the organization that handles existing products.[12] There are two reasons for this line of thinking. First, executives involved with ongoing products are more likely to have a short-term outlook. Their time is taken up with the day-to-day problems of existing products, and consequently they may tend to put new products on the back burner, so to speak. Second, managers of successful existing products often are reluctant to assume the risks involved in the marketing of new products that have uncertain market acceptance.

Product-Planning Committee

A number of companies utilize a committee, with heavy representation from top management, to guide new-product planning and development activities. The members usually include the company president and executives from major departments—marketing, production, finance, engineering, and research. After the product has successfully passed through the introductory stages of development, the marketing responsibility for it is taken over by another unit—perhaps a product manager or a new-product department.

---

[12]See, for example, David W. Nylen, "New-Product Failures: Not Just a Marketing Problem," *Business*, September–October 1979, especially pp. 4–6.

In a committee, the ideas and wisdom of several executives can be pooled. Any new product that results is likely to win the approval of the administrators who took part in its development. On the other hand, committee activity takes much valuable executive time and slows the decision-making process.

New-Product Department

To support new-product development as a full-time activity, several well-known manufacturers have established new-product departments. Generally, these units are small, consisting of four or five people or, frequently, only one person. Usually, the department head reports to the president. Typically, such a department is responsible for setting up new-product programs and guiding new products through the developmental stages. When a product is ready for full-scale commercial marketing, it is turned over to the appropriate operating department.

An innovative version of the new-product department has been implemented in a number of large North American companies. This department is responsible for generating new products *quickly* by such means as (1) reviving old patents, (2) contracting with outside product brokers who can match other companies' products with the firm's needs or product strategies, or (3) farming out ideas to firms specializing in new-product development. This new-style department has another unusual job — that of selling-off products, inventions, and technology that the company has developed but cannot market right now for one reason or another. Rather than sit on the product for several years, management gets some immediate payoff for its research and development investment.

Product Manager

In many companies a product manager — sometimes called a brand manager or a merchandise manager — is the executive responsible for planning related to *new* products as well as to *established* ones. A large company may have several product managers, who report to a top marketing executive. The wealth of discussion in business regarding the product manager's function is some indication of management's interest in this organizational structure.

In many large firms—Procter & Gamble and General Foods, for example — the product manager's job is quite broad. This executive is responsible for *planning the complete marketing program* for a brand or group of products. Thus, he or she may be concerned with new-product development as well as the improvement of established products. Responsibilities include setting marketing goals, preparing budgets, and developing plans for advertising and field-selling activities. At the other extreme, some companies limit product managers' activities essentially to the area of selling and sales promotion.

Probably the biggest problem in the product-manager system is that a company will assign great responsibility to these product managers, yet it will *not* give them the corresponding authority. They must develop the field-selling plan, but they have no line authority over the sales force. Product managers do not select advertising agencies, yet they are responsible for developing advertising plans. They have a profit responsibility for their brands, yet they are often denied any control over product costs, prices, or advertising budgets. Their effectiveness depends largely on their ability to influence other executives to cooperate with their plans.[13]

Venture Team

The venture team is a relatively new, rapidly growing organizational concept for managing product innovation from idea stage to full-scale marketing. A venture team is a small, multidisciplinary group, organizationally segregated from the rest of the firm. It is composed of representatives from engineering, production, finance, and marketing research. The team operates in an entrepreneurial environment, in effect being a separate small business. Typically the group reports directly to top management and has one goal — to enter a new market profitably.

Once a new product is found to be commercially viable, it is typically turned over to another group — an existing unit, a new division, or even a new subsidiary company. The venture team usually is then disbanded. However, in some cases it may continue on as the management nucleus when a new company is established.

A venture team is designed to avoid the product-development problems found in traditional organizational structures — problems of bureaucratic foul-ups, reluctance to change, and lack of authority to move a product through the developmental stages.[14]

Why do some products fail while others succeed? In the various research studies regarding this question, we find some consistently recurring themes. The key reasons typically cited for the failure of new products are as follows.[15]

WHY NEW PRODUCTS FAIL OR SUCCEED

---

[13]For an evaluation of the product-manager structure and what can be done to improve it, see Richard T. Hise and J. Patrick Kelly, "Product Management on Trial," *Journal of Marketing*, October 1978, pp. 28–33; see also Kelly and Hise, "Industrial and Consumer Goods Product Managers Are Different," *Industrial Marketing Management*, November 1979, pp. 325–332, and Christopher K. Bart, "Product Management: After 56 Years the Questions are Still Unanswered," *Proceedings* of the Marketing Division of the Administrative Sciences Association of Canada, 1984, pp. 11–20.

[14]See Richard M. Hill and James D. Hlavacek, "The Venture Team: A New Concept in Marketing Organization," *Journal of Marketing*, July 1972, pp. 44–50. For opposing points of view on the effectiveness of new-venture groups, see Dan T. Dunn, Jr., "The Rise and Fall of Ten Venture Groups," pp. 32–41, and William R. Osgood and William E. Wetzel, Jr., "A Systems Approach to Venture Initiation," pp. 42–53, both in *Business Horizons*, October 1977. Also see Shelby H. McIntyre and Meir Statman, "Managing the Risk of New Product Development," *Business Horizons*, May–June 1982, pp. 51–55.

[15]See David S. Hopkins, *New Product Winners and Losers*, The Conference Board, New York, report no. 773, 1980, pp. 12–20; and Graham Denton, "How to Develop Successful New Products," *Business Quarterly*, Winter 1983, pp. 62–65.

poor

1. *Inadequate marketing research.* It is essential that detailed marketing research be undertaken before any new product is introduced. Failure to do this research often means that a product is rushed to market by an enthusiastic developer or that necessary modifications are not made. Misjudging what the market wanted, overestimating potential sales, and failing to obtain information concerning consumer buying motives and behaviour will generally contribute to new-product failure.

2. *Technical problems in the new product's design or in its production.* Poor product quality and performance, products that were too complicated, and especially products that did not offer any significant advantage over competing items already on the market. Failure to offer consumers a significant point of difference means that they have no good reason to switch from their current brand to the new one.

3. *Poor timing in product introduction.* Delays in bringing the product to the market; or, conversely, rushing the product too quickly to the market.

4. *Indistinct image.* The most successful new products of the 1980s not only sell the product but spend a great deal of time and money cultivating the appropriate image so that it has definite appeal for the market segment to which it is directed. This positive image is created through appropriate advertising and packaging, as well as by the physical product itself.

5. *Improper targeting.* Some products are technically quite acceptable, but have simply been marketed incorrectly by being targeted at the wrong market segment. The IBM PCjr was introduced as a rather expensive home computer, but was later re-targeted at the low end of the office computer market.[16]

6. *Other poor management practices.* Lack of a well-defined new-product strategy; lack of a strong, long-term commitment by top management to new-product development; ineffective organization for new-product development.

Now let's look at the good news. Corrective actions to remedy these deficiencies have increased the systemization and effectiveness of the new-product development process. Specifically, we can attribute new-product success to these product factors and management characteristics.[17]

1. The product satisfies one or more market needs.

2. The product is technologically superior, and it enjoys a competitive cost advantage.

3. The product is compatible with the company's internal strengths in key functional areas such as selling, distribution, and production.

4. Top management makes a long-term commitment to new-product development. The experience thus gained enables management to

---

[16]See Eric Reguly, "Marketing's Biggest Blunders," *Financial Times*, October 8, 1984, p. 1.
[17]*New Products Management for the 1980s, op. cit.*, pp. 17–23.

improve its performance in introducing new products over a period of years.

5. Strategies for new products are clearly defined. They enable a company to generate and select new products that specifically meet internal strategic needs and external market needs.

6. There are an effective organization and a good management style. The organization structure is consciously established to promote new-product development. The management style encourages new-product development and can adjust to changing new-product opportunities.

One authority on new products observed that in the history of every successful product he studied, he always found at least one of three advantages — a product advantage, a marketing advantage, or a creative advertising advantage. Without at least one of these three, it appeared there simply was no chance for success. Here are some examples of these features as developed by companies you'll probably recognize.[18]

1. *Product advantage.* Polaroid ("Here's a camera that takes a picture, develops it, and gives you a print in 60 seconds") and Xerox ("Here's a machine that copies anything in seconds — no chemicals or special paper needed").

2. *Marketing advantage.* Coleco obtained a distinct marketing advantage over the competition with the introduction of the Cabbage Patch Kids line of children's dolls. Each product was differentiated by being physically different and accompanied by its own birth certificate. In addition to producing associated lines to accompany the main product (clothing, and even pets, for the Cabbage Patch Kids), Coleco even sends birthday cards for the dolls to their proud owners.

3. *Creative advertising advantage.* Pepsi-Cola, Jell-O, Kellogg's cereals, and Avis all were number 2 or lower in their field. Then they developed, through advertising, a jingle, cartoon, slogan, or some other distinctive feature that rocketed them to the top, or at least to a very strong number 2 position.

SUMMARY

If the first commandment in marketing is "Know thy customer," then the second is "Know thy product." A firm can fulfil its socioeconomic responsibility to satisfy its customers by producing and marketing truly want-satisfying products or services. In light of a scarcity of resources and a growing concern for our environment, socially responsible product innovation becomes even more important. The new products or services marketed by a firm are a prime determinant of that company's growth rate, profits, and total marketing program.

To manage their product assortments effectively, marketers should understand the full meaning of the term *product* and the different concepts of what a *new product* is.

[18]Harry W. McMahan, "Alltime Ad Triumphs Reveal Key Success Factors behind Choice of '100 Best,'" *Advertising Age*, April 12, 1976, p. 72.

There are seven steps in the development process for new products, starting with a clear statement of the intended new-product strategy. The early stages in this process are important. If a firm can make an early (and proper) decision to drop a product, a lot of money and labour can be saved. In its decision regarding whether to accept or reject a new product, there are several criteria for a manufacturer or a middleman to consider. The product should fit in with marketing, production, and financial resources. But the key point is that there *must* be an adequate market demand for the product.

Organizational relationships are typically reported as a major problem in new-product planning and development. Top management must be deeply committed to product innovation and must support this activity in a creative fashion. Most firms that report reasonable success in product innovation seem to use one of these four organizational structures for new-product development: product-planning committee, new product department, product-manager system, or venture team. Successful products typically have an advantage in at least one of three areas — as a want-satisfying product, in their marketing program, or in their advertising.

KEY TERMS AND CONCEPTS

Product 219

New product 219

Product planning 221

Product development 221

Merchandising 222

Relation of sales volume and profit over life of a product 223

Conspicuous consumption 225

New-product development process 227

New-product strategy 227

Product-concept testing 229

Test marketing 229

Product-planning committee 231

New-product department 232

Product manager 232

Venture team 233

QUESTIONS AND PROBLEMS

1. In what respects are the products different in each of the following cases?
   a. An Arrow shirt sold by a local men's clothing store and a similar shirt sold by Sears under its own brand name. Assume that the same manufacturer makes both shirts.
   b. A Sunbeam Mixmaster sold by a leading department store and the same model sold by a discount house.

2. a. Explain the various interpretations of the term *new product*.
   b. Give some examples, other than those stated in this chapter, of products in each of the three new-product categories.

3. Bring to class three advertisements that stress product benefits. Also bring three that stress some part of the product rather than the benefits to be derived from the product.

4. What factors account for the growing importance of product planning?

5. In planning developing new products, how can a firm make sure that it is being socially responsible in regard to scarce resources and our environment?

6. What are some of the questions that management is likely to want answered during the business-analysis stage of new-product development?

7. Assume that the following organizations are considering the stated additions to their product lines. In each case, should the proposed product be added?
   a. Automobile manufacturer — outboard motors
   b. Firm such as Xerox Corporation — office dictating machines
   c. Supermarket — wallpaper
   d. Manufacturer of electronic parts and equipment — automatic garage-door opener

8. Under what conditions might a firm profitably use a separate department for new-product development?

9. What are some of the problems typically connected with the product-manager type of organizational structure for new-product development?

10. Why do so many new products turn out to be failures in the market?

Chapter

9 | Product-Mix Strategies

CHAPTER GOALS

At any given time, a firm may be marketing some new products and some older products, while others are being planned and developed. This chapter is concerned with the managing of the entire range of products. After studying the chapter, you should understand:

1. *The difference between product mix and product line*
2. *The major product mix strategies, such as:*
   a. *Expansion*
   b. *Contraction*
   c. *Alterations*
   d. *Positioning*
   e. *Trading up and trading down*
3. *Product differentiation and market segmentation*
4. *A product's life cycle and its management*
5. *Planned obsolescence, including:*
   a. *Style and fashion*
   b. *The fashion-adoption process*

The Head Ski Company introduces a new line of high-quality running clothing and the Bata Shoe Company opens a chain of Athlete's World stores, both to take advantage of the North American fascination with physical fitness and running, in particular. Procter & Gamble adds a line of orange soft drinks and Eaton's, Sears, and The Bay all expand into the travel agency business. Carling O'Keefe repositions its Trilight brand of light beer as the "taste of moderation." Howick jeans expands its lines to include the André Michel designer label. Danskin, originally a company specializing in dance wear, expands into "activewear" — leotards, tights, and legwarmers. And Calvin Klein brings out a line of underwear for women, including jockey

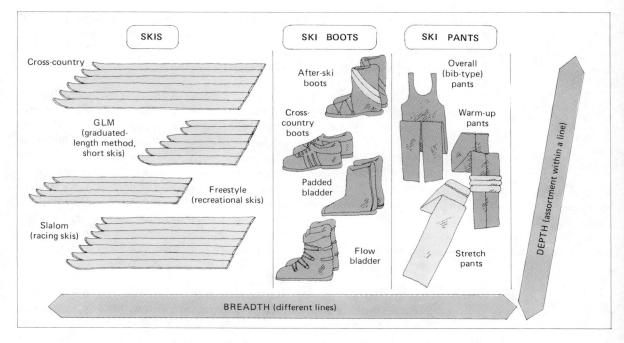

| SKIS | SKI BOOTS | SKI PANTS |

Cross-country

GLM
(graduated-
length method,
short skis)

Freestyle
(recreational skis)

Slalom
(racing skis)

After-ski
boots

Cross-
country
boots

Padded
bladder

Flow
bladder

Overall
(bib-type)
pants

Warm-up
pants

Stretch
pants

DEPTH (assortment within a line)

BREADTH (different lines)

Figure 9-1
BREADTH AND
DEPTH.

Part of a ski retailer's
product mix, illustrating
breadth and depth of mix.

briefs and T-shirts. Carlton Cards introduces battery-powered singing greeting cards. All of these cases have one thing in common — they are all examples of strategies and policies relating to the firm's assortment of products and services.[1]

PRODUCT MIX AND PRODUCT LINE

A broad group of products, intended for essentially similar uses and possessing reasonably similar physical characteristics, constitutes a **product line**. Wearing apparel is one example of a product line. But in a different context, say, in a small specialty shop, men's furnishings (shirts, ties, and underwear) and men's ready-to-wear (suits, sport jackets, topcoats, and slacks) would each constitute a line. In another context, men's apparel is one line, as contrasted with women's apparel, furniture, or sporting goods (see Fig. 9-1).

The **product mix** is the full list of all products offered for sale by a company. The structure of the product mix has dimensions of both breadth and depth. Its *breadth* is measured by the *number* of product lines carried; its *depth*, by the assortment of sizes, colours, and models offered *within* each product line.

[1] For an overview of strategies for consumer products and industrial products as stated by fourteen business executives and consultants, see Earl L. Bailey (ed.), *Product-Line Strategies*, The Conference Board, New York, report no. 816, 1982, especially pp. 25–76.

MAJOR PRODUCT-MIX STRATEGIES

Several major strategies used by manufacturers and middlemen in managing their product mix are discussed below. A discussion of planned obsolescence as a product strategy, and of fashion as an influence on the product mix, is, however, deferred until later in the chapter.

Expansion of Product Mix

A firm may elect to expand its present product mix by increasing the number of lines and/or the depth within a line. New lines may be related or unrelated to the present products. Labatt Brewing Company added two light beers (Labatt's Lite and Blue Light) and a premium beer (John Labatt Classic) to meet the competition from other brewers and to take advantage of a market trend toward lighter beers. Coca-Cola and Pepsi added caffeine-free variations of their major brands and Scripto introduced a disposable lighter in competition with the market leader, Bic. Expanding into less obviously related lines, Canada's telephone companies began selling computer equipment, such as printers, to their business clients who used the telephone lines for the transmission of data. Canada's major department stores, Eaton's and The Bay, added various financial services.

Contraction of Product Mix

Another product strategy is to thin out the product mix, either by eliminating an entire line or by simplifying the assortment within a line. The shift from fat and long lines to thin and short lines is designed to eliminate low-profit products and to get more profit from fewer products. In the 1970s, Xerox, RCA, and General Electric all dropped their lines of computers. Gillette dropped digital watches from its product mix as price competition eroded the profitability of that product. Some firms discontinued manufacturing roller skates as the market for that product became saturated.

The practice of slimming the product mix has long been recognized as an important product strategy. However, since the late 1970s it has been used quite extensively as many companies moved to delete unprofitable products in the face of rising prices and growing competition. A wide variety of industries has been forced to retreat from (1) the full-line product concept, with its emphasis on more products and greater sales volume, to (2) a product position that emphasizes profits and efficient use of materials and energy.

Alteration of Existing Products

As an alternative to developing a completely new product, management should take a fresh look at the company's existing products. Often, improving an established product can be more profitable and less risky than developing a completely new one.

For industrial goods especially, *redesigning* is often the key to the product's renaissance. The market for a hospital centrifuge was expanded by redesigning it so that it harmonized architecturally with modern cabinetry. *Packaging* has been a very popular area for product alteration, particularly in consumer products. Even something as mundane as thread, glue, or cheesecloth can be made more attractive by means of creative packaging and display. The apparently simple addition of a twist cap gave Labatt's Blue a definite advantage over competitive brands of beer.

Management's ability to position a product appropriately in the market is a major determinant of company profits. A product's **position** is the image that the product projects in relation to competitive products and to other products marketed by the same company. Unfortunately, the term *product positioning* has no generally accepted definition, so this important concept in product management is loosely applied and difficult to measure.

Marketing executives can choose from a variety of positioning strategies. These strategies may be grouped into the following six categories:[2]

Positioning the Product

A product may be positioned relative to various attributes.

1. *Positioning in relation to a competitor*. For some products (American subcompact cars, for example), the best position is directly against the competition. Thus, the Chevrolet Chevette and the Ford Escort were positioned to compete head-to-head with low-priced foreign imports. For other products, head-to-head positioning is exactly what *not* to do, especially when a competitor has a strong market position. Avis became successful only after it stopped positioning itself directly against Hertz, readily admitted it was number 2, and advertised that it must try harder. Midas Muffler, going head-to-head with Speedy Muffler King, termed its mechanics "the top guns." Burger King took a swipe at McDonald's by advising its customers that they could have Burger King hamburgers "any way you want."

2. *Positioning by product attribute*. A company can associate its product with some product feature or customer benefit. Consider, for example, how foreign car manufacturers have used this positioning strategy. Toyota and Nissan stress economy and reliability. Volvo emphasizes durability, and BMW's position is based on European craftsmanship. In toothpaste, Crest is known as the family's cavity fighter, while Aim's position is based on cavity prevention as well as on a taste that children will like. The soft drink 7-Up tried to distance itself from Coke and Pepsi by labelling the brand "the Uncola."

3. *Positioning by price and quality*. Some retail stores are known for their high-quality merchandise and high prices (Harry Rosen, Birks). Positioned at the other end of the price and quality scale are discount stores such as K-Mart and The Met.

   Trying to reposition a company on the price and quality spectrum can be a tricky proposition. In the 1970s, Woolco and other discount department stores tried to upgrade their fashion and quality image by adding lines of brand-name fashion clothing, while at the same time trying to retain their image for low price and "good value for the money." The move met with varying degrees of success, serving in some cases to blur the corporate image and to confuse some customers. Zellers, similarly, has been working on trading-up its image toward becoming

---

[2]Adapted from David A. Aaker and J. Gary Shansby, "Positioning Your Product," *Business Horizons*, May–June 1982, pp. 56–58. For another classification of positioning strategies along with a good discussion, see F. Beavin Ennis, "Positioning Revisited," *Advertising Age*, March 13, 1982, p. M–43.

a family department store, rather than a discount store. Zellers has added designer-label clothing lines to the store's own labels and has introduced well-known brand names in a new cosmetics section.

4. *Positioning in relation to product use.* Cow Brand baking soda sales increased tremendously after the long dormant product was repositioned as an effective odour-killing agent for use in refrigerators.

5. *Positioning in relation to a target market.* In the face of a declining birthrate, Johnson & Johnson repositioned its mild baby shampoo for use by mothers, fathers, and people who must wash their hair frequently. Labatt Breweries introduced the first light beer into the Canadian market. Labatt's Special Lite (the "Special" was later dropped) was introduced as a low-calorie beer and appealed to diet-conscious consumers who drank relatively little beer. In contrast, Molson Light was introduced as a light beer with the taste of a regular beer—a beer with "heart." Later, Carlsberg Light was introduced to trade on the "European" image of the Carlsberg parent brand and to appeal to an up-scale, sophisticated market segment. More recently, Carling O'Keefe's Trilight has been repositioned to appeal to beer customers who are concerned about moderation.

6. *Positioning in relation to a product class.* Sometimes a company's positioning strategy involves associating its product with (or disassociating it from) a common class of product. Most cigarette manufacturers introduced low tar and nicotine brands in the 1970s as health concerns had a major impact on that industry. Much the same phenomenon has had a similar effect in the food products business as many companies have introduced product lines with little or no salt added. Del Monte, Green Giant, and Aylmer have packaged salt-free canned vegetables. Heinz baby food and Nabisco Shredded Wheat also promote on their labels the fact that neither salt nor sugar has been added to the product. These items are positioned against the food products that are packaged with the conventional amounts of salt. Soft-drink manufacturers also took advantage of a trend by adding caffeine-free brands to their lines in the early 1980s.

As we move further into the 1980s, positioning for social accountability is an interesting development likely to be adopted by many firms. This move is an attempt by business to increase its credibility, build a reputation for reliability, and generally satisfy a broader market spectrum over the long run. In this vein, many food processors are stressing nutritional information on their labels. And many companies in a variety of industries are advertising various ways we can conserve energy.[3]

---

[3]For a step-by-step procedure to follow in selecting a positioning strategy, see Aaker and Shansby, *op. cit.*, pp. 58–62; and William D. Neal, "Strategic Product Positioning: A Step-by-Step Guide," *Business*, May–June 1980, pp. 34–42. A detailed interpretation of the concept of positioning is to be found in Jack Trout and Al Reis, *Positioning: The Battle for Your Mind*, McGraw-Hill Book Company, New York, 1980.

As product strategies, trading up and trading down involve, essentially, an expansion of the product line and a change in product positioning. **Trading up** means adding a higher-priced, prestige product to a line in the hope of increasing the sales of existing lower-priced products. In the automobile industry some years ago, Ford introduced the Thunderbird, and Chevrolet the Corvette. More recently, we have seen the Toyota Cressida and the Honda Prelude, all positioned in such a way that the lower-priced cars produced by these companies will benefit from the reflected image of the higher-priced models.

When a company embarks upon a policy of trading up, at least two avenues are open with respect to promotional emphasis: (1) The seller may continue to depend upon the older, lower-priced product for the bulk of the sales volume and promote it heavily, or (2) the seller may gradually shift promotional emphasis to the new product and expect it to produce the major share of sales volume. In fact, the lower-priced line may be dropped altogether after a transition period.

A company is said to be **trading down** when it adds a lower-priced item to its line of prestige products. The company expects that people who cannot afford the original product will want to buy the new one because it carries some of the status of the higher-priced good. In line with this strategy, major manufacturers of 35mm single lens reflex (SLR) cameras, such as Pentax, Canon, and Minolta, have in recent years introduced smaller, simplified cameras for photography buffs who want to be seen to be using the major brands but who do not want to be bothered with the intricacies of 35mm photography. Mont Blanc, the West German manufacturer of the "world's most famous fountain pen," introduced a lower-priced ballpoint pen, thereby allowing its purchasers to own a Mont Blanc without having to pay more than $300 for the top-of-the-line fountain pen.

Trading up and trading down are perilous strategies because the new product may simply confuse buyers, so that the net gain is negligible. Nor is any useful purpose served if sales of the new item are generated at the expense of the older products. When *trading down* is used, the new article may permanently hurt the firm's reputation and that of its established high-quality product. This is exactly what happened years ago to the Packard Motor Car Company — which produced the "Cadillac" of its day. Packard introduced a low-priced car that looked just like its higher-priced luxury model, and this move destroyed the market for Packard.

In *trading up*, on the other hand, the seller's major problem is to change the firm's image enough so that new customers will accept the new, higher-priced product. At the same time, the seller does not want to lose its present customers. The real risk is that the company will lose *both* customer groups through this change in its product positioning: The former customers may become confused because the company has clouded its image, and the new target market may not believe that the company is marketing high-quality merchandise. Many women, for example, will never believe that they can buy high-quality, high-fashion clothing in women's ready-to-wear chain stores. The reason is that these stores have, through the years,

Trading Up and Trading Down

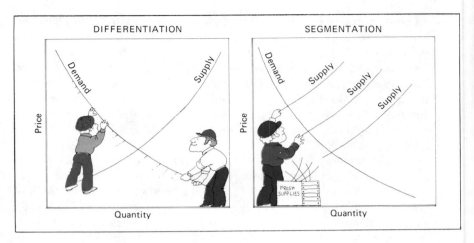

Figure 9-2
PRODUCT DIFFEREN-
TIATION AND MARKET
SEGMENTATION.

The object of differentiation is to fit the market to
the product; segmentation
is an attempt to fit a
product line to the market.

projected an image that denotes low-priced merchandise. This is what happened to a number of discount retailers in North America in the 1970s. It
remains to be seen whether discounters such as Woolco, K-Mart, and Zellers
can pull off a similar trading-up strategy in the 1980s.

Product
Differentiation
and Market
Segmentation

Product differentiation and market segmentation are two related *product
strategies.*[4] They may be employed by firms who wish to engage in nonprice
competition in markets characterized by imperfect or monopolistic competition. Market segmentation was introduced in Chapter 4 in connection
with the identification and analysis of target markets.

Differentiation

Product Differentiation involves promoting an awareness of differences
between one company's product and those of competitors. The strategy is
used so that a company can remove itself from price competition. If it works,
the company can compete on the nonprice basis that its product is different from, or better than, competitors' products. Sometimes a company will
differentiate the design of the product, or the only differentiation may be
in the brand or packaging. Frequently, two products are virtually identical
in a physical and chemical sense; the difference between them is trivial
and sometimes only psychological. This strategy is often used by companies selling reasonably standardized products, such as soap, cigarettes, or
toothpaste, to a broad market that is fairly homogeneous in its demand for
the given item.[5]

---

[4]Much of this section is based on the classic analysis of these strategies by Wendell R. Smith.
See his "Product Differentiation and Market Segmentation as Alternative Marketing Strategies,"
Journal of Marketing, July 1956, pp. 3–8.

[5]See "Warring Toothpaste Makers Spend Millions Luring Buyers to Slightly Altered Products,"
The Wall Street Journal, September 21, 1981, p. 33.

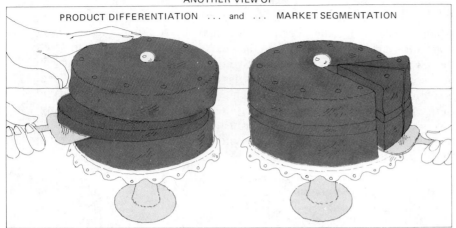

ANOTHER VIEW OF

PRODUCT DIFFERENTIATION ... and ... MARKET SEGMENTATION

In the language of economic theory, the seller (product differentiator) assumes that there is a single demand curve for its product. Any variations in the wants of individual consumers regarding that product will be offset by extensive promotion that emphasizes the product's broad market appeal. Essentially, as Wendell R. Smith has said, "product *differentiation* is concerned with the bending of demand to the will of supply."

Inexorable market pressures work against the seller that attempts to *expand* a firm's market by using the strategy of product differentiation. The broader the market, the more difficult it becomes to satisfy all consumers' wants with the single product. Any competing product is apt to satisfy more precisely the wants of some group in this broadened range of consumers. The seller must then resort to increased promotional expenditures or reduced prices, or both, in attempting to offset the fact that some consumers prefer variations of one sort or another in the product.

Segmentation

In employing the strategy of **market segmentation**, a seller recognizes that a firm's total heterogeneous market is made up of many smaller homogeneous segments. Each of these smaller segments has a different set of wants, motivations, and other characteristics. The market is seen as a *series* of demand curves rather than the *single* curve of product differentiation (see Fig. 9-2). The seller then attempts to develop different products, each one suited to one or more of these market segments. Tailor-made products are extreme examples of this strategy in action.

Market segmentation attempts to penetrate a limited market in *depth*, whereas product differentiation seeks *breadth* in a more generalized market. Smith says, "The differentiator seeks to secure a layer of the market cake, whereas one who employs market segmentation strives to secure one or more wedge-shaped pieces."

A firm may first employ the strategy of market segmentation but soon be forced by competition to combine that strategy with product differentiation. A firm that makes electric razors may divide the market into two segments—men and women—and then develop separate products to meet the specific wants of each segment. Eventually the women's segment will be recognized as a separate market by this firm's competitors, each of which will bring out an electric razor for women. Soon all these sellers will have to resort to differentiation to maintain their separate identities. Thus any given segmentation of a market is a transitory phenomenon, and competitive conditions force sellers constantly to seek new ways of segmenting their markets.

> ## FIRST WE HAD NO SUGAR AND NOW WE HAVE NO SALT— IN SOME FOODS, THAT IS—OR HOW TO IMPLEMENT THE STRATEGY OF MARKET SEGMENTATION
>
> For many years now, various food processors have been marketing products with no sugar added, for the market segments that are weight-conscious, tooth-cavity-conscious, or diabetic. Thus we have diet (sugar-free) soft drinks (Tab, Diet Pepsi), sugar substitutes (Sweet'n Low, Equal), and no-sugar-added canned fruits and vegetables.
>
> Then, in the early 1980s, to cater to the market segment that wants to reduce its salt intake, several food manufacturers introduced low-salt products. So now we can buy no-salt-added canned fruit and vegetables from Green Giant, Aylmer, and Del Monte. We can get Nabisco Shredded Wheat and Christie's Triscuits without salt, and many Heinz baby food products are now available without salt or sugar. Tuna fish and even some types of potato chips are now being packed with a much-reduced salt content.

Product differentiation on the basis of no-salt content.

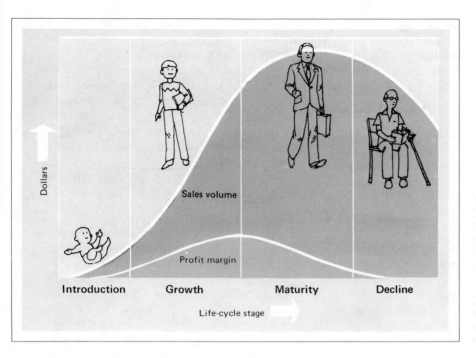

Figure 9-3
SALES VOLUME CURVE
AND PROFIT MARGIN
CURVE IN RELATION-
SHIP TO A PRODUCT'S
LIFE.

Profit margin usually
starts to decline while a
product's sales volume is
still increasing.

CONCEPT OF THE PRODUCT LIFE CYCLE

This concept was introduced briefly in Chapter 8. There we noted that products have life cycles that can be divided into five stages: introduction, growth, maturity, decline, and possible abandonment. A company's marketing success can be affected considerably by its ability to understand and manage the life cycle of its products.

The product life cycle can be illustrated with the sales-volume and profit curves, as in Fig. 9-3. The *shapes* of these curves will vary from product to product. However, the basic shapes and the relationship between the two curves are usually as illustrated. (The relationship between these two curves was explained in Chapter 8 in connection with Fig. 8-1.) The *length* of the life cycle also varies among products. It will range from a few weeks or a short season (for a fad or a clothing fashion) to several decades (for, say, autos or telephones).

Figure 9-3 suggests that the life-cycle stages cover nearly equal periods of time, although actually that is *not* the case. The different stages in any given product's life cycle usually last for *different* periods of time.[6] Also, the duration of each stage will vary among products. Some products take years to pass through the introductory stage, while others are accepted in a few weeks. Moreover, not all products go through all the stages. Some may fail in the introductory stage, and others may not be introduced until

[6]See John O. King, "Revised Graph of Product Life Cycle Theory Could Eliminate Confusion in Marketing Texts," *Marketing News*, July 24, 1981, p. 26.

the market is in the growth or maturity stage. In virtually all cases, however, decline and possible abandonment are inevitable, because (1) the need for the product disappears (as when frozen orange juice generally eliminated the market for juice squeezers); (2) a better or less expensive product is developed to fill the same need (plastics are replacing wood, metal, and paper in many products); or (3) a competitor does a superior marketing job.

Characteristics of Each Stage

It is quite important that management recognize what part of the life cycle its product is in at any given time. The competitive environment and the resultant marketing strategies ordinarily will differ depending upon the stage.

Introduction

During the first stage of a product's life cycle, it is launched into the market in a full-scale production and marketing program. It has gone through the embryonic stages of idea evaluation, pilot models, and test marketing. The entire product may be new, like a machine that cleans clothes electronically without using any water. Or, the basic product may be well known but have a new feature or accessory that is in the introductory stage — a gas turbine engine in an automobile, for example. Or the product may be well accepted in some market segments but be in the pioneering stage in other markets. Introductory promotion was needed (and in many cases still is) to sell automatic dishwashers and home freezers to consumers long after these products were well accepted in some industrial markets.

There is a high percentage of product failures in this period. Operations in the introductory period are characterized by high costs, low sales volume, net losses, and limited distribution. In many respects, the pioneering stage is the most risky and expensive one. However, for really new products, there is very little direct competition. The promotional program is designed to stimulate *primary*, rather than *secondary*, demand. That is, the *type of product*, rather than the *seller's brand*, is emphasized.

Growth

In the growth, or market-acceptance, stage, both sales and profits rise, often at a rapid rate. Competitors enter the market — in large numbers if the profit outlook is particularly attractive. Sellers shift to a "buy-my-brand" rather than a "try-this-product" promotional strategy. The number of distribution outlets increases, economies of scale are introduced, and prices may come down a bit.

Maturity

During the first part of this period, sales continue to increase, but at a decreasing rate. While sales are levelling off, the profits of both the manufacturer and the retailers are starting to decline. Marginal producers are forced to drop out of the market. Price competition becomes increasingly severe. The producer assumes a greater share of the total promotional effort in the fight to retain dealers and the shelf space in their stores. New models are introduced as manufacturers broaden their lines, and trade-in sales become significant.

PAC MAN, SPACE INVADERS, AND THE PRODUCT LIFE CYCLE

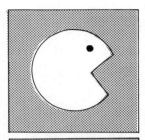

Through the years, many teenagers and young adults played pinball machines in stores, restaurants, and amusement arcades. Meanwhile, other individuals and families often sat passively in front of their TV sets. But in the 1970s a new product — video-game machines — began to change the leisure-time habits of both these groups. This new product replaced pinball machines in most commercial amusement arcades, gave rise to new arcades, and appeared in a growing number of homes that had television sets.

Video games went through the introductory stage of their product life cycle in the 1970s as games such as Pac-Man, Space Invaders, and Asteroids were introduced and grew in popularity. Then, along about 1981 to 1983, video games really boomed into the growth stage of their life cycle, even though those were recession years. The *factory* sales volume for these machines was estimated at about $2 billion in 1982 — double the 1981 sales figure. In 1981, *consumers* spent three times as much on video games (at home and in arcades) as they spent on movies . There were over 300 different games on the market in early 1983, with more expected to come.

About 14 to 15 million TV homes had game consoles by the end of 1982. That was double the number at the end of 1981. The industry forecasted that about half the United States homes with a TV set would have a game console by 1985.

In the early part of the growth stage, the main market was 8- to 18-year-old males. However, the industry intended to broaden its base by expanding into other market segments. Women and families became target markets. Preschoolers were reached with entertainment and educational games featuring Mickey Mouse, and other Disney characters, and the Sesame Street gang. Also, there were plans to expand into the European market.

Initially, video games were marketed by only a few companies. In 1981 it was estimated that Atari had 65 to 75 percent of the market and Mattel (Intellivision) had about 15 percent. But once the product advanced into its growth stage, a number of other firms moved in for a piece of the action. Several companies added game machines to their line. Other firms added only the software (game cartridges) because they were higher-profit items. Still other firms introduced satellite items such as printed T-shirts and books on how to master the games.

So far, video games have been a classic example of a product moving through its life cycle — in terms of the market's behaviour and the marketer's response to this behaviour. Some industry analysts predicted that the sales curve would flatten out in the mid-1980s, indicating that video games played on TV sets would be in the maturity stage of their life cycle at that time. This forecast was based on the prediction that home computers would grow in popularity and, consequently, people would play these games on their personal computers.

Decline and Possible Abandonment

For virtually all products, obsolescence sets in inevitably as new products start their own life cycles and replace the old ones. Cost control becomes increasingly important as demand drops. Advertising declines, and a number of competitors withdraw from the market. Whether the product has to be abandoned, or whether the surviving sellers can continue on a profitable basis, often depends upon management's abilities.

Management of the Product Life Cycle

The shape of a product's sales and profit curves is not predetermined. To a surprising extent, the shape can be controlled by effective managerial action. One key to successful life-cycle management is (1) to predict the shape of the proposed product's cycle even before it is introduced, and then, at each stage, (2) to anticipate the marketing requirements of the following stage. The introductory period, for instance, may be shortened by broadening the distribution or by increasing the promotional effort. A product's life may be extended in the maturity stage if the product is revitalized through new packaging, repricing, or product modifications. The makers of nylon, Jell-O, and Scotch tape, for example, all have employed three different strategies to expand sales: (1) increase the frequency of the product's use, (2) attract new users, and (3) find new uses for the product.

Some products may be revitalized once they reach the maturity stage through design changes or modifications in form or package. Raleigh, a leading manufacturer of quality bicycles, having capitalized on the international fascination with racing (10-speed) bicycles in the 1960s and 1970s, further changed with the times and introduced a successful line of BMX bicycles for children and, more recently, mountain bikes. Procter & Gamble, manufacturer of Ivory Soap, has recently taken steps to extend the life cycle of this successful old product by producing a liquid soap that is packaged in a container equipped with a pump.

Perhaps it is in the sales-decline stage that a company finds its greatest challenges in life-cycle management. At some point in the product's life, management may have to consider whether to abandon the product. The costs of carrying profitless products go beyond the expenses that show up on financial statements. The real burdens are the insidious costs accruing from managerial time and effort that are diverted to sick products. Unfortunately, management often seems reluctant to discard a product. Sometimes, the reasons are emotional and sentimental. At other times, executives rationalize (1) that they need the item to round out the product line or (2) that the decline is temporary and they soon will hit the jackpot.

When sales are declining, management has the following alternatives, some of which are reflected in "A 10-Point Vitality Test . . . " in the nearby box:

1. Improve the product in a functional sense, or revitalize it in some manner.

2. Make sure that the marketing and production programs are as efficient as possible.

3. Streamline the product assortment by pruning out unprofitable sizes and models. Frequently, this tactic will *decrease* sales and *increase* profits.

4. "Run out" the product; that is, cut all costs to the bare-minimum level that will optimize profitability over the limited remaining life of the product.

5. Abandon the product.

A 10-POINT VITALITY TEST FOR OLDER PRODUCTS, OR HOW TO GET THAT SALES CURVE TO SLOPE UPWARD AGAIN

1. Does the product have new or extended uses? Sales of Cow Brand baking soda increased considerably after the product was promoted as a refrigerator deodorant.

2. Is the product a generic item that can be branded? Sunkist put its name on oranges and lemons, thus giving a brand identity to a formerly generic item.

3. Is the product category "underadvertised"? Tampons were in this category until International Playtex and Johnson & Johnson started spending large advertising appropriations, particularly on television ads.

4. Is there a broader target market? Procter & Gamble increased the sales of Ivory soap by promoting it for adults, instead of just for babies.

5. Can you turn disadvantages into advantages? Several small regional Canadian companies have been able to prove to customers that, while they may not have the extensive product line of a national company, they almost certainly know the needs of their region better.

6. Can you build volume and profit by cutting the price? This is what has happened with many of the new technologies of recent years. Sales of digital watches and home computers increased dramatically as prices fell.

7. Can you market unused by-products? Lumber companies market sawdust as a form of kitty litter.

8. Can you sell the product in a more compelling way? Procter & Gamble's Pampers disposable diapers were only a moderate success in the market when they were sold as a convenience item for mothers. Sales increased, however, after the advertising theme was changed to say that Pampers kept babies dry and happy.

9. Is there a social trend to exploit? Many companies have been successful in taking advantage of the national interest in fitness and nutrition. Yoplait yogourt and Fleischmann's corn-oil margarine are merely two examples of products that have been successful as a result of an increased diet-consciousness among Canadians.

10. Can you expand distribution channels? Hanes Hosiery Company increased its sales of L'eggs panty hose by distributing this product through supermarkets.

Source: Adapted from *The Wall Street Journal*, February 18, 1982, p. 25.

Knowing when and how to abandon products successfully may be as important as knowing when and how to introduce new ones. Certainly management should develop a systematic procedure for phasing out its weak products.[7]

PLANNED OBSOLESCENCE AND FASHION

Consumers seem to be on a constant quest for the "new" but not "*too* new." The market wants newness — new products, new styles, new colours. However, people want to be moved gently out of their habitual patterns, not shocked out of them. This has led many manufacturers to develop the product strategy of planned obsolescence. Its objective is to make an existing product out of date and thus to increase the market for replacement products.

Nature of Planned Obsolescence

The term **planned obsolescence** has been used to mean several different things:

1. *Technological or functional obsolescence.* Significant technical improvements result in a more effective product. For instance, jet engines made propeller-driven aircraft technologically obsolete. This type of obsolescence is generally considered to be socially and economically desirable.

2. *Postponed obsolescence.* Technological improvements are available, but they are not introduced until the market demand for present models decreases and a new market stimulus is needed.

3. *Style obsolescence.* This is sometimes called "psychological" or "fashion" obsolescence. Superficial characteristics of the product are altered so that the new model is easily differentiated from the previous model. The intent is to make people feel out of date if they continue to use old models.

When people criticize planned obsolescence, they are usually referring to this last interpretation — style obsolescence. In our discussion, planned obsolescence will mean only style obsolescence, unless otherwise stated.

Nature of Style and Fashion

Although the words *style* and *fashion* are often used interchangeably, there is a clear distinction between the two. A **style** is defined as a distinctive manner of construction or presentation in any art, product, or endeavour (singing, playing, behaving). Thus we have styles in automobiles (sedans, station wagons), in bathing suits (one-piece, bikinis), in furniture (Early American, French Provincial), and in music (rock, new wave, C & W).

A **fashion** is any style that is popularly accepted and purchased by several successive groups of people over a reasonably long period of time.

---

[7]For a review and excellent bibliography of the research on product life cycles, see David R. Rink and John E. Swan, "Product Life Cycle Research: A Literature Review," *Journal of Business Research*, vol. 7, 1979, pp. 219–242. Some of this research suggested that there may be as many as eleven differently shaped life-cycle curves, each calling for different marketing strategies. See Swan and Rink, "Fitting Marketing Strategy to Varying Product Life Cycles," *Business Horizons*, January–February 1982, pp. 72–76.

Not every style becomes a fashion. To be rated as a fashion, or to be called "fashionable," a style must become popularly accepted.

A **fad** normally does not remain popular so long as a fashion, and it is based on some novelty feature.

Basic styles never change, but fashion is always changing. Fashions are found in all societies, including primitive groups, the great Oriental cultures, and the societies of ancient and medieval Europe.

Fashion is rooted in sociological and psychological factors. Basically, people are conformists. At the same time, they yearn to look, act, and be a little different from others. They are not in revolt against custom; they simply wish to be a bit different and still not be accused of bad taste or insensitivity to the code. Fashion discreetly furnishes them the opportunity for self-expression.

Origin of Fashion[8]

Stanley Marcus, then president of Neiman-Marcus, the high-fashion women's store in Dallas, Texas, observed:[9]

> *If, for example, a dictator decreed feminine clothes to be illegal and that all women should wear barrels, it would not result in an era of uniformity, in my opinion. Very shortly, I think you'd find that one ingenious woman would color her barrel with a lipstick, another would pin paper lace doilies on the front of hers, and still another would decorate hers with thumbtacks.* This is a strange human urge toward conformity, but a dislike for complete uniformity.

Another sociopsychological factor underlying the growth of fashion in our society is boredom, fostered by leisure time and monotonously specialized activity. To break the monotony, people seek change. Still another factor involves a person's ego. Basic human needs for reassurance and recognition lie behind the emphasis on clothing styles, according to fashion psychologist Ernest Dichter.[10]

Fashion-Adoption Process

The fashion-adoption process reflects the concepts of (1) large-group and small-group influences on consumer buying behaviour and (2) the diffusion of innovation, as discussed in Chapter 5. People usually try to imitate others in the same social stratum, or those on the next higher level. They do so by purchasing the fashionable product. This shows up as a wave of buying in that particular social stratum. The fashion-adoption process then is a series of buying waves that arise as the given style is popularly accepted in one group, then another and another, until it finally falls out of fashion. This wavelike movement, representing the introduction, rise, popular culmination, and decline of the market's acceptance of a style, is referred to as the **fashion cycle**.

---

[8]Part of this section is drawn from Edward Sapir, "Fashion," *The Encyclopedia of the Social Sciences*, The Macmillan Company, New York, 1931, vol. VI, pp. 139–144.

[9]Stanley Marcus, "Fashion Merchandising," a Tobé lecture on retail distribution, Harvard Graduate School of Business Administration, Cambridge, Mass., March 10, 1959, pp. 4–5.

[10]As quoted in "Why People Follow the Dictates of Designers," *U.S. News & World Report*, April 9, 1979, p. 53.

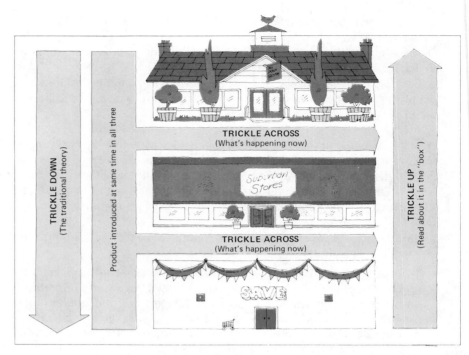

Figure 9-4
FASHION-ADOPTION
PROCESSES.

Three theories of fashion adoption are recognized (see Fig. 9-4):

1. **Trickle-down**, where a given fashion cycle flows *downward* through several socioeconomic classes.

2. **Trickle-across**, where the cycle moves *horizontally* and *simultaneously within* several social classes.

3. **Trickle-up**, where the cycle is initiated in lower socioeconomic classes, then later the style becomes popular among higher income and social groups.

Traditionally, the trickle-down theory has been used as the basic model to explain the fashion-adoption process. As an example, designers of women's apparel first introduce a style to the leaders — the tastemakers who usually are the social leaders in the upper-income brackets. If they accept the style, it quickly appears in leading fashion stores. Soon the middle-income and then the lower-income markets want to emulate the leaders, and the style is mass-marketed. As its popularity wanes, the style appears in bargain-price stores and finally is no longer considered fashionable.

To illustrate the trickle-across process, let us again use the example of women's apparel. Within a few weeks at the most, at the beginning of the fall season, the same style of dresses appears (1) in small, exclusive dress shops appealing to the upper social class, (2) in large department stores appealing to the middle social class, and (3) in discount houses and low-priced women's ready-to-wear chain stores, where the appeal is to the upper-lower social class. Price and quality mark the differences in the dresses sold on the three levels — *but the style is basically the same. Within each*

THE "TRICKLE-UP" PROCESS

Blue jeans, denim jackets, T-shirts, and "soul" food in the 1980s. Years earlier there were popular styles of music we call jazz and the blues. These all have one thing in common. They are styles that *trickled up* in popularity; that is, they were popular first with lower socioeconomic groups. Later, their popularity trickled up as these styles gained wide acceptance among higher-income markets. T-shirts—once the domain of beer-drinking blue-collar workers, radicals, and Marlon Brando as Stanley Kowalski in *A Streetcar Named Desire*—have moved up considerably in social respectability and price. Now they are designed by Yves Saint Laurent, Calvin Klein, Ralph Lauren, and others.

class the dresses are purchased early in the season by the opinion leaders —the innovators. If the style is accepted, its sales curve rises as it becomes popular with the early adopters, and then with the late adopters. Eventually, sales decline as the style ceases to be popular. This cycle or flow is a horizontal movement occurring virtually simultaneously within each of several social strata.

Today the trickle-across concept best reflects the adoption process for most fashions. Granted, there is some flow downward, and obviously there is an upward influence. But market conditions today seem to foster a horizontal flow. By means of modern production, communication, and transportation methods, we can disseminate style information and products so rapidly that all social strata can be reached at about the same time. In the apparel field particularly, manufacturing and marketing programs tend to foster the horizontal movement of fashions. Manufacturers produce a wide *variety* of essentially one style. They also produce various *qualities* of the same basic style so as to appeal to different income groups simultaneously. When an entire cycle may last only one short season, sellers cannot afford to wait for style acceptance to trickle down. They must introduce it into many social levels as soon as possible.

When a firm's products are subject to the fashion cycle, management must know what stage the cycle is in at all times. They must decide at what point to get into the cycle, and when they should get out.

Accurate forecasting is of inestimable value in achieving success in fashion merchandising. This is an extremely difficult task, however, because the forecaster is often dealing with complex sociological and psychological factors. Frequently a retailer or a manufcturer operates largely on intuition and inspiration, tempered by considerable experience.[11]

The executives also must know what market they are aiming for. Ordinarily, a retailer cannot successfully participate in all stages of the fashion cycle at the same time. A high-grade specialty store selling apparel—whose

Marketing Considerations in Fashion

[11]For the suggestion that fashion changes follow a fairly regular cycle and are reasonably easy to predict, see Dwight E. Robinson, "Style Changes: Cyclical, Inexorable, and Foreseeable," *Harvard Business Review*, November–December 1975, pp. 121–131.

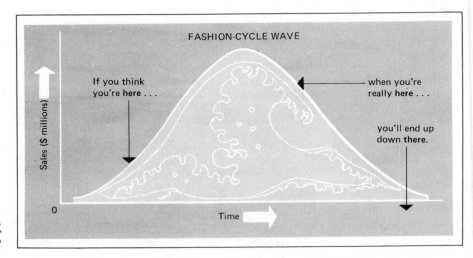

FASHION-CYCLE WAVE

If you think you're **here** . . .

when you're really **here** . . .

you'll end up down **there**.

Sales ($ millions)

Time

0

**MANAGING THE
FASHION CYCLE?**

stocks are displayed discreetly in limited numbers without price tags — will want to get in at the start of a fashion trend. A department store appealing to the middle-income market will plan to enter the cycle in time to mass-market the style as it is climbing to its peak of popularity.

**Evaluation of
Planned
Obsolescence**

Style obsolescence is one of the most controversial aspects of modern marketing. As is true of most social complaints against marketing, much of the criticism of style obsolescence is neither all true nor all false. One criticism is that fashion designers are dictators (especially in women's ready-to-wear), and that people buy whatever the designers decree will be fashionable. This is true only in a very superficial sense. The designers themselves obey many masters. First and foremost, the designs must be profitable to the manufacturers. Also, the designers are controlled by established custom and cannot depart too far from it. A designer just cannot combat a firmly established fashion trend.

Professor Sapir, along with other writers, has noted that throughout history there have been both social and economic criticisms of fashion. Social critics object to fashion — particularly women's ready-to-wear — because it calls attention to the human body. Actually, the criticism is valid. Women's apparel generally is intended to draw attention to the human form. This fits in with human psychology. People want to be as expressive — even as immodest, perhaps — as society will allow. Fashion helps them to achieve this objective.

Supporters of the strategy of style obsolescence point out that it satisfies the consumers' desire to have something new. It also maintains our economy at a higher level than would be possible if consumers used a product until it wore out physically. Furthermore, people who cannot afford to buy, say, new automobiles or appliances, have an opportunity to satisfy their wants for these products by purchasing used models. These would not be

---

ANOTHER "LAW OF FASHION"

The same dress is indecent 10 years before its time, daring 1 year before its time, chic in its time, dowdy 3 years after its time, hideous 20 years after its time, amusing 30 years after its time, romantic 100 years after its time, and beautiful 150 years after its time.

Source: James Laver, British costume historian, in *Today's Health*, October 1973, p. 69.

---

available if other consumers had not traded in their older models when acquiring the latest ones.

Planned obsolescence — both functional and style — is a characteristic of a free and expanding economy. In any economy controlled by the state or by cartels, product obsolescence and innovation are likely to take place slowly.

No matter how marketing people try to answer the criticisms, many individuals, including businesspeople, still have a nagging conscience about style obsolescence. Two basic issues seem to keep coming up. First, does our prevailing system of style obsolescence make sensible use of our resources and productive capacity? The second, and related, issue concerns whether planned obsolescence results in an artificially short life for the products, thus creating some sort of disutility. One cannot help asking why marketers cannot be just as aggressive with functional innovation as they are with superficial styling and prestige appeals.

SUMMARY

To make the product-planning phase of a company's marketing program most effective, it is imperative that management select appropriate strategies for the company's product mix. One strategy is simply to expand the product mix by increasing the number of lines and/or the depth within a line. An alternative is to prune out the product mix by eliminating an entire line or by simplifying the assortment within a line. Another strategy is to alter the design, packaging, or other features of existing products. Still another is appropriate "positioning" of the product, relative to competing products or to other products sold by the firm.

In other strategies, management may elect to trade up or trade down, relative to its existing products. Management may strive to differentiate its products from competitive models, at the same time selling to a broad market. Or, the decision may be to identify separate market segments and then develop different products, each tailored for a different segment.

Executives need to understand the concept of a product's life cycle and the characeristics of each stage in the cycle. The task of managing a product as it moves through its life cycle presents both challenges and opportunities — perhaps most frequently in the sales decline stage.

An especially controversial product strategy is that of planned obsolescence, built around the concepts of style, fashion, and the fashion cycle. Fashion—essentially a sociological and psychological phenomenon—follows a reasonably predictable pattern. With advances in communications and production, the fashion-adoption process has moved away from the traditional trickle-down pattern. Today the process is better described as trickle-across. There are also some noteworthy examples of fashions trickling up. Style obsolescence, in spite of its critics, is based on consumer psychology and is associated with a free-market economy.

KEY TERMS AND CONCEPTS

Product line 239

Product mix 239

Product-mix breadth and depth 239

Expansion of product mix 240

Contraction of product mix 240

Product positioning 241

Trading up/trading down 243

Product differentiation 244

Market segmentation 245

Product life cycle 247

Planned obsolescence 252

Fashion obsolescence 252

Style 252

Fashion 252

Fashion-adoption process 253

Trickle-down 254

Trickle-across 254

Trickle-up 254

QUESTIONS AND PROBLEMS

1. "It is inconsistent for management to follow concurrently the product-line strategies of *expanding* its product mix and *contracting* its product mix." Discuss.

2. "Trading up and trading down are product strategies closely related to the business cycle. Firms trade up during periods of prosperity and trade down during depressions or recessions." Do you agree? Why?

3. How might the manufacture of each of the following articles implement the product strategy of market segmentation? Of product differentiation?
   a. Shoes   c. Tape recorders
   b. Paint   d. Typewriters

4. Name some products that you believe are in the introductory stage of their life cycles. Identify the market that considers your examples to be new products.

5. Give examples of products that are in the stage of market decline. In each case, point out whether you think the decline is permanent. What recommendations do you have for rejuvenating the demand for the product?

6. How might a company's pricing strategies differ, depending upon whether its product is in the introductory stage or maturity stage of its life cycle?

7. What advertising strategies are likely to be used when a product is in the growth stage?

8. What products, other than wearing apparel and automobiles, stress fashion and style in marketing? Do styles exist among industrial products?

9. Select a product and trace its marketing as it moves through a complete fashion cycle. Particularly note and explain the changes in the distribution, pricing, and promotion of the product in the various stages of the cycle.

10. Is the trickle-across theory applicable in describing the fashion-adoption process in product lines other than women's apparel? Explain, using examples.

11. Planned obsolescence is criticized as a social and economic waste because we are urged to buy things we do not like and do not need. What is your opinion in this matter? If you object to planned obsolescence, what are your recommendations for correcting the situation?

12. What effects might a recession have on:
    a. Product life cycles
    b. Planned obsolescence
    What marketing strategies might a firm employ to counter (or take advantage of) these effects?

Chapter 10

Brands, Packaging, and Other Product Features

CHAPTER GOALS

The title of this chapter could be "Product Presentation" — because the way in which a physical product is presented to potential customers is very much a part of the product itself. After studying this chapter, you should understand:

1. *The nature and importance of brands, including the characteristics of a good brand and the problem of generic brand names*
2. *Brand strategies of manufacturers and middlemen*
3. *The "battle of the brands"*
4. *The nature and importance of packaging*
5. *Major packaging strategies*
6. *Types of labelling*
7. *Major legislation regarding packaging and labelling*
8. *The marketing implications in some other product features — design, colour, quality, warranty, and servicing*

Why do people use certain products and not others? Some factory managers insist on Texaco oils and greases while others prefer Esso or Gulf lubricants. Some consumers choose Aylmer canned peaches; others buy Libby's or Del Monte. Some families like York french fries, others prefer McCain's. Yet many consumers insist that there are no significant differences among the well-known brands of french fries or canned peaches. The buyer's choice may be influenced by the guarantee offered or by an attractive package. Frequently, the brand, the colour and design, and other product characteristics combine to project an image to the prospective consumer. Consequently, these features are important in a marketing program.

INFLUENCES OF PRODUCT FEATURES ON BUSINESS FUNCTIONS

Branding, packaging, and the other product features are interrelated with, and affect, the production and financial functions of a firm as well as other marketing activities. If a product is manufactured in six colours instead of one, the *production* runs are shorter, there are more of them, and therefore they are more costly. A product made in small units and packaged in an attractive wrapper is ordinarily more costly than one put up in large, bulk-packaged units.

Financial risks increase as the variety of sizes and colours is increased. Packaging products in special Christmas containers exposes a company to a financial loss on merchandise that is unsold by December 26. A business that offers a generous warranty—"Double your money back if not entirely satisifed"—has greater financial risks than a firm whose policy is "All sales are final."

Product features are also interrelated with other marketing elements. A company that manufactures products to be sold on a self-service basis must devote attention to packaging and labelling, to attract the customer at the point of purchase. And, normally, branding increases price rigidity. At the same time, however, well-known brands are most likely to have their prices cut to attract customers to the seller's establishment.

BRANDS

The word brand is comprehensive term, and it includes other, narrower terms. A **brand** is a name, term, symbol, or special design, or some combination of these elements, that is intended to identify the goods or services of one seller or a group of sellers. A brand differentiates one seller's products or services from those of the competitors.[1] A brand **name** consists of words, letters, and/or numbers that can be *vocalized*. A brand **mark** is the part of the brand that appears in the form of a symbol, design, or distinctive colouring or lettering. It is recognized by sight but is not expressed when a person pronounces the brand name. Ski-Doo, Du Maurier, and Labatt's 50 are brand names. The distinctive signature of Coca-Cola and the stylized CN logo of Canadian National are brand marks.

A trademark may be defined as a brand that is given legal protection because under the law it has been appropriated exclusively by one seller. Thus *trademark* is essentially a legal term. All trademarks are brands and thus include the words, letters, or numbers that may be pronounced. They may also include a pictorial design (brand mark). Some people erroneously believe that the trademark is only the pictorial part of the brand.

One major method of classifying brands is on the basis of who owns them—producers or middlemen. IBM, Arrow, Bick's, and York are producers' brands, while Domino, Viking, Pride of Arabia, Kenmore, Coldspot, Birkdale, and Ann Page are middlemen's brands.

Although the terms *national* and *private* brands have been used to describe producer and middleman ownership, respectively, marketing people prefer the producer-middleman terminology. To say that the brand of a small manufacturer of poultry feed who markets his produce in two or three provinces is a national brand, while the brands of Eaton's, Loblaws, The Bay, Woodward's, and Dominion Stores are private brands, seems to be stretching the meaning of the terms *national* and *private*.

Various parts of a brand.

---

[1] Adapted from *Marketing Definitions: A Glossary of Marketing Terms*, American Marketing Association, Chicago, 1960, p. 8.

Importance of Branding

Brands make it easy for consumers to identify products or services. Brands also assure purchasers that they are getting comparable quality when they reorder.

For sellers, brands are something that can be advertised and that will be recognized when displayed on shelves in a store. Branding also helps sellers to control their share of the market because buyers will not confuse one product with another. Branding reduces price comparisons because it is hard to compare prices on two items with different brands. Finally, for sellers, branding can add a measure of prestige to otherwise ordinary commodities (Sunkist oranges, Robin Hood Flour, McCain's french fries, Sifto salt, Highliner fish products, Schwartz vinegar).

Reasons for Not Branding

Many firms do not brand their products because they are unable or unwilling to assume the two major responsibilities inherent in brand ownership: (1) to promote the brand and (2) to maintain a consistent quality of output.

Some items are not branded because of the difficulty of differentiating the products of one firm from those of another. Clothespins, nails, and industrial raw materials (coal, cotton, wheat) are examples of goods for which product differentiation is generally unknown. The physical nature of some items, such as fresh fruits and vegetables, may discourage branding. However, now that these products are often packaged in typically purchased quantities, brands are being applied to the packages.

Producers frequently do not brand that part of their output that is below their regular quality. Products graded as seconds or imperfects are sold at a cut price and are often distributed through channels different from those used for regular quality goods.

Selecting a Good Brand Name

Selecting a good brand name is one of the most difficult tasks facing marketing management. In spite of the acknowledged importance of a brand, it is surprising how few really good brand names there are. In a study made many years ago, it was found that only 12 percent of the names helped sell the product; 36 percent actually hurt sales, and 52 percent were "nonentities — contributing nothing to the sales appeal of the product." There is no reason to believe that the situation has improved materially since this study was made.[2]

Sometimes distinctiveness is sufficient in a brand. (*Photograph by Harold M. Lambert; courtesy Miller Services Ltd.*)

Characteristics of a Good Brand

A good brand should possess as many of the following characteristics as possible. It is extremely difficult, however, to find a brand that has all of them. A brand should:

[2]For a report on the brand-selection process used by large manufacturers of consumer goods, see James U. McNeal and Linda M. Zeren, "Brand Name Selection for Consumer Products," *MSU Business Topics*, Spring 1981, pp. 35–39.

1. Suggest something about the product's characteristics — its benefits, use, or action. Some names that suggest desirable benefits include Coldspot, Wear-Ever, Easy-Off, Mor-Power, Craftsman, and Beautyrest. Product use and action is suggested by Spic and Span, Pop-Tarts, Minute Maid, Ultra Brite, and Dream Whip.

2. Be easy to pronounce, spell, and remember. Simple, short, one-syllable names such as Tide, Gleem, Crest, Ban, and Raid are helpful.

3. Be distinctive. Brands such as National, Presto, Star, and Standard fail on this point.

4. Be adaptable to new products that may be added to the product line. An innocuous name like Heinz, Adidas, or Jelinek may serve the purpose better than a highly distinctive name suggestive of product benefits. Frigidaire is an excellent name for a refrigerator and other cold-image products. But when the manufacturer expanded this line of home appliances and added Frigidaire kitchen ranges, the name lost some of its sales appeal.

5. Be capable of being registered and legally protected under the Trade Marks Act and other statutory or common laws.[3]

Generic Usage of Brand Names

Over a period of years some trademarks become so accepted that the brand name is substituted for the generic or descriptive name of the particular product. People associate the name with the product and not with the producer-owner of the brand. A number of product names such as shredded wheat and linoleum were originally trademarks limited to use by the owner, but they have long since lost their distinctiveness and any firm may use them.

A company may lose the right to exclusive use of a brand name for a number of reasons. Under protection of a patent, a manufacturer's brand name may become so closely associated with the product that, upon expiration of the patent, that brand name is used by the public to describe all brands of the product, regardless of manufacturer. There is simply no better name available to the public to describe the product class.

More often, trademark protection is lost simply because a company has done an outstanding job of marketing its product. In these cases, a product becomes so successful that its brand name becomes synonymous with the type of product. Where the brand name falls into such common usage that it ceases to be distinctive or to distinguish the product of one manufacturer from those of others, then the original owner of the brand name is in danger of losing the legal right to exclusive use of the brand. A number of brand names would appear to be in danger of becoming generic. These might include such brands as Band-Aid, Ski-Doo, Kleenex, and Xerox. All

---

[3]See Douglas Deeth, "The Trade Mark: Cornerstone of the Franchise," *The Financial Post*, October 17, 1981, p. F14.

Figure 10-1
EXAMPLES OF
CORPORATE AND
PRODUCT SYMBOLS.

WHEN IS LITE NOT LIGHT?

When Labatt's Breweries introduced Canada's first light beer into the Ontario market just before Christmas 1977, they likely were not expecting to have to pull the product off the market. The federal government challenged Labatt's product name "Special Lite," arguing that "Lite" really means "Light." Under federal labelling laws, a beer can not be called a "light beer" unless it contains fewer than 70 calories and less than 2.5% alcohol by volume. The new Labatt's Special Lite product contained 99 calories and 4% alcohol.

A judge of the Federal Court later ruled that Special Lite is not likely to be mistaken for a light beer and Labatt's resumed production and advertising for the product. This ruling opened the door to the introduction of "light" beers by most Canadian brewers.

---

of these are extremely successful brand names but have been promoted so well that consumers tend to use them generically. Ideally, a firm wants its brand to be preferred and even insisted upon by consumers, but it does not want its brand name to become generic.

It is the responsibility of the trademark owner to assert his rights in order to prevent the loss of the distinctive character of his trademark. A number of strategies are employed to prevent the brand name from falling into generic usage. The most common strategy is to ensure that the words "trade mark" or the letters "TM"® appear adjacent to the brand name wherever it appears. Coca-Cola Limited often uses the following phrase in its advertising: "Coca-Cola is a registered trade mark which identifies only the product of Coca-Cola Limited." Such phrases give evidence to the public and to competitors that the brand name has been registered.

A second strategy is to use two names — the brand name together with either the company's name or the generic name of the product. An example of this is the name "Thermos Vacuum Bottle," which is designed to suggest to the public that "Thermos" is but one brand of vacuum bottle and that the name "Thermos" should not be applied to all products in that product category.

A third strategy for protecting a trademark involves the incorporation into the trademark of a distinctive signature or logo. Many companies have adopted distinctive ways of presenting the brand name of their products so that the consumer is able to identify their products whenever they encounter the particular brand written in a certain script or type face. Some examples of such signatures and logos are presented in Fig. 10-1.

Finally, the owner of a registered trademark must be willing to prosecute any other companies attempting to market products under a brand name that is identical to or similar to the registered brand name. By prosecuting such infringements of the trademark protection, the owner is demonstrating to the courts that he is actively protecting his right to use of the brand and is guarding against its falling into generic usage. If the owner fails to prosecute infringements, even if he decides to prosecute at a later

Just a little reminder from Xerox.   XEROX

You may have heard a phrase like. "I Xeroxed the recipe for you" or "Please Xerox this for me." And they may seem harmless enough.

But they're not. Because they overlook the fact that Xerox is a registered trademark of Xerox Corporation. And trademarks should not be used as verbs.

As a brand name, Xerox should be used as an adjective followed by a word or phrase describing the particular product.

Like the Xerox 1075 Copier. The Xerox 640 Memorywriter. Or the Xerox 9700 Electronic Printing System.

Our brand name is very valuable to us. And to you, too. Because the proper use of our name is the best way to ensure you'll always get a Xerox product when you ask for one.

So, please remember that our trademark starts with an "X."

And ends with an "®."

Figure 10-2
TRADEMARK
PROTECTION
ADVERTISING.

*(Courtesy Xerox
Canada.)*

date after other companies have adopted his brand, the distinctive character of his trademark will be lost and the courts are likely to rule that the original owner no longer has exclusive right to use of the brand name, as it is in the public domain. Some companies seek to show competitors or others who wish to make use of registered trademarks that they are willing to take legal action to protect their trademarks. An example of advertising that is designed to achieve this purpose is presented in Fig. 10-2.

Brand Policies and Strategies

Manufacturers' Strategies

Manufacturers must decide whether to brand their products and whether to sell any or all of their output under middlemen's brands.

Marketing Entire Output under Manufacturers' Own Brands   Companies that market their entire output under their own brands typically are very large, well financed, and well managed. Polaroid, Maytag, and IBM are examples. They typically have broad product lines, well-established distribution systems, and large shares of the market. Probably only a small percentage of manufacturers follow this policy, and their number seems to be decreasing.

Many of the reasons for adopting this policy have already been covered in the section on the importance of branding to the seller. In addition, middlemen often prefer to handle manufacturers' brands, especially when the brands have high consumer acceptance.

Branding of Fabricating Parts and Materials   In a strategy similar to the one described just above, some producers of industrial fabricating materials and parts (products used in the further manufacturing of other goods) will brand their products. This strategy is used in the marketing of Domtar building materials, Fiberglas insulation, Pittsburgh glass, Pella windows, Du Pont's Dacron fibres, and in marketing many automobile parts, such as Purolator oil filters and Champion spark plugs.

WOULD YOU BUY A USED NISSAN? OR, SHOULD A COMPANY DROP A WELL-ESTABLISHED, WELL-ACCEPTED BRAND NAME?

For several years, in North America the Datsun was a popular and highly respected brand of automobile. This car was manufactured by the Nissan Company in Japan. In fact, it was marketed in Japan under the Nissan brand.

Then in 1981, the Nissan Company decided to abandon the Datsun name in North America and to substitute Nissan as the brand name for these autos. This move was part of Nissan's global branding strategy. The company planned to phase in the new name gradually in Canada and the United States, starting with the 1982 models. That year the company introduced the Nissan Stanza model, but it still carried the Datsun emblem. At that time, marketing research showed that 85 percent of the people recognized the Datsun brand versus only a 10 to 15 percent recognition of the Nissan name.

Do you agree with Nissan's decision? (Would you buy a used Nissan?) Or, should the entire company's name be changed to Datsun to parallel a move that has been made by Sony, Sunbeam, Del Monte, Talon (zippers), and other owners of popular brand names?

Underlying this strategy is the seller's desire to develop a market preference for its branded part or material. For instance, the Du Pont Company wants to build a market situation in which customers will insist on a shirt made with Dacron or Qiana (both are Du Pont–brand materials). In addition, the parts manufacturer wants to persuade the producer of the finished item that using the branded materials will help sell the end product. In our example, the Du Pont Company hopes to convince shirt manufacturers that their sales will increase if their shirts are made with Dacron polyester or Qiana nylon.

Certain product characteristics lend themselves to the effective use of this strategy. First, it helps if the product is also a consumer good bought for replacement purposes. This factor encourages the branding of Champion spark plugs and Fram oil filters, for example. Second, the seller's situation is improved if the item is a major part of the finished product — a television picture tube, for example.

Marketing under Middlemen's Brands   A widespread strategy is for manufacturers to brand part or all of their output with the brands of their middlemen customers. For the manufacturer, this middlemen's-brand business generates additional sales volume and profit dollars. Orders typically are large, payment is prompt, and a manufacturer's working-capital position is improved. Also, manufacturers may utilize their production resources more effectively, including their plant capacities. Furthermore, refusing to sell under a retailer's or wholesaler's brand will not eliminate competition from this source. Many middlemen want to market under their own brands; if one manufacturer refuses their business, they will simply go to another.

Middlemen can sell their brands at a lower price and a higher gross margin. However, they often use "sales" of manufacturers' brands to attract customers to their stores.

Probably the most serious limitation to marketing under middlemen's brands is that a manufacturer may be at the mercy of the middlemen. This problem grows as the proportion of that producer's output going to middlemen's brands increases.

Middlemen's Strategies

The question of whether or not to brand must also be answered by middlemen.

Carry Only Manufacturers' Brands

Most retailers and wholesalers follow this policy because they are not able to take on the dual burdens of promoting a brand and maintaining its quality. Even though manufacturers' brands usually carry lower gross margins, they often have a higher rate of turnover and a better profit possibility.

Carry Middlemen's Brands Along with Manufacturers' Brands

Many large retailers and some large wholesalers have their own brands. Middlemen may find it advantageous to market their own brands for several reasons. First, it increases their control over their market. If customers prefer a given middleman's brand, they can get it only at that middleman's store. Furthermore, middlemen can usually sell their brands at prices below those of manufacturers' brands and still earn higher gross margins. This is possible because middlemen can buy at lower costs. The costs may be lower because (1) manufacturers' advertising and selling costs are not included in their prices, or (2) producers are anxious to get the extra business to keep their plants running in slack seasons.

Middlemen have more freedom in pricing products sold under their own labels. (Some manufacturers give a retailer virtually no price flexibility in selling the manufacturers' brands. In other instances, prices on manufacturers' brands can be cut drastically by competing stores.) Products carrying middlemen's brands become differentiated products, and this hinders price comparisons that might be unfavourable to the middlemen.

Strategies Common to Manufacturers and Middlemen

Manufacturers and middlemen alike must adopt some strategy with respect to branding their product mix and branding for market saturation.

Branding a Line of Products

At least four different strategies are widely used by firms that sell more than one product.

1. The same "family" or "blanket" brand may be placed on all products. This policy is followed by Heinz, Campbell, Libby, and others in the food field, as well as by Westinghouse and General Electric.

2. A separate name may be used for each product. This strategy is employed by General Foods, Procter & Gamble, and Lever Brothers.

3. A separate family brand may be applied to each grade of product or to each group of similar products. Sears, for example, groups its major home appliances under the name Kenmore, its paints and home furnishings under the Harmony House label, its tools under Craftsman, and its tires and insurance under the name Allstate.

4. The company's trade name may be combined with an individual name for the product. Thus, there is Kraft Cracker Barrel, Kellogg's Corn Flakes, Molson Golden, and Moosehead Export.

When used wisely, a family-brand strategy has considerable merit. It is much simpler and less expensive to introduce new related products to a line. Also, the general prestige of a brand can be spread more easily if it appears on several products rather than on one. A family brand is best suited for a marketing situation where the products are related in quality, in use, or in some other manner. Canada Packers does not associate its Maple Leaf and York food brands with its Shur-Gain brand of livestock and poultry feeds.

On the other hand, the use of family brands places a greater burden on the brand owner to maintain consistent quality among all products. One bad item can reflect unfavourably, and even disastrously, on all other goods carrying the same brand.

Branding for Market Saturation

Frequently, to achieve a greater degree of market saturation, a firm will employ a multiple-brand strategy. Often one type of sales appeal is built around a given brand. To reach another segment of the market, the company will use other appeals and other brands. Procter & Gamble's two detergents, Tide and Ivory Snow, illustrate this point. Some people feel that if Tide is strong enough to clean dirty work clothes, it cannot be used on lingerie and other fine clothing. For these people, Procter & Gamble has marketed Ivory Snow, a detergent whose image is more gentle than that of Tide.

The use of multiple brands on the same or similar products affords a seller some flexibility in pricing. A competitor may have an attractively priced item. Rather than cut the price on their *known* brands, manufacturers may come out with other "fighting brands" priced to beat those of their competitors. For example, Robin Hood multifoods markets Bick's and Rose brand pickles, the latter being a "fighting brand."

The Battle of the Brands

Middlemen's brands have proved to be eminently successful in competing with manufacturers' brands. However, neither group has demonstrated a convincing competitive superiority over the other in the marketplace. Consequently, the "battle of the brands" shows every indication of continuing and becoming more intense.

In the late 1970s, many supermarket chains introduced products sold under their generic names. That is, the products were simply labelled as pork and beans, peanut butter, cottage cheese, paper towels, and so on. Thus generic-labelled products became, in effect, a "no-brand" brand name. Generic products now account for a large enough share of total sales in their respective product lines to be a major factor in the battle of the brands.[4]

Several factors account for the success of middlemen's brands and generic-labelled products. The thin profit margins on manufacturers' brands have encouraged retailers to establish their own labels. The improved quality of retailers' brands has boosted their sales. Consumers have become more sophisticated in their buying, and their brand loyalty has declined, so they do consider alternative brands. It is quite generally known that middlemen's brands are usually produced by large, well-known manufacturers. Generic labels, with their low-price, no-frills approach, appeal to price-conscious consumers during periods of inflation.

Manufacturers do have some effective responses they can use to combat generic labels and retailers' brands. Producers can devote top priority to product innovation and packaging, an area in which retailers are not as strong. Manufacturers' research and development capacity also enables them to enter the market in the early stages of a product's life cycle, whereas retailer brands typically enter after a product is well established.

---

[4]See Patricia Lush, "Loblaw Expects Generics to Lead in Profit Growth," *Globe and Mail*, April 22, 1981; B. Portis, T. Deutscher, and J. Rasmussen, "Trial and Satisfaction with Generic Grocery Products in Canada," in *Proceedings* of the Marketing Division of the Administrative Sciences Association of Canada, 1980, pp. 280–288; Kent L. Granzin, "An Investigation of the Market for Generic Products," *Journal of Retailing*, Winter 1981, pp. 39–55; J. L. Bellizzi, H. F. Krueckeberg, J. R. Hamilton, and W. S. Martin, "Consumer Perception of National, Private, and Generic Brands," *Journal of Retailing*, Winter 1981, pp. 56–70; and Jo Marney, "On Brand Preference," *Marketing*, September 19, 1983, p. 9.

BATTLE OF THE BRANDS.

Middlemen's brands are usually less expensive than manufacturers' brands. No-brand products are somewhat lower in price and quality than branded goods.

. . . AND NOW WE HAVE AN INFLATION FIGHTER — LOW-COST GENERIC PRODUCTS, THE "NO-BRAND" BRAND:

Catsup, spaghetti, dry beans, strawberry jam, peanut butter, canned tuna fish, ice cream, several different types of canned fruits and vegetables, packages of fresh fruits and vegetables, paper towels, and napkins — all with plain white labels and black letters carrying no brand name — only the generic name of the product. These are just some of the more than sixty generic, unbranded products introduced in competition with manufacturers' and middlemen's branded products in supermarkets in the late 1970s. And the number keeps growing. Unbranded products generally sell for 30 to 40 percent less than manufacturers' brands and 20 percent less than retailer's brands.

While they are the nutritional equivalent of branded products, the generics (graded "standard" in industry terms) may not have the colour,size, and appearance of the branded items (graded "fancy").

First introduced in the Carrefour chain of giant supermarkets in France, generic products now are sold in most supermarket chains in Canada. Some chains give these products a brand name, but most of the chains sell these products completely unbranded — referring to them as "generic" or "generic products" in the store's advertising. In effect, "generic" becomes an unofficial brand name in that it is the identifying name used by the stores and consumers.

The generics are immensely successful. They account for a substantial share of the store's sales in the particular product category. Generics seem to be hurting the sales of manufacturers' brands more than retailers' brands. The gross margin on generics is comparable to (or even better than) the margin on branded products. The comparable gross margins on the generics are possible, even with lower selling prices, because the supermarkets can buy the products at such low prices from producers. The producers closely control all their production and distribution costs. They use low-cost raw materials and have long (low-cost) production runs. No advertising or selling expenses are charged to generics, and packaging costs are low.

PACKAGING

Packaging may be defined as all the activities involved in designing and producing the container or wrapper for a product. There are three reasons for packaging:

1. Packaging serves several *safety* and *utilitarian purposes.* It protects a product on its route from the producer to the final customer, and in some cases even while it is being used by the customer. For example, effective packaging can help to prevent ill-intentioned persons from tampering with products, as occurred in the pain-reliever poisonings in the United States in 1982. Some protection is provided by "child-proof" closures on containers of medicines and other products that are potentially harmful to children. Also, compared with bulk items, packaged goods generally are more convenient, cleaner, and less susceptible to losses from evaporation, spilling, and spoilage.

2. Packaging may implement a company's marketing program. Packaging helps to identify a product and thus may prevent substitution of competitive goods. A package may be the only significant way in which a firm can differentiate its product. In the case of convenience goods or industrial operating supplies, for example, most buyers feel that one well-known brand is about as good as another. Also, changing the package is an inexpensive way to imply that the product itself has been changed.

   Retailers recognize that effective protection and promotion features in a package can cut their costs and increase sales. At the point of purchase, the package serves as a silent salesperson.

   Some features of the package may serve as a sales appeal — for example, a no-drip spout, a self-applicator, or a re-usable jar. Furthermore, the package advertising copy will last as long as the product is being used in its packaged form.

3. Management may package its product in such a way as to increase profit possibilities. A package may be so attractive that customers will pay more just to get the special package — even though the increase in price exceeds the additional cost of the package. Also, an increase in ease of handling or a reduction in damage losses, due to packaging, will cut marketing costs, again increasing profit.

Packaging for ease of display and product visibility — packaging that sells.

Importance of Packaging in Marketing

Historically, packaging was a production-oriented activity in most companies, performed mainly to obtain the benefits of protection and convenience. In recent years, however, the marketing significance of packaging has been increasingly recognized; and today, packaging is truly a major competitive force in the struggle for markets. The widespread use of self-service selling and automatic vending means that the package must do the selling job at the point of purchase. Shelf space is often at a premium, and it is no simple task for manufacturers even to get their products displayed in a retail outlet. Most retailers are inclined to cater to producers who have used effective packaging. In addition, the increased use of branding and the public's rising standards in health and sanitation have contributed to the importance of packaging.

Safety in packaging has become an especially important marketing and social issue in recent years. The pain-reliever poisoning deaths highlighted the need for more effective "tamper-proof" packaging to protect many products and their users. Since those tragedies, several firms in their promotional programs have stressed the safety features incorporated into the packaging of their products.

New developments in packaging, occurring rapidly and in a seemingly endless flow, require management's constant attention to packaging design. We see new packaging materials replacing the traditional ones, new shapes and sizes, new closures, and other new features (measured portions, metered flow). These all make for increased convenience for consumers and additional selling points for marketers.

Changing the Package

Packaging Strategies

In general, management has two reasons for considering a package change: to combat a decrease in sales, and to expand a market by attracting new groups of customers. More specifically, a firm may want to correct a poor feature in the existing container, or a company may want to take advantage of new materials. Some companies change their containers to aid in promotional programs, such as the new tall bottles and twist caps introduced by the Canadian brewing industry. A new package may be used as a major appeal in advertising copy, or because the old container may not show up well in advertisements.

In Canada, manufacturers of many packaged consumer products had to initiate changes in package design in order to conform with the requirements of the Consumer Packaging and Labelling Act relating to metrication. Since Canada has adopted the metric system of measurement, it is now a requirement of this Act that all food products must be labelled in metric units. Some companies changed the labels on their existing packages and containers so that the labels bear both the metric and imperial units of measure. Other manufacturers took the route of "hard conversion," in which the container was actually redesigned to a rounded metric capacity. For example, most soft drink bottlers replaced their 10 ounce bottles with new 300 millilitre bottles.

Packaging the Product Line

A company must decide whether to develop a family resemblance in the packaging of its several products. **Family packaging** involves the use of identical packages for all products or the use of packages with some common feature. Campbell's Soup, for example, uses virtually identical packaging on its condensed soup products. Management's philosophy concerning family packaging generally parallels its feeling about family branding. When new products are added to a line, promotional values associated with old products extend to the new ones. On the other hand, family packaging should be used only when the products are related in use and are of similar quality.

Re-Use Packaging

Another strategy to be considered is re-use packaging. Should the company design and promote a package that can serve other purposes after the original contents have been consumed? Glasses containing cheese can later be used to serve fruit juice. Baby-food jars make great containers for small parts like nuts, bolts, and screws. Re-use packaging also should stimulate repeat purchases, as the consumer attempts to acquire a matching set of containers.

Multiple Packaging

For many years there has been a trend toward multiple packaging, or the practice of placing several units in one container. Dehydrated soups, motor oil, beer, golf balls, building hardware, candy bars, towels, and countless other products are packaged in multiple units. Test after test has proved that multiple packaging increases total sales of a product.

Criticisms of Packaging

Packaging is in the socioeconomic forefront today because of its relationship to environmental pollution issues. Perhaps the biggest challenge facing packagers is how to dispose of used containers, which are a major contributor to the solid-waste disposal problem. Consumers' desire for convenience (in the form of throw-away containers) conflicts with their desire for a clean environment.

Other socioeconomic criticisms of packaging are:

1. Packaging depletes our natural resources. This criticism is offset to some extent as packagers increasingly make use of recycled materials. Another offsetting point is that effective packaging reduces spoilage (another form of resource waste).

2. Packaging is excessively expensive. Cosmetic packaging is often cited as an example here. But even in seemingly simple packaging — beer, for example — half the production cost goes for the container. On the other hand, effective packaging reduces transportation costs and losses from product spoilage.

3. Health hazards occur from some forms of plastic packaging and some aerosol cans. Government regulations have banned the use of several of these suspect packaging materials.

4. Packaging is deceptive. Government regulation plus improvements in business practices regarding packaging have reduced the intensity of this criticism, although it still is heard on occasion.

Truly, marketing executives face some real challenges in satisfying these complaints while at the same time retaining the marketing-effectiveness, consumer-convenience, and product-protection features of packaging.

LABELLING

Labelling is another product feature that requires managerial attention. The **label** is the part of a product that carries verbal information about the product or the seller. A label may be part of a package, or it may be a tag attached directly to the product. Obviously there is a close relationship between labelling and packaging, and between labelling and branding.

Types of Labels

Typically, labels are classed as brand, grade, and descriptive. A **brand label** is simply the brand alone applied to the product or to the package. Thus some oranges are brand-labelled (stamped) Sunkist or Jaffa, and some clothes carry the brand label Sanforized. A **grade label** identifies the quality of the product by a letter, number, or word. For example, in Canada, beef is grade-labelled A, B, or C, and each grade is subdivided by number from 1 to 4, indicating an increasing fat content. The letters indicate the age of the animal, with A and B indicating young beef. **Descriptive labels** give objective information about the use, construction, care, performance, or other features of the product. On a descriptive label for a can of corn there will be statements concerning the type of corn (golden sweet), the style (creamed or in niblet kernels), and the can size, number of servings, other ingredients, and nutritional contents.

Relative Merit

Brand labelling creates very little stir among critics. While it is an acceptable form of labelling, its severe limitation is that it does not supply sufficient information to a buyer. The real fight centres on grade versus descriptive labelling, and whether grade labelling should be mandatory.

The proponents of grade labelling argue that it is simple, definite, and easy to use. They also point out that if grade labels were used, prices would be more related to quality, although grade labelling would not stifle competition. In fact, they believe that grade labelling might increase competition, because consumers would be able to judge products on the basis of both price and known quality. The cost of grade labelling is very low, so it would not place a great burden on the manufacturer.

Those who object to grade labelling point out that it is not possible to grade differences in flavour and taste, or in style and fashion. A very low score on one grading characteristic can be offset by very high scores on other factors. Companies selling products that score high *within* a given grade would be hurt by grade labelling. It would not be possible for these companies to justify a higher price than that charged for another Grade A product that scored very low in the Grade A quality range. Some people feel that grades are an inaccurate guide for consumer buying because the characteristics selected for grading, the weights assigned to them, and the means of measuring them are all established on an arbitrary basis.[5]

---

[5]For a report on labelling programs and research, including an extensive summary of the literature on this subject, see John A. Miller, *Labeling Research: The State of the Art*, Marketing Science Institute, Cambridge, Mass., report no. 78–115, 1978.

Statutory Labelling Requirements

The importance of packaging and labelling in terms of its potential for influencing the consumer's purchasing decision is reflected in the large number of federal and provincial laws that exist to regulate this marketing activity. At the federal level, the Combines Investigation Act has for a number of years regulated the area of misleading advertising and a number of companies have been convicted of misleading advertising for the false or deceptive statements that have appeared on their packages. In this case, the information that appears on a package or label has been considered to constitute an advertisement.

The Hazardous Products Act was passed in 1969, giving the federal government the power to regulate the sale, distribution, advertising, and labelling of certain consumer products that are considered dangerous. A number of products have been banned from sale under this Act and since 1971 all hazardous products, such as cleaning substances, chemicals, and aerosol products, must carry on their labels a series of symbols that indicate the danger associated with the product and the precautions that should be taken with its use. The symbols illustrate that the product is poisonous, inflammable, explosive, or corrosive in nature.

Similarly the federal Food and Drugs Act regulates the sale of food, drugs, cosmetics, and medical devices. Under this Act, regulations exist that deal with the manufacture, sale, advertising, packaging, and labelling of such products. Certain misleading and deceptive packaging and labelling practices are specifically prohibited.

The Textile Labelling Act requires that manufacturers label their products, including wearing apparel, yard goods, and household textiles, according to the fibre content of the product. In the past, more than 700 fabric names have appeared on products, but most of these were brand names of individual companies. For example, the fibre known generically as polyester has been labelled as Terylene, Trevira, Dacron, Kodel, Fortrel, Tergal, Tetoron, and Crimplene, all of which are manufacturers' brand names for polyester. In order to reduce confusion among the buying public, products now have to be labelled according to the generic fibre content, with the percentage of each fibre in excess of 5 percent listed.

There also exist in Canada two government-sponsored consumer product labelling schemes that are informative in nature. These programs are the Canada Standard Size program and the Textile Care Labelling program. The Textile Care Labelling program involves the labelling of all textile products with symbols that indicate instructions for washing and dry cleaning the product.

The Consumer Packaging and Labelling Act came into effect in 1974 and regulates all aspects of the packaging and labelling of consumer products in this country. The regulations that have been passed under this Act require that most products sold in Canada must bear bilingual labels. The net quantity of the product must appear on the label in both metric and imperial units. If the quantity of a food product is expressed in terms of a certain number of servings, the size of the servings must also be stated. Where artificial flavourings are used in the manufacture of a food product, the

A typical nutritional content label.

label must contain the information that the flavour is imitation or simulated. The Act also makes provision for the standardization of container sizes. The first set of regulations to be passed under the Act set down the standard package sizes for toothpaste, shampoo, and skin cream products and it is in contravention of the regulations to manufacture these products in other than the package sizes approved. It is likely that this program of standardization of package sizes will be extended to other product categories in the future.

The requirements of the Consumer Packaging and Labelling Act have caused many manufacturers of consumer products, especially in the food industry, to undertake the redesign of their product's packages and labels. Since the passage of the packaging and labelling regulations in 1974, manufacturers have had to incorporate the bilingual and metric requirements into the design of their labels. At the same time, most manufacturers added the Canadian Grocery Product Code to the design of their labels.

The provinces have also moved into the field of regulating packaging and labelling. A number of provinces have passed legislation regarding misleading advertising and any information that appears on a package or label is considered an advertisement. In Quebec, that province's Official Language Act requires that all labels be written in French or in French and another language. If both English and French appear on the label, at least equal prominence must be given to the French.[6]

A well-rounded program for product planning and development will include a company policy on several additional product attributes: product design, colour, quality, guarantee, and servicing.

One way to build an image of a product is through its design. In fact, a distinctive design may be the only feature that significantly differentiates a product. Many firms feel that there is considerable glamour and general promotional appeal in product design and the designer's name. In the field of industrial products, *engineering* design has long been recognized as extremely important. Today there is a realization of the marketing value of *appearance* design as well. Office machines and office furniture are examples of industrial products that reflect recent conscious attention to product design, often with good sales results. The marketing significance of design has been recognized for years in the field of consumer products, from big items like automobiles and refrigerators to small products like fountain pens and apparel.

Good design can improve the marketability of a product in many ways. It can make the product easier to operate. It can upgrade the product's quality or durability. It can improve product appearance and reduce manufacturing costs.

OTHER IMAGE-BUILDING FEATURES

Product Design

---

[6]Imported goods do not always conform to Canadian packaging and labelling laws. See Martin Mehr, "Marketers Want Rules Applying to All," *The Financial Post*, March 7, 1981, p. 19.

Colour Colour often is the determining factor in a customer's acceptance or rejection of a product, whether that product is a dress, a table, or an automobile. Colour by itself, however, is no selling advantage because many competing firms offer colour. The marketing advantage comes in knowing the right colour and in knowing when to change colours. If a garment manufacturer or a retail store's fashion coordinator guesses wrong on what will be the fashionable colour in women's clothing, this error can be disastrous.

Marketers must appreciate the importance of colour as both a psychological and a sociological factor. The careful use of colour can increase sales, raise worker productivity, reduce eyestrain, and generally affect emotional reactions.

Product Quality In recent years, manufacturers have been increasingly concerned about the quality of their products. And well they should be! For many years, a major consumer complaint has concerned the poor quality of some products — both materials and workmanship. Some foreign products — Japanese cars, for example — have made serious inroads into the Canadian market because these products are perceived as being of better quality than their North American counterparts.[7]

The quality of a product is extremely important, but it is probably the most difficult of all the image-building features to define. Users frequently disagree on what constitutes quality in a product, from a cut of meat to a piece of music. Personal tastes are deeply involved. Nevertheless, a marketing executive must make several decisions about product quality. First, the product should reach only that level of quality compatible with the intended use of the item; it need not be any better. In fact, *good* and *poor* are misleading terms. *Correct* and *incorrect* or *right* and *wrong* would be much more appropriate. If a person is making a peach cobbler, grade B or C peaches are the correct quality. They are not neessarily the *best* quality, but they are *right* for the intended use. It is not necessary to pay Grade A prices for large, well-formed peaches when these features are destroyed in making the cobbler.

Product Warranty The general purpose of a warranty is to give buyers some assurance that they will be compensated in case the product does not perform up to reasonable expectations. In years past, courts seemed generally to recognize only **express warranties** — those stated in written or spoken words. Usually these were quite limited in what they covered and seemed mainly to protect the seller from buyers' claims.

But times have changed! Consumer complaints have led to a governmental campaign to protect the consumer in many areas, one of which is product

---

[7]L. A. Heslop and P. M. Cross, "Marketers as a Communication Link in the 'Quality Era'," in Robert Wyckham (ed.), *Marketing 1981: In Pursuit of Excellence*, proceedings of the Annual Conference of the Administrative Sciences of Canada — Marketing Division, vol. 2, part 3, 1981, pp. 142–151.

liability. Today, courts and government agencies are broadening the scope of warranty coverage by recognizing the concept of **implied warranty** — that is, the idea that warranty was *intended* by the seller, although not actually stated. Manufacturers are being held responsible, even when the sales contract is between the retailer and the consumer. Warranties are considered to "run with the product." Manufacturers are held liable for product-caused injury, whether or not they are to blame for negligence in manufacturing. It all adds up to "Let the seller beware."[8]

In recent years manufacturers have responded to legislation and consumer complaints by broadening and simplifying their warranties. Many sellers are using their warranties as promotional devices to stimulate purchases by reducing consumers' risks. The effective handling of consumers' complaints related to warranties can be a significant factor in strengthening a company's marketing program.[9] As a dimension of competitive strategy, a promotional warranty policy will probably be most effective when:

1. The unit price of the product is high.
2. The product is purchased infrequently.
3. The product is perceived by consumers as being complex.
4. The buyer does not have much knowledge of the product; he cannot judge the product's quality by inspecting it; or, as in mail-order selling, the purchasing decision (and maybe the payment) must be made in advance of seeing the product.
5. The seller's share of the market is small or the product is not well known.

The Hazardous Products Act indicates how the law has changed regarding product liability and injurious products. This law prohibits the sale of certain dangerous products and requires that other products which may be potentially dangerous carry an indication on their labels of the dangers inherent in their use. As further indication of the growing interest on the part of consumer groups and governments in the protection that existing forms of warranties offer the consumer, the Ontario Law Reform Commission in 1972 issued its Report on Consumer Warranties and Guarantees in the Sale of Goods. This report recommended broad and sweeping changes in the law respecting warranties and guarantees, which would provide the consumer with greater protection. Since the mid-1970s, two provinces, Saskatchewan and New Brunswick, have passed Consumer Products Warranty Acts. The Saskatchewan Act provides for statutory warranties that are deemed to be given by the retailer to the original purchaser and to subsequent owners. It also prescribes the form that written warranties must take.

---

[8]See "Packagers Accept New Regulations," *Marketing*, July 4, 1983, p. 4.
[9]See C. L. Kendall and Frederick A. Russ, "Warranty and Complaint Policies: An Opportunity for Marketing Management," *Journal of Marketing*, April 1975, pp. 36–43.

Product Servicing

A related problem is that of adequately providing the services guaranteed by the warranty. Product servicing requires management's attention as products become more complex, service facilities seem unable to keep pace, and consumers grow increasingly dissatisfied and vocal. To cope with these problems, management can consider several courses of action. For instance, a producer can establish several geographically dispersed factory service centres, staff them with well-trained company employees, and strive to make servicing a separate profit-generating activity. Or the producer can shift the main burden to middlemen, compensate them for their efforts, and possibly even train their service people.

Today the provision of adequate product servicing should be high on the list of topics calling for managerial action. A perennial major consumer complaint is that manufacturers and retailers do *not* provide adequate repair service for the products they sell. Oftentimes, the situation is simply that the consumers wish to be *heard*; that is, they simply want someone to listen to them regarding their complaints. In response to this situation, a number of manufacturers have established toll-free (800-number) telephone lines to their customer services departments.

SUMMARY

The management of the various features of a product—its brand, package, labelling, design, colour, quality, warranty, and servicing — is an integral part of effective product planning. A *brand* is a means of identifying and differentiating the products or services of an organization. Branding aids sellers in managing their promotional and pricing activities. Brand ownership carries the dual responsibilities of promoting the brand and maintaining a consistent level of quality. Selecting a good brand name — and there are relatively few really good ones — is a difficult task. A good name should suggest a product's benefits, be easy to pronounce and remember, lend itself to product-line additions, and be eligible for legal registration and protection.

Manufacturers must decide whether to brand their products and whether to sell under a middleman's brand. Middlemen must decide whether to carry manufacturers' brands alone, or whether to establish their own brands as well. Both groups of sellers must set policies regarding branding of groups of products and branding for market saturation.

Packaging is becoming increasingly important as sellers recognize the problems as well as the marketing opportunities, involved in packaging. *Labelling* is a related activity. Marketers should understand the merits and problems of grade labelling and of descriptive labelling. The social significance of labelling is also important to a company. Many consumer criticisms of marketing have involved packaging and labelling, and there are several federal laws regulating these marketing activities.

Companies are now recognizing the marketing value of product *design* — especially appearance design. Two related factors are product *colour* and product *quality*. Selecting the right colour is a marketing advantage.

Projecting the appropriate quality image is essential. In addition, *warranties* and *servicing* require considerable management attention these days because of consumer complaints and governmental regulations in these areas.

QUESTIONS AND PROBLEMS

1. List five brand names that you think are good ones, and five that you consider poor. Explain the reasoning behind your choices.

2. Evaluate each of the following brand names in light of the characteristics of a good brand, indicating the strong and weak points of each name:
   a. Xerox (office copiers)
   b. IBM (business machines)
   c. Mustang (automobiles)
   d. Hush Puppies (shoes)
   e. A-1 (steak sauce)
   f. Hotpoint (appliances)

3. Suggest some brands that are on the verge of becoming generic. What course of action should a company take to protect the separate identity of its brand?

4. Under what conditions would you recommend that a manufacturer brand a product that will be used as a part or material in the production of another product?

5. In which of the following cases should the company adopt the strategy of family branding?
   a. A manufacturer of men's electric razors introduces a model for women.
   b. A manufacturer of women's cologne and deodorants adds men's after-shave lotion to the product lines.
   c. A producer of mattresses introduces a line of electric blankets.

6. Suppose you are employed by the manufacturer of a well-known brand of skis. Your company is planning to add ice skates and water skis to its product line. It has no previous experience with either of these two new products. You are given the assignment of selecting a brand name for the ice skates and water skis. Your main problem is in deciding whether to adopt a family-brand policy. That is, should you use the ski brand name for either or both of the new products? Or, should you develop separate names for each of the new items? You note that Campbell's (soups) and Heinz (pickle products) use family brands. You also note that Sears and Procter & Gamble generally do the opposite. They use different names for each *group of products* (Sears) or each *separate product* (P&G). What course of action would you recommend? Why?

7. A manufacturer of a well-known brand of ski boots acquired a division of a company that marketed a well-known brand of skis. What brand strategy should the new organization adopt? Should all products (skis and boots) now carry the boot brand? Should they carry the ski brand? Is there still some other alternative that you feel would be better?

8. Why do some firms sell an identical product under more than one of their own brands?

9. Assume that a large department-store chain proposed to the manufacturers of Maytag washing machines that Maytag supply the department store with machines carrying the store's brand. What factors should Maytag's management consider in making a decision? If the product were General Foods' Jell-O, to what extent would the situation be different?

10. Give examples of products that are excellently packaged. Mention some that are very poorly packaged.

11. What changes would you recommend in the typical packaging of these products?
   a. Cornflakes   c. Pepsi-Cola
   b. Toothpaste   d. Typing paper

12. If grade labelling is adopted, what factors should be used as bases for grading the following products?
   a. Sheets and pillowcases
   b. Suntan lotion
   c. Canned peaches

13. Give examples of products for which the careful use of the colour of the product has increased sales. Can you cite examples to show that poor use of colour may hurt a company's marketing program?

14. Explain the relationship between a product warranty on small electric appliances and the manufacturer's distribution system for these products.

15. How would the warranty policies set by a manufacturer of skis differ from those adopted by an automobile manufacturer?

Case 8
Dumore Stapler Company

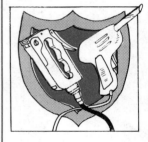

Adding a New Product

The owner and general manager of the Dumore Stapler Company, Klaus Seel, recently was approached by a representative of Becton Adhesives Company. The representative wanted Dumore to distribute Becton's new product — a hot-melt, epoxy-glue gun.

The Dumore Stapler Company was an exclusive distributor for the Viking brand of industrial pneumatic fasteners. When Mr. Seel started the Dumore Company twenty-five years ago, Viking's product line consisted of one pneumatic stapling tool that was used in furniture upholstering operations. Through the years, Viking expanded its line of staplers. Currently, Dumore could provide an assortment and quality of pneumatic tools necessary for performing all the fastening operations in a wide variety of industries. The availability of this wide assortment of fastening tools helped Dumore to increase its sales of the fasteners themselves. Actually, the fasteners were part of the product line that accounted for the largest share of sales revenues and profits. In fact, Dumore provided both the pneumatic staplers and a maintenance service free of charge to very large accounts. Dumore's high volume of staples and other fasteners sold to these accounts justified that firm's investment in the tools and servicing.

Dumore was the exclusive distributor of Viking products in a territory comprising most of southern and eastern Ontario, excluding the City of Toronto. Major offices with merchandising inventories were located in Hamilton and Kingston. Smaller sales and service offices were located in three other cities. Dumore employed twelve sales representatives. Some of these reps did only selling or only product servicing. Other reps performed both sales and servicing activities. Dumore's sales volume last year was about $2.5 million. Mr. Seel estimated that his firm held about 25 percent of the market in his region.

Most of that sales volume came from sales to manufacturers of trailers, campers, mobile homes, and furniture. The construction industry, after years of resisting pneumatic fasteners, was beginning to use these products in increasing numbers.

While new uses for fasteners were being discovered all the time, competition in this field continued to be very keen. Dumore's strongest competitor was the Bostitch Company. Other major competitors were Swingline, Senco, Paslode, and a German company.

Dumore's sales of the Viking line of fasteners had been increasing steadily and quite satisfactorily over the past several years. In fact, Mr. Seel was afraid he might be doing too well — Viking had a history of eliminating (bypassing) distributors that had done exceptionally well in developing their territories. That is, after a distributor had built up the business, Viking would use its own sales forces to sell directly to this market. Thus, that distributor was eliminated from the Viking distribution channel.

Currently, however, Dumore was experiencing a slump in sales, primarily because of an economic slowdown that had particularly affected the furniture and mobile home industries. In light of these two factors — Mr. Seel's fear of losing the Viking franchise, plus his heavy dependence on these key industries — he was considering adding a new product to his company's product mix. Mr. Seel knew several independent Viking distributors who carried non-Viking packaging products such as tape, boxes, and steel banding. In fact, in the past Mr. Seel had carried some non-Viking products himself.

The representative from the Becton Adhesive Company was trying to interest Mr. Seel in an exclusive distributorship for the hot-melt, epoxy-glue guns. Hot-melt plugs of epoxy glue, which resemble stubby candles, were inserted into the gun, and the glue was melted right in the gun. Application was easy — just point the gun and squeeze the trigger. The nature of epoxy glue caused glue buildup in the gun, which required regular servicing to stay operable. Epoxy glue is very strong, and it can be used in a number of fastening operations such as packaging, carpentry, and assembly. The gun would sell for $400 to users. This price was comparable with that of similar competitive products.

Mr. Seel felt that the convenience of use, plus the labour-saving feature of the glue gun, would make it attractive to potential users. He anticipated, however, that the market-education job would take some time and expense. He also believed that it would be difficult to make an accurate estimate of the volume potential for the product in Dumore's territory. He thought the product could be used especially in cabinetry and packaging operations.

Mr. Seel anticipated that he could sell the glue gun to some of his present accounts. However, some of that new business would come at the expense of staple sales, which would continue to be the backbone of Dumore's business. Consequently, Mr. Seel also realized that he would have to generate new accounts not currently buying from Dumore.

One question in Mr. Seel's mind was whether he could use his existing sales force to sell the glue gun. Another Viking distributor had set up a separate sales force to handle a product similar to the glue gun. Seel wondered about the costs of organizing, selecting, and training a new sales force in a partly new market.

Mr. Seel also was concerned about what Viking's reaction would be if Dumore added the Becton glue gun. Currently, Dumore's line consisted almost entirely of Viking products. Also, the glue gun would compete directly with some of the Viking products. While Mr. Seel did not approve of all Viking's policies, he had a generally good relationship with this supplier. This relationship was important, because in the past he had had some unhappy experiences with other suppliers.

Mr. Seel preferred to investigate the Becton offer in more depth. However, there was not much time. He had to give Becton an answer soon, or run the risk that the offer would be withdrawn and perhaps made to a competing distributor in Dumore's market area.

Question

Should Mr. Seel add the Becton glue gun to the Dumore product mix?

Adding a New Line of Products

Julie Gibson, the founder and owner of the Peter Rabbit Toy Shoppe, was considering the feasibility of expanding into juvenile furniture. The city in which her toy store was located currently had no full-line children's furniture store. Julie felt the time was right and the market was right for Peter Rabbit to add the new line. At the same time, however, she realized that, potentially, there were some significant problems connected with this proposed expansion.

The Peter Rabbit Toy Shoppe was located in Rockwood Mall, a small shopping centre in Port Moody, British Columbia. Port Moody is only 30 kilometres from downtown Vancouver. The store had opened a little over four years ago.

Last year Peter Rabbit recorded a net profit of 5 percent on sales of $450,000. Ms. Gibson expected that this year's sales volume would exceed the half-million mark. The main reason for this projected increase was that a major competitor in the area had moved to another city. Julie was hoping to capture the market share previously held by this store.

Julie felt that her store was in reasonably good financial condition. Each year Peter Rabbit's earnings were reinvested in the firm. Most of the initial bank loan had been paid off. This was a loan (along with Julie and her husband's own capital) that had been invested in opening inventory and the necessary furniture and fixtures. Neither Julie nor her husband Kerry, who helped to operate the store, had drawn any salaries since the store opened. If all went well this year, however, Ms. Gibson hoped to start drawing a salary next year.

Peter Rabbit carried only those toys that fitted in with Julie Gibson's philosophy about toys and children. She believed that "toys should be emotionally healthy for children and should be something they are able to love." Thus, for example, her store did not carry guns or soldiers. The products that she did carry were unique, hard to find, durable, and of high quality. She did not carry toys that were nationally advertised, because the local discount stores could sell these products at prices lower than those at which she could buy them.

The line of products that Ms. Gibson was considering adding included a full range of children's furniture and accessories for ages up to fourteen. The furniture assortment would range from cribs, high chairs, and diapering tables to bunkbeds, desks, and dressers. The accessories would include bedding items, lamps, and wall decorations.

Most of the proposed inventory would reflect the quality image that Peter Rabbit tried to project in its selection of toys. Ms. Gibson intended to carry some expensive, unique items even if they did not sell quickly. She felt that products of this nature would attract the higher-income clientele and perpetuate her desired store image. At the same time, she intended to stock in depth the basic items that would account for the bulk of the sales volume. She also wanted to attract lower-income buyers by carrying some articles that would appeal to that segment. She planned to import from foreign suppliers, as well as buy from Canadian companies. Most of the inventory would carry a markup of 50 percent of the retail selling price — the customary markup in furniture retailing.

To expand into juvenile furniture, Peter Rabbit would have to double its present floor space to 900 square metres. The shopping centre developers agreed to add this additional floor space by constructing a new building that would be connected with the present Peter Rabbit store. The additional space would rent annually for $180 per square metre. Gibson estimated she would need capital of $150,000 for the new inventory and store furniture and fixtures.

Julie intended to display the furniture and accessories in room groupings. This would help shoppers visualize how a baby's, child's, or teenager's room would look. By grouping the furniture in this manner, Julie thought the customer would be more likely to buy an entire ensemble.

At the present time, no specialty juvenile furniture stores existed in the Port Moody area. Most stores offered only fragmented lines of children's furniture, with no accessories and usually of low quality. To purchase children's furniture, area residents had three options — to buy through a mail-order catalogue, to shop at the local discount stores, or to drive to Vancouver. Since there were no local full-line stores, most people did drive to Vancouver.

Julie and Kerry Gibson were reviewing some of the market data they had collected. In 1981, the Vancouver Census Metropolitan Area, in which Port Moody is located, had a population of 1,268,000. The population of Port Moody itself was 15,000. Port Moody is a middle-income community and a large number of young professional people live there, generally commuting to their jobs in Vancouver. The city is located at the end of Burrard Inlet and is surrounded by Burnaby (population 137,000) and Coquitlam (population 61,000). A large part of Port Moody's economy was dependent on the logging industry and on Simon Fraser University, which is located nearby.

Looking further at national demographic data, Julie noticed that juvenile furniture sales were directly related to the number of women giving birth to their first child. About one-half of all first-born children were born to parents who had been married three years or less. Also, about one-half of all women giving birth were under twenty-five years of age. In many of the families with young children in the Port Moody area, both parents were working. Through the late 1980s the birthrate was expected to remain close to the relatively low level of the 1970s and early 1980s. Government agencies had forecast a slowly expanding market for child-related industries into the 1990s.

Kerry Gibson did not think that Peter Rabbit should add the proposed line of juvenile furniture. Although both toys and furniture were intended for the same ultimate users — children — he felt that they were not a compatible combination in the same store. He feared that people would not think of buying good furniture in a toy shop. Furthermore, he was afraid that by adding a line of furniture, Peter Rabbit would blur its image as a high-class toy store.

He questioned whether Peter Rabbit had the executive know-how to buy and market furniture. "Even the company name does not project a satisfactory image for furniture retailing," he said. Both he and Julie also were concerned about their projected cash flow and other financial considerations. Furniture typically was considered a big-ticket item (high unit value), and the average furniture store had a low rate of stock turnover.

Question

Should the Peter Rabbit Toy Shoppe add the proposed line of juvenile furniture?

Brand Strategy

Case 10 Dependable Drugs*

Two brothers, Ed and Jim Henderson, owned and operated a chain of five retail drugstores, doing business under the name of Dependable Drugs. From the time they started in business, Ed and Jim had consistently followed the policy of carrying only nationally branded merchandise — that is, well-known manufacturers' brands. In recent months, however, they had come to realize that inflation was making the customers increasingly price-conscious. The brothers also had observed that some supermarket chains had introduced, with apparent success, a line of products being sold without any brand name. These products were simply labelled with the generic name of the article — beans, peanut butter, or paper towels, for example. As a result of these various developments, the Henderson brothers were wondering whether they should add a line of products under their own store name — in effect, their own "private brand."

The Dependable Drugs stores were located in small shopping centres and residential areas in the Halifax-Dartmouth metropolitan area of Nova Scotia. Ed Henderson was a registered pharmacist, and his brother, Jim, had a degree in Business Administration from a local university.

The brothers started in business about twenty years ago when they purchased their father's drugstore, which was located in an old, established residential neighbourhood. Several years later, an uncle, who also owned a retail drug business, died very suddenly. His widow offered his store to Ed and Jim at a relatively low price. The remaining three units in the Dependable Drugs chain were started as new stores in nearby suburban shopping centres.

The first two stores in the Dependable Drugs chain were being successfully operated as full-service businesses when the Henderson brothers acquired them. The other three stores, however, had presented quite a different business situation. These stores were started from scratch as far as location, customers, fixtures, reputation, and managerial policies were concerned. Consequently, they had presented a series of challenging elements of entrepreneurship not experienced in the first two stores.

---

*This case has been adapted from the original, prepared by Walter F. Rohrs. Used with permission.

Business in the new stores initially was slow, despite elaborate "grand opening" promotional efforts. During succeeding months, the sales volume increased moderately. However, neither the sales volume nor the profit had yet come up to the owners' expectations.

The original store had a large cellar, which the company still used as its main storage area. For two reasons, however, this storage area was rapidly becoming overcrowded. First, Dependable Drugs had to buy some products in large amounts in order to obtain the quantity discounts that helped meet the keen price competition. Second, there was a stream of new sizes, colours, and varieties of existing products, plus a flow of new products, which the Henderson's felt they had to carry.

The Hendersons believed that their policy of stocking only national (manufacturers') branded merchandise was a good one. With such a policy, they could trade on the general consumer acceptance of national brands as well as the fine reputation of large, well-known organizations. Furthermore, these products typically were heavily advertised and otherwise promoted by the manufacturers.

Over the past several months, clerks in all the Dependable Drugs stores had observed that customers were becoming very price-conscious. In some instances, they even brought in newspaper ads of other local retailers showing nationally branded products at prices considerably lower than those charged by Dependable Drugs. Some customers said they did not mind paying a few cents more at Dependable Drugs, but 15 to 20 percent on an item was just too much. Consequently, the sales of some proprietary (nonprescription) medicines had been declining.

During their recent regular Friday afternoon business meetings, Ed and Jim had been discussing this problem of lost sales caused by intense price competition. They had explored several options, one of which was to market a line of products under their own private brand — the Dependable Drugs brand. At the same time, however, they were uncertain regarding whether or not they should go the private-brand route.

Jim had gathered detailed information and samples from a number of sources that could provide top-grade products under the Dependable Drugs brand. The prices of these products were generally much lower than the prices of similar products carrying the manufacturers' brands. This was the case even though the product-quality specifications on the private-branded merchandise were as good as, or better than, the specifications for the national brands.

Jim and Ed recognized there were advantages to their marketing a group of products under the Dependable Drugs brand. These products could be sold at lower prices than the nationally branded items. Also, by using a private brand, Dependable Drugs largely eliminated price comparisons with competitive products. The Hendersons were impressed by the fact that the large national drug chains, such as Shoppers Drug Mart, had been marketing under a private brand for years. In fact, the brothers were enthusiastic enough to have selected a brand name — "Double D" — in the event they decided to go the private-brand route.

At the same time, Ed and Jim recognized they were likely to encounter problems with a private brand. Ed pointed out that consumer resistance was likely to be strong, at least in the beginning. He said that strong emotional considerations were involved in the purchase of many drugstore products. Dependable Drugs would have to educate its customers and build consumer confidence in the Double D brand. Store personnel would have to explain to customers that Dependable Drug's products were, by law, at least the equivalent of the better-known national brands. Ed also stressed that Dependable Drugs would need a carefully planned promotional effort and a strong money-back guarantee of quality.

Both brothers were concerned with the potential warehousing, inventory control, and financing problems that they might face. Already their cellar warehouse often was close to being full. Financing pressures might increase because private-brand suppliers often required large minimum orders.

Jim then raised another question. "Supposing we decide to go the private-brand route," he said. "Then we have to consider how extensively we should apply the Double D brand. Do we put it on just a few products where we face the greatest price competition? Or, do we use our brand over a wider range of products and product lines?"

Ed suggested they might start by using the Double D brand on about twenty fast-moving items such as vitamins, rubbing alcohol, and talcum powder.

Jim recalled the experiences of a drug retailer in another city who had plunged in with a private brand on a broad assortment of products. And, he pointed out, the guy had been pretty successful at it.

Ed was wondering if Dependable Drugs could draw on the recent experiences that supermarket chains were having with generic brands. "They started out with only a few items," he observed, "and now they have generic toothpaste, suntan lotion, paper products, and lots of other non-food items. Should we follow their policy?"

Questions

1. Should Dependable Drugs adopt a private-brand policy?
2. If your decision is yes, what products should carry the Double D brand?
3. Should Dependable Drugs add a line of generic "branded" products?

Product Strategies for a New Brand

Mr. Don Evans, president of The Newfoundland Tea Company, had just received confirmation that his bank had agreed in principle to provide a limited line of credit for the development and marketing of his new consumer brand, Bentley Fresh Brew Tea; final approval would depend on its perceived viability, as evidenced by the marketing plan he was to produce prior to their next meeting. The main task facing him at present was to plan and develop the actual product itself, and to finalize various product strategies for Bentley Fresh Brew Tea. Information on consumers' brand choice criteria is presented in Table B-1.

Case 11
Bentley
Fresh Brew
*Tea (B)**

*Refer to Part (A) of this case for essential background and statistical information on the market, competition, and the brand.

Table B-1   MOST IMPORTANT BRAND CHOICE CRITERIA

("What is the most important reason why you buy your regular brand of tea bags rather than any other brand?")

	Low Price	Strong Taste	Dark Colour	Fresh	Quick Brew	Other
I *Age**						
Less than 25	31%	0%	4%	18%	26%	21%
25 to 34	12	32	6	32	14	4
35 to 49	10	40	7	28	8	7
50 or more	7	46	9	24	6	8
II *Household Consumption Per Month*						
Light	8%	28%	4%	31%	7%	22%
Medium	12	35	6	26	15	6
Heavy	6	54	7	20	9	4
III *"Regular" Brand**						
Tetley Users	11%	36%	6%	24%	16%	7%
Red Rose Users	4	47	3	28	0	18
Users of Other Brands	9	50	7	21	9	4
IV *Total Sample*	10%	40%	6%	24%	12%	11%

*indicates chi-square statistic significant at the 0.05 level.

The first major product strategy decision facing Mr. Evans was to determine the actual composition of the product. He had obtained samples of many varieties of tea from various tea plantations and agents throughout the world; each tea was distinctive in some characteristic (such as taste, colour, or price) and therefore the number of combinations and blends was endless. In simplest terms, there were three broad possible strategies: develop a blend that was slightly inferior to one or more competitors, develop a superior blend, or match the competition.

Each product composition alternative had far-reaching implications for each of the other elements of the marketing mix (distribution, promotion, and particularly price), as well as the overall "positioning" of the brand. The first alternative, to use a blend of cheaper and slightly lower-quality teas, would reduce product costs — and reduced costs would permit Bentley Fresh Brew to attain adequate profit margins while selling at lower retail prices than Tetley and Red Rose (one store manager had suggested that the new brand should be priced low because consumers were becoming more and more price sensitive). Alternatively, the savings in cost could be used to increase the profits of the firm, or to engage in more aggressive advertising and promotional activities.

A second strategy, as noted above, might be to develop a superior blend of quality teas. According to many industry observers, the overall quality of teas marketed in the western world has decreased over the years — a factor that may have contributed to the current situation of decreasing per capita consumption. Being something of a tea connoisseur, Mr. Evans had a slight preference for this strategy; however, he realized the difficulty

Table B-2 USUAL PACKAGE SIZE PURCHASED

	Small (less than 60 bags) %	**Medium** (60 to 72 bags) %	**Large** (more than 72 bags) %
I *Age**			
Less than 25	4%	96%	0%
25 to 34	0	78	22
35 to 49	0	70	30
50 or more	8	75	17
II *"Regular" Brand**			
Tetley	3%	76%	21%
Red Rose	8	64	28
Other	10	48	42
III *Total Sample*	6%	68%	26%

*indicates chi-square statistic significant at the 0.05 level.

of ascertaining whether a "superior" tea would be perceived as such by consumers. In addition, any attempt to upgrade quality above the levels of existing brands would result in either higher retail prices or decreased profit margins.

A third strategy, often termed the "me too" approach by marketers, would be to match the competition on one or more characteristics; unfortunately, this strategy does not foster any differentiation of brand preference among consumers, although it could reduce risk of failure by catering to existing taste preferences. However, one uncertainty here would be which brand to match: Red Rose, Tetley, King Cole, or others?

One potential advantage for Bentley Fresh Brew, notwithstanding the choice of the abovementioned alternatives, is freshness; given his direct contact with tea plantations and agents, and his company's small size and physical proximity to the market, Mr. Evans felt Bentley could be from two to eight months fresher than any other brand at the time of purchase by consumers. However, he feared that such an advantage might not be discerned by the average tea drinker.

Type of overwrap (i.e. material used to contain the tea) for the individual tea bags was also yet to be determined. The existing plant equipment could package Bentley Fresh Brew in a number of different overwrap materials: (1) a synthetic gauze covering, as used by Red Rose and King Cole; (2) a perforated webbing, as used and advertised by Tetley; and (3) a paper-based material, as used primarily by polybag brands. All three types were readily available from suppliers; however, the paper-based overwrap was only one-half the cost of the other two materials, which were similarly priced.

Package design was another critical product decision yet to be made. Cost estimates ranged from $600 for a simple, two-colour design without illustrations, photography, or elaborate graphics and up to $12,000 for a professionally produced and appealing four-colour design utilizing illustrations and photography of a place setting, shadings of colour from the centre to edges of the front panel, and distinctive layout and graphics. Another packaging alternative was to use a package with a distinctive shape or size (rather than the normal rectangular box) or one that was re-usable or collectable. In addition, he considered using a "flash" on the front panel of whichever package design was adopted; such a "flash" was sometimes used by national brands to announce "NEW," "COUPON INSIDE," or some other message in an effort to increase the visibility of the package on the supermarket shelf. During the course of his investigations, he talked to several women at the nearby Co-op supermarket; one felt strongly that package design did not influence her choice of brand for any product, remarking "Who cares about the package? It's what's inside that counts!"

Another critical product strategy decision yet to be made related to package size: how many different sizes of packages to offer, as well as the actual number and sizes of tea bags for each package size. Mr. Evans was pondering the implications of introducing one "regular" package size versus following the practice of the major brands by having up to seven different sizes of packages. Another key decision had to be made regarding the actual number of tea bags in each package size. Should Mr. Evans have the same number of tea bags per package as one of the existing brands, or should he introduce Bentley Fresh Brew with different numbers of tea bags per package than currently available? A related strategic decision had to be made regarding the amount of tea to package in each bag: the standard two-cup size of the major brands; a smaller amount, to decrease costs; or a larger amount such as a three-cup bag? Selected consumer research results are presented in Tables B-1 and B-2.

Questions

1. What would you recommend to Mr. Evans in each of the following product strategy areas? Substantiate your recommendations.
     (i)   Product composition/blend
    (ii)   Product "positioning"
   (iii)   Type of overwrap
   (iv)   Package design
    (v)   Number of package sizes (depth)
   (vi)   Number of tea bags for each package size
  (vii)   Size/weight of each tea bag

2. Are there any other decisions Mr. Evans needs to make in the product strategy area? What are they?

The Price

THE DEVELOPMENT AND USE OF A PRICING STRUCTURE
AS PART OF THE FIRM'S MARKETING MIX

We are in the process of developing a strategic marketing mix to reach our target markets and achieve our marketing goals. With our product planning completed, we now turn our attention to the pricing ingredient in the marketing mix. In the strategic planning for — and development of — the pricing structure, we face two broad tasks. First, we must determine the base price for a product, including a decision on our pricing objectives. These topics are covered in Chapters 11 and 12. Second, we must decide on the strategies (such as discounts) to employ in modifying and applying the base price. These strategies are discussed in Chapter 13.

Chapter 11

Pricing Objectives and Price Determination

CHAPTER GOALS

In this chapter we discuss the role of price in the marketing mix — what it can do and how it can be used. After studying the chapter, you should understand:

1. *The meaning of price*
2. *The importance of price in our economy and in an individual firm*
3. *The major pricing goals*
4. *A procedure for price determination*
5. *The idea of an "expected" price*
6. *"Skimming" pricing and "penetration" pricing as alternative pricing strategies*

"How much do you think we ought to sell it for?" This is a question frequently asked by executives who have the responsibility for pricing the products or services they are marketing. The question would be more accurately worded if they asked, "How much do you think people will pay for this item?" or "How much should we ask for it?" The question would then be in accord with the generalization that *prices are always on trial*. A price is simply an offer or an experiment to test the pulse of the market. If customers accept the offer, then the price is fine. If they reject it, the price usually will be changed quickly, or the product may even be withdrawn from the market. Before being concerned with actual price determination, however, executives should understand the meaning and importance of price, and they should decide on their pricing goals.

IMPORTANCE OF PRICE

In the Economy

Pricing is considered by many to be the key activity within a free-enterprise system. The market price of a product influences wages, rent, interest, and profits. That is, the price of a product influences the price paid for the factors of production — labour, land, capital, and entrepreneurship. Price thus is a basic regulator of the economic system because it influences the allocation of these factors of production. High wages attract labour, high interest rates attract capital, and so on. In its role as an allocator of scarce resources, price determines what will be produced (supply) and who will get how much of the goods and services that are produced (demand).

Pricing takes on added importance during periods of inflation and recession, such as we have been experiencing for the past several years in Canada as well as in other countries. Consumer confidence in the economy, consumer buying psychology, and consumer buying behaviour are especially affected by price movements during such periods.

Criticism of the economic system, and the public's demand for further restraints, are often triggered by a reaction to price or to pricing policies.

The price of a product or service is a major determinant of the market demand for the item. Price affects the firm's competitive position and its share of the market. As a result, price has a considerable bearing on the company's revenue and net profit.

In the Individual Firm

The price of a product also affects the firm's marketing program. In product planning, for example, management may decide to improve the quality of its product or add differentiating features. This decision can be implemented only if the market will accept a price high enough to cover the costs of these changes.

At the same time, there usually are forces that limit the importance of pricing in a company's marketing program. Differentiated product features or a favorite brand may be more important to consumers than price. In fact, as noted in Chapter 10, one object of branding is to decrease the effect of price on the demand for a product. Such forces tend to make prices more rigid or "sticky" — that is, less responsive to changes in demand or supply. Thus, the traditional, theoretical role of price as an allocator of scarce resources is modified somewhat in today's economic system.

To put the role of pricing in a company's marketing program in its proper perspective, then, let us say that price is important, but not all-important, in explaining marketing success. The current state of the economy has a considerable influence on the importance that business executives attach to pricing relative to other marketing activities. When economic conditions are good and consumers feel relatively affluent, then price is not rated as important as product planning or promotional activity. During periods of recession and inflation, however, executives consider that pricing is an extremely important activity contributing to marketing success.[1]

Some of the psychological aspects of pricing should also be understood by marketing executives. For instance, consumers rely heavily on price as an indicator of a product's quality, especially when they must make purchase decisions with incomplete information. Studies have consistently shown

Price and Product-Quality Relationship

---

[1]See William B. Wagner, "Changing Industrial Buyer-Seller Pricing Concerns," *Industrial Marketing Management*, April 1981, pp. 109–117.

that consumers' perceptions of product quality vary directly with price.[2] Thus, the higher the price, the better the quality is perceived to be. Consumers make this judgement particularly when no other clues as to product quality are available. Consumers' quality perceptions can, of course, also be influenced by store reputation, advertising, and other variables.

MEANING OF PRICE

Undoubtedly, many of the difficulties associated with pricing start with the rather simple fact that often we do not really know what we are talking about. That is, we do not know the meaning of the word *price*, even though it is true that the concept is quite easy to define in familiar terms.

In economic theory, we learn that price, value, and utility are related concepts. **Utility** is the attribute of an item that makes it capable of want-satisfaction. **Value** is the quantitative measure of the worth of a product to attract other products in exchange. We may say the value of a certain hat is three baseball bats, or a box of red Delicious apples, or 30 litres of gasoline. Because our economy is not geared to a slow, ponderous barter system, we use money as a common denominator of value. And we use the term *price* to describe the money value of an item. **Price** is value expressed in terms of dollars and cents, or any other monetary medium of exchange.

Practical problems arise in connection with a definition of price, however, when we try to state simply the price of a quart of fresh strawberries, or an office desk. Suppose Helen paid $1.10 for a carton of strawberries, while Bill paid only 55 cents for a carton and was allowed to eat all the additional strawberries he wanted at the seller's location. And suppose the price quoted to Helen for an office desk was $325, while Bill paid only $175.

At first glance it looks as if Bill got the better deal in each example. Yet, when we get all the facts, we may change our opinion. Helen bought her strawberries at the local supermarket. Bill responded to a strawberry grower's advertisement that stated that if one came out to the farm and picked the berries, they would cost 55 cents a carton. The grower allowed Bill to eat all he wanted while he was berry picking. Helen's desk was delivered to her office, she had a year to pay for it, and it was beautifully finished. Bill bought a partially assembled desk with no finish on it. (He was a do-it-yourself fan.) He had to assemble the drawers and legs and then painstakingly stain, varnish, and hand-rub the entire desk. He arranged for the delivery himself, and he paid cash in full at the time of purchase. Now let us ask who paid the higher price in each case. The answer is not as easy as it seemed at first glance.

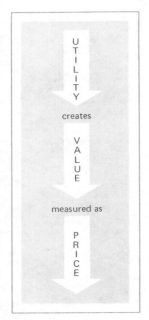

U T I L I T Y

creates

V A L U E

measured as

P R I C E

[2]For a summary of several of these studies, see Kent B. Monroe, "Buyers' Subjective Perceptions of Price," *Journal of Marketing Research*, February 1973, pp. 70–80; also see Peter C. Riesz, "Price versus Quality in the Marketplace," *Journal of Retailing*, Winter 1978, pp. 15–28.

For the contention that price often is not a good indicator of product quality, see Ruby T. Morris and Claire S. Bronson, "The Chaos of Competition Indicated by Consumer Reports," *Journal of Marketing*, July 1969, pp. 26–34; and John E. Swan, "Price-Product Performance Competition between Retailer and Manufacturer Brands," *Journal of Marketing*, July 1974, pp. 52–59.

These examples illustrate how difficult it is to define price in an everyday business situation. Many variables are involved. The definition hinges on the problem of determining exactly what is being sold. This relates to a problem posed in Chapter 8, that of trying to define a product. In pricing, we must consider more than the physical product alone. A seller usually is pricing a combination of the physical product and several services and want-satisfying benefits. Sometimes it is difficult even to define the price of the physical product alone. On one model of automobile, a stated price may include radio, power steering, and power brakes. For another model of the same make of car, these three items may be priced separately.

In summary, **price** is the amount of money (plus possibly some goods) that is needed to acquire some combination of a product and its accompanying services.

NEW FLEXIBILITY IN PRICING[3]

Traditionally, the pricing structure in most large companies, especially in manufacturing firms, was rather rigid. Some companies added a fixed markup percentage onto their costs to arrive at a selling price, even during periods of declining demand. Other firms tended to follow the customary price charged by the industry leader. Still other companies set a price that they believed would bring them a certain percentage return on their investment over the long run.

Obviously, competition would force some deviations from these rigid structures. Nevertheless, the aim was to have a structure in which price generally held firm, and any price changes were predictable. But, since the late 1970s, many companies have found themselves caught by inflationary costs, stagnant demand, and increasing competition from foreign companies. One net result of these external forces has been to move companies away from their past policy of price rigidity.

---

[3]This section is adapted in part from "Flexible Pricing," *Business Week*, December 12, 1977, p. 78.

Today, many of these firms are finding that pricing is a different ball game. Today, the key word is *flexibility* — a willingness to cut prices to hold a market share. There is less rigid adherence to a fixed markup over cost or a follow-the-industry-leader policy. In effect, marketers are adding price to their kit of aggressive marketing tools, along with promotion and new-product planning.

Look at a few illustrative examples. Modified government reglations have caused airlines to feature a variety of discount fares. Gasoline pricing has shifted considerably from the days when the major brands in one market all charged the same price and minor brands were two or three cents a gallon less. Some smaller steel companies cut the price on some items below the level set by the industry's price leaders.

As we shall see in the next section, companies still are setting the traditional pricing goals. But today management is employing a more flexible approach in achieving these goals.

PRICING OBJECTIVES

Every marketing task — including (and perhaps, especially) pricing — must be directed toward the achievement of a goal. In other words, management should decide on its pricing *objective* before determining the price itself. Yet, as logical as this may be, very few firms consciously establish, or explicity state, their pricing objective.

The main goals in pricing are oriented either toward profit, toward sales, or toward maintaining the status quo. They are:

- Profit-oriented, to:
  a. Achieve target return on investment or on net sales
  b. Maximize profit

- Sales-oriented, to:
  a. Increase sales
  b. Maintain or increase market share

- Status quo–oriented, to:
  a. Stabilize prices
  b. Meet competition

The pricing goal that management selects should be entirely compatible with the goals set for the company and its marketing program. To illustrate, let's assume that the company's goal is to increase its return on investment from the present level of 15 percent to a level of 20 percent at the end of a three-year period. Then it follows that the pricing goal during this period must be to achieve some stated percentage return on investment. It would not be logical, in this case, to adopt the pricing goal of maintaining the company's market share or of stabilizing prices.

Profit-Oriented Goals

By selecting profit maximization or a target return, management focuses its attention on profit generation. Profit goals may be set for either the short run or for longer periods of time.

WHAT YOU PAY IS THE PRICE FOR WHAT YOU GET

"That which we call a rose by any other name would smell as sweet."
—*Romeo and Juliet*, Act II, Scene 2

Tuition	Education
Interest	Use of money
Rent	Use of living quarters or a piece of equipment for a period of time
Fare	Taxi or bus ride
Fee	Services of a physician or lawyer
Retainer	Lawyer's services over a period of time
Toll	Long-distance phone call or travel on some highways
Salary	Services of an executive or other white-collar worker
Wage	Services of a blue-collar worker
Commission	Salesperson's services
Honorarium	Guest speaker
Dues	Membership in a union or a club

— then in socially undesirable situations, some people pay a price called blackmail, ransom, or bribery.

Source: Suggested, in part, by David J. Schwartz, *Marketing Today: A Basic Approach*, 2d ed., Harcourt Brace Jovanovich, New York, 1977, p. 520.

Achieve Target Return

A firm may price its products or services to achieve a certain percentage return on its *investment* or on its *sales*. Such goals are used by both middlemen and manufacturers.

Many retailers and wholesalers use target return on *net sales* as a pricing objective for short-run periods. They set a percentage markup on sales that is large enough to cover anticipated operating costs plus a desired profit for the year. In such cases, the *percentage* of profit may remain constant, but the *dollar* profit will vary according to the number of units sold. In retailing and wholesaling, the typical return on net sales is low. On the average, wholesalers earn about 2 percent on net sales. Retail supermarkets earn about 1 percent, and department stores get about 3 to 4 percent return on net sales.

Achieving a target return on *investment* is typically selected as a goal by manufacturers that are leaders in their industry — companies such as General Motors and Union Carbide (Prestone antifreeze, Eveready batteries). Typical target-return percentages range from 10 to 20 percent after taxes.

The reasoning behind the frequent use of target-return pricing by industry leaders is as follows: A dominant firm can set its pricing goals more independently of competition than can the smaller "follower" firms in the industry. Also, in large multidivisional companies, a target-return goal gives management an objective basis for evaluating the performance of the various divisions.

Maximize Profits

The pricing objective of making as much money as possible is probably followed by a larger number of companies than any other goal. The trouble with this goal is that the term *profit maximization* has an ugly connotation. It is connected in the public mind with profiteering, high prices, and monopoly. In economic theory or business practice, however, there is nothing wrong with profit maximization. Theoretically, if profits become unduly high because supply is short in relation to demand, new capital will be attracted into the field. This will increase supply and eventually reduce profits to normal levels. In the marketplace, it is difficult to find many situations where profiteering has existed over an extended period of time. Substitute products are available, purchases are postponable, and competition can increase to keep prices at a reasonable level. Where prices may be unduly high and entry into the field is severely limited, public outrage soon balances the scales. If market conditions and public opinion do not do the job directly, government restraints will soon bring about moderation.

A profit maximization goal is likely to be far more beneficial to a company and to the public if practised over the *long run*. Pricing by a company that cannot see beyond the end of next month's profit-and-loss statement often results in repercussions that may be detrimental to the firm. Practised over the long run, however, profit maximization should result in a socially desirable allocation of resources. Efficient firms are rewarded, and inefficient firms disappear. Profits attract new capital into the field. Prices tend to remain at a reasonable level, and supply is sufficient to satisfy market demands.

To maximize profits over the long run, firms may have to accept short-run losses. A firm entering a new geographic market or introducing a new product frequently does best by setting low prices to build a large clientele. Such companies often do not expect to show a profit for the first few years, but they are laying a solid foundation for adequate profits over the long run.

The goal should be to maximize profits on *total output* rather than on each single item marketed. A manufacturer may maximize total profits by practically giving away some articles that will attract the buyer's attention or stimulate sales of other goods. For many years, through its sponsored broadcasts and telecasts of athletic events, Gillette frequently promoted razors at very low, profitless prices. Management hoped that once customers acquired Gillette razors, they would become long-term profitable customers for Gillette blades. In this way the company would maximize profits in total but not on each product in its mix. A retailer often finds that the best way to maximize profits for the entire store is to offer well-known items as "leaders." These are sold at a very small profit or even at a loss. But they attract so many customers to the store — customers who stay to buy other items — that the overall profit picture of the store is enhanced considerably.

In some companies, management's pricing attention is focused on sales volume rather than on profits. In these situations, the pricing goal may be to increase sales volume or to maintain or increase the firm's market share.

Sales-Oriented Goals

Increase Sales Volume

This pricing goal is usually stated as a percentage increase in sales volume over some period of time, say, one year or three years. Retailers typically use such a goal as they strive to beat last year's sales volume by some given percentage. However, to increase sales volume may or may not be consistent with the marketing concept that advocates *profitable* sales volume. In one case, a company's goal may be to increase sales volume, but still to maintain its profitability. In another case, management may decide to increase its volume by discounting or some other aggressive pricing strategy, perhaps incurring a loss. Thus, management is willing to take a short-run loss if the increased sales enable the company to get a foothold in its market.

Maintain or Increase Market Share

In some companies, both large and small, the major pricing objective is to maintain or increase the share of the market held by the firm. One factor that makes this a workable goal is that a company can usually determine what share of the market it enjoys. In some respects, market share is a better indicator of corporate health—and thus a better pricing goal—than target return on investment. This is true especially when the total market is growing. Then a firm might be earning what management considers a reasonable return. But if management is not aware that the market is expanding, the company may be getting a decreasing share of that market.

These two closely related goals—to stabilize prices and to meet competition—are the least aggressive of any of the pricing goals.

Status Quo Goals

Stabilize Prices

Price stabilization often is the goal in industries with a price leader. Especially in industries where demand can fluctuate frequently and sometimes considerably, large companies will try to maintain stability in their pricing. Such price leadership does not necessarily mean that all firms in the industry charge the same price as that set by the leader. Price leadership means only that there is some relationship between the leader's prices and those charged by other firms.

A major reason for seeking stability in pricing is to avert price wars, whether demand is increasing or declining. As we noted in the section on pricing flexibility, however, adherence to the industry leader's prices is not as rigid today as it used to be, especially during periods of sluggish demand. In some instances, smaller firms are cutting below the industry price and are not suffering reprisals from the large firms in the industry.

Meet Competition

Countless firms, regardless of size, consciously price their products simply to meet the competition. Large rubber companies, such as Goodyear, for example, believe that they can generally exercise only very little influence on the market-determined price. And, in industries where there is a price leader and where the product is highly standardized, most firms have a follow-the-leader policy.

FACTORS INFLUENCING PRICE DETERMINATION

Knowing their objective, executives can move to the heart of price management—the actual determination of the base price of a product or service. By **base price** (or list price) we mean the price of one unit of the product at its point of production or resale. This is the price before allowance is made for quantity discounts, delivery charges, or any other modification involving pricing strategies such as those discussed in Chapter 13.

The same general procedure is followed in pricing both new and established products. However, the pricing of an established product usually involves little difficulty, because the exact price or a narrow range of prices may be dictated by the market. In the pricing of new products, though, the decisions called for throughout the pricing process typically are important and difficult.

In the price-determination process, several factors usually influence the final decision. The key factors that management should consider are as follows:

1. Demand for the product
2. Target share of the market
3. Competitive reactions
4. Use of skimming pricing or penetration pricing
5. Other parts of the marketing mix—the product, distribution channels, and promotion
6. Costs of producing or buying the product

We shall discuss the first five of these factors in this chapter, and the sixth one in the next chapter.

Estimated Demand for the Product

An important step in pricing a product is to estimate the total demand for it. This is easier to do for an established product than for a new one. Two practical steps in demand estimation are, first, to determine whether there is a price that the market expects and, second, to estimate the sales volumes at different prices.

The "Expected" Price

The "expected" price for a product is the price at which customers consciously or unconsciously value it—what they think the product is worth.

It is almost impossible to estimate an expected price as one specific dollar amount; often the expected price is simply a range. It might be "between $250 and $300" or "not over $10."

Customers sometimes can be surprisingly shrewd in evaluating a product. A new product, however, has little direct competition or price comparability during its early life. Consequently, manufacturers have considerably more latitude in setting prices for new products than for older ones.

A producer must also consider the middlemen's reaction to the price. Middlemen are more likely to give an article favourable treatment in their stores if they approve of its price. Retail or wholesale buyers can frequently examine an item and make an accurate estimate of the selling price that the market will accept.

It is possible to set a price too low. If the price is much lower than what the market expects, sales may be lost. For example, it would probably be a mistake for a well-known cosmetics manufacturer to put a 19-cent price tag on lipstick or to price its imported perfume at $1.29 an ounce. Either customers will be suspicious of the quality of the product, or their self-concepts will not let them use such low-priced merchandise. More than one seller has raised the price of a product and experienced a considerable increase in sales. In terms of market-demand curves, this situation is referred to as **inverse demand** — the higher the price, the greater the unit sales.

Inverse Demand:

Sales go up
with the price.

How do sellers determine expected prices? They may submit articles to experienced retailers or wholesalers for appraisal. A manufacturer of industrial products sometimes approaches engineers working for prospective customers. By showing models or blueprints, the manufacturer can solicit informed judgements on what the price "ought to be." Another possibility is to observe prices of comparable competitive products. A third alternative is to survey potential customers. They may be shown the article and asked what they would pay for it. This approach can bring misleading answers because often there is a considerable difference between what people say the product is worth and what they will actually pay. A much more effective approach is to market the product in a few limited test areas. By trying different prices under controlled research conditions, the seller can determine at least a reasonable range of prices.

Estimates of Sales at Various Prices

It is extremely helpful to estimate what the sales volume will be at several different prices. Here experience with the product or with like products is the best source of information. By estimating the demand for its product at different prices, management is, in effect, determining the demand curve for the item and thus its demand elasticity. A product with an elastic market demand should usually be priced lower than an item with an inelastic demand. These estimates of sales at different prices are important also in determining break-even points, which are discussed in the next chapter.

Target Share of Market   The market share targeted by a company is a major factor to consider in determining the price of a product or service. A company striving to increase its market share may price more aggressively (lower base price, larger discounts) than a firm that wants to maintain its present market share.

The expected share of the market is influenced by present production capacity and ease of competitive entry. It would be a mistake for a firm to aim for a larger share of the market than its plant capacity can sustain. Suppose that a new product is priced low in an attempt to gain a broad market. Then, if the market response is extremely favourable, the company may not be able to fill its orders. So, if management is not interested in expanding its plant because ease of competitive entry will drive down future profits, the initial price should be set relatively high.

Competitive Reactions   Present and potential competition is an important influence in determining a base price. Even a new product is distinctive for only a limited time, until the inevitable competition arrives. The threat of *potential* competition is greatest when the field is easy to enter and the profit prospects are encouraging. Competition can also come from three other sources:

1.   Directly similar products—General Mills Wheaties versus Kellogg's Corn Flakes or General Foods Post Toasties

2.   Available substitutes — steel versus aluminum or plastics

3.   Unrelated products seeking the same consumer dollar

Profit-oriented pricing goals are particularly susceptible to competitive reactions. On the other hand, in a company with status quo pricing goals, management is likely to set its price at the competitive level.

Skimming Pricing versus Penetration Pricing   In the course of pricing a product, especially a new product, management should consider whether to enter the market with a high price or a low price. These opposite alternatives are popularly referred to as *skimming pricing* and *penetration pricing*.[4]

Skimming Pricing

The skimming strategy involves setting a price that is high in the range of expected prices. The seller may continue with this strategy for an indefinite period, or later lower the price to tap other segments of the market. Skimming pricing is particularly suitable for new products because:

1.   In the early stages of a product's life cycle, price is less important, competition is minimal, and the product's distinctiveness lends itself to effective marketing.

---

[4]See Joel Dean, "Pricing Policies for New Products," *Harvard Business Review*, November 1950, pp. 45–53; or the reprint of this article as a *Harvard Business Review* "classic," November–December 1976, pp. 141–153.

2. This strategy can effectively segment the market on an income basis. At first, the product is marketed to that segment that responds to distinctiveness and exclusiveness in a product and is relatively insensitive to price. Later, the seller can lower the price and appeal to segments of the market that are highly sensitive to price.

3. The strategy acts as a strong hedge against a possible mistake in setting the price. If the original price is too high and the market does not respond, management can easily lower it. But it is very difficult to raise a price that has proven to be too low to cover costs.

4. High initial prices can be used to keep demand within the limits of a company's productive capacity.

Penetration Pricing

In penetration pricing, a low initial price is set to reach the mass market immediately. This strategy can also be employed at a later stage in the product's life cycle. Many a firm has saved its product from a premature old age or death simply by switching to penetration pricing from skimming pricing.

Penetration pricing is likely to be more satisfactory than skimming pricing when the following conditions exist:

1. The quantity sold is highly sensitive to price. That is, the product has a highly elastic demand.

2. Substantial reductions in unit production and marketing costs can be achieved through large-scale operations.

3. The product is expected to face very strong competition soon after it is introduced to the market.

4. The high-income market is not large enough to sustain a skimming price.

The nature of the potential competition will critically influence management's choice between the two pricing strategies. If competitors can enter a market quickly, and if the market potential for the product is very promising, management probably should adopt a policy of penetration pricing. Low initial pricing may do two things. First, it may discourage other firms from entering the field. The required investment in production and marketing may be too great relative to the anticipated low profit margin. Second, low initial pricing may give the innovator such a strong hold on its share of the market that future competitors cannot cut into it.[5]

On the other hand, skimming may be more feasible where the market is not large enough to attract the big competitors. While percentage margins may be attractive, the total dollar profits could be too small to attract large firms.

---

[5]See Robert E. Weigand, "'Buying In' to Market Control," *Harvard Business Review*, November–December 1980, pp. 141–149.

Other Parts of the Marketing Mix

In the course of determining the base price, management should consider the other major parts of its marketing mix.

The Product

We have already observed that the price of a product is influenced substantially by whether it is a new item or an older, established one. The importance of the product in its end use must also be considered. To illustrate, there is little price competition among manufacturers of packaging materials or producers of industrial gases, and a stable price structure exists. These industrial products are only an incidental part of the final article, so customers will buy the least expensive product consistent with the required quality. In another product situation, a manufacturer will charge a lower price for a product sold under a middleman's brand than for the same product sold under that manufacturer's brand. The reason is that the middleman's branded item costs less to produce. For example, the costs connected with promoting the manufacturer's own brand usually will not be allocated to the middleman's branded goods.

Channels of Distribution

The channels selected and the types of middlemen used will influence a manufacturer's pricing. A firm selling both through wholesalers and directly to retailers often sets a different factory price for each of these two classes of customers. The price to wholesalers is lower because they perform activities (services) that the manufacturer otherwise would have to perform itself — activities such as providing storage, granting credit to retailers, and selling to small retailers.

Promotional Methods

The promotional methods used, and the extent to which the product is promoted by the manufacturer or middlemen, are still other factors to consider in pricing. If major promotional responsibility is placed upon retailers, they ordinarily will be charged a lower price for a product than if the manufacturer advertises it heavily. Even when a manufacturer promotes heavily, it may want its retailers to use local advertising to tie in with national advertising. Such a decision must be reflected in the manufacturer's price to these retailers.

This chapter and the next one are designed to show how a company can determine a base price for its product or service. So far, we have discussed pricing goals, estimates of expected prices, and some major factors that will influence the price-determination process. In the next chapter, we shall narrow the range of possible prices by discussing the major methods of setting a specific selling price.

In our economy, price is a major regulator because it influences the alloca- **SUMMARY** tion of scarce resources. In individual companies, price is one important factor in determining marketing success. For consumers who lack other information, price often is used as an indicator of quality. The problem is that it is difficult to define price. A rather general definition is this: Price is the amount of money (plus possibly some goods or services) needed to acquire, in exchange, some assortment of a product and its accompanying services. Today, firms show more flexibility in their pricing structures, in contrast to the policy of price rigidity that generally prevailed in the past.

Before setting the base price on a product, management should decide what it is trying to accomplish with its price structure — that is, it should identify its pricing goals. Major pricing objectives are (1) to earn a target return on investment or on net sales, (2) to maximize profits, (3) to increase sales, (4) to gain or hold a target share of the market, (5) to stabilize prices, and (6) to meet competition's prices.

Once a pricing goal has been selected, management should consider several key factors in the course of determining the base price for its product. These influencing factors are:

1. Demand for the product
2. Desired share of the market
3. Competitive reactions
4. Whether to use a skimming or a penetration-pricing strategy
5. Other major parts of the marketing mix
6. Cost of producing or buying the product (as discussed in Chapter 12)

Price 296

Relationship between price and product quality 296

New flexibility in pricing 297

Pricing objectives 298

Target return 299

Maximize profit 300

Market share 301

Price stability 301

Meet competition 302

Base price 302

List price 302

Expected price 302

Inverse demand 303

Skimming pricing 304

Penetration pricing 304

KEY TERMS AND CONCEPTS

QUESTIONS AND PROBLEMS

1. What market factors or forces have served to reduce the importance of the price-setting function in many companies today?
2. Two students paid $1.29 for identical tubes of toothpaste at a leading department store. Yet, one student complained about paying a much higher price than the other. What might be the basis for this complaint?
3. Explain how a firm's pricing objective may influence the promotional program for a product. Which of the six pricing goals involves the largest, most aggressive promotional campaign?

4. "The goal of stabilization is marked by nonaggressive marketing strategies and is usually found only in mature companies." Discuss.

5. What marketing conditions might logically lead a company to set "meeting competition" as a pricing objective?

6. Is profit maximization compatible with each of the other major pricing goals? Explain.

7. What is the expected price for each of the following articles? How did you arrive at your estimate in each instance?
    a. A new type of carbonated cola beverage that holds its carbonation long after it has been opened; packaged in 12-ounce (355 ml) and 2-litre bottles
    b. A nuclear-powered 23-inch table-model television set, guaranteed to run for years without replacement of the original power-generating component; requires no battery or electric wires
    c. An automatic garage-door opener for residential housing

8. Name at least five products for which you think an inverse demand exists. For each product, within which price range does this inverse demand exist?

9. Give some examples of products that have an elastic demand; then name some with an inelastic demand.

10. For each of the following products, do you recommend that the seller adopt a skimming or a penetration-pricing strategy? Support your decision in each instance.
    a. Original models of women's dresses styled and manufactured by Dior
    b. A new wonder drug
    c. An exterior house paint that wears twice as long as any competitive brand
    d. A cigarette *totally* free of tar and nicotine
    e. A tablet that converts a litre of water into a litre of automotive fuel

Basic Methods of Setting Prices

Chapter 12

CHAPTER GOALS

In this chapter we consider price setting relative to product costs, market demand, and competitive prices. The chapter is somewhat more difficult and quantitative than previous chapters. After studying the chapter, you should understand:

1. *The several types of costs that are incurred in producing and marketing a product*
2. *How production and marketing costs are affected by changes in the quantity produced*
3. *The cost-plus method of setting a base price*
4. *The use of break-even analysis in setting a price*
5. *Prices established by considering both supply and demand (costs and anticipated revenues)*
6. *Prices established in relation only to the competitive market price*

In the price-determination discussion in the preceeding chapter, we stopped short of choosing a specific selling price. The next step is to do just that. Over the years, many different methods have been used by individual companies to establish base prices for their products. Most of these approaches to price setting are variations of the following methods:

1. Prices are based on total cost plus a desired profit.
2. Prices are based on a balance between estimates of market demand and of supply (the costs of production and marketing).
3. Prices are based on competitive market conditions.

COST-PLUS PRICING

In its simplest form, cost-plus pricing means setting the price of one unit of a product equal to the unit's total cost plus the desired profit on the unit. As an example, suppose a contractor figures that the labour and materials required to build and sell ten houses will cost $500,000, and that the other expenses (office rent, depreciation on equipment, wages of management, and so on) will equal $100,000. On this total cost of $600,000, the contractor desires a profit of 10 percent of cost. The cost plus the profit amount to $660,000, so each of the ten houses is priced at $66,000.

Table 12-1   EXAMPLE OF COST-PLUS PRICING

Actual results often differ from the original plans because the various types of costs react differently to changes in output.

Costs, Selling Prices, Profit	Number of Houses Built and Sold	
	Planned = 10	**Actual = 8**
Labour and material costs ($50,000 per house)	$500,000	$400,000
Overhead (fixed) costs	$100,000	$100,000
Total costs	$600,000	$500,000
Total sales at $66,000 per house	$660,000	$528,000
Profit: Total	$ 60,000	$ 28,000
Per house	$ 6,000	$ 3,500
As % of sales	10%	5.3%

While this is a very simple and easily applied pricing method, it has one serious limitation. It does not account for the fact that there are different types of costs, and that these costs are affected differently by increases or decreases in output. In our housing example, suppose the contractor built and sold only eight houses at the cost-plus price of $66,000 each. Total sales would be $528,000. Labour and material chargeable to the eight houses would total $400,000 ($50,000 per house). Since the contractor would still incur the full $100,000 in overhead expenses, however, the total cost would be $500,000. This would leave a profit of only $28,000, or $3,500 per house instead of the anticipated $6,000. On a percentage basis, the profit would be only 5.3 percent rather than the desired 10 percent. This example of the cost-plus pricing of the houses is summarized in Table 12-1.

The Cost Concepts

The total unit cost of a product is made up of several types of costs. These costs react differently to changes in the quantity produced. Thus, the total unit cost of the product changes as output expands or contracts. A more sophisticated approach to cost-plus pricing takes such changes into consideration.

The cost concepts in the nearby box are important to our discussion. These nine cost concepts and their interrelationships may be studied in Table 12-2 and in Figs. 12-1 and 12-2, which are based on the table. Figure 12-1 shows that the *total* of all costs is the sum of fixed costs and variable costs. The *fixed* costs are represented by a horizontal line because they are constant within the short run. As the output increases, the total cost increases by the amount of *variable* cost incurred by each unit. Thus the total cost curve rises to the right.

The interrelationships among the various *average unit* costs is displayed graphically in Fig. 12-2 and explained briefly as follows (again the data come from Table 12-2):

1. The **average fixed cost curve** declines as output increases because the total of the fixed costs is spread over an increasing number of units.

THE DIFFERENT KINDS OF COSTS

A **fixed cost** is an element, such as rent, executive salaries, or property tax, that remains constant regardless of how may items are produced. Such a cost continues even if production stops completely. It is called a fixed cost because it is difficult to change in the short run (but not in the long run, over several years).

Total fixed cost is the sum of all fixed costs.

Average fixed cost is the total fixed cost divided by the number of units produced. It is the amount of the total fixed cost that is allocated to each unit.

A **variable cost** is an element, such as labour or material cost, that is directly related to production. Variable costs can be controlled in the short run simply by changing the level of production. When production stops, for example, all variable production costs become zero.

Total variable cost is the sum of all variable costs. The more units produced, the higher this cost is.

Average variable cost is the total variable cost divided by the number of units produced. Average variable cost is usually high for the first few units produced. It decreases as production increases, owing to such things as quantity discounts on materials and more efficient use of labour. Beyond some optimum output it increases, owing to crowding of production facilities, overtime pay, etc.

Total cost is the sum of total fixed cost and total variable cost (for a specific quantity produced).

Average total cost is the total cost divided by the number of units produced.

Marginal cost is the cost of producing and selling one more unit; it is the cost of the last unit produced. Usually the marginal cost of the last unit is the same as the variable cost of that unit.

2. The **average variable cost curve** usually is U-shaped. It starts high because average variable costs for the first few units of output usually are high. The variable costs per unit then decline as the company realizes efficiencies in production. Eventually the average variable cost curve reaches its lowest point, reflecting the optimum output as far as variable costs (not total costs) are concerned. In Fig. 12-2, this point is at six units of output. Beyond that point, the average variable cost rises, reflecting the increase in unit variable costs caused by overcrowded facilities and other inefficiencies. If the variable costs per unit were constant, then the average variable cost curve would be a horizontal line at the level of the constant unit variable cost.

3. The **average total cost curve** is the sum of the first two curves — average fixed cost and average variable cost. It starts high, reflecting the fact that total *fixed* costs are spread over so few units of output. As output increases, the average total cost curve declines, because the unit fixed cost and unit variable cost are decreasing. Eventually, the point of lowest total cost per unit is reached (eight units of output in

Table 12-2 COSTS FOR INDIVIDUAL FIRM

Total fixed costs never change, despite increases in quantity. These are costs that are incurred for land rent, executive salaries, and other items that remain constant no matter what quantity is produced. **Variable costs** are the costs of inputs — materials, labour, power. Their total increases as production quantity rises. **Total cost** is the sum of all fixed and variable costs. The other measures in the table are simply methods of looking at costs per unit; they always involve dividing a cost by the number of units produced.

(1)	(2)	(3)	(4)	(5)	(6)	(7)	(8)
					Average	Average	Average
	Total	Total	Total	Marginal	Fixed	Variable	Cost
Quantity	Fixed	Variable	Costs	Cost	Cost	Cost	per Unit
Output	Costs	Costs	(2) + (3)	per Unit	(2) ÷ (1)	(3) ÷ (1)	(4) ÷ (1)
0	$256	$ 0	$256		Infinity	$ 0	Infinity
				$ 64			
1	256	64	320		$256.00	64	$320.00
				20			
2	256	84	340		128.00	42	170.00
				15			
3	256	99	355		85.33	33	118.33
				13			
4	256	112	368		64.00	28	92.00
				13			
5	256	125	381		51.20	25	76.20
				19			
6	256	144	400		42.67	24	66.67
				31			
7	256	175	431		36.57	25	61.57
				49			
8	256	224	480		32.00	28	60.00
				73			
9	256	297	553		28.44	33	61.44
				103			
10	256	400	656		25.60	40	65.60

Fig. 12-2). Beyond that optimum point, diminishing returns set in and the average total cost curve rises.

4. The **marginal cost curve** has a more pronounced U-shape than the other curves in Fig. 12-2. That marginal cost curve slopes downward until the fifth unit of output, at which point the marginal costs start to increase.

Now note the relationship between the marginal cost curve and the average cost curve. The average total cost curve slopes downward *as long as the marginal cost is less than the average total cost.* Even though the marginal cost increases after the fifth unit, the average total cost curve continues to slope downward until after the eighth unit. This is so because marginal cost — even when it is going up — is still less than average total cost.

The marginal cost curve and the average total cost curve intersect at the lowest point of the average total cost curve. Beyond that point (the eighth

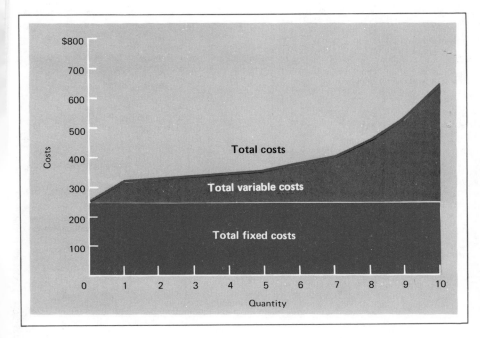

Figure 12-1
TOTAL COST CURVES
FOR AN INDIVIDUAL
FIRM.

This graph shows the
relationships among total
fixed costs, total variable
costs, and total costs. The
effect of total variable
costs in this example is to
make total cost a slowly
ascending curved line.

unit in the example), the cost of producing and selling the next unit is higher
than the average cost of all units. Therefore, from then on the average
total cost rises. The reason for this is that the average variable cost is increasing faster than the average fixed cost is decreasing. Table 12-2 shows
that producing the ninth unit reduces average fixed cost by $3.56 (from
$32 to $28.44), but causes average variable cost to rise by $5.

Refinements in Cost-Plus Pricing

Once management understands that not all costs react in the same way to
output increases or decreases, refinements in cost-plus pricing are possible.
Let's assume that the desired profit is included either in the fixed cost or in
the variable cost schedule. That is, profit is included as a cost in Table 12-2
and Figs. 12-1 and 12-2. Then management can refer to the table or graphs
to find the appropriate price, once a decision has been made regarding
output quantity. If the executives decide to produce six units in our example,
the selling price will be $66.67 per unit. A production run of eight units
would be priced at $60 per unit (refer to Table 12-2 or Fig. 12-2).

The user of this pricing method assumes that all the intended output will
be produced and sold. If fewer units are produced, each would have to sell
for a higher price in order to cover all costs and show a profit. But, obviously,
if business is slack and output must be cut, it is not wise to raise the unit
price. Thus the difficulty in this pricing approach is that no attention is paid
to market demand. For this reason, the method has limited application for
producers.

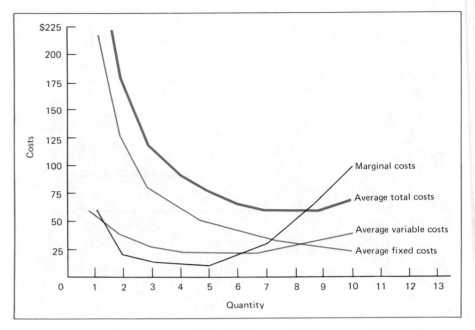

**Figure 12-2
UNIT COST CURVES
FOR AN INDIVIDUAL
FIRM.**

This figure is based on data in Table 12-2. Here we see how *unit* costs change as quantity increases. Using cost-plus pricing, four units of output would be priced at $92 each, while eight units would sell at $60 each.

Prices Based on Marginal Costs Only

Another approach to cost-plus pricing is to set a price that will cover only the marginal costs, not the total costs. Refer again to the cost schedules shown in Table 12-2 and Fig. 12-2, and assume that a firm is operating at an output level of six units. Under marginal cost pricing, this firm can accept an order for one unit at $31, instead of the total unit cost of $66.67. The firm is then trying to cover only its variable costs. If the firm can sell for any price over $31 — say, $33 or $35 — the excess contributes to the payment of fixed costs.

Obviously, not all orders can be priced to cover only variable costs. Marginal cost pricing may be feasible, however, if management wants to keep its labour force employed during a slack season. Marginal cost pricing may also be used when one product is expected to attract business for another. A department store, for example, may price meals in its tearoom at a level that covers only the marginal costs. The reasoning is that this tearoom will bring shoppers to the store, where they will buy other merchandise.

Cost-Plus Pricing by Middlemen

Cost-plus pricing is widely used by retailing and wholesaling middlemen. At least it seems this way at first glance. A retailer, for example, pays a given amount to buy products and have them delivered to the store. Then the retailer adds an amount (a markup) to the acquisition cost. This markup is estimated to be sufficient to cover the store's expenses and still leave a reasonable profit. To simplify pricing and accounting, the retailer may add the same *percentage* markup to every product. This is an average markup that the retailer's experience has shown is large enough to cover the costs

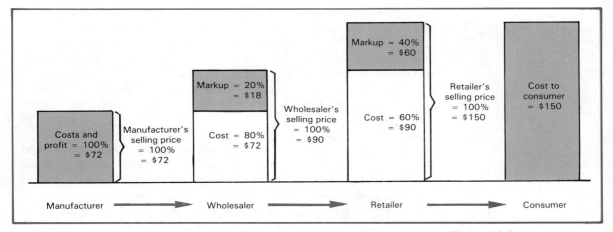

Figure 12-3
EXAMPLES OF
MARKUP PRICING BY
RETAILERS AND
WHOLESALERS.

and profit for the store. Thus, a clothing store may buy a garment for $30 including freight, and then price the item at $50. The price of $50 reflects a retailer markup of 40 percent based on the selling price, or 66⅔ percent based on the merchandise cost. Different types of retailers will require different percentage markups because of the nature of the products handled and services offered. A self-service supermarket has lower costs and thus a lower average markup than a full-service delicatessen. Fig. 12-3 shows an example of markup pricing by middlemen. The topic of markups is discussed in more detail in Appendix A.

To what extent is cost-plus pricing truly used by middlemen? At least three significant indications suggest that what seems to be cost-plus pricing is really market-inspired pricing:

1. Most retail prices set by applying average percentage markups are really only price offers. If the merchandise does not sell at the original price, that price will be lowered until it reaches a level at which the merchandise will sell.

2. Many retailers do not use the same markup on all the products they carry. A supermarket will have a markup of 6 to 8 percent on sugar and soap products, 15 to 18 percent on canned fruit and vegetables, and 25 to 30 percent on fresh meats and produce. These different markups for different products definitely reflect competitive considerations and other aspects of the market demand.

3. The middleman usually does not actually set a base price but only adds a percentage to the price that has already been set by the manufacturer. The manufacturer's price is set to allow each middleman to add the customary markup and still sell at a retail price that is in line with the competitive market. That is, the key price is set by the manufacturer, with an eye on the market.

Evaluation of
Cost-Plus Pricing

We have emphasized that a firm must be market-oriented and must cater to consumers' wants. Why, then, are we now considering cost-plus pricing? Actually, it provides a good point of departure for our discussion of price determination. Also, cost-plus pricing is mentioned so widely in business that it must be understood. Adherents of cost-plus pricing point to its simplicity and its ease of determination. They say that costs are a known quantity, whereas attempts to estimate demand for pricing purposes are mainly guesswork.

This opinion is questionable on two counts. First, it is doubtful whether adequate, accurate cost data are available. We know a fair amount about cost-volume relationships in production costs, but what we know is still insufficient. Furthermore, our information regarding marketing costs is woefully inadequate. Second, it is indeed difficult to estimate demand — that is, to construct a demand schedule that shows sale volume at various prices. Nevertheless, sales forecasting and other research tools can do a surprisingly good job in this area.

Critics of cost-plus pricing do not say that costs should be disregarded in pricing. Costs should be a determining influence, they maintain, but not the only one. Costs are a floor under a firm's prices. If goods are priced under this floor for a long time, the firm will be forced out of business.

Companies using target return on net sales as a pricing goal typically prefer cost-plus pricing, at least as a starting point in price determination. Management can add its desired profit percentage to the firm's total costs for a given product. In other situations, management can determine a tentative base price, using the cost-plus method, and then adjust this price in light of the pricing goal or other factors discussed in Chapter 11. To illustrate, management may arrive at a cost-plus price of $250 for a given product. If the company's goal is to meet competition, and the price of the competing product is $240, management may reduce its price to $240. In another situation, management's cost-based price of $250 may fall in the middle of the expected price range. Then management may adopt a skimming strategy and go to the upper end of that range.

Thus, we may conclude that costs provide a good point from which to start computing a base price. But when used by itself, cost-plus pricing is a weak and unrealistic method because it completely ignores the influences of competition and market demand.

BREAK-EVEN ANALYSIS

One way to use market demand as a basis for price determination, and still consider costs, is to approach pricing through a break-even analysis and a determination of break-even points. A break-even point is that quantity of output (number of units produced) at which the sales revenue equals the total costs, *assuming a certain selling price*. Thus, there is a different break-even point for each different selling price. Sales of quantities above the break-even output result in a profit on each unit. The further the sales are above the break-even point, the higher the total and unit profits. Sales below the break-even point result in a loss to the seller.

Table 12-3 COMPUTATION OF BREAK-EVEN POINT

At each of several prices, we wish to find out how many units must be sold to cover all variable costs plus total fixed costs. At a unit price of $100, the sale of each unit contributes $70 to cover the overhead expenses. We must sell about 3.6 units to cover the $250 fixed cost. See Figs. 12-4 and 12-5 for a visual portrayal of the data in this table.

(1)	(2)	(3)	(4)	(5)
		Contribution	Overhead	Break-Even
	Unit Variable	to Overhead	(Total Fixed	Point
Unit Price	Costs, AVC	(1) − (2)	Costs)	(4) ÷ (3)
$ 60	$30	$ 30	$250	8.3 units
$ 80	$30	$ 50	$250	5.0 units
$100	$30	$ 70	$250	3.6 units
$150	$30	$120	$250	2.1 units

Determining the Break-Even Point

The method of determining the break-even point is illustrated in Table 12-3 and Figs. 12-4 and 12-5. In our hypothetical situation, the company's fixed costs are $250, and its variable costs are constant at $30 a unit. Recall that in our earlier example (Table 12-2 and Figs. 12-1 and 12-2), we assumed that the unit variable costs were *not* constant; they fluctuated. Now to simplify our break-even analysis, we are assuming that the unit variable costs *are* constant.

Thus the total cost of producing one unit is $280. For five units the total cost is $400 ($30 multiplied by 5, plus $250). In Fig. 12-4 the selling price is $80 a unit. Consequently, every time a unit is sold, $50 is contributed to overhead (fixed costs). That is the variable costs are $30 per unit, and these costs are incurred in producing each unit. But any revenue over $30 can be used to help cover the fixed costs. At a selling price of $80, the company will break even if five units are sold. This is so because a $50 contribution from each of five units will just cover the total fixed costs of $250.

Stated another way, the variable costs for five units are $150 and the fixed costs are $250, for a total cost of $400. This is equal to the revenue from five units sold at $80 each. So, for an $80 selling price, the break-even volume is five units.

The break-even point may be found with the formula

$$\text{Break-even point in units} = \frac{\text{total fixed costs}}{\text{unit contribution to overhead}}$$

$$= \frac{\text{total fixed costs}}{\text{selling price} - \text{average variable cost}}$$

It is important to note the assumptions underlying the computations in the preceding paragraph and in Fig. 12-4. First, we assume that total fixed

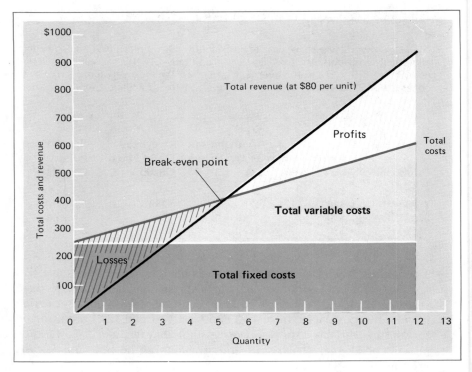

Figure 12-4
BREAK-EVEN CHART
WITH SELLING PRICE
OF $80 PER UNIT.

Here the break-even point is reached when the company sells five units. Fixed costs, regardless of quantity produced and sold, are $250. The variable cost per unit is $30. If this company sells five units, total cost is $400 (variable cost of 5 × $30, or $150, plus fixed cost of $250). At a selling price of $80, the sale of five units will yield $400 revenue, and costs and revenue will equal each other. At the same price, the sale of each unit above five yields a profit.

costs are constant. This is true only over a short period of time and within a limited range of output. It is reasonably easy, however, to develop a break-even chart wherein the fixed costs, and consequently the total costs, are stepped up at several intervals. A second assumption in our example is that the variable costs remain constant per unit of output. In the earlier discussion of the cost structure of the firm, we noted that the average variable costs in a firm usually fluctuate. Thus the total costs were shown as a curved line in Fig. 12-1, and the average variable cost line in Fig. 12-2 was curved and sloped rather than straight and horizontal.

Another limitation of Fig. 12-4 is that it shows a break-even point only if the unit price is $80. It is highly desirable to compute the break-even points for several different selling prices. Therefore, in Fig. 12-5 the break-even point is determined for four prices — $60, $80, $100, and $150. Fig. 12-5 is also based on Table 12-3. If the price is $60, it will take sales of approximately 8.3 units to break even; at $150, only about 2.1 units. Every differ-

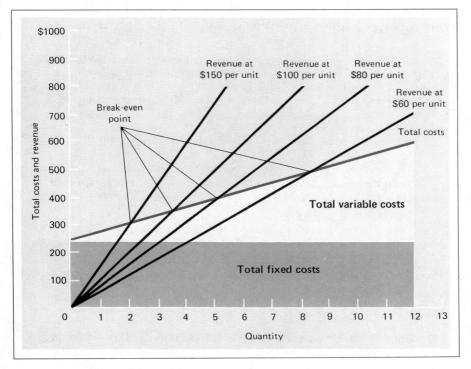

Figure 12-5
BREAK-EVEN CHART
SHOWING FOUR
DIFFERENT SELLING
PRICES.

Here the company is experimenting with several different prices in order to determine which is the most appropriate. There are four different prices and four break-even points. At a price of $60, the company will start making a profit after it has sold 8.3 units. At the opposite extreme, the break-even point for a price of $150 is about 2.1 units.

ent selling price will result in a different break-even point. A company could use these break-even points as the basis for setting the selling price — say, by choosing the price that results in the most reasonable break-even point.

The major limitation of break-even analysis as a realistic pricing tool is that it ignores the market demand at the various prices. It is still essentially a tool for cost-plus pricing. The revenue curves in Figs. 12-4 and 12-5 show only what the revenue will be at the different prices *if* (and it is a big if) the given number of units can be sold at these prices. The completed break-even charts show only the amount that must be sold at the stated price to break even. The charts do not tell us whether we *can* actually sell this amount. The amount the market will buy at a given price could well be below the break-even point. For instance, at a selling price of $80 per unit, the break-even point is five units. If the market will buy only three or four units, the firm will not break even; it will show a loss.

Break-Even Analysis Related to Market Demand

Table 12-4   RELATIONSHIPS BETWEEN BREAK-EVEN ANALYSIS,
                        TOTAL REVENUE FROM MARKET DEMAND, AND PROFIT

By comparing market demand and break-even point at each unit price, we find
which price will maximize profits. Note that at a $60 price, the break-even point
is 8.3 units. Yet the market will buy only 7 units at the price, so a loss would result.
Explain why there is a $50 profit at the $80 price. This is shown graphically in
Fig. 12-6.

(1) Unit Price	(2) Market Demand at the Price, in Units	(3) Total Revenue (1) × (2)	(4) Break-Even Point	(5) Total Cost of Units Sold	(6) Total Profit (3) − (5)
$ 60	7	$420	8.3	$460	$ − 40
80	6	480	5.0	430	50
100	5	500	3.6	400	100
150	2	300	2.1	310	10

*Computed from cost data in Table 12-3. (Unit variable costs are $30, and total fixed costs are $250.)

This deficiency in break-even analysis can be remedied by estimating
the total demand that actually exists at each of several different selling
prices. Then this market information can be superimposed on our break-
even chart. The procedure is illustrated in Table 12-4 and Fig. 12-6. Management first constructs a demand schedule, that is, its estimate of the quantities it can sell at various prices. Columns 1 and 2 of Table 12-4 show this
information. From these figures, total revenue at each price is determined
—column 3—and this information is plotted on a graph. The total-demand
curve DD in Fig. 12-6 is the result.

You may be more familiar with the traditional demand curve, which slopes
downward to the right. The difference is that the usual demand curve shows
average revenues, while the DD curve in Fig. 12-6 represents *total* revenues.
Basically, the curves are developed from the same demand schedule. In
fact, a traditional demand curve could be plotted fron the figures in columns
1 and 2 of Table 12-4.

As in Fig. 12-6, the DD curve is superimposed on the break-even chart,
which shows several revenue lines representing different unit selling prices.
To maximize profit, management finds the point on the demand curve that
is the greatest vertical distance above the total cost curve. In Fig. 12-6, this
is point b. The best selling price is the one represented by the revenue line
that intersects this point on the DD curve. The optimum level of output is
also determined by this intersection. In our example, $100 is the best selling
price, and five units is the output that will maximuze profit (at $100). An
$80 price will sell six units and bring a profit of $50. The other two prices,
$60 and $150, will result in losses of $40 and $10, respectively. Demand at
these prices is less than that needed to break even.

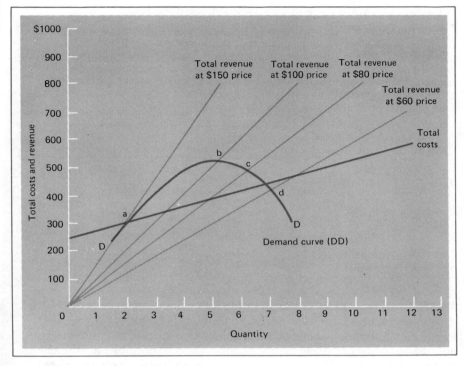

Superimposing the total demand curve on the break-even chart graphically shows which price will maximize profit. We seek the point at which the demand curve is the greatest vertical distance above the total cost line (point b in this case). Then we determine the price represented by the total revenue line that intersects the demand curve at this point. Our price is $100. Note that the lower price of $60 would result in a loss of $40 (point d is below the total cost line).

Evaluation of Break-Even Analysis

Certainly no one should claim that break-even analysis is the perfect pricing tool. Many of its underlying assumptions are unrealistic in a practical business operation. It assumes that costs are stable (that is, nonfluctuating). Thus, break-even analysis has limited value in companies where the average (unit) cost fluctuates frequently. Regarding the market demand estimates, break-even analysis often oversimplifies the demand (revenue-producing) situation facing the firm. That is, management may lightly say, "At an $80 price, we'll break even at five units." In truth, the company will break even *if* it can sell five units at $80. Management seems to take lightly the fact that competition and a volatile market demand situation may prevent its actually selling those five units.

These limitations, however, should not lead management to dismiss break-even analysis as a pricing tool. While it is not perfect, it is extremely valuable, especially when used in conjunction with an analysis of total demand. Even in its simplest form, break-even analysis is very helpful because, in the short run, many firms are faced with reasonably stable cost and demand structures.

Table 12-5   DEMAND SCHEDULE FOR INDIVIDUAL FIRM

At each market price, a definite quantity of the product will be demanded at any given time. Thus, changing the unit price upward or downward will result in a differing number of units sold and a differing amount of total revenue. Marginal revenue is simply the amount of additional money gained by selling one more unit. In this example the company no longer gains marginal revenue after it has sold the sixth unit at a price of $60.

Units Sold	Unit Price (Average Revenue)	Total Revenue	Marginal Revenue
1	$80	$ 80	
2	75	150	$ 70
3	72	216	66
4	68	272	56
5	65	325	53
6	60	360	35
7	50	350	−10
8	40	320	−30

PRICES BASED ON A BALANCE BETWEEN SUPPLY AND DEMAND

Another method of price setting involves balancing demand with costs to determine the best price for profit maximization. This method of price determination is thus best suited for companies whose pricing goal is to maximize profit. However, companies with other pricing goals should also understand this method. These firms might use this method in special situations or perhaps to compare prices determined by different methods.

In discussing demand, we should distinguish between the demand curve or schedule facing an individual seller and the one facing the entire industry. Theoretically, when a firm operates in a market of perfect competition, its demand curve is horizontal at the market price. That is, the single seller has no control over the price. And the seller's entire output can be sold at the market price. However, the industry as a whole has a downward-sloping curve. That is, the industry can sell more units at lower prices than at higher prices.

The market situation facing most firms in Canada today — as well as most countries outside the communist bloc — is one of monopolistic, or imperfect, competition. This is characterized by product differentiation and nonprice competition. By differentiating its products, an individual firm gains some control over its prices. In effect, each firm becomes a separate "industry"; its product is to some extent unlike any other. Thus an individual firm in monopolistic competition has a downward-sloping demand curve. That is, it will attract some buyers at a high price, but to broaden its market and to sell to more people, it must lower the price.

Determining the Price

To use this pricing method, the price setter must understand the concepts of average and marginal revenue, in addition to average and marginal cost. **Marginal revenue** is the income derived from the sale of the last unit — the marginal unit. **Average revenue** is the unit price at a given level of

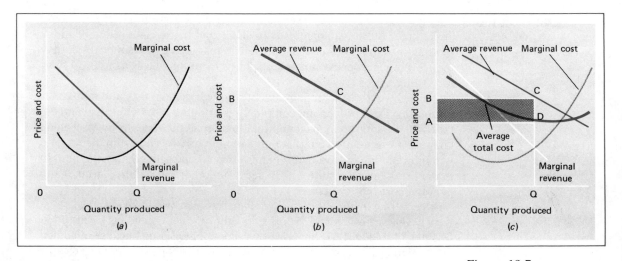

Figure 12-7
PRICE SETTING AND
PROFIT MAXIMIZA-
TION THROUGH
MARGINAL ANALYSIS.

unit sales. It is calculated by dividing total revenue by the number of units sold. Referring to the hypothetical demand schedule in Table 12-5, we see that the company can sell one unit at $80. To sell two units, it must reduce its price to $75 for each unit. Thus, the company receives an additional $70 (marginal revenue) by selling two units instead of one. The fifth unit brings a marginal revenue of $53. After the sixth unit, however, total revenue declines each time the unit price is lowered to sell an additional unit. Hence, there is a negative marginal revenue.

The price-setting process that involves the balancing of supply and demand is illustrated in the three-part Fig. 12-7. We assume that a firm will continue to produce and sell more units as long as the revenue from the last unit sold exceeds the cost of producing this last unit. That is, output continues to increase as long as marginal revenue exceeds marginal cost. At the point where they meet (quantity Q in Fig. 12-7a) output theoretically should cease. Certainly management will not want to sell a unit at a price less than the out-of-pocket (variable) costs of production. Thus the **volume of output** is the quantity for which **marginal** costs equal marginal revenue or quantity Q.

The **unit price** is determined by locating the point on the average revenue curve that represents an output of Q units. Remember that average revenue represents the unit price. The average revenue curve has been added in Fig. 12-7b. The unit price at which to sell quantity Q is represented by point C. It is the price B in Fig. 12-7b.

The average total (unit) cost curve has been added in Fig. 12-7c. It shows that, for output quantity Q, the average unit cost is represented by point D. This average unit cost is A. Thus, with a price of B and an average unit cost of A, the company enjoys a unit profit given by AB in the future. The total profit is represented by area ABCD (quantity Q times unit profit AB).

Evaluation of Supply-Demand Pricing

Supply and demand analysis as a basis for price setting has enjoyed only limited use. Businesspeople usually claim that better data are needed for plotting the curves exactly. Supply and demand analysis can be used, they feel, to study past price movements, but it cannot serve as a practical basis for setting prices.

On the brighter side, management's knowledge of costs and demand is improving. Data processing equipment is bringing more complete and detailed information to management's attention all the time. In the preceding chapter, it was pointed out that management usually can estimate demand within broad limits, and this is helpful. Also, experienced management in many firms can do a surprisingly accurate job of estimating marginal and average costs and revenues.

Price setting by means of marginal analysis can also have practical value if management will adjust the price in light of some conditions discussed in Chapter 11. In Fig. 12-7, the price was set at point B. But, because of limited production facilities, management may prefer to adopt a skimming strategy and price above B. Or, in the short run, management may price below B, or even below A, adopting an aggressive pricing strategy to better penetrate the market or to discourage competiton.

PRICES SET IN RELATION TO MARKETING ALONE

Cost-plus pricing is one extreme among pricing methods. At the other end of the scale is a method whereby a firm's prices are set in relation to *only* the competitive market price. The seller's price may be set right at the market price to meet the competition, or it may be set either above or below the competitive market price.

Pricing to Meet Competition

Management may decide to price a product right at the competitive level in several situations. A firm is most likely to use this pricing method when the market is highly competitive and the firm's product is not differentiated significantly from competing products. To some extent, this method of pricing reflects market conditions that parallel those found under perfect competition. That is, effective product differentiation is absent, buyers and sellers are well informed about market conditions, and the seller has no discernible control over the selling price. Most producers of agricultural products, manufacturers of grey goods in the textile industry, and small firms producing well-known, standardized products ordinarily use the market-based method of pricing.

The market-based method of pricing is also used when a traditional or "customary" price level exists. Candy bars, soft drinks, and chewing gum, for example, were traditionally priced in this manner. When rising costs placed pressure on the customary price, sellers often tailored their costs to the customary market price by reducing the quantity or the quality of the product. (Recently, in most markets, however, rising costs have raised "customary" prices to new levels.)

The sharp drop in revenue that occurs when the price is raised above the customary level indicates that the individual seller faces a kinked demand

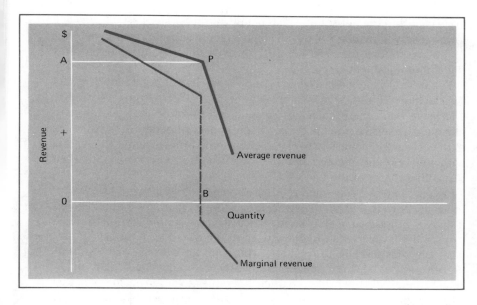

Figure 12-8
KINKED DEMAND
CURVE FACING
MANUFACTURER OF
PRODUCT SOLD AT
CUSTOMARY PRICE
(THE SAME TYPE OF
CURVE FACES
INDIVIDUAL
OLIGOPOLIST).

The kink occurs at the point representing the customary price A. Above A, demand declines rapidly as the price is increased. A price set below A results in very little increase in volume, so revenue is lost. That is, the marginal revenue is negative.

(see Fig. 12-8). The customary price is at A. If the seller tries to go above that price, the demand for the product drops sharply, as indicated by the flat average revenue curve above point P. At any price above A, then, the demand is highly elastic. Below price A, the demand is highly inelastic, as represented by the steeply sloping average revenue curve and the negative marginal revenue curve. That is, the total revenue decreases each time the price is reduced to a level below A. The customary price is strong. Consequently, a reduction in price by one firm will not increase the firm's unit sales very much, certainly not enough to offset the loss in average revenue.

Up to this point in our discussion of pricing to meet competition, we have observed market situations that involve many sellers. Oddly enough, the same pricing method is often used when the market is dominated by only a few sellers. This type of market is called an **oligopoly**. The products of all manufacturers are reasonably similar, and the demand is usually inelastic. The demand curve facing an individual seller in an oligopoly is a kinked one, as in Fig. 12-8.

An oligopolist must price at market level to maximize profits. Selling *above* market price will result in a drastic reduction in total revenue because the average revenue curve is so elastic above point P. If an oligopolist cuts its price *below* the market price, all other members of the oligopoly must respond immediately. Otherwise the price cutter will enjoy a substantial increase in business. Therefore, the competitors do retaliate with comparable price cuts, and the net result is that a new market price is established at a lower level. All members of the oligopoly end up with about the same share of the market that they had before. However, unit revenue is reduced by the amount of the price cut.

Theoretically, oligopolists gain no advantage by cutting their prices. For their own good, they should simply set their prices at a competitive level and leave them there. In reality, price wars are often touched off in an oligopoly because it is not possible to fully control all sellers of the product. In the absence of collusion, every so often some firm will enter the market with a price reduction, and all others will usually follow to maintain their respective shares of the market.

Pricing to meet competition is rather simple to do. A firm ascertains what the going price is, and after allowing for customary markups for middlemen, it arrives at its own selling price. To illustrate, a manufacturer of men's dress shoes is aware that retailers want to sell the shoes for $69.95 a pair. The firm sells directly to retailers, who want an average markup of 40 percent of their selling price. Consequently, after allowing $27.98 for the retailer's markup, the firm's top price is about $42. It then decides whether $42 is enough to cover its production and marketing expenses and still leave it a reasonable profit. Sometimes it faces a real squeeze in this regard, particularly when its costs are rising but the market price is holding firm.

Pricing Below Competitive Level

A variation of market-based pricing is to set a price at some point *below* the competitive level. This method of pricing is typically used by discount retailers. These stores offer fewer services, and they operate on the principle of low markup and high volume. They typically price nationally advertised brands 10 to 30 percent below the suggested retail list price, or the price actually being charged by full-service retailers. Even full-service retailers may price below the competitive level by eliminating specific services. In recent years, for example, some gas stations began to offer a discount to customers who paid cash instead of using a credit card, or who used the self-service pumps.

Pricing Above Competitive Level

Manufacturers or retailers sometimes set their prices above the market level. This may be done by a producer that follows a strategy of skimming. Usually, above-market pricing works only when the product is distinctive or when the seller has acquired prestige in its field. Most cities have a prestige clothing or jewellery store where price tags are noticeably above the competitive level set by other stores that handle similar products.

SUMMARY

The base (list) price for a product or service may be set on the basis of:

1. Total cost plus desired profit
2. A balance between market demand and product costs (supply)
3. Competitive market conditions

For cost-plus pricing to be at all useful or effective, a seller must consider the several types of costs and their different reactions to changes in the quantity produced. The differences among fixed, variable, and marginal costs must be understood. A producer usually sets a price to cover total cost. In some cases, however, the best policy may be to set a price that covers marginal cost only. The major weakness in cost-plus pricing is that it completely ignores the market demand.

To partially offset this weakness, a company may use break-even analysis as a tool in price setting. Break-even computations do take into consideration the factor of market demand. The demand estimates, however, assume that a given quantity can be sold at a stated price.

In real-life situations, virtually *all* price setting is market-inspired to some extent. Consequently, marginal analysis is a useful method for setting a price. A company continues to produce more of a product as long as the marginal revenue exceeds the marginal cost. Prices are set and output level is determined at the point where marginal cost equals marginal revenue.

For many products, price setting is a relatively easy job because management simply sets the price at the market level established by the competition. This pricing method is used both in markets where there are many small sellers and in oligopolistic markets. There are two variations of market-level pricing. One is to price *below* the competitive level. This is typically done by discount sellers. The other variation is to price *above* the competitive level — a policy followed for distinctive products or prestigious stores.

Table 12-6 outlines 16 criteria that executives can use as practical guidelines in price setting. Many of these generalizations were discussed in Chapters 11 and 12, so Table 12-6 also can serve as a meaningful summary.

Table 12-6 SUMMARY OF CRITERIA FOR SETTING PRICES

Custom-made products are priced higher than mass-produced ones (no. 3). Long-lived products can be priced lower because costs can be amortized over a longer period (no. 5).

Low Price When	Pricing Criteria	High Price When
Little	1. Promotion	Much
Commodity	2. Product type	Proprietary
Mass-produced	3. Manufacture	Custom-made
Intensive	4. Market coverage	Selective
Long-lived	5. Product obsolescence	Short-lived
Slow	6. Technological change	Rapid
Capital-intensive	7. Production	Labour-intensive
Large	8. Market share	Small
Short	9. Channels of distribution	Long
Mature	10. Stage of market	New
Long-term	11. Profit perspective	Short-term
Single-use	12. Product versatility	Multiple-use
Much	13. Promotional contribution to line	Little
Few or none	14. Ancillary services	Many
Short	15. Product life in use	Long
Fast	16. Turnover	Slow

Source: William J. E. Crissy and Robert Boewadt, "Pricing in Perspective," *Sales Management*, June 15, 1971, p. 44.

QUESTIONS AND PROBLEMS

1. In Fig. 12-2, what is the significance of the point where the marginal cost curve intersects the average total cost curve? Explain why the average total cost curve is declining to the left of the intersection point and rising beyond it. Explain how the marginal cost curve can be rising, while the average total cost curve is still declining.

2. In Table 12-1, what is the marginal cost of the seventh unit produced?

3. "Without exception, the marginal cost is always equal to the variable cost of the marginal unit." Do you agree? Explain.

4. What are the merits and limitations of the cost-plus method of setting a base price?

5. In a break-even chart, is the total *fixed* cost line always horizontal? Is the total *variable* cost line always straight? Explain.

6. In Table 12-3 and Fig. 12-4, what would be the break-even points at prices of $50 and $90, if the variable costs are $40 per unit and the fixed costs remain at $250?

7. In Table 12-3 and Fig. 12-4, find the break-even point for selling prices of $60 and $100 if the fixed cost totals $400.

8. A small manufacturer sold ballpoint pens to retailers at $8.40 per dozen. The manufacturing cost was 50 cents for each pen. The expenses, including all selling and administrative costs except advertising, were $19,200. How many dozen must the manufacturer sell to cover these expenses and pay for an advertising campaign costing $6,000?

9. "Beyond the break-even point, all revenue from sales is pure profit. Consequently, once the break-even point has been achieved, sellers should increase their advertising and personal selling efforts to get more of these profitable, above-break-even-point sales." Discuss.

10. Does supply and demand analysis in relation to pricing have any practical value for the business executive? Explain.

11. In Fig. 12-7, why would the firm normally stop producing at quantity Q? Why is the price set at B and not at F or D?

12. Are there any stores in your community that generally price above the competitive level? How are they able to do this?

13. A soft-drink manufacturer has been pricing its 280 ml canned drink to sell for 25 cents at retail. The product has a strong market acceptance in its regional market, competing with Coal-Cola, Pepsi-Cola, 7-Up, and other well-known brands. For some time, production and marketing costs have been increasing, and management must now take some action. Which of the following courses of action should the company follow? Can you propose a better alternative?
    a. Raise the price to 30 cents or two cans for 55 cents.
    b. Reduce the quality of the beverage.
    c. Reduce the quantity to 250 ml.
    d. Curtail the advertising.

Pricing Strategies and Policies

CHAPTER GOALS

This chapter is concerned with the ways in which a base price can (and sometimes must) be modified. After studying the chapter, you should understand:
1. *Price discounts and allowances*
2. *Geographic pricing strategies*
3. *One-price and variable-price strategies*
4. *Unit pricing*
5. *Price lining*
6. *Resale price maintenance*
7. *"Leader" pricing*
8. *Psychological pricing*
9. *Pricing in periods of inflation*
10. *Price competition versus nonprice competition*

In managing the price portion of a company's marketing mix, management first decides on its pricing goal, and then sets the base price for a product or service. The next task is to develop the appropriate strategies and policies concerning several aspects of the price structure. What kind of discount schedule should be adopted? Will the company occasionally absorb freight costs? If such strategies and policies have already been set for other products, then management must decide which of these are to apply to a new product. In this chapter we shall discuss ten areas that require strategy decisions and policy making. We shall also consider some of the legal aspects of these activities.

Because we shall be using the terms *policy* and *strategy* so frequently in this chapter, let's review the meaning of these terms as they were defined in Chapter 2: A **strategy** is a broad plan of action by which an organization intends to reach its goal. A **policy** is a managerial guide to future decision making when a given situation arises. Thus a policy becomes the course of action followed routinely any time a given strategic or tactical situation arises. To illustrate, suppose management adopts the *strategy* of offering certain quantity discounts in order to achieve the goal of a 10 percent increase in sales next year. Then, routinely, every time the company receives an order of a given size, it is company *policy* to grant the customer the quantity discount prescribed for that particular order size.

RETAILERS, TOO,
OFFER QUANTITY
DISCOUNTS.

(©Van Bucher 1983)

DISCOUNTS AND ALLOWANCES

Quantity Discounts

Discounts and allowances result in a deduction from the base (or list) price. The deduction may be in the form of a reduced price or some other concession, such as free merchandise.

Quantity discounts are deductions from the list price offered by a seller to encourage customers to buy in larger amounts or to make most of their purchases from that seller. The discounts are based on the size of the purchase, either in dollars or in units.

A **noncumulative** discount is based upon the size of an *individual order* of one or more products. Thus a retailer may sell golf balls at $1 each or at three for $2.50. A manufacturer or wholesaler may set up a quantity discount schedule such as the following, which was used by a manufacturer of industrial adhesives.

Boxes Purchased on Single Order	% Discount from List Price
1-5	0.0
6-12	2.0
13-25	3.5
Over 25	5.0

Noncumulative quantity discounts are expected to encourage large orders. Many expenses, such as billing, order filling, and the salaries of salespeople, are about the same whether the seller receives an order totalling $10 or $500. Consequently, selling expense as a percentage of sales decreases as orders become larger. The seller shares such savings with the purchaser of large quantities.

Cumulative discounts are based on the total volume purchased *over a period of time*. These discounts are advantageous to a seller because they tie customers more closely to that seller. They are really patronage discounts, because the more total business a buyer gives a seller, the greater is the discount. Cumulative discounts are especially useful in the sale of perishable products. These discounts encourage customers to buy fresh supplies frequently so that the merchandise will not grow stale.

Quantity discounts can help a manufacturer effect real economies in production as well as in selling. Large orders can result in lower-cost production runs and lower transportation costs. A producer's cumulative discount based on total orders from all the stores in a retail chain may increase orders from that chain substantially. This enables the producer to make much more effective use of production capacity, even though the individual orders are small and do not generate savings in marketing costs.

Trade Discounts

Trade discounts, sometimes called *functional* discounts, are reductions from the list price offered to buyers in payment for marketing functions that they will presumably perform. A manufacturer may quote a retail list price of $400 with trade discounts of 40 percent and 10 percent. This means that the retailer pays the wholesaler $240 ($400 less 40 percent), and the wholesaler pays the manufacturer $216 ($240 less 10 percent). The wholesaler is given the 40 and 10 percent discounts. The wholesaler is expected to keep the 10 percent to cover the costs of the wholesaling functions and to pass on the 40 percent discount to the retailers. Note that the 40 and 10 percent discounts do not constitute a total discount of 50 percent off the list price. Each discount percentage in the "chain" is computed on the amount remaining after the preceding percentage has been deducted.

Cash Discounts

A **cash** discount is a deduction granted to buyers for paying their bills within a specified period of time. The discount is computed on the net amount due after first deducting trade and quantity discounts from the base price. Let's say a buyer owes $360 after the other discounts have been granted and is offered terms of 2/10, n/30 on an invoice dated November 8. This buyer may deduct a discount of 2 percent ($7.20) if the bill is paid within 10 days after the date of the invoice (by November 18). Otherwise the entire bill of $360 must be paid in 30 days (by December 8).

Every cash discount includes three elements: (1) the percentage discount itself, (2) the time period during which the discount may be taken, and (3) the time when the bill becomes overdue (see Fig. 13-1). There are many different terms of sale because practically every industry has its own traditional combination of elements.

Normally, most buyers are extremely eager to pay bills in time to earn cash discounts. The discount in a 2/10, n/30 situation may not seem like very much. But management must realize that this 2 percent is earned just for paying 20 days in advance of the date the entire bill is due. If buyers fail to take the cash discount in a 2/10, n/30 situation, they are, in effect, borrowing money at 36 percent annual rate of interest. (In a 360-day year,

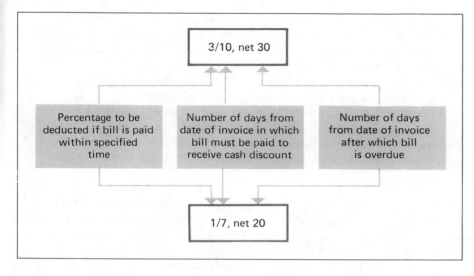

Figure 13-1
THE PARTS OF A
CASH DISCOUNT.

(*Source:* Don L. James,
Bruce J. Walker, and
Michael J. Etzel, *Retailing
Today*, 2d ed., Harcourt
Brace Jovanovich, Inc.,
New York, 1981, p. 199.)

there are 18 periods of 20 days. Paying 2 percent for one of these 20-day periods is equivalent to paying 36 percent for an entire year.)

The inflation and high interest rates in the 1980s have made marketing and financial executives extremely sensitive to the financial terms of sale, especially bill payments. In many cases, we are seeing changes in the traditional pattern of paying bills early to take advantage of cash discounts. Instead, buyers are passing up the cash discounts and are delaying their bill payments as long as possible. These buyers are, in effect, using the sellers' funds as a source of capital. This situation is occurring at all levels in the distribution channels, even including household consumers. To meet this challenge, sellers seek strategies that will reach the two goals of (1) effectively coping with the late payments, and (2) minimizing conflicts that may occur in channels of distribution as buyers and sellers each look to their own self-interest.[1]

Other Discounts and Allowances

A firm that produces articles, such as air conditioners, that are purchased on a seasonal basis may consider the policy of granting a **seasonal** discount. This is a discount of, say, 5, 10, or 20 percent given to a customer who places an order during the slack season. Off-season orders enable manufacturers to make better use of their production facilities.

Forward dating is a variation of both seasonal and cash discounts. A manufacturer of fishing tackle, for example, might seek and fill orders from wholesalers and retailers during the winter months. But the bill would be

---

[1]See Michael Levy and Dwight Grant, "A Flexible Approach to Determining Financial Terms of Sale," *Industrial Marketing Management*, February 1981, pp. 11–16; and Levy and Grant, "Financial Terms of Sale and Control of Marketing Channel Conflict," *Journal of Marketing Research*, November 1980, pp. 524–530.

dated, say, April 1, with terms of 2/10, n/30 offered as of that date. Orders that the seller fills in December and January help to maintain production during the slack season for more efficient operation. The forward-dated bills allow the wholesale or retail buyers to wait to pay their bills until after the season has started and some sales revenue has been generated.

Promotional allowances are price reductions granted by a seller in payment for promotional services performed by buyers. To illustrate, a manufacturer of builders' hardware gives a certain quantity of "free goods" to dealers who prominently display its line. Or, a clothing manufacturer pays one-half the space charge of a retailer's advertisement that features the manufacturer's product.

Brokerage Allowances

When the services of a broker as a wholesaling middleman are employed in the producer's channel of distribution, the broker is paid a certain percentage of the sales volume it generates. This payment is called a *brokerage allowance* and is really just another form of trade discount. Because of the legal implications in certain types of brokerage arrangements, these allowances are noted separately instead of being included with trade discounts. Many times in the past, the commission which the seller normally paid a broker was *instead* paid to large-scale buyers who performed the services usually ascribed to brokers.

Legal Regulation of Discounts and Allowances

The discounts and allowances discussed in this section may result in different prices for different customers. Whenever price differentials exist, there is price discrimination; the terms are synonymous. In certain situations, price discrimination is prohibited under the Combines Investigation Act. This is one of the most important federal laws affecting a company's marketing program.

Background of the Act

Anticombines legislation in Canada was first introduced in 1888. Small businessmen who suffered from the monopolistic and collusive practices in restraint of trade by large manufacturers pressured Parliament into setting up a Combines Investigation Commission. Investigators attempting to verify the allegations of the small tradesmen unearthed a widespread range of restrictive practices and measures.

The results of the investigation led Parliament in 1889 to pass an Act for the Prevention and Suppression of Combinations Formed in Restraint of Trade. The intent of the Act was to declare illegal monopolies and combinations in restraint of trade. Athough the Act was incorporated into the Criminal Code as section 520 in 1892, it proved ineffectual, because to break the law an individual would have to commit an illegal act within the meaning of the "common law." In 1900 the Act was amended to remove this loophole and undue restriction of competition became, in itself, a criminal offence.

Additional legislation was passed in 1910 after a rash of mergers involving fifty-eight business firms, to complement the Criminal Code and assist in the application of the Act. In 1919 the Combines and Fair Prices Act was passed, which prohibited undue stockpiling of the "necessities of life" and also prohibited the realization of exaggerated profits through "unreasonable" prices.

In 1923, Canadian combines legislation was finally consolidated. The most important sections of the Combines Investigation Act of 1923 are still operative. Following the presentation of a report by the Economic Council of Canada in 1969,[2] the Government of Canada introduced into Parliament, in 1971, Bill C-256 (the Competition Bill), which contained a number of important amendments to the Combines Investigation Act and which was to form the basis for a new competition policy for Canada. First-stage amendments to the Combines Investigation Act were finally passed by Parliament in December 1975 and became law on January 1, 1976.[3]

Predatory Pricing as an Offence

The provisions respecting predatory pricing are contained in paragraph 34(1)(c) of the Combines Investigation Act, which states:

34.(1) *Every one engaged in a business who*
(c) *engages in a policy of selling products at prices unreasonably low, having the effect or tendency of substantially lessening competition or eliminating a competitor, or designed to have such effect;*
is guilty of an indictable offence and is liable to imprisonment for two years.

In order for a conviction to result under paragraph 34(1)(c), it must be shown that prices are unreasonably low and that such prices have the effect of reducing competition. Such conditions are difficult to prove and, as a result, very few predatory pricing charges have been laid. The amendments to the Combines Investigation Act that were passed in December 1975 extended the predatory pricing provisions to the sale of both articles and services. The word "products" is now defined in the Combines Investigation Act to include articles *and* services.

---

[2]Economic Council of Canada, *Interim Report on Competition Policy*, Queen's Printer, Ottawa, July 1969.

[3]The materials presented in this section are adapted from the Act itself, from selected portions of presented papers by D. H. W. Henry (The Director of Investigation and Research under the Act) as reproduced in M. D. Beckman and R. H. Evans (eds.), *Marketing: A Canadian Perspective*, Prentice-Hall Canada Ltd., Scarborough, 1972, pp. 102–125; and from D. H. W. Henry, "The Combines Investigation Act," as reproduced in B. Mallen and I. A. Litvak (eds.), *Marketing: Canada*, 2d ed., McGraw-Hill Book Co., Toronto, 1968, pp. 184–211.
A detailed examination of the proposed amendments to the Combines Investigation Act and of the Competition Bill in general is contained in Department of Consumer and Corporate Affairs, *Proposals for a New Competition Policy for Canada*, Information Canada, Ottawa, November 1973.

Price Discrimination as an Offence

At present, price discrimination is regulated under paragraph 34(1)(*a*) of the Combines Investigation Act, which states:

> **34.**(1) *Every one engaged in a business who*
> *(a) is a party or privy to, or assists in, any sale that discriminates to his knowledge, directly or indirectly, against competitors of a purchaser of articles from him in that any discount, rebate, allowance, price concession or other advantage is granted to the purchaser over and above any discount, rebate, allowance, price concession or other advantage that, at the time the articles are sold to such purchaser, is available to such competitors in respect of a sale of articles of like quality and quantity;*
> *is guilty of an indictable offence and is liable to imprisonment for two years.*

This section goes on to state in paragraph 34(2):

> *(2) It is not an offence under paragarph (1)(a) to be a party or privy to, or assist in any sale mentioned therein unless the discount, rebate, allowance, price concession or other advantage was granted as part of a practice of discriminating as described in that paragraph.*

The following conditions must, therefore, be met in order for a conviction to be registered for price discrimination: (1) a discount, rebate, allowance, price concession, or other advantage must be granted to one customer and not to another; (2) the two customers concerned must be *competitors*; (3) the price discrimination must occur in respect of *articles* of like quality and quantity; (4) the act of discrimination must be part of a *practice* of discrimination.

Not all price discrimination is, *per se*, an offence. It is lawful to discriminate in price on the basis of quantities of goods purchased. The cost justification defence — that of a seller differentiating his price to a favoured competitor because of a difference in the costs of supplying that customer — is not viewed as an acceptable basis for discrimination. On the other hand, a seller does not have to demonstrate a cost difference in order to support a quantity discount structure. Rather, the basis for such price discrimination is accepted only on a quantity of goods purchased basis. Establishing volume discount pricing structures that are available to competing buyers who purchase in comparable quantities is a major basis for discriminating under the provision.

It is also of note that the buyer is seen as being as liable as the seller in cases of discrimination. The legislation applies to those who are party to a sale and this includes both buyer and seller. This wording was intended to restrain large-scale buyers from demanding discriminatory prices. In addition, the buyer (as well as the seller) must know that the price involved is discriminatory. From a practical standpoint, it is difficult for the Crown to prove that a buyer "knowingly" received a discriminatory price. While the intent of the legislation is to prevent price discrimination, the difficulty involved in proving that the various provisions of paragraphs 34(1)(*a*) and 34(2) have been met has contributed to the fact that there has never been a conviction for price discrimination in Canadian courts.

Granting Promotional Allowances as an Offence

The Combines Investigation Act in section 35 requires that promotional allowances be granted proportionately to all competing customers. This section states:

> **35.***(1) In this section "allowance" means any discount, rebate, price concession or other advantage that is or purports to be offered or granted for advertising or display purposes and is collateral to a sale or sales of products but is not applied directly to the selling price.*
>
> *(2) Every one engaged in a business who is a party or privy to the granting of an allowance to any purchaser that is not offered on proportionate terms to other purchasers in competition with the first-mentioned purchaser, (which other purchasers are in this section called "competing purchasers"), is guilty of an indictable offence and is liable to imprisonment for two years.*
>
> *(3) For the purposes of this section, an allowance is offered on proportionate terms only if*
>
> *(a) the allowance offered to a purchaser is in approximately the same proportion to the value of sales to him as the allowance offered to each competing purchaser is to the total value of sales to such competing purchaser,*
>
> *(b) in any case where advertising or other expenditures or services are exacted in return therefor, the cost thereof required to be incurred by a purchaser is in approximately the same proportion to the value of sales to him as the cost of such advertising or other expenditures or services required to be incurred by each competing purchaser is to the total value of sales to such competing purchaser, and*
>
> *(c) in any case where services are exacted in return therefor, the requirements thereof have regard to the kinds of services that competing purchasers at the same time or different levels of distribution are ordinarily able to perform or cause to be performed.*

The Competition Bill Amendments, passed in December 1975, extended the provisions of section 35 to the sale of both articles and services. This amendment is not likely to alter the fact that price discrimination through the use of promotional allowances is difficult to prove. While discrimination in the granting of promotional allowances is a *per se* offence, not requiring proof of the existence of either a practice of discrimination or a lessening of competition, there have been no convictions under section 35. A marketer who wishes to discriminate among his customers may do so through the legal practice of granting quantity discounts.

Geographic pricing strategies allocate freight costs between seller and buyers. Increasing costs have emphasized the importance of these strategies.

GEOGRAPHIC PRICING STRATEGIES

In its pricing, a seller must consider the freight costs involved in shipping the product to the buyer. This consideration grows in importance as freight becomes a larger part of total variable costs. Pricing policies may be established whereby the buyer pays all the freight, the seller bears the entire costs, or the two parties share the expense. The chosen strategy can have an important bearing on (1) the geographic limits of a firm's market, (2) the location of its production facilities, (3) the source of its raw materials, and (4) its competitive strength in various market areas.

F.O.B. Point-of-Production Pricing

In one widely used geographic pricing strategy, the seller quotes the selling price at the factory or other point of production, and the buyer pays the entire cost of transportation. This is usually referred to as **f.o.b. mill** or **f.o.b. factory** pricing. Of the four strategies discussed in this section, this is the only one in which the seller does not pay *any* of the freight costs. The seller pays only the cost of loading the shipment aboard the carrier — hence the term **f.o.b.**, or **free on board**.

Under the f.o.b. factory price policy, the seller nets the same amount on each sale of similar quantities. The delivered price to the buyer varies according the freight charges. Such a policy has important economic and marketing implications. In effect, f.o.b. mill pricing tends to establish a geographic monopoly for a given seller because freight rates prevent distant competitors from entering the market. The seller in turn is increasingly priced out of more distant markets.

Uniform Delivered Pricing

Under the **uniform delivered pricing** strategy, the same delivered price is quoted to all buyers regardless of their locations. This strategy is sometimes referred to as "postage stamp pricing" because of its similarities to the pricing of first-class mail service. The net revenue to the seller varies, depending upon the shipping cost involved in each sale.

A uniform delivered price is typically used where transportation costs are a small part of the seller's total costs. This strategy is also used by many retailers who feel that "free" delivery is an additional service that strengthens their market position.

Under a uniform delivered price system, buyers located near the seller's factory pay for some of the costs of shipping to more distant locations. The counterargument is that an f.o.b. factory system gives an undue advantage to buyers located near the factory. Critics of f.o.b. factory pricing are usually in favour of a uniform delivered price. They feel that the freight expense should not be isolated and charged to individual customers any more than any other single marketing or production expense should be.

Zone Delivered Pricing

Under a **zone delivered pricing** strategy, a seller's market is divided into a limited number of broad geographic zones, and a uniform delivered price is set within each zone. Zone delivered pricing is similar to the system used in pricing parcel post services and long-distance telephone service. A firm that quotes a price and then says, "Slightly higher west of the Lakehead," is using a two-zone pricing system. The freight charge built into the delivered price is approximately an average of the charges at all points within a zone area.

When a zone delivered pricing strategy is employed, the seller must walk a neat tightrope to avoid charges of illegal price discrimination among buyers or among customers of the buyers. This means that the zone lines must be drawn so that all buyers who compete for a particular market are in the same zone. Such a condition is most easily met where markets are widely distributed.

Freight Absorption Pricing

A **freight absorption pricing** strategy may be adopted to offset some of the competitive disadvantages of f.o.b. factory pricing. With an f.o.b. factory price, a firm is at a price disadvantage when it tries to sell to buyers located in markets nearer to competitors' plants. To penetrate more deeply into such markets, a seller may be willing to absorb some of the freight costs. Thus, seller A will quote to the customer a delivered price equal to (1) A's factory price plus (2) the freight costs that would be charged by the competitive seller located nearest the customer.

A seller can continue to expand the geographic limits of its market as long as its net revenue after freight absorption is larger than its marginal cost for the units sold. Freight absorption is particularly useful to a firm whose fixed costs per unit of product are high and whose variable costs are low. In these cases, management must constantly seek ways to cover fixed costs, and freight absorption is one answer.

The legality of freight absorption is reasonably clear. The strategy is legal if it is used independently and not in collusion with other firms. Also, it must be used only to meet competition. In fact, if practised properly, freight absorption can have the effect of strengthening competition because it can break down geographic monopolies.

ONE-PRICE VERSUS VARIABLE-PRICE STRATEGY

Rather early in its pricing deliberations, management should decide whether to follow a one-price strategy or a variable-price strategy. While adopting one does not necessarily preclude the use of the other, normally it is not wise to waver back and forth.

Under a **one-price** strategy, the company charges the same price to all similar customers who purchase similar quantities of the product. Under a **variable-price** strategy, the company might sell similar quantities to similar buyers at different prices; the price is usually set as a result of bargaining.

In general, the one-price policy has been followed more than variable pricing, particularly at the retail level. In the marketing of any product where a trade-in is involved, however, variable pricing abounds. Thus a one-price policy is virtually unknown in automobile retailing, even though window-posted list prices may suggest that the same price is charged to all buyers.

A one-price policy builds customer confidence in a seller, whether at the manufacturing, wholesaling, or retailing level. Weak bargainers need not feel they are at a competitive disadvantage. A variable-price policy also has its advantages. For example, the seller may wish to make price concessions to woo a buyer away from a competitor. Or, a seller may want to give a buyer a better deal because that customer shows promise of becoming a large-scale buyer in the future. During recessionary times, more variable pricing appears at the instigation of both buyers and sellers. As conditions improve, the incidence of variable pricing decreases.

On balance, however, a variable-price strategy is generally less desirable than a one-price strategy. In sales to business firms, but not to consumers, variable pricing is likely to be in violation of the Combines Investigation Act. Variable pricing may also generate considerable ill will when the word gets around that some buyers acquired the product at lower prices.

UNSLTD PEANUTS

UNIT PRICE   RETAIL PRICE
$4.52   **$3.89**
PER KILOGRAM

Unit-pricing shelf labels reduce prices to a common basis.

UNIT PRICING

Unit pricing is a retail price-information strategy that, to date, has been employed largely by supermarket chains. The method is, however, adaptable to other types of stores and products. The strategy is a business response to consumer protests concerning the proliferation of package sizes, especially in grocery stores. Prior to metrication, the practice made it virtually impossible to compare the prices of similar products. Regarding canned beans, for example: Was a can labelled "15½ avoirdupois ounces" for 39 cents a better deal than two "1 pound 1 ounce (482 grams)" cans for 89 cents? After metrication, at least the measurement units became standardized — if not well understood. The comparison of different packages in grams or millilitres is certainly easier than pound and ounce combinations. With more standard package sizes, consumers have an even easier task.

Now with unit pricing, for each separate product and package size there is a shelf label that states (1) the price of the package and (2) this price expressed in dollars and cents per metric unit of standard measure.

Unit pricing was instituted in the 1970s. The hope is that as a result, consumers are making more knowledgeable purchases.[4] The cost of installing and maintaining unit pricing is presumably offset by societal benefits.

18200 00902

The universal product code label from a beer six-pack.

ALL
DRESSES

$ 39⁹⁵
$ 44⁹⁵
$ 49⁹⁵

Periods of continuing
inflation, like that of the
1970s and early 1980s,
can be a problem for
stores featuring
price lines.

To an increasing extent, supermarkets and other retail stores are using
electronic scanners at the checkout stands to read the Universal Product
Code on products. Some of these retailers are no longer price-marking each
individual item in a store. In such situations, which are becoming more
common, unit-pricing shelf signs clearly are important, if not absolutely
essential, to provide consumers with price information.

Price lining is used extensively by retailers of all types of apparel. It consists of selecting a limited number of prices at which a store will sell its
merchandise. Thus, a shoe store may sell several styles of shoes at $39.95
a pair, another group at $49.95, and a third assortment at $59.95.

For the consumer, the main benefit of price lining is that it simplifies
buying decisions. From the retailer's point of view, the strategy is advantageous because it helps store owners plan their purchases. A dress buyer,
for example, can go into a market looking for dresses that can be retailed
for $59.95, $69.95, or $89.95.

Rising costs can put a real squeeze on price lines because a company
hesitates to change its price line every time costs go up. But if costs increase and prices remain stationary, profit margins are compressed, and
the retailer may be forced to seek products with lower costs. Where price
lines are traditional, as they are for candy bars, manufacturers may reduce
the product's size or quality (and thus its cost) to enable retailers to hold
prices at existing levels.

PRICE LINING

---

[4]See J. Edward Russo, "The Value of Unit Price Information," *Journal of Marketing Research*,
May 1977, pp. 193–201; also Bruce F. McElroy and David A. Aaker, "Unit Pricing Six Years
after Introduction," *Journal of Retailing*, Fall 1979, pp. 44–57.

RESALE PRICE MAINTENANCE

Some manufacturers want control over the prices at which retailers resell the manufacturers' products. This is most often done in Canada by following a policy of providing manufacturers' suggested list prices, where the price is just a guide for retailers. It is a list price on which discounts may be computed. For others, the suggested price is "informally" enforced. Normally, enforcement of a suggested price, termed resale price maintenance, has been illegal in Canada since 1951.[5] In this country, attempts on the part of the manufacturers to control or to influence upward the prices at which their products are sold by retailers have been considered akin to price fixing.

Section 38 of the Combines Investigation Act prohibits a manufacturer or supplier from requiring or inducing a retailer to sell a product at a particular price or not below a particular price. On occasion, a supplier may attempt to control retail prices through the use of a "suggested retail price." Under section 38, the use of "suggested retail prices" is permitted *only* if the supplier makes it clear to the retailer that the product *may* be sold at a price below the suggested price and that the retailer will not in any way be discriminated against if the product is sold at a lower price. Also, where a manufacturer advertises a product, and in the advertisement mentions a certain price, the manufacturer must make it clear in the advertisement that the product *may* be sold at a lower price.

Prior to 1975 it was legal in Canada for a manufacturer to refuse to supply a product to a retailer if that retailer was selling that product as a loss leader or was using the product in "bait advertising" to attract people to his or her store. The 1975 amendments to the Combines Investigation Act eliminated this provision, and it is now illegal for a manufacturer to refuse to supply a product to a retailer because of the pricing policies of the retailer. In other words, a retailer is free to sell a product at whatever price he or she deems appropriate, and the manufacturer of that product is not permitted to exert any pressure on the retailer to sell at a particular price.

In recent years, Canadian courts have dealt with a large number of cases involving alleged efforts on the part of suppliers to influence resale prices. In these cases, convictions have resulted in the imposition of fines as large as $15,000. There is, however, some question concerning the effectiveness of the legislation and this activity in the courts in reducing the incidence of resale price maintenance. Cases involving this practice do not reach the courts unless a retailer is willing to register a complaint against a supplier. There is some evidence that, despite the provisions of section 38, some suppliers still employ certain measures that ensure that prices are maintained at the retail level.

LEADER PRICING AND UNFAIR-PRACTICES ACTS

Many firms, primarily retailers, temporarily cut prices on a few items to attract customers. This price and promotional strategy is called **leader pricing**, and the items whose prices are cut are called **loss leaders**. These leader items should be well-known, heavily advertised articles that are purchased frequently.

---

[5]For excellent background information on the regulation of resale price maintenance in Canada, the reader is referred to *Restrictive Trade Practices in Canada*, L. A. Skeoch (ed.), McClelland and Stewart, Limited, Toronto, 1966, pp. 156–157.

The idea is that customers will come to the store to buy the advertised leader items and then stay to buy other regularly priced merchandise. The net result, the firm hopes, will be increased total volume and total profit.

Three provinces, British Columbia, Alberta, and Manitoba, have had legislation dealing with loss leader selling. The approach has been to prohibit a reseller from selling an item below invoice cost, including freight, plus a stated markup, which is usually 5 percent at retail. No prosecutions had taken place under these provincial statutes up to time of writing.[6]

The general intent of these laws is commendable. They eliminate much of the predatory type of price-cutting; however, they permit firms to use loss leaders as a price and promotional strategy. That is, a retailer can offer an article below full cost but still sell above cost plus 5 percent markup. Under such Acts low-cost, efficient businessmen are not penalized, nor are high-cost operators protected. Differentials in retailers' purchase prices can be reflected in their selling prices, and savings resulting from the absence of services can be passed on to the customers.

On the other hand, the Acts have some glaring weaknesses. In the first place, the provinces do not establish provisions or agencies for enforcement. It is the responsibility and burden of the injured party to seek satisfaction from the offender in a civil suit. Another limitation is that it is difficult or even impossible to determine the cost of doing business for each individual product. The third weakness is that the laws seem to disregard the fundamental idea that the purpose of a business is to make a profit on the total operation, and not necessarily on each sale of each product.

PSYCHOLOGICAL PRICING — ODD PRICING

We have already briefly discussed some pricing strategies that might be called **psychological pricing**. For example, there is price lining, prestige pricing above competitive levels, and *raising* a too-low price in order to *increase* sales. At the retail level, another psychological pricing strategy is commonly used. Prices are set at odd amounts, such as 49 cents, 89 cents, and $19.95. Automobiles are priced at $8,995 rather than $9,000, and houses sell for $89,950 instead of $90,000.

In general, retailers believe that pricing items at odd amounts will result in larger sales. Thus, a price of 49 cents or 98 cents will bring greater revenue than a price of 50 cents or $1. Furthermore, retailers believe that buying psychology is such that odd prices will bring more sales volume than the next *lower* even-numbered price. That is, at 49 cents or 97 cents, a firm will sell more units than at 48 cents or 96 cents. If this is true, the seller's average revenue curve will have the zigzag shape shown in Fig. 13-2.

There is little concrete evidence to support retailers' belief in the value of odd prices. Various studies have reported inconclusive results.[7] Odd pricing is often avoided in prestige stores or on higher-priced items. Thus, expensive men's suits are priced at $450, not $449.95.

---

[6]See L. A. Skeoch, "Canada" in B. S. Yamey (ed.), *Resale Price Maintenance*, Weidenfeld and Nicolson, London, 1966, pp. 62–63.

[7]For example, see Zarrel V. Lambert, "Perceived Prices as Related to Odd and Even Price Endings," *Journal of Retailing*, Fall 1975, pp. 13–22ff.

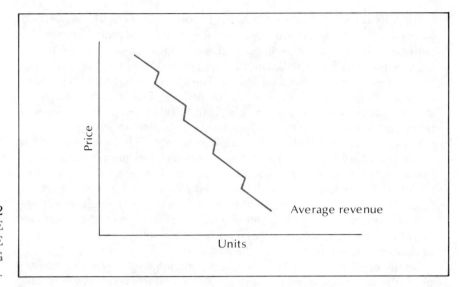

Figure 13-2
DEMAND CURVE
PRESUMED TO FACE
A FIRM USING
ODD PRICING.

Some segments of the curve slope negatively. That is, as the price declines, volume also decreases. The zig-zag shape reflects the idea that a familiar odd price will bring more sales volume than the even-numbered prices immediately below these figures. Do you agree? What types of stores use odd pricing? What products lend themselves to odd pricing?

PRICING IN PERIODS OF INFLATION

The inflation that has plagued the Canadian economy (and many foreign economies as well) for several years is moderating but can return in the foreseeable future. Inflation presents some real problems to executives in their management of a marketing program—especially in the area of pricing. Management must develop innovative and creative pricing strategies to meet the continuing challenge of inflation.

The management of price-increase strategies involves the timing, size, and method of implementing the increase. Here are a few examples:

1. Some companies have "unbundled" their prices and now charge extra for services that once were included as part of the base price. A firm may now charge extra for delivery, repairs, or some types of credit sales.

2. Management may reduce the percentage of cash or quantity discounts.

3. Long-term sales contracts may include various renegotiation and price-escalator clauses. These clauses provide for price and terms-of-sale changes in line with increases in the government index of consumer prices or wholesale prices.

4. Some firms simply add a flat percentage surcharge to prices quoted in catalogues, menus, or other printed price lists.

Prices generally are raised during inflation because a firm's costs have increased. So another series of managerial challenges involves ways to control (and even to reduce) some costs, thus reducing the upward pressure on prices. One such cost-control strategy is to eliminate low-profit products from a company's product mix. However, care must be taken not to drop products that customers expect the seller to carry as a normal part of the product mix. Also, the remaining products must absorb the share of fixed costs formerly carried by the eliminated products.

Another cost-control approach is to conduct an analysis of a company's marketing costs to identify high-cost customers, sales territories, and products. Then measures can be taken to reduce these costs or to drop particular customers, territories, or products. (Marketing cost analysis is discussed in Chapter 24.)

In the course of developing its marketing program, management has a choice of emphasizing price competition or nonprice competition. This choice can affect various other parts of the firm's marketing system.

PRICE VERSUS NONPRICE COMPETITION

Price Competition

In our economy today, there still is a considerable amount of price competition. A firm can effectively engage in price competition by regularly offering prices that are as low as possible. Along with this, the seller usually offers a minimum of services. In their early years, discount houses and chain stores competed in this way. A firm can also use price to compete by (1) changing its prices and (2) reacting to price changes made by a competitor.

Price Changes by the Firm

Any one of several situations may prompt a firm to change its price. As costs increase, for instance, management may decide that the best course of action is to raise the price, rather than to cut quality or aggressively promote the product and still maintain the price. If a company's share of the market is declining because of strong competition, its executives may react initially by *reducing* their price. In the long run, however, their best alternative may be to improve their own marketing program, rather than to rely on the price cut. *Temporary* price cuts may be used to correct an imbalance in inventory or to introduce a new product.

From the seller's standpoint, the big disadvantage in price cutting is that competitors will retaliate. This is especially true in oligopolistic market situations. The net result can be a price war, and the price may even settle permanently at a lower level. Note that "oligopoly" does not necessarily imply *large* firms. Oligopoly means "a few sellers." Thus a neighbourhood group of small merchants — barbers, for instance — can constitute an oligopoly. These merchants will try to avoid price competition, because if one reduces prices, all must follow.

Reaction to Competitors' Price Changes

Any firm can assume that its competitors will change their prices. Consequently, every firm should at least be ready with some policy guidelines on how it will react, or, better yet, have an established plan for reacting. Advance planning is particularly necessary in the case of a competitive price *reduction*, since time is then of the essence. If a competitor *boosts* prices, a reasonable delay in reacting will probably not be perilous. In fact, it may turn out to be the wise thing to do if this increase was a mistake.

Nonprice Competition

In nonprice competition, sellers maintain stable prices. They attempt to improve their market position by emphasizing other aspects of their marketing programs. Of course, competitive prices still must be taken into consideration, and price changes will occur over time. Nevertheless, in a nonprice competitive situation the emphasis is on something other than price.

By using terms familiar in economic theory, we can differentiate nonprice competition from price competition. In price competition, sellers attempt to move up or down their individual demand curves by changing prices. In nonprice competition, sellers attempt to *shift* their demand curves to the right by means of product differentiation, promotional activities, or some other device. This point is illustrated in Fig. 13-3. The demand curve faced by the producer of a given model of skis is DD. At a price of $150, the producer can sell 35,000 pairs a year. On the basis of price competition alone, sales can be increased to 55,000 if the producer is willing to reduce the price to $130. The demand curve is still DD.

However, the producer is interested in boosting sales without any decrease in selling price. Consequently, the firm embarks upon a promotional

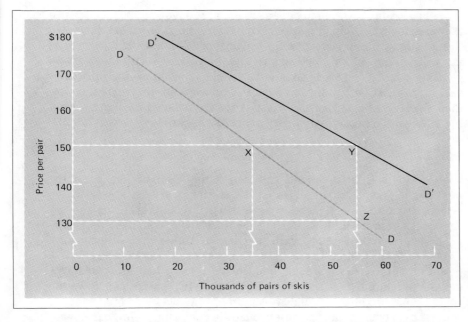

Figure 13-3
SHIFT IN DEMAND
CURVE FOR SKIS.

The use of nonprice competition can shift the demand curve for a product. A company selling skis used a promotional program to sell more skis at the same price, thus shifting DD to D′D′. Volume increased from 35,000 to 55,000 units at $150 (point X to point Y). Besides advertising, what other devices might this firm use to shift its demand curve?

program—a form of nonprice competition. Suppose enough new customers are persuaded to buy at the original $150 price so that unit sales increase to 55,000 pairs a year. In effect, the firm's entire demand curve has been shifted to position D′D′.

Nonprice competition is being used increasingly in marketing. Companies want, at least to some extent, to be the masters of their own destiny. In nonprice competition, a seller's entire advantage is not removed when a competitor decides to undersell. Furthermore, there is little customer loyalty when price is the only feature that distinguishes the seller. Buyers will stick only as long as that seller offers the lowest price.

Two of the major methods of nonprice competition are **promotion** and **product differentiation**. In addition, some firms emphasize the **variety and quality of their services**.

The use of **trading stamps**—which can be exchanged for gifts or cash— as a method of nonprice competition has fluctuated over the years. Trading stamps hit a peak of popularity in the late 1960s but declined more than 50 percent in *product* marketing in the early 1970s. Gasoline shortages and a drive to lower food prices generally eliminated the two largest buyers of stamps — gas stations and supermarkets. Some of this decline was offset by an increased use of stamps by *service* marketing firms—banks, travel agencies, and others.

Trading stamps do seem to offer a competitive advantage to the first firm that uses them in a given market. When many firms use them, however, this advantage disappears. Stamps usually cost the retailers 2 percent of sales. (They pay $2 for 1,000 stamps and then give 1 stamp for every 10 cents' worth of purchases.) Obviously, retailers must raise their prices or absorb this cost by cutting some other expenses. Or, they may increase their sales volume so that *unit fixed* costs are reduced enough to offset the 2 percent increase in *unit variable* costs.

SUMMARY

After deciding on pricing goals and then setting the base (list) price, the next task in pricing is to establish specific strategies in several areas of the pricing structure. One of these areas relates to discounts and allowances— deductions from the list price. Management has the option of offering quantity discounts, trade discounts, cash discounts, and other types of deductions. The factor of freight costs must also be considered in pricing strategy. A producer can pay all the freight (uniform delivered price) or let the buyer pay the freight bill (f.o.b. factory price). Or, the two parties can share the cost in some proportion (freight absorption). Any decisions involving discounts or freight allowances must be made in conformity with the relevant sections of the Combines Investigation Act. This is the major legislation relating to price discrimination and other aspects of a company's marketing program.

Management should decide whether to offer the same price to all similar buyers (one-price strategy) or to adopt a variable pricing strategy. Unit pricing—a relatively new development—can affect a company's marketing program. Some firms, especially retailers, have adopted price lining as a marketing strategy. Many retailers use leader pricing to stimulate sales. Odd pricing is a psychological pricing strategy commonly used by retailers.

An inflationary economy presents real challenges to marketing executives, especially in the management of the pricing sector of their marketing mixes. Consequently, companies need to develop pricing strategies designed especially to counter the effects of inflation. A basic decision facing management is whether to engage primarily in price competition or in nonprice competition. Most firms prefer to use promotion, product differentiation, and other nonprice marketing activities, rather than to rely only on price as a sales stimulant.

KEY TERMS AND CONCEPTS

Quantity discount 331

Trade discount 332

Cash discount 332

Combines Investigation Act 334

F.o.b. factory price 338

Uniform delivered price 338

Zone delivered price 339

Freight absorption 339

QUESTIONS AND PROBLEMS

1. Carefully distinguish between cumulative and noncumulative quantity discounts. Which of these two types of quantity discounts has the greater economic and social justification? Why?

2. A manufacturer of appliances quotes a list price of $500 per unit for a certain model of refrigerator and grants trade discounts of 35, 20, and 5 percent. What is the manufacturer's selling price? Who might get these various discounts?

3. Two families living in the same apartment house each purchased a set of dining room furniture from the same retailer. One family was charged $25 more than the other. Is this a violation of the Combines Investigation Act?

4. Company A sells to all its customers at the same published price. A sales executive finds that company B is offering to sell to one of A's customers at a lower price. Company A then cuts its price to this customer but maintains the original price for all other customers. Is this a violation of the Combines Investigation Act?

5. Name some products that might logically be sold under a uniform delivered price system.

6. "An f.o.b. point-of-purchase price system is the only geographic price system that is fair to all buyers." Discuss.

7. An eastern firm wants to compete in western markets, where it is at a significant disadvantage with respect to freight costs. What pricing alternatives can it adopt to help it overcome the freight differential?

8. Under what marketing conditions is a company likely to use a variable-price strategy? Can you name some firms that employ this strategy, other than when a trade-in is involved?

9. What effects is unit pricing likely to have on a manufacturer's marketing program?

10. Distinguish between leader pricing and predatory price cutting.

11. Explain the reasoning underlying the zigzag shape of the demand curve in Fig. 13-2. Does this demand phenomenon actually exist in real life?

12. How should a manufacturer of prefinished plywood interior wall panelling react if a competitor cuts prices?

13. What factors account for the increased use of nonprice competition?

14. On the basis of the topics covered in this chapter, establish a set of price strategies for the manufacturer of a new glass cleaner that is sold through a broker to supermarkets. The manufacturer sells the product at $8 for a case of a dozen 454-ml bottles.

15. Suppose you are president of a company that has just developed a camera and film process somewhat comparable to Polaroid's. The camera is designed

to be used only with film produced by your firm. The chief marketing executive recommended that the camera be priced relatively low and the film relatively high. The idea was to make it easy to buy the camera, because from then on the customer would have to buy the company's film. The company's chief accountant said "no" to that idea. He wanted to price both camera and film in relation to their full cost plus a reasonable profit. You are mulling over these alternative strategies and also wondering whether there is not a third alternative, better than either of those two. Which pricing strategy would you adopt for the new camera and film?

Case 12
Green Valley Landscaping Co. Ltd.

Pricing a Service in a New Company

Last spring, Martin Dixon and Harvey Scully decided to become partners in a lawn-care business. Both had college degrees in horticulture. Eventually they wanted to grow into the business of landscape gardening or landscape architecture—hence their conservative choice of a company name. (Their original idea for a name was "Marty and Harvey—The Twin Clippers," accompanied by the slogan "You grow it, we mow it.")

However, Marty and Harvey realistically acknowledged that they would have to start out at a more modest level. They also realized that initially most of their business would involve mowing and trimming lawns. Consequently, one of their first concerns was how to price their mowing and trimming services.

Green Valley Landscaping was located in a small city (population 20,000) near Calgary. The initial services offered by the company included weekly mowing at a grass height of 6 cm, catching the grass clippings, and trimming the edges of the lawn. As soon as they could become better established, Dixon and Scully intended to provide such services as weed control, fertilizing, aerating, power raking, pruning, laying sod, installing sprinkler systems, and specialized landscape design.

Currently, their were three other lawn-care firms operating in Green Valley's market area. One specialized in liquid fertilizing and offered a mowing service on the side. A second competitor specialized in lawn care for commercial accounts such as apartment complexes. The third firm—Foster's Lawn Service—maintained a variety of accounts, but was not accepting any new business at the present time.

Marty Dixon identified the following four market segments as the best target markets for Green Valley:

1. Senior citizens who were physically unable to mow their lawns. Because most of these people were living on a fixed income, price was very important to them.

2. People who were too busy to cut their own grass. This segment included households where both the husband and wife were working. Dixon felt that price was important in this market also.

3. Higher-income people who could afford more services, who were concerned with the appearance of their yards, and who liked the prestige of having their own lawn service. These people were not very price-conscious.

4. Owners of commercial property — office buildings, stores, industrial sites, apartment complexes — that had lawns to maintain. These owners generally expected to pay for lawn-care service.

Dixon and Scully spent $2,500 for tools and equipment. They also bought a very used pickup truck for $2,800. They planned to amortize these costs over a three-year period. Administrative overhead expenses were estimated to be $1,500 a year. Salaries and wages were expected to be $2,300 each month during the May-to-October growing and operating seasons. The cost of operating the truck was 25 cents per mile. Other operating expenses (gasoline, oil, equipment maintenance) for mowing and trimming a lawn were estimated to be $1.25 per 1,000 square metres of lawn.

The partners planned to spend $600 on promotion during the first season. They planned to distribute pamphlets to homes in the higher-income areas of the city. They also wanted to run some display ads in the local papers and were considering running a classified ad in a local business directory.

Both partners realized the importance of developing a clientele that would use Green Valley's services throughout the entire growing season. The partners were willing to mow lawns on a one-time basis. However, they felt that they should charge more for this sporadic type of service than for repeat business. Repeat business would present fewer scheduling problems and could be done at a lower cost. Also, when a customer used Green Valley's mowing service on a regular basis, the customer was more likely to use other company services, such as pruning, fertilizing, and weed control.

The partners were somewhat at a loss as to (1) what pricing *method* they should use and (2) what general price *level* they should charge for their mowing and trimming service. Marty thought that they should base their charges on a fixed hourly rate. Harvey was in favour of charging at some rate per 1,000 square metres of lawn. Then they wondered whether they should offer some type of discount to stimulate new business. They talked about possibly offering a discount to senior citizens, or a referral discount to existing customers who brought them new customers.

The partners next calculated that they needed to charge a minimum of $28 per 1,000 square metres of lawn cutting to cover expenses. They then bid ten jobs at that price but landed only one of them. People whom they contacted in this bidding process generally seemed to think that $28 per 1,000 square metres of lawn was extremely high. Scully said he knew that many people hired neighbourhood kids to mow their lawns for $10 to $15, but both men agreed that Green Valley would not compete in what they called "this low-end market."

The men both realized they had to charge reasonable prices or they would not land many jobs. On the other hand, there had to be enough profit in the business for them to earn a decent wage and a satisfactory return on their investment. They also believed that the pricing of their mowing and trimming service was going to have a substantial influence on the success of the other services they intended to provide later.

Question

How should Dixon and Scully price their mowing and trimming service?

Pricing a New Product

A few months ago, Mr. Aaron Harber, the president of Life-Lite Safety Products, was completing his marketing plans for the introduction of a new bicycle light. The product, called Laser-Lite, was ready for the market. All that remained to be determined were the suggested retail price and the wholesale price.

Laser-Lite was a green fluorescent bicycle light. The colour green was selected because it was found to be one of the colours most visible to the human eye. Laser-Lite produced 360 degrees of illumination and was considered a significant improvement in nighttime bicycling safety.

The light, about the size of a bicycle air pump, featured a 200 mm-long safety tube — a glass tube within a plastic tube. It weighed 700 grams and was both break- and weather-resistant. The light was activated by a small generator that produced power from the revolution of the bicycle wheels, starting at very low speeds (about 5 kph).

It was fairly easy to assemble the Laser-Lite. The light itself was attached to the frame of the bicycle under the seat, and the generator was attached to the frame in the rear. The product had been tested for up to ten years of normal usage (3,000 hours) and was fully guaranteed for ninety days.

The Life-Lite Company purchased the Laser-Lites from an assembler. Life-Lite then repackaged and distributed the product. The delivered price to Life-Lite was $6 a light. Additional expenses to Life-Lite were (1) the packages, which cost $1.15 each; (2) advertising, estimated at $30,000 a year; and (3) annual overhead of $15,000, which included the rent and salaries charged to the Laser-Lite project.

No statistics were published on annual bicycle-light sales. However, from conversations with people in the bicycle industry, Mr. Harber estimated that about 5 percent of *all* bicycles and 15 percent of *new* bicycles were equipped with lighting systems. If future legislation were to require light systems on all new bicycles sold, Mr. Harber realized that the bicycle-light industry would be booming. A relatively small amount of advertising was done by the manufacturer of bicycle lights. Mr. Harber estimated that with an effective advertising campaign, his company could achieve a 10 percent market share in the bicycle-light industry.

Because the demand for bicycle lights is derived from the demand for bicycles, Mr. Harber also realized that he should investigate the bicycle market in some depth.

Both the sale of bicycles and bicycling as an adult activity enjoyed a boom during the 1970s. During the late 1970s, sales of new bikes ran at the rate of 9 to 10 million units a year, according to industry trade association figures. The same source indicated an increase of 8 to 10 percent per year through the 1980s. Industry figures in 1960 indicated that, of the new bikes sold, less than 12 percent were for adult use. By 1980, two-thirds to three-quarters of new-bike purchases were for adult use.

One major deterrent to an even greater public commitment to the bicycle was the safety factor. Each year more bike riders were killed in traffic accidents. The hazards associated with bike riding prompted regulatory

*Adapted from case prepared by Randi Silverman, University of Colorado student.

organizations to establish stringent standards covering the manufacture and sale of bicycles. One of these standards included the requirement for reflectors.

Many local governments required both reflectors and lights for night-time riding, but these requirements had not been strictly enforced in the past. Because of the increase in accidents, however, Mr. Harber came to the conclusion that many local governments would soon be enforcing their safety standards more strictly. The general opinion among bicycle retailers was that in the near future, every bicycle would be required to have a lighting system. Mr. Harber estimated that if that situation were to occur, the primary demand for bicycle lights would be increased to about five times its present level.

On the basis of customers' reasons for buying, Mr. Harber identified three market segments for bicycle lights. The first was a small group of people who purchased a bike light *only* for the safety factor. Price was not an important buying consideration for these people. The second group were young people who were interested in the Laser-Lite purely as a novelty item, and price was of paramount importance. The third, and largest, group were attracted to the product for both safety and novelty reasons. These people needed to feel they were extremely visible when riding at night. At the same time, the novelty feature was important because there was no other *green* bike light on the market.

Following up on this segmentation analysis, Mr. Harber pinpointed four target markets for the Laser-Lite:

1.   People who commuted by bicycle to and from work. Laser-Lite was effective in twilight hours — both dawn and dusk.

2.   School and college students (and, to a lesser extent, other members of college communities) who rode extensively during twilight and dark hours.

3.   Children and teenagers who were attracted by the novelty of the product.

4.   Parents who were concerned about the safety of their bike-riding children.

Both battery-powered and generator-powered bicycle lights provided effective competition for the Laser-Lite. The battery-powered lights ranged from $2 to $18 in retail price. The most popular model was an 8 mm lightweight plastic light that was strapped to the cyclist's leg. Battery-powered lights also came in the traditional models that were attached to the front or the back of the bike.

Generator-powered lights — the category that was more directly comparable to the Laser-Lite — were a little more expensive, with a retail price between $10 and $20. These lights operated on power that was generated by the revolving wheels. The lights were attached to the frame of the bicycle. The power-generation mechanism caused some resistance while pedaling. It was this feature that sometimes made the generator-powered models less appealing to serious bicyclists. Laser-Lite minimized this drawback with its low-drag feature.

Eventually the company hoped to sell Laser-Lite directly to bike manufacturers that would include it as part of a bicycle that was fitted with accessories. In the meantime, however, the Laser-Lite would be marketed as a separate product.

Life-Lite planned to distribute its new product nationally, using two channels of distribution. In the first channel, the product would be sold directly to mass merchandisers such as Canadian Tire, K Mart, and Sears. This group of retailers accounted for about 50 percent of the sales of new bicycles. In the other major channel, Laser-Lite would be distributed through wholesalers, that, in turn, would sell to bicycle specialty stores and to department stores that carried a small assortment of bicycles.

For a product like bicycle lights, the usual markup was 20 percent to wholesalers and 40 to 50 percent to retailers. (These markups are stated as a percentage of the given firm's selling price.)

In the course of arriving at a suggested price schedule, Mr. Harber was wondering how elastic the demand would be for a product like Laser-Lite. He also wondered whether the company should adopt a pricing strategy of skimming or penetration pricing.

In an earlier test-marketing experiment, Laser-Lite had been introduced in Florida, but with limited promotion and only limited sales success. During this market trial, the retail price ranged from $19.95 to $24.95.

A limited marketing research project also was conducted to learn something about consumers' price expectations and perceptions. Consumers under 18 years of age felt that the product should be priced at $5 to $10. Those between the ages of 18 and 24 generally priced the product between $15 and $25.

Mr. Harber wanted to come up with a price structure for Laser-Lite that would best suit the product in the long run.

Question

What should be the manufacturer's selling price for Laser-Lite? The wholesaler's selling price? The retailer's selling price?

Price Determination

Wilson Electronics was an industrial supplier of small electronic components used by other manufacturing firms. The company prided itself on the quality of its products and on its ability to manufacture to the precise specifications of industrial customers.

One of Wilson's major customers was a producer of a varied line of equipment and appliances. This customer, Magnus Manufacturing Ltd., purchased a wide line of Wilson products. Magnus had contracted with Wilson to purchase an intricate thermostatic switch. To produce the requested item, known as Model K-50, Wilson developed a specialized stamping machine

Case 14
Wilson
Electronics
Co. Ltd. *

*Case prepared by Prof. Barry J. Hersker, Florida Atlantic University. Used with permission.

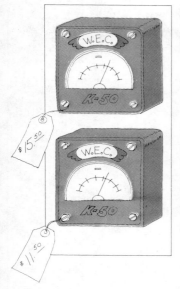

that could not be readily used for any other purpose, at an investment of almost $250,000. At the time the decision was made, Magnus Manufacturing agreed to purchase at least 10,000 units of K-50 yearly at a price not to exceed $16 per unit for a minimum of five years. Wilson estimated that the cost of production of K-50, including depreciation on the specialized machinery, would approximate this price. That is, Wilson only expected to break even on K-50, but the Magnus account was believed to be so important that Wilson undertook to produce this item as a service to this customer. The possibility of selling additional quantities of K-50 to others was considered to be rather remote. However, the physical capacity to increase output existed, and such production would not require any additional capital investment.

A problem in quality control developed with K-50 during the third contract year. To settle the resulting dispute, Wilson agreed to lower the price of K-50 units to $15.50 each. Mr. Maxwell, president of Wilson, stated, "We are determined to maintain the loyal patronage of Magnus Manufacturing. Their volume of purchases is considerable. We must remember that the machinery and equipment currently used on K-50 cannot readily be used for any other production. It cannot be permitted to remain idle."

The following year, the purchasing director of Rigbee Controls, which was not a customer of Wilson, contacted the firm about an unusual requirement for a thermostatic switch. The Wilson engineers discovered that with minor changes in specifications, K-50 would adequately fulfil Rigbee's requirements. Rigbee then asked Wilson to quote a price for quantities of 15,000 units annually. Rigbee also said that it would contract for delivery in these quantities for several years to come.

Wilson engineers reconfirmed the fact that ample capacity existed to expand production of K-50. The comptroller, Fred Shaw, indicated that production costs would be lower at this increased volume. He estimated that the reduced costs could permit Wilson to earn a profit estimated at $3.68 per K-50 unit. It was decided to offer K-50 to Rigbee at $15.50 each.

Rigbee's executives responded that they could not use K-50 at any price higher than $11.50 per unit. They said they would be better off substituting another apparatus entirely if that price could not be met. Rigbee's executives also admitted that they probably never would be a large purchaser of Wilson products other than K-50. The Wilson engineers confirmed the fact that Rigbee could not afford K-50 at more than $11.50 and that Rigbee would probably never purchase any other items from Wilson. They also confirmed that Magnus would not use more than 10,000 of the K-50 units annually, no matter how low Wilson set the price. One Wilson vice president said that maybe the Rigbee price would be acceptable. He thought the increased volume would lower production costs enough to offset the small loss resulting from the sale of K-50 to Magnus at $15.50.

"You're not suggesting that we sell to Rigbee at $11.50 and to Magnus at $15.50, are you?" exclaimed Mr. Ernest Bennett, the vice president of the sales division. "This line of reasoning is out of the question! Most Rigbee and Magnus executives are friends. How would Magnus react if we charge our good customer more than we charge Rigbee? This conduct is highly questionable on both a legal and an ethical basis."

Mr. Maxwell interrupted the dispute and asked the vice president of sales for his specific suggestions on the matter. "Well, let's look at it this way," Mr. Bennett responded. "K-50 has been an apparent loser. The reason — sales were too low! We've got the chance to add 15,000 more units, and we believe we could sell still another 25,000 units if we priced realistically! The specifications of K-50 lend themselves to a wider range of industrial applications than we thought. Five more of our accounts would be willing to buy this item, which would push our volume to 50,000 units per year. This is, admittedly, our current productive capacity, but I feel sure we could reach this level within one year."

"Mr. Bennett, your job is to sell our products," Mr. Maxwell interrupted, "but why haven't we exploited this market potential long ago?"

"Well, to hit a capacity volume of 50,000 units, we need to offer K-50 at a competitive price. If we can offer the item for $10, I know this volume can be reached," Mr. Bennett replied.

"Pardon the interruption," broke in Alfred Horn, assistant to the president. "Wouldn't this price be below our cost of production?"

"I have asked the treasurer to bring the detailed cost data for capacity volume. Did you, Fred?" Mr. Bennett asked.

Fred Shaw, the treasurer, was the next to speak. "Ernest, I'm sorry that I did not have time to go over this with you in greater detail before. Costs are lower toward capacity, but these savings are not as great as you evidently assumed. I prepared a cost schedule to make it easier for us to view the situation at various volumes. I calculated unit costs and charges at 10,000, 25,000, and 50,000 unit levels of production. Labour charges per unit are constant, since this is a machine operation and output varies directly with the time of the run. We experience some economies on material by purchasing in larger quantities, and our subcontractor will be able to plate the necessary components at half the price if we hit 50,000 units. But, on the other hand, we must remember that capacity volume will require more frequent servicing. We'll lose some ground here — 3 cents in indirect charges, to be exact, between 25,000 and 50,000 units. But, of course, that is only an added expenditure of $1,500."

"You'll have to slow up, Fred, I'm afraid this grey head can't absorb your calculations quite so quickly," Mr. Maxwell interrupted.

"I'm sorry, Mr. Maxwell — perhaps I'd better distribute the data. If we sell and produce K-50 at a capacity output, our costs per unit only fall to $10.56. I've itemized these details for you on the cost sheet I've prepared for each of you." (At this point, Mr. Shaw distributed the cost data that are presented in Table 1.)

The executives examined the cost data for a few moments. Mr. Horn was the first to speak. "Perhaps I'd better summarize what Mr. Shaw appears reluctant to point out. He is saying that Mr. Bennett would have us lose 56 cents on every item of K-50 we sell at this 50,000 volume! Or at least we would, in fact, lose 32 cents per item if we even sell to Rigbee and hit a total of 25,000 units! I say, just sell only to Magnus as a favour at $15.50 and let the sleeping dogs lie."

"Never mind," exclaimed Mr. Maxwell angrily. "We here at Wilson have an obligation to our stockholders as well as to our customers. It appears that I was the one who made all the decisions on the K-50 from the very beginning. So I'll make this one, too. This meeting is adjourned!"

Table 1   UNIT COSTS FOR MODEL K-50 AT VARIOUS PRODUCTION
VOLUMES

Costs	Unit Costs at Output of:		
	10,000	25,000	50,000
Labour	$ 3.18	$ 3.18	$ 3.18
Material	1.52	1.48	1.44
Plating	.10	.08	.05
Indirect charges*	.48	.48	.51
Depreciation allowance†	4.00	1.60	.80
Overhead‡	1.06	1.06	1.06
Total factory production cost	$10.34	$ 7.88	$ 7.04
Selling and administration charges§	5.17	3.94	3.52
Total costs per unit	$15.51	$11.82	$10.56

*Indirect charges include supplies, repairs, and routine maintenance on specialized equipment, electric power, etc., expressed on a per-unit-of-output basis.

†Depreciation is straight-line basis over life of Magnus contract, less residual value, computed per unit of output.

‡Allocation to cover fixed factory overhead costs, charged at the rate of 33.3% of direct labour.

§Allocation to cover selling and administrative expenses, charged at the rate of 50% of total factory production costs.

Questions

1. Analyse the cost data, especially considering the fixed and variable costs and the allocation bases.
2. What action should Mr. Maxwell take regarding the Rigbee offer and the pricing of the K-50 switch?

Case 15 Bentley Fresh Brew Tea (C)*

Pricing Strategies for a New Brand

Mr. Don Evans, president of The Newfoundland Tea Company, was preparing the pricing section of his marketing plan for Bentley Fresh Brew Tea. He realized pricing was a critical factor to the success of the brand for three reasons: (1) it strongly influenced consumer demand levels, (2) it determined gross revenue, and therefore strongly influenced net profit, and (3) it was a key factor in the "positioning" of the brand in consumers' minds. The pricing decision was further complicated by its strong interrelationship with the three other elements of the marketing mix and their costs: product and packaging, advertising and promotion, and distribution channels. Among the key decision areas to be addressed were: (1) pricing objectives, (2) suggested retail price levels, (3) discounts and profit margins for channel middlemen, (4) promotional discounts and allowances, (5) quantity and other discounts, and (6) other pricing policies.

A major constraint to the pricing decision was the lack of complete

*Refer to Part (A) of this case for essential background and statistical information on the market, competition, and the brand.

information on fixed and variable costs. Overhead costs were incomplete because key decisions had yet to be made in areas such as: (1) advertising expenditures, (2) costs of recruiting, compensating, and managing a sales-force, if agents are not to be utilized in the distribution channel, (3) amount of plant and equipment costs to be allocated to Bentley, and (4) inventory levels and costs. Variable costs were also unknown, as no decision had been finalized on the actual composition and cost of the tea blend to be used; however, Mr. Evans felt certain that The Newfoundland Tea Company could keep comparable total variable costs per unit to within 10 percent of his competitors. Given the abovementioned costing deficiencies, it was not possible to accurately forecast profits or to conduct a break-even analysis at this stage of the planning process.

Being a small and new organization, The Newfoundland Tea Company had not formalized pricing objectives. Mr. Evans had a desire to generate an "adequate" profit and return on investment in the long run, and was willing to endure a small loss in the short term to enable Bentley Fresh Brew to become established. However, he was considering market share as one pricing objective. With an objective of obtaining a higher market share, he would probably need to price at low levels, and/or promote at special discounts frequently; production facilities, however, would need to be expanded significantly if the share increased beyond 25 percent. Alternately, a lower market share objective could possibly permit higher prices and greater gross profit per unit.

A key pricing decision yet to be made involved suggested retail price levels. While retailers are free by law to set their own selling prices, they often adopt manufacturers' suggested list prices to ensure their prices are not widely different from those of competing retailers. Mr. Evans realized that there were a number of key influences to consider before arriving at a final decision: consumer brand loyalty, if any; consumer price sensitivity; and competitors' pricing levels and practices. These areas are discussed in Part (A) of this case.

Mr. Evans was considering three broad pricing strategies for Bentley Fresh Brew. First, he could employ "penetration" pricing to encourage higher consumer trial and usage of the brand. This aggressive strategy of pricing low in the expected range of prices would probably mean shelf prices in the neighbourhood of $1.99 per "regular size" package. While it offered the potential of increasing volume, this strategy would reduce profit margins. A second strategy was "skimming," pricing high in the expected range of prices; this strategy would probably result in shelf prices of $2.49 or higher per "regular size" package. Potential advantages of such a strategy included higher unit profits; a hedge against cost miscalculations and/or pricing mistakes; positioning the brand as premium quality, given the price-quality relationship perceived by consumers in some situations; and allowing use of a higher-quality and higher-priced blend of teas without reducing profit margins.

A third pricing strategy open to Mr. Evans is often referred to as "meeting the competition." This strategy is sometimes felt to have the least risk, since consumers are conditioned to this "regular" price; however, as noted by Mr. Evans, such a strategy might suggest to consumers that Bentley was no different from the existing brands and therefore it offered no incentive to change from their "regular" brand.

An additional important consideration in the pricing decision was choice of distribution channel and types of middlemen used. As discussed in Part (D) of this case, manufacturers' agents (which would be used in lieu of a company-owned sales force) would require a commission of 5 percent to 8 percent of sales; wholesalers (which would stock and distribute the brand) normally require a profit margin of 9 percent to 14 percent of sales revenue. Retailers are reported to take a profit margin of 20 percent with the Tetley and Red Rose brands. Should Mr. Evans increase the profits/commissions to middlemen so as to ensure greater acceptance of and support for Bentley Fresh Brew? Such a decision would result in lower profit margins for The Newfoundland Tea Company, a loss that might be necessary and that could possibly be recouped by increased sales.

In addition to the abovementioned strategic pricing decisions, Mr. Evans also had to decide on various pricing policies for Bentley Fresh Brew. One policy area, promotional discounts and allowances, was particularly important. Tetley had offered discounts up to 15 percent for two-week periods on approximately ten occasions during the past year; partially as a result of this, supermarkets frequently promoted Tetley as an advertised special at prices ranging from $1.49 to $1.89 for the 72-bag package. Red Rose and King Cole were rarely promoted at special prices. Should Mr. Evans offer similar promotional discounts for Bentley and, if so, of what size and frequency?

Another area under consideration by Mr. Evans was the use of quantity discounts; while these had not been used to any extent by competitors, he felt both cumulative and noncumulative discounts had potential advantages for Bentley. In addition, he also had to make decisions on cash discounts, freight charges, if any, and merchandising allowances.

While analysing the facts before him in an effort to complete the pricing strategies section of his marketing plan, Mr. Evans contemplated one other essential area that could affect his decision: competitive retaliation. What reactions should he expect from competitors to counteract the introduction of Bentley Fresh Brew, and what contingency plans should he adopt to minimize their impact?

Question

What pricing strategies and policies would you recommend for Bentley Fresh Brew Tea? Why?

Part 5

Distribution

RETAILING AND WHOLESALING INSTITUTIONS, THE CHANNELS OF DISTRIBUTION FROM PRODUCER TO USER, AND THE PHYSICAL DISTRIBUTION OF A COMPANY'S PRODUCTS

We are in the process of developing a marketing program to reach the firm's target markets and to achieve the goals established in strategic marketing planning. So far, we have considered the product and the pricing structure in that marketing program. Now we turn our attention to the distribution system — the means for getting the product to the market.

Our discussion of the distribution ingredient in the marketing mix will include three broad topics: (1) the retailing and wholesaling institutional structure used in distribution (Chapters 14 and 15), (2) strategies for selecting and operating channels of distribution (Chapter 16), and (3) physical distribution systems for moving materials and supplies to production facilities and then moving finished products and services to target markets (Chapter 17).

Chapter 14

The Retail Market and Retailing Institutions

CHAPTER GOALS

The distribution of consumer products begins with the producer and ends with the ultimate consumer. Between the two there usually is at least one middleman — a retailer — who is the subject of this chapter. After studying the chapter, you should understand:

1. *What is a channel of distribution*
2. *The functions and importance of middlemen*
3. *The nature of the retail market*
4. *The differences between large-scale and small-scale retailing*
5. *The classification of retailers by:*
   a. *Product lines carried*
   b. *Form of ownership*
6. *The methods of selling in retailing*
   a. *Full-service, in-store*
   b. *Supermarket*
   c. *Discount*
   d. *Nonstore*
7. *Current trends in retailing*

Even before a product is ready for its market, management should determine what methods and routes will be used to get it there. This task involves the establishment of a strategy covering channels of distribution and the physical distribution of the product. Because retailing and wholesaling institutions are important parts of the distribution system, we shall discuss them first — in this chapter and the next. We begin by defining the terms *middleman* and *channel of distribution*, which we have already used in a more or less intuitive sense.

MIDDLEMEN AND CHANNELS OF DISTRIBUTION

What Are Middlemen?

A **middleman** is an independent business concern that operates as a link between producers and ultimate consumers or industrial users. Middlemen render services in connection with the purchase and/or sale of products

(a)   (b)

A middleman is an independent business concern that either (*a*) purchases products from producers and then resells them to consumers or to other middlemen, or (*b*) actively assists in the sale of the products without actually owning them.

moving from producers to consumers. Middlemen either take title to the merchandise as it flows from producer to consumer or actively aid in the transfer of ownership.

The essence of middlemen's operations is their active and prominent role in negotiations involving the buying and selling of goods. Their income arises directly from the proceeds of these transactions. Their involvement in the transfer of ownership is what differentiates middlemen from other business institutions, such as banks, insurance companies, and transportation firms. These other institutions help in the marketing process, but they do not take title and are not actively involved in purchase and sale negotiations. A middleman may or may not actually handle the products. Some middlemen store and transport merchandise, while others do not physically handle it at all.

Middlemen are commonly classified on the basis of whether or not they take title to the products involved. **Merchant** middlemen actually take title to the goods they are helping to market. **Agent** middlemen never actually own the goods, but they do actively assist in the transfer of title. Real estate brokers and manufacturers' agents are two example of agent middlemen. The two major groups of merchant middlemen are wholesalers and retailers. It should be noted particularly that retailers are merchant middlemen.

A **channel of distribution** (sometimes called **trade channel**) for a product is the route taken by the *title* to the product as it moves from the producer to the ultimate consumer or industrial user. A channel always includes both the producer and the final customer for the product, as well as all middlemen involved in the title transfer. Even though agent middlemen do *not* take actual title to the goods, they are included as part of a distribution channel. Again, this is done because they play such an active role in the transfer of ownership.

A trade channel does *not* include firms such as railroads and banks, which render marketing services but play no major role in negotiating purchases and sales. If a consumer buys apples from the grower at a roadside stand, or if a manufacturer sells a shirt by mail directly to a college student, the

What Is a Channel of Distribution?

channel is from producer to consumer. If the shirt manufacturer sold to a department store that in turn sold to the college student, the channel would be producer → retailer → consumer.

Sometimes we need to distinguish between the channel for the *title* to the goods and the channel for the *physical movement* of the goods. Frequently, these routes are partially different. A contractor might order a large load of sand or gravel from a local building supply house. The product would be shipped directly from the sand and gravel producer to the contractor to minimize freight and handling costs. The channel for the title (and for the invoice), however, would be producer → building supply house → contractor.

The channel for a product extends only to the last person who buys it without making any significant change in its form. When its form is altered and another product emerges, a new channel is started. When lumber is milled and then made into furniture, two separate channels are involved. The channel for the *lumber* may be lumber mill → broker → furniture manufacturer. The channel for the *finished furniture* may be furniture manufacturer → retail furniture store → consumer.

How Important Are Middlemen?

Middlemen are very important in many cases — in fact, in virtually *all* cases where consumers are involved. Usually, it simply is not practical for a producer to deal directly with ultimate consumers. Think for a moment how inconvenient it would be if there were no retail middlemen — no drugstores, newspaper stands, supermarkets, or gasoline stations.

There is an old saying in marketing that "you can eliminate the middlemen, but you cannot eliminate their functions (activities)." Someone has to perform those activities — if not the middlemen, then the producers or the final customers. Middlemen serve as purchasing agents for their customers and as sales specialists for their suppliers (see Fig. 14-1). Middlemen frequently provide various financial services for both their suppliers and their customers. The storage service of middlemen, their bulk-breaking activities (dividing large shipments into smaller quantities for resale), and the market information they provide benefit suppliers and customers alike.

In the next two chapters, we shall discuss the economic services provided by particular types of middlemen — services that justify their existence and demonstrate their importance. For now, let's look at a couple of broad concepts that illustrate the important role of middlemen in our economy.

Concentration, Equalization, Dispersion

Frequently, the quantity and assortment of goods produced by a firm are out of balance with the variety and amounts wanted by consumers or industrial users. A business needs paper, pencils, typewriters, and desks. A homeowner wants grass seed, topsoil, fertilizer, a rake, and eventually a lawn mower. No single firm produces all the items either of these users wants. And, no producer could afford to sell any of them in the small quantity the user desires. Obviously there is a need for someone to match what

BUYING for consumers
- Anticipates wants
- Bulk-breaking
- Storage and transportation
- Installation and repair
- Financing
- Guarantees the product

RETAILING MIDDLEMEN

SELLING for producers
- Sales specialist
- Advertises
- Interprets wants
- Acts as buffer
- Bulk-breaking
- Financing
- Storage

Figure 14-1
THE RETAILER
PROVIDES SERVICES
FOR CONSUMERS ON
ONE HAND, AND FOR
PRODUCERS AND
WHOLESALERS ON
THE OTHER.

various producers turn out with what the final customers want. This is part of the task of middlemen.

The job to be done involves (1) collecting or *concentrating* the outputs of various producers, (2) subdividing these outputs into the amounts desired by customers and then putting the various items together in the assortment wanted (which together are called *equalizing*), and (3) *dispersing* this assortment to consumers or industrial buyers. In a few cases, these concentrating, equalizing, and dispersing tasks are simple enough to be done by the producer and the final customer working closely together. A copper mine may sell directly to a smelting firm; coal producers may sell directly to steel mills. In most cases, however, the producer and the consumer are not able to work out the proper quantity and assortment. A specialist in concentration, equalization, and dispersion is needed, and this is the middleman.

Creation of Utility

Middlemen aid in the creation of time, place, and possession utilities. In classical economic theory, production is defined as the creation of utility, and several types of utility are recognized. One is **form utility**, which results from chemical or physical changes that make a product more valuable. When lumber is made into furniture or flour into bread, form utility is created. Other utilities are equally valuable to the final user. Furniture located in Kitchener, Ontario, in April is of little value to people in Edmonton who want to give the furniture as Christmas presents. Transporting the furniture from Ontario to Alberta increases its value: **place utility** is added. Storing it from April to December adds another value—**time utility**. Finally, **possession utility** is created when the Alberta families buy the items.

If a supermarket sells some floor wax to a gift-shop operator to polish the shop floor, is this a retail sale? When a gas station advertises that tires are being sold at the wholesale price, is this retailing? Can a wholesaler or manufacturer engage in retailing? Obviously, we need to define the terms *retailing, retail store, retail sales*, and *retailers*, to avoid misunderstandings in later discussions.

Retailing includes all activities directly related to the sale of goods or services to the ultimate consumer for personal, nonbusiness use. While

NATURE OF RETAIL MARKET

Table 14-1 TOTAL RETAIL TRADE IN CANADA, 1961-1981

Retail sales have increased almost six-fold since 1961. Even after allowing for increases in population and price levels, there has been a huge increase in the volume of merchandise sold. In contrast, there has been a remarkable stability in the number of retail establishments since 1961.

	1961	1971	1981
Number of stores (000)	152.6	158.2	163.6*
Total sales ($000,000)	$ 16,072	$ 32,080	$ 94,293
Average sales per store	$105,504	$202,781	$576,363*

* estimates.
Source: Statistics Canada.

most retailing is done through retail stores, retailing may be done by any institution. A manufacturer selling brushes or cosmetics door-to-door is engaging in retailing, as is a farmer selling vegetables at a roadside stand. Any firm—manufacturer, wholesaler, or retail store—that sells something to ultimate consumers for their nonbusiness use is making a **retail sale**. This is true regardless of *how* the product is sold (in person or by telephone, mail, or vending machine) or *where* it is sold (in a store or at the consumer's home).

A **retailer** or a **retail store** is a business enterprise that sells *primarily* (over one-half the store's sales volume) to household consumers for nonbusiness use. The word *dealer* generally is synonymous with *retailer*. In contrast, a *distributor* is a wholesaling middleman.

Ease of Entry into Retailing

It is easier to go into retailing than virtually any other trade, profession, or line of business. To practise medicine or law, one must pass state licensing examinations. To start a manufacturing firm, one must have a substantial sum of money to acquire a plant, equipment, and materials. To enter a labour trade in many parts of the country, one must acquire union membership, and some unions have strict apprenticeship provisions. But to operate a retail store no examinations are required, and the necessary business licences are easy to acquire. Furthermore, many people entering retailing have the idea that no real training or special experience is needed.

There are important economic and social implications in the ease with which people may enter retailing. Often, underfinanced, poorly qualified people come into the field. They soon fail, thus causing economic waste and inefficient use of human and economic resources. Mortality is higher among retail establishments than in any other classification of business and industry.

On the bright side, ease of entry results in fierce competition and better value for the consumer. Except perhaps in a small town, it is rather difficult to establish an unregulated, monopolistic position in retailing. Certainly large-scale enterprises exist in retailing, and in some markets a relatively few large firms account for most of the business. Yet, these giants usually compete with one another, so the consumer still benefits.

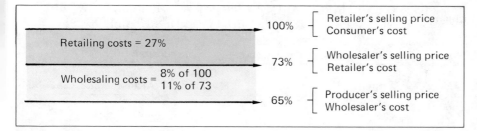

Figure 14-2
AVERAGE COSTS OF
RETAILING AND
WHOLESALING.

To get into retailing is easy. To be forced out is just as easy. Consequently, to survive in retailing, a company must do a satisfactory job in its primary role — catering to the consumer — and in its secondary role — serving producers and wholesalers. This dual responsibility is both the justification for retailing and the key to success in retailing.

Economic Justification for Retailing

There are more than 160,000 retail stores in Canada, and their total annual sales volume in 1981 was almost $95 billion (see Table 14-1). In spite of the population increase and rising consumer incomes over the past three decades, there has been no appreciable change in the number of retail stores. The increase in total sales volume, however, has been tremendous — about a six-fold increase from the early 1960s to 1981. Even if adjustment is made for the big rise in the price level and the increase in population, we find that total retail sales, and per capita retail sales, have gone up considerably. That is, there has simply been a huge increase in the physical volume of merchandise sold at retail.

Size of Retail Market

Information regarding the costs of retailing is very meagre. By gleaning data from several sources, however, we can make some rough generalizations.

Costs and Profits of Retailers

Total Costs and Profits

As nearly as can be estimated, the total average operating expense for all retailers combined is about 25 to 27 percent of retail sales. Wholesaling expenses are estimated at about 8 percent of the *retail* dollar or about 10 to 11 percent of *wholesaling* sales. Thus, retailing costs are about 2½ times the costs of wholesaling, when both are stated as a percentage of sales of the middlemen in question (see Fig. 14-2).

The proportionately higher retailing costs are generally related to the expense of dealing directly with the consumer. In comparison with wholesalers' customers, consumers demand more services. The average retail sale is smaller, the rate of merchandise turnover is lower, merchandise is bought in smaller lots, rent is higher, and expenses for furniture and fixtures are greater. And retail salespeople cannot be used efficiently because customers do not come into retail stores at a steady rate.

Table 14-2   GROSS MARGIN AND NET PROFIT, AS A PERCENTAGE OF
NET SALES, FOR SELECTED TYPES OF RETAILERS, 1981

How do you account for the difference across types of retailers?

Type of Business	Gross Margin %	Net Profit % After Income Tax
Food stores	20.6	1.2
Department stores	32.5	1.1
Variety stores	26.8	3.9
General merchandise	19.9	2.1
Auto accessories and parts	28.3	2.7
Gasoline service stations	17.5	1.7
Motor vehicle dealers	12.4	0.6
Motor vehicle repair shops	48.5	4.0
Shoe stores	39.6	2.7
Men's clothing stores	39.0	2.8
Women's clothing stores	42.5	3.7
Dry goods stores	37.9	5.3
Hardware stores	29.8	2.4
Furniture and appliance stores	32.5	2.4
Electrical appliance repairs	53.5	5.2
Drug stores	31.1	2.9
Book and stationery stores	38.7	2.8
Florists' shops	51.7	2.9
Fuel dealers	17.7	2.4
Jewellery stores	47.5	5.5
Tobacconists	40.0	0.4
TOTAL RETAIL TRADE	25.9	3.3

Source: Statistics Canada, *Corporation Financial Statistics*, 1981, cat. no. 61-207.

Costs and Profits by Kind of Business

The expense ratios of retailers vary from one type of store to another.
Table 14-2 shows average gross margins as a percentage of sales for different kinds of stores. These margins range from 12.4 percent for auto dealers to 53.5 percent for electrical appliance repair shops. Table 14-2 also
shows average net profit after taxes as a percentage of gross sales for each
type of store.

Retailing Structure in Metropolitan Areas

As we might expect, retail sales and retailer location tend to follow the
population. The bulk of retail sales is concentrated in very small land masses
— the Census Metropolitan Areas. In Canada there are 24 Census Metropolitan Areas, which account for over 56 percent of the nation's population
and 62 percent of the retail trade in 1983.

Within the central city and its adjacent suburbs in a metropolitan area,
there are several discernible types of shopping districts. Together these
constitute a retailing structure that should be recognized by marketers.
The hub of retailing activity has traditionally been the central downtown
shopping district — the location of the main units of department stores,
major apparel specialty stores, jewellery stores, and other shopping goods
stores.

In older, larger cities we often find a secondary shopping district with branches of downtown stores. A third type of shopping district is a "string-street" development, or a cluster of small, neighbourhood stores. None of these three types of shopping districts is planned or controlled for marketing purposes. Thus they are different from planned suburban shopping centres.

Suburban Shopping Centres

Since the 1940s, another significant type of shopping district has been developed in metropolitan areas—the suburban shopping centre. Such a centre differs from all other shopping districts in that it is planned, developed, and controlled by one organization. These planned centres range from (1) a *neighbourhood* centre built around a supermarket, through (2) a *community* centre featuring a discount store or junior department store, to (3) a *regional* centre anchored by a branch of one or two downtown department stores. In the regional centre, ideally there is at least one limited-line store to compete with each department in the department stores.

(Courtesy Cadillac-Fairview, Toronto)

Many of the regional centres are giant-sized; in effect, they are miniature downtowns. These supercentres may have as many as five department stores, plus many small stores and service operations. They may also include hotels, banks, office buildings, churches, and theatres. These centres integrate retail, cultural, and commercial activies, all enclosed under one roof.

In the late 1970s, the building of giant regional centres slowed considerably as the market for shopping centres became saturated in many parts of the country. In the 1980s, energy shortages and concern for more efficient land use have further discouraged the development of outlying shopping centres. At the same time, increased attention is being devoted to in-city shopping facilities. Many cities, both large and small, already have built traffic-limited downtown shopping malls as part of their urban renewal programs.[1]

The success of suburban shopping centres lies essentially in their conformity with consumer buying patterns. A wide selection of merchandise is available; stores are open evenings; an informal atmosphere encourages shoppers to dress informally and bring the children; plenty of free parking space is available. By coordinating their promotional efforts, all stores benefit; one builds traffic for another. Many stores in these centres are too small to do effective, economical advertising on their own. But they can make good use of major media by tying in with the overall shopping centre advertising.

Retail trade is concentrated in relation to population and reflects the buying power of various regions of the country. For example, Table 14-3 indicates that the Atlantic Provinces (New Brunswick, Newfoundland, Nova Scotia, and Prince Edward Island) accounted for approximately 9.1 percent of the Canadian population in 1983, but because of a lower average per capita

---

[1]Frances Phillips, "Picking Location More Vital than Ever for Retailing," *The Financial Post*, October 16, 1982, p. 11.

Table 14-3 PROVINCIAL SHARES OF POPULATION AND RETAIL
SALES, 1983

Province	% of Canadian Population 1983	% of Total Retail Sales
Alberta	9.44	10.61
British Columbia	11.34	11.33
Manitoba	4.21	3.89
New Brunswick	2.84	2.66
Newfoundland	2.32	1.85
Nova Scotia	3.45	3.32
Ontario	35.42	37.27
Prince Edward Island	0.50	0.46
Quebec	26.21	24.25
Saskatchewan	3.99	4.08
Yukon and Northwest Territories	0.28	0.28

Source: "The Canadian People and Their Markets—Buying Power Indices, 1983," *The Financial Post Canadian Markets 1984*, Maclean-Hunter Limited, Toronto, 1983, pp. 66-77.

income in this region, these four provinces accounted for only about 8.3 percent of total Canadian retail sales for that year. Conversely, the higher than average per capita incomes of Ontario, Alberta, and British Columbia explain the fact that these provinces accounted for a larger share of retail sales (59.2 percent) than would be warranted by population alone. Thus an analysis of the geographic location of retail trade can be used to evaluate regional market potential for many products.

Classification of Retailers

To better explain the role of retailing middlemen in the channel structure, we shall classify and discuss retailers on four bases:

1. Size of store, by sales volume
2. Extent of product lines handled
3. Form of ownership
4. Method of operation

Any given store can be classed according to all four of these bases. We have done this below, using Sears and a neighbourhood paint store as examples. See also Fig. 14-3.

SEARS	CLASSIFICATION BASE	PAINT STORE
Large	1. Size of store	Small
General merchandise	2. Product lines carried	Single line of merchandise
Corporate chain	3. Form of ownership	Independent owner
Both in-store and mail order; supermarket method and full service depending on product department	4. Method of operation	In-store selling; full service

CLASSIFICATION OF RETAILERS

BY SALES VOLUME	BY PRODUCT LINES CARRIED	BY FORM OF OWNERSHIP	BY METHOD OF OPERATION
Large-scale retailers Small-scale retailers	General merchandise stores: Department stores Variety stores Limited-line stores (shoes, furniture, hardware, bakery, apparel)	Corporate chain Independents—unaffiliated Associations of independent retailers	Full-service retailing Supermarket retailing Discount retailing Nonstore retailing (door-to-door, mail-order, vending machines)

Figure 14-3
RETAILERS MAY BE
CLASSIFIED IN
SEVERAL WAYS.

RETAILERS CLASSIFIED BY SALES VOLUME

Sales volume is a useful basis for classifying retail stores, because stores of different sizes (in terms of sales) present different management problems. Buying, promotion, financing, personnel relations, and expense control are influenced significantly by whether a store's sales volume is large or small. And, as you will see, on the basis of store sales volume, retailing is both a small-scale and a large-scale operation.

Quantitative Measurement

Most retail establishments are very small. Unfortunately, Statistics Canada has not been collecting data relating to the size of retail stores in Canada since 1971. At that time, 46 percent of the retail stores operating in Canada had an annual sales volume of less than $100,000. These stores accounted for only 4 percent of total retail sales in the country. At the same time, there is a high degree of concentration in retailing. The largest retail chains account for only about 1 percent of the stores, but likely generate more than one-third of all retail sales in Canada.

But looking at *individual store sales* does not convey a true picture of concentration in retailing. When we examine *individual company* volume, we get a better understanding of just how much of Canadian retail sales volume is accounted for by just a few companies. A single company may operate a large number of retail outlets, as is the case with national chain stores such as Eaton's, The Bay, Canadian Tire, Birks, and the Dylex Group. When retail sales are analysed by companies, the high degree of concentration becomes more evident. From Table 14-4, we see that the 25 largest retailers in Canada in 1983 had retail sales in excess of $41 billion, or more than one-third of all retail sales in Canada. The small size of the annual profit of these companies — often less than 1 percent of sales — may surprise some people who feel that retailers make large profits.

Table 14-4   25 LARGEST RETAILERS IN CANADA, 1983
(BY SALES VOLUME)

Company	Sales ($000)	Net Income as % of Sales
Loblaws	6,091,019	0.85
Hudson's Bay Co.[1]	4,370,528	N/A
Provigo	3,891,151	0.68
Canada Safeway	3,437,683	2.25
Steinberg	3,352,851	0.36
Simpsons-Sears	3,314,113	1.04
Oshawa Group	2,434,985	1.06
Dominion Stores	2,204,972	1.23
Canadian Tire	1,903,378	2.51
F.W. Woolworth	1,738,820	1.81
Kelly, Douglas & Company	1,583,999	1.09
Groupe Metro-Richelieu	1,325,307	0.88
K-Mart Canada	1,001,979	1.11
Consumers Distributing	898,916	1.79
Dylex[2]	822,404	3.82
Sobeys Stores	558,251	0.94
Gendis[3]	435,913	4.38
Grafton Group	420,654	4.32
Acklands	332,246	1.02
Automotive Hardware	304,077	0.41
Reitmans (Canada)	282,347	4.92
Marks and Spencer Canada	276,648	2.76
Henry Birks and Sons	265,092	2.80
Kinney Shoes of Canada	247,433	1.99
Becker Milk	233,113	2.16

[1]Includes The Bay, Simpsons, and Zellers.

[2]Combined sales of Braemar, Fairweather, Suzy Shier, Ruby's Shoes, Town and Country, Thrifty's, Family Fair, BiWay, Tip Top Tailers, Harry Rosen, and Big Steel Man.

[3]Formally General Distributors of Canada.

Source: The Financial Post 500, Summer 1984, p. 112; and "The 1983 Performance Scorecard," *Canadian Business,* June 1984, p. 191.

Competitive Positions of Large and Small Retailers

The relative competitive strengths and weaknesses of large and small retailers may be evaluated as follows:

BASES FOR EVALUATION	COMPETITIVE ADVANTAGE IS GENERALLY WITH:
1. Division of labour and specialization of management.	1. Large-scale retailers. This is their major advantage.
2. Flexibility of operations – merchandise selection, services offered, store design, reflection of owner's personality.	2. Small retailers. This is their biggest advantage.

3.	Buying power.	3.	Large retailers. They can buy in bigger quantities and thus get lower prices.
4.	Effective use of advertising — especially in citywide media.	4.	Large retailers. Their markets fit better with media circulation.
5.	Development and promotion of retailer's own brand.	5.	Large retailers.
6.	Feasibility of integrating wholesaling and manufacturing with retailing.	6.	Large retailers.
7.	Opportunity to experiment with new products and selling methods.	7.	Large retailers can better afford the risks and can supply the necessary executive specialists.
8.	Cost of operations.	8.	Small stores generally have lower expense ratios and lower overhead costs. Large stores pay a price for executive specialization and the large number of employees in non-selling jobs.
9.	Financial strength.	9.	Large-scale retailers. This advantage also underlies some of the advantages noted above — integration, experimentation, purchase discounts, effective advertising, and executive specialization.
10.	Public image and legal considerations.	10.	Small local independent merchants enjoy public support and sympathy. But often this same public votes with its pocket book for (that is, shops at) the big store. Large-scale retailers have been a major target of restrictive legislation.

With the above evaluation adding up so heavily in favour of large-scale retailing, you might well wonder why so many small retailers seem to be succeeding. We find the answer in several developments among both large and small firms. One such development has been the voluntary association of retailers in a chainlike form of organization. This gives the individual members the features of specialized management, buying power, and other advantages of scale listed above. A second development has been the expansion of franchising operations in many fields (by Holiday Inn, Tim Horton's, Japan Camera, Pizza Delight, and Harvey's hamburgers, for instance). Franchising enables small-scale business people to operate their own businesses under the name and guidance of a large company. This gives some small entrepreneurs the best of both worlds. (Franchising and voluntary associations are discussed later in this chapter.)

Change in the consumer market is another factor working for the smaller retailer. On one hand, huge supermarket-type stores carrying a wide variety of merchandise are catering to consumers' wants. At the same time, small specialty shops are growing in number and apparently doing well, in

Improved Position of Small Retailers

response to another facet of consumer buying behaviour. Small retailers who take advantage of their flexibility can adapt their merchandise lines to their market. They can also establish an individual personality for their stores by means of unusual store layout and design. The relative position of small stores also is improved when large retailers suffer from the usual problems of large-scale operation—retailing or otherwise. High overhead costs, restrictive union contracts, difficulty in motivating salespeople, and organizational inflexibilities all limit the competitive position of the large-scale retailer.[2]

RETAILERS CLASSIFIED BY PRODUCT LINE

In classifying retailers according to the product lines they carry, we group them into two categories — general merchandise stores and limited-line stores.

General Merchandise Stores

As the name suggests, **general merchandise** stores carry a large variety of product lines, usually with some depth of assortment in each line. Department stores are the type of general merchandise stores with the largest sales volume. Variety stores (Woodworth's, Zellers) are also included in this category.

Department Stores

Department stores are large retailing institutions that carry a *very wide* variety of product lines, including apparel, other soft goods, furniture, and home furnishings. These stores are highly organized business enterprises. Merchandising (product planning), headed by a general merchandising manager, is usually the key to a store's success. Under the merchandising manager are the department buyers. In effect, each department is a business in itself, and the buyer has considerable autonomy.

In addition to the general advantages and drawbacks of large-scale retailing (specialized management, buying power, and so on), department stores have some other significant merits and limitations. These stores offer a wider variety of products and services than any other type of retail institution where the customer comes to the store. (The mail-order house — a form of nonstore retailing—may carry more lines than a department store.) On the other hand, their operating expenses are considerably higher than those of most other kinds of retail business, running about 35 percent of sales. One of the features of department stores — their many services — contributes significantly to this high operating expense.

A substantial problem confronting department stores has been their location — typically in the heart of the downtown shopping district. The population exodus to the suburbs and the traffic problems downtown have combined to force many department stores to open branches in the suburbs. The big downtown store, with its large investment, high-tax location, and

---

[2]Ernest Hillen, "The Little Shop on Main Street," *The Financial Post Magazine*, July/August 1981, pp. 23–25.

(Courtesy Woodward's, Edmonton)

high-cost operations, must be maintained. But it reaps a decreasing share of the total business in the area. Of course, for many years the department stores have been well aware of the "downtown problem." In many cities, working with other downtown merchants, the department store have spearheaded movements to revitalize the downtown areas. Also, as mentioned earlier, energy shortages, land-use concern, and inner-city decay all are forces that are spurring urban renewal programs in the 1980s. These programs, in turn, are revitalizing downtown shopping areas, thus benefiting downtown department stores.

Department stores face strong competition on other fronts as well. Some examples of these challenges are (1) the continued expansion of discount selling, (2) the growth of chains of small specialty apparel stores (Dalmys, Harry Rosen, Le Chateau), and (3) the development of specialty stores catering to hobbies, sports, and other leisuretime activities. The recent slowdown in population growth, the greater number of working women, and other demographic changes have made department store retailing in the 1980s different from what it was in the 1960s.

Those big-market, easy-growth years may be gone, but department stores are displaying some innovative, aggressive strategies to meet the competitive challenges. To illustrate, stores are using marketing research extensively to determine current purchasing motives, attitudes, and life-styles. Rather than try to be all things to all people, many stores are trying to appeal to a limited number of market segments — especially the younger, more fashion-conscious groups. These retailers are reducing their merchandise mix — stressing fashion and exclusiveness rather than carrying products in a wide variety of price lines. Many department stores have converted entire floors into groups of specialty shops. Each of these shops features a different line of merchandise, and each has a different decorative display theme or motif. Bargain basements are being revitalized to counter the lower prices in discount stores. Some department stores have adopted strategies of selling through warehouse outlets or through the mail. Some will also encourage their customers to shop by telephone and will arrange local home delivery. A few department stores have even tried their hands at operating their own discount subsidiaries or have opened catalogue outlets, with varying degrees of success.[3]

Limited-Line Stores

Limited-line stores carry a considerable assortment of goods, but in only one or a few related lines. We identify these stores by the names of the individual products they feature — food stores, shoe stores, furniture stores, hardware stores, and so on.

This identification is still useful for some types of stores — those selling apparel, furniture, or building materials, for instance. For other types, such as food stores and drugstores, however, to include a single type of product in the store name is inaccurate and misleading. This is the result of a major trend toward **scrambled merchandising** — the practice of adding new, unrelated lines to the products customarily sold in a particular type of store. Moreover, it is a mistake to interpret food store sales, for example, as being equal to total sales of food products. Supermarkets carry many nonfood lines. Food products, in turn, are sold in drugstores, gas stations, and department stores.

The limited-line category also includes what we call **specialty stores**. These are tobacco shops, bakeries, dairy stores, and furriers, for example — stores that typically carry a very limited variety of products. The name "specialty stores" is an unfortunate, and perhaps even misleading, title. Specialty *stores* should *not* be confused with specialty *goods*. Actually, specialty shops do *not* often carry specialty goods. Using the word *specialty* in describing the store implies that it carries a limited line of merchandise.

Limited-line stores usually carry an excellent assortment of goods. In the apparel field, they often feature the newest fashions. Frequently they are the exclusive dealers for certain brands in a given market. Because they limit their merchandise to one or a few lines, these stores can often buy in large quantities and thus secure favourable prices.

RETAILERS CLASSIFIED BY FORM OF OWNERSHIP

The major store-ownership categories are *independent* stores and *corporate chain* stores. A third group consists of *voluntary associations of independents* that band together in chainlike fashion in order to compete more effectively with corporate chain-store organizations.

Corporate Chain Store

A **corporate chain-store system**, according to Statistics Canada's definition, is an organization of four or more stores, centrally owned and managed, that generally handle the same lines of products on the same level in the distribution structure. Technically, four or more units may constitute a chain, although today many merchants who consider themselves small-scale in-

---

[3]David B. Stewart, "The Nature of Competition Amongst Department Stores: An International Comparison," *Proceedings* of the Marketing Division, Administrative Sciences Association of Canada, vol. 4, part 3, 1983, pp. 334–340; and Ellen Roseman, "Retail Giants Slipping in Service, Share of Market," *The Globe and Mail*, July 12, 1984, p. 12.

dependents have more than four units that they have opened up in shopping centres and newly popluated areas. These retailers ordinarily do not think of themselves as a chain. Consequently, it might be more meaningful to consider a larger number of units to be a reasonable minimum when categorizing a store as a chain. For census purposes, Statistics Canada defines a chain-store organization as one that operates four or more retail outlets in the same kind of business under the same legal ownership. Those operating two or three stores are termed multiples and, together with the single stores, are referred to as independent stores. All department stores are considered chain-store organizations regardless of whether they own one or more outlets.

Central ownership is the key factor that differentiates corporate chains from voluntary associations of independent wholesalers or retailers. The third element in our definition of a chain-store system is central management. Individual units in a chain have very little autonomy. Buying is highly centralized with respect to both the physical purchasing and the determination of what will be bought. Centralized management also leads to considerable standardization in operating policies among the units in the chain.

Many chains are also vertically integrated, but this feature is not essential for definitional purposes. Dominion Stores, the large grocery chain, maintains large distribution centres where they buy from producers, do their own warehousing, and then distribute to their own stores in their own trucks. Some chain organizations, such as Eaton's, actually own and operate manufacturing plants to supply some of their needs. Another form of vertical integration has resulted in *manufacturer-owned* retail chains, such as shoe stores (Bata Shoe), sewing machines (Singer), and gasoline outlets (Imperial Oil).

An example of a national chain store. *(Courtesy Tip Top Tailors)*

Importance

Organizations with four or more stores did more than 40 percent of retail trade in 1982. The importance of chains varies considerably from one type of commodity to another (see Table 14-5). Chains account for more than 80 percent of total sales in the general merchandise and variety stores categories. Among hardware stores and furniture stores, however, chains account for less than 20 percent of total retail sales. In the food field, there are several giant chain firms, yet chains still account for less than 60 percent of total food store sales.

Chain store companies have increased their share of the total retail market since the early 1960s, but the growth has not been uniform in all fields. In the food store category, for example, since 1966 chain stores have increased their share of total food sales from 44.9 percent to just under 60 percent. On the other hand the share of variety store sales accounted for by chains has in fact decreased since 1966. The growth of chains in the drug store field reflects the way these stores have expanded into a wide variety of products. Further growth in drug chains is likely as they capitalize on potential government-sponsored business and the fact that the over-65 market is increasing in size and in buying power.

Table 14-5   CHAINS' SHARE OF TOTAL SALES VOLUME BY KIND OF
BUSINESS, 1966, 1974, 1979, AND 1982

	Percent of Sales			
Kind of Business	**1966**	**1974**	**1979**	**1982**
Total retail sales	33.4	41.1	41.5	43.8
Grocery and combination stores	44.9	57.5	60.4	58.7
Other food stores	8.7	8.1	8.5	7.1
Department stores*	100.0	100.0	100.0	100.0
General merchandise	74.7	80.4	79.8	80.6
Variety stores	86.7	83.2	76.3	82.4
Men's clothing	13.2	18.6	34.3	44.8
Women's clothing	26.5	40.9	53.3	58.7
Family clothing	21.9	28.5	49.9	52.8
Shoe stores	45.0	51.8	66.0	68.0
Hardware stores	15.5	19.0	N/A	N/A
Furniture stores	19.2	19.2	19.5	19.9
Pharmacy stores	13.4	18.5	22.4	26.9
Jewellery stores	33.7	39.4	45.4	48.9

*All department stores are considered chains by Statistics Canada.

Source: Statistics Canada, *Market Research Handbook*, 1975, cat. no. 63-224, pp. 66-67;
1980, cat. no. 63-224, pp. 124-125; 1983, cat. no. 63-224, pp. 201, 204.

Competitive Strengths and Weaknesses

Chain-store organizations are large-scale retailing institutions. As such, they
are subject to the general advantages and limitations of all large retailers
we discussed earlier in this chapter. Let's look at a few of these points,
especially as they relate to chain stores.

Lower Selling Prices   Chain stores have traditionally been credited with
selling at lower prices than independents. But the claim of lower prices
needs careful scrutiny because it can be misleading. It was probably more
justified in the past than it is today. Many independents have pooled their
buying power so that, in many instances, they can buy products at the
same price as the chains.

   It is very difficult to compare the prices of chains with those of independents. The merchandise is often not exactly comparable, because many
chains sell items under their own brands. It is difficult to compare the prices
of Del Monte peaches and Loblaws or Steinberg's brand of peaches. Also, it
is not accurate to compare the price of the product sold in a cash-and-carry,
no-customer-service store with the price of an identically branded product
in a full-service store. The value of services should be included in the
comparison.

Multistore Feature of Chains   Chain stores do not have all their eggs in
one basket (or in one store). Even large-scale independent department stores
or supermarkets cannot match this advantage of the chain. A multiunit

operation has automatically *spread its risks* among many units. Losses in one store can be offset by profits in other units. Multistore organizations can *experiment* quite easily. They can try a new store layout or a new type of merchandise in one store without committing the entire firm.

A chain can make more *effective use of advertising* than even a giant single-unit independent store. To illustrate, a grocery chain may have fifteen medium-sized stores blanketing a city. An independent competitor may have one huge supermarket doing three to four times the business of any single unit of the chain. Yet the chain can use the metropolitan daily newspaper as an advertising medium with much less waste in circulation than the independent can. Many chains can also make effective use of national advertising media.

On the Negative Side   Standardization, the hallmark of a chain-store system and a major factor in its success, is a mixed blessing. *Standardization also means inflexibility*. Often a chain cannot adjust rapidly to a local market situation. Chains are well aware of this weakness, however, and have consequently given local store managers somewhat greater freedom to act in various situations.

Franchise Systems Involving Small, Independent Retailers

A major competitive factor facing corporate chains is the increased effectiveness of independent retailers and wholesalers that have copied chain-store marketing methods. Independents have adopted self-service methods in many types of stores; they have improved store appearance and layout; they have sought better locations, including suburban shopping centres; they have improved their merchandising practices by eliminating some slow-moving items and keeping fresh stock; and they have improved their accounting and inventory-control systems.

Probably the most effective measure adopted by small independents is their practice of voluntarily associating with wholesalers, manufacturers, or other retailers in some form of contractual franchise system. These associations sometimes resemble a corporate chain so closely that about the only significant difference is that the member stores are not centrally owned.

Nature and Extent of Franchise Systems

In our discussion here, we use a broad interpretation of franchising. It includes any contractual arrangement between *franchisers* (suppliers, that may be manufacturers or wholesalers) and independent *franchisees* (either wholesalers or retailers). The franchiser grants the right to sell certain goods or services in a stated geographic market. The franchiser usually provides equipment, the products or services for sale, and managerial services. In return, the franchisee agrees to market the product or service in a manner established by the supplier. Within this broad definition we find two main types of franchising systems — one is a voluntary association of retailers; the other is a retailer network sponsored by a producer.

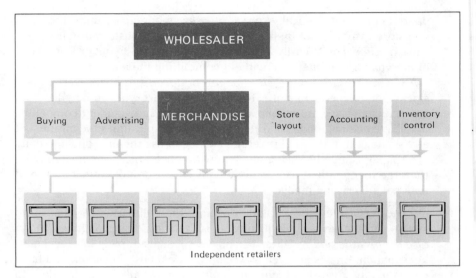

Figure 14-4
VOLUNTARY CHAIN.

In a voluntary chain, a
wholesaler provides
services and sells
merchandise to a group
of independent retailers.

Associations of Independent Retailers

The two main forms of voluntary associations of independent retailers are
voluntary chains (sponsored by wholesalers) and **retailer cooperative
chains** (sponsored by retailers). Both forms have the same basic purpose
— namely, to enable independent wholesalers and retailers to meet more
effectively the competition from corporate chain stores. By combining the
buying power of their many retailer members, these associations can buy
at prices competitive with those of the corporate chains (see Figs. 14-4 and
14-5).[4]

Some differences between the two groups are as follows:

VOLUNTARY CHAIN	RETAILER COOPERATIVE CHAIN
1. Most prevalent in grocery field (IGA). These chains also exist in hardware (Home Hardware), auto supplies (Western Auto), and variety stores.	1. Quite significant in grocery field (local areas), but not in other lines.
2. Sponsored by wholesalers. A contract is the connecting link between wholesalers and independent retailer members.	2. Sponsored by retailers. They combine to form and operate a wholesale warehouse corporation.
3. Wholesaler provides a wide variety of management services — buying, advertising, store layout, accounting, and inventory control. Retailers agree to buy all (or almost all) their merchandise from wholesaler. Members agree to use common store name and design, and to follow common managerial procedures.	3. Services to retailer members are primarily large-scale buying and warehousing operations. Members maintain their separate identities.

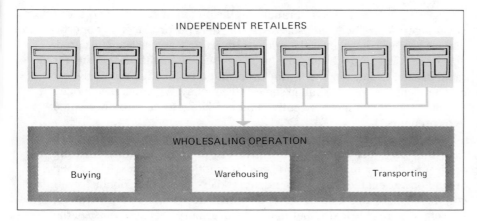

Figure 14-5
RETAILER
COOPERATIVE CHAIN.

In a retailer cooperative chain, independent retailers combine to operate an efficient buying, warehousing, and transporting organization for their own use only.

Producer-Sponsored Systems

In producer-sponsored systems of franchising, a manufacturer (or other producer) sets up a network of retail outlets by contracting with independent retailers. The contract may cover:

1. Only one brand within a department (Zenith televisions or Maytag appliances)

2. An entire department in a store (Ziggy's Deli)

3. The entire retail outlet (auto dealerships or gas stations, McDonald's, Speedy Muffler, Harvey's hamburgers, Holiday Inns, Hertz auto rentals)

We can distinguish between two concepts in producer-sponsored franchise systems. One features franchising as a form of *exclusive distribution* of a product or line. This type has existed for years and often involves a large-scale retailer. The other concept is the rise of *entrepreneurship franchising*. This practice is relatively new, and it typically has involved small-scale retailers. Enterprise franchising has especially proliferated in the fast-foods industry (Pizza Delight, Harvey's hamburgers) and in service industries (recreation, auto rentals, motels, auto repairs).

The concept of a producer franchising an entire retail outlet (as contrasted with a single department or one brand within a department) is not new — automobile manufacturers have done this for years. What is new, however, is its substantial growth since about 1950 and its spread into many new fields. In addition to fast-food services, today producer-sponsored franchise selling also embraces such products and services as auto mufflers, putting greens, paint, part-time office help, hearing aids, motels, and dance studios.[5]

---

[4]John Dart, "Voluntary Retail Groups: Performance and Promise," *Proceedings* of the Marketing Division, Administrative Sciences Association of Canada, vol. 1, part 3, 1980, pp. 117–125.

[5]K.V. Gadd, "Franchising Revives Role of Independent Grocer," *The Canadian Business Review*, Autumn 1982, pp. 16–18; and Laird O'Brien, "There's a Fortune in Franchises," *The Financial Post Magazine*, September 15, 1981, pp. 27–30.

Competitive Advantages   Franchising has many economic and social advantages. A producer-sponsored system offers the producer an opportunity for greater control over the pricing, advertising, and selling of its products or services. Franchising also provides suppliers with the means for rapid market expansion and a wide distribution system at a relatively low cost. Franchisees typically put up some of the money. With their own money at stake, they have more incentive and are likely to be more dedicated entrepreneurs.

When the retailers are identified as a group (through a producer's name), then that producer can make effective use of cooperative advertising programs, display materials, and other promotional features. The group buying power enables the independent retailer-members to obtain lower-cost merchandise and a better selection of the latest products. Furthermore, the retailers are able to do a better job of store management because of the administrative services furnished by the sponsor.

In a producer-sponsored network particularly, franchising enables many people to realize their dream of owning their own business. Also, the franchisees' investment is relatively small, and it is easier for them to borrow the necessary funds when big national firms are behind them. They may be independent, small-scale retailers, but they are backed by the buying power, promotional programs, and management know-how of big companies.

Limitations   In the authors' opinion, the biggest single competitive weakness of all independent retailers, whether affiliated or not, is their assumption that the sole advantage of the chain is its buying power. The real strength of a large-scale institution, however, lies in its superior management personnel and specialized management practices.

Ignorance or disregard of this fact places major limitations on voluntary associations of independents. Too often these retailers reject the management advice given by sponsors. Many retailers think of the association as a buying aid only, and make little use of advertising, accounting, and other association services.

The rapid expansion of producer-sponsored franchising systems during the past twenty-five years has also brought its share of problems. One is the charge that the franchising agreements are terribly one-sided — all in favour of the franchisor. To the extent that this charge is true, any imbalance can be minimized if both parties carefully analyse all appropriate criteria when selecting a franchising partner. Also, legislation has been established to generate fairness in franchising agreements.

Perhaps the major threat to the continued successful expansion of franchising is the practice whereby the producer-sponsor takes over the ownership of successful units in its franchise system. This, in effect, turns the independent units into a corporate chain system. One unfortunate aspect of this trend is to reduce the numbers of successful, small, independent entrepreneurs.[6]

---

[6]For a summary of franchising, including a good bibliography, see Shelby D. Hunt, "Franchising: Promises, Problems, Prospects," *Journal of Retailing*, Fall 1977, pp. 71–84.

The four types of retailers, classified by method of operation, are listed in Fig. 14-3. The traditional form, *in-store full-service* retailing, is still quite prevalent, although its use has declined considerably over the past thirty years. It probably will continue to be important in retailing high-fashion products and products that require explanation or fitting. The use of the remaining three classes — supermarket, discount, and nonstore retailing (door-to-door selling, mail-order selling, and automatic vending) — has increased during the last three decades.

It is somewhat difficult to analyse supermarket retailing because there is no universally accepted definition of the term. To some people a supermarket is a *type* of retail store found in the grocery business. To others, the term describes a *method* of retailing and can be used in connection with stores in any product line.

In this discussion, a **supermarket** will be defined as a large-scale departmentized retailing institution offering a variety of merchandise (including groceries, meats, produce, and dairy products). Such a store operates largely on a self-service basis with a minimum of customer services, and features a price appeal and (usually) ample parking space.

Development of Supermarkets

Supermarkets, as we know them today, had their start in the Depression days of the 1930s. They were owned and operated by the independents attempting to compete with chain food stores. The self-service supermarket approach to food retailing soon became a success and was adopted by chain stores as well as by other full-service independents. Supermarkets are overwhelmingly the dominant institution in food retailing today. It is increasingly rare to find a full-service grocery store.

Through the years, the supermarkets competed fiercely with one another because a new supermarket had to attract much of its business from existing stores. Much of this competition involved nonprice considerations such as trading stamps (although these were never as popular in Canada as they were in the United States), games with cash awards, longer store hours (many have now turned to Sunday or twenty-four-hour opening), and other incentives. These forms of nonprice competition did, of course, increase operating costs and selling prices, but unfortunately not profits.

The 1970s were not good years for conventional supermarkets. Costs increased (sometimes dramatically), inflation hurt, competition intensified, and both profits and productivity declined. Now, in the 1980s, supermarket management is facing the challenge of reversing these trends — especially the decline in profits and productivity. This challenge is being met in quite different ways. Many chains are cutting costs and stressing their low prices by offering limited services, no frills, and generic brands. A few supermarket organizations are going the opposite route — featuring a wider assortment of products and services and higher-quality products at higher prices. Both groups are using technological innovations at the checkout stands, in packaging, and elsewhere in the store. Perhaps the strongest challenge to

RETAILERS CLASSIFIED BY METHOD OF OPERATION

Supermarket Retailing

Bulk food bins, one form of
no-frills retailing, are
becoming more popular in
supermarkets.
(Courtesy Miller Services)

supermarket management is the task of encouraging the adopting of a greater number of these technological innovations at a faster rate than in previous years.[7]

Discount Supermarkets

The inviting vacancy at the bottom of the supermarket pricing structure soon generated discount selling in food and the rise of the *discount supermarket*. This discount food retailer operates with fewer services, no trading stamps, lower gross margins, and lower prices than conventional supermarkets. A number of food chains have converted some or all of their stores to discount operations.

The **warehouse store** (also called a **box store**) is a form of discount supermarket operation that has appeared in recent years. This type of food store offers a limited assortment of brands and commonly used products on a no-frills basis. There is, especially, a limited offering of fresh produce, fresh meats, frozen foods, and other perishable goods. The products are displayed on pallets or shelves in the original packing boxes whose tops or sides have been cut off. To further reduce costs, these stores typically use computerized price-scanning equipment and other labour-saving equipment.[8]

[7]Philip Rosson, "Point-of-Sale Scanning in Supermarkets: Developments and Issues," *Proceedings* of the Marketing Division, Administrative Sciences Association of Canada, vol. 1, part 3, 1980, pp. 320–330.

[8]See Jonathan N. Goodrich and Jo Ann Hoffman, "Warehouse Retailing: The Trend of the Future?" *Business Horizons*, April 1979, pp. 45–50; "Food Stores with Few Services Spring Up to Lure Increasingly Frugal Consumers," *The Wall Street Journal*, January 23, 1981, p. 42; and "Hunger Waning for No-Frills Food Stores," *Advertising Age*, October 19, 1981, p. 56.

Convenience Stores

Other innovative competitors of conventional supermarkets are the **convenience stores** (7-Eleven, Mac's Milk, Beckers, and others). These stores, interestingly enough, have higher prices and a more limited product assortment and are smaller in size. But they do have longer shopping hours and more convenient locations, and they can provide the fill-in type of merchandise when other food stores are closed. In some ways they are the throwback to the corner grocery store of years past.

In recent years, increasing numbers of convenience stores have been adding gasoline and fast foods to their product assortments. In so doing, these stores provide one-stop shopping for customers. Thus they have become effective competition for gas stations and fast-food chains as well as for conventional supermarkets.

Superstores

The newest and possibly the toughest innovative competitor of the conventional supermarket is the **superstore** — also called a hypermarket or a super-supermarket. Unlike most modern retailing innovations, the superstore concept did not originate in North America; it was imported from France.

Supermarkets and the newer superstores are alike in that they both are low-cost, high-volume, limited-service operations. The key difference between the supermarket and the superstore concepts lies in the breadth of consumer needs to be filled. The supermarket strives mainly to fulfil the consumers' needs for food, laundry, and home-cleaning products. The superstore is designed to provide those same products and to fill other *routine* purchasing needs as well. For example, superstores carry personal-care products, tobacco products, some apparel, low-priced housewares and hardware items, gasoline, consumable lawn and garden products, stationery and sewing supplies, some leisure-time products (books, records, hobby items), and household services (laundry, dry cleaning, shoe repair).

Superstores are usually larger than conventional supermarkets and may generate sales at levels three or four times that of the supermarket. Customer traffic is much greater and average sales per square foot often double the levels experienced in the supermarket. In Canada, the superstore leader is Provigo, Inc. of Quebec. In late 1984, Provigo opened its fourth superstore in the Montreal area, a 50,000 square-foot store in Longueuil.[9]

Because of the market saturation by supermarkets and discount stores, the superstore development in North America is likely to occur in two forms. First, a relatively few true superstores will be built. And second, the smaller, established supermarkets and discount houses will incorporate as many of the superstore's features as possible.

---

[9]"Provigo is Set for Superstore," *The Globe and Mail Report on Business*, November 14, 1984, p. B2.

Discount Retailing and the Discount House

The development of the modern discount house in the decade following World War II is quite significant. This institution or method of selling entered the retailing field as a brash innovator and forced an examination of traditional pricing structures and operating methods.

In this section we really are talking about two things. One is the type of retailing *institution* (the discount house), and the other is a *method* of retail selling that is applicable to almost any type of store. Actually, there is nothing new about discount selling — the practice of selling below the list price or the regular advertised price. There is also nothing new about discount houses; they have existed in some form for many years. The discount houses that emerged after World War II, however, and that upset traditional retailers so much, are quite different from their predecessors. The modern **discount houses** are large stores that are open to the public. They advertise widely, and they carry a reasonably complete selection of wearing apparel and well-known brands of hard goods (appliances, home furnishings, sporting goods, jewellery). They consistently sell below nationally advertised list prices, and they offer a minimum of customer services.

Growth of Discount Retailing

Two major factors led to the success of the modern-day discount houses. Those factors were (1) the traditional retail markups on appliances and other products that typically are not discounted, and (2) the consumers' receptivity to a low-price, no-service appeal.

As products that were relatively new in the 1930s (and generally classed as luxuries), electric home appliances required an intensive selling effort by retailers. Consequently, manufacturers had to offer retailers large markups — 30 to 40 percent — to encourage them to stock these products and then to advertise, explain, and service them.

By the 1950s, however, the marketing situation regarding these products had changed considerably. The role of the retailer was played down as these products were presold to consumers through national advertising by manufacturers. Also, the products were of better quality, so the manufacturer's guarantee was sufficient for the consumer.

Also by the 1950s, the vast middle-income market had emerged, composed largely of people who had been in low-income groups before World War II. These people were price-conscious. Supermarket methods of selling had conditioned them for discount selling — low prices and few services.

The situation thus was ripe for major changes in retailing. Most retailers, however, maintained their traditional markup policies. On the other hand, the discount sellers saw the tremendous possibilities in a low-margin, high-turnover type of operation, with few services but big price reductions. Their operating methods enabled them to limit expenses to 12 to 18 percent of sales, compared with the 30 to 40 percent in department and limited-line stores. The combination of willing customers and effective marketing re-sulted in a very profitable method of retailing.

Recent Developments in Discount Retailing

Discount selling has led to a revision of traditional retailing methods. Manufacturers have altered their channels of distribution to include dis-counting retailers. Small-scale retailers have been forced to drop discounted products or else to meet the discount-house price by offering fewer ser-vices and adopting more efficient marketing methods. Large-scale retail-ers, such as department stores, have realistically lowered their markups on discounted products and have even dropped some of these items.

The discount houses themselves are changing. Some are upgrading their image to that of "promotional department stores," and some have opened stores in suburban shopping centres. In general, all discounters are trading up in products and services. Today many have added soft goods, including a line of wearing apparel. In fact, reasonably expensive, high-fashion women's ready-to-wear is carried in a number of large discount houses. Separate dis-count department stores have been established by "conventional" retailers such as Woolworth (Woolco) and Kresge (K Mart).

The discount sellers' risks and operating costs do increase, of course, as they add more expensive merchandise, move into fancier buildings and locations, and add more services. Intensified competition is also causing financial problems for some discounters, and there has been a slowdown in the rate of entry into the field.

The **catalogue showroom** is a form of discount retailing that has ex-panded considerably in recent years. The showroom features attractive displays of all the merchandise carried in the company's catalogue. Cus-tomers can examine the products at their lesuire. They place orders by filling out order forms and presenting the forms at a desk. Orders are filled immediately from inventory stock in the store's warehouse area. A limited number of salespeople are available to help customers with products such as photographic equipment, television sets, and jewellery. Catalogue show-rooms advertise extensively and use their low prices on nationally branded products as their primary selling appeal. In Canada, the undisputed leader in the catalogue showroom area is Consumers Distributing Limited. Al-though other retailers have tried to break into the market pioneered by Consumers Distributing, none has really succeeded. On the other hand, Consumers has solidified its position in the market and has expanded its product line to include fashion jewellery.

Discount sellers' risks and operating costs do increase, of course, as they add more expensive merchandise, move into fancier buildings and locations, and add more services. In the 1980s, high interest rates, inflation, and in-tense competiton have caused financial problems for some discounters. However, prospects look favourable for discount department stores in gen-eral through the remainder of the 1980s.

Nonstore Retailing   In-Home Selling

Door-to-door selling is one of the oldest retailing methods in history. Sometimes it simply involves house-to-house canvassing, without any advance selection of prospects. More likely, however, there is an initial contact in a store or by phone, or a mailed-in coupon. "**Party-plan**" selling is also included in this category. A hostess invites some friends to a party. These guests understand that a salesperson — say for a cosmetics or housewares company — will be making a sales presentation at the party. The sales representative has a larger prospective market under more favourable conditions than if the "guests" were approached individually on a house-to-house basis. And these guests get to do their shopping in a pleasant, friendly atmosphere. The best-known of the party-plan retailers are Tupperware, Mary Kay cosmetics, and Stanley Home Products.

Door-to-door selling is practised both by producers and be retailers. You probably know of some manufacturing firms that use this method — Avon cosmetics, Electrolux vacuum cleaners, World Book encyclopedias, Fuller brushes, and Amway household products, for example. Drapery and home-heating departments in department stores often have their salespeople call directly on consumers at their homes.

In-home selling offers consumers the convenience of buying at home, but the merchandise assortment is limited and there is no opportunity to shop and compare products. For the seller, door-to-door selling allows the most aggressive form of retail selling, as well as the chance to demonstrate a product in the customer's home.[10]

On the negative side, door-to-door selling is the most expensive form of retailing. Sales-force commissions alone usually run as high as 40 to 50 percent of the retail price. Through the years, this method of selling has acquired a bad reputation because some salespeople have been nuisances or even fraudulent. Finally, managing a door-to-door sales force is a real problem because good salespeople are extremely hard to find and the turnover rate is very high.

There are some indications that telephone shopping — a long-existing method of in-home retailing — will increase in the 1980s as consumers put higher values on time saving and convenience in shopping. The real growth in nonstore retailing during the next decade, however, is expected to be in the area of computer- and television-assisted shopping. "Teleshopping" provides the consumer with a two-way communication channel between home and store. Although some consultants and observers of the retail industry predict that as much as 20 percent of retail sales in some areas by 1990 will be made through television and computer-based information systems, others are predicting that success will come far more slowly.[11] Experience

---

[10]Ann Silversides, "Soaring Direct Sales Turn Big Profits," *The Financial Post*, May 20, 1981.

[11]"The Home Information Revolution," *Business Week*, June 29, 1981, p. 74. Also see Larry J. Rosenberg and Elizabeth C. Hirschman, "Retailing without Stores," *Harvard Business Review*, July-August 1980, pp. 103–112; and "With Video Shopping Services, Goods You See on the Screen Can Be Delivered to Your Door," *The Wall Street Journal*, July 14, 1981, p. 48.

to date with experimental computer-shopping systems have met with mixed success. In some cases, the systems have been used far more for entertainment purposes than to access information or to shop. Greater success is anticipated in the future, when such systems will be installed in large shopping-office-hotel complexes. In larger cities, for example, office workers may access a computer shopping system from their offices or hotel guests from their hotel rooms. Merchandise may be ordered and either delivered to the office or room or picked up from the retail store in the same complex of buildings.

Mail-Order Selling

In addition to ordering merchandise from the traditional catalogue, mail-order buying also includes any ordering by mail from an ad or from a direct-mail appeal. Originally designed primarily to reach rural markets, mail-order retailing today is appealing with success to urban buyers. It is especially appealing to those buyers who want to avoid traffic and shopping congestion and who want the convenience of in-home shopping.

Some of the mail-order houses, such as Sears, are *general merchandise* houses that offer an exceptionally wide variety of product lines. Other mail-order institutions might be termed *specialty* houses in that they limit the number of lines they carry — Book-of-the-Month-Club, Columbia House Records, Dominion Seed House, for example.

Mail-order retailing enjoys some competitive advantages. Operating costs and prices usually are lower than for in-store retailing. A wide variety of merchandise is offered by general merchandise houses. Also, the consumer can shop at leisure from the catalogue and then place an order without the inconvenience of going to a store.

On the other hand, customers must place their orders without actually seeing the merchandise (unless the items are displayed at catalogue stores). This disadvantage is counteracted to some extent by liberal return privileges, guarantees, and excellent catalogue presentations. Mail-order houses have little flexibility. Catalogues are costly and must be prepared long before they are issued. Price changes and new merchandise offerings can be announced only by issuing supplementary catalogues, which are a weak selling tool.

Automatic Vending

Today an amazingly wide variety of products is sold through coin-operated machines that automatically sell merchandise (or services) without the presence of a sales clerk. According to *Vend* magazine, products sold through vending machines account for about 1.5 percent of total retail trade. The bulk of this volume comes from cigarettes, soft drinks, candy, and hot beverages. Such products and others sold through vending machines typically have low unit value and low markups, so they are relatively inexpensive to sell through stores.

Vending machines can expand a firm's market by reaching customers where and when it is not feasible for stores to do so. In addition, many stores use vending machines as a complementary form of retailing. Another major market for automatic vending is in-plant feeding, that is, the provision of meals for employees of factories and offices. Several companies now provide mobile canteen services to employees of construction companies "on site" and to office employees of companies that do not have their own cafeteria or coffee facilities.

The outlook for this "robot retailing" is promising, but automatic vending still faces major problems. Operating costs are high, and there is a continual need for machine repair. The prices of automatically vended products are frequently higher than store prices for the same products. Products that can be sold successfully by machine must be well-known, presold brands with a high rate of turnover. They must be reasonably low in unit value, small and uniform in size and weight, and generally of a convenience-goods nature. Only a limited amount of processing can be accomplished at the vending machine, although some vending companies have now installed microwave ovens near their vending machines so that food may be heated, thereby expanding the range of products that may be supplied through these machines.

THE FUTURE IN RETAILING

In the 1980s, retailing management faces challenges perhaps unequalled since the Depression of the 1930s. Population increases and economic growth have slowed down considerably since the 1960s. The costs of capital and energy have soared, and unemployment and inflation have been at uncomfortably high levels. Consumerism and government restrictions affecting retailing are likely to increase. The demographic and psychographic aspects of consumer markets are changing, and at a greater pace than in the past. These forces underlie several broad, significant trends in retailing.[12]

One of these trends is toward **more professional management**. Traditionally, store presidents came up through the merchandising ranks and were "good merchants." Today's economic and competitive conditions call for executives with a more rounded managerial capability, along with the traditional merchandising skills. Companies are especially stressing profit-performance measures (return on investment, for example) and other internal financial controls. Prior to the mid-1980s, strategic planning generally had not been adopted by retailing executives. However, now there seems to be a modest but growing awareness of the value of this management tool.[13]

---

[12]Gary Lamphier, "Baby Boomers are Reshaping Markets," *The Financial Times*, November 5, 1984, p. 3; David S. Litvack, "Retail Institutions in a Changing Environment," *Proceedings* of the Marketing Division, Administrative Sciences Association of Canada, vol. 4, part 3, 1983, pp. 161–170; and Frances Phillips, "Mixed Future for Retailers," *The Financial Post*, April 24, 1982, p. 13.

[13]Frances Phillips, "Strengthening Marketing Strategy," *The Financial Post*, April 10, 1982, p. 16.

Out of dangerously low profit margins is also coming an intensified drive for **increased productivity** in retailing. To this end, virtually all kinds of consumer products are being sold, at least to some extent, on a self-service basis. This permits retailers to reduce their salary and wage cost, which typically is their largest single operating expense. Automated materials-handling systems are helping to cut physical distribution expenses. Computers are making retailers' information systems—for accounting, inventory control, and marketing research—more effective. In fact, better information systems are leading to improved information management in all phases of operations in many retailing organizations.

Another trend is the continuing move toward **scrambled merchandising**, which results in more intense competition among traditionally different types of stores. That is, in the constant search for higher-margin items, one type of store will add products that traditionally were handled by other types of outlets. This forces wholesalers and manufacturers to change their channel systems and retailers to adjust their marketing programs to meet the challenge of scrambled merchandising. With the introduction of **advanced technology in retailing**, managers generally have much more information available to them than has ever been the case in the past. In theory at least, a retailer should be in a much better position today to make sound management decisions, especially where scanning systems at the checkouts provide up-to-date detailed information on stock movements and inventory positions.

An interesting **polarity in store size and merchandise assortment** is developing in retailing. At one pole are the huge mass-merchandising operations of discount stores and department stores, with their tremendously wide variety of products. At the other pole is the small specialty shop — the boutique type of store. As retailers more carefully identify and segment their markets, these specialty stores are increasing in numbers and importance.

A further development bound to have an impact in Canada in the near future is the **extension of store opening hours**. In some parts of Canada, most retailers have been forced to close on Sundays under legislation usually known as the Lord's Day Act. With the increasing level of competition found in retailing today, many store owners have been arguing for the right to open their doors on Sundays, or indeed, at any time they wish. In some areas, these laws have already been repealed and stores are now staying open seven days a week. In the latter half of the 1980s, we will likely see more stores adopt this policy and, in order to remain competitive, some will start to stay open twenty-four hours a day.

We can anticipate a considerable increase in **nonstore retailing** in the coming years. Mail-order sales (in some cases tied-in with catalogue showrooms) and telephone sales are expected to increase. On the horizon is buying through television systems coupled with computer systems. Consumers will be able to do much of their buying at home, using a telephone after seeing the merchandise on a television screen. The phone order is

Buying at home
via television is
close to reality.
(Warner Amex/QUBE)

placed through a computerized system that arranges for product delivery and automatic payment from the customer's bank account.[14]

Changing life-styles — especially among women, who, incidentally, still do most of the shopping — are a major factor stimulating the growth in nonstore-retailing. Close to 60 percent of all married women are employed outside the home and have little time to shop. So the timesaving convenience and the product information provided by nonstore retailing are attractive to this growing market segment.

Through the years, many of the evolutionary changes in retailing have followed a cyclical pattern called the **wheel of retailing**. As M. P. McNair has succinctly explained it:[15]

> *The cycle frequently begins with the bold new concept, the innovation. The innovator has an idea for a new kind of distributive enterprise. At the outset he is ridiculed, condemned as "illegitimate." Bankers and investors are leery of him. But he attracts the public on the basis of a price appeal made possible by the low operating costs inherent in his innovation. As he goes along he trades up, improves the quality of his*

---

[14]See Robert A. Sawyer, "The Shape of Things to Come," *Advertising Age*, January 18, 1982, p. S–1; also see "How the Telemarketing Revolution Will Affect Marketing Managers and Top Management," *Marketing News*, July 10, 1981, p. 10. For the cautionary notion that nonstore retailing may not grow as fast as several optimistic forecasts predict, see John A. Quelch and Hirotaka Takeuchi, "Nonstore Marketing: Fast Track or Slow?" *Harvard Business Review*, July-August 1981, pp. 75–84.

[15]M. P. McNair, "Significant Trends and Developments in the Postwar Period," in A. B. Smith (ed.), *Competitive Distribution in a Free, High-Level Economy and Its Implications for the University,* The University of Pittsburgh Press, Pittsburgh, 1958, pp. 17–18. Also see Dillard B. Tinsley, John R. Brooks, Jr., and Michael d'Amico, "Will the Wheel of Retailing Stop Turning?" *Akron Business and Economic Review*, Summer 1978, pp. 26–29. For another conceptual approach to evolution in retailing, see Rom J. Markin and Calvin P. Duncan, "The Transformation of Retailing Institutions: Beyond the Wheel of Retailing and Life Cycle Theories," *Journal of Macromarketing*, Spring 1981, pp. 58–66.

merchandise, improves the appearance and standing of his store, at-
tains greater responsibility. Then, if he is successful, comes the period
of growth, the period when he is taking business away from the estab-
lished distribution channels that have clung to the old methods. Repeat-
edly something like this has happened in American distribution. . . .

The maturity phase soon tends to be followed by top-heaviness, too
great conservatism, a decline in the rate of return on investment, and
eventual vulnerability. Vulnerability to what? Vulnerability to the next
revolution of the wheel, to the next fellow who has the bright idea and
who starts his business on a low-cost basis, slipping in under the um-
brella that the old-line institutions have hoisted.

Several instances of this familiar cycle can be observed in the past 100 years. First the department stores supplanted small retailers in the cities during the late 1800s and early 1900s. In the 1920s, mail-order houses hit their peak. In that same decade the chain stores grew at the expense of independents, particularly in the grocery store field. In the 1930s, the independents retaliated with supermarkets, which proved so successful that the chain stores copied the method. In the 1950s, the discount houses — young innovaters — placed tremendous pressure on department stores, which had become staid, mature institutions. By the early 1960s, the discount houses had passed the youthful stage. In the 1970s, we observed substantial growth in warehouse retailing (catalogue showrooms, furniture warehouse showrooms) and the spread of supermarket-type retailing. Now we wait to see what will be the innovation in the late 1980s — perhaps it will be automated retailing. Manufacturers must keep abreast of the inevitable changes in the retailing institutional scene and be ready to appraise the potential of any retailing innovators. Established retailers must be alert to meet the challenge with innovations of their own. Truly, a retailer must be willing to innovate, for the alternative is to die.[16]

SUMMARY

Middlemen balance producers' outputs and consumers' wants through the activities of concentration, equalization, and dispersion. They aid considerably in creating time, place, and possession utilities. Truly, one may eliminate middlemen, but not their functions. Middlemen play a significant role in our social and economic system.

Producers and wholesalers of consumer products must understand the retail market before they can intelligently develop distribution strategies. Retailing is selling to people who are buying for personal, nonbusiness reasons. It is easy to get into retailing, but the mortality rate among retail stores is very high. The national average cost of retailing is about 27 percent of the retail selling price. Costs vary considerably, however, among the different types of retailers, and profits (as a percentage of sales) generally are very low. Retailers tend to locate where the market is, mainly in metropolitan areas. In such areas, there are several types of shopping districts, the newest being planned suburban shopping centres.

---

[16]Jurgen W. Lindhorst, "Can We Cope with Prosperity? Just Give Us a Chance! — W. Dean Muncaster," *Business Life*, April 1983, pp. 19–28.

We have classified retailers in four ways. First we looked at the competitive positions of large and small retailers. In the second classification (products carried), we examined the positions of department stores and limited-line stores. The third classification (type of ownership) provided an opportunity to discuss corporate chain stores and independents — especially the associations formed by small independents to compete with the large chains. Franchising in its various forms can also be attractive to independent retailers. In the fourth classification (method of operation), we discussed supermarket retailing, discount selling, and the major types of nonstore retailers.

It is obvious that retailing institutions will continue to change in the future (perhaps at an increasing rate). Retailers' success will depend to a great extent upon their ability to adapt to such change.

KEY TERMS AND CONCEPTS

Middleman 362

Merchant and agent middlemen 363

Channel of distribution 363

Concentration, equalization, and dispersion of middlemen 364

Time and place utilities 365

Retailing 365

Retail sale 366

Retailer 366

Downtown shopping district 368

Planned suburban shopping centre 369

Department store 374

Limited-line store 376

Scrambled merchandising 376

Specialty store 376

Corporate chain store 376

Voluntary chain (wholesaler-sponsored) 380

Retailer cooperative chain 380

Producer-sponsored franchise system 381

Entrepreneurship franchising 382

Supermarket retailing 383

Discount retailing 386

Door-to-door retailing 388

Mail-order selling 389

Automatic vending 389

Wheel-of-retailing concept 392

QUESTIONS AND PROBLEMS

1. "You can eliminate middlemen, but you cannot eliminate their functions." Discuss.

2. Which of the following institutions are middlemen? Explain.
   a. Stockbroker
   b. Real estate broker
   c. Department store
   d. Railroad
   e. Advertising agency
   f. Chain supermarket
   g. Bank
   h. Hardware wholesaler
   i. Mary Kay cosmetics salesperson
   j. Radio station

3. Explain how time and place utility may be created in the marketing of the following products. What business institutions might be involved in creating these utilities?
   a. Sewing machines
   b. Fresh peaches
   c. Hydraulic grease racks used in garages and service stations

4. Explain the terms *retailing, a retail sale*, and *a retailer* in light of the following situations:
   a. Avon cosmetics salesperson selling door-to-door
   b. Farmer selling produce door-to-door
   c. Farmer selling produce at a roadside stand
   d. Sporting goods store selling uniforms to a professional baseball team

5. How do you account for the wide differences in operating expenses among the various types of retail stores shown in Table 14-2?

6. What is the relationship between the growth and successful development of planned suburban shopping centres and the material you studied in Chapters 4 to 6 regarding the consumer?

7. "Retailing is typically small-scale business." "There is a high degree of concentration in retailing today; the giants control the field." Reconcile these two statements, using facts and figures when appropriate.

8. Of the criteria given in this chapter for evaluating the competitive positions of large-scale and small-scale retailers, which show small stores to be in a stronger position than large-scale retailers? In light of your finding, how do you account for the numerical preponderance of small retailers?

9. What courses of action might small retailers follow to improve their competitive position?

10. What can department stores do to offset their competitive disadvantages?

11. In what ways does a corporate chain (Dominion, Loblaws, or Eaton's) differ from a voluntary chain such as IGA?

12. With all the advantages attributed to voluntary associations of independents, why do you suppose some retailers are still unaffiliated?

13. "The only significant competitive advantage that chains have over independents is greater buying power. If buying power can be equalized through antichain legislation or by having the independents join some voluntary association, then independents can compete equally with the chains." Discuss.

14. "The supermarket, with its operating expense ratio of 20 percent, is the most efficient institution in retailing today." Do you agree? In what ways might supermarkets reduce their operating expenses?

15. Name some discount houses in your community or in a nearby large city. Is there a distinction between "discount selling" and a "discount house"?

16. "House-to-house selling is the most efficient form of retail selling because it eliminates wholesalers and retail stores." Discuss.

17. "The factors that accounted for the early growth of mail-order retailing no longer exist, so we may expect a substantial decline in this form of selling." Discuss.

18. The ease of entry into retailing undoubtedly contributes to the high mortality rate among retailers, with the resultant economic waste. Should entry into retailing be restricted? If so, how could this be done?

19. What recommendations do you have for reducing the costs of retailing?

20. By 1990, most of our retail purchases will be made through television-linked computer systems. Do you agree? Why?

Chapter 15

The Wholesale Market and Wholesaling Middlemen

CHAPTER GOALS

The wholesaling middlemen are the "other" middlemen, the ones that consumers rarely see. After studying this chapter, you should understand:

1. *The nature and importance of wholesaling*
   a. *The meaning of the term* wholesaling
   b. *The economic justification of wholesaling*
   c. *What wholesalers are and how they differ from wholesaling middlemen*
2. *The major classes of wholesaling middlemen*
3. *The costs and profits in wholesaling*
4. *Full-service merchant wholesalers and the services they render*
5. *The functions of rack jobbers and limited-service wholesalers*
6. *The several types of agent wholesaling middlemen and the services they provide*

"Let's eliminate the middleman" and "The middleman makes all the profit" are cries that have been echoed by consumers, businesspeople, and legislators through the years. These complaints are most often focused on the wholesaling segment of the distribution structure. Historically, the wholesaler has been a truly powerful figure in North American marketing. During the past 25 to 50 years, however, many manufacturers and retailers have made successful attempts to eliminate the wholesaler from their trade channels. Yet, wholesaling middlemen continue to be important, and in many cases dominant, in the distribution system.

NATURE AND IMPORTANCE OF WHOLESALING

Wholesaling Broadly Defined

Wholesaling or **wholesale trade** includes the sale, and all activities directly incident to the sale, of products or services to those who are buying for resale or for business use. Thus, *broadly viewed*, sales made by one manufacturer to another are wholesale transactions, and the selling manufacturer is engaged in wholesaling. A retail variety store is engaged in wholesaling when it sells pencils or envelopes to a restaurant. That is, wholesaling includes sales by any firm to any customer except to an ultimate consumer who is buying for personal, nonbusiness use. As in our definition of retailing, the only real criterion is the purchaser's purpose for buying.

While this general definition of wholesaling is accurate, it is too broad to be useful in (1) understanding the role of wholesaling middlemen and (2) establishing channels of distribution. For analytical convenience, the definition must be limited. We are concerned here with companies that are engaged *primarily* in wholesaling. Therefore, we shall ignore retailers who occasionally make a wholesale sale. We shall also exclude the sales of manufacturers and farmers, because they are primarily engaged in production (creating form utility), and not in wholesaling.

The Narrower Definition of Wholesaling

A **wholesaling middleman** is a firm engaged primarily in wholesaling. The more restrictive term **wholesaler** applies only to *merchant* middlemen engaged in wholesaling activities. (Recall that merchant middlemen are those who take title to the goods they handle.) *Wholesaling middlemen* thus is the all-inclusive term, covering both wholesalers and other wholesaling middlemen, such as agents and brokers, that do not take title to the merchandise. Thus a food broker or a manufacturers' agent is not a wholesaler but, rather, a wholesaling middleman.

Sometime one hears the terms *jobber and distributor*. Although usage varies from trade to trade, in this book these terms are considered synonymous with *wholesaler*. Figure 15-1 shows these distinctions.

Wholesalers and Wholesaling Middlemen

Most manufacturing companies in Canada are small and specialized. They don't have the capital needed to maintain a sales force large enough to contact the many small retailers who are their customers. Even for manufacturers that have sufficient capital, output often is too small to justify the necessary sales force. On the other hand, most retailers buy in small quantities and have only a limited knowledge of the market and sources of supply. Thus there is a gap between the retailer (buyer) and the producer (seller). The wholesaler can fill this gap by pooling the orders of many retailers and so furnish a market for the small manufacturer. At the same time, the wholesaler is performing a buying service for small retailers.

From a macromarketing point of view, wholesaling brings to the total distribution system the economies of skill, scale, and transactions. Wholesaling middlemen are marketing specialists. Their wholesaling *skills* are efficiently concentrated in a relatively few hands. This saves the duplication of effort that would occur if the many producers had to perform the wholesaling functions themselves. Economies of *scale* result from the specialization of the wholesaling middleman who performs functions that might otherwise require several small departments run by producing firms.

Economic Justification of Wholesaling

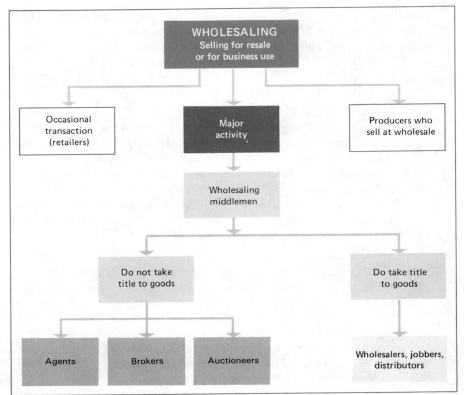

Figure 15-1
WHOLESALING
INSTITUTIONS.

How the general definition
of wholesaling leads to our
definition of wholesaling
middlemen, wholesalers,
and agents and brokers.

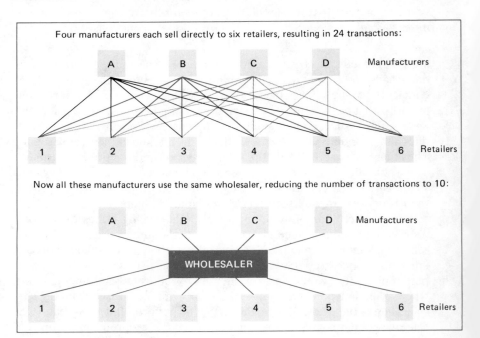

Figure 15-2
THE ECONOMY OF
TRANSACTIONS IN
WHOLESALING.

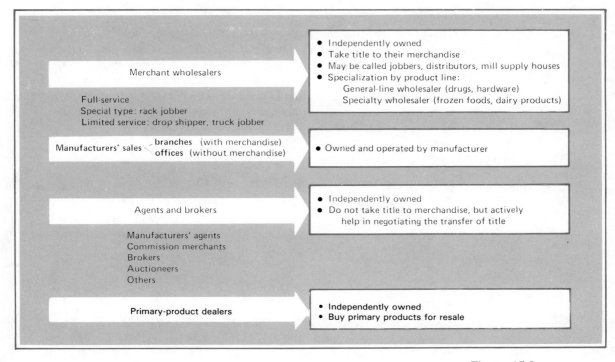

Figure 15-3
TYPES OF
WHOLESALING
INSTITUTIONS.

Wholesalers typically can perform the wholesaling functions at an operating-expense percentage lower than most manufacturers can. *Transaction economies* come into play when wholesaling middlemen are introduced between producers and their customers. To see this, assume four manufacturers want to sell to six retailers. Without a wholesaling middleman, there are 24 transactions. With one wholesaler, the number of transactions is cut to 10. That is, 4 transactions occur when the producers all sell to the wholesaler and another 6 occur when the wholesaler sells to all the retailers (Fig. 15-2).

Any attempt to classify wholesaling middlemen in a meaningful way is a precarious project. It is easy to get lost in a maze of categories, because these middlemen vary greatly in (1) the products they carry, (2) the markets they sell to, and (3) the methods of operation they use. In an attempt to minimize the confusion, we will use the classification scheme shown in Fig. 15-3. There, all wholesaling middlemen are grouped into only four broad categories — wholesale merchants, manufacturers' sales branches, agents and brokers, and primary-product dealers. These four groups are the classifications used by Statistics Canada, which is the major source of quantitative data on wholesaling institutions and markets.

Classification of
Wholesaling
Middlemen

Wholesale Merchants

These are the firms we usually refer to as wholesalers, jobbers, or industrial distributors. They typically are independently owned, and they take title to the merchandise they handle. They form the largest single segment of wholesaling firms when measured either by sales or by number of establishments. Statistics Canada reports that wholesale merchants, along with manufacturers' sales branches and primary-product dealers, discussed below, account for about 80 percent of total wholesale trade.

Manufacturers' Sales Branches and Offices

These establishments are owned and operated by manufacturers, but they are physically separated from the manufacturing plants. The distinction between a sales branch and a sales office is that a branch carries merchandise stock and an office does not.

Agents and Brokers

Agents and brokers do *not* take title to the merchandise they handle, but they do actively negotiate the purchase or sale of products for their principals. The main types of agent middlemen are manufacturers' agents, commission merchants (in the marketing of agricultural products), and brokers. As a group, agents and brokers represent approximately 20 percent of total wholesale trade.

Primary-Product Dealers

These firms are principally engaged in buying for resale primary products such as grain, livestock, furs, fish, tobacco, fruit, and vegetables from the primary producers of these products. On occasion, they will act as agents of the producer. Cooperatives that market the primary products of their members are also included in this category.

Some other subcategories used in classifying the wholesaling business are reflected in Fig. 15-3. For example, wholesaling middlemen may be grouped by:

- *Ownership of products* — wholesale merchants versus agent middlemen
- *Ownership of establishment* — manufacturers' sales branches versus independent merchants and agents
- *Range of services offered* — full-service wholesalers versus limited-service firms
- *Depth and breadth of the line carried* — general-line wholesalers (drugs, hardware) versus specialty firms (frozen foods, dairy products)

Table 15-1 WHOLESALE TRADE IN CANADA, 1982

	Number of Establishments	Number of Locations	Sales Volume ($ millions)
Wholesale merchants	44,513	54,742	142,983.9
Agents and brokers	5,009	5,183	27,077.1
Total	49,522	59,925	170,061.0

Note: For purposes of data presentation, Statistics Canada includes manufacturers' sales branches and primary-product dealers in the wholesale merchants category.

Source: Statistics Canada, cat. no. 63-226.

Size of the Wholesale Market

In 1982, there were about 50,000 wholesaling establishments in Canada, with a total annual sales volume of more than $170 billion. This represents a major increase in the number of establishments over the course of the past thirty years or so. The 1982 sales figure represents an increase of more than 250 percent from the estimated sales for wholesale establishments in 1973. Part of this increase is accounted for by increases in prices that have occurred in the past decade, but even if sales were expressed in constant dollars, we would still see a substantial increase.

The statistics presented in Table 15-1 reflect the number of companies engaged in wholesaling in the two major categories of wholesale merchants and agents and brokers. Over the course of the past ten years or so, a major increase in the sales of these wholesaling establishments is noted. Defining precisely what the trends have been has been complicated, however, by the fact that Statistics Canada in 1981 changed the manner in which it measures wholesale data. Prior to 1981, Statistics Canada collected data in odd years from a sample of companies in the wholesale merchants category and in even years from a sample of agents and brokers. As a result, data from the period preceding 1981 are estimates only.

Nevertheless, it is safe to conclude that the sales of wholesalers have been increasing dramatically. Also, over the past decade, the percentage of total sales accounted for by each of the two major categories of wholesalers has remained fairly stable — wholesale merchants accounting for approximately 80 percent of wholesale sales, and agents and brokers for 20 percent. This has occurred despite the fact that there has been a substantial increase in the number of companies in the wholesale merchants category, while the number of agents and brokers has remained fairly stable. As market potential has increased in various areas, a number of manufacturers have established sales branches in territories that once were served by agents or brokers. Despite this, the agents and brokers category has been able to retain a stable share of total wholesale sales.

Customers of Wholesaling Middlemen

One might expect that total retail sales would be considerably higher than total wholesale trade, because the retail price of a given product is higher than the wholesale price. Also, many products sold at retail never pass through a wholesaler's establishment and so are excluded from total wholesale sales.

Total sales figures belie this particular line of reasoning (see Table 15-2). In each year, the volume of wholesale trade is considerably higher than total retail sales.

The explanation for this seemingly upside-down situation may be found in an analysis of the customers of wholesaling middlemen (Table 15-3).

Most wholesale merchants' sales are made to customers other than retailers. That is, large quantities of industrial products are now sold through wholesale merchants. Moreover, sales by the other types of wholesaling middlemen show this same pattern. Thus, overall, sales to retailers account for less than one-half of total sales by wholesale merchants.

Another trend that has become obvious in recent years is the increase in the percentage of consumer goods sold directly to retailers by manufacturers. Yet, in spite of this increased bypassing of the wholesaler, wholesaling is on the increase, an indication of the usefulness of wholesaling to the business world.

Table 15-2   TOTAL WHOLESALE AND RETAIL TRADE, 1971–1983

Year	Wholesale Trade[1]	Retail Trade
1971	$ 36,892.6	$ 31,390.1
1975	55,284.4	51,408.5
1976	61,176.1	57,166.9
1977	66,541.5	61,651.3
1978	77,231.7	68,859.2
1979	109,633.7*	76,992.5
1980	128,932.6*	84,026.6
1981	176,852.7	95,240.2
1982	170,061.0	97,638.5
1983	not available	106,243.0

[1]Wholesale figures for 1971 through to 1978 are for the wholesale merchants category only. This figure represents approximately 80 percent of total wholesale trade.

*Estimates

Source: Statistics Canada, *Market Research Handbook*, cat. no. 63-224 (annual); *Canadian Statistical Review*, cat. no. 11-003E (monthly); *Corporation Financial Statistics, 1981*, cat. no. 61-207; and *Wholesale Trade Statistics, 1981 and 1982*, cat. no. 63-226.

Table 15-3   DISTRIBUTION OF SALES OF WHOLESALE MERCHANTS, 1982

Type of Customer	Percentage of Total Wholesale Trade
Retailers (for resale)	36.9
Industrial, commercial and other users	29.8
Exports (to foreign markets)	13.3
Other wholesalers (for resale)	11.3
Farmers (for use in farm production)	5.0
Household consumers	3.7
Total	100.0

Source: Statistics Canada, unpublished data.

The average total operating expenses for all wholesaling middlemen combined has been estimated at about 17 percent of *wholesale* sales. It has also been estimated that operating expenses of retailers average about 25 percent of *retail* sales (omitting bars and restaurants, which do some processing of products) (see Table 15-4). Therefore, on a broad average, the expenses of wholesaling middlemen take less than 8 percent of the consumer's dollar.

Operating Expenses and Profits of Wholesaling Middlemen

Expenses by Type of Operation

Table 15-5 shows operating expenses as a percentage of net sales for selected categories of wholesaling middlemen. Wholesalers of industrial equipment have the highest average operating expenses at 27.9 percent.

Table 15-4 REVENUE AND EXPENSES: WHOLESALE AND RETAIL TRADE, 1981

| | Wholesale Trade | | Retail Trade | |
	$ millions	%	$ millions	%
Income	120,837.5	100.0	95,240.2	100.0
Expenses				
Materials	97,157.1	80.4	67,799.9	71.2
Operating	21,026.9	17.4	24,022.1	25.2
Total	118,184.0	97.8	91,822.0	96.4
Net profit before taxes	3,021.7	2.5	3,723.7	3.9
Net profit after taxes	1,932.0	1.6	3,048.7	3.2

Source: Statistics Canada, *Corporation Financial Statistics, 1981*, cat. no. 61-207

Table 15-5 OPERATING EXPENSES AND NET PROFIT AFTER TAXES AS PERCENTAGE OF TOTAL INCOME FOR CATEGORIES OF WHOLESALERS, 1981

Type of Operation	Operating Expenses as Percentage of Total Income	Net Profit After Taxes as Percentage of Total Income
Industrial equipment	27.9%	2.2%
Scrap and waste dealers	26.8	n/a
Furniture and furnishings	24.8	1.6
Electrical machinery	24.6	2.8
Drug and toilet preparations	22.9	1.7
Motor vehicles and parts	19.7	2.5
Hardware, plumbing, and heating	19.7	1.6
Lumber and building products	19.6	1.6
Apparel and drygoods	19.1	2.0
Farm machinery	16.0	1.6
Metal products	14.4	1.3
Livestock	11.8	0.5
Food	10.9	1.2
Petroleum products	10.6	1.7
Paper	8.2	1.2
ALL WHOLESALERS	17.8	1.6

Source: Statistics Canada, *Corporation Financial Statistics, 1981*, cat. no. 61-207.

Faster-moving, low-margin products such as food and livestock produce much lower levels of operating expenses as a percentage of total income.

Care should be exercised when interpreting these figures. For instance, we should not conclude that wholesalers of petroleum products, paper, and food are highly efficient because their operating expenses are low and that wholesalers of industrial equipment and electrical machinery are inefficient. The cost differentials are attributable to the differences in the nature of the products handled and to the nature of the services provided by the various wholesalers. Were more data available, we would likely find that agents and brokers have much lower levels of operating expenses than do wholesale merchants. Similarly, we generally find that manufacturers' sales branches and offices have lower operating expenses as a percentage of sales. Even when merchant wholesalers in given product lines (paper products, machinery) are compared with manufacturers' sales branches in the same line, the branch ordinarily shows a lower operating cost ratio. Careful analysis shows that the comparison is often "loaded" in favour of the manufacturers' branch operations. Branches and sales offices are located only in the markets offering the highest potential sales and profits. Thus the manufacturers' operations would get more sales per dollar of effort. Often, too, a branch is not allocated its full share of costs. Many indirect administrative expenses are charged in full to the home office, even though the branches share in the benefit. Finally, costs of manufacturers' sales branches and merchant wholesalers are not always comparable because of differences in services provided.

Net profits

Net operating profits after taxes, expressed as a percentage of total income, is extremely modest for wholesaling middlemen and is considerably lower than that for retailing middlemen. Data collected by Statistics Canada from wholesalers in 1981 showed an average after-tax profit of only 1.6 percent. This compares with an average of 3.2 percent profit after taxes among retailers (see Table 15-4). The highest after-tax profits were reported by wholesalers of electrical machinery and of motor vehicles and parts. Several categories of wholesalers reported after-tax profits of less than 1.5 percent of total income. These included metal-products wholesalers, and those engaged in the wholesaling of paper, food, and livestock products.

FULL-SERVICE WHOLESALERS

Full-service (also called full-function) wholesalers are independent merchant middlemen who generally perform a full range of wholesaling functions. These are the firms that fit the layman's image or stereotype of wholesalers. They may be called simply "wholesalers," or they may be listed as "distributors," "mill supply houses," "industrial distributors," or "jobbers," depending upon the usage in their line of business. They may handle consumer and/or industrial products, and these goods may be manufactured or nonmanufactured, and imported or exported.

Wholesale merchants have accounted for well over one-half of total whole-sale trade in Canada for many years. Thus, the full-service wholesalers have held their own in the competitive struggles within the distribution system. In fact, their market share has been relatively constant in the recent past, despite increasing competition from agents and brokers and from direct-selling manufacturers and their sales offices and branches. A presumption is that the wholesalers' existence is maintained by the services they provide both to their customers and to their suppliers (see Table 15-6).

This picture of stability in the full-service wholesaler's share of the market may be a bit misleading. It hides the volatility and shifting competitive positions within various industries. Wholesalers have increased their market share in some industries but have lost ground in other markets where they once dominated. Certainly the aggregate market-share figures are misleading in industries where wholesalers are, and always have been, used very little.

Table 15-6 WHOLESALERS' SERVICES TO CUSTOMERS AND TO
PRODUCER-SUPPLIERS

1. *Buying:* Act as purchasing agents for customers. Anticipate customers' needs and have good knowledge of market and sources of supply. Enable customers to deal with only a few salespeople rather than representatives of many producers.

2. *Selling:* Provide a sales force for producers to reach small retailers and industrial users, at a lower cost than producers would incur to reach these markets. Customers often know and trust their local wholesalers more than distant suppliers.

3. *Dividing, or bulk-breaking*: Wholesalers buy in carload and truckload lots and then resell in case lots or less, thus providing a saving and a service to customers and producers.

4. *Transportation*: Provide quick, frequent delivery to customers, thus reducing their risks and investment in inventory. Reduce producers' and customers' freight costs by buying in large quantities.

5. *Warehousing*: Provide a service to both customers and suppliers by reducing inventory risks and costs. Wholesalers can warehouse more efficiently than any single customer or producer.

6. *Financing*: Grant credit to customers, sometimes for extended periods of time, thus reducing their capital requirements. Producers usually would not offer comparable credit aid to small retailers. Wholesalers also aid producers by ordering well ahead of season and by paying bills on time.

7. *Risk bearing*: We already mentioned some of the ways wholesalers reduce risks for customers and producers. In addition, simply by taking title to products, wholesalers reduce a producer's risk. Losses due to spoilage or fashion obsolescence are then borne by wholesalers.

8. *Market information*: For their customers, wholesalers supply information regarding new products, competitors' activities, special sales by producers, etc.

9. *Management services and advice*: By offering managerial services and advice, especially to retailer customers, wholesalers have significantly strengthened their own position in the market. The existence of full-service wholesalers is dependent upon the economic health and well-being of small retailers. Therefore, by helping the retailers, the wholesalers really help themselves.

Special Types of Wholesale Merchants

Within the broad category of wholesale merchants, there are a few subclassifications worth observing because of the special nature of their operations. Their titles reflect either the specialized nature of their work or the limited range of wholesaling services they offer (recall Fig. 15-3).

Rack Jobbers

These firms (often called rack merchandisers) are wholesale merchants that began operations after World War II, primarily to supply grocery supermarkets with nonfood items. Since then, rack jobbers have expanded to serve drugstores, hardware stores, variety stores, and other stores that have instituted the self-service method of retailing. The many general-line wholesalers carrying these nonfood lines could not easily sell to supermarkets for at least three reasons. First, the wholesalers' regular customers, such as drugstores or hardware stores, would complain loudly and probably withdraw their business. Second, too many different wholesalers would have to call on the supermarket to fill all the nonfood lines, and the retailer would object to seeing so many wholesalers. Third, a single supermarket ordinarily orders too small a quantity in any one nonfood line to make it profitable for a wholesaler to service that line.

One rack jobber (or a very few) can furnish all the nonfood items in a supermarket. Rack jobbers furnish the racks or shelves upon which to display the merchandise, and they stock only the fastest-moving brands on these racks. They are responsible for maintaining fully stocked racks, building attractive displays, and price-marking the merchandise. In essence, the retailers merely furnish floor or shelf space and then collect the money as the customers go through the checkout stands.

Limited-Function Wholesalers

A small group of wholesale merchants who have received attention in marketing literature through the years, possibly more attention than their numerical importance merits, are the limited-function wholesalers. These are merchant middlemen who do not perform all the usual wholesaling functions. The activities of most of these wholesalers are concentrated in a few product lines. The major types of limited-function wholesalers are truck jobbers, drop shippers, and retailer cooperative warehouses. The retailer cooperative warehouse was discussed in the preceding chapter.

Truck distributors or jobbers (sometimes still called "wagon jobbers" in memory of the days when they used a horse and wagon) are specialty wholesalers, chiefly in the food field. Each jobber carries a nationally advertised brand of fast-moving and perishable or semi-perishable goods, such as candies, dairy products, potato chips, and tobacco products. The unique feature of their method of operation is that they sell and deliver merchandise during their calls. Their competitive advantage lies in their ability to furnish fresh products so frequently that retailers can buy perishable goods in small amounts to minimize the risk of loss. The major limitation of truck

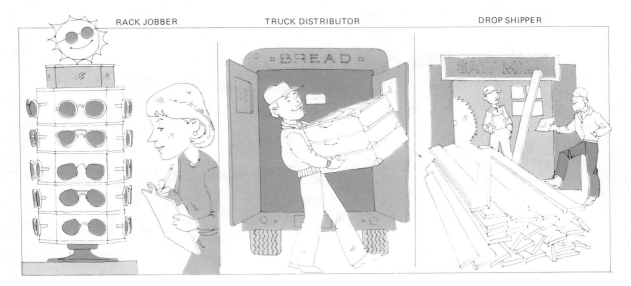

RACK JOBBER   TRUCK DISTRIBUTOR   DROP SHIPPER

jobbers is their high operating cost ratio. This is caused primarily by the small order size and the inefficient use of delivery equipment. A truck is an expensive warehouse.

Drop shippers, sometimes called "desk jobbers," get their name from the fact that the merchandise they sell is delivered directly from the manufacturer to the customer and is called a "drop shipment." Drop shippers take title to the products, but do not physically handle them. They operate almost entirely in coal and coke, lumber, and building materials. These products are typically sold in carload quantities, and freight is high in comparison to unit value. Thus it is desirable to minimize the physical handling of the product.

Another important group of wholesaling middlemen consists of agents and brokers. These middlemen are distinguished from wholesale merchants in two important respects: Agent middlemen do *not* take title to the merchandise, and they typically perform fewer services for their clients and principals (see Table 15-7). For these reasons, the average operating expenses for agents and brokers is only 3 to 4 percent, compared to approximately 17 percent for service wholesalers. On the basis of sales volume, the major types of agent middlemen are manufacturers' agents, brokers, and commission merchants. Other types include auction companies, selling agents, import agents, and export agents.

The total number of agents and brokers engaged in wholesale trade has not changed appreciably over the past forty years, but their market share has dropped somewhat. In the wholesaling of agricultural products, agent middlemen are being replaced by wholesale merchants or by direct sales to retailers and food processors. In the marketing of manufactured goods, the agent middlemen are being supplanted by manufacturers' sales branches and offices. As manufacturers become larger and their markets grow in

AGENT WHOLESALING MIDDLEMEN

Table 15-7   SERVICES PROVIDED BY AGENT
WHOLESALING MIDDLEMEN

Services	Manufacturers' Agents	Selling Agents	Brokers	Commission Merchants
Provides buying services	Yes	Yes	Some	Yes
Provides selling services	Yes	Yes	Yes	Yes
Carries inventory stocks	Sometimes	No	No	Yes
Delivers the products	Sometimes	No	No	Yes
Provides market information	Yes	Yes	Yes	Yes
Sets prices and terms of sale	No	Yes	No	No
Grants credit to customers	No	Sometimes	No	Sometimes
Reduces producers' credit risks	No	Yes	No	No
Sells producers' full line	Sometimes	Yes	Sometimes	No
Has continuing relationship with producer throughout the year	Yes	Yes	No	No
Manufacturer uses own sales force along with agents	Sometimes	No	No	No
Manufacturer uses same agent for entire market	No	Yes	No	No

sales potential, they no longer have to rely on manufacturers' agents or brokers to reach customers in these markets. From a marketing point of view, it is more effective for manufacturers to establish their own outlets and sales force in these markets.

Manufacturers' Agents

Manufacturers' agents (frequently called manufacturers' representatives) are agents commissioned to sell part or all of a producer's products in particular territories. The agents are independent and are in no way employees of the manufacturers. They have little or no control over the prices and terms of sale; these are established by the manufacturer. Because a manufacturers' agent sells in a limited territory, each producer typically uses several agents. Unlike brokers, manufacturers' agents have continuing, year-round relationships with their principals. Each agent usually represents several noncompeting manufacturers of related products. The agent can pool into one profitable sale the small orders that otherwise would go to several individual manufacturers.

Manufacturers' agents are used extensively in the distribution of many types of consumer and industrial products. The main service offered to manufacturers by agent middlemen is selling. They seek out and serve markets that manufacturers cannot profitably reach. Furthermore, because a manufacturers' agent does not carry nearly so many lines as a full-service wholesaler, the agent can offer a higher-calibre, more aggressive selling service. Operating expenses depend upon the product sold and whether the merchandise is stocked. Some representatives operate on a commission as low as 2 percent, while others charge as much as 20 percent. These commissions cover operating expenses and net profit. On an overall basis, the operating expense ratio is about 8 percent for these agents.

There are some limitations to the use of manufacturers' agents. Many agents do not carry merchandise stocks. Also, many agents cannot furnish customers adequate technical advice and repair service, nor are they equipped to install major products.

Manufacturers' agents are most helpful in three characteristic situations:

1. When a small firm has a limited number of products and no sales force, manufacturers' agents may do all the selling.

2. When a firm wants to add a new and possibly unrelated line to its existing product mix, and the present sales force either is not experienced in the new line or cannot reach the new market, then the new line may be given to manufacturers' agents. Thus a company's own sales force and its agents may cover the same geographic market.

3. When a firm wishes to enter a new geographic market that is not yet sufficiently developed to warrant sending its own sales force, manufacturers' agents familiar with that market may be used.[1]

Brokers are agent middlemen whose prime responsibility is to bring buyers and sellers together. They furnish considerable market information regarding prices, products, and general market conditions. Brokers do not physically handle the goods. Nor do they work on a continuing basis with their principals. Most brokers work for sellers, although about 10 percent represent buyers. Brokers have no authority to set prices. A broker simply negotiates a sale and leaves it up to the seller to accept or reject the buyer's offer. Because of the limited service provided, brokers operate on a very low cost ratio — about 3 percent of net sales.

Brokers

Brokers are most prevalent in the food field. Their operation is typified by a seafood broker handling the pack from a salmon cannery. The cannery is in operation for possibly three months of the year. The canner employs a broker each year (the same one if relationships are mutually satisfactory) to find buyers for the salmon pack. The broker provides information regarding market prices and conditions, and the canner then informs the broker of the desired price. The broker seeks potential buyers among chain stores, wholesalers, and others. When the entire pack has been sold, the agent-principal relationship is discontinued until possibly the following year.

An evolutionary development in the food brokerage field should be noted. Through the years, many brokers have established permanent relationships with some principals. These brokers are now performing activities that would more accurately classify them as manufacturers' agents. They still call themselves "food brokers," however, and they are classed as brokers by Statistics Canada.

---

[1] For further discussion, see Stanley D. Sibley and R. Kenneth Teas, "The Manufacturers' Agent in Industrial Distribution," *Industrial Marketing Management*, November 1979, pp. 286–292.

Commission Merchants

In the marketing of many agricultural products, a widely used middleman is the commission merchant, also called a *commission man* or *commission house*. (The term *commission merchant* is actually a misnomer. This handler is really an agent middleman who, in many transactions, does not take title to the commodities that are handled.)

The commission method of operation, mainly found in large central markets, may be described briefly as follows: Assemblers in local markets (possibly local resident produce buyers or grain elevators) consign shipments to commission merchants in central markets. These firms usually have established working relationships over a period of years. The commission merchants meet trains or trucks and take charge of the shipments. It is their responsibility to handle and sell the goods. They arrange for any necessary storage, grading, and other services prior to the sale. They find buyers at the best possible prices, make the sales, and arrange for the transfer of shipments. They deduct their commissions, freight charges, and other marketing expenses, and then remit the balance as soon as possible to the local market shippers.

Auction Companies

Auction companies provide the auctioneers who do the selling and the physical facilities for displaying the products of sellers. In this way, auction companies help the assembled buyers and sellers to complete their transactions. Auctioneers account for a very small percentage of total wholesale trade. Yet they are extremely important in the wholesaling of some agricultural products (tobacco, livestock, fruit, and furs). Their operating expenses usually are quite low — about 3 percent of the sales they handle.

Selling Agents

A selling agent is an independent middleman who essentially takes the place of a manufacturer's entire marketing department. These agents typically perform more marketing services than any other type of agent middleman. They also have more control and authority over their clients' marketing programs. A manufacturer will employ one selling agent to market the full output of the firm over its entire market. Although selling agents account for a very small percentage of total wholesale trade, they are quite important in the marketing of textile products and coal. They are also found to some extent in the distribution of apparel, food, lumber, and metal products. Their operating expenses average about 3 percent of sales.

FUTURE OF THE WHOLESALER

In the 1930s, it was frequently forecast that the full-function merchant wholesaler was a dying institution. Statistics in this chapter and elsewhere, however, show that wholesale merchants have enjoyed a resurgent growth rate during the past forty years. Today they hold a strong and significant position in the economy.

There are two basic reasons for the comeback of wholesalers. One is a fuller realization of the true economic worth of their services. The other is the general improvement of their management methods and operations. The bandwagon to eliminate the wholesaler proved to be a blessing in disguise. Innumerable firms tried to bypass the wholesaler and came to

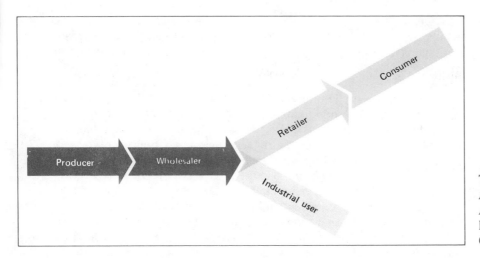

THE WHOLESALER IS
ALIVE AND WELL
AND LIVING IN MANY
DISTRIBUTION
CHANNELS.

realize that the net result was unsatisfactory. In many cases, it became evident that the wholesaler was able to provide manufacturers and retailers with better services, and at a lower cost, than these firms themselves could do.

Wholesalers are still the controlling force in the channels used by many firms. We must not conclude, however, that only low-cost wholesalers can survive in the competitive market. Even seemingly high-cost wholesalers are thriving. A high operating cost ratio is not necessarily the result of inefficiency. Instead, it is usually the result of more and better service.

Wholesalers, admittedly slow to adopt modern business methods and attitudes, are striving to catch up in this respect. Moreover, the already evident trends shaping the future of wholesale distribution suggest that the wholesaler (1) is responsive to the business environment and (2) can effectively adapt to pressures from both suppliers and customers for lower-cost distribution.

SUMMARY

Wholesaling is the sale, and all activities directly related to the sale, of products and services to those who are buying (1) to use the items in their business or (2) to resell them. Thus, in a broad sense, all sales are either wholesale sales or retail sales. The difference depends only on the purchaser's purpose in buying: Is it a business or a nonbusiness use?

On a narrower scale, the definition of wholesaling encompasses only companies that are *primarily* engaged in wholesaling. Excluded are sales by farmers, retailers, manufacturers (except for their sales branches), and other firms usually called producers (in contrast to resellers).

The institutional structure of wholesaling middlemen (the all-inclusive term) may be divided into four groups: (1) wholesale merchants, (2) manufacturers' sales offices and branches, (3) agents and brokers, and (4) primary-product dealers. Total operating expenses of all wholesaling middlemen average about 17 percent of *wholesale* sales and less than 10 percent of *retail* sales (the consumer's dollar). Net profits in wholesaling average less than 2 percent of sales. Less than 40 percent of wholesale sales are made to retailers, and approximately the same percentage go to industrial users and other wholesalers.

Wholesale merchants (also called jobbers or distributors) generally fit the layman's stereotype of a wholesaler. They constitute the largest category of wholesaling middlemen, in both sales volume and number of companies. These middlemen offer the widest range of wholesaling services and consequently incur the highest operating expenses of the four major groups of wholesaling middlemen. Wholesale merchants have consistently accounted for well over 50 percent of all wholesale sales over the past forty years. In spite of persistent attempts to "eliminate the middleman" (namely, the wholesale merchant), middlemen continue to grow and thrive, thus attesting to their real economic value in our economy.

The use of agents and brokers has decreased over the years, as these middlemen have been replaced in distribution channels by manufacturers' sales offices and branches. Agent wholesaling middlemen (manufacturers' agents, brokers, and others) remain strong in certain industries, and in geographic areas where the market potential is still too small for a producer's sales force.

KEY TERMS AND CONCEPTS

Wholesaling 396

Wholesaling middleman 397

Wholesaler 397

Manufacturer's sales office 400

Manufacturer's sales branch 400

Distributor 404

Jobber 404

Rack jobber 406

Limited-function wholesaler 406

Agent wholesaling middleman 407

Manufacturer's agent 408

Broker 409

Commission merchant 410

Auction company 410

Selling agent 410

QUESTIONS AND PROBLEMS

1. A large furniture warehouse is located in a major city in Saskatchewan. The following conditions exist with respect to this firm:
   a. All merchandise is purchased directly from manufacturers.
   b. The warehouse is located in the low-rent, wholesaling district.
   c. Merchandise remains in original crates; customers use catalogues and swatch books to see what the articles look like and what fabrics are used.
   d. About 90 percent of the customers are ultimate consumers, and they account for 85 percent of the sales volume.
   e. The firm does quite a bit of advertising, pointing out that consumers are buying at wholesale prices.
   f. Crates are not price-marked. Salespeople bargain with customers.
   g. Some 10 percent of sales volume comes from sales to furniture stores. Is this firm a wholesaler? Explain.

2. Which of the following are wholesaling transactions?
   a. A farmer sells fresh produce to a restaurant.
   b. A chemical manufacturer sells chemicals to a fertilizer manufacturer.
   c. A drug wholesaler sells drugs to a hospital; to a drug retailer.
   d. A retail lumberyard sells plywood to a building contractor; to a home-owner for a "do-it-yourself" project.

3. What conditions account for the fact that manufacturers' sales offices and branches have maintained a steadily increasing share of total wholesale trade, while the agents' and brokers' share has declined somewhat over the past thirty years?

4. How do you account for the substantial variation in operating expenses among the major types of wholesalers shown in Table 15-5?

5. In comparing the operating expense ratio for retailers and for wholesalers in Table 15-4, we see that wholesalers typically have lower operating expenses. How do you account for this?

6. What activities could full-service wholesalers discontinue in an effort to reduce operating costs?

7. What service does a full-function wholesaler provide for a manufacturer?

8. What types of retailers, other than supermarkets, offer reasonable fields for entry by the rack jobber? Explain.

9. Why would a manufacturing firm prefer to use manufacturers' agents instead of its own company sales force?

10. Why is it that manufacturers' agents often can penetrate a market faster and at a lower cost than a manufacturer's sales force?

11. What is the economic justification for the existence of brokers, especially in light of the few functions they perform?

12. Which type of agent middleman, if any, is most likely to be used by each of the following? Explain your choice in each instance.
    a. A small manufacturer of a liquid glass cleaner to be sold through supermarkets
    b. A small manufacturer of knives used for hunting, fishing, and camping
    c. A small independent fish processor in Newfoundland, producing high-quality crab and salmon for the restaurant market
    d. A small-tools manufacturing firm that has its own sales force selling to the industrial market and that wishes to add backyard barbecue equipment to its line
    e. A Quebec textile mill producing unbranded towels, sheets, pillowcases, and blankets

13. Looking into the future, which types of wholesaling middlemen do you think will increase in importance, and which ones will decline? Explain.

Chapter 16

Channels of Distribution: Conflict, Cooperation, and Management

CHAPTER GOALS

A distribution channel is a system—often with very independent parts that may be in conflict. To work effectively, a distribution channel must be well designed and well managed. After studying this chapter, you should understand:

1. *The distribution channel as a total system*
2. *The nature of the conflicts in channels of distribution:*
   a. *Between manufacturers and wholesalers*
   b. *Between manufacturers and retailers*
3. *Vertical marketing systems*
4. *The major channels of distribution*
5. *The factors affecting the selection of a channel*
6. *The concept of intensity of distribution*
7. *The choice of individual middlemen*
8. *The legal considerations in channel management*

Distribution-channel design and management are among the most difficult tasks faced by marketing executives. This difficulty is due in part to the dynamic nature of the distribution structure and its tendency to change. Moreover, producers frequently have little or no control over their middlemen. And wholesalers, in turn, have little control over their retailers. Each is, in fact, an independent business firm.

The task of choosing and managing a distribution channel often begins with a manufacturer or producer. For that reason, we shall approach our discussion of channel design largely from the vantage point of the producer. As you will see, however, the channel problems faced by middlemen are similar to those of a producer. Furthermore, the control of the channels used by manufacturers and the freedom of choice regarding these channels may actually rest with middlemen.

A channel of distribution should be treated as a unit—a total system of action. Producers and middlemen alike should understand that each of them is one component of a total systematic organization that is designed to maximize marketing effectiveness in selling to the final customer. Thus there is a real need for coordination throughout the channel. A properly operated distribution system is a significant competitive advantage for each firm that is part of that system.

Unfortunately, a trade channel too often is treated as a fragmented assortment of competing, independently operating organizations. Manufacturers may view their own retailers as competitors. Or middlemen may be in conflict with their suppliers, rather than recognizing that the real threat is other middlemen or the distribution systems of other manufacturers. That is, the real competition is between distribution systems of different producers, rather than among the organizational units within one producer's system.

One possible reason why producers have problems with their channels of distribution is that in most organizations nobody is in charge of the channels. There is no executive with the title of "distribution channels manager" in the same sense that there is an advertising manager or a general sales manager. In fact, the distribution system is the *only* major element in the marketing mix that typically does not have anyone directly in charge. Perhaps it is time for manufacturers to establish the position of channels manager in their marketing executive structure. The person in this position would be directly responsible for the managerial activities of planning, coordination, and evaluation as they are related to the firm's distribution channels.[1]

The systems concept of distribution suggests a need for cooperation among channel members. Yet power structures do exist in trade channels, and there is a continuous tug-of-war among channel members. At the root of this struggle is institutional change, several examples of which were observed in our study of retailing and wholesaling institutions. It is axiomatic that change begets conflict, and that conflict very often results in change.

Competitive conflicts in channels of distribution may involve middlemen on the same level of distribution (horizontal conflict) or firms on different levels of distribution (vertical conflict).

CONFLICT AND COOPERATION IN DISTRIBUTION CHANNELS

Nature of the Conflicts

Firms on the Same Level of Distribution

Horizontal conflicts may occur:

- Between middlemen of the same type — hardware store versus hardware store, or
- Between different types of middlemen on the same level — hardware store versus paint store.

Perhaps the main source of horizontal conflict has been the competition caused by **scrambled merchandising** — that is, the practice whereby middlemen diversify their product assortments by adding new, nontraditional

---

[1]Donald W. Jackson, Jr., and Bruce J. Walker, "The Channel Manager: Marketing's Newest Aide?" *California Management Review*, Winter 1980, pp. 52–58.

merchandise lines. Grocery supermarkets, for example, have added toiletries, drugs, clothing, magazines, small appliances, records, alcoholic beverages, and other nonfood lines. The retailers who traditionally sell these lines have become irritated both at the grocery stores for diversifying and at manufacturers for using these "unorthodox" channels.

Product proliferation, and the resultant crossing of traditional channel lines, may stem from the market, the middleman, or the manufacturer. Consumers (the *market*) prefer convenient, one-stop shopping, so stores broaden their product offerings to satisfy this want. *Middlemen* constantly seek to add new products with higher gross margins or to add new lines in the hope of increasing customer traffic. *Manufacturers* add new types of outlets to expand their markets or to reduce unit production costs. All these efforts toward product or channel expansion only intensify the degree of channel conflict.

Firms on Different Levels of Distribution

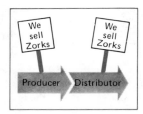

Perhaps the most severe competitive conflicts in distribution systems today are of a vertical nature — that is:

- *Between retailer and wholesaler.* Retailers may make some sales to institutions and other industrial users, thus competing with wholesaling middlemen. Stationery stores will sell office supplies to other retail stores, for example.

- *Between producer and retailer.* Producers compete with retailers by selling house to house or by selling through their producer-owned retail stores.

- *Between producer and wholesaling middleman.* Manufacturers may alienate agent middlemen by placing their own (manufacturers') sales forces in markets previously developed and covered by the agents.

The remainder of this section on conflict is devoted to the *vertical* types of conflict.

Who Controls the Channels?

In marketing literature, authors have generally taken a manufacturer-oriented approach to channels of distribution. The implication is that manufacturers are the ones that make the decisions regarding type of outlet, number of outlets, and even the selection of individual outlets. This is a one-sided point of view. Actually, middlemen have considerable freedom to make their own choices in establishing channels. Certainly the name Eaton's, Loblaws, or The Bay means more to consumers than most of the brands sold in these stores. Large retailers today are challenging manufacturers for channel control, just as the manufacturers challenged wholesalers fifty to sixty years ago. Even small retailers may be quite influential in local markets because their prestige may be greater than that of their suppliers.

Actually, the questions of who *is* the channel leader and who *should* be remain largely unsettled. The position that supports leadership by the manufacturer is production-oriented. That is, manufacturers create the new products, and they need increasing sales volumes to derive the benefits of large-scale operations. One can also argue that the retailers are the natural leaders under the marketing concept — standing closes to the consumers, knowing their wants, and being their purchasing agents. Perhaps the best answer to the channel-control questions is a compromise — a balance of power — rather than domination by any one level of a distribution channel.

During the past sixty years, a significant channel conflict has occurred between the manufacturer and the wholesaler. The conflict stems from manufacturers' attempts to bypass wholesalers and deal directly with retailers. Ordinarily, this battle is between the producers and wholesalers of manufactured *consumer* products. It usually does not involve wholesaling middlemen for industrial products because there is a tradition of direct sale in industrial marketing. Where middlemen *are* used, the need for their services has long been recognized.

Manufacturer versus Wholesaler

Nor does this conflict involve *agent* middlemen for consumer goods to any great extent. The relationships between manufacturers and their agent middlemen are relatively peaceful for two reasons. First, these relationships are established on a temporary basis. Brokers work with a manufacturer only part of the year. Manufacturers' agents know in advance that they may lose their franchise as soon as the territory can support the manufacturer's sales force. Second, agent middlemen offer fewer services than wholesalers. This means that there are fewer points of possible conflict with manufacturers.

Historical Background of the Conflict

The clash of interests between wholesalers and manufacturers can best be understood by reviewing (1) the position of the wholesaler before 1920, (2) the changing position of the manufacturer over the years, (3) the changing position of the retailers since 1920, and (4) the net effect these changes have had on the wholesalers and manufacturers.

Historically, *wholesalers* have occupied a position of major importance in distribution systems. Before 1920, they were dominant because both manufacturers and retailers were small and poorly financed. In addition, retailers were widely dispersed over the country. In effect, the wholesaler served as the sales force of the manufacturer and as the purchasing agent for the retailer.

As a result of the risks they took and the broad scale of their services, the wholesalers had high operating costs. To cover these costs, they needed a wide margin of profit. Through the nineteenth century and the early part of the twentieth, wholesaler institutions became complacent. They suffered

Conflicts between manufacturers and wholesalers may stem from attempts by the producer to bypass the wholesaler.

increasingly from inertia and a lack of flexibility in management. These firms did not adjust to changing economic and social conditions.

During the last half of the nineteenth century and the first part of the twentieth, the position of the *manufacturer* changed substantially. Manufacturing became more efficient. Furthermore, manufacturers were beginning to realize that it was better to make a small profit on the sale of many units than a large margin on the sale of a few units. They were quick to learn that the best means of achieving increased volume was through a change in marketing methods. Aggressive selling effort, lower prices, product identification through branding, and advertising were recognized as keys to mass markets. Once the manufacturers embarked upon these programs, they balked at giving wholesalers their customary wide margin on sales — sales that the manufacturers' policies were now stimulating.

After World War I, the position of the *retailer* changed considerably. Large-scale retailing institutions developed in great numbers, and retail markets became more concentrated in and around metropolitan centres. Large-scale operations entailed increased buying power, well-financed retailers, and better-managed firms. Large-scale retailers thus were economically able to assume many wholesaling functions. All these factors encouraged retailers to purchase their merchandise directly from manufacturers.

Wholesalers were caught between large-scale, direct-buying retailers on the one hand and large-scale, direct-selling manufacturers on the other. The wholesalers saw their importance being reduced. Yet, they realized they could not afford to promote aggressively the products of any manufacturer, and they resented any cut in their discount margin.

The View from Each Side Today

When manufacturers prefer to bypass wholesalers and sell directly to retailers or consumers, it is basically because (1) the manufacturers are dissatisfied with the wholesalers' services or (2) the market conditions call for direct sale. The wholesalers, in turn, are often unhappy with the actions of manufacturers. The arguments voiced by each side are summarized in Table 16-1.

Table 16-1   MANUFACTURERS VERSUS WHOLESALERS:
THE CONTROVERSY TODAY

From Manufacturers' Point of View
1. Wholesalers fail to promote products aggressively. Wholesalers generally concur with this charge. Since they usually carry thousands of items, it is not possible for their sales forces even to *mention* each item to a prospective customer, much less try to *sell* each item.
2. Wholesalers no longer perform the storage services that producers were accustomed to. Improvements in transportation and communication enable wholesalers to carry smaller inventories, thus shifting the storage function back to the manufacturers.
3. Some wholesalers promote their own brands in direct competition with manufacturers' brands.
4. Wholesalers' services cost too much. The manufacturers believe they can do the job at a lower cost. However, this may be a mistaken assumption. Many producers have learned the hard way that bypassing wholesalers may actually *increase* the cost of marketing or result in poor market coverage.
5. Manufacturers want closer market contact. They want control over their products for a greater part of the route to the customer.
6. Some products may need rapid physical distribution because they are perishable or are subject to fashion obsolescence, and the producer → retailer channel is faster.
7. Large-scale retailers usually prefer to buy directly from manufacturers.

From Wholesalers' Point of View
1. Manufacturers do not understand that the primary obligation of wholesalers is to serve their customers. Serving the manufacturer is only secondary.
2. Manufacturers expect too much. Wholesalers' discounts are not high enough to justify the level of warehousing and promotion expected by producers.
3. Manufacturers skim the cream off the market. That is, they use wholesalers only in the early stages of territorial development or in the least profitable segments of the market. In the concentrated, profitable areas or after a new market has been developed, manufacturers bypass the wholesalers and sell directly to retailers or industrial users. This observation is accurate. However, wholesalers should understand that their real value lies in their being able to reach markets the manufacturers themselves cannot penetrate profitably.

Courses of Action Open to Manufacturers

If manufacturers wish to bypass wholesalers, there are four possible courses of action to choose from. Each of these alternatives places a greater financial burden on manufacturers and adds immeasurably to their management problems. They must operate their own sales force and handle the physical distribution of their products. And direct-selling manufacturers face competition from their former wholesalers, which are now selling competitive products.

1. **Sell directly to retailers** Under certain market and product conditions, selling directly to retailers is a reasonable alternative. An ideal retail *market* for direct selling is one made up of large-scale retailers who buy in large quantities from central buying offices. In addition, it is often profitable to sell directly to specialty stores (shoes, clothing,

photographic equipment) that buy large quantities of a limited line of products.

Direct selling is advantageous when the *product* (1) is subject to physical or fashion perishability, (2) carries a high unit price, (3) is custom-made, or (4) requires mechanical servicing and installation.

2. **Establish sales offices or branches**   This variation of the first alternative is frequently adopted by a producer with a large sales force that can be managed more effectively on a decentralized basis. For such a sales force to operate profitably, essentially the same market and product conditions are required as for the direct-selling course of action.

3. **Sell directly to consumers**   In Chapter 14 we discussed various direct-to-consumer distribution methods. Producers may employ house-to-house or mail-order selling. They may establish their own retail stores or sell directly to consumers at the point of production.

4. **Use a missionary sales force**   As a compromise, when manufacturers prefer to use wholesalers but also want aggressive selling, they may employ missionary salespeople. Also known as promotional salespeople, detail men, or factory representatives, these missionary salespeople perform a number of services. Typically, a missionary salesperson calls upon a retailer and aggressively promotes the product of the manufacturer. Any orders the salesperson secures are passed on to the jobber, who receives the normal commission. Missionary salespeople may be used to install point-of-purchase displays in retail stores to introduce new items to retailers. Because employing a missionary sales force is one step short of establishing a sales office or branch, it is less expensive and presents fewer management problems.

Courses of Action Open to Wholesalers

Wholesalers too can adopt measures to improve their competitive position. These alternatives are attempts (1) to improve the wholesaler's efficiency to such a level that neither suppliers nor customers find it profitable to bypass the wholesaler, and (2) to tie the retailers to the wholesaler.

1. **Improve internal management**   Many wholesalers have modernized their establishments and upgraded the calibre of their management. New, functional, single-storey warehouses have been built outside the congested downtown areas, and mechanized materials-handling equipment has been installed. Electronic data processing equipment has streamlined accounting and reduced inventory losses. Many wholesalers have adopted selective selling. That is, less profitable accounts are visited less frequently, and some customers may be solicited only by mail or telephone. These and other innovations have generally lowered operating costs or have given far better service for the same money.

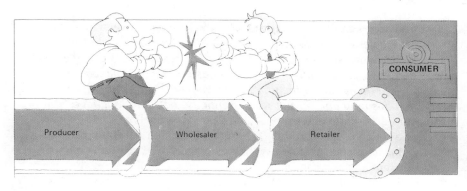

Conflicts between manufacturers and retailers are most often a struggle for control of the distribution channel.

2. **Provide management assistance for retailers**   Wholesalers generally realize that anything they can do to improve retailers' operations is really in the wholesalers' interest. They can help retailers improve store layouts and install better accounting and inventory-control systems. They can also help retailers in selecting and promoting their merchandise.

3. **Form voluntary chains**   In a voluntary chain (discussed in Chapter 14), a wholesaler enters into a contract with several retailers, agreeing to furnish management services and large-volume buying advantages. In turn, the retailers agree to do all, or almost all, their buying from the wholesaler.

4. **Develop and promote their own brands**   Many large wholesalers have successfully established their own brands. If a wholesaler is connected with a voluntary chain of retailers, the chain provides the wholesaler's brand with a built-in market.

5. **Seek legislative aid**   While the authors do not recommend legislative aid as a long-run solution, it seems to be favoured by many wholesalers. Wholesalers' organizations typically lobby vigorously for unfair trade practices legislation. One intent of these laws was to neutralize the tremendous buying power of giant retailers. A fundamental error made by many middlemen — wholesalers and retailers alike — is to believe that the *only* advantage corporate chains have over smaller independents is buying power. Even if all stores bought merchandise at the same price, the other advantages of large-scale enterprises would clearly enable them to dominate the smaller merchants.

    In the authors' opinion, legislative aid can help the wholesaler only temporarily. It obscures the basic problems and therefore postpones their effective long-range solution. The wholesalers' real salvation and opportunity for growth lie in their ability (1) to improve the internal management of their establishments and (2) to help small-scale retailers become more effective marketers.

Manufacturer versus Retailer

Today, perhaps even more significant than the conflict between manufacturers and wholesalers is the struggle for channel control that goes on between manufacturers and retailers. A very basic reason for the conflict is this: *"The people who manufacture the goods and the people who move the goods into the hands of the ultimate consumer do not share the same business philosophy and do not talk essentially the same language."*[2] In manufacturing corporations, the executives' point of view is typically characterized as a psychology of *growth*. Their goals are essentially dynamic and evolving. In sharp contrast, the psychology of small and medium-sized retailers is essentially *static* in nature. Their goals are well defined and are far more limited than those of manufacturing corporation executives. At some point, the retailer attains (and tends to maintain) a continuously satisfying plateau.

Domination versus Cooperation

Each group has weapons it can use in its efforts to dominate the other. Manufacturers can use their promotional programs to build strong consumer preferences for their products. Legal weapons are available to them in the form of franchise contracts, consignment selling, or outright ownership of retail stores. Occasionally, the manufacturer may be justified in refusing to sell to uncooperative retailers. However, in this case the manufacturer runs some risk of violating certain provisions of the Combines Investigation Act. This legislation essentially states that it is illegal for a manufacturer to refuse to sell to a retailer unless that retailer has promoted the products of the manufacturer in such a manner that the image of the products would be impaired.

Retailers are not necessarily unarmed. By advertising effectively or by establishing their own brands, they can develop consumer preferences for their stores. They can either concentrate their purchases with one supplier or spread their buying among many sources, depending upon which strategy is most effective for them. Over the past several years, retailers, especially the large ones, have strengthened their position in channels of distribution. Retailers have upgraded the quality of their management, improved their computerized information systems, and generally employed more sophisticated marketing programs. As a result, these retailers have generally become stronger and more independent in distribution systems.

On the other side of the coin, fortunately, channel members seem to realize that the returns from cooperating with one another do outweigh any reasons for conflict. Perhaps manufacturers and retailers alike understand that it is in their own best interests to treat a distribution channel as a total system. They must consider the channel as an extension (forward or backward, as the case may be) of their own internal organizations. To implement this concept, manufacturers should do the sort of things for retailers that they do for their own marketing organizations. That is, manufacturers can provide advertising aids, training for dealer salespeople, managerial assistance, and so on. Retailers can reciprocate by carrying adequate inventories, promoting the products, and building consumer goodwill.

Table 16-2   TYPES OF VERTICAL MARKETING SYSTEMS

Type of System	Control Maintained By	Examples
Corporate	Ownership	Tip Top Tailors clothes, CIL paints, Singer sewing machines
Administered	Economic power	Levis, Scott lawn products, Samsonite luggage
Contractual:		
Wholesaler-sponsored voluntary chain	Contract	IGA, Super Valu (food stores), Home Hardware
Retailer-owned cooperative	Stock ownership by retailers	Associated Grocers
Franchise systems	Contract:	
	Manufacturer-sponsored retailers	Auto dealers
	Manufacturer-sponsored wholesalers	Soft-drink bottlers
	Marketers of services	Harvey's, Hertz, Avis, Howard Johnson, Delta Inns

Vertical Marketing Systems

Institutional changes in distribution during the past twenty to thirty years have led to the development of vertical marketing systems.[3] These newer vertical marketing systems offer significant economies of scale and increased coordination in distribution. They also eliminate duplication of marketing services. Instead, they enable any given marketing activity to be performed at the most advantageous position in the system.

Vertical marketing systems may be characterized as corporate, administered, or contractual (see Table 16-2). In **corporate** vertical marketing systems, the production and marketing facilities are owned by the same company. As manufacturers, for example, Singer Sewing Machines and the Florsheim Shoe Company each operate a number of their own retail stores. Many large food chains own some processing facilities. Sears has ownership interests in manufacturing firms that supply Sears. In these integrated systems, to refer to the corporate owner as a manufacturer or a retailer oversimplifies the real situation.

In **administered vertical marketing systems**, the coordination of production and marketing activities is achieved essentially through the domination of one powerful channel member. This type of distribution is exemplified by Levis in jeans, Samsonite in luggage, General Foods, and Canadian General Electric. The manufacturer's brand and market position are strong enough to get the voluntary cooperation of retailers in matters of advertising, pricing, and store display.

In **contractual vertical marketing systems**, independent institutions —producers, wholesalers, and retailers—are banded together by contract to achieve the necessary economic size and coordination of effort. Three types of contractual systems can be identified: wholesaler-sponsored voluntary chains, retailer-owned cooperatives, and franchise systems. All three were discussed in Chapter 14.

---

[2]Warren J. Wittreich, "Misunderstanding the Retailer," *Harvard Business Review*, May-June 1972, p. 147.

[3]Much in this section is drawn from the works of Professor Bert C. McCammon, Jr., of the University of Oklahoma.

SELECTING CHANNELS OF DISTRIBUTION

With the background of the previous sections, we can now look at the major channels used by producers. Then we can discuss the factors that most influence a company's choice of its trade channels.

Major Channels of Distribution

Even to describe the major channels is risky because it may suggest an orthodoxy that does not exist. Nevertheless, what follows is an outline of the most frequently used channels for consumer products and industrial goods. Refer to Fig. 16-1 while reading the following section.

Figure 16-1
MAJOR MARKETING CHANNELS AVAILABLE TO PRODUCERS.

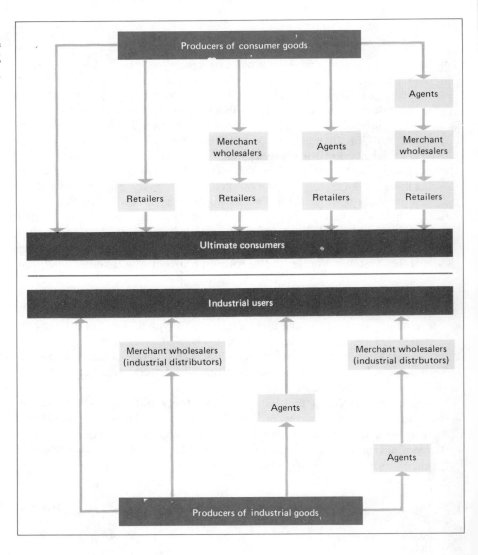

Distribution of Consumer Goods

Five channels are widely used in the marketing of consumer products. In each, the manufacturer also has the alternative of using sales branches or sales offices. Obviously, our suggestion that there are only five major channels is an oversimplification, but one that seems necessary if we are to discuss this unwieldy subject in a few paragraphs.

1. **Producer → consumer** The shortest, simplest channel of distribution for consumer products is from the producer to the consumer, with no middlemen involved. The producer may sell from house to house or by mail.

2. **Producer → retailer → consumer** Many large retailers buy directly from manufacturers and agricultural producers.

3. **Producer → wholesaler → retailer → consumer** If there is a "traditional" channel for consumer goods, this is it. Small retailers and small manufacturers by the thousands find this channel the only economically feasible choice.

4. **Producer → agent → retailer → consumer** Instead of using wholesalers, many producers prefer to use a manufacturers' agent, a broker, or some other agent middleman to reach the retail market, especially *large-scale* retailers. For example, a manufacturer of a glass cleaner selected a food broker to reach the grocery store market, including the large chains.

5. **Producer → agent → wholesaler → retailer → consumer** To reach *small* retailers, the producers mentioned in the preceding paragraph often use agent middlemen, who in turn call on wholesalers that sell to small stores.

Distribution of Industrial Products

Four types of channels are widely used in reaching industrial users. Again, a manufacturer may use a sales branch or a sales office to reach the next institution in the channel, or two levels of wholesalers may be used in some cases (again see Fig. 16-1).

1. **Producer → industrial user** This direct channel accounts for a greater *dollar* volume of industrial products than any other distribution structure. Manufacturers of large installations, such as airplanes, generators, and heating plants, usually sell directly to users.

2. **Producer → industrial distributor → user** Producers of operating supplies and small accessory equipment frequently use industrial distributors to reach their markets. Manufacturers of building materials and air-conditioning equipment are two examples of firms that make heavy use of the industrial distributor.

3. **Producer → agent → user** Firms without their own marketing departments find this a desirable channel. Also, a company that wants to introduce a new product or enter a new market may prefer to use agents rather than its own sales force.

4. **Producer → agent → industrial distributor → user** This channel is similar to the preceding one. It is used when, for some reason, it is not feasible to sell through agents directly to the industrial user. The unit sale may be too small for direct selling. Or decentralized inventory may be needed to supply users rapidly, in which case the storage services of an industrial distributor are required.

SOME GENERALIZATIONS ABOUT DISTRIBUTION CHANNELS

1. Channel design should begin with the final customer and work backward to the producer, because channels of distribution should be determined by consumer buying habits.

2. The channels finally selected must be totally appropriate to the basic objectives of the firm's marketing program. If management sets as its goal the widest possible distribution of its product line, then obviously an exclusive franchise policy at the retail level is *not* an appropriate strategy.

3. The channels should provide a firm with access to a predetermined share of the market. A manufacturer of golfing equipment seeking the broadest possible market would make a mistake by using a channel strategy that includes only large department stores and sporting goods stores at the retail level.

4. The channels must be flexible enough so that the use of one channel does not permanently close off another. A manufacturer of small appliances (irons, toasters), for example, distributed only through appliance wholesalers, which in turn distributed to appliance retailers. The company had an offer from a drug chain to buy the products directly from the manufacturer. The appliance retailers threatened to discontinue the line if the manufacturer placed it in drugstores. The producer decided to turn down the drug chain's offer. Subsequently, a competitive manufacturer accepted a similar offer and profited considerably.

5. There is a high degree of interdependence among all firms in the channel for any given product. There can be no weak link in the chain if it is to be successful.

6. Channels of distribution and middlemen are always on trial, and changes occur constantly. Middlemen survive only when the existence is economically sound and socially desirable. Furthermore, new middlemen and channels arise to do new jobs or to do the existing jobs better. *

*For an interesting discussion of ten conceptual generalizations regarding distribution systems, see Michael M. Pearson, "Ten Distribution Myths," *Business Horizons*, May-June 1981, pp. 17–23. Pearson contends that the ten points he discusses are commonly accepted assumptions that have not been validated by any quantitative measurements.

Because a channel of distribution should be determined by customer buying patterns, the nature of the market is the key factor influencing management's choice of channels. Other major considerations are the product, the middlemen, and the company itself. Basically, when selecting its channels of distribution, a company should follow the criteria of the three C's — channel *control*, market *coverage*, and a *cost* that is consistent with the desired level of customer service.

Factors Affecting Choice of Distribution Channels

Market Considerations

Perhaps the most obvious point to consider is whether the product is intended for the consumer or industrial market. If it is going to the industrial market, of course retailers will not be included in the channel. In either case, other significant market variables should be considered:

1. **Number of potential customers** With relatively few potential customers, a manufacturer may use its own sales force to sell directly to consumers or industrial users. For a large number of customers, the manufacturer would more likely use middlemen. A related point is the

---

THE XEROX STORE — A "SUPERMARKET" FOR AUTOMATED OFFICES — OR, HOW A CHANGING MARKET CHANGED THE CHANNELS FOR ELECTRONIC OFFICE EQUIPMENT

Even for a giant like the Xerox Corporation, a changing market can force the company to alter its channels of distribution. Through the years, Xerox used its own sales force to sell its line of copiers directly to its market of industrial users.

But in the latter part of the 1970s, the market environment changed considerably. Japanese competitors introduced smaller, lower-priced office copiers. Also, the small-business market for electronic office equipment was growing. However, Xerox felt it could not reach this growing market profitably with the company's direct sales force.

Consequently, in 1980, Xerox opened the first of a chain of stores selling automated office equipment for small businesses. The company also added to its product mix an assortment of smaller copiers, word processors, and other items to serve this growing market. And, for the first time, in these stores Xerox sold products manufactured by other firms — Apple small-business computers, Hewlett-Packard calculators, and Matsushita dictating machines, for example. Then, a couple of years later, Xerox stated that it intended eventually to use *independent* retail stores and distributors to sell its new line of copiers.

IBM and Digital Equipment Company also changed their distribution channels in response to the expanding market for electronic office equipment. Like Xerox, these companies had formerly used only their own sales forces to sell direct to industrial users. Then, in the early 1980s, these two firms opened their own stores to sell computers and other products to the small-business market. In contrast to the Xerox equipment, however, the IBM stores sold *only* IBM products, and some of the stores were located on upper floors of large office buildings.

number of different *industries* to which a firm sells. One company, marketing drilling equipment and supplies only to the oil industry, sold directly to users. A paper products manufacturer, on the other hand, made extensive use of industrial distributors to reach many different industries.

2. **Geographic concentration of the market**   Direct sale to the textile or the garment manufacturing industry is feasible because most of the buyers are concentrated in a few geographic areas. Even in the case of a national market, some segments have a higher density rate than others. Sellers may establish sales branches in densely populated markets, but they would use middlemen in the less concentrated markets.

3. **Order size**   A food products manufacturer would sell directly to large grocery chains because the large order size and total volume of business make this channel economically desirable. The same manufacturer, however, would use wholesalers to reach the small grocery stores whose orders are usually too small to justify direct sale.

Product Considerations

1. **Unit value**   The unit value of a product affects the amount of funds available for distribution. Thus, the lower the unit value, the longer, usually, are the channels of distribution. However, when products of low unit value are sold in large quantities or are combined with other goods so that the total order is large, shorter channels may be economically feasible.

2. **Perishability**   Products subject to physical or fashion perishability must be speeded through their channels. The channels are usually short.

3. **Technical nature of a product**   An industrial product that is highly technical is often distributed directly to users. The producer's sales force must provide considerable presale and postsale service; wholesalers normally cannot do this.

   Consumer products of a technical nature provide a real distribution challenge for manufacturers. Ordinarily, manufacturers cannot sell the goods directly to the consumer. As much as possible, manufacturers try to sell directly to retailers, but even then the servicing of the product often poses problems.

Middlemen Considerations

1. **Services provided by middlemen**   Each producer should select middlemen that will provide those marketing services that the producer either is unable to provide or cannot economically perform.

2. **Availability of desired middlemen**   The middlemen whom a producer desires may not be available. They may be carrying competitive products and may not wish to add another line.

| MARKET | PRODUCT | MIDDLEMEN | COMPANY |

3. **Attitude of middlemen toward manufacturer's policies** Sometimes, manufacturers' choices of channels are limited because their marketing policies are not acceptable to certain types of middlemen. Some retailers or wholesalers, for example, are interested in carrying a line only if they can get an exclusive franchise in a territory.

THE FOUR INFLUENCES ON THE CHOICE OF DISTRIBUTION CHANNELS.

Company Considerations

1. **Financial resources** A financially strong company needs middlemen less than one that is financially weak. A business with adequate finances can establish its own sales force, grant credit, or warehouse its own products. A financially weak firm would have to use middlemen who could provide these services.

2. **Ability of management** Channel decisions are affected by the marketing experience and ability of the firm's management. Many companies lacking marketing know-how prefer to turn the distribution job over to middlemen.

3. **Desire for channel control** Some producers establish short channels simply because they want to control the distribution of their products, even though the cost of the more direct channel may be higher. By controlling the channel, producers can achieve more aggressive promotion and better control both the freshness of merchandise stocks and the retail prices of their products.

4. **Services provided by seller** Often producers' channel decisions are influenced by the marketing services they can provide in relation to those demanded by middlemen. For example, often a retail chain will not stock a given product unless it is presold through heavy manufacturer advertising.

A manufacturer is likely to use multiple channels (also called **dual distribution**) to reach *different* markets when selling:

Use of Multiple Channels of Distribution

- The same product (sporting goods, typewriters) to both the consumer and the industrial markets
- Unrelated products (margarine and paint, or rubber products and plastics)

Dual distribution is also often used to reach a *single* market, but one in which there are differences in (1) the size of the buyers or (2) the densities within parts of the market. A manufacturer of food products will sell directly to large grocery chains but use wholesalers to reach smaller stores. A producer of industrial machinery may use its own sales force to sell directly to users in concentrated markets. But it may employ manufacturers' agents to reach customers in sparsely populated markets.

A significant development in dual distribution (and a source of channel conflict) has been the *increased* use of competing channel systems by manufacturers to sell the *same* brand to the *same* market. A paint manufacturer or a tire manufacturer, for instance, may distribute through a series of retail stores that it owns. At the same time, this producer will use conventional channels of independent wholesalers and retailers to reach the same market. Manufacturers may open their own stores (thus creating dual distribution) when they are not satisfied with the market coverage provided by existing retail outlets. Or, manufacturers may establish their own stores primarily as testing grounds for new products and marketing techniques.

DETERMINING INTENSITY OF DISTRIBUTION

After selecting their distribution channels, manufacturers should next decide upon the number of middlemen—the intensity of distribution—to be employed at the wholesale and retail levels. There are three strategies to choose from here, but they are not neatly compartmentalized. Instead, they form a continuum, or points on a scale, running from *intensive* distribution through *selective* distribution to *exclusive* distribution (see Fig. 16-2).

Intensive Distribution

Ordinarily the strategy of **intensive distribution** is used by manufacturers of consumer convenience goods. Consumers demand immediate satisfaction with this class of product and will not defer purchases to find a particular brand. Retailers often control the extent to which the strategy of intensive distribution can be implemented. For example, a new manufacturer of toothpaste may want distribution in all supermarkets, but the retailers may limit their assortment to the four fastest-selling brands. Intensive distribution places most of the burden of advertising and promotion on the shoulders of the manufacturer. Retailers will not pay to advertise a product that is sold by all their competitors.

Selective Distribution

Selective distribution covers a wide range of distribution intensity. A business that adopts this strategy may have only a few outlets in a particular market, or it may have a large number but still have something short of intensive distribution. Selective distribution lends itself especially well to consumer shopping and specialty goods and industrial accessory equipment, for which most customers have a brand preference.

A company may decide to adopt a selective distribution strategy after some experience with intensive distribution. The change usually hinges upon the high cost of intensive distribution or the unsatisfactory performance of some middlemen. Certain customers perennially order in small,

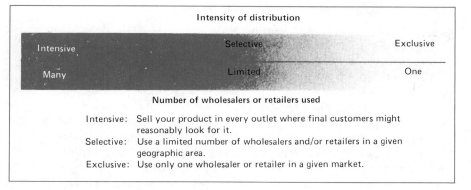

Intensity of distribution

Intensive	Selective	Exclusive
Many	Limited	One

Number of wholesalers or retailers used

Intensive: Sell your product in every outlet where final customers might reasonably look for it.

Selective: Use a limited number of wholesalers and/or retailers in a given geographic area.

Exclusive: Use only one wholesaler or retailer in a given market.

Figure 16-2
THE INTENSITY-OF-
DISTRIBUTION
CONTINUUM.

unprofitable amounts. Others may be poor credit risks. Eliminating such marginal middlemen may reduce the number of outlets, but it can increase a company's sales volume substantially. Many companies have found this to be the case simply because they were able to do a more thorough selling job with a smaller number of accounts.

Under an **exclusive distribution** strategy, the supplier agrees to sell only to a particular wholesaling middleman or retailer in a given market. Under an exclusive distributorship (with a wholesaler) or an exclusive dealership (with a retailer), the middleman is sometimes prohibited from handling a directly competing product line.

> Exclusive
> Distribution

Exclusive dealerships are frequently used in the marketing of consumer specialty products such as expensive suits. Producers also often adopt an exclusive distribution strategy when it is essential that the retailer carry a large inventory. This form of distribution is also desirable when the dealer or distributor must furnish installation and repair service. Manufacturers of farm machinery and large construction equipment frequently use exclusive distributorships for this reason.

Evaluation from Manufacturer's Standpoint

An exclusive distribution policy helps a manufacturer control the retail segment of its channels. The producer is better able to set the retail prices of its products, and it is in a position to approve advertisements featuring its products. The dealers are more likely to be cooperative and to promote these products aggressively, realizing that their future is tied to the success of the manufacturer.

On the other hand, in using this distribution strategy, a company substantially limits the number of its sales outlets. Also, the producer will suffer if its exclusive dealers don't serve their customers well. Essentially, the manufacturer has all its eggs in one basket in each market. The producer is pretty much dependent on its retailers. And if the manufacturer later wants to terminate the exclusive arrangement, a great deal of ill will may develop.

Evaluation from Retailer's Standpoint

A significant advantage of being an exclusive dealer is that the dealer reaps all the benefits of the manufacturer's marketing activities in the particular market and gets all the repeat sales.

The main drawback to being an exclusive dealer is that the dealer (retailer) may become too dependent upon the manufacturer. If the producer does a good job with the product, the dealer may prosper. But if the manufacturing firm fails, the dealer is powerless to do anything but sink with it, as far as that product is concerned. Dealership agreements often require the retailer to invest a considerable sum of money in equipment and facilities. If the agreement is then cancelled, the retailer stands to lose a major investment. Another hazard is that once the volume has been built up in a market, the manufacturer may add other dealers. The retailer thus is often at the mercy of the manufacturer. It is a one-sided arrangement in this respect, particularly if the brand is strong and the franchise is valuable.

SELECTING AND WORKING WITH INDIVIDUAL MIDDLEMEN

When all is said and done, middlemen can often make or break a manufacturer. Middlemen are the ones who personally contact the final customers — the ultimate consumers or industrial users. Thus the success of manufacturers' distribution efforts depends ultimately upon how well (1) manufacturers select their individual middlemen and then (2) work with these distributors and dealers.

MANUFACTURERS AND MIDDLEMEN: A PERFECT WORKING RELATIONSHIP

The perfect middleman:

1. Has access to the market that the manufacturer wants to reach.
2. Carries adequate stocks of the manufacturer's products and a satisfactory assortment of other products.
3. Has an effective promotional program — advertising, personal selling, and product displays. Promotional demands placed on the manufacturer are in line with what the manufacturer intends to do.
4. Provides services to customers — credit, delivery, installation, and product repair — and honours the product-warranty conditions.
5. Pays its bills on time and has capable management.

The perfect manufacturer:

1. Provides a desirable assortment of products — well designed, properly priced, attractively packaged, and delivered on time and in adequate quantities.
2. Builds product demand for these products by advertising them.
3. Furnishes promotional assistance to its middlemen.
4. Provides managerial assistance for its middlemen.
5. Honours product warranties and provides repair and installation service.

The perfect combination:

1. Probably doesn't exist.

When selecting a middleman, the key factor to consider is whether the middleman sells to the market that the manufacturer wants to reach. Then, the manufacturer should determine whether the middleman's product mix, promotional activities, and customer service are all compatible with the manufacturer's needs.

There is a community of interests in what each organization — manufacturer and middleman — expects from the other in terms of support for an effective total marketing program. A series of rewards and penalties may be instituted by either party to encourage the other to perform as expected. The major reward for either party is increased profit. Probably the most powerful penalty a manufacturer can impose is to terminate a sales agreement with a dealer. A middleman, in turn, can penalize a manufacturer by not promoting products adequately, by pushing a competitor's products, or ultimately by dropping the manufacturer's line entirely.

To improve the coordination of their intrachannel activities, manufacturers and their middlemen should develop a communication system, such as the one illustrated in Fig. 16-3. This system provides an information exchange

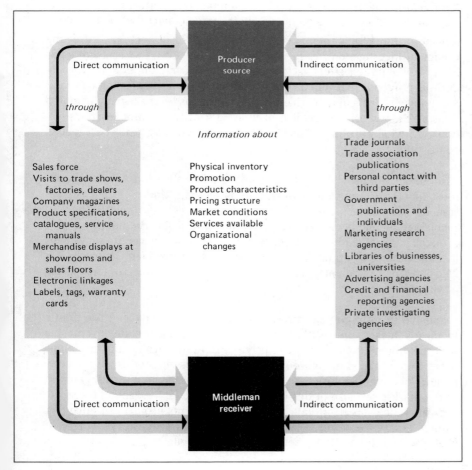

Figure 16-3
MODEL OF CHANNEL COMMUNICATION SYSTEMS.

(Adapted from Walter Gross, "Profitable Listening for Manufacturers and Dealers," *Business Horizons*, December 1968, p. 39.)

on inventory stocks, market conditions, and other marketing data important in day-to-day working relationships.

LEGAL CONSIDERA- TIONS IN CHANNEL MANAGEMENT

In various ways, companies may try to exercise control over the distribution of their product as it moves through the channel. Generally speaking, any attempts to control distribution may be subject to legal constraints. In this section we shall briefly discuss four control methods that are frequently considered by suppliers (usually manufacturers):

1. *Dealer selection.* The manufacturer wants to select its customers, and possibly refuse to sell to some middlemen.

2. *Exclusive dealing.* The manufacturer prohibits its dealers from carrying products of the manufacturer's competitors.

3. *Tying contracts.* The manufacturer sells a product to a middleman only under the condition that this middleman also buys another (possibly unwanted) product from the manufacturer. Or at least the middleman agrees not to buy the other product from any other supplier.

4. *Exclusive (closed) territories.* The manufacturer requires each middleman to sell *only* to customers within the middleman's assigned territory.

None of the arrangements is automatically illegal. Section 31.4 of the Combines Investigation Act specifically states, however, that such contracts are unlawful if their effect is "to substantially lessen competition." It is under this provision that unreasonably restrictive exclusive dealing contracts and tying contracts may be ruled illegal. Questions on the legality of closed sales territories usually involve section 31.4 of the Combines Investigation Act, which prohibits unfair competition that may result in reduced competition.

Dealer Selection

Also, under the provisions of the Combines Investigation Act, it is illegal for a supplier to refuse to deal with a middleman. Under certain circumstances, however, a manufacturer may refuse to sell its products to certain retailers if the middlemen engage in a practice of selling the manufacturer's product as a loss leader, fail to provide adequate postpurchase service, or in some other way do not adequately support the product. Generally, it is illegal to drop a middleman for carrying competitors' products or for resisting a tying contract.

Exclusive Dealing

Exclusive dealing contracts have been declared unlawful if the manufacturer's sales volume is a substantial part of the total volume in a market or if the volume done by the exclusive dealers is a significant percentage of the total business in an area. That is, the law is violated when the competitors of a manufacturer are essentially shut out from a substantial part of the market because of this manufacturer's exclusive dealing contract.

By inference, it is clear that exclusive dealing is not illegal in all situations. In fact, where the seller is just getting started in a market or where its share of the total market is so small as to be negligible, its negotiation of exclusive dealing agreements may not only improve its competitive position but also strengthen competition in general.

Ordinarily there is no question of legality when a manufacturer agrees to sell to only one retailer or wholesaler in a given territory, provided there are no limitations on competitive products. Also, a manufacturer can sell to dealers who do not carry competitors' products, as long as this is a voluntary decision on the part of the franchise holder.

A supplier is likely to push for a tying agreement when:

Tying Contracts

1. There are shortages of a desired product, and the supplier also wants to push products that are less in demand.

2. The supplier grants a franchise (as in fast-food services) and wants the franchisee to purchase all necessary supplies and equipment from this supplier.

3. The supplier has exclusive dealers or distributors (in appliances, for example) and wants them to carry a full line of the supplier's products.

With regard to tying contracts, apparently a dealer can be required to carry a manufacturer's full line as long as this does not impede competition in the market. The arrangement may be questionable, however, if a supplier forces a dealer or a distributor to take slow-moving, less attractive items in order to acquire the really desirable products.

Closed sales territories may be illegal because they restrict competition. They may also tend to create a monopoly for a product in a given territory in that buyers cannot play exclusive dealers in different territories against one another. Perhaps the safest policy is to assign each reseller a geographic area of primary responsibility rather than a closed sales territory.

Exclusive Territories

These limitations on closed sales territories are likely to foster vertical marketing systems, where the manufacturer retains ownership of the product until it reaches the final buyer. That is, the manufacturer could either (1) own the retail or wholesale outlet or (2) consign products on an agency basis to the middlemen but retain ownership. In either of these situations, exclusive territories are quite legal.

With an understanding of the retailing and wholesaling institutional structure as a foundation, marketing executives are in a position to design and manage distribution-channel systems for their companies. These tasks are likely to be easier if executives realize that a trade channel is a living structure that should be developed as a total system. Channel design and management are often a problem, however, because middlemen in the channel are independent organizations, frequently with goals that conflict with those of the manufacturer.

SUMMARY

Conflicts in channels of distribution can occur on the same level of distribution (horizontal conflict) or between different distribution levels (vertical conflict). Probably the most intensive struggle is between producers and wholesalers of manufactured consumer products. Manufacturers may use alternative channels that bypass the wholesalers. Wholesalers, in turn, can strive to improve their efficiency and to provide services for their retailer customers. Manufacturers and retailers are often in conflict, because there are fundamental differences in the goals and business philosophies of the two groups.

To offset the disadvantages of the traditional, fragmented approach to distribution, many firms (producers, wholesalers, and retailers) are developing vertical marketing systems. These systems are typically controlled by means of corporate ownership, economic power, or formal contract.

In establishing channels of distribution, management faces three tasks. The first is to select the basic channel. This choice is influenced by the market, the product, the middlemen, and the company itself. The second step is to determine the intensity of distribution. How many middlemen will be used on each distribution level in a given market? The third step is to select the individual middlemen and then develop a cooperative working relationship with each of them. Throughout the channel-management activity, executives should be aware of the legal constraints affecting their ability to control their product as it goes through the channel.

KEY TERMS AND CONCEPTS

Conflicts on the *same* level of distribution   415

Scrambled merchandising   415

Conflicts between *different* levels of distribution   416

Channel leader   416

Missionary salespeople   420

Vertical marketing systems   423
  a. Corporate   423
  b. Administered   423
  c. Contractual   423

Selection of a channel   424

Dual distribution   429

Intensive distribution   430

Selective distribution   430

Exclusive distribution   431

Management of a channel   434

Exclusive dealing   434

Tying contracts   435

Exclusive (closed) territories   435

QUESTIONS AND PROBLEMS

1. "Large manufacturers always control the channels used to reach local markets." Do you agree? In your community, are there big manufacturers that are unable to tap the local market except through local independent retailers?

2. Explain the role played by each of the following factors in the conflict between manufacturers and wholesalers, particularly in the marketing of consumer products:
   a. Traditional position of the wholesaler before 1920
   b. Changing position of the manufacturer since the late 1800s
   c. Changing position of the retailer since 1920

3. Why is there considerably less friction between manufacturers and wholesalers in the industrial goods field than in the consumer goods field?

4. Explain the reasons why manufacturers are dissatisfied with the performance of wholesalers. Do you agree with the manufacturers' point of view?

5. Why are full-service wholesalers relatively unimportant in the marketing of women's high-fashion wearing apparel, furniture, and large electrical equipment?

6. "The use of a missionary sales force is a compromise between the use of the wholesaler and the elimination of the wholesaler." Discuss this idea, showing how missionary salespeople can offset manufacturers' objections to wholesalers.

7. "The future of wholesalers depends upon their ability to increase their own efficiency and to furnish managerial aids to their retailers." Discuss, pointing out the alternatives if the wholesaler fails to meet this challenge.

8. Explain, using examples, the differences among the three major types of vertical marketing systems — corporate, administered, contractual. Which is the best kind?

9. Which of the channels illustrated in Fig. 16-1 is most apt to be used for each of the following products? Defend your choice in each case.
   a. Life insurance   d. Refrigerators
   b. Single-family residences   e. Toothpaste
   c. Farm tractors   f. Women's shoes

10. "The great majority of industrial sales are made directly from the producer to the industrial user." Explain the reason for this in terms of the nature of the market, then in terms of the product.

11. A small manufacturer of fishing lures is faced with the problem of selecting its channel of distribution. What reasonable alternatives does it have? Consider particularly the nature of its product and the nature of its market.

12. Is a policy of intensive distribution consistent with consumer buying habits for convenience goods? For shopping goods? Is intensive distribution normally used in the marketing of any type of industrial goods?

13. Assume that a manufacturer of builders' hardware wants to change from an intensive to a selective distribution system. How would it go about determining which accounts to keep and which to eliminate?

14. From a manufacturer's viewpoint, what are the competitive advantages of exclusive distribution?

15. What are the drawbacks to exclusive selling from a retailer's point of view? To what extent are these alleviated if the retailer controls the channel for the particular brand?

16. A manufacturer of a well-known brand of men's clothing has been selling directly to one dealer in an Ontario city for many years. For some time, the market has been large enough to support two retailers very profitably. Yet, the present holder of the franchise objects strongly when the manufacturer suggests adding another outlet. What alternatives does the manufacturer have in this situation? What course of action would you recommend?

17. "Manufacturers should always strive to select the lower-cost channel of distribution." Do you agree? Should they always try to use the middlemen with the lowest operating costs? Explain.

Chapter

17

Management of Physical Distribution

CHAPTER GOALS

In the last chapter we set up a distribution channel. In this chapter we physically move the goods through that channel. After studying this chapter, you should understand:

1. *What physical distribution is*
2. *The total-system concept of physical distribution*
3. *The total-cost approach to physical distribution*
4. *The use of physical distribution to strengthen a marketing program and to reduce marketing costs*
5. *The five major subsystems within a physical distribution system:*
   a. *Inventory location and warehousing*
   b. *Materials handling*
   c. *Inventory control*
   d. *Order processing*
   e. *Transportation*

After the channels of distribution have been established, a firm can turn its attention to the physical distribution of its product through these channels. **Physical distribution** consists of all the activities concerned with moving the right amount of the right products to the right place at the right time.

IMPORTANCE OF PHYSICAL DISTRIBUTION MANAGEMENT

In recent years, North American business management has placed increasing emphasis on physical distribution activities. A major reason for all this attention is that physical distribution expenses are quite substantial in many industries. For some products, the largest group of operating expenses comprises those involved in physical distribution. For other products, as much as one-half the wholesale cost is incurred in performing transportation and warehousing activities. The rising cost of energy and high interest rates (which especially affect inventory costs) are additional forces that spotlight the need for efficient physical distribution systems.

Through the years, management has made substantial progress toward reducing production costs. Cost reductions have also been effected in many areas of marketing. Physical distribution is the new (and perhaps the last) major frontier of cost cutting. And the dollars saved in physical distribution have a considerable leverage effect on profit. In a supermarket operation, for instance, the net profit on sales may be 1 percent. Then every $1 saved in physical distribution costs has the same effect on profit as an *increase of $100* in sales volume.

Physical Distribution and Customer Service

Perhaps the most important contribution of physical distribution to the total marketing effort in a firm stems from its close relationship to customer service.[1] In a landmark study, it was reported that customer service was considered by top management to be a key element in a company's marketing mix. The surveyed executives stated that the physical distribution function comes closest to their customers' views regarding what constitutes customer service. That is, physical distribution activities constitute the major part of customer service. And effective customer service is not possible without effective physical distribution. Moreover, the study suggested that (1) top management should set customer-service standards in a firm, and (2) the physical distribution people should be responsible for maintaining these standards.[2]

TOTAL-SYSTEM CONCEPT OF PHYSICAL DISTRIBUTION

Physical distribution in marketing is essentially a problem in logistics. An army cannot afford to have a battalion in position with guns but no ammunition, or with trucks but no gasoline. By the same token, a private business is in a weak position when it has orders but no merchandise to ship, or when it has a warehouse full of goods in Toronto but insistent customers in Winnipeg. These examples point up the importance of *location* in marketing, especially as regards merchandise. The appropriate assortment of products must be in the right place at the right time to maximize the opportunity for profitable sales.

   Physical distribution, then, is the physical flow of products. **Physical distribution management** is the development and operation of efficient flow systems for products. In its full scope, physical distribution for manufacturers would involve (1) the movement of *finished goods* from the end of the production line to the final customer and (2) the flow of *raw materials* from their source of supply to the production line. Similarly, middlemen would manage the flow of goods *onto* their shelves as well as *from* their shelves to customers' homes or stores.

---

[1]This paragraph is adapted from Bernard J. LaLonde and Paul H. Zinszer, *Customer Service: Meaning and Measurement*, National Council of Physical Distribution Management, Chicago, 1976, executive summary.

[2]For additional insights on how a firm can better plan its management of customer services, see William B. Wagner and Raymond LaGarce, "Customer Service as a Marketing Strategy," *Industrial Marketing Management*, February 1981, pp. 31–41.

Transportation

Order processing

Requirements forecasting

Production planning

Sales forecasting

SALES

Plant and warehouse location

Inventory control

Protective packaging

MANAGER

WHAT THE MANAGER
OF PHYSICAL
DISTRIBUTION
WORRIES ABOUT.

The task of physical distribution may be divided into five parts—in effect, five subsystems:

1. Inventory location and warehousing
2. Materials handling
3. Inventory control
4. Order processing
5. Transportation

A decision regarding any one of these parts affects all the others. The location of a warehouse influences the selection of transportation methods and carriers; the decision on carriers influences the optimum size of shipments; and so on. Later in this chapter we shall examine each of these five tasks in more detail.

From time to time in this book, it has been pointed out that marketing is a total system of business action, and not a fragmented series of operations. Nowhere is this idea seen more clearly than in the matter of physical

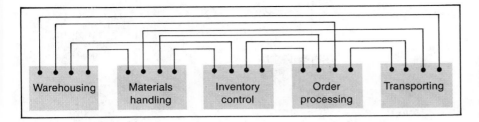

Each of the five activities in physical distribution is "wired" to the others. A decision in any one area affects the others.

distribution. But it has not always been this way. Traditionally—and unfortunately this is still true in many firms—the activities involved in physical distribution have been fragmented. Managerial responsibility for these activities has been delegated to various units that often have conflicting, and even diametrically opposite, goals. The production department, for instance, sets the production schedule. This group is interested in long production runs to minimize unit manufacturing costs, even though the result may be abnormally high inventory costs. The traffic department looks at the freight rates rather than at the total cost of physical distribution. Thus, carriers with low ton-mile charges are often selected, even though this may mean undue time spent in transit and require larger inventories to fill the long pipelines. The finance department wants a minimum of funds to be tied up in inventories. At the same time, the sales department wants to have a wide assortment of products available at locations near the customers. Under such conditions, it is impossible to optimize the flow of products. However, the systems approach to physical distribution can cut through the problem and result in the effective coordination of these activities.

In physical distribution, management must deal with a large number of readily measurable variables. Such problems lend themselves nicely to solution by statistical and mathematical techniques. For instance, operations research—a technique involving the use of statistical models and methods—is a particularly helpful tool. It has been used in determining the number and location of warehouses, the optimum size of inventories, and the best transportation routes and methods. Computers are used to rapidly process the large quantities of data needed in these analyses. In our survey treatment in this chapter, however, we shall not be concerned with the quantitative methods used to solve such problems. Instead, we shall discuss the conceptual aspects of physical distribution management.

As part of the systems concept, executives should apply a **total-cost approach** to the management of physical distribution. A firm can choose from alternative methods of shipping, of storing, and of handling its products. Administrators should seek the *total* set of alternatives that optimizes the cost-profit relationship for the *entire* physical distribution system, rather than consider the separate costs of individual activities.

Too often, executives attempt to minimize the cost of only one aspect of physical distribution—transportation, for example. They might be upset by the high cost of shipment by air freight. But their efforts to reduce that

The Total-Cost Approach

The total-cost approach entails the balancing of each distribution cost with all the others, and the total distribution cost with customer satisfaction.

Physical distribution system

Target market

transportation expense may result in an increase in warehousing expenses that more than offsets the saving in freight costs.

The airlines particularly have been conscious of the total-cost concept. This is so because unit freight rates are appreciably higher for air transportation than for land or sea shipment. A leading pharmaceutical company found that the higher costs of air freight were more than offset by the savings from (1) lower inventory costs, (2) less insurance and interest expense, (3) lower crating costs, and (4) fewer lost sales due to depletion of stock. The company eliminated all except one warehouse, cut inventories by 50 percent, boosted the rate of stock turnover, and found it could supply markets that had previously been inadequately served.

The point here is *not* that air freight is the best method of transportation. (In fact, the company later substantially reduced its business with airlines in some parts of the country.) Rather, the idea is that physical distribution should be viewed as a *total* process and its costs analysed accordingly.

Optimization and Cost Trade-offs

Implicit in the total-cost concept is the idea that management should strive for an optimal balance between total cost and customer services. This is what we call the concept of **optimization** in physical distribution. That is, rather than seek *only* to minimize the total costs of physical distribution, executives should also consider customer want-satisfaction. Actually, it may be necessary to increase physical distribution costs somewhat in order to reach the desired level of customer service.

Achieving this optimal balance leads us to the idea of **cost trade-offs**. To illustrate this concept, let's assume that management wants to minimize both its warehousing expenses and its transportation costs. But these prove to be conflicting goals. In order to accumulate a large enough shipment to get low-cost carload freight rates, the shipper may have temporarily to increase its warehouse stocks. This, in turn, will increase both warehousing and inventory costs. Management then must decide at what point it will trade off its higher warehousing and inventory costs for its lower transportation expenses. In another example, a seller may want to provide quick and frequent deliveries to customers. This seller will have to consider the trade-off between (1) the better service to customers and (2) the higher costs of processing and transporting the small orders.

Trade-off decisions call for careful managerial analysis. In effect, management is seeking that point where there is an even trade-off between (1) the seller's cost and (2) the value received for providing the service.

THE STRATEGIC USE OF PHYSICAL DISTRIBUTION

The strategic use of business logistics may enable a company to strengthen its market position by providing more customer satisfaction and by reducing operating costs. The management of physical distribution can also affect a firm's marketing mix — particularly its product-planning, pricing, and distribution channels.[3]

Improve Customer Service

A well-run logistics system can improve the distribution service a firm provides its customers — whether they are middlemen or ultimate users. And the level of customer service directly affects demand. This is especially true in the marketing of nondifferentiated products (chemicals, building materials) where effective customer service may be a company's only significant competitive advantage. As regards service, physical distribution systems have generally stressed *spatial* considerations (warehouse location, for example). *Temporal* factors may be equally important. That is, buyers are influenced by service-time and delivery-time differences among suppliers.

Reduce Distribution Costs

Many avenues to cost reductions may be opened by the effective management of a company's physical distribution activities. Effectively systematizing these activities may lead to simplifications, such as the elimination of unneeded warehouses. Inventories — and their attendant carrying costs and capital investment — may be reduced by consolidating stocks at fewer locations and by shortening the replenishment cycle in warehouses.[4]

Generate Additional Sales Volume

A properly designed logistics system can also help to generate additional sales volume. Such a system minimizes out-of-stock conditions, thereby increasing both sales and customer satisfaction. A responsive system can shorten the order cycle and thus reduce inventory requirements. The cost savings can then be passed on to customers in the form of lower prices, again leading to increased sales. Increased efficiencies in physical distribution often enable sellers to expand their geographic markets.

---

[3]For a report on the use of logistics in developing competitive strategies in business, see James L. Heskett, "Logistics — Essential to Strategy," *Harvard Business Review*, November-December 1977, pp. 85–96.

[4]For an insight into the potential to be realized by effectively managing the physical distribution system, see: Douglas Lambert and Robert Quinn, "Increase Profitability by Managing the Distribution Function," *Business Quarterly*, vol. 46, no. 1, Spring 1981, pp. 56–64; and James Dingwall, "The Hidden Dollars in Distribution," *Canadian Business*, May 1982, pp. 110–122.

Adjust to Differences in Production and Consumption: Create Time and Place Utilities

The economic value of storage (as a key part of warehousing) is the fact that it creates **time utility**. A product may be properly located with respect to its market, but the timing may be such that there is no present demand for it. Management adds precious value to this item simply by holding and properly preserving it in storage until the demand rises. Time utility is created and value is added when bananas are picked green and allowed to ripen in storage, or when meat is aged or tobacco is cured in storage.

Storage is essential to correct imbalances in the timing of production and consumption. An imbalance can come about when there is year-round consumption but only seasonal *production*, as in the case of agricultural products. Proper use of warehousing facilities enables a producer to store the seasonal surplus so that it can be marketed long after the harvest has ended.

In other instances, warehousing helps to adjust year-round *production* to seasonal *consumption*, as in the case of skis. Manufacturers prefer to produce on a year-round basis, to operate their plants more efficiently. For this, enough surplus stock must be stored during the off-season to meet the peak-season demand without requiring overtime operation or additional plant capacity.

In an economic sense, the main function of the transportation subsystem in physical distribution is to add value to products through the creation of **place utility**. A fine suit hanging on a garment manufacturer's rack in Montreal has less value to a retailer or consumer in Regina than a similar suit displayed in the retailer's store. Transporting the suit from Montreal to the retailer in Regina creates place utility and thus adds value to the product.

Stabilize Prices

Careful management of warehousing and transportation facilities can help to stabilize prices for an individual firm or for an entire industry. If a market is temporarily glutted with a certain product, sellers can store the product until supply and demand conditions are more in balance. This managerial use of warehousing facilities is common in the marketing of agricultural products and other seasonally produced goods. The judicious movement of products from one market to another may (1) enable a seller to avoid a market with depressed prices, or (2) allow a seller to take advantage of a market that has a shorter supply and higher prices.

Affect Choice of Channels and Location of Middlemen

Decisions regarding inventory management have an important bearing on a manufacturer's selection of trade channels and the location of middlemen. Logistical considerations may become paramount, for example, when a company decides to decentralize its inventory. Now management must determine (1) how many sites to establish and (2) whether to use wholesalers, its own branch warehouses, or public warehouses. One manufacturer may select merchant wholesalers that perform storage and other warehousing services. Another may prefer to use a combination of manufacturers' agents and public warehouses. These agents can solicit orders and provide aggressive selling, while the ordered products can be physically distributed through the public warehouses.

One point should be kept in mind, however. Rarely are channels selected primarily on the basis of physical distribution considerations. Instead, logistics is only one of several factors to consider. Recall from the previous chapter that the nature of the market and other factors heavily influence channel design.

Good traffic managers see to it that their companies enjoy the fastest routes and the lowest rates for whatever methods of transportation they use. The pricing of transportation services is one of the most complicated parts of the Canadian business scene. The rate, or tariff, schedule is the carrier's price list. To read one properly is a real art that requires considerable practice. As a simple example of some of the difficulties that are involved, shipping rates vary for different types of goods. Moreover, the classes of goods overlap, so that a particular product may be in two or more classes with different freight rates.

Ensure Lowest Costs via Traffic Management

Another service that traffic managers can render their companies is the auditing (checking) of freight bills. This is necessary because carriers sometimes charge a higher rate than the one that should apply. They are not intentionally trying to defraud the shipper. They are simply misinterpreting the complex rate schedule.

Good traffic managers can also negotiate with carriers to get their products reclassified or to get special rates. A company may offer to ship larger quantities on a given carrier if lower rates are granted. Traffic managers should investigate the possibility of having their companies operate their own private carrier, especially their own trucking system. If this possibility seems reasonable for a shipper, it can be an effective bargaining tool in dealing with common carriers.

An effective physical distribution system is built around five subsystems. There is much interaction and interdependence among these subsystems. Consequently, each of them must be carefully coordinated with the others.

MAJOR TASKS IN PHYSICAL DISTRIBUTION MANAGEMENT

The name of the game in physical distribution is inventory management. Executive judgement must be exercised regarding the size, location, handling, and transporting of inventories. Decision making in these four areas is interrelated. The number and locations of inventory sites, for example, influence inventory size and transportation methods. These interrelationships are often quite complex.

Inventory Location and Warehousing

Storage versus Warehousing

We should distinguish carefully between these two activities in physical distribution. **Storage** is the marketing activity that involves holding and preserving products from the time of their production until their sale.

Warehousing embraces storage plus a broad range of functions, such as assembling, dividing (bulk-breaking), and preparing products for reshipping. Warehousing is therefore a broader concept than storage. Storage is more passive by nature; warehousing involves more activity.[5]

Inventory: Centralized or Dispersed?

Basic to the inventory location problem is the company's intended strategy regarding inventory deployment. Is inventory to be heavily concentrated or dispersed throughout the market? Each strategy has its merits and limitations. A centralized inventory can be smaller in total size, can be better controlled, and is more responsive to unusual requests. Efficiency in warehousing and materials handling should be increased. On the other hand, centralizing the stocks often means higher total transportation charges and slower delivery to some segments of the market. Dispersing the inventory presents the other side of the coin on each of these points.

The Distribution-Centre Concept

An effective inventory location strategy may be a compromise — the establishment of one or more *distribution centres*. Such centres are planned around markets rather than transportation facilities. The basic idea is to develop under one roof an efficient, fully integrated system for the flow of products — taking orders, filling them, and delivering them to customers. The distribution centre is a relatively new idea in warehousing, but the concept has been adopted by many well-known firms.[6]

A number of large companies have reduced their number of warehouses dramatically by replacing them with large regional distribution centres. This is especially the case in the food industry, but the same patterns have been followed in other industries. The distribution of the Canadian population over a very large land area makes it difficult for distribution centres to be strategically located to serve a large population. The concept has been used, however, in areas of relatively high population density, especially in the Windsor-Quebec corridor. In the retail food business, Dominion Stores has established centralized distribution centres to serve a large number of its retail stores. Canadian Tire has followed the same practice in providing inventory to concentrations of stores.

The use of distribution centres has lowered distribution costs by reducing the number of warehouses, cutting excessive inventories, and eliminating out-of-stock conditions. Storage and delivery time have been cut to a minimum. This puts into practice the adage that companies are in business to sell goods, not to store them.

---

[5]For some guides to improving productivity in warehousing, see Kenneth B. Ackerman and Bernard J. LaLonde, "Making Warehousing More Efficient," *Harvard Business Review*, March-April 1980, pp. 94–102.

[6]For a discussion of the distribution-centre concept, see David Aronchik and Stanley J. Shapiro, "The Ontario Grocery Chains: Efficient Food Distributors or Oligopolistic Extortionists?" in S. J. Shapiro and Louise Heslop (eds.), *Marketplace Canada: Some Controversial Dimensions*, McGraw-Hill Ryerson Limited, Toronto, 1982, pp. 132–149.

Ownership and Types of Warehouses

A firm (manufacturer, wholesaler, or retailer) has the option of operating its own private warehouse or using the services of a public warehouse. A **private warehouse** is more likely to be used if (1) a company moves a large volume of products through a warehouse, and (2) there is very little, if any, seasonal fluctuation in this flow. **Public warehouses** offer storage and handling facilities to any interested individual or company. Public warehousing costs are a variable expense. Customers pay only for the space they use, and only when they use it. Additional services typically provided by public warehouses are noted in the following box. Major types of public warehousing facilities include:

1. *General merchandise warehouses*, which store practically any product that needs to be protected from the weather but has no special temperature, humidity, or handling requirements

2. *Special commodity warehouses*, which are used for particular agricultural products such as grains, wool, fruit, or tobacco

3. *Cold-storage warehouses*

BESIDES THE SERVICES MENTIONED BELOW, PUBLIC WAREHOUSES CAN PROVIDE:

A SUBSTITUTE FOR COMPANY WAREHOUSES OR WHOLESALERS

Public warehouses will provide office and display space, and accept and fill orders for sellers. Manufacturers can ship in carload quantities to a public warehouse, just as they ship to their own branches or wholesalers. Sellers thus have flexibility in their inventory locations. If they wish to change locations, they simply change public warehouses.

PROTECTION THROUGH GOVERNMENT LEGISLATION

In some jurisdictions, laws regulate the services of public warehouses. These laws are the guarantee that makes public-warehouse receipts acceptable as bank collateral. The laws also curtail abuses by warehouse operators.

FINANCIAL SERVICES

Warehouse receipts covering stored products may be used as collateral for bank loans.

The field (custodian) warehousing service operates as follows: Assume that some products are stored in the owner's private warehousing facilities. The owner wants to get a bank loan on the merchandise without the expense of moving it to a public warehouse. So the owner leases to a public warehouse company a section of the private warehouse that contains the merchandise in question. (A field warehouse need not be a portion of a regular private warehouse. It can be an office cabinet, locked desk drawer, office safe, open yard, or some other storage facility.) The warehouse company then issues a receipt for the goods, and this receipt serves as collateral for a bank loan. The leased area, in effect, becomes a public warehouse, and the goods cannot be removed until the receipt is redeemed.

Materials Handling

The selection of the proper equipment to physically handle products is an important aspect of physical distribution management. Proper equipment can minimize losses from breakage, spoilage, and theft. Efficient equipment can reduce handling *costs* as well as the *time* required for handling.

In this discussion of materials-handling equipment, we include the warehouse building itself. Historically, warehouses have been multistorey buildings located in congested parts of town. Their operation has been characterized by the use of elevators, chutes, and other highly expensive *vertical* methods of moving products. Modern warehouses are huge one-storey structures. They are located in outlying parts of town where land is less expensive and loading platforms are easily accessible to motor trucks and railroad spurs. Forklift trucks, conveyor belts, motor scooters, and other mechanized equipment are used to move merchandise. In some warehouses the order fillers are even equipped with roller skates.

"Containerization" is a cargo-handling system that is gaining increasing acceptance in physical distribution. The system involves enclosing a shipment of products in large containers of metal, wood, or some other material. The containers are then transported unopened from the time they leave the shipper until they reach their destination.

Inventory Control

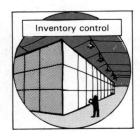

The key activity in any physical distribution system is maintaining control over the size and composition of the inventories. Inventory represents a sizable investment for many companies. The goal of inventory control is to minimize both the investment and the fluctuations in inventories, while at the same time filling customers' orders promptly and accurately.

Perhaps the greatest boon to inventory control in recent years has been the improvements in computer technology. These have enabled management to shorten the order-delivery time and to substantially reduce the size of inventories.

Inventory size is determined by balancing market needs and costs. Market demands on inventory can be anticipated through sales forecasts. The more accurate the forecasts, the greater the probability of optimizing inventory size. Inventory costs include (1) acquisition costs, that is, the costs of making or buying the products to put in inventory, and (2) carrying or holding costs — warehousing expenses, interest on investment, losses due to spoilage and pilferage, inventory taxes, and so on.

Inventory size is also influenced considerably by the desired level of customer satisfaction. That is, what percentage of orders does the company expect to fill promptly from inventory on hand? Out-of-stock conditions result in lost sales, loss of goodwill, and sometimes even the loss of customers. Yet, to be able to fill 100 percent of the orders promptly may require an excessively large and costly inventory. Authorities estimate that about 80 percent *more* inventory is required to fill 95 percent of the orders than to fill only 80 percent.

Related to the size question is the need to establish the optimal quantity to reorder (make or buy) when it is time to replenish inventory stocks. The

Table 17-1 DISTRIBUTION OF INTERCITY FREIGHT TRAFFIC IN
CANADA AMONG THREE MAJOR FREIGHT CARRIERS

	Millions of ton-miles		
	1978	1980	1982
Railroads	141,736	156,248	139,559
Trucking	24,931	28,585	n/a
Airlines	926	1,121	1,151

Source: Statistics Canada, cat. no. 52-207, 53-224, 51-002, and 52-007.

determination of this "economic order quantity" (EOQ) for a manufacturer moves us back into production scheduling. Once again we see the total-system aspect of physical distribution. The size of the EOQ is determined by balancing acquisition costs, carrying costs, and the desired level of satisfaction in filling customers' orders.[7]

Order Processing

Still another part of the physical distribution system is a set of procedures for handling and filling orders. This should include provision for billing, granting credit, preparing invoices, and collecting past-due accounts. Consumer ill will can result if a company makes mistakes or is slow in filling orders.

Methods of Transportation

A major part of the physical distribution system in many companies involves the shipping of products to customers. Management must decide on both the form of transportation to use and the particular carriers. In this discussion, we are concerned primarily with *intercity* shipments.

The five major forms of transportation are railroads, trucks, water vessels, pipelines, and airplanes. In Canada, most domestic freight is carried by rail and road. Relatively little intercity freight movement is accounted for by ships, although this mode of transportation is, of course, important to the movement of imports and exports and for coastal traffic on the east and west coasts and in the St. Lawrence Seaway. Similarly, pipelines carry the bulk of oil and natural gas to the major markets in Canada and for export to the United States.

Railroads are still by far the major intercity freight carrier. Although their relative position has been stable or declining for decades, the actual number of ton-miles of freight carried by rail has been increasing and is still far larger than the volume of intercity freight carried by trucks. In 1982, for example, railroads in Canada carried almost 140 billion ton-miles of freight (see Table 17-1). During 1980, on the other hand, trucks carried only 29 billion ton-miles of intercity freight. In that same year, airlines carried slightly more than one billion ton-miles. These figures, while interesting, understate the true value of airlines and truck carriers in the transportation industry.

[7]For a method that can be used to determine inventory carrying costs, and for some managerial uses of this information, see Bernard J. LaLonde and Douglas M. Lambert, *Journal of Physical Distribution*, vol. 6, no. 1 (1975), pp. 51–63.

Table 17-2   COMPARISON OF TRANSPORTATION METHODS

Selection Criteria	Transportation Method				
	Rail	**Water**	**Highway**	**Pipeline**	**Air**
Speed (door-to-door time)	Medium	Slowest	Fast	Slow	**Fastest**
Cost of transportation	Medium	**Lowest**	High	Low	Highest
Reliability in meeting delivery schedules	Medium	Poor	Good	**Excellent**	Medium
Flexibility (variety of products carried)	**Widest variety**	Widest variety	Medium	Very limited, very inflexible	Somewhat limited
Number of geographic locations served	Very many, but can go only where track is laid	Limited	**Unlimited, very flexible**	Very limited	Many
Products most suitable	Long hauls of carload quantities of bulky products, when freight costs are high in relation to product's value	Bulky, low-value, nonperishable	Short hauls of high-value goods	Oil, natural gas, slurried products	High-value, perishable, where speed of delivery is all-important

Airlines are principally passenger carriers, but represent a valuable mode of transportation for small, fragile, and high-value items. Trucks represent the principal means of transporting freight within cities and their use for transporting intercity freight has been increasing dramatically in recent years.

In Table 17-2 the major transportation methods are compared on the basis of some criteria likely to be used by physical distribution management in the transportation selection process.

Special Services Offered by Railroads

Despite the trend shown in Table 17-1, railroads are still the lowest-cost, most efficient method of transportation for many products and in many marketing situations. To meet the increased competition from other carriers, especially trucks, the railroads have instituted several special services and freight rates.

Carload versus Less-Than-Carload Freight Rates
Railroads offer substantial savings to firms that ship on carload (c.l.) quantities rather than less-than-carload (l.c.l.) amounts. For many items, the c.l. freight rate is as much as 50 percent less than the l.c.l. rate. This is a tremendous incentive to shippers of large quantities of products — especially minerals, agricultural products, and similar goods for which freight expenses are a significant percentage of total value.

Combined Shipments
Long ago the railroads realized that they were vulnerable to competition from other types of carriers when it came to

handling l.c.l. shipments. Consequently, the railroads have introduced several measures designed to reduce the cost of l.c.l. shipments and to speed them up. These measures provide for combining into a carload quantity the freight from one or more companies that are shipping products to customers located in one area. The pooled freight can go at carload rates and can be delivered much more rapidly than if its component parts were sent separately in l.c.l. units.

In-Transit Privileges   Two in-transit privileges offered by railroads are (1) diversion in transit and (2) the opportunity to process some products en route. **Diversion in transit** allows a seller to start a shipment moving in one direction and to change destination while the car is en route, just as long as the new destination involves no backtracking. The charges are computed on the basis of the through rate or long-haul rate from the point of origin to the ultimate destination, plus a small charge for diversion. This is a valuable service to shippers of perishable products that are subject to price variations from one city to another on any given day.

B.C. Tree Fruits may want to ship McIntosh apples to eastern markets. Several carloads will be shipped from Kelowna to Toronto, or they may be shipped eastward with the specific destination to be determined some time after the shipment leaves Kelowna. Before the shipment reaches Toronto, the shipper may receive word that prices in the Toronto market are temporarily depressed because of a heavy supply in relation to the demand but that there is a good market in Montreal. Consequently, at the appropriate "diversion point" (probably Toronto in this case) the cars will be rerouted to Montreal. The freight charges will be based on the through rate from Kelowna to Montreal. A shipment may be diverted several times before reaching its final destination.

Under the privilege of *processing in transit*, a shipper may have his product unloaded, graded, manufactured, or otherwise processed in some manner while en route, and then have it shipped on to its final destination. As an example, livestock may be shipped from Alberta to Toronto. En route the animals may be unloaded, watered, and fattened in feedlots, but the through rate to Toronto will apply. Wheat may be shipped from Saskatchewan to Winnipeg, where it may be made into flour shipped to Toronto. Again, the shipper has the privilege of processing in transit. The through rate is usually substantially less than the combined rates from origin to processing point and from processing point to destination.

Piggyback and Fishyback Services   **Piggyback** service involves carrying truck trailers on railroad flatcars. Products can be loaded on trucks at the seller's shipping dock. The truck *trailer* is later transported by train to the destination city where it is trucked to the buyer's receiving station. This combination service provides (1) more flexibility than railroads alone can offer, (2) lower freight costs than trucks alone, and (3) less handling of the goods.

Fishyback service involves transporting loaded trailers on barges or ships. The trailers may be carried piggyback fashion by railroad to the dock, where they are transferred to the ship. Then, at the other end of the water trip, the trailers are loaded back onto trains for the completion of the haul. In an alternative use of the fishyback service, railroads are not used at all. Merchandise is trucked directly to ports, where the trailer vans are loaded on barges. At the end of the water journey, the vans are trucked to the receiving station.

Freight Forwarders

The **freight forwarder** is a specialized marketing institution that has developed through the years to serve firms that ship in l.c.l. quantities. Freight forwarders do not own their own transportation equipment, but they do provide a valuable service in physical distribution. Their main function is to consolidate l.c.l. shipments, or less-than-truckload shipments, from several shippers into carload and truckload quantities. Their operating margin is generally the spread between c.l. and l.c.l. rates. That is, the shipper pays l.c.l. rates, and the freight forwarder transports the products at c.l. rates. The freight forwarder also picks up the merchandise at the shipper's place of business and arranges for delivery at the buyer's door. The l.c.l. shipper also benefits from the speed and minimum handling associated with c.l. shipments, but does pay l.c.l. rates. Also, freight forwarders provide the small shipper with traffic management services, such as selecting the best transportation methods and routes.

THE FUTURE IN PHYSICAL DISTRIBUTION

Executives involved in physical distribution face tremendous challenges and opportunities in the years ahead. These pressures stem both from within their companies and from external environmental forces.

Within most firms there is a need to coordinate physical distribution activities more effectively so that they function as a system. Essentially, this is a problem in organization. If you ask, "Who is in charge of physical distribution?" all too often the answer is, "No one." Instead, managerial responsibility is fragmented among units that may have conflicting goals. Fortunately, there is a trend toward the establishment of a separate department responsible for all physical distribution activities.[8]

It is imperative that top management view logistics as one of its prime responsibilities. Physical distribution costs are the largest simple operating cost in many firms. For countless companies, effective customer service (which involves physical distribution activities primarily) can mean the difference between a strong and a weak marketing position. Once the top

---

[8]For an analysis of alternative organizational structures for managing the physical distribution function in a company, see Bernard J. LaLonde, "Strategies for Organizing Physical Distribution," *Transportation and Distribution Management*, January-February 1974, pp. 21–25.

executives become aware of the stakes, they are likely to play an active role in logistics management. If these internal conditions are not sufficient incentive to ensure effective management, then certainly the macro-environmental forces should be.

Urban population congestion, soaring energy costs, and rising concern for the environment all greatly affect physical distribution management. The entire transportation system in Canada is on the brink of massive changes. Mass urban transportation is getting increasing political attention. There is a real possibility of a major overhaul in the government regulation of railroad and trucking operations, and the freight rates of both types of carriers. Air pollution controls, highway speed limits, and soaring fuel costs are altering many traditional patterns in physical distribution. Truly, the 1980s are imposing some formidable challenges for physical distribution executives. But, at the same time they also are bringing unlimited opportunities for innovative management.

SUMMARY

Physical distribution involves the flow of products from supply sources to the firm, and from the company to its customers. Executives who manage physical distribution are responsible for developing and operating efficient flow systems. Their goal is to move the right amount of the right products to the right place at the right time. Physical distribution costs are a substantial part of total operating costs in many firms. Moreover, physical distribution is probably the only remaining source of major cost reductions in many companies.

Physical distribution should be treated as a total system of business action. In the past (and unfortunately even now in too many firms), physical distribution activities have been fragmented operationally and organizationally. Applying the systems concept also means applying the total-cost approach — that is, reducing the cost of the entire system, rather than the costs of individual elements in the system. Thus, management might decide to use expensive air freight if its high cost could be more than offset by savings in warehousing and inventory carrying costs. However, management should *not* strive for the lower total cost of physical distribution. Instead, the goals should be to effect the best balance between level of customer service and total cost. Sometimes a company can improve its market position by providing a higher level of customer service, even though this means an increase in physical distribution costs.

The actual operation of a physical distribution system requires management's attention and decision making in five areas: (1) inventory location and warehousing, (2) materials handling, (3) inventory control, (4) order processing, and (5) transportation. Again, these areas should not be approached as individual activities, but as subsystems of the whole — the physical distribution system.

KEY TERMS AND CONCEPTS

QUESTIONS AND PROBLEMS

1. In some companies, activities such as processing and shipping orders, maintaining an inventory control system, and locating inventory stocks throughout the market are treated as separate, fragmented tasks. What are some of the administrative and operational problems that are likely to occur in this type of arrangement?

2. "The goals of a modern physical distribution system in a firm should be to operate at the lowest possible *total* costs." Do you agree?

3. Name some products for which the physical distribution constitutes at least one-half of the total price of the goods at the wholesale level. Can you suggest ways of decreasing the physical distribution cost of these products?

4. Explain how marketing managers can use transportation and warehousing facilities to stabilize the prices of their products.

5. "A manufacturer follows an inventory-location strategy of concentration rather than dispersion. This company's inventory size will be smaller, but its transportation and warehousing expenses will be larger, than if its inventory were dispersed." Do you agree? Explain.

6. "The use of public warehouse facilities makes it possible for manufacturers to bypass wholesalers in their channels of distribution." Explain.

7. How are transportation decisions related to packaging policies?

8. Why are l.c.l. shipments so much slower and more costly than c.l. shipments?

9. Assume that a manufacturer must ship in l.c.l. quantities. However, the competitive price structures for this company's products are such that it cannot afford to pay the high l.c.l. freight rates. What alternatives does this firm have regarding the transportation of its products?

10. As traffic manager of a large department store in the city nearest your campus, you are asked to determine the best transportation method and route for the shipment of each of the following items to your store. In each case your store is to pay full freight charges. Unless specifically noted, time is not important.

    a. Fresh salmon from Prince Rupert, B.C. Total shipment weighs 100 kg.

    b. An assortment of various types of large appliances from Hamilton, Ontario. Total weight is 10,000 kg.

    c. A refill order of 200 dresses from Winnipeg. This is a "hot" fashion item, so speed is of the essence.

    d. Sheets, pillowcases, and towels from a mill in Sherbrooke, Quebec. Total weight is 50 kg.

    e. Ten sets of dining-room furniture from Napanee, Ontario.

11. Under what conditions is a company apt to select air freight as the main method of transporting its finished goods?

Case 16
Rexford Company

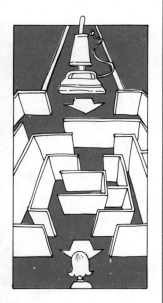

Selecting a Distribution Channel to Minimize Conflict

About nine months ago, the Rexford Company began to import a new model of vacuum cleaner from West Germany. Rexford's president and owner, Thomas Herff, originally had intended to sell this new product only to the company's existing industrial market. However, the more he thought about it, the more Mr. Herff believed that the vacuum cleaner could also be sold very successfully in the consumer market. The problem was that the Rexford Company had never sold any products to the consumer market. Consequently, Mr. Herff did not know what channels of distribution he should use to reach this market. He also was concerned that, by selling the vacuum cleaner as a consumer product, he might antagonize the middlemen now being used to reach Rexford's industrial market.

The Rexford Company was an Ontario firm that manufactured and marketed two lines of carpet cleaners for industrial uses. One line consisted of six different models of a steam carpet cleaner, known in the industry as an "extractor." The other product line was a series of vacuum cleaners. Rexford manufactured all these except the new import from Germany.

The extractors consisted of (1) a basic unit (the motor and a bucket containing the cleaning solution), (2) hoses to carry the cleaning solution to the carpet and back, and (3) a series of end-of-hose tools such as brushes, gleaners, and nozzles. Rexford's selling price on these extractors ranged from $1,500 to $11,000.

The vacuums that Rexford manufactured had to be used with one of the extractors, since the extractor contained a bucket that held the debris. The vacuums did not have a bag of their own like most vacuum cleaners. This tended to make the vacuuming a slower process. However, the vacuums were extremely efficient because of the tremendous suction power from the extractors.

The new German import was the usual upright type of vacuum cleaner with a bag attached. However, the vacuum also possessed some unique features, which Herff believed would make it one of Rexford's best-selling products. For example, unlike most conventional uprights, the German model had two motors. One powered the vacuum itself and the other operated the brush. Also, the brush and the belt were protected by a special clutch system. If the brush or the belt became obstructed by a hairpin or some other object, the clutch would disengage the brush motor automatically, thus preventing damage to the belt or motor. As a result, the vacuum would last for a longer period of time without repairs. The vacuum also had a hose nozzle that could easily be removed from the vacuum unit, and that could be used to vacuum hard-to-get-at places such as corners, tops of cabinets, and stairs. This made the vacuum more versatile that just a carpet sweeper would be. The vacuum was lightweight and easy to maintain. Mr. Herff planned to sell the industrial models to distributors for about $500, but consumer models would be priced much lower. All in all, Mr. Herff was excited about the market prospects for the new vacuum cleaner. He believed it had a great potential in both the industrial and the consumer market.

The channel of distribution for Rexford's products was from Rexford to industrial distributors to industrial users. The distributors usually were janitorial supply houses. They took an average markup of 15 percent on their cost (Rexford's selling price). Most of the industrial users were janitorial maintenance firms that cleaned carpets in office buildings, schools, hospitals, and hotels and motels. The distributors also sold to building contractors and to companies (other than supermarkets) that rented out carpet-cleaning equipment.

Rexford defined itself strictly as a supplier of steam carpet-cleaning equipment, and therefore the company defined its competition in the same way. It did not consider itself to be competing with companies that sold floor polishers and other carpet-cleaning accessories. Within this definition, most of Rexford's competitors were much larger firms. Yet, Tom Herff believed that his company had about 25 percent of the market.

Herff attributed his company's market success to three factors: (1) the variety in its product line, (2) the product design that made the unit easy to use, and (3) the fact that Rexford had its own sales force. Most of the competition used manufacturers' agents. Rexford also used six of these agents, but the company really depended on its own sales force for an effective selling effort.

Rexford had a sales force of ten people who reported to the sales manager, Terry Fletcher. These sales reps were paid at straight commission of 10 percent of their net sales. The salespeople paid their own expenses except for intercity transportation, which was paid by the Rexford Company.

The job of a Rexford sales representative consisted primarily of two sets of activities. The first involved finding distributors (janitorial supply houses) and selling them the Rexford products. The second set of job duties consisted of activites intended to make the distributor's selling effort more effective.

In order to get a distributor to carry the Rexford line, a sales rep often would bring orders to that distributor. This is the way it worked. The sales rep would first go to a janitorial service that cleaned several office buildings. The rep would go through a sales presentation which included a demonstration of the product, and secure an order. The rep then took this order to the distributor. With orders from the final user already secured, it was an easy task to get the distributor to carry the Rexford line.

Once the distributor had agreed to handle Rexford's products, it was the sales rep's job to keep that distributor actively and effectively selling those products. Most of the distributors also carried other brands of carpet cleaners besides Rexford. Consequently, the reps were constantly trying to persuade the distributors to promote the Rexford line over competitors' brands. This meant that the Rexford reps had to make frequent calls on their distributors.

Mr. Herff did not believe there would be any problems in setting up a distribution channel to sell the German vacuum cleaner to the industrial market. He planned to have the Rexford salespeople sell the machine to Rexford's existing industrial distributors—the janitorial supply houses. These distributors would then sell to the janitorial maintenance firms that would be actual users of the vacuum cleaner.

But to reach the consumer market — Mr. Herff realized that was an entirely different situation. One channel of distribution Mr. Herff was considering was the traditional channel for home appliances. That is, the Rexford sales force would sell to appliance wholesalers that in turn would sell to retail appliance stores. A variation of this channel would be for Rexford to sell directly to large retailers, such as department stores and discount merchandisers, such as Zellers and K-Mart.

At a meeting to discuss the matter, Terry Fletcher reminded Mr. Herff that Rexford would have to do more advertising to support distribution through these channels. Advertising expenses currently ran about 3 percent of sales. The company advertised in trade journals, primarily to generate inquiries from janitorial maintenance firms. Then these leads were given to the distributors in the hope that they would follow up the leads and generate sales of Rexford products. Mr. Fletcher also questioned whether the Rexford sales force was sufficiently familiar with the wholesale market for consumer appliances. He also suggested the possibility of using the present wholesale distributors — janitorial supply houses — to sell to appliance retailers.

Edward Jerrold, who was Rexford's director of sales training and also the director of the company's selling seminars for its distributors, then became involved in the discussion. He liked the idea of selling the German vacuum cleaner as a consumer product. However, he wanted to use a trade channel that would not compete with Rexford's existing janitorial supply distributors that were selling to the industrial market.

Jerrold said, "Suppose one of the appliance retailers runs a price special on the new cleaner. Some of the cleaning services and other janitorial maintenance firms that now buy from our distributors then might end up buying at the retail store. Or, at least they will question the distributor's price when they see the reduced price at a retail store."

Jerrold continued, "How about this idea — let's get into the consumer market in an indirect way. Let's sell to professional carpet-cleaning firms that clean carpets in private homes. Then, when people at home see the vacuum cleaner in action, a few may buy one at a local store. However, mainly what we'll be doing is to sell to home carpet-cleaning firms that service the consumer market. This business will parallel our sales to janitorial maintenance firms that service the industrial market."

After listening to Ed Jerrold's ideas, Mr. Herff realized that Jerrold had not indicated how their salespeople would reach the professional home-cleaning firms. Would Rexford have to increase the size of its sales force and sell directly to these firms, or would Rexford sell through some kind of a distributor? Mr. Herff also wondered what promotional requirements would be needed to support Jerrold's suggested trade channels.

Question

What channel of distribution should the Rexford Company use to sell the German vacuum cleaner in the consumer market?

Selection of Channels of Distribution for a New Product

The two founders of the Clarkson Cold Products Company, Anthony Clarkson and Everett Iversen, recently developed a new product to add to their line. Now the two men, especially Mr. Iversen, who was in charge of marketing, were wondering what channels of distribution they should use to reach the market for this product.

The Clarkson Company was a small Quebec firm whose main product was a defrosting unit. The unit was a small device designed to be installed in refrigerators and freezers of all sizes, both domestic and commercial. Its function was to defrost the cooling coils during a defrost cycle. Clarkson held the patents on these units. The company manufactured and marketed them to small and medium-sized manufacturing companies on a contract basis. Clarkson also marketed to jobbers who in turn sold the products to refrigeration service firms. Clarkson's annual sales volume was about $1.4 million.

The new product that was posing a channels problem for Mr. Iversen was a portable cooling unit, popularly called an "ice chest." Rather than using ice to keep the temperature down, however, a cooling coil had been placed in the box. This coil could be connected to, and disconnected from, an automobile air-conditioner compressor. When the air conditioner in the car was turned on, the coils in the box were also charged. With only a one-hour charge, foods and liquids could be kept cold and fresh for twenty-four hours. A device was also available to allow a person to charge the portable cooling unit without having to run the air-conditioning unit inside the car.

The cooler was 33 cm wide, 22 cm long, and 40 cm high. Its walls were 2.5 cm thick and were made of aluminum-encased insulating foam. The product was to be priced to the consumer at about 20 percent above competitive models, which used ice for cooling. The competition consisted of several branded and unbranded ice chests, with the Coleman brand probably being the best known. Actually, however, Clarkson's marketing studies indicated that brand recognition and brand preference generally were low for portable coolers.

Mr. Iversen believed that the competitive advantages of the Clarkson cooler were many: no more having to locate and buy ice; no more large pieces of ice taking up room in the ice chest; no more having to dump water when the ice begins to melt. The weight of a loaded cooler was reduced because of the no-ice factor. Furthermore, much lower temperatures could be reached and maintained with the new Clarkson unit than with any other unit.

Marketing studies indicated a good market potential for the cooler, and a wide range of potential customers. Increased leisure time in the North American market, coupled with a desire to get out in the country, meant that many people were potential users of a portable cooler. Furthermore, the product was considered to be relatively "recession-proof." That is, even during an economic decline, people still engaged in recreational activities such as picnicking, camping, and auto travelling. These activities led to a demand for a portable cooler for food and drinks.

Consequently, the Clarkson executives believed that their new cooler unit would be carried in recreational vehicles and mobile homes. It also would be used in boats, summer cottages, and automobiles. Even the above-market-level price was considered *not* to be a limiting factor, once a potential user had learned of the advantages of the Clarkson unit.

Research further indicated that different buying patterns existed among the segments of the recreation industry that Clarkson hoped to reach. Large manufacturers of recreational vehicles such as campers, vans, and trailers usually preferred to buy their component parts directly from the producers. Once a supplier's salesperson had demonstrated and sold a part to the recreational vehicle manufacturer, little servicing of this account was needed. Once a year new bids were made and new purchase contracts were prepared.

Medium-sized manufacturers of recreational vehicles also preferred to deal directly with the producers of equipment and parts. However, the smaller these parts orders became, the more likely it was that the parts manufacturers would prefer to sell through wholesalers, rather than directly to recreational vehicle manufacturers.

Wholesalers played a major role in supplying recreational vehicle parts and supplies to small manufacturers and to retailers of sporting goods. Large retailers preferred to buy directly from manufacturers.

To market its defrosting devices, the Clarkson Company had three sales-people who serviced existing accounts and solicited new accounts. Each salesperson worked in a different part of Canada and reported directly to Iversen. The three did a good job of contacting their manufacturing accounts about once a month and their jobbers about twice a month, if they felt it was necessary. They were on the road about twenty-two days a month and very seldom got back to the home office. Because of the large number of jobbers, as well as the limits on company funds, however, many potential jobbers accounts were not called on at all.

Question

What channels of distribution should the Clarkson Company use for its new portable cooler?

Case 18 Foodland Super-markets Limited*

Conversion of a Supermarket to a Discount Operation

Stephen Glass is president of Foodland Supermarkets Limited. Mr. Glass is currently facing a number of important decisions which will shape the future of his company.

Foodland Supermarkets Limited operates two large food stores in an eastern Canadian city which has a total population of approximately 100,000. The company was established in 1959 as a furniture retailer that operated a large furniture store on Westdale Road at the western end of the city. Within a year or so of its establishment, management of the company decided to convert approximately half of the furniture store to accommodate a grocery business. Partially related to the fact that very few other food retailers were operating in the area, the experiment with grocery products

---

*Case prepared by Professor James G. Barnes. Intended to stimulate classroom discussion of a management problem and not to illustrate either effective or ineffective management. Copyright 1982.

was so successful that within a year the furniture side of the business was phased out and the entire store was converted to a large modern supermarket.

In 1963 a second supermarket was opened on Mill Road, 3 km or so east of the existing store, in an established residential-commercial neighbourhood. In 1976 the original supermarket on Westdale Road was demolished and replaced by a larger, more modern supermarket with 2,100 square metres of gross floor area. In December 1980 the retail selling area in the Mill Road store was extended from 2,000 to 2,900 square metres by incorporating an existing 800 square metres of warehouse space into the retail selling area. The total gross floor area of the Mill Road store is 3,000 square metres.

Mr. Glass had recently commissioned trading area studies, which showed that the Westdale Road store drew its customers not only from its immediate area but also from Glendale Park, a large suburb of 20,000 population located west of the city. Because Foodland's Westdale Road store was situated on a major traffic artery leading out of the city, it relied, for a large percentage of its sales, on customers who drove relatively long distances to shop there. On the other hand, the Mill Road store was located in an older, middle-class area of the city and more than 80 percent of the people who shop there live in the immediate area. The clientele of the Mill Road store were, on average, older and of lower income than those who shopped at the Westdale Road outlet. This characteristic is partially related to the fact that the Mill Road store is located in an established working class neighbourhood in which is situated a large senior citizens' complex, only several hundred metres from the store itself.

Both supermarkets had been operated since their establishment on a conventional basis, although Mr. Glass took considerable pride in the fact that his stores were among the cleanest in the city and that his staff were known for their friendliness and rapport with customers. The major competition for the two Foodland stores came from eight Dominion Stores outlets and five stores of a major regional chain (see Exhibit 1). In addition, there was one other independent supermarket and a Co-op store serving the area, as well as numerous small corner grocery stores.

In late 1979 Mr. Glass, realizing the existence of current trends in the food retailing industry toward the establishment of no-frills stores and having seen such stores in operation in the United States and in Europe, began to consider a plan for converting the Foodland store on Mill Road to a low-price, high-volume food retail operation. His deliberations on this point were motivated by the fact that the Mill Road store at present was not drawing customers from outside its immediate trading area. Mr. Glass wished to expand its trading area and to increase average transaction size and attract a younger clientele. He had been looking for a suitable location in the east end of the city for several years with a view to opening a third supermarket. Having had no success in acquiring a suitable location, and considering the cost of constructing a new store, he decided that his next best alternative was to expand his existing operations. Although two small "box stores" were presently operating in the city, there were no large discount supermarkets in operation.

Planning for the conversion of the Mill Road store took almost a year. Working with a local marketing consultant, Mr. Glass wished to change the entire image of the existing Foodland store. He considered a new name and a totally new concept in food retailing: one with which residents of the city would not be familiar. The "new store" was not to be a modification of the existing Foodland store but a totally different concept.

The marketing consultant developed a list of possible names for the new store and, following a series of focus group interviews, the name Shop and Save was selected. This name was considered to be friendly in tone, playing upon a "low price" theme, and offered many possibilities for creative advertising strategy. A red-and-white colour scheme was decided upon, and detailed planning for the conversion of the store began. A new logo was designed; new exterior and interior signs, staff uniforms, and in-store advertising materials were ordered; and construction began to expand the selling area of the store from the existing 2,000 to 2,900 square metres. The entire planning process involved only Mr. Glass, the consultant, and Foodland's management group. The conversion of the Mill Road store was to be a surprise to the shoppers of the city.

The actual transformation of the Foodland Mill Road store took place over a three-day period in December 1980. Shoppers and staff of the store were advised that the store would be closed for that period. Since some construction and painting had been ongoing for a number of weeks, the impression was given that the store would be closed to make changes in the layout of aisles and fixtures. No mention had been made of Shop and Save. The only promotion carried out in the period immediately prior to the conversion was a "teaser" advertising campaign, which ran in local newspapers for two weeks before the opening of the new store.

The Mill Road store was closed as a Foodland store at 6:00 p.m. on Saturday, December 6, 1980, and a team of carpenters, painters, and some employees worked for three days to convert the store. The 800 square metres of new selling space was opened. New fixtures and freezers were installed, including a much expanded frozen food department. The prices on all items in the store were reduced, the entire store was repainted in the red-and-white design of Shop and Save, and new exterior and interior signs were installed. Checkout staff and grocery personnel were called in on Tuesday to be outfitted with new uniforms and to be briefed on the opening of the new store. The Mill Road store reopened at 10:00 a.m. on Wednesday, December 10, as Shop and Save: a much larger, brighter store with much lower prices. Tuesday newspapers announced the grand opening with a full-page ad proclaiming that "Shop and Save has declared war on inflation."

The new store was visibly larger than the Foodland outlet had been, and the layout had been altered. Some new products had been added, including more white-label products, but several had also been discontinued. Aisles were wider but the personnel were unchanged, although their new red-and-white uniforms bore the Shop and Save logo, as did new shopping bags. Prices were now lower than those charged by any other store in the area, and some customer services had been discontinued. Customers could no longer order custom cuts of meat, and they were now expected to bag and carry out their own groceries.

Mr. Glass had decided that the low-price policy of the new store was to be implemented across all product categories. The low-price, high-volume

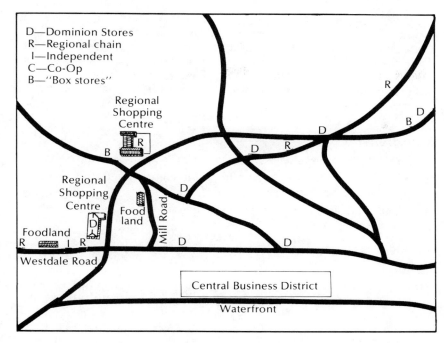

D—Dominion Stores
R—Regional chain
I—Independent
C—Co-Op
B—"Box stores"

Regional Shopping Centre

R

B

R

D

B

D

R

D

Regional Shopping Centre

Food land

Mill Road

D

D

Foodland

R   I   R

Westdale Road

D

D

Central Business District

Waterfront

Exhibit 1
MAP OF FOODLAND
AND OTHER RETAIL
FOOD STORES.

strategy was designed to draw new customers to the Mill Road store. Not only was Shop and Save offering better prices on "specials," but Mr. Glass was determined to ensure that its prices were lower "across the board," so that his customers could be guaranteed of saving on their total food bills by shopping there. Radio and newspaper advertising was used to promote the opening and the low prices.

Mr. Glass realized that not all existing Mill Road customers would be happy with the conversion. Some of the store's regular customers complained about having to bag their own groceries and about the fact that they could no longer obtain custom cuts of meat. Several objected to the fact that Foodland had apparently sold out, believing that a new company had taken over the store. Some switched to new supermarket and several began to patronize the Foodland store on Westdale Road, rather than shop at Shop and Save. During the conversion of the Mill Road store, the Westdale Road Foodland outlet continued to carry on business as usual.

From a company point of view, the conversion of the Mill Road store from a Foodland operation to Shop and Save was a success. Sales volume in the first few weeks following the grand opening was the highest in the company's history. Sales continued at this high level and in the first six months following the opening, sales in the Mill Road store were double the volume for the same period a year earlier. A follow-up trading area study showed that customers at Shop and Save were coming from all areas of the city and from some neighbouring towns. Mr. Glass estimated that the total share of the retail grocery market accounted for by his two stores had increased considerably.

Mr. Glass now faced some additional difficult decisions, the principal one being whether or not to convert the Foodland store on Westdale Road to a Shop and Save operation as well. At present the two stores operated quite independently. The Westdale Road store was operated as a full-service conventional supermarket. Although its prices were quite competitive with other local supermarkets, they were not as low as prices at Shop and Save.

Questions

1. Evaluate Mr. Glass's decision to convert the Mill Road store.
2. Evaluate also the process he followed in converting from a Foodland operation to Shop and Save.
3. Should Mr. Glass convert the Westdale Road store to a Shop and Save operation as well?

Case 19 Blue Mountain Herb Teas Company

Conflict in Distribution Channels

"Health food stores constituted our first significant group of customers, and they still remain one of our major markets. Consequently, I think that we had better figure out some way to handle their growing discontent — even hostility — toward us." These thoughts were expressed recently by Cary Penfold, the vice president of sales, to another executive at the Blue Mountain Herb Teas Company.

The Blue Mountain Herb Teas Company was started by two young men, Bart Wilcox and Fred Easton, in British Columbia in the late 1960s. In the eyes of these two founders, their company was part of the growing "natural foods" industry. With this philosophy, initially they sold their products only to health food stores.

During its relatively short life span, Blue Mountain experienced phenomenal market success. Sales volume last year was about $5 million. Management forecast that sales would increase about 25 percent a year over the next five years. Currently, Blue Mountain's teas were sold throughout Canada and in the northern United States. Mr. Penfold stated that the company was planning to enter some overseas markets within the next two years.

Blue Mountain produced fifteen different blends of herb teas, packaged in tea bags and in bulk (loose) form. Three of these blends accounted for a little over half the company's total sales. Some of the teas were blended for use at a certain time of the day — morning, afternoon tea-time, and bedtime. Other blends were designed to appeal to two broad and growing markets — people who wanted natural foods, and people who were seeking alternatives to regular tea or coffee.

The company used a different brand name for each blend and tried to select names that were catchy and that appealed to young adults. Blue Mountain stressed the purity of its teas. Only natural ingredients were used, and only the morning tea contained any caffeine. The herbal ingredients were imported from several different countries.

Blue Mountain teas faced competition from several different sources. The company's major direct competitor was the Celestial Seasonings Herb Teas company, which was located in Boulder, Colorado, and was marketing its teas very successfully throughout the United States and Canada. Other major competition came from: (1) the standard teas and coffees, (2) decaffeinated coffees, and (3) a growing number of specially flavoured teas and coffees (General Foods' line of International Coffees and Twining's teas, for example).

Originally, Blue Mountain's teas were sold directly to health food stores in British Columbia and the northwest United States. As the company grew and its geographic market was expanded, the company broadened its distribution patterns. Currently, to reach its ultimate consumers, Blue Mountain was selling through three groups of retailers or institutional users — health food stores, grocery stores, and institutions such as restaurants, hospitals, colleges, and universities.

Blue Mountain sold directly to the large grocery chains and institutional users. However, the company used wholesalers to reach the health food stores and the smaller grocery stores and institutional buyers. Cary Penfold managed a sales force of twelve people who sold to these wholesalers, large retailers, and large institutional buyers. Each of these sales reps had a separate geographic territory and called on all types of customers in that territory.

For some time now, Mr. Penfold realized he had a problem growing in his distribution system. The health food store operators were becoming increasingly unhappy as they saw the retail herb-tea business shift from their stores to grocery supermarkets. The health food retailers felt that, since they were the first to carry the Blue Mountain teas, they should have exclusive rights to continue selling these teas. Penfold knew he had to do something to minimize this discontent, but he was at a loss as to what course of action would be best.

As noted above, when Blue Mountain started in business, the company sold only to health food stores. These retailers still accounted for a substantial share of Blue Mountain's sales. Penfold estimated that 80 to 90 percent of the health food stores carried at least part of the Blue Mountain line of teas.

In recent years, however, the share of Blue Mountain's sales accounted for by health food stores was *declining*, as grocery supermarkets *increased* their share of Blue Mountain's sales. Penfold believed that the grocery stores provided the greatest growth opportunities for Blue Mountain's products. Grocery stores were increasing the number of products they carried that directly competed with the health food stores. Some grocery stores even had a separate health food department. In grocery stores, the Blue Mountain teas were stocked either with the health foods or in the regular coffee and tea department, or sometimes in both places. Grocery stores usually sold the same products at a lower price than in the health food stores. This situation occurred because the large grocery stores bought directly and in larger quantities, from the manufacturers. The health food stores usually bought through wholesalers.

Although the major growth prospects might lie in the grocery store field, Penfold also realized that his company needed the support of the health food stores. Blue Mountain's image was improved when its teas were carried by health food stores. These stores were also needed for the introduction of new products in the future. Health food stores would have to show that a new product had market acceptance before the grocery stores would provide shelf space for it.

To stop Blue Mountain's distribution expansion into grocery stores, the health food retailers threatened to stop buying from wholesalers who were selling the herb teas both to health food stores and to grocery stores. Actually, some health food retailers did boycott their wholesalers, and these distributors then had to choose between supplying one or the other type of store.

At first, Mr. Penfold considered redistributing his sales force so that there would be two sales reps in a given territory. One rep would deal exclusively with grocery stores, and the other would call on health food retailers and wholesalers. This move would entail hiring additional salespeople. Blue Mountain's president objected to the additional selling costs, and he also feared there would be other inefficiencies in distribution. Another executive suggested that the company should do some direct-mail advertising or some type of dealer-relations activity with the health food retailers to explain Blue Mountain's position.

Some of the sales reps thought the problem was temporary—that it would go away as soon as the health food retailers realized that the consumer market for each type of store (grocery and health food) was different. These reps felt that people who buy herb teas in health food stores would not shop in grocery stores for these teas. Blue Mountain's advertising mentioned that the teas can be found in health food stores as well as in grocery stores. Some reps stated that Blue Mountain teas might even draw new customers to health food stores, and then these people would buy other health foods. Finally, the sales reps argued that health food retailers knew that it would be unwise to discontinue a product that was so well liked by their customers, as well as being profitable.

Mr. Penfold was considering these alternatives, but he also was wondering whether there was a better solution.

Question

What should Cary Penfold do to reduce the conflict in his company's distribution channels?

Case 20 Bentley Fresh Brew Tea (D)*

Distribution Strategies for a New Brand

Don Evans, president of The Newfoundland Tea Company, was considering a number of alternative channel structures in planning the distribution strategies section of his marketing plan for Bentley Fresh Brew Tea. Decisions had to be made concerning the intensity of distribution, channel structure, the geographic scope of initial as well as future distribution, and the type and size of specific retail stores. In considering the alternatives, he realized the importance of coordinating distribution strategies with the other three elements of the marketing mix for Bentley Fresh Brew.

There were a number of alternative channel structures available for Bentley Fresh Brew. Some of these included: (1) distribute directly to retailers, hiring a sales force to arrange listings and to promote the brand at the

---

*Refer to Part (A) of this case for essential background and statistical information on the market, competition, and the brand.

retail level; (2) distribute through independent wholesalers to retailers, hiring a (smaller) sales force to promote the product at the retail level; (3) utilize independent manufacturers' representatives, rather than his own sales force, to promote Bentley Fresh Brew at the wholesale and retail level. Channel (1) would require that The Newfoundland Tea Company hire a sales force of two to four individuals (depending on the geographic scope of distribution), arrange physical distribution, and carry higher inventories —as many retail stores carry minimum stocks, and expect up to two deliveries per week for fast moving items.

Channel (2) would shift some of the above responsibilities to an independent wholesaler, who would expect to obtain between 9 and 14 percent profit margin when selling to retailers. However, since wholesalers carry many products from different manufacturers, it could still be necessary to hire one or more salespeople to promote the brand at the retail level: to ensure listings, adequate inventories, good shelf position and facings, and special displays. Based on his experience in the industry, Mr. Evans estimated that it would cost approximately $35,000 annually per salesperson, to cover salary, bonuses, and expenses.

Channel (3) would utilize independent, commission sales agents/manufacturers' representatives rather than a company sales force; such agents normally represent a number of noncompeting products of other manufacturers and, while not taking title to the product, are active in promoting them to both wholesalers and retailers. Several such agents had expressed some interest in promoting Bentley Fresh Brew to wholesalers and/or retailers for a commission of approximately 5 to 8 percent of sales.

Another key distribution decision yet to be made for Bentley Fresh Brew was intensity of distribution: intensive, selective, or exclusive. Should Mr. Evans concentrate on having Bentley available in selected supermarkets or other stores only, or in as many stores of all sizes and types as possible? To obtain distribution in a chain store, the first step is to make a presentation to their buyer; the buyer then makes a recommendation regarding acceptance to the chain's buying committee. If approved, the product is "listed," i.e. authorized as an approved product that individual store managers or buyers may order and stock if they wish (hence the need for sales representation in individual retail stores). Only rarely would a product be given automatic distribution (an initial order to all stores initiated by head office).

The food retailing business was extremely competitive in Newfoundland, as well as in Canada as a whole. As a result, most supermarket chains often required a "listing allowance" of up to $2,500 from new brands as a condition for being listed. One consideration in Mr. Evans's mind, therefore, was what other inducements might be necessary to obtain listings for Bentley Fresh Brew — particularly considering that *per capita* consumption of tea was decreasing and that some stores stocked up to ten different brands of tea bags. For example, should the retailers' suggested profit margin be higher than the normal 20 percent? Would other discounts and allowances be necessary?

Related to the question of distribution intensity was geographic scope of initial and future distribution for Bentley Fresh Brew. Should The Newfoundland Tea Company concentrate initially on the St. John's metropolitan area (population of 150,000), or should distribution be extended to cover the entire Avalon Peninsula area (located within a 160 km radius of St. John's and containing a population of 250,000) or the entire province (with a population of 575,000)? See Tables A-2, A-3, A-4, and the map in Part (A) of this case. In addition, Mr. Evans was considering whether Bentley Fresh Brew should be marketed in the three Maritime Provinces of Nova Scotia, New Brunswick, and Prince Edward Island, and/or in the remaining provinces of Canada. A related decision had to be made regarding the timing or schedule of distribution outside the province: should he expand to all areas at the same time, so as to lessen the effects of competitive retaliation, or should distribution be expanded on a gradual basis over a longer period of time?

Question

Which distribution channels and strategies would you recommend for Bentley Fresh Brew? Why?

Promotion

6

THE DESIGN AND MANAGEMENT OF A MARKETING SUB-
SYSTEM FOR THE PURPOSE OF INFORMING AND PERSUAD-
ING PRESENT AND POTENTIAL CUSTOMERS

So far, we have developed three of the four parts of a marketing mix to reach the organization's target markets and achieve
its marketing goals. We have considered strategies regarding
the product, the pricing structure, and the distribution system.
To complete the marketing mix, we now turn to the task of
developing a promotional program.

In Chapter 18 we discuss promotion as a communication
process, the concepts of the promotional mix and a promotional campaign, and finally, the governmental regulation of
promotional activities. Chapter 19 covers the personal selling
process and the management of a sales force. Chapter 20 is
devoted to the management of advertising and sales promotion.

The Promotional Program

CHAPTER GOALS

This chapter is, essentially, a discussion of what promotion is and how it fits into a firm's complete marketing system. After studying the chapter, you should understand:

1. *Promotion and its relation to selling and non-price competition*
2. *Promotion as a communication process*
3. *The concept of the promotional mix*
4. *The factors that shape a company's promotional mix*
5. *The problems and methods involved in determining the promotional appropriation*
6. *The concept of a promotional campaign*
7. *Government regulation of promotional activities*

Product planning, pricing, and distribution are marketing activities that are performed mainly within the company, or between the company and its marketing "partners." However, in its promotional activities, the firm gets its chance to communicate with potential customers, to "beat the drum" about its product. Chapters 18 to 20 deal with the management of the **promotional mix**—that is, the combination of advertising, personal selling, sales promotion, and other promotional tools used to help reach the goals of the marketing program.

The statement "Nothing happens until somebody sells something" expresses rather well the place of promotional activities in today's business scene. Yet, promotion is the most criticized of all the marketing activities—and perhaps deservedly so. Without question, some advertisements are misleading, and some salespeople act in poor taste. However, we should not confuse the tool with the user. Misuses are not the fault of promotion as a tool, but of the people who use it improperly.

Unfortunately, it is human nature to blame the tool itself. A person hammers a nail crookedly and blames the poor quality of the nail, or hits a finger and blames the hammer. But you don't throw away the hammer just because you hit your finger with it. Nor should we get rid of promotion because some people use it improperly.[1]

---

[1]See James U. McNeal, "You Can Defend Advertising — But Not Every Advertisement," *Business Horizons*, September-October 1981, pp. 33–37.

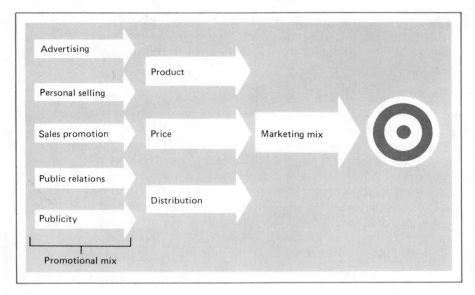

Figure 18-1
THE ROLE OF
PROMOTION IN THE
MARKETING MIX.

To reach your target
market, coordinate the
elements in the promo-
tional mix, and coordinate
promotion with the other
elements in your
marketing mix.

MEANING AND IMPORTANCE OF PROMOTION

Many people consider selling and marketing to be synonymous terms, when, actually, selling is only one of the many components of marketing. We shall treat selling and promotion as synonymous terms, although **promotion** is preferred. For many people, selling suggests only the transfer of title or only the activities of salespeople and does not include advertising or other methods of stimulating demand. In our definition, promotion includes advertising, personal selling, and all other selling tools. Together, they are basic factors in the marketing mix (see Fig. 18-1).

Promotional Methods

The two most widely used methods of promotion are **personal selling** and **advertising**. Other forms of promotion are:

1. **Sales promotion**, which is designed to supplement and coordinate personal selling and advertising efforts. Sales promotion includes such activities as setting up store displays, holding trade shows, and distributing samples, premiums, or "cents-off" coupons.

2. **Publicity**, which is a nonpersonal form of demand stimulation and is not paid for by the person or organization benefiting from it. Typically, publicity takes the form of a favourable news presentation — a "plug" — for a product, service, or organization. The plug is made in print, on radio or television, or in some form of public address.

3. **Public relations**, which is a planned effort by an organization to influence some group's attitude or opinion toward that organization. The target market of the public relations effort may be any given "public," such as customers, a government agency, or people living near the promoting organization.[2]

---

[2]See Jonathan N. Goodrich, Robert L. Gildea, and Kevin Cavanaugh, "A Place for Public Relations in the Marketing Mix," *MSU Business Topics*, Autumn 1979, pp. 53–57.

In addition, there is a group of marketing strategies, discussed in earlier chapters, that are in part promotional. Such strategies as product differentiation, market segmentation, trading up or trading down, and branding belong in this group.

Basic Nature of Promotion

Basically, promotion is an exercise in information, persuasion, and communication. These three are related, because to inform is to persuade, and conversely, a person who is persuaded is also being informed. And persuasion and information become effective through some form of communication. Many years ago, Prof. Neil Borden pointed up the pervasive nature of persuasion (influence) in our socioeconomic system. He said that "the use of influence in commercial relations is one of the attributes of a free society, just as persuasion and counterpersuasion are exercised freely in many walks of life in our free society — in the home, in the press, in the classroom, in the pulpit, in the courts, in the political forum, in legislative halls, and in government agencies for information."[3]

Promotion and Imperfect Competition

Our marketplace today operates under conditions of imperfect competition. That means there is product differentiation, nonrational buyer behaviour, and less-than-complete market information. Under these conditions, promotional activities are essential. That is, a company needs promotion to aid in differentiating its product, to persuade the buyers, and to bring more information into the buying-decision process.

In economic terms, the basic purpose of promotion is to change the location and shape of the demand (revenue) curve for a company's product. (See Fig. 18-2 and recall the discussion of nonprice competition in Chapter 13.) Through the use of promotion, a company hopes to increase a product's sales volume at any given price. It also hopes that promotion will affect the demand elasticity for the product. The intent is to make the demand *inelastic* when the price increases, and *elastic* when the price goes down. In other words, management wants the quantity demanded to decline very little when the price goes up (inelastic demand). However, when the price goes down, management would like sales to increase considerably (elastic demand).

Need for Promotion

Several factors point up the need for promotion today. In the first place, as the distance between producers and consumers increases, and as the number of potential customers grows, the problem of market communication becomes significant.

Once middlemen are introduced into a marketing pattern, it is not enough for a producer to communicate only with the ultimate consumers or industrial users. It becomes essential that the middlemen, too, be informed about products. Wholesalers, in turn, must promote the products to retailers, and retailers must communicate with consumers. In other words, even the most useful and want-satisfying product will be a marketing failure if no one

---

[3]Neil H. Borden, *The Economic Effects of Advertising*, Richard D. Irwin, Inc., Homewood, Ill., 1942, p. 802.

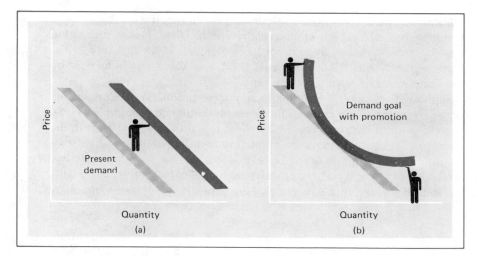

Figure 18-2
THE GOAL OF
PROMOTION: TO
CHANGE THE PAT-
TERN OF DEMAND
FOR A PRODUCT.

Through promotion a
company attempts to (a)
shift a product's demand
curve to the right and
(b) change the shape
of the curve.

knows it is available. A basic purpose of promotion is to disseminate information — to let potential customers know!

The intense competition among different industries, as well as among individual firms within an industry, has placed tremendous pressures on the promotional programs of individual sellers. In our economy, want-satisfaction has generally replaced the necessity of fulfilling only basic physiological requirements. Consequently, customers are more selective in their buying choices, and a good promotional program is needed to reach them.

Oddly enough, promotion is also needed during periods of shortages — the opposite of abundance. During periods of shortages, advertising can stress product conservation and efficient uses of the product. The sales force can direct its efforts toward servicing accounts and helping customers solve their shortage-induced problems. Other promotional activities can be used to aid consumers in "making do" and, incidentally, help build the company image.

Any economic recession quickly points up the importance of selling. During such a period, there are no major problems in product planning. Channels remain essentially the same, and the pricing structure is basically unchanged. The key problem is selling. Promotion is needed to maintain the high material standard of living and the high level of employment that we have traditionally enjoyed in this country.

In line with the systems approach, a company should treat all its promotional efforts as a complete subsystem within the total marketing system. This means coordinating sales-force activities, advertising programs, and other promotional efforts. Unfortunately, today in many firms these activities still are fragmented, and advertising managers and sales-force managers often are in conflict.[4] Of course, for an effective marketing program,

**Promotion and
Strategic Marketing
Planning**

[4]See Alan J. Dubinsky, Thomas E. Barry, and Roger A. Kerin, "The Sales-Advertising Interface in Promotion Planning," *Journal of Advertising*, vol. 10, no. 3 (1981), pp. 35–41.

the total promotional effort also must be coordinated with the product planning, pricing, and distribution subsystems in a firm. That is, promotion must be coordinated with the other three elements of the marketing mix. Moreover, as is true of those elements, promotion is strongly influenced by the firm's strategic marketing planning.

Suppose, for example, that a company faces production limitations imposed by materials shortages. This firm's marketing goal is simply to hold onto its present customers and its present market share — at least in the short run. Its strategic marketing planning and the strategic planning for its promotional program would be geared toward attaining that objective. And, a set of promotional strategies would be called for that would be quite different from that of a company where a newly developed technology offered bright prospects for market expansion.

THE COMMUNICATION PROCESS

As noted earlier, promotion is basically an exercise in communication. Executives who understand something of the theory of communication should be able to better manage their firm's promotional program.

ON THE LIGHTER SIDE IN BUSINESS COMMUNICATION

Speaking the other person's language is one of the prime requirements of good communications. An even more valuable asset, however, is being able to understand what people are really saying. These definitions of common business terms, from *Steel* and *Reporting* magazines, may prove helpful:

- *A Program.* Any assignment that can't be completed by one telephone call.
- *To expedite.* To confound confusion with commotion.
- *Coordinator.* The guy who has a desk between two expediters.
- *Consultant (or expert).* Any ordinary guy more than 50 miles from home.
- *To activate.* To make carbons and add more names to the memo.
- *Under consideration.* Never heard of it.
- *Under active consideration.* We're looking in the files for it.
- *Reliable source.* The guy you just met.
- *Informed source.* The guy who told the guy you just met.
- *Unimpeachable source.* The guy who started the rumour in the first place.
- *We are making a survey.* We need more time to think of an answer.
- *Note and initial.* Let's spread the responsibility for this.
- *See me, or let's discuss.* Come down to my office; I'm lonesome.
- *Give us the benefit of your present thinking.* We'll listen to what you have to say as long as it doesn't interfere with what we've already decided to do.
- *Will advise you in due course.* If we figure it out, we'll let you know.
- *We are confident that.* We're keeping our fingers crossed.

The word **communication** is derived from the Latin word *communis*, meaning "common." Thus, when you communicate, you are trying to establish a "commonness" with someone. Through the use of verbal or nonverbal symbols, you as the source send a message through a channel to a receiver, in an effort to share information. Fundamentally, the communication process requires only four elements — a **message**, a **source** of this message, a communication **channel**, and a **receiver**. However, in practice, additional elements come into play. The information that the sending source wants to share must first be *encoded* into transmittable form, *transmitted*, and then *decoded* by the receiver. Another element to be reckoned with is **noise**, which is anything that tends to distort the message at any stage in the system. The final element in the process — **feedback**—tells the sender whether the message was received and how it was perceived by the target. The feedback is also the basis for planning ahead. The sender learns how the communication may be improved by determining how well the message was received.

These elements constituting a general communication system may be conceptualized as in Fig. 18-3.[5] The information source may be a person with an idea to communicate. This person will encode the idea into a transmittable form by putting it into written or spoken words. Or, perhaps the sender uses a gesture of some sort (waving the arms or dimming bright lights). The coded message is then carried by print media, sound waves,

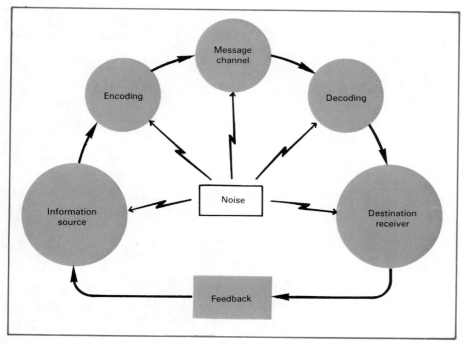

Figure 18-3
A GENERALIZED
COMMUNICATION
SYSTEM.

[5]Adapted from David K. Berlo, *The Process of Communication*, Holt, Rinehart and Winston, Inc., New York, 1960, pp. 30–32.

or light waves (the channel) to the destination — an individual, a church audience, or a university class, for example. The receivers decode (interpret) the message in light of their individual experiences or frames of reference. The closer the decoded message is to its encoded form (assuming it was encoded fully and accurately), the more effective the communication is. By evaluating the receiver's words or actions (feedback), the sender can judge how well the message got through. This same model, as adapted to the promotional activities in a company's marketing program, is illustrated in Fig. 18-4.

Let us illustrate the process with a marketing example. An executive wants to communicate a selling message to consumers. The message is encoded into a radio commercial and carried to the consumers via a radio program and a receiving set. The consumers hear the commercial and interpret it. Through marketing-research feedback, the sender tries to determine how effectively the message came through and how much it moved the consumers to action.

At any point in the process, interfering noise may reduce the effectiveness of the system. While the radio commercial is on, children may be making noise in the house or the doorbell may ring. Competitive promotion is also a form of noise. The sender can counteract the noise by preparing an especially good commercial or by running it at a time when doorbells, children, and competitors are likely to be quiet.

Figure 18-4
A MARKETING
COMMUNICATION
SYSTEM
ILLUSTRATING
ACTIVITIES IN
PROMOTIONAL
PROGRAM.

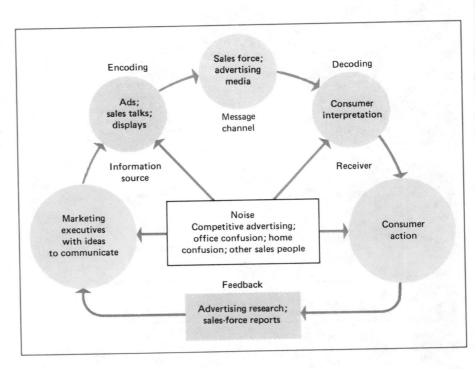

Management has to determine what combinations of advertising, personal selling, and other promotional tools will make the most effective promotional program for a company. This is a tough job. Executives simply do not know exactly how much the advertising or any other promotional tool will help achieve the goals of the marketing program.

Four factors should be taken into account in deciding on the promotional mix. They are (1) the amount of money available for promotion, (2) the nature of the market, (3) the nature of the product, and (4) the stage of the product's life cycle.

DETERMIN-ATION OF PROMOTIONAL MIX

Factors Influencing Promotional Mix

Funds Available

Regardless of what may be the most desirable promotional mix, the amount of money available for promotion is the real determinant of the mix. A business with ample funds can make more effective use of advertising than an enterprise with limited financial resources. Small or financially weak companies are likely to rely on personal selling, dealer displays, or joint manufacturer-retailer advertising. Lack of money may even force a company to use a less efficient promotional method. For example, advertising can carry a promotional message to far more people and at a lower cost *per person* than a sales force can. Yet, the firm may have to rely on personal selling because it lacks the funds to take advantage of advertising's efficiency.

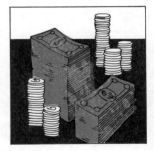

FUNDS

Nature of the Market

As is true in most problem areas in marketing, decisions on the promotional mix will be greatly influenced by the nature of the market. This influence is felt in at least three ways.

1. *Geographic scope of the market*: Personal selling may be adequate in a small local market, but as the market broadens geographically, greater stress must be placed on advertising.

2. *Type of customers*: The promotional strategy is influenced by whether the organization is aiming its promotion at industrial users, household consumers, or middlemen. To illustrate, a promotional program aimed at retailers will probably include more personal selling than a program designed to attract household consumers. In many situations, the middlemen may strongly influence the promotional strategy used by a manufacturer. Often a retail store will not even stock a product unless the manufacturer agrees to do a certain amount of advertising.

3. *Concentration of the market*: The total number of prospective buyers is one consideration. The fewer potential buyers there are, the more effective personal selling is, compared with advertising.

MARKET

Another consideration is the *number* of different *types* of potential customers. A market with only one type of customer will call for a different promotional mix from that of a market with many different customer groups. A firm selling large power saws used only by lumber manufacturers may be able to use personal selling effectively. In contrast, a company selling hand tools used by thousands of consumers and virtually all types of industrial firms probably will include liberal portions of advertising in its mix. Personal selling would be prohibitively expensive in reaching the many customers.

Finally, even though a firm sells nationally, it may find its market concentrated in relatively few spots. In this type of market concentration, emphasis on personal selling may be feasible. But it would be unrealistic if the potential customers were widely distributed all over the country.

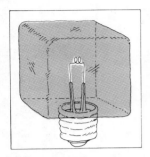

PRODUCT

Nature of the Product

Consumer products and industrial goods frequently require different strategies. Within the category of consumer goods, a promotional mix is influenced by whether the product is generally considered a convenience, shopping, or specialty item. With regard to industrial goods, installations are not promoted in the same way as operating supplies.

Firms marketing convenience goods will normally rely heavily on manufacturers' advertising in addition to dealer displays. Personal selling plays a relatively minor role. This mix is best because a convenience product is widely distributed and needs no special demonstration or explanation.

In the field of industrial goods, the promotional strategy used to market installations usually features heavy emphasis on personal selling. The market for such products is more easily pinpointed than the market for other types of industrial products. Also, the unit sales are typically large, products are often made to the customer's specification, and considerable presale and postsale personal service is necessary.

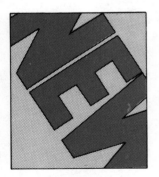

LIFE-CYCLE STAGE

Stage of the Product's Life Cycle

Promotional strategies for a product are influenced by the life-cycle stage that a product is in at any given time. Table 18-1 shows how these strategies change as the product moves through its life cycle.

Questions of Basic Promotional Strategy

By asking and then answering six questions regarding promotional strategy, we can set some guidelines for determining a company's promotional mix. The answers are related to the four factors that influence the mix.[6]

---

[6]This question approach to promotional strategy was first noted in the writings of Prof. James D. Scott, University of Michigan.

When Should Personal Selling be the Main Ingredient?

Personal selling will ordinarily carry the bulk of the promotional load (1) when the company has insufficient funds with which to carry on an adequate advertising program, (2) when the market is concentrated, or (3) when the personality of a salesperson is needed to establish rapport. Personal selling will also be emphasized when the product (4) has a high unit value, (5) requires demonstration, (6) must be fitted to the individual customer's needs, as in the case of securities or insurance, or (7) involves a trade-in.

Table 18-1 PROMOTIONAL STRATEGY AND PRODUCT LIFE-CYCLE STAGE

Market Situation	Promotional Strategy
Introductory Stage	
Customers are unaware of the product. They do not understand how it will benefit them.	Inform and educate potential customers. Tell them that the product exists, how it might be used, and what want-satisfying benefits it provides. In this stage, a seller must stimulate **primary demand**—the demand for a type of product—as contrasted with **selective demand**—the demand for a particular brand. For example, manufacturers had to sell consumers on the value of microwave kitchen ovens in general before it was feasible to promote Tappan or some other brand. Normally, heavy emphasis must be placed on personal selling. Trade shows are also used extensively in the promotional mix. Rather than call on customers individually, the company can promote its new product at some type of trade show where prospective customers come to the seller's exhibit. Manufacturers also rely heavily on personal selling to attract middlemen to handle a new product.
Growth Stage	
Customers are aware of product benefits. The product is selling well, and middlemen want to handle it.	Stimulate selective (brand) demand. Increase the emphasis on advertising. Middlemen share more of the total promotional burden.
Maturity Stage	
Competition intensifies and sales level off.	Advertising is used as a tool of persuasion rather than only to provide information. Intense competition forces sellers to devote larger sums to advertising and thus contributes to the declining profits experienced in the maturity stage.
Sales Decline Stage	
Sales and profits are declining. New and better products are coming into the market.	All promotional effort should be cut back substantially, except when attempting to revitalize the product.

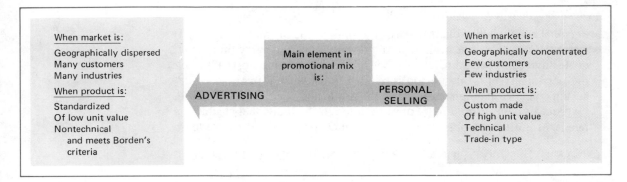

When market is:
Geographically dispersed
Many customers
Many industries

When product is:
Standardized
Of low unit value
Nontechnical
    and meets Borden's
    criteria

Main element in
promotional mix
is:

ADVERTISING   PERSONAL
                     SELLING

When market is:
Geographically concentrated
Few customers
Few industries

When product is:
Custom made
Of high unit value
Technical
Trade-in type

WHEN TO STRESS
ADVERTISING AND
WHEN TO STRESS
PERSONAL SELLING:
A SUMMARY.

When Should Advertising be the Main Ingredient?

If the market for the product is widespread, as in the case of a national consumer market, advertising should receive heavy emphasis. Advertising also works best when the seller wishes to inform many people quickly, as in the case of an announcement of new store hours or a special sale.

Certainly not every product lends itself to advertising. Many years ago, Prof. Neil H. Borden identified five criteria that can serve as guides for management in determining the "advertisability" of its product.[7] If all five of these criteria are met, normally there is an excellent opportunity to advertise. However, this ideal situation rarely exists. Ordinarily, a product meets some, but not all, of these conditions. Then the decision on whether to advertise becomes more difficult.

The five criteria are as follows:

1. The primary demand trend for the product should be favourable. In spite of some opinion, advertising cannot successfully sell a product that people do not want. Nor can advertising reverse a basic declining primary demand.

2. There should be considerable opportunity to differentiate the product. Then it is easier to advertise because the company has something to say. For this reason, automobiles or cosmetics are easier to advertise than salt or sugar. Products that are not easy to differentiate by *brand* may still be advertised by a trade association, such as the Canadian Dairy Bureau or the Pork Products Marketing Board.

3. The product should have hidden qualities. This condition affords the seller grounds for educating the market through advertising. On this point, a sofa or a mechanical device is easier to advertise than greeting cards.

4. Powerful emotional buying motives should exist for the product. Then buying action can be stimulated by appeal to these motives. It is easier to build an effective advertising campaign for Weight Watchers than for articles such as clotheslines or hammers.

[7]Borden, *op. cit.*, pp. 424–428.

5. The company must have sufficient funds to support an advertising program adequately.

When Should Promotional Efforts by Retailers be Stressed?

If the product has important qualities that can be judged at the point of purchase, or if it is a highly standardized item, it lends itself to dealer display. So do products that are purchased on impulse. And retailer promotion is particularly important when the retailer is better known in the market than the manufacturer.

When Should Manufacturer-Retailer Cooperative Advertising be Used?

There are really three questions involved here. These queries and some brief answers follow:

1. When should a manufacturer list its dealers' names and addresses in advertisements? The retailers' names should be mentioned particularly when the manufacturer employs selective or exclusive distribution policies. It then becomes important to tell the market where the product may be obtained.

2. Under what conditions should a manufacturer pay a retailer to mention the manufacturer's product in the retailer's advertisements? The manufacturer may have to pay the retailer's advertising cost just to get the retailer to carry the commodity. Also, the retailer may be in a position to demand payment when the retailer's name has better selling power than the manufacturer's.

3. When should a retailer emphasize the manufacturer's product in the store's advertising and display? A retailer should promote the manufacturer's products when the manufacturer's name is very important.

Is Retailer Promotion Needed Even When the Manufacturer Emphasizes Advertising or Personal Selling?

The answer to this question is yes. Personal selling, advertising, and merchandise display done by the retailer can be quite effective. No matter how much advertising is done, the manufacturer can always benefit from high-calibre selling at the retail level. When a retail store operates on a self-service basis, dealer display is almost essential to move the product.

Should Promotional Activity be Continued When Demand is Heavy or Exceeds Capacity?

The answer is a definite yes. It is important that a manufacturer's name is kept before the public. A market is a dynamic institution, and customer loyalty is a "sometime thing." Old customers leave and new customers must be won. If conditions of high demand persist, they are certain to attract competitors. In any event, the nature of the advertising message may change. When demand is heavy in relation to supply, the advertiser will probably switch to institutional or indirect-action advertising.

Examples of
Promotional Mix

The business applications of some of the points we have just examined are reflected in Table 18-2, which shows the promotional mix used by twenty different companies. The amounts spent for advertising, sales promotion, and personal selling are shown as a percentage of sales.

The table also shows the differences in the promotional mixes used by various industries. Cosmetics and toiletries manufacturers typically rely much more heavily on advertising than on sales promotion or personal selling. These firms need to develop brand acceptance in a highly competitive national market. The personal selling cost in these industries probably stems mainly from the heavy use of manufacturer-financed demonstrator salespeople in retail stores. On the other hand, the insurance firm (number 9 in the table) relied much more on its personal sales force.

All the firms selling industrial products placed more reliance on a sales force than on advertising. Some of the firms reported a very high ratio of

Table 18-2   PROMOTIONAL COSTS AS PERCENTAGE OF SALES,
BY INDIVIDUAL COMPANY

Note the wide variations in the promotional mixes used by different firms. Compare the cosmetics firm (Number 1) and the insurance company (Number 9). In the industrial field, sales-force expenditures usually are much higher than advertising costs.

Type of Product	Advertising	Sales Promotion	Sales Force
Consumer Goods Firms			
1. Cosmetics	22.0	2.0	10.0
2. Paints	10.0	2.0	15.0
3. Soft drinks	5.0	3.0	1.0
4. Pianos	4.0	0.3	5.0
5. Baby foods	2.7	2.6	6.0
6. Hand tools	2.5	0.9	7.1
7. Appliances	2.5	1.5	4.0
8. Photographic equipment	1.3	0.7	3.0
9. Insurance	1.0	0.5	17.5
10. Textiles	1.0	1.0	0.5
Industrial Goods Firms			
11. Instruments	2.0	0.9	9.0
12. Graphic arts	1.5	0.5	16.0
13. Metal-cutting tools	1.2	n.a.	5.6
14. Industrial machinery	1.0	2.0	7.0
15. Automotive parts	1.0	0.5	4.5
16. Die cutting	1.0	n.a.	10.0
17. Hand tools	0.5	0.2	2.4
18. Textiles	0.5	n.a.	12.0
19. Automotive	0.5	n.a.	0.5
20. Plate steel fabrication	0.4	0.5	0.5

n.a.: not available.
Source: Adapted from Dale Houghton, "Marketing Costs: What Ratio to Sales?" *Printers' Ink.*, February 1, 1957, pp. 24, 54–55.

personal selling to advertising. For example, a textile manufacturer (number 18) had a 24:1 ratio, and a die-cutting firm (number 16) a 10:1 ratio.

It is extremely difficult to establish promotional appropriations. Management lacks reliable standards for determining (1) how much to spend on advertising or personal selling in total or (2) how much to spend on specific activities within each area. An even more serious problem is that management normally cannot assess the results of its promotional expenditures. A firm may decide to add ten salespeople or increase its trade-show budget by $200,000 a year. But it cannot determine what increase in sales or profits is to be expected from these moves. Nor can anyone measure the relative value of the two expenditures.

Promotional activities usually are budgeted as current operating expenses, implying that their benefits are used up immediately. Joel Dean and others have proposed that advertising (and presumably other promotional efforts) should be treated as a capital investment. Their reasoning is that the benefits and returns on these investments often (1) are not immediately evident and (2) are spread over several years.

There are four basic methods of determining the appropriation for promotion. These methods are frequently discussed in connection with the advertising appropriation alone, but they may also be applied to the total promotional appropriation.

DETERMINATION OF TOTAL PROMOTIONAL APPROPRIATION

Methods of Determining Appropriation

Relation to Income

The promotional appropriation may be related in some way to company income. The expenditures may be set as a percentage of past or anticipated sales. However, some businesses prefer to budget a fixed amount of money per *unit* of past or expected future sales. Manufacturers of products with a high unit value and a low rate of turnover (automobiles or appliances, for example) frequently use the unit method.

This percentage-of-sales method is probably the most widely used of all those discussed here. It has achieved broad acceptance because it is simple to calculate. It also sets the cost in relation to sales income and thus has the effect of being a variable expense rather than a fixed expenditure.

Actually, the method is unsound and logically inconsistent. By setting promotional expenditures on the basis of past sales, management is saying that promotion is a *result* of sales when, in fact, it is a *cause* of sales. Even when promotion is set as a percentage of *future* sales, this method is logically indefensible. By forecasting *future* sales and then setting the promotional appropriation, management is still considering advertising and personal selling to be a *result* of sales. If sales depend upon promotion, as is truly the case, they cannot be forecast until the promotional appropriation has been determined. Another undesirable result of this method is that it reduces promotional expenditures when sales are declining. And this is just when promotion is most needed.

Task or Objective

A much sounder basis for determining the promotional budget is to decide what tasks the promotional program must accomplish, and then to determine what this will cost. Various forms of this method are widely used today. The *task method* forces management to define realistically the goals of its promotional program.

Sometimes this approach is called the *buildup method* because of the way it operates. For example, as one goal, a company may elect to enter a new geographic market. The executives then decide that this venture will require ten additional salespeople. Compensation and expenses of these people will cost a total of $270,000 per year. Salary for an additional sales supervisor and expenses for extra office and administrative needs will cost $35,000. Thus, in the personal selling part of the promotional mix, an extra $205,000 must be appropriated. Similar estimates can be made for the anticipated cost of advertising, sales promotion, and other promotional tools to be used. Thus the promotional appropriation is *built up* by adding up the costs of the individual promotional tasks needed to reach the goal of entering a new territory.

Use of All Available Funds

A new company frequently plows all available funds into its promotional program. The objective here is to build sales for the first one to five years. After that period, management expects to earn a profit and be able to budget for promotion in a different manner.

Follow Competition

A weak method of determining the promotional appropriation, but one that is used enough to be noted here, is to match the promotional expenditures of competitors. Sometimes only one competitor is followed. In other cases, management will have access to industry averages through its trade association, and these will become company bench marks. The system is weak on at least two counts. First, a firm's competitors may be just as much in the dark regarding how to set a promotional budget. Second, one company's promotional goals and strategies may be quite different from those of its competitors because of differences in the firms' strategic marketing planning.

THE CAMPAIGN CONCEPT: AN EXERCISE IN STRATEGIC PLANNING

In planning the total promotional program for an organization, management should make use of the campaign concept. A **campaign** is a coordinated series of promotional efforts built around a single theme and designed to reach a predetermined goal. In effect, a campaign is an exercise in strategic planning.

Although the term *campaign* is probably thought of most often in connection with advertising, we should apply the campaign concept first to the entire promotional program. Then the total promotional campaign can be subdivided into its advertising, personal selling, and sales promotion components. These subcampaigns can then be planned in more detail, to work toward the program goal.

Many types of promotional campaigns may be conducted by a company, and several may be run concurrently. Geographically, a firm may have a local, regional, or national campaign, depending upon the available funds and objectives. One campaign may be aimed at consumers, and another at wholesalers and retailers. The stage of a product's life cycle may determine whether a pioneering or a competitive campaign will be conducted.

In developing a promotional campaign, a firm should first establish the campaign goal. This goal, and the buying motives of the customers, will determine what selling appeals will be stressed. Assume that the goal of a promotional campaign put on by an airline is to introduce its new jumbo jet service. Then the appeals might be to the customers' desire for speed, a quiet and restful trip, or fine food and courteous service. The same airline might want to increase its plane loadings of air freight. Then the ads and the personal selling might stress speed of delivery, reduction in losses due to spoilage and handling, or convenient schedules.

A campaign revolves around a central idea or focal point. This "theme" permeates all promotional efforts and tends to unify the campaign. A **theme** is simply the promotional appeals dressed up in a distinctive, attention-getting form. It expresses the product's benefits. Frequently the theme takes the form of a slogan, such as Coutts-Hallmark's "When you care enough to send the very best" or DeBeers' "A diamond is forever." Some companies use the same theme for several campaigns; others develop a different theme for each new campaign.

For a promotional campaign to be successful, the efforts of the participating groups must be coordinated effectively. This means that:

- The *advertising program* will consist of a series of related, well-timed, carefully placed ads that reinforce the personal selling and sales promotional efforts.

- The *personal selling effort* will be coordinated with the advertising program. The sales force will explain and demonstrate the product benefits stressed in the ads. The salespeople will also be fully informed about the advertising part of the campaign — the theme, the media used, and the schedule for the appearance of ads. The salespeople, in turn, should carry this information to the middlemen so that they can become effective participants in the campaign.

- The *sales promotional devices*, such as point-of-purchase display materials, will be coordinated with the other aspects of the campaign. For each campaign, new display materials must be prepared. They should reflect the ads and appeals used in the current campaign, to maximize the campaign's impact at the point of sale.

- *Physical distribution management* will ensure that adequate stocks of the product are available in all outlets prior to the start of the campaign.

REGULATION OF PROMOTIONAL ACTIVITIES

Because the primary objective of promotion is to sell something by communicating with a market, promotional activities attract attention. Consequently, abuses by individual firms are easily and quickly noted by the public. This situation in turn soon leads to (1) public demand for correction of the abuses, (2) assurances that they will not be repeated, and (3) general restraints on promotional activities. To answer this demand, regulations have been established by the federal government and most provincial governments. In addition, many private business organizations have established voluntary guideposts for the direction of promotional activities.

The Federal Role

A number of departments of the federal government administer Acts aimed at controlling various aspects of promotion, particularly advertising. The Broadcasting Act established the Canadian Radio-Television and Telecommunications Commission (CRTC) in 1968 and provided for sweeping powers of advertising regulation. Under section 16 of the Act, the Commission may make regulations concerning the character of broadcast advertising and the amount of time that may be devoted to it. While the potential for substantial control exists, the Commission did not in reality pass on each commercial message. What it has done is to delegate authority in certain fields to other agencies such as the Health Protection Branch of the Department of National Health and Welfare and the Combines Investigation Branch of the Department of Consumer and Corporate Affairs.

The Health Protection Branch deals with advertising in the fields of drugs, cosmetics, and devices (officialese for birth-control products), and it has sweeping powers to limit, control, rewrite, or ban promotion for the products under its authority. The authority itself is embodied in such Acts, and regulations associated with them, as the Health and Welfare Department Act, the Proprietary or Patent Medicine Act, the Food and Drug Act, the Criminal Code of Canada, and the Broadcast Act. The various Acts and regulations result in general types of prohibition aimed at preventing the treatment, processing, packaging, labelling, advertising, and selling of foods, drugs, and devices in such a manner as to mislead or deceive, or even be "likely to create an erroneous impression as to their character, value, quantity, composition, merit or safety."[8]

The Branch also prevents the advertising of whole classes of drugs. It has developed a list of diseases or conditions for which a cure may not be advertised under any circumstances. This prohibition stands even if a professionally accepted cure exists. The logic for the prohibition of advertising, in spite of the existence of a cure, is that the Branch does not wish members of the general public to engage in self-diagnosis of the condition that can be treated.

By virtue of the powers delegated to it by the Commission, the Branch has absolute control over radio and television advertisements for the products under its jurisdiction. All such advertisements must be submitted to it

---

[8]*Report of the Special Senate Committee on Mass Media*, vol. II, Ottawa, 1970, p. 155.

at least fifteen days prior to airing, and no medium can air an ad without its having been approved by the Branch and, thereby, the Commission. In practical terms, the Health Protection Branch, even though an appeal route to the CRTC is available, has complete authority and advertisers have no recourse of any consequence.

In contrast to the delegated review powers the Health Protection Branch has over advertisements using the broadcast media, its position with reference to the print media is weak. Its formal control is in terms of alleged Food and Drug violations, which must be prosecuted in court. Given the lack of jurisprudence in this area, the Branch is loath to go to court in case it loses and thus sets a precedent or in case its regulations (many of which have not been tested in court) are founded to be illegal. What the Branch does is advise advertisers of its opinion of advertisements that are prepared for the print media. This opinion is not a ruling, and ads submitted, as well as those that are not, are still subject to the regulations for which the Branch has responsibility. This does not mean that the Branch does not monitor the print media. Newspapers and magazines are sampled and advertisements examined.

The Department of Consumer and Corporate Affairs has substantial and major responsibility in the area of regulating promotion. The Combines Investigation Branch of the Department carries the major burden of promotional regulation. The Acts administered include: (1) the Hazardous Products Act (concerning poisonous compounds for household use), (2) the Precious Metals Marketing Act (i.e., definitions of sterling and carat weight), (3) the Trade Marks Act, (4) the Consumer Packaging and Labelling Act, and of greatest significance, (5) the Combines Investigation Act. Within the Combines Investigation Act, a number of sections pertain directly to the regulation of advertising and promotional activities. Section 35, for example, requires that manufacturers or wholesalers who offer promotional allowances to retailers must offer such allowances on proportionate terms to all competing purchasers. Section 36 of the Act regulates misleading advertising in general, while section 37 pertains specifically to "bait and switch" advertising.[9]

Section 36 of the Combines Investigation Act makes it illegal for an advertiser to make any false or misleading statement to the public in advertising or promotional materials or with respect to warranties. This section also regulates the use of false statements regarding the expected performance or length of life of a product and the use of testimonials in advertising. Section 36.2 of the Act regulates the use of "double ticketing" in retail selling and requires that, where a retailer promotes a product at two different prices or where two prices appear on a product or at the point of sale, the

---

[9]For a review of court decisions in misleading advertising cases in Canada, refer to James G. Barnes, "Advertising and the Courts," *The Canadian Business Review*, Autumn 1975, pp. 51–54. The Misleading Advertising Division of the Department of Consumer and Corporate Affairs also publishes a quarterly review of misleading advertising cases entitled the *Misleading Advertising Bulletin*. Persons interested in receiving this bulletin can have their names placed on the mailing list simply by writing to the Department of Consumer and Corporate Affairs.

retailer must sell the product at the lower of the prices. Businesses or individuals who are convicted of violating section 36 are subject to fines as large as $25,000 or to imprisonment for up to one year.

Paragraph 36(1)(*d*) of the Combines Investigation Act regulates "sale" advertising and would apply particularly to retail advertisers. Section 37 requires that an advertiser who promotes a product at a "sale" price have sufficient quantities of the product on hand to satisfy reasonable market demand. Section 37.1 prohibits an advertiser from selling a "sale" item at a price higher than the advertised "sale" price. Finally, section 37.2 regulates the conduct of contests, lotteries, and games of chance. This section requires that advertisers who promote such contests disclose the number and value of prizes and the areas in which prizes are to be distributed, and further requires that prizes be distributed on a basis of skill or on a basis of random selection.

The provisions of the Combines Investigation Act relating to misleading advertising do not apply to publishers and broadcasters who actually distribute the advertising in question to the general public, provided that these publishers have accepted the contents of the advertising in good faith. In essence, this means that a newspaper cannot be prosecuted for misleading advertising if it accepted the advertising on the assumption that its contents were not misleading. Although no newspaper can be prosecuted for misleading advertising if it accepted the advertising in good faith, there is still some question concerning whether media production departments and advertising agencies, which actually participate with the advertiser in the production of misleading advertising, might not in the future be considered jointly responsible with the advertiser for the contents of the offending advertisement. This is a question with which the Canadian courts may deal in the future.

The Provincial Role

In each of the provinces, a considerable variety of legislation exists that is aimed at controlling various promotional practices. For instance, in Ontario, various degrees of control are exercised by the Liquor Control Board of Ontario, the Ontario Board of Film Censors, the Ontario Superintendent of Insurance, the Ontario Human Rights Commission, the Ontario Securities Commission, the Ontario Police Commission, the Ontario Racing Commission, various ministries of the Ontario government responsible for financial, commercial, consumer, and transportation functions and services, and yet more. Most of the provinces have similar sets of legislation, regulatory bodies, and provincial departments. While much of the federal regulation must in the end result in argument and prosecution in a courtroom, the provincial machinery would appear to be much more flexible and potentially regulatory in nature, and if pursued, may have a more substantial effect on undesirable practices.

The powers of provincial governments in relation to the regulation of misleading advertising have been increased considerably in recent years.

Since 1974 a number of provinces have passed new legislation dealing with unfair and unconscionable trade practices. The "trade practices" Acts passed by British Columbia, Alberta, and Ontario contain "shopping lists" of practices that are made illegal by these Acts. In reality, these pieces of legislation write into law practices that have been considered illegal by federal prosecutors for a number of years. Relating to advertising, these Acts prohibit such practices as advertising a product as new when it is in fact used; advertising that fails to state a material fact, thereby deceiving the consumer; and advertising that gives greater prominence to low down payments or monthly payments rather than to the actual price of the product. The Alberta Unfair Trade Practices Act also contains a provision for corrective advertising. This provision means that a court, upon convicting an advertiser for misleading advertising, can order that advertiser to devote some or all of his advertising for a certain period to informing his customers that he had been advertising falsely in the past and to correcting the misleading information that had been communicated in the offending advertisements.

The Province of Quebec has within its Consumer Protection Act a section that regulates quite stringently advertising directed at children. This section forbids the use of exaggeration, endorsements, cartoon characters, and statements that urge children to buy. Quebec's Official Language Act also contains a number of sections that govern the uses of French and English in advertising in that province.

Regulation by Private Organizations

Several kinds of private organizations also exert considerable control over promotional practices of businesses. Magazines, newspapers, and radio and television stations regularly refuse to accept advertisements that they feel are false, misleading, or generally in bad taste, and in so doing they are being "reasonable" in the ordinary course of doing business. Some trade associations have established a "code of ethics" that includes points pertaining to sales-force and advertising activities. Some trade associations regularly censor advertising appearing in their trade or professional journals. Better Business Bureaus located in major cities all over the country are working to control some very difficult situations. The Advertising Advisory Board administers the Canadian Code of Advertising Standards and also administers, through the Advertising Standards Council, a number of other advertising codes, including the Broadcast Code for Advertising to Children (on behalf of the Canadian Association of Broadcasters) and a code regulating the advertising of over-the-country drugs, which was developed by the CAAB in cooperation with the Proprietary Association and Health and Welfare Canada.

SUMMARY

This is the first of three chapters dealing with promotion — the final major component of a company's total marketing mix (along with product planning, pricing, and distribution). Promotion is synonymous with selling. Its intent is to inform, persuade, and influence people. It is a basic ingredient in nonprice competition, and it is an essential element in modern marketing.

The three major forms of promotion are personal selling, advertising, and sales promotion.

The promotional activity in marketing is basically an exercise in communication. Fundamentally, the communication process consists of a source sending a message through a channel to a receiver. Some sort of noise is usually present, which tends to interfere with the transmission of the message. For effective promotion, marketers must understand the makeup of their communication channels and the effects of this noise.

When deciding on the appropriate promotional mix (the combination of advertising, personal selling, and other promotional tools), management should be influenced by four factors: (1) money available, (2) nature of the market, (3) nature of the product, and (4) stage of the product's life cycle. A series of questions relating to basic promotional strategy can be of help when applying the four factors to develop a promotional mix.

It is difficult to set a dollar figure for the total promotional appropriation. The most commonly used method is to set the appropriation as a percentage of sales. Unfortunately, this is an illogical method. A better approach is to decide what promotional goals are to be achieved, and then figure out how much this will cost. These funds and the promotional efforts of the firm should be coordinated into a campaign built around a single theme and designed to reach a predetermined goal.

As a result of continuous criticism, government regulations affecting promotion have been passed. The main federal laws are the Combines Investigation Act and the Broadcasting Act. The Department of Consumer and Corporate Affairs has substantial responsibility for the regulation of promotion.

KEY TERMS AND CONCEPTS

Promotional mix   470

Promotion   471

Selling   471

Advertising   471

Personal selling   471

Publicity   471

Public relations   471

Sales promotion   471

Nonprice competition   472

Using promotion to shift the demand curve   472

Communication process   475

Primary demand   479

Selective demand   479

Promotional appropriation   483

Percentage-of-sales method   483

Task or objective method   484

Promotional campaign   484

Campaign theme   485

Federal legislation regulating promotion   486

1. What is the difference between selling and marketing?

2. Explain and illustrate a communication system using the following situations:
    a. A teenage girl trying to sell her father on the idea that she should get contact lenses instead of glasses
    b. A salesperson talking to a prospect about buying a small electric automobile as a second car in the family

3. Explain how the *nature of the market* would affect the promotional mix for the following products:
    a. Oil-well drilling   c. Golf clubs
    b. Plywood   d. Cigarettes

4. Explain how the promotional mix is likely to be affected by the life-cycle stage in which each of the following products is situated.
    a. Portable electric typewriters
    b. Telephoto telephones
    c. Freeze-dried coffee

5. Using Borden's criteria, evaluate the advertisability of each of the following products. Assume that sufficient funds are available in each case.
    a. Car batteries   c. Wall mirrors
    b. Mattresses   d. Small power tools

6. Explain why personal selling is, or is not, likely to be the main ingredient in the promotional mix for each of the following products:
    a. Life insurance being considered by a young, newly married couple
    b. Living-room furniture
    c. Burglar alarm system for an industrial plant
    d. Oversized tennis rackets

7. Explain why retailer promotional efforts should or should not be stressed in the promotional mix for the following:
    a. Expensive men's suits sold through exclusive distribution
    b. Chiquita-brand bananas
    c. A line of expensive cosmetics for women
    d. Steel-belted radial tires

8. Why is the percentage-of-sales method so widely used to determine the promotional appropriation when, in fact, most authorities recognize the task or objective method as the most desirable one?

9. Identify the central idea — the theme — in some current promotional campaigns.

10. Assume you are marketing a liquid that removes creosote (and the danger of fire) from chimneys used for wood-burning stoves. Briefly describe the roles you would assign to advertising, personal selling, sales promotion, and publicity in your promotional campaign.

11. Explain the term "proportionally equal basis" in connection with manufacturers granting advertising allowances. Consider especially the situations where retailers vary in size.

12. Do you think we need additional legislation to regulate advertising? To regulate personal selling? If so, explain what you would recommend.

Chapter 19

Management of Personal Selling

CHAPTER GOALS

In this chapter we look at personal selling from both the sales manager's and the salesperson's viewpoint.
1. *The importance of personal selling in our economy and in a company's marketing program*
2. *How sales jobs are different from other jobs*
3. *The wide variety of sales jobs*
4. *The steps involved in the selling process — that is, in making a sale*
5. *The steps involved in staffing and operating a sales force*
6. *A little about the evaluation of a salesperson's performance*

Selling is essential to the health and well-being of our economic system, and it probably offers more job opportunities than any other single vocation today. Yet, personal selling is frequently criticized, and it is very hard to attract qualified young people into selling jobs. Truly, the task of managing a sales force is a difficult one. But the level of success in this task often has a direct bearing on the level of success of a company's total marketing program.

NATURE AND IMPORTANCE OF PERSONAL SELLING

The goal of all marketing efforts is to increase profitable sales by offering want-satisfaction to the market over the long run. Personal selling is by far the major promotional method used to reach this goal. The number of people employed in advertising is in the thousands. In personal selling, the number is over a million. In many companies, personal selling is the largest single operating expense, often equaling 8 to 15 percent of net sales. In contrast, advertising costs average 1 to 3 percent of sales. Expenditures for salespeople's salaries, commissions, and travel expenses, the costs of operating sales branches, and the expenses of managing these salespeople all add up to a tidy sum.

Relative Merits

Personal selling consists of individual, personal communication, in contrast to the mass, impersonal communication of advertising, sales promotion, and the other promotional tools. Consequently, compared with these other tools, personal selling has the advantage of being more flexible in operation. Salespeople can tailor their sales presentations to fit the needs and behaviour of individual customers. Also, salespeople can see the customer's reaction to a particular sales approach and then make the necessary adjustments on the spot. A second merit of personal selling is that it permits a minimum of wasted effort. In advertising, much of the cost is devoted to sending the message to people who are in no way real prospects. In personal selling, a company has an opportunity to pinpoint its target market far more effectively than with any other promotional device.

Personal selling is promotion on an individual basis.

In most situations it is personal selling that results in the actual sale. Advertisements can attract attention and arouse desire. But usually they do not arouse buying action or complete the transfer of title. And salespeople can perform for management many other services that are not strictly selling jobs. They can collect credit information, reflect customer attitudes, and relay complaints to management.

The major limitation of personal selling is its high cost. It is true that the use of a sales force enables a business to reach its market with a minimum of wasted effort. However, the cost of developing and operating a sales force is high. Another disadvantage is that personal selling is often limited by a company's inability to get the calibre of people needed to do the job. At the retail level, many firms have abandoned their sales forces and shifted to self-service for this very reason.

Nature of the Sales Job

The sales job of today is quite different from that of years gone by. The old type of salesman — the cigar-smoking, back-slapping, joke-telling man epitomized by Harold Hill in *The Music Man* and Willy Loman in *Death of a Salesman* — generally has disappeared.

True, high-pressure selling still exists and may always have a role in some fields, but it is no longer typical. Instead, to implement the marketing concept in a manufacturing firm, for example, we see a new type of salesperson — a territorial marketing manager. Rather than just push whatever the factory has to sell, our new breed of salespeople interpret customers' wants. The sales reps either fill these wants with existing products or relay the wants to the producer so that appropriate products may be developed. They engage in a *total* selling job — missionary selling, servicing customers, being territorial profit managers, and acting as a mirror of the market as they feed back marketing information.

In this new position, salespeople occupy many roles with many divergent role partners, a situation that makes heavy emotional demands on these sellers.[1] Among their other roles, they are persuaders, service people, information gatherers, expediters, coordinators, problem definers, travellers,

---

[1]This paragraph and the following one are adapted from James A. Belasco, "The Salesman's Role Revisited," *Journal of Marketing*, April 1966, pp. 6–11; see also Orville C. Walker, Jr., Gilbert A. Churchill, Jr., and Neil M. Ford, "Organizational Determinants of the Industrial Salesman's Role Conflict and Ambiguity," *Journal of Marketing*, January 1975, pp. 32–39.

Salespeople must be able to identify easily with several groups of people: the company management, their customers, and often their customers' customers.

display arrangers, and customer-ego builders. Their operations are socially, psychologically, and physically independent of the usual worker-supervisor relationship. In this performance, salespeople face role conflicts of identification and advocacy. They must identify first with their companies and then with their customers. In so doing, they are subject to conflicts regarding whose position—the company's or the customer's—they are advocating. The several groups with whom salespeople interact often have differing and conflicting expectations.

Salespeople's jobs, then, involve a wide range of behaviours and varying degrees of social contact. The emotional and interactional demands are great for two reasons: There is a high level of role conflict, and salespeople must handle the behavioural ambiguities pretty much on their own.

Sales Jobs Are Different from Other Jobs

Sales jobs usually are quite different from other jobs in several ways:

- Salespeople represent their company to the outside world. Consequently, opinions of a company and its products are often formed from impressions left by the sales force. The public ordinarily will not judge a firm by its office or factory workers.

- Other employees usually work under close supervisory control, whereas a sales force typically operates with little or no direct supervision. Moreover, to be successful, salespeople often must work hard physically and mentally. They must be creative and persistent and show great initiative — and all of this requires a high degree of motivation.

- Salespeople probably need more tact, diplomacy, and social poise than other employees in an organization. Many sales jobs require the sales person to mix socially with customers, who frequently are high-level executives. The salesperson also must display considerable social intelligence in dealing with buyers.

- Salespeople are among the few employees authorized to spend company funds. They spend this money for entertainment, transportation, and their other business expenses.

- Sales jobs frequently require a considerable amount of travelling and much time spent away from home and family. Being in the field puts salespeople in enemy territory, so to speak. There they deal with an apparently endless stream of customers who seem determined not to buy the sellers' products. These mental stresses, coupled with the physical demands of long hours and travelling, combine to require a degree of mental toughness and physical stamina rarely demanded in other types of jobs. Selling is hard work!

Salespeople as Strategic Planners

Earlier in this chapter we referred to the modern professional salesperson as a territorial marketing manager. Truly, today's sales reps may very well do much of the strategic planning for their individual territories. Salespeople typically operate with little or no direct supervision. They usually are given a reasonably well-defined geographical territory, a product mix, and a price structure. They also may have been through a company training program. They probably are assigned performance goals in the form of a sales volume, gross margin, or activity quota.

Within those general guidelines, however, the reps may have to develop their own specific strategies and tactics to reach their goals. They will make their own strategic decisions regarding (1) what target markets they will solicit, (2) how they will deal with each market segment, and (3) what particular products they will push.

Wide Variety of Sales Jobs

No two selling jobs are alike. Even when sales jobs are grouped on some basis, we find that the types of jobs and the requirements needed to fill them cover a wide spectrum. Consider, for example, the job of a soft-drink driver-salesperson who calls in routine fashion on a group of retail stores. That job is in a different world from the job of a computer salesperson who sells a system for storing and retrieving information to an automobile manufacturer. An Avon representative selling cosmetics door to door has a job only remotely related to that of an airplane manufacturer's rep selling executive-type aircraft to large firms.

A useful way to classify the many different types of sales jobs is to array them on the basis of the creative skills required in the job, from the very simple to the highly complex. One such classification is the following.[2]

---

[2]Adapted from Robert N. McMurry, "The Mystique of Super-Salesmanship," *Harvard Business Review*, March-April 1961, p. 114.

1. Positions in which the job is primarily to deliver the product — for example, a *driver-salesperson* for soft drinks, milk, or fuel oil. The selling responsibilities, if any, are secondary.

2. Positions in which the salespeople are primarily *inside order takers* — for example, retail clerks standing behind counters. Most of the customers have already decided to buy; the sales clerks only serve them. The clerks may sell through suggestion, but ordinarily they cannot do much more.

3. Positions in which the salespeople are primarily *outside order takers* going to the customers in the field — for example, wholesale hardware or office supply salespeople who call on retail stores.

4. Positions in which the salespeople are not expected or permitted to solicit orders. Their job is to build goodwill, perform promotional activities, or provide services for customers. These are the *missionary salespeople* for a distiller, for example, or the *detail salespeople* for a pharmaceutical manufacturer.

5. Positions in which the major emphasis is on the salesperson's technical product knowledge — for example, a *sales engineer*.

6. Positions that demand *creative selling of tangible products*, such as vacuum cleaners, airplanes, encyclopedias, or computers. Customers may not be aware of their need for the product. Or they may not realize how the new product can satisfy their wants better than the product they are now using. When the product is of a technical nature, this category may overlap that of the sales engineer.

7. Positions that require *creative selling of intangibles*, such as insurance, advertising services, consulting services, or communication systems. Intangibles are typically difficult to sell because they cannot easily be demonstrated.

THE STRATEGIC PERSONAL SELLING PROCESS

Sales executives are in a position to develop effective strategies for their sales force to follow, if they understand the theories underlying the interaction between buyer and seller. These theories are based upon research in the behavioural sciences and upon knowledge obtained from years of selling experience in practical market settings.

Coupling their marketing knowledge with other research findings in interaction theory, Robertson and Chase derived the following set of predictions relative to the sales process.[3]

1. The more closely matched the physical, social, and personality characteristics of customer and salesperson are, the more likely it is that a sale will result.

2. The more believable and trustworthy the customer perceives a salesperson to be, the more likely it is that a sale will result.

The closer the match, the more likely the sale.

---

[3]Thomas S. Robertson and Richard B. Chase, "The Sales Process: An Open Systems Approach," *MSU Business Topics*, Autumn 1968, pp. 49–50.

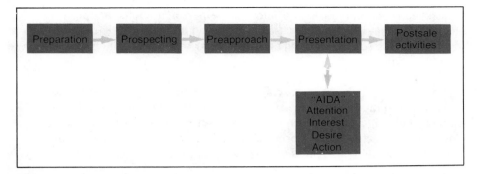

Figure 19-1
THE PERSONAL
SELLING PROCESS:
THE 5 P'S.

3. The more persuadable a customer is, the more likely it is that a sale will result.

4. The more a salesperson can make prospective buyers view themselves favourably, the more likely it is that a sale will result.

5. The second salesperson to call on a prospect will generally have an advantage over the first one.

At this point we shall summarize one procedure, or strategy, that can be used in personal selling. See Fig. 19-1 for the 5 P's that constitute the selling process.

Presale Preparation

In the chain of events that — it is hoped — will lead to a sale, the first step is to make certain that the salesperson is prepared. This means that he or she must be well acquainted with the product, the market, the competition, the techniques of selling — everything that conceivably could pertain to the sale.

Prospecting, or Locating Potential Buyers

The salesperson is now ready to locate customers. This second step toward a sale involves drawing up a profile of the ideal prospect. The salesperson can examine records of past and present customers in an effort to determine the characteristics of such prospects. From this profile the seller may develop a list of people or companies that are logical potential buyers of the product.

There are other ways in which salespeople can acquire a list of prospects. Their sales manager may prepare a list for them; present customers may suggest new leads; present users may want later or different models of the product. And a little thought will often suggest logical prospects. For instance, sellers of home furnishings or telephone equipment find prospects in the regularly published lists of building permits issued. Sellers of many products find leads among birth or engagement announcements in newspapers.

Preapproach to Individual Prospects

Before calling on prospects, salespeople should learn all they can about the persons or companies to whom they hope to sell. They might want to know what products the prospects are now using and the prospects' reactions to these products.

Salespeople should also try to find out the personal habits and preferences of the prospect. In general, salespeople should try to get all the information they can so that they will be able to tailor their presentations to the individual buyers.

Presentation   The actual sales presentation will start with an attempt to attract the prospect's attention. The salesperson will try to hold the customer's interest while building a desire for the product. Then the salesperson will try to close the sale. All through the presentation, the salesperson must be ready to meet any hidden or expressed objections that the prospect may have.

Attract Attention — The Approach

Several approaches may be used to attract the prospect's attention and start the presentation. The simplest is merely to greet the prospect and state what you are selling. While this is direct, in many situations it is not so effective as other approaches. If the salesperson was referred to the prospect by a customer, the right approach might be to start out by mentioning this common acquaintance. Sometimes this is called the "Joe sent me" approach. The salesperson might suggest the product benefits by making some startling statement. One sales-training consultant often greets a prospect with the question, "If I can cut your selling costs in half, and at the same time double your sales volume, are you interested?" A fourth approach, which can be effective if the salesperson has a new product, is simply to walk in and hand the product to the prospect. While the prospect looks it over, the salesperson can start the sales presentation.

Hold Interest and Arouse Desire

After attracting the prospect's attention, the salesperson can hold this interest and stimulate a desire for the product by means of the sales talk itself. There is no common pattern here. Usually, however, a product demonstration is invaluable. Whatever pattern is followed in the talk, the salesperson must always show how the product will benefit the prospect.

Many companies insist that their salespeople use a "canned" sales talk. That is, all representatives must give the same presentation, verbatim or with only very minor changes. Although many people may feel that this is a poor practice, it has been proved time and again that a canned sales talk can be effective. Salespeople can still project their own individual personalities, even though they all say essentially the same thing. These presentations ensure that all points are covered. They employ tested techniques, and they facilitate the sales training job considerably.[4]

Meet Objections and Close the Sale

After explaining the product and its benefits, the salesperson should try to close the sale and write up an order. As part of the presentation, the

[4]See Marvin A. Jolson, "The Underestimated Potential of the Canned Sales Presentation," *Journal of Marketing,* January 1975, pp. 75–78.

salesperson may periodically venture a *trial close* to sense the prospect's willingness to buy. By posing some "either-or" questions, a salesperson can start to bring the presentation to a head. That is, the salesperson may ask, "Would you prefer the grey or the green model?" or "Would you plan to charge this or pay cash?"

The trial close is important because it gives the salesperson an indication of how near the prospect is to a decision. A salesperson may lose a sale by talking too much. The prospect may be ready to buy at the beginning, and then have a change of mind if the salesperson insists on a full presentation. Sometimes sales are lost *simply because the representative fails to ask for the order*.

The trial close also tends to bring out the buyer's objections. A salesperson should encourage buyers to state their objections. Then the salesperson has an opportunity to answer these objections and to bring out additional product benefits or re-emphasize previously stated points.

The toughest objections to answer are those that are unspoken. A salesperson must uncover the real objections before hoping to make a sale. Another difficult situation occurs when the prospect wants to "think it over." The salesperson must close the sale then and there, or the chances are that it will be lost.

Textbooks on selling discuss different types of sales-closing techniques. The *assumptive close* is probably used as much as any other, and it can be used in a wide variety of selling situations. In this closing technique, the salesperson assumes that the customer is going to buy. So it is just a case of settling the details and asking such questions as, "When do you want this delivered?" "Is this a charge sale?" or "What colour have you decided upon?"

Postsale Activities

An effective selling job does not end when the order is written up. The final stage of the selling process is a series of postsale services that can build customer goodwill and lay the groundwork for future business. If mechanical installation is necessary, the representative should make certain the job is done properly.

In general, all these activities by the salesperson serve to reduce the customer's postdecision anxiety — or cognitive dissonance. The theory of cognitive dissonance holds that after a person has made a buying decision, anxiety (dissonance) will usually occur. This happens because the buyer knows the alternative selected has some disagreeable features, as well as advantages. Consequently, the buyer seeks reassurance that the correct choice was made. Conversely, the buyer wants to avoid anything that suggests that one of the discarded choices really would have been better.

In this final stage of the selling process, it is the salesperson's job to minimize the customer's dissonance. The salesperson should reassure the customer that the right decision was made by (1) summarizing the product's benefits, (2) repeating why it is better than the discarded alternative choices, and (3) pointing out how satisfied the customer will be with the product performance.

STRATEGIC SALES-FORCE MANAGEMENT

Management of the personal selling function is simply a matter of applying the three-stage management process (planning, implementing, evaluating) to a sales force and its activities. The process begins when the sales executives set their sales goals and do the strategic planning of sales-force activities. This step involves the forecasting of sales, preparation of sales budgets, establishment of sales territories, and setting of quotas for the salespeople.

Then the sales force must be organized, staffed, and operated so as to carry out those plans and reach the predetermined goals. The final stage — performance evaluation — includes evaluating the performance of individual salespeople, as well as appraising the total sales performance.

Sales-force management strategies are shaped and limited by a company's strategic marketing planning and its overall promotional planning. For example, a firm that relies heavily on personal selling in its promotional mix will use different sales-force strategies from those of a company that depends primarily on advertising.

As another illustration, assume that two companies both have the same marketing goal — to increase their sales volume by 30 percent over the next two years. But they may plan to use different marketing strategies to reach that goal. Company A's strategy may be to open new geographic markets and sell to new classes of customers. Company B's strategy may be to intensify its coverage of its present markets. These different marketing strategies will call for different strategies in such sales-force management activities as quota setting, training, supervision, compensation, and expense payments.

OPERATING A SALES FORCE

Most sales executives spend the bulk of their time in staffing and operating their sales forces. Consequently, in this section we shall look briefly at the major tasks that are involved in this managerial activity. These tasks are outlined in Fig. 19-2.

Selecting the Sales Force

The key to success in managing a sales force is to select good salespeople. In the authors' opinion, *personnel selection* (staffing) is the most important activity in the management process in any organization. This is true whether the organization is a sales force, an athletic team, a college faculty, a political party, or any other group.

Several benefits accrue from having a good sales-personnel selection program. First, it increases a company's chance of getting the type of sales representative it needs. This is important because there is a shortage of good salespeople, and they are hard to find. Second, when running a sales force, a sales manager's performance can be no better than the material he or she has to work with. No matter how well managed a sales force may be, if it is distinctly inferior in quality to that of a competitor, the competitor will win out. Third, if a sales force is well selected, many other tasks in sales management, such as training and supervision, are made easier. Fourth, a well-selected sales force will be more productive and will build better customer relations than a poorly chosen group.

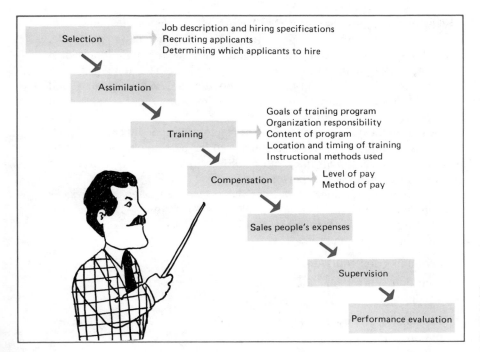

Figure 19-2
STAFFING AND
OPERATING A
SALES FORCE.

Scope of Selection Task

The three major steps in sales-force selection are:

1. Determine the number and type of people wanted. This step includes the preparation of a written job description. Management must also determine what specific qualifications are needed to fill the job as it is described.
2. Recruit an adequate number of applicants.
3. Select the qualified persons from among the applicants.

What Makes a Good Salesperson?

The key to success in the first step is to establish the proper hiring specifications, just as if the company were purchasing equipment or supplies instead of manpower. To establish these specifications, management must first know what the particular sales job entails. This calls for a detailed job analysis and a written description. It should include specific statements regarding job duties and applicant qualifications. This written description will later be invaluable in training, compensation, and supervision.

Determining the qualifications needed to fill the job is the most difficult part of the selection function. We still really do not know all the characteristics that make a good salesperson. We cannot measure to what degree each quality should be present. Nor do we know to what extent an abundance of one can offset the lack of another.

Over the years, many myths have arisen about what traits lead to success in selling. A good sales representative was supposed to be aggressive, extroverted, articulate, well groomed, and endowed with a great physique. Yet, in actual fact many outstanding salespeople have been mild-mannered and introverted. Other good ones have been somewhat inarticulate and carelessly dressed. Many good salespeople are of average or even small size.

The search for the qualities that make a good salesperson continues. As one approch, some companies have analysed the personal histories of their past sales representatives in an effort to determine the traits common to successful (or unsuccessful) performers.

One psychologist, Robert McMurry, who has worked extensively in sales management, concluded that people who are outstanding sales successes inevitably possess these traits:[5]

- A high level of energy
- Abounding self-confidence
- A chronic hunger for money, status, and the good things in life
- A well-established habit of industry
- The habit of perseverance — each objection or resistance is a challenge
- A natural tendency to be competitive

Moreover, McMurry maintains that the *sine qua non* of sales success is an intangible, largely intuitive sensitivity to people. Supersalespeople are, in effect, constant and habitual "wooers." They have an inherent flair for winning the acceptance of others.

In another approach to the question of what makes a good salesperson, Mayer and Greenberg concluded after some years of research that two personality traits are basic to sales success.[6]

1. *Empathy:* The ability to identify with customers and their feelings
2. *Ego drive*: The personal need to make a sale, and a measure of self-fulfilment and not just for the money

Recruiting Applicants

A planned system for recruiting a sufficient number of applicants is the next step in selection. A good recruiting system has these characteristics:

1. It operates continuously, not only when there are vacancies on the sales force.
2. It is systematic, reaching and exploiting all appropriate sources of applicants.
3. It provides a continuous flow of qualified applicants in greater numbers than the company can use.

---

[5]McMurry, *op. cit.*, pp. 117–118.

[6]David Mayer and Herbert M. Greenberg, "What Makes a Good Salesman?" *Harvard Business Review*, July-August 1964, pp. 119–125.

4. It is set up so that the mechanical, initial steps can be delegated and do not require the attention of the high-level executive.

Matching Applicants with Hiring Specifications

Sales managers should use all available selection tools in their effort to determine which applicants possess the desired qualifications. These tools include application banks, interviews, references, credit reports, psychological tests, and physical examinations. Probably all companies use application blanks. They serve as records of personal histories and can be used to implement interviewing.

The interview is the other most widely used selection device. Virtually no salesperson is hired without at least one personal interview, and it is desirable to have several. Ideally, these should be conducted in different physical settings and by different people. The effect of one person's possible bias is reduced by gathering several opinions. And interviewing in different locations allows interviewers to see how the recruit acts under different conditions. Usually an interview can help an employer to determine (1) how badly applicants want the job, (2) whether the company can assure them of the success they want, and (3) whether they will work to their fullest capacity. Patterned interviews are usually considered most desirable because they overcome many weaknesses found in the typical interviewing process. A patterned interview is one that is planned in advance by preparing a list of questions to ask the applicant.

Assimilating New Salespeople into the Organization

When salespeople are hired, management should pay close attention to the task of integrating them into the company family. Often this step is overlooked entirely. Potential salespeople are carefully selected and are wined and dined in order to recruit them into the firm. Then, as soon as they are hired, the honeymoon is over, and they are left to shift for themselves. In such cases, the new people often become discouraged and may even quit. A wise sales manager will recognize that the new people know very little about the details of the job, their fellow workers, or their status in the firm. A vital need exists to maintain open, two-way channels of communication between new sales personnel and management.

Training the Sales Force

Another major aspect of sales-force operation is training. New salespeople obviously need careful indoctrination and guidance. But even experienced reps need some training periodically. Setting up a training program involves answering the questions listed below. In each instance, decisions will be influenced by the kind of training program involved — indoctrination program, refresher course, or some other type.

1. What are the goals of the program? In very general terms, the aim of the program is to increase productivity and stimulate the sales force. In addition, executives must determine what specific ends they wish to accomplish. For instance, the goal may be to increase sales of high-margin items, or to improve prospecting methods for developing new accounts.

2. Who should do the training? The training program may be conducted by line sales executives, by a company staff-training department, or by outside training specialists.

3. What should be the content of the program? A well-rounded sales-training program should cover three general topics: product knowledge, information about company policies, and selling techniques.

4. When and where should training be done? Some companies believe in fully training new people before they go into the field. Others let new people prove that they have some desire and ability to sell, and then bring them back into the office for intensive training.

   Firms may employ either centralized or decentralized training programs. A centralized program may involve a periodic meeting attended by all salespeople. A decentralized program may be held in branch offices or during on-the-job training. Decentralized programs generally cost less than centralized programs. The big problem with decentralized programs is that the quality of instruction is often inferior.

5. What instructional methods should be used? The lecture method may be employed to inform trainees about company history and practices. Demonstrations may be used to impart product knowledge or selling techniques. Role playing is an excellent device for training a person in proper selling techniques. On-the-job training may be used in almost any phase of the program.

Compensating the Sales Force

To compensate their sales forces, companies offer both financial and non-financial rewards. The *nonfinancial rewards* involve opportunities for advancement, recognition of efforts, and a feeling of belonging. *Financial rewards* may take the form of *direct* monetary payment or of *indirect* monetary payment (paid vacations, pensions, and insurance plans).

Establishing a compensation system really involves decisions concerning both the *level* of compensation and the *method* of compensation. The *level* refers to the total dollar income that a salesperson earns over a period of time. The *method* refers to the system or plan by which the salesperson will reach the intended level. The level is influenced by the type of person required and the competitive rate of pay for similar positions.

There are three widely used methods of compensating a sales force: straight salary, straight commission, and a combination plan. Today, well over half the firms in the country use some kind of combination plan.

The **straight-salary** plan offers a maximum of security and stability of earnings for a salesperson. Management can expect its salespeople to perform any reasonable work assignment because they receive the same pay regardless of the task performed. Under a straight salary, the sales reps can consider the customers' best interests, and the reps are less likely to use high-pressure selling tactics.

A commonly stated drawback of the straight-salary plan is that it does not offer adequate incentive. Thus, management has the added burden of motivating and directing the salespeople. The pay plan itself does not provide any appreciable direction or control. Also, under this plan, compensation is a fixed cost unrelated to sales revenue. Straight-salary plans typically are used:

1. To compensate new salespeople or missionary salespeople.
2. When opening new territories.
3. When sales involve a technical product and a lengthy period of negotiation.

A **straight commission** tends to have just the opposite merits and limitations. It provides tremendous incentive for salespeople, and the commission costs can be related directly to sales or gross margin. Sales representatives have more freedom in their work, and their level of income is determined largely by their own efforts. On the other hand, it is difficult to control the salespeople and to get them to do a fully balanced sales job. It is particularly difficult to get them to perform tasks for which no commission is paid. There is always the danger that they will oversell customers or otherwise incur ill will. Straight-commission plans may work well if:

1. Great incentive is needed to get the sales.
2. Very little nonselling missionary work is required.
3. The company is financially weak and must relate its compensation expenses directly to sales or gross margin.
4. The company is unable to supervise the sales force.

The ideal combination plan has the best features of both the straight-salary and the straight-commission plans, with as few of their drawbacks as possible. To come close to the ideal, the combination plan must be tailored to the particular firm, product, market, and type of selling.

An important element in the financial affairs of salespeople is reimbursement for business expenses they incur in travelling or selling. The importance of sales-force expense control is difficult to overrate. It is essential that sales executives develop a plan both to control these costs and to reimburse the salespeople fairly. In principle, salespeople should not make or lose money because of their expense accounts. Nor should they forgo any beneficial sales activities because they will not be adequately reimbursed for the attendant expenses.

Supervising the Sales Force

The Supervision of a sales force is both difficult and important. It is difficult because salespeople often work where they cannot be closely and continually supervised. It is important because supervision serves both as a method of continuation training and as a device to ensure that company policies are being carried out. Still another value of sales-force supervision is that it affords a two-way channel of communication between management and the sales force. Personal supervision by a field supervisor or some other sales executive typically is the most effective supervisory method. Other methods of supervision involve the use of correspondence, reports, and sales meetings.

EVALUATING A SALESPERSON'S PERFORMANCE

Managing a sales force includes the job of evaluating the efforts of the salespeople. Until executives know what their sales force is doing, they are in no position to make constructive proposals for improvement. By studying salespeople's activities and by establishing standards of performance, management should be able to upgrade the sales force's efforts in general.

Performance analysis can help salespeople improve their own efforts. People with poor sales records may know that they are doing something wrong. But they cannot determine what it is if they have no objective standards by which to measure their performance.

Performance evaluation can be of help in determining what should be included in a training program, and it can aid in sales supervision. A supervisor who knows some of the specific strengths and weaknesses of each salesperson can do a better job of directing and training. Performance evaluation can also help management decide on salary increases and promotions for individual salespeople.

Bases for Evaluation

Both quantitative and qualitative factors should be used as the bases for performance evaluation. The quantitative bases generally have the advantage of being specific and objective. Qualitative factors, unfortunately, require the subjective judgement of the evaluators. For both types of appraisal factors, however, management has the difficult task of setting the standards against which performance can be measured.

Quantitative Bases

Sales performance should be evaluated on the basis of both input (or efforts) and output (or results). A person's selling effectiveness is a combination of the two — output as measured by sales volume, gross margin, etc., and input as indicated by call rate, nonselling activities, etc.

The importance of output factors in a performance evaluation is readily recognized. Sometimes, however, the value of input factors is underestimated. Actually, an analysis of the input factors often is effective in locating trouble spots. If a person's output performance is unsatisfactory, very often the cause lies in the handling of the various input factors over which the salesperson has control.

Some *output* (result) factors that ordinarily are quite useful as quantitative evaluation bases are:

1. Sales volume — by products, customer groups, etc.
2. Sales volume as a percentage of quota or territorial potential
3. Gross margin by product line, customer group, etc.
4. Orders:
   a. Number
   b. Average size (dollar volume)
   c. Batting average (orders divided by calls)
5. Accounts:
   a. Percentage of accounts sold
   b. Number of new accounts called on and sold

Some useful *input* (effort) factors to measure are:

1. Calls per day (call rate)
2. Direct selling expense, in dollars or as a percentage of sales volume
3. Nonselling activities:
   a. Advertising displays set up
   b. Number of training sessions held with dealers and/or distributors

One key to a successful evaluation program is to appraise the salesperson's performance on as many different bases as possible. Otherwise, management may be misled. A high daily call rate may look good, but it tells us nothing about how many orders per call are being written up. A high batting average (orders divided by calls) may be camouflaging a low average order size or a high sales volume on low-profit items.

Qualitative Bases

It would be nice if the entire performance evaluation could be based only on quantitative factors, thus minimizing the subjectivity and personal bias of the evaluators. Unfortunately, this cannot be done. Too many qualitative factors must be considered because they influence a salesperson's performance. These factors include:

1. Knowledge of the product, company policies, and the competition
2. Management of the salesperson's own time and the preparation for calls
3. Customer relations
4. Personal appearance and health
5. Personality and attitudinal factors, such as:
   a. Cooperation
   b. Resourcefulness
   c. Ability to analyse logically and make decisions

This concludes our coverage of the management of the personal selling effort in a company's promotional mix. In the next chapter we shall consider the other two widely used promotional tools — advertising and sales promotion.

SUMMARY

Personal selling is the major promotional method used in Canadian business — whether measured by people employed, by total expenditures, or by expenses as a percentage of sales. The sales job today is not what it used to be. A new breed of professional salesperson has been developing over the past few decades. Today the sales jobs are quite different from other jobs in a company. There is a variety of different sales jobs. They range from that of a driver-salesperson, through jobs like inside order takers, missionary seller, and sales engineer, to the positions that call for highly creative selling of tangible goods and intangible services.

There are five steps in the actual sale of a product or service. The first three involve presale preparation, prospecting for potential buyers, and preapproaching these prospects. Then a salesperson is ready to make a sales presentation. This fourth step involves approaching the customer and creating some customer interest. The actual sales talk may be canned or individually tailored for each prospect. The salesperson must be prepared to meet customer objections and then try to close the sale. Finally, postsale activities are needed to satisfy the customer and reduce his or her anxieties concerning the purchase.

Strategic sales-force management involves planning and operating a sales force within the guidelines set by the strategic marketing planning. The tasks involved in staffing and operating a sales force present managerial challenges in several areas. The key to successful sales-force management is to do a good job in selecting the salespeople. Then plans must be made for assimilating these new people into the company. Sales-training and supervision programs have to be developed. Management needs to set up plans for compensating salespeople and reimbursing them for their business expenses.

The final stage in strategic sales-force management is to evaluate the performance of the individual salespeople.

KEY TERMS AND CONCEPTS

New type of salesperson 493

Classification of sales jobs 495

AIDA (Fig. 19-1) 497

Presale preparation 497

Prospecting for new customers 497

Preapproach 497

The approach 498

Canned sales talk 498

Meeting objections in sales talk 498

Cognitive dissonance 499

Postsale activities 499

Sales-force selection tasks 500

Decisions in sales training 503

Financial compensation 504

Nonfinancial compensation 504

Straight-salary compensation 504

Straight-commission compensation 505

Bases for evaluating salespeople 506

QUESTIONS AND PROBLEMS

1. The cost of a double-page, full-colour advertisement in one issue of *Playboy* magazine is much more than the cost of employing one salesperson for a full year. A sales-force executive is urging her company to eliminate a few of these ads and, instead, to hire a few more salespeople. This executive believes that one good salesperson working for an entire year can sell more than one ad in one issue of *Playboy*. How would you answer her?

2. "The salesperson occupies many roles with many divergent role partners, and this entails heavy emotional demands." Explain.

3. Refer to the seven-way classification of sales jobs in this chapter, and answer the following questions:
   a. In which types of jobs is the salesperson most free from close supervision?
   b. Which types are likely to be the highest paid?
   c. Which are likely to involve the most travelling?
   d. For which jobs is a high degree of motivation necessary?

4. What information would you seek as part of your presale preparation to sell each of the following products? In each case, assume you are selling to the users of the product.
   a. Snowmobiles
   b. Desk-top office copiers
   c. Nets for public tennis courts
   d. Mopeds or motor scooters

5. What are some of the sources you might use to acquire a list of prospects for the following products?
   a. Automobiles
   b. Baby furniture
   c. Life insurance
   d. Room air conditioners

6. What can a salesperson do when customers object that the price of a product is too high?

7. "A good selection program is desirable, but not essential. Improper selection of salespeople can be counterbalanced by a good training program, by a good compensation system, or by fine supervision." Discuss.

8. What sources should be used for recruiting sales applicants in each of the following firms? Explain your reasoning in each instance.
   a. A company selling executive airplanes to a manufacturer of paper products
   b. A firm selling cosmetics door-to-door
   c. A dress manufacturer selling high-fashion dresses to department stores and exclusive specialty shops.

9. "It is best to hire experienced salespeople because they do not require any training." Discuss.

10. What factors should be considered in determining the *level* of sales compensation?

11. Compare the merits of a straight-salary plan and a straight-commission plan of sales compensation. Name some types of sales jobs in which each plan might be desirable.

12. How might a firm determine whether a salesperson is using high-pressure selling tactics that may injure customer relations?

13. How can a sales manager evaluate the ability of salespeople to get new business?

Chapter 20

Management of Advertising and Sales Promotion

CHAPTER GOALS

This chapter is a discussion of nonpersonal selling, as distinguished from the personal selling of the last chapter. After studying this chapter, you should understand:

1. *The nature of advertising and its importance in our economy and in an individual firm*
2. *The major types of advertising*
3. *How to develop an advertising campaign and select the advertising media*
4. *How to evaluate the effectiveness of advertising*
5. *Sales promotion — its nature, importance, and services rendered*

Hunters do not ordinarily use a rifle to hunt ducks. They need a device that reaches a wider area than a rifle without expending additional effort. Thus, duck hunters ordinarily use a shotgun. By the same token, mass communication is needed to reach mass markets at a reasonable cost. Advertising and sales promotion are just the tools for this job. It is too costly and time-consuming to try to do the job with salespeople alone.

NATURE OF ADVERTISING

Advertising consists of all the activities involved in presenting to a group a nonpersonal, oral or visual, openly sponsored message regarding a product, service, or idea. This message, called an **advertisement**, is disseminated through one or more media and is paid for by the identified sponsor.

We should note some important points in connection with this definition. First, there is a significant distinction between advertising and an advertisement. The advertisement is the message itself. Advertising is a process—it is a program or a series of activities necessary to prepare the message and get it to the intended market. Another point is that the public knows who is behind the advertising because the sponsor is openly identified in the advertisement. Also, payment is made by the sponsor to the media that carry the message. These last two considerations differentiate advertising from propaganda and publicity.

Marketing executives should understand the various classes of advertising because the type of advertising used depends on the company's objectives in its advertising program.

Product and Institutional Advertising

All advertising may be classed as either product or institutional. In **product advertising**, advertisers are informing or stimulating the market about their products or services. Product advertising is often further subdivided into direct-action and indirect-action advertising. With *direct-action advertising*, sellers are seeking a quick response to their advertisements. An advertisement with a coupon may urge the reader to send immediately for a free sample. *Indirect-action advertising* is designed to stimulate demand over a longer period of time. Such advertising is intended to inform customers that the product exists and to point out its benefits. The idea is that when customers are ready to buy the product, they will look favourably upon the seller's brand.

Institutional advertising is designed to create a proper attitude toward the seller and to build goodwill, rather than to sell a specific product or service. Institutional advertising may be subdivided into three subtypes:

- **Patronage.** Presents information about the advertiser's business. A retail store advertises its new store hours or a change in its delivery policy.
- **Public relations.** Presents information about the advertiser's role in the community. A manufacturer's ads tell what the company is doing to reduce the stream pollution caused by its factory.
- **Public service.** Shows the advertiser as a "good citizen." A company's ads urge the public to support a Red Cross campaign or to drive carefully.

National and Local Advertising

National (general) advertising is sponsored by manufacturers or other producers. **Local (retail)** advertising is placed by retailers. Although the terms *national* and *local* are used synonymously with *general* and *retail* in the advertising business, this is an unfortunate and inexact comparison. It is true that most manufacturers sell in more than one local market, and it is also true that a retailer's market is usually confined to one locality. As used in the trade, however, the term *national advertising* refers only to the level of the advertiser and has no relation to geographic coverage. If a manufacturer places a single ad in only one city, this is still referred to as national advertising.

Another purposeful distinction may be drawn between manufacturers' and retailers' advertising. A manufacturer's advertising is designed to build the demand for its products. The producer does not care where the items are purchased, as long as customers buy its brand. In retailers' advertising, the stress is on the store. A given retailer does not care what products or brands you buy, so long as you buy them at that retailer's store. Therefore, retailers' advertisements often feature appeals to patronage motives, showing you why it is to your advantage to buy at their particular stores.

Nature of Market

Advertising also may be classified according to the target market at which it is directed. To illustrate:

MARKET	MESSAGE
Consumer	"Buy this product for your personal use and enjoyment."
Middleman	"Buy this product to resell in your store at a profit."
Industrial user	"Buy this product to use in your business."
Professional	"Specify this product for use by your clients or patients."

Cost of Advertising   Advertising in one form or another is used by virtually all manufacturers and retailers in the country. The importance of advertising may be indicated by its cost.

Advertising Expenditures in Total and by Media

One quantitive indication of the importance of advertising is the total amount spent on advertising in Canada. In 1984, the revenues of Canadian advertising media were approximately $5 billion. Table 20-1 shows the percentage of the total accounted for by each of the major media. For years, newspapers have been the most widely used medium, based upon total advertising dollars invested. About 80 percent of the expenditures for advertising in Canadian daily newspapers goes for local and classified

Table 20-1   PERCENT SHARES OF NET ADVERTISING REVENUES BY INDIVIDUAL SECTORS IN BROADCAST AND PRINT, 1974 to 1982

	1974	1976	1978	1980	1982*
Radio	10%	11%	11%	10%	10%
Television	13	14	16	16	17
Daily newspapers	30	31	28	27	26
Weekly and other newspapers	5	5	5	6	5
General magazines	3	3	4	4	5
Business papers	3	4	3	4	4
Directories	6	6	6	6	7
Religious, school, and other publications	—	—	1	1	1
Direct mail, catalogues	21	19	20	20	20
Outdoor	8	7	7	6	6

*estimates by Maclean-Hunter Research Bureau.

Note: Totals may not add up to 100% due to rounding.

Source: Maclean-Hunter Research Bureau, *A Report on Advertising Revenues in Canada,* Toronto, November 1980.

advertising rather than for national advertising. The revenues generated by television networks and stations and periodicals have increased quite well between 1974 and 1982.

Another perspective on advertising expenditures can be obtained by some international comparisons of outlays in dollar terms, on a per capita basis, and as a proportion of Gross National Product. Table 20-2 shows these comparisons. In 1980, expenditures on advertising in the United States totalled $54.58 billion, as compared with $3.03 billion in Canada. When these amounts are translated into ratio terms, an interesting picture develops. Although some Canadians have been critical of the volume of advertising in this country, when Canadian and other advertising expenditures are compared, we find that in Canada only $127 was spent per capita on advertising in 1980, as compared with $241 per capita in the United States. In Canada, 1.27 percent of GNP is devoted to advertising expenditures as compared with slightly over 2 percent in the United States. Japan, in terms of expenditures as a percentage of GNP, is not too far behind Canada, while its per capita rate is approximately three-quarters that of ours. The United Kingdom per capita expenditure is quite similar to ours and is a much higher proportion of GNP.

Advertising Revenues as a Percentage of Company Sales

When gauging the importance of advertising, it is often more meaningful to measure expenditures against a benchmark rather than simply to look at the total in an isolated position. Frequently, advertising expenses are expressed as a percentage of a company's sales. Table 20-3 shows the fifty largest advertisers in Canada for 1983. Some of the advertisers who spend a large dollar amount on advertising actually devote a *very* small percentage of sales to advertising. Table 20-4 presents data that permit a comparison of various industries in terms of the percentage of sales devoted to advertising expenses. The data for 1965 (the last year for which Statistics Canada produced figures, but still indicative of the patterns, since 1981 U.S. data are also quite similar) show that the heaviest expenditures, on a

Table 20-2   ADVERTISING EXPENDITURES IN SEVEN MAJOR INDUSTRIAL COUNTRIES, 1980

	Total Expenditures (Millions of $U.S.)	Expenditure Per Capita ($U.S.)	Expenditure as % of GNP
United States	54,580	241	2.08
Japan	11,243	96	1.00
United Kingdom	6,620	118	1.83
West Germany	6,018	98	0.81
France	4,420	82	0.80
Italy	3,893	68	1.25
Canada	3,029	127	1.27

Source: World Advertising Expenditures, 1981, Starch INRA Hooper, Mamaroneck, N.Y., 1981, pp. 11, 16, 17.

Table 20-3   FIFTY LARGEST ADVERTISERS IN CANADA, 1983

	1983 Advertising Expenditures
1. Government of Canada	$53,006,553
2. Procter & Gamble	37,971,891
3. John Labatt Limited	37,667,366
4. Rothmans of Canada	29,879,148
5. Dart & Kraft	27,491,123
6. Ontario Government	27,172,073
7. General Motors of Canada	26,738,953
8. Nabisco Brands	25,838,150
9. The Molson Companies	24,249,966
10. General Foods	21,478,320
11. Chrysler Canada	17,440,268
12. Unilever	17,439,530
13. Kellogg Salada Canada	17,362,341
14. American Home Products	16,989,689
15. Ford Motor Co. of Canada	15,448,136
16. CP Enterprises	15,023,643
17. Imasco Holdings Canada	14,400,316
18. The Thomson Group	14,234,204
19. Warner Lambert Canada	13,280,397
20. Dairy Bureau of Canada	12,704,655
21. Quebec Government	11,810,896
22. Coca-Cola	11,480,959
23. Imperial Oil	11,271,455
24. CNR	10,574,927
25. Nestle Enterprises	10,457,697
26. Bristol-Myers Canada	10,302,115
27. Ralston Purina Canada	10,085,460
28. Gillette Canada	10,077,443
29. Canadian Tire Corporation Ltd.	9,881,186
30. Canada Packers	9,701,408
31. Bank of Montreal	9,645,206
32. Rowntree Mackintosh Canada	9,612,630
33. Macdonald Restaurants Canada	9,174,589
34. Nissan Automobile of Canada	8,812,817
35. The Irwin Group	8,632,404
36. Union Carbide Canada	8,538,157
37. Quaker Oats of Canada	8,427,292
38. Johnson & Johnson	8,208,253
39. Telecom Canada	7,660,515
40. General Mills Canada	7,633,277
41. Pepsico	7,627,794
42. Gulf Canada	7,539,662
43. Canadian Imperial Bank of Commerce	7,440,656
44. Eatons of Canada	7,440,586
45. Simpsons-Sears	7,438,125
46. Toyota Canada	7,429,001
47. Kodak Canada	7,321,950
48. Mattel Canada	7,216,851
49. Commodore Business Machine	7,100,226
50. S.C. Johnson & Son	7,095,535

Source: Marketing, vol. 89, no. 17, April 23, 1984, p. 22.

ratio basis, are by the toilet preparations (No. 29) and the soap and cleaning compounds manufacturers (No. 25). At the other extreme are the sugar refiners (No. 28) at 0.19 percent of sales and pulp and paper mills (No. 23) with 0.24 percent. It is clear from the table that, in general, the consumer goods industries are spending more per sales dollar than are industrial goods manufacturers. It is also interesting to note the change in ratios from 1954 to 1965. Pharmaceutical and medicines manufacturers (No. 22) have increased their spending ratio; the manufacturers of toys and games (No. 30) have increased spending substantially; and industries such as agricultural

Table 20-4 SELECTED ADVERTISING RATIOS, 1954 AND 1965

	Ratio of Advertising to Sales	
	1954	1965
	(%)	
1. Agricultural implement	1.20	0.98
2. Artificial ice manufacturers	0.96	0.15
3. Battery manufacturers	2.34	1.20
4. Boiler and plate works	0.91	0.36
5. Breweries	2.19	6.56
6. Broom, brush, and mop industry	2.01	2.65
7. Button, buckle, and fastener industry	0.94	1.36
8. Carpet, mat, and rug	0.87	1.11
9. Clock and watch manufacturers	3.88	6.70
10. Confectionery manufacturers	2.68	4.78
11. Distilleries	3.50	2.74
12. Electric lamp and shade	1.14	0.31
13. Flour mills	1.14	2.11
14. Foundation garments	6.38	5.42
15. Fur goods	2.55	0.26
16. Hardware, tool, and cutlery manufacturers	1.20	3.41
17. Heating equipment manufacturers	2.23	0.81
18. Hosiery mills	1.63	2.01
19. Linoleum and coated fabrics	3.26	1.27
20. Pen and pencil manufacturers	6.24	7.35
21. Petroleum refining	0.88	1.17
22. Pharmaceuticals and medicines manufacturers	6.07	8.65
23. Pulp and paper mills	0.10	0.24
24. Scientific and professional equipment manufacturers	1.32	2.06
25. Soap and cleaning compounds manufacturers	11.26	10.85
26. Sporting goods	1.80	1.37
27. Statuary, art goods, regalia, etc.	1.62	0.86
28. Sugar refineries	0.07	0.19
29. Toilet preparations manufacturers	15.86	15.22
30. Toys and games	0.95	6.50
31. Umbrella manufacturers	0.28	0.98
32. Wineries	2.89	3.99
33. Wire and wire products	0.51	0.21
34. Women's clothing factories	0.30	0.45

Source: Advertising Expenditures in Canada, 1965, cat. no. 63-216, Table 19. Reproduced with permission of Information Canada.

implements have moved in the opposite direction. Shifts such as these continue. Within each industry, of course, a variance exists, with some firms spending quite heavily compared with the industry average and others relying on nonadvertising forms of promotional variables and spending a small amount compared with the industry average.

Sometimes it may seem as if the public is bombarded on all sides by advertising; however, the total amount spent is usually small in relation to sales volume.

One representative study showed that manufacturers of consumer products spend about 3 percent of sales for advertising purposes, while manufacturers of industrial goods spend less than 1 percent. In a summary report, the Conference Board showed advertising as a percentage of sales for various types of manufacturers, retailers, and service industries. In the majority of these industries, advertising was less than 2 percent of sales.

Cost of Advertising versus Cost of Personal Selling

While we do not have accurate totals for the costs of personal selling, we do know they far surpass advertising expenditures. In manufacturing, only a few industries, such as drugs, toiletries, cleaning products, tobacco, and beverages, have advertising expenditures higher than those for personal selling. In countless companies, advertising runs from 1 to 3 percent of net sales. But, in many firms, the expenses of recruiting and operating a sales force run from 8 to 15 percent of sales.

At the wholesaling level, advertising costs are very low. Personal selling costs may run 10 to 15 times as high. Even among retailers in total — and this includes those with self-service operations — the cost of personal selling runs substantially higher than advertising.

OBJECTIVES OF ADVERTISING

Fundamentally, the only purpose of advertising is to help sell something — a product, a service, or an idea. Stated another way, the real goal of advertising is effective communication. That is, the ultimate effect of advertising should be to modify the attitudes and/or behaviour of the receiver of the message.

Specific Objectives

This broad goal of advertising is better reached by setting specific objectives that can be incorporated into individual advertising campaigns. Of course, specific advertising objectives will be determined by the company's overall marketing strategies — especially the strategies related to the firm's promotional program. A few examples of specific goals are as follows:

1. Support personal selling. Advertising may be used to open customers' doors for salespeople, and to acquaint prospects with the sellers' company (see Fig. 20-1).

2. Reach people inaccessible to the sales force. Salespeople may be unable to reach top executives, or they may not be certain who makes the buying decisions in a company. In either case, there is a good chance that these executives will read a journal that carries the ads.

Figure 20-1

(*Source:* McGraw-Hill Publications)

3. Improve dealer relations.

4. Enter a new geographic market or attract a new group of customers.

5. Introduce a new product.

6. Increase sales of a product. An advertising campaign may be designed to lengthen the season for the product (as has been done in the case of soft drinks); increase the frequency of replacement (as is done in campaigns for spark plugs and light bulbs); increase the variety of product uses; or increase the units of purchase.

7. Expand the industry's sales.

8. Counteract prejudice or substitution.

9. Build goodwill for the company and improve its reputation (a) by rendering a public service through advertising or (b) by telling of the organization behind the product.

DEVELOPING AN ADVERTISING CAMPAIGN

Once a company decides to advertise (based on the factors discussed in Chapter 18), management can get on with the job of developing an advertising campaign. An advertising campaign is simply one part of a total promotional campaign — identified in Chapter 18 as an exercise in strategic planning. It is a coordinated series of promotional efforts built around a central theme and designed to reach a specific goal.

Initial Planning

The planning in an *advertising* campaign must be done within the framework of the overall strategic marketing plan and the *promotional* campaign planning. Therefore, at the time the advertising campaign is being planned, presumably management already has made decisions in several areas. For example, the specific promotional goals have been established. Also, management has decided what the central campaign theme will be, and what appeals will be stressed in light of consumer buying motives and habits. The total promotional appropriation has been determined and has been allocated among the various promotional tools. And the role of advertising in the promotional campaign has been determined. Management can now make decisions involving (1) the selection of the advertising media and (2) the creation and production of individual advertisements.

Selecting the Media

Three levels of decision making are required in the selection of advertising media. First, management must determine what general types of media to use. Will newspapers, television, or magazines be used? Second, if magazines are to be used, will they be of the special-interest type (for example, exploration magazines such as *Equinox*, or business magazines such as *Canadian Business*), or of the general-interest type? Finally, the specific medium must be chosen. The company that decides first on radio and then on location stations now must decide what specific station to use in each city. Some of the factors to consider in making media decisions are as follows:

1. *Objective of the advertisement.* Media choices are influenced both by the purpose of a specific advertisement and by the goal of an entire campaign. For example, if the goal of the campaign is to generate appointments for salespeople, the advertising company will probably use direct mail. If an advertiser wants to place an ad inducing action within a day or two, newspapers or radio may be used. Magazines are not so good for this purpose, because the ad must be placed weeks before the date of publication.

2. *Media circulation.* Media circulation must match the distribution patterns of the product. Consequently, the *geographic* scope of the market will influence the choice of media considerably. Furthermore, media should be selected that will reach the desired *type* of market with a minimum of waste circulation.

    Today many media—even national and other large-market media—can be targeted at smaller, specialized market segments. This reduces waste circulation for an advertiser. For example, some national magazines publish regional editions. Trade and professional journals exist in many fields. Large metropolitan newspapers publish suburban editions and regional editions within the big city. Some radio stations specialize in rock, country, middle-of-the-road, or classical music.

3. *Requirements of the message.* The medium should fit the message. For example, meat products, floor coverings, and apparel are ordinarily best presented in pictorial form. If the advertiser can use a very brief message, as is possible in advertising salt, beer, or sugar, then billboards may be the best choice.

4. *Time and location of buying decision.* The medium should reach prospective customers near the time they make their buying decisions and the places where they make them. For this reason, outdoor advertising often does well for gasoline products. Many grocery store ads are placed in newspapers on Wednesdays or Thursdays in anticipation of heavy weekend buying.

5. *Cost of media.* The costs of the advertising media should be considered in relation to (a) the amount of funds available and (b) the circulation of the media. In the first instance, the amount of funds available could rule out television as a choice. Or, possibly the advertiser can afford local television but not a national network. On the second count, the advertiser should try to develop some relationships between the cost of the medium and the size of the audience it will reach.

Characteristics of Major Types of Media

In the process of selecting the media to use in a campaign, management must consider the advertising characteristics of the main classes of media. The term *characteristics* is carefully chosen instead of *advantages* and *disadvantages*. To illustrate, one characteristic of radio as an advertising medium is that it makes its impression through the ear. For many products, this feature is an advantage. For products that benefit from a colour photograph, however, this characteristic of radio is a drawback.

Newspapers   As an advertising medium, newspapers are flexible and timely. They can be used to cover one city or several urban centres. Ads can be cancelled on a few days' notice or inserted on one day's notice. Newspapers also give an advertiser an intense coverage of a local market because almost everybody reads newspapers. The local feature also helps in that the ads can be adapted to local social and economic conditions. Circulation costs per prospect are low. On the other hand, the life of a newspaper advertisement is very short.

Magazines   Magazines are an excellent medium when high-quality printing and colour are desired in an advertisement. Magazines can be used to reach a national market at a relatively low cost per prospect. Through the use of special-interest magazines or regional editions of national magazines, an advertiser can reach a selected audience with a minimum of waste circulation. Magazines are usually read in a leisurely fashion, in contrast to the

SPECIAL-INTEREST
MAGAZINES REACH
SELECTED
AUDIENCES.

(*Source:* A Gregg/McGraw-
Hill publication.)

haste with which other print media are read. This feature is particularly valuable for the advertiser who must present a message at some length. Some of the less favourable characteristics of magazines are their inflexibility and the infrequency with which they reach the market, as compared with other media.

Direct Mail   Direct mail is probably the most personal and selective of all the media. Because it reaches only the market that the advertiser wishes to contact, there is a minimum of waste circulation. Direct mail is not accompanied by articles or other editorial matter, however, unless the advertiser provides it. That is, most direct mail is pure advertising. As a result, a direct-mail ad creates its own circulation and attracts its own readers. The cost of direct mail per prospect reached is quite high compared with other media. But other media reach many people who are not real prospects and thus have higher waste-circulation costs. A severe limitation of direct mail is the difficulty of getting and maintaining good mailing lists. Direct-mail advertising also suffers from the stigma of being classed as "junk mail."

Radio   Radio is enjoying a renaissance as an advertising and cultural medium and as a financial investment. When interest in television soared, radio audiences (especially for national network radio) declined so much that people were predicting radio's demise. But for the past ten years or so, this medium has been making a real comeback. Local radio (as contrasted with national networks) is especially strong. To a large extent, new developments in programming and technology have led to this revival of interest in radio.

As an advertising medium, radio's big advantage is its relatively low cost. You can reach almost 100 percent of the people with radio. At the same time, with special-interest programming, some segmented target markets can be pinpointed quite effectively.

On the other hand, radio makes only an audio impression. So it is useless where visual impact is needed. As with direct mail, radio advertisers must create their own audiences. And the exposure life of a given radio message is extremely short. Also, audience attention often is at a low level, especially when the radio is being used mainly to provide background for driving, studying, or some other activity.

Television   Television is probably the most versatile medium. It makes its appeal through both the eye and the ear; products can be demonstrated as well as explained. It offers considerable flexibility in terms of the geographic market covered and the time of message presentation. By making part of its impression through the ear, television can take advantage of the personal, dramatic impact of the spoken word.

On the other hand, television is an extremely expensive medium. The message is not permanently recorded for the message receiver. Thus the prospect who is not reached the first time is lost forever, as far as a particular message is concerned. Television does not lend itself to long advertising copy, nor does it present pictures so clearly as magazines do. As with direct mail and radio, television advertisers must create their own audiences.

Outdoor   Outdoor advertising is a flexible and relatively low-cost medium. Because it reaches virtually the entire population, it lends itself nicely to widely used consumer products that require only a brief selling statement. It is excellent for the reminder type of advertising, and it carries the impact of large size and colour. There is flexibility in geographic coverage and in the intensity of market coverage within the area. However, unless the advertised product is a widely used consumer good, considerable waste circulation will occur. While the cost of reaching an individual prospect is low, the total cost of a national campaign is quite high. There also is considerable public criticism of the clutter and landscape-defacing aspects of outdoor advertising.

Creating the Advertisements

Remember once again that the main purpose of advertising is to help sell something and that the ad itself is a sales message. The ad may be a high-pressure sales talk, as in a hard-hitting, direct-action ad. Or it may be a very long-range, low-pressure message, as in an institutional ad. In any case, it is trying to sell something. Consequently, it involves the same kind of selling procedure as sales talks delivered by personal salespeople. That is, the ad must first attract attention, and then hold interest long enough to stimulate a desire for the product, service, or idea. Finally, the ad must move the prospect to some kind of action.

Creating an advertisement involves the tasks of writing the copy, selecting the illustrations, preparing the layout, and arranging to have the advertisement reproduced for the selected media.

The **copy** in an advertisement is defined as all the written or spoken material in it. Copy includes the headline, coupons, and advertiser's name and address, as well as the main body of the message. The **illustration** is a powerful feature in a printed advertisement. Probably the main points to consider with respect to illustrations are (1) whether they are the best alternative use of the space and (2) whether they are appropriate in all respects to the ad itself. The **layout** is the physical arrangement of all the elements in an advertisement. A good layout can be an interest-holding device as well as an attention getter. It should lead the reader through the entire advertisement in an orderly fashion.

EVALUATING THE ADVERTISING EFFORT

As part of the management of its advertising program, a company should carefully evaluate the effectiveness of (1) what has been done and (2) what is planned for the future.

Importance of Evaluation

Advertising typically is one of the most highly criticized parts of our marketing system. While advertising has been improved greatly through the years, much still remains to be done. We need to increase the effectiveness of advertising, and we must find better ways to evaluate this effectiveness. Management needs to test advertising, to know not only *which* ads are better than others, but also *why* they are better.

Shrinking profit margins and increasing competition, both foreign and domestic, are forcing management to appraise all its expenditures carefully. Top executives want more proof than they now have that advertising really does pay. They want to know whether dollars spent on advertising can be associated with proportionately as many sales as dollars spent on other activities.

Difficulty of Evaluation

It is very difficult to measure the effectiveness of advertising. One problem is our inability to identify the results of any given advertisement or even an entire campaign. Except in the case of mail-order advertising, we cannot attribute a given unit of sales to any specific advertisement or campaign. By the very nature of the marketing mix, all elements—including advertising—are so intertwined that measurement of any one by itself is impossible. Many factors besides advertising influence sales success.

Essentially, there are only two parts to an advertisement—*what* is said and *how* it is said.[1] One part deals with product attributes to be explained, and the other is made up of the headlines, illustrations, and layouts. A great deal has been done to improve the manner of presentation (the "how"). This has been possible because research has been able to establish criteria to measure its effectiveness. The most commonly used evaluation methods measure the number of people who note, read, and remember the advertisements. But little has been done to aid management in its evaluation of the "what" part of an ad.

---

[1] Clarence E. Eldridge, "Advertising Effectiveness: How Can It Be Measured?" *Journal of Marketing*, January 1958, pp. 242–243.

> "I know that about half of my advertising is wasted, but I don't know which half."
>
> "I spent $2 million for advertising, and I don't know if that is half enough or twice too much."
>
> — John Wanamaker

Many individual advertisements, and even entire campaigns, do not aim primarily at immediate sales results. For example, some advertisements simply announce new store hours or new service policies. Other institutional advertising is intended to build goodwill or to create a company image. It is very difficult to measure the effectiveness of these kinds of advertising.

Methods Used to Measure Effectiveness

In spite of the difficulties, advertisers do attempt to measure advertising effectiveness simply because they must do so — some knowledge is better than none at all. The effectiveness of an advertisement may be tested before the advertisement is presented to the public, while it is being presented, or after it has completed its run. The sales results test attempts to measure the sales volume stemming directly from the advertisement or series of advertisements being tested.

Most other types of tests are *indirect* measurements of effectiveness. One group consists of tests called "readership," "recognition," or "recall" tests. They involve showing respondents part or all of a previously run advertisement. This is done to determine (1) whether the ad was read, (2) what parts in it were remembered, and (3) whether the respondent knows who sponsored it. The theory underlying these tests is this: The greater the number of people who see, read, and remember an advertisement, the greater will be the number who do as the advertisement urges them. Another type of test involves measuring the number of coupons or other forms of inquiries that were received from certain advertisements.

Sometimes marketing people use a consumer panel to appraise a group of advertisements. With respect to radio and television advertising, several techniques are used to measure the size and makeup of program audiences. The theory is that the number of people who will buy the sponsor's products varies proportionately with the number who watch or hear the program.

The basic goal of advertising is to help sell something — to modify consumer attitudes or behaviour. Note, however, that most tests measure effectiveness through some variable other than sales. We should be more concerned with measuring advertising's ability to influence attitudes and behaviour than with measuring consumers' recall of given advertisements.

ORGANIZING FOR ADVERTISING

Now let's consider the organization needed to perform and manage the advertising activities in a company. Management has three alternatives. It may (1) develop a company advertising campaign, (2) use an outside advertising agency, or (3) use both a company department and an advertising agency. Regardless of which alternative is selected, generally the same specialized skills are needed to do the advertising job. Creative people are needed to do the copywriting, generate the illustrative material, and prepare the layouts. Media experts are needed to select the appropriate media, buy the time and space, and arrange for the scheduled appearance of the ads. Managerial skills are needed to plan and administer the entire advertising program.

Within the Company

All these advertising tasks, only some of them, or none of them can be performed within a company department. When advertising is a substantial part of the marketing mix, a company is likely to have its own advertising department. The head of this department should report to the marketing manager, if the company is to implement the marketing concept. Large retailers, for example, often have their own advertising departments and do not use an advertising agency at all.

Advertising Agency

Many companies, especially producers, use an advertising agency to do some or all of the advertising job. An **advertising agency** is an independent company set up to render specialized services in advertising in particular and in marketing in general. Today, the term *agency* is a misnomer. These firms are not agents in the legal sense but, instead, are independent companies.

Many agencies offer a broad range of services. In the field of advertising alone, they plan and execute entire advertising campaigns. In radio and television, some agencies produce the entertainment as well as the commercials. Many of these firms are becoming *marketing* agencies, offering services that heretofore were performed by other outside specialists or by the advertisers themselves.

Why Use Both a Department and an Agency?

Many producers have their own advertising department but also use an advertising agency. The advertising department acts as liaison between the agency and the company. It approves the agency's plans and advertisements, and has the responsibility of preparing and administering the advertising budget. The department also handles direct-mail advertisements, dealer displays, and other activities not handled by an agency.

Using an agency along with a department has other advantages for a company. The agency usually has more advertising specialists than does the company. Also, a company can benefit from the agency's experience with many other products and clients. An agency often can do more for the same amount of money, because the agency can spread the costs of its staff over many accounts.

SALES PROMOTION

In Chapter 8, *merchandising* and *sales promotion* were called the two most loosely used terms in the marketing vocabulary. What, then, is sales promotion? The American Marketing Association says its preferred definition is: "those marketing activities, other than personal selling, advertising, and publicity, that stimulate consumer purchasing and dealer effectiveness, such

SHOWS FEATURING CONSUMER PRODUCTS BOTH INFORM POTENTIAL CUSTOMERS AND STIMULATE BUYER INTEREST.

(*Ray Ellis/Photo Researchers, Inc.*)

as displays, shows and expositions, demonstrations, and various noncurrent selling efforts not in the ordinary routine."[2] In effect, a major function of sales promotion is to serve as a bridge between advertising and personal selling — to supplement and coordinate efforts in these two areas.

Traditionally, advertising has been the "glamorous" promotional tool, attracting much managerial attention in many firms. In contrast, the sales promotion manager of a major oil company once referred to sales promotion as "muddled, misused, and misunderstood." But this situation seems to be changing. In recent years, expenditures for sales promotion have increased more rapidly than outlays for advertising. Currently, annual expenditures for sales promotion are estimated to parallel or exceed those for advertising. Sales promotion is also being integrated into the total marketing strategy in many firms. It is being introduced at the inception of a campaign, and not tacked on afterward.

Changes in the marketing environment are exerting upward pressure on the demand for sales promotion. As the number of brands increases, for example, the competitive pressures for display space in retail stores intensify for manufacturers. These forces increase retailers' demands for more sales promotional effort from their suppliers.[3]

Importance of Sales Promotion

---

[2]Committee on Definitions, *Marketing Definitions: A Glossary of Marketing Terms*, American Marketing Association, Chicago, 1960, p. 20. In this set of definitions, however, the American Marketing Association also observes that in retailing, sales promotion is interpreted to cover "all methods of stimulating customer purchasing including personal selling, advertising, and publicity." Thus, in retailing, *sales promotion* is used in a broad sense and is virtually synonymous with *promotion*, as the term is used in this book and also by most manufacturers.

[3]For an excellent review of the status of sales promotion and the management of sales-promotional activities, see Roger A. Strang, "Sales Promotion — Fast Growth, Faulty Management," *Harvard Business Review*, July–August 1976, pp. 115–124.

Today, much consumer dissatisfaction with respect to retail selling could be alleviated by a good sales promotion program. The trend away from the use of retail salespeople — and toward self-service — also points up the need for sales promotion. Sales-promotional devices are often the only promotional materials available at the point of purchase. Advertising media reach potential customers at their homes, at their places of business, or in their travels. When the time for buying arrives, the impact of the advertisements may have worn off (or the prospect may not even have seen the advertisement). However, sales-promotional devices at the point of purchase inform, remind, or otherwise stimulate the buyer. People who see the promotional devices are excellent prospects. They are usually in a buying frame of mind, or they would not be in that store.[4]

Services Rendered by Sales Promotion

The sales promotion personnel of a manufacturer may work with three different groups — consumers, dealers and distributors, and other sections of the marketing department. Similarly, retailers engage in sales-promotional activities aimed at consumers. A manufacturer's sales-promotional program that is directed toward consumers may be divided into two groups of activities — those intended to *inform* consumers and those intended to *stimulate* them. To inform consumers, companies will prepare booklets, give demonstrations, and offer free consulting services. To stimulate consumers, many firms give away samples and premiums or conduct contests. In recent years, there has been a real boom in the consumers' use of "cents-off" and refund coupons issued by manufacturers.

Services rendered to dealers and distributors include such activities as conducting training programs for the middlemen's sales forces, giving managerial advice, and installing point-of-purchase displays. The objective is to increase the dealers' interest in the product and thus enhance their effectiveness as merchants.

Within the manufacturer's marketing department, the sales promotion division can prepare sales manuals, demonstration kits, and other selling aids used by the salespeople. Also, in the field, the sales force can concentrate on product selling, while the sales-promotion people do all the missionary work with dealers. The sales-promotion department can aid the advertising people by preparing displays and other point-of-purchase advertising materials.

For all these reasons, marketing managers must carefully consider the role that sales promotion can play in the marketing mix. The activity should not be submerged in other departments that are concerned primarily with advertising or the personal sales force.

SUMMARY

Advertising is the impersonal-selling, mass-communications component in a company's promotional mix. The company has the option of running product or institutional types of advertising. The product ads may call for

---

[4]For a study on the promotional effectiveness of various types of in-store signs, see Gary F. McKinnon, J. Patrick Kelly, and E. Doyle Robinson, "Sales Effects of Point-of-Purchase In-Store Signing," *Journal of Retailing*, Summer 1981, pp. 49–63.

direct or indirect action. Another useful classification of advertising is national-local (or manufacturer-retailer). Advertising expenditures are large in total, but the cost of advertising in a firm is only 1 to 3 percent of sales, on the average. This is considerably less than the average cost of personal selling. Most advertising dollars are spent in newspaper media; second place goes to television.

Management should develop an advertising campaign as part of the firm's total promotional program. The first step here is to set the specific goals for the particular campaign. A major task in developing a campaign is to select the advertising media — both the broad media class and the specific individual media. The selection should be based on the characteristics of the media and the way they fit the product and the market. The advertising message — as communicated to the market through the advertising copy, illustrations, and layout — is an integral part of a campaign.

A particularly important, yet difficult, task in advertising management is to measure (evaluate) the effectiveness of the advertising effort — both the entire campaign and individual ads. Several methods are widely used. However, except for the sales results test, the commonly used techniques measure only the extent to which the ad was read or remembered.

To operate an advertising program, a firm may use its own advertising department, retain an advertising agency, or combine the two organizational structures. Sales promotion is the third major promotional tool, and the one used to coordinate and supplement the advertising and sales-force programs.

KEY TERMS AND CONCEPTS

Advertising   510

An advertisement   510

Product advertising   511

Institutional advertising   511

National (manufacturer) advertising   511

Local (retail) advertising   511

Advertising campaign   518

Advertising media   518

Advertising copy and layout   522

Sales results test   523

Readership or recall tests   523

Advertising agency   524

Sales promotion   524

QUESTIONS AND PROBLEMS

1. How do you account for the variation in advertising expenditures as a percentage of sales among the different types of companies in Table 20-4?

2. Several specific objectives of advertising were outlined early in the chapter. Bring to class some advertisements that illustrate at least four of these goals. Or, be prepared to describe a current radio or television advertisement that is an attempt to achieve these objectives.

3. Which advertising medium is best for advertising the following products?
   a. Life insurance
   b. Plastic clothespins
   c. Auto seat covers
   d. Suntan lotion
   e. Women's hosiery
   f. Industrial valves and gauges

4. Many grocery products manufacturers and candy producers earmark a good portion of their advertising appropriations for use in magazines. Is this a wise choice of media for these firms? Explain.

5. Why do department stores use newspapers so much more than local radio as an advertising medium?

6. Why is it worthwhile to pretest advertisements before they appear in the media? Suggest a procedure for pretesting a magazine ad.

7. What procedures can a firm use to determine how many sales dollars resulted from a given ad or from an entire campaign?

8. Many advertisers on television use program ratings to determine whether to continue the sponsorship of a program. These ratings reflect the number of families that watch the program. Are program ratings a good criterion for evaluating the effectiveness of advertising? Does a high rating indicate that sales volume will also be high? Discuss.

9. If a manufacturing firm finds a good advertising agency, should it discontinue its own advertising department?

10. Visit a supermarket, a clothing store, and a hardware store, and then make a list of all the sales-promotional devices that you observed in each store. Which of these devices do you feel are particularly effective?

11. Is sales promotion effective for selling expensive consumer products such as houses, automobiles, or backyard swimming pools? Is your answer the same for expensive industrial products?

12. Explain how sales promotion can be used to offset weaknesses in personal selling in retail stores.

Designing a Promotional Program

Eric Hale, the chief marketing executive for Skyways Pacific, was wondering what promotional program he should adopt to increase business on his company's flights to the South Pacific. Skyways was a major airline with both domestic and international routes. Its domestic flights served large cities in Canada, and it had flights to several foreign countries including Australia and New Zealand. During the past three years, Skyways Pacific, like virtually all major international airlines, had posted a net loss.

Within the company, the South Pacific route also operated at a net loss. However, management definitely intended to continue flying the South Pacific routes for two major reasons. First, these routes covered their marginal costs and contributed greatly to the company's much-needed cash flow. Second, management viewed the South Pacific — especially Australia and New Zealand — as growth markets with much potential for Skyways Pacific. Eric Hale said, "Now all we have to do is figure out how to achieve this revenue potential, and at a profit."

Skyways flew several times a week from Vancouver to Auckland, New Zealand, and from Vancouver to Sydney, Australia. Each of these routes included an intermediate stop in Honolulu, Hawaii. Four years ago, Skyways bought a new series of McDonnell-Douglas DC-10 aircraft that could fly nonstop from Honolulu to either Auckland or Sydney. Prior to that time, Skyways' planes had to stop for refueling at Pago Pago or at Nadi, Fiji.

Skyways' main competitors on the South Pacific routes were Qantas Airways, Air New Zealand, Continental Airlines, and Pan American Airlines. Qantas and Air New Zealand were owned by their respective governments. When matched against these airlines in Australia or New Zealand, Skyways faced some competitive disadvantages in scheduling, routing, and equipment. For example, Air New Zealand flew to Auckland more frequently than Skyways did, and Qantas had more flights to Sydney. Pan American also had more flights to Auckland than Skyways, and a better mix of nonstop and one-stop service. For flights to or from other cities in Australia and New Zealand (besides Sydney and Auckland), Qantas and Air New Zealand had feeder flights. But Skyways could use *only* the Auckland and Sydney airports.

All Skyways' major competitors used the Boeing 747 aircraft on the South Pacific Routes. On long-haul flights, these planes provided larger passenger capacity, lower seat-mile cost, and the opportunity to use lounges and sleeper chairs.

Skyways Pacific's major competitive advantage was that it had a large domestic route system in Canada to provide feeder flights to the south.

This was a big factor in Skyways' favour because the Canada–South Pacific round-trip passengers originated far more often in Canada than in either Australia or New Zealand.

To get some background information for his promotional program, Hale reviewed some of the findings from marketing research studies. Currently, the company had a market share of 20 to 25 percent for air travel between Canada and Sydney or Auckland. Visitors from Canada tended to be older (over 45), affluent (over $30,000 annual income), travelling with someone else (usually a spouse), and travelling for pleasure (75 percent as against 25 percent for business). Travellers northbound from the South Pacific to Canada had basically those same characteristics. Air travel to the South Pacific was highly seasonal, with the peak occurring during the Northern Hemisphere winter.

Regarding a passenger's choice of a specific airline, Skyways Pacific's research showed that four factors were decisive. The first two were the routes (does the airline go where you want to go?) and the flight schedules (are they convenient?). The third factor — and a very important one for long-distance flights — was the ticket price. Finally, travel agents played a very significant role in a person's choice of airlines to the South Pacific. Some 75 to 80 percent of Skyways' South Pacific passengers bought their tickets through a travel agent.

Skyways' passenger traffic to the South Pacific did not meet the company's expectations. Several reasons were advanced for this poor performance. In the early 1980s, all major airlines had experienced a recession, escalating costs, depressed traffic, and uncertainties brought about by airline deregulation.

Hale further pointed out that Skyways was often identified as a domestic and North American carrier. The company was better known for its multistop routes to many places in Canada and the United States than for its long-haul routes over the Pacific. Consequently, travel agents did not always think of Skyways as a passenger carrier to Australia or New Zealand. Hale realized that this had a devastating effect on Skyways' South Pacific business, because travel agents accounted for such a large percentage of this business. Another problem was that many people (including travel agents) were not aware that Skyways now had the planes to fly nonstop from Honolulu to Auckland or Sydney.

As with most airlines in the 1980s, a significant percentage of Skyways' passengers bought tickets at various discounted fares. It was difficult to fill seats at the regular higher fares. At one point, Skyways tried to penetrate the South Pacific market by introducing *considerably* lower fares. However, this move was blocked by the Australian and New Zealand governments as they sought to protect the market position of Qantas and Air New Zealand.

Hale realized that his company needed an effective promotional program to strengthen its market position. Even though they were operated at a net loss, the South Pacific routes did bring in a considerable amount of cash. Furthermore, any additional plane seats sold contributed heavily to profits. Approximately the same costs are incurred whether a plane is 30 percent, 60 percent, or 100 percent full. Hale felt that the South Pacific market was in the early part of its growth stage. Consequently, he wanted to firmly establish Skyways Pacific's position in this market before a wave of new competitors entered the scene.

To stimulate increased passenger traffic on its South Pacific routes, Hale knew that Skyways would require a major promotional program with heavy promotional expenditures. Yet, the company's current financial situation was such that funds for promotion must be allocated carefully and used effectively. Hale received several suggestions, some of which were conflicting, from other company executives. For example, regarding the target market, one executive urged Hale to increase sales by persuading travellers to switch from competing airlines to Skyways. Hale himself felt that Skyways should seek to expand the total market for South Pacific travel — in other words, to expand primary demand. That is, Hale would promote the destinations (Australia and New Zealand) rather than just the carrier.

Another executive suggested that the company capitalize on its reputation for trained, courteous personnel, on-time flights, and generally high-quality service. Among those passengers who knew Skyways, the company enjoyed a fine reputation for its service. This same executive also suggested that Hale should cut down on promotion to ultimate consumers and concentrate his promotional efforts on travel agents.

Eric Hale's proposals for next year's promotional program were due in the president's office in two weeks.

Question

What promotional program should Skyways Pacific use to stimulate increased passenger use of its South Pacific routes?

Determining the Promotional Mix

Case 22
The Stork
and Cradle
Shop

The owners of the Stork and Cradle Shop, Sybil and Brad Arnett, were analysing the operating results covering the eight-month period since they opened their new store. Because these results were not up to their expectations, Sybil and Brad realized they had to do something to increase (1) the customer traffic in the store and (2) the sales volume.

The Stork and Cradle Shop was a small store specializing in clothes for very young children — infants up to six-year-olds. The store was located in a large shopping centre in a western suburb of Toronto. The store did *not* have a prime location in this shopping centre. It was situated in one of the walkways off the main mall, and thus was separated from the mainstream of mall shopper traffic.

Because each of the Arnetts held another full-time job, they did not have time to operate the Stork and Cradle Shop. They had hired Brenda Toyad, aged 30 and a long-time family friend, to run the store and to handle some of the managerial duties. Brenda had no previous managerial experience, but she had worked in a small clothing store for the past three years. Later, Brenda hired a younger woman to work as a sales clerk and to help in other store activities.

The Stork and Cradle Shop carried a line of infant clothes such as pyjamas, small outfits, and booties. The store also carried infant items such as diapers, blankets, and food-warming dishes and utensils. It also offered clothes for older preschool children. Among the brands sold were Levis and a line of Buster Brown clothes and shoes. In addition, toys and stuffed animals were sold in the store.

Sybil and Brad estimated they needed a sales volume that would average $5,000 per month to break even. The gross margin on this volume would be about $2,000 a month. Earlier they had obtained a bank loan for $10,000 to buy the initial inventory. The rent on the store was $700 per month, and they paid $200 per month for an advertisement in the Yellow Pages of the telephone directory. Payroll, utilities, and other expenses ran to about $1,000 per month.

Since its opening, the store had averaged less than $5,000 a month in sales. In fact, December was the only month in which sales volume was satisfactory. Sales varied considerably by product line. Toys and stuffed animals sold well. Sales of infant clothes had been disappointing, but other infant items (blankets, food warmers, and so on) had sold well. Sales of clothing for preschool children were only fair.

The competition facing the Stork and Cradle Shop came primarily from the two department stores in the shopping centre, and from two other department stores located in another major shopping centre just two miles away. Stork and Cradle accepted Master Card and Visa credit cards, and the shop's prices were comparable to prices in the department stores. Another competitor was a nearby K Mart discount store, where prices were slightly lower than at the Stork and Cradle.

Except for the month of December (Christmas), sales volume had been below the Arnett's expectations. The two department stores in the shopping centre did generate a large amount of customer traffic, but not enough of this traffic was going into the Stork and Cradle Shop. Part of the problem was the store's location — off the main mall. To offset this limitation, the Arnetts placed a sign in the main mall to direct customers to their shop. The sign had little effect, apparently, because customer traffic increased only slightly.

The Arnetts believed that they had to increase their promotional efforts to offset the department store and K Mart competition, and to generate additional customer traffic and sales volume. Both Sybil and Brad felt that they needed to develop a store theme, such as "A specialty shop especially for your special baby." This would give parents and grandparents more reason to shop at the Stork and Cradle. The Arnetts wanted to communicate to the public the benefits of the personal service, the warm friendly atmosphere, and the product expertise that people would receive at the Stork and Cradle.

To date, the store's only advertising had been a small "grand opening" ad in local newspapers and the continuing ad in the Yellow Pages. Otherwise, the Arnetts relied solely on mall exposure to bring in business. They had no measure of the effectiveness of their advertising.

After much discussion, the Arnetts decided to obtain a bank loan of $3,000 for a promotion campaign. Brad felt this sum was too high, but Sybil wanted to have enough money "to do the job right," as she put it. She looked upon the campaign as their last big effort to generate business for the store. She believed that if they could get people to try the store, then these people would develop into repeat purchasers.

Brad and Sybil next were faced with the problem of how they should allocate this money. That is, they were wondering what their promotional mix should be. Brad was in favour of heavy advertising in the local newspaper. He felt that newspapers were a good medium (1) for product advertising and (2) for creating a favourable consumer attitude toward the store. He believed that their initial newspaper ads had been poor. Also, they had not been run frequently enough, nor over a long enough period of time, to be effective. He felt that some kind of sales training was needed to increase the effectiveness of the personal selling effort in the store. He even liked the idea of spot television commercials, but he did not know whether they had enough money for TV advertising.

Sybil, on the other hand, wanted to engage more in the area of consumer promotions — "sales promotion," as a textbook might call it. She wanted to begin with a mail campaign, by sending invitations (to visit the store) with discount coupons enclosed. These invitations would go to new parents and parents with preschool children throughout the local area. Sybil felt that the invitations and discount offers would motivate prospects to try the store, and thus would stimulate sales. She also wanted to mix the mail campaign with some newspaper advertising that would emphasize the store's new "specialty shop" theme.

Question

What promotional program should be adopted by the Stork and Cradle Shop?

Promotional Program in Expanding Industrial Market

Case 23 Crown Specialty Steel Co. Ltd.

Mr. Oscar Meade, president of Crown Specialty Steel of Hamilton, Ontario, realized that potential sales in the Hamilton area far exceeded the area's supply of specialty steel products and services. Moreover since the end of the recession, the market was showing signs of expansion. Consequently, Mr. Meade was wondering what kind of a program his firm should develop (1) to take advantage of the growing market opportunities and (2) to minimize the effects of competition, which were sure to intensify.

Crown Specialty Steel's sole line of business was to provide Hamilton-area industries with custom-made, alloyed steel products capable of withstanding heavy, excessive abuse in specialized use situations. Basically, Crown was a service organization. The company did not produce any of the products it sold; instead, it acted as a liaison between steel users and steel producers. During regular calls on prospective customers, Crown salesmen would seek to identify problem situations calling for specialty steel products. Or when a user — even a large concern such as Ford or General Motors — encountered a problem that might feasibly be solved by the use of high-strength, alloyed steel, that company would initiate the contact with a specialty steel company like Crown. A Crown representative would analyse the problem and recommend the particular type of steel needed in the situation.

An order was then forwarded to a steel manufacturer. There the mill's metallurgists formulated the processes and components that would yield the desired products. Typically some material (tungsten, silicon, manganese, or nickel) was mixed with the molten steel to form an alloy that would give the desired hardness, toughness, tensile strength, or ability to withstand temperature extremes.

Extra-high-stength steel is most useful in heavy-wear areas in a factory or in situations requiring materials that can withstand heavy blows and stresses over long periods of time. Alloyed steel is commonly used in conveyor systems, blast furnaces, and certain machine parts. For example, the conveyor hooks that attach to a car body during automobile assembly must be small, but extremely strong, to provide adequate life while not impairing assembly. These small conveyor hooks are made from a special nickel-alloy, high-strength steel. Conveyors carrying gravel are subject to heavy wear and are also constructed of special steel alloys. Machine parts typically produced with specialty steels include gears, bearings, shafts, connecting rods, blades, springs, pins, and cutting units.

Through the years there had been increasing industrial needs for specialized, high-strength steel products. Two specific reasons, however, explain why the specialty steel suppliers developed to satisfy these needs, rather than the major users going directly to large steel producers to get these products. First, the major users of special steel found that they did not use this type of product often enough to warrant having a separate facility for its procurement. But when the users *did* need the specialty product, determining its specifications and procuring it were complex tasks. Second, the greatly expanded list of steel alloys available meant that considerable expertise was needed to ensure correct product choice.

Crown's primary market was the heavily industrialized area within a 100 km radius of Hamilton. This included the Toronto area. However, the company did consider that its total market extended out 300 km from Hamilton. The company held 22 percent of the specialty steel market within that 300 km limit, according to Mr. Meade. Crown faced three competitors in this market. The competitors' market shares and number of salespeople were as follows:

	Market Share (percent)	Number of Salespeople
Company A	30	11
Company B	28	9
Company C	20	8
Crown	22	8

Competition in the specialty steel industry was usually on a nonprice basis because steelmill suppliers maintained comparable prices. An important part of the product-service mix of a specialty steel firm was the ability of its salespeople to analyse a user's problem and to recommend a steel alloy that would provide the required service at a reasonable cost to the user. However, all Crown's competitors could provide this service. Competition was also affected by the personal relations that salespeople built with their customers and by other promotional efforts designed to strengthen the company image and customer loyalty.

In its relatively short life Crown had experienced some significant ups and downs in its sales history. From its beginning in 1952 until the late 1950s the company showed gradually increasing sales and profits. In the late 1960s, however, Crown's sales leveled off and even declined during four consecutive years. The reason for the decline was Crown's failure to provide fast, reliable delivery on its orders. A steel mill may receive ten to fifty orders a week from the specialty steel companies, and often will delay production of a certain order for weeks or even months. Crown's former president, Mr. Michael Latrobe, ordered from several different suppliers. Consequently, he did not enjoy a favoured position with any one, nor did he maintain adequate contact with them so as to ensure prompt production of his orders.

In 1975 Mr. Meade took over as president of Crown, since when sales increased annually to the present level of about $2 million. Net operating profit increased to 7 percent of net sales. Mr. Meade credited much of this successful turnaround to his methods of working with suppliers. He selected only one mill supplier — Dofasco — and he maintained intensive written and personal contact with the manufacturer. The result was that Dofasco filled Crown's orders promptly; consequently, Mr. Meade was usually able to provide faster service than any of his competitors.

Crown's market position had progressed to the point where Mr. Meade estimated that the four specialty steel companies could handle only 80 percent of the potential business in the Hamilton area, and furthermore the market was expanding rapidly. Crown had built a clientele of steady customers in the automotive, cement, and gravel industries. The account list included Ford, General Motors, Oxford Gravel Works, and some smaller cement companies. But most important, new users and new uses of specialty steel offered opportunities for both replacing lost markets (automotive industry problems) and market expansion. Local chemical companies and machine parts makers, for instance, were potential customers.

Crown's main promotional efforts were through the company's eight salespeople. Sometimes Mr. Meade made the initial contact with a customer, but from then on a salesperson handled Crown's work with that customer. Further promotion consisted of customer entertainment. No advertising was done at all. In fact, only one of Crown's three competitors used any advertising, and then only in a very small amount.

With demand outrunning supply in the specialty steel market, Crown's market prospects looked good. Mr. Meade was smart enough to realize, however, that the current market situation could very well be a short-lived phenomenon. Such a market was bound to attract additional competitors and to draw a more aggressive, better-trained selling effort from existing firms. Consequently, he was wondering how he might improve and intensify Crown's promotional efforts in order to capture a satisfactory share of the expanding market.

As one alternative, Mr. Meade considered budgeting $80,000 to $100,000 for an advertising program during the coming year. He consulted a Toronto advertising agency, which indicated that a program of direct-mail advertising, plus placing advertisements in selected trade journals and Southern Ontario newspapers, would have several advantages, some of which were:

1. It would make salespeople's efforts more efficient by using advertising to make the initial customer contact.

2. It would establish company identity and image.

3. It would reach customer personnel now inaccessible to the sales force.

Another alternative was to use the same amount of money to hire, train, and compensate three additional salespeople. The total cost per person would be about $35,000, depending on the amount of training they needed — which in turn would depend to some extent upon whether experienced people were hired, thus reducing training costs. Any unallocated funds could be used (1) to further train the present salespeople and (2) to equip the sales force with better sales tools (catalogues, samples, etc.).

An informal market investigation, which Mr. Meade conducted, revealed the following interesting facts about the purchase decision for specialty steel products:

1. The initial purchase idea comes from a first level of management — a foreperson or general foreperson — which is in close contact with a company's problems.

2. Buying decisions for specialty steels are made quickly when a need arises, and then the buyer seeks the assistance of a specialty steel company; the purchase is not a long-range, planned affair.

Question

What promotional program should the Crown Company use to expand its sales effectively and profitably?

Case 24
Bentley
Fresh Brew
Tea (E)*

Promotion Strategies for a New Brand

The final decision confronting Mr. Don Evans, president and owner of The Newfoundland Tea Company, was the promotion element of the marketing plan for Bentley Fresh Brew Tea. Many alternatives had been identified by both himself and various associates, including personnel from his marketing research agency. He realized that any promotion decision could only be effective if it was coordinated with strategies for the other three elements of the marketing mix: product, pricing, and distribution.

Given the nature of the market and the actions of Tetley and Red Rose (as outlined in Part (A) of this case), Mr. Evans felt that an extensive advertising and promotion campaign would probably be necessary for the success of Bentley Fresh Brew. However, as reminded by his bank manager, financial resources were limited, and therefore he should consider introducing the brand without the heavy expense of producing ads and buying media time and space; indeed, noted the bank manager, "if the product is good, then people will buy it — with or without advertising."

A related question, should Mr. Evans decide to conduct an advertising campaign, was how much money would be spent. His accountant estimated that national companies with related product lines spent 2 to 4 percent of factory sales on advertising; however, Mr. Evans felt that, since his sales during the first year would be very low, an advertising budget based on this percentage of sales method might not be adequate.

A critical advertising decision centred on the advertising appeal or theme to use, should a campaign be undertaken. Several associates suggested

*Refer to Part (A) of this case for essential background and statistical information on the market, competition, and the brand.

Table E-1   USE OF COUPONS FOR PURCHASE OF ANY FOOD PRODUCT
DURING THE PAST SIX MONTHS

		Yes	No
I	*Household Size**		
	1 or 2 persons	44%	66%
	3 or 4 persons	33	67
	5 or more persons	77	23
II	*Age**		
	Less than 25	17%	83%
	25 to 34	52	48
	35 to 49	65	35
	50 or more	40	60
III	*Occupation**		
	Professional	59%	41%
	White Collar	64	36
	Skilled Labour	57	63
	Unskilled Labour	14	86
	All Other	40	60
IV	*"Regular" Brand**		
	Tetley Users	58%	42%
	Red Rose Users	29	71
	All Other Users	42	58
V	*Household Tea Consumption Per Month*		
	Light	38%	62%
	Medium	64	36
	Heavy	48	52
VI	*Total Sample*	47%	53%

*indicates chi-square statistics significant at 0.05 level.

that he attempt to persuade consumers to switch from coffee and other beverages to tea, by promoting tea's advantages of lower cost and lower caffeine levels per cup, or by promoting tea as "today's drink." Of course, such ads would identify Bentley Fresh Brew as the sponsor. Mr. Evans felt that "taste" or "freshness" should be the key advertising message; however, he also realized that the target market, as well as actual product composition and strategies should be key inputs into the advertising appeal decision. As noted in Table B-1, there were a number of other appeals available as well, ranging from low price or good value to colour of the tea to the speed of the tea bag in steeping (i.e. releasing its flavour and colour into the water). (See Part (A) of the case for details on competitors' advertising activities.)

One final advertising decision to be made concerned media strategy. Which media class should Mr. Evans choose: television, radio, newspaper, or magazine? One 30-second spot on either of the two provincewide television stations during prime time (7:00 pm to 11:00 pm) cost approximately $200 to $300. Radio advertising was less expensive than television, with 30-second spots costing from $20 to $40 on either of the two province-wide AM radio stations. A one-page ad in the St. John's evening newspaper cost $750, while the same space in the morning paper cost $500;

to have complete provincewide coverage in newspapers, however, would require purchasing space in up to ten other (mostly weekly) newspapers, where one-page ads cost from $200 to $400 each. The province's only wide-distribution magazine, *The Newfoundland Herald*, also contained a comprehensive TV guide and entertainment schedule; a regular one-page ad cost $300, while an outside back cover location cost $600. Related to the task of determining media classes and vehicles was the choice of media scheduling and concentration: at what periods throughout the year should the advertising campaign run, and should the advertising be concentrated in one medium to gain impact or scattered throughout two or more media classes to increase reach?

The manager of his marketing research agency suggested that advertising alone might not be sufficient to induce consumer trial of the brand; he suggested that Mr. Evans consider sampling (in-store or door-to-door, with a package of five or ten teabags), couponing (in newspapers or magazines, door-to-door, in-store, or in-package), contests (such as Tetley had used successfully for years), or in-package premiums (such as Red Rose had previously used). (See Table E-1.) Mr. Evans was considering the advantages and disadvantages of these sales promotional strategies; one major constraint was cost. He wondered which was the most efficient and effective approach, and whether there was not some other means of promoting Bentley Fresh Brew Tea.

Questions

1. Will it be necessary to engage in an advertising campaign for Bentley Fresh Brew? Why or why not?

2. If Mr. Evans does decide to engage in an advertising campaign, how should he determine the brand's advertising budget? Why?

3. Which advertising appeal would be most appropriate for Bentley Fresh Brew? Why?

4. Which media class(es) should Mr. Evans choose? Why? What period(s) of the year should the campaign run? Why?

5. Will it be necessary for Mr. Evans to use sales promotion tools for the successful introduction of Bentley Fresh Brew? Why or why not? If yes, which tools would you recommend? Why?

Marketing in Special Fields

Part

7

MARKETING PROGRAMS FOR MARKETERS OF SERVICES,
NONBUSINESS ORGANIZATIONS, AND FIRMS MARKETING
IN FOREIGN COUNTRIES

So far in this book, our discussion has dealt largely with the *domestic marketing of products* by *profit-seeking businesses*. Here we rectify that imbalance a bit as we consider strategies in three special areas of marketing. The first is the marketing of intangible services, as contrasted to physical products (Chapter 21). The second is the marketing activity in nonprofit organizations and in organizations that are not usually considered as businesses — hospitals and art museums, for example (Chapter 22). And the third is multinational marketing — that is, the marketing of products and services across national boundaries (Chapter 23).

Strategic marketing planning as applied in these three areas is *fundamentally* the same as we first outlined in Chapter 2 and have been discussing throughout the book. That is, the service, nonprofit, or international organization should first identify its mission. Next, the company should define its overall company goals and its marketing goals. Management then can identify its target markets. Finally, the organization should develop and implement a strategic marketing mix that will reach the target markets and achieve the organization's goals.

However, the results of marketing planning in these special fields often are quite different from those for profit-seeking domestic product marketers. It is these differences — plus the tremendous importance of service, nonprofit, and international organizations in our society and economy — that make these three chapters essential in this book.

Chapter
21

Marketing of Services

CHAPTER GOALS

The special nature of services — especially their intangibility — leads to special marketing problems. After studying this chapter, you should understand:

1. *What services are and are not*
2. *The importance of services in our economy*
3. *The characteristics of services, and the marketing implications in these characteristics*
4. *The marketing concept in service marketing*
5. *A program for the marketing of services*
6. *The future outlook in service marketing*

Some people might argue that there is no such thing as service marketing, but only marketing in which the service element is greater than the product element. We do recognize that there are both a product component *and* a service component in the sale of most, if not all, goods. However, many service organizations (such as insurers, consultants, and barbers) do not think of themselves as producers or sellers of goods. They see themselves (as do most of their customers) as providers of services.[1]

NATURE AND IMPORTANCE OF SERVICES

In concept, product marketing and service marketing are essentially the same. In each case, the marketer must select and analyse its target markets. Then a marketing program must be built around the parts of the marketing mix — the product (or service), the price structure, the distribution system, and the promotional program. Moreover, there often are substantial similarities in practice. At the same time, however, the basic characteristics that differentiate services from products usually lead to a quite different marketing program in a service organization. The strategies and tactics used in conventional product marketing often are inappropriate for service marketing.[2]

---

[1]The contributions of Professor Milton M. Pressley, University of Mississippi, to this chapter when it was being prepared for an earlier edition of this book are again acknowledged. Many of his contributions are retained in this edition.

It is unfortunate that we still do not have general agreement regarding what service marketing encompasses. Here is the definition of services that we shall use in this chapter.

Definition and
Scope of Field

> **Services** are those separately identifiable, essentially intangible activities that provide want-satisfaction, and that are not necessarily tied to the sale of a product or another service. To produce a service may or may not require the use of tangible goods. However, when such use is required, there is no transfer of the title (permanent ownership) to these tangible goods.

Now let's elaborate a bit on that definition, to reduce any possibility of confusion:

- We include such activities as medical care, entertainment, and repair services (but not the medicines or repair parts purchased).

- We *exclude* credit, delivery, and other services that exist only when there is the sale of a product or another service.

- The consumer of a service can take only *temporary* possession or make only *temporary* use of any goods required in the production of the service —a hotel room or a rented car, for example. (An exception here would include such tangible goods as insurance policies, legal papers, or a consultant's reports that supplement but do not comprise the service.) Service organizations are those that do not have as their *principal* aim the production of tangible products that buyers will possess permanently.

Product marketing

The definitional problem will continue. Some statistics on services may be misleading because it is becoming more difficult to separate products and services in our economy. We rarely find situations in which services are marketed without any product involvement whatsoever. Most products are accompanied by services, and most services require supporting products. It is this product-service mix that really is growing in importance in our economy.

We are concerned here primarily with the services marketed by business or professional firms with profit-making motives—commercial services— in contrast to those of nonbusiness organizations, such as churches, public schools, and the government. One useful classification of commercial services is given below. No attempt is made to separate these into consumer and industrial services, as we did with products. In fact, most are purchased by both market groups.[3]

---

[2]See John E. G. Bateson, "Do We Need Service Marketing?" (his conclusion is yes) in *Marketing Consumer Services: New Insights*, Marketing Science Institute, Cambridge, Mass., report no. 77-115, 1977, pp. 1–30. Also see Leonard L. Berry, "Services Marketing Is Different," *Business*, May-June 1980, pp. 24–29; Dan R. E. Thomas, "Strategy Is Different in Service Businesses," *Harvard Business Review*, July-August 1978, pp. 158–165; and G. Lynn Shostack, "Breaking Free from Product Marketing," *Journal of Marketing*, April 1977, pp. 73–80.

[3]See Duane L. Davis, Joseph P. Guiltinan, and Wesley H. Jones, "Service Characteristics, Consumer Search, and Classification of Retail Services," *Journal of Retailing*, Fall 1979, pp. 3–23.

Services marketing

1. Housing (includes rentals of hotels, motels, apartments, houses, and farms)

2. Household operations (includes utilities, house repairs, repairs of equipment in the house, landscaping, and household cleaning)

3. Recreation (includes rental and repair of equipment used to participate in recreation and entertainment activities; also admission to all entertainment, recreation, and amusement events)

4. Personal care (includes laundry, dry cleaning, beauty care)

5. Medical and other health care (includes all medical service, dental, nursing, hospitalization, optometry, and other health care)

6. Private education

7. Business and other professional services (includes legal, accounting, management consulting, and computer services)

8. Insurance and financial (includes personal and business insurance, credit and loan service, investment counselling, and tax services)

9. Transportation (includes freight and passenger service on common carriers, automobile repairs and rentals)

10. Communications (includes telephone, telegraph, and specialized business communication services)

Importance of Services

It is common these days for social commentators to see us moving beyond the industrial economy stage to the point where we are becoming part of the world's new service economy. Almost three-quarters of the nonfarm labour force is employed in supplying services, and service jobs typically hold up better in a recession than do jobs in the goods-producing industries.

Roughly 42 percent of personal consumption expenditures are for the purchase of services. These expenditures have increased in absolute dollar terms every year from 1975 to 1981 (see Table 21-1). As a proportion of personal consumption expenditures, the increase has been roughly 2.5 percent, and as a proportion of Gross National Product it has been about 1 percent. Furthermore, projections indicate that services will attract an even larger share of consumer spending and employment. Unfortunately, one

---

THE SERVICE ECONOMY

For a fee, there are now companies that will balance your budget, baby-sit your philodendron, wake you up in the morning, drive you to work, or find you a new home, job, car, wife, clairvoyant, cat feeder, or gypsy violinist. Or perhaps you want to rent a garden tractor? A few cattle? Some original paintings? Or maybe some trendies to decorate your next cocktail party? If it is business services you need, other companies will plan your conventions and sales meetings, design your products, or supply temporary secretaries or even executives.

Source: "Services Grow While the Quality Shrinks," *Business Week*, October 30, 1971, p. 50.

feature of the service-economy boom is that the prices of most services have been going up at a considerably faster rate than the prices of most products. You are undoubtedly aware of this if you have had your car or TV set repaired or your shoes half-soled, or paid a dental bill in recent years.

When we say that services account for close to one-half of *personal consumption expenditures*, we still grossly understate the economic importance of services. These figures do not include the vast amounts spent for *business and industrial services*. By all indications, spending for business services has increased even more rapidly than spending for consumer services.

To understand the reasons for the growth in *consumer services*, we must understand what has been happening in our economy during the past forty years. The long period of general prosperity has meant higher incomes, increased leisure time, and an overall rise in living standards. In the early stages of a period such as this, people first expend their rising incomes on goods. This was particularly true after World War II, when there was a huge backlog of product demand. Products were denied to consumers in the 1930s because of the Depression, and in the early 1940s because of the war. Then, as the years go by, the average consumer becomes relatively well stocked with goods. Consumers increasingly turn to services that heretofore they either could not afford or did not desire — services such as travel, education, personal grooming, and medical care.

The growth of *business services* may be attributed to the fact that business has become increasingly complex, specialized, and competitive. As a consequence, management has been forced to call in experts to provide services in research, taxation, advertising, labour relations, and a host of other areas.

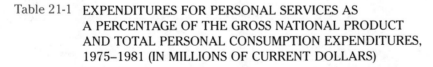

Table 21-1   EXPENDITURES FOR PERSONAL SERVICES AS A PERCENTAGE OF THE GROSS NATIONAL PRODUCT AND TOTAL PERSONAL CONSUMPTION EXPENDITURES, 1975–1981 (IN MILLIONS OF CURRENT DOLLARS)

| | | | | Service Expenditure as Percentage of | |
Year	Services	Total Personal Consumption Expenditure	Gross National Product	Personal Consumption Expenditures	Gross National Product
1975	38,825	96,995	165,343	40.03	23.48
1976	45,722	110,886	191,031	41.23	23.93
1977	51,438	122,530	208,868	41.98	24.63
1978	57,065	135,153	230,490	42.22	24.76
1979	62,915	150,521	261,576	41.80	24.05
1980	71,324	168,395	291,869	42.36	24.44
1981	81,064	191,025	331,338	42.44	24.47

Source: Statistics Canada, *Market Research Handbook*, Ottawa, 1983, table 5.1, pp. 336, 337; table 5.4, p. 342.

The rate of growth has not been uniform for all categories of consumer services. As disposable personal incomes have increased and household and family structure and life-styles have changed, the demand for some services has grown relatively faster than for others. Expenditures for out-of-home eating have increased greatly, and expenditures for municipal transportation have increased relatively as people make less use of their private autos. Projections to 1990 suggest that high growth rates in jobs and spending will occur especially in the health-care industry, auto repairs, retail trade, and the banking and finance fields.

To capitalize on the emerging service potential, product *manufacturers* have diversified into services. Some product *retailers* have done the same. Sears in Canada now has some forty nonmerchandise offerings, including an insurance company (Allstate) and a car rental agency.

Characteristics of Services

The special nature of services stems from several distinctive characteristics. These characteristics create special marketing challenges and opportunities. They also often result in strategic marketing programs that are substantially different from those found in product marketing.

Intangibility

Since services are essentially intangible, it is impossible for customers to sample — to taste, feel, see, hear, or smell — services *before* they buy them. This feature of services places some strain on a marketing organization. The burden falls mainly on a company's promotional program. The sales force and the advertising department must concentrate on the *benefits* to be derived from the service, rather than emphasizing the service itself. An insurance company thus may promote service benefits such as guaranteed payment of a child's university expenses or a retirement income of so many dollars per month. The communications companies tell us how business users can cut selling and inventory costs by using long-distance calling.[4]

Inseparability

Services often cannot be separated from the person of the seller. Moreover, some services must be created and dispensed simultaneously. For example, dentists create and dispense almost all their services at the same time.

From a marketing standpoint, inseparability frequently means that direct sale is the only possible channel of distribution, and a seller's services cannot be sold in very many markets. This characteristic also limits the scale of operation in a firm. One person can repair only so many autos in a day or treat so many medical patients.

As an exception to the inseparability feature, the service may be sold by a person who is representing the creator-seller. A travel agent, insurance broker or agent, or rental agent, for instance, may represent and help promote the service that will be sold by the institution producing it.

---

[4]For suggestions on how to offset the marketing problems created by intangibility in services (and also in products), see Theodore Levitt, "Marketing Intangible Products and Product Intangibles," *Harvard Business Review*, May-June 1981, pp. 94–102.

Heterogeneity

It is impossible for a service industry, or even an individual seller of services, to standardize output. Each "unit" of the service is somewhat different from other "units" of the same service. For example, an airline does not give the same quality of service on each trip. All repair jobs a mechanic does on automobiles are not of equal quality. An added complication is the fact that it is often difficult to judge the quality of a service. (Of course, we can say the same for some products.) It is particularly difficult to forecast the quality in advance of buying a service. A person pays to see a football game without knowing whether it will be an exciting one, well worth the price of admission, or a dull performance.

Service companies should therefore pay particular attention to the "product-planning" stage of their marketing programs. From the beginning, management must do all it can to ensure consistency of quality and to maintain high levels of quality control.[5]

Perishability and Fluctuating Demand

Services are highly perishable, and they cannot be stored. Unused electric power, empty seats in a stadium, and idle mechanics in a garage all represent business that is lost forever. Furthermore, the market for services

---

[5]See Jeremy Main, "Toward Service without a Snarl," *Fortune*, March 23, 1981, pp. 58ff.

fluctuates considerably by season, by day of the week, and by hour of the day. Many ski lifts lie idle all summer, and most golf courses go unused in the winter. The use of city buses fluctuates greatly during the day.

There are some notable exceptions to this generalization regarding the perishability and storage of services. In life insurance, for example, the service is purchased. Then it is held by the insurance company (the seller) until needed by the buyer or the beneficiary. This holding constitutes a type of storage.

The combination of perishability and fluctuating demand offers product-planning, pricing, and promotion challenges to service company executives. In some companies, they might look for new uses for idle plant capacity in off-seasons. Through advertising and reduced fares, public transport executives can show consumers the advantages of using city transportation facilities during nonpeak hours. In an attempt to level demand, telephone companies offer lower rates at night and on weekends.

THE MARKETING CONCEPT AND SERVICE MARKETING

The growth in services has generally not been due to marketing developments in service industries, but rather, to the maturation of our economy and our changes in life-styles and standards of living. Traditionally, executives in our service companies have not been marketing-oriented. They have lagged behind sellers of products in accepting the marketing concept, and have generally been slow in adopting promotional methods, "product" strategies, and other marketing techniques. Marketing management in service firms has not been especially creative. Innovations in service marketing have come typically from product-associated companies.

We can identify some of the reasons for this lack of marketing orientation. No doubt, the intangibility of services creates more difficult marketing challenges for service sellers than for product sellers. In many service industries — particularly professional services — the sellers think of themselves as producers or creators, and not as marketers, of the service. They are proud of their ability to repair a car, diagnose an illness, or provide a good hairstyle. They do not think of themselves as businesspeople — particularly those in small businesses.

The all-encompassing reason, however, is that top management does not yet understand (1) what marketing is or (2) its importance to a company's success. These executives seem to equate marketing with selling, and they fail to consider other parts of the marketing system. They also do not effectively coordinate their marketing activities. Many service firms lack an executive whose sole responsibility is marketing — the counterpart of the vice president of marketing in a goods-producing company.

There are, of course, exceptions to these negative generalizations. Some extremely successful firms have adopted modern marketing techniques. The success of such organizations as Holiday Inn and Avis is traceable in large part to their marketing orientation.

BANKING THEN AND NOW.

The changes (and increased revenues) came about as bankers became more marketing-oriented.

The banking industry provides an interesting example of a service industry that was not marketing-oriented in the past but has, in recent years, been struggling to make the transition to modern times. For years, commercial banks made customers feel that they should be honoured to have their money in a checking account with no interest, but with a service charge. And savings accounts earned very low interest rates. Banks were marble mausoleums; tellers were faceless people behind protective bars; the banker was the "black-hatted and caped villain" of song and story.

Most banks have worked to change those images, and the market situation in banking has changed appreciably. Competition from both within and outside the industry has intensified. To meet the challenge, many banks finally started to do a little marketing to go along with their advertising. In fact, some banks moved aggressively to shorten the transition period by pirating marketing executives from consumer-product companies. Banks are developing their marketing departments, conducting sales-training programs, and engaging in marketing research. They are running hard-sell "product" ads, expanding their service (product) mix, and sending their employees to bank-marketing executive-development programs.[6]

Banks are making concerted efforts to attract retail (consumer) business. Buildings and internal layouts are now designed to project an image of warmth, friendliness, and informality. Bank credit cards and automatic teller services have been initiated for consumer convenience (and, incidentally, additional revenues). Other new services include stock purchasing, personal financial counselling, payment of customers' monthly bills, and 24-hour outside deposit and withdrawal facilities. Who knows — perhaps the next step will be to offer full-service banking during evening hours and on weekends.[7]

---

[6]See "New Bankers Turn to a Hard Sell Pitch," *Business Week*, September 21, 1981, p. 66.

[7]For a report on another service industry that traditionally has been *very* nonmarketing-oriented but that is slowly changing its ways, see Donna K. Darden, William R. Darden, and G. E. Kiser, "The Marketing of Legal Services," *Journal of Marketing*, Spring 1981, pp. 123–134; also see Bernie Whalen, "Legal Services Marketing Enters New Era with Ad Co-op's 'Slick,' Professional TV Commercial," *Marketing News*, March 5, 1982, p. 1.

A STRATEGIC PROGRAM FOR THE MARKETING OF SERVICES

Because of the characteristics of services (intangibility, etc.), the task of developing a total marketing program in a service industry is often uniquely challenging. However, as in product marketing, management first should define its marketing goals and select its target markets. Then management must design and implement marketing-mix strategies to reach its markets and fulfil its marketing goals.

Target Market Analysis

The task of analysing a firm's target markets is essentially the same, whether the firm is selling a product or a service. Marketers of services should understand the components of population and income — the demographic factors — as they affect the market for the services. In addition, marketers must try to determine, for each market segment, why customers buy the given service. That is, what are their customers' buying *motives*? Also, sellers must determine the buying patterns for their services — when, where, and how do customers buy, who does the buying, and who makes the buying decisions? The psychological determinants of buying behaviour — attitudes, perceptions, personality, etc. — are as pertinent in the marketing of services as in product marketing. In like manner, the sociological factors of social-class structure and small-group influences are market determinants for services. The fundamentals of the adoption and diffusion of product innovation are also relevant in the marketing of services.

Some of the trends pointed out in Chapters 4 to 7 are particularly worth watching because they carry considerable influence in the marketing of services. As an example, increases in disposable income and discretionary buying power mean a growing market for personal counselling, insurance, and transportation services. More leisure time plus greater income mean increased markets for recreation and entertainment services.

Planning and Developing the Service

New services are just as important to a service company as new products are to a product-marketing firm. Similarly, the improvement of existing products and the elimination of unwanted, unprofitable services are also key goals.

Product planning and development has its counterpart in the marketing program of a service industry. Management must select appropriate strategies regarding (1) what services will be offered, (2) what will be the length and breadth of the service mix offered, and (3) what, if anything, needs to be done in the way of service attributes such as branding or providing guarantees.

The high perishability, fluctuating demand, and inability to store services make product planning critically important to service marketers. A service industry can expand or contract its "product mix," alter existing services, and trade up or down. The reasons for these moves are familiar. The company may want to increase its total volume, reduce seasonal fluctuations in volume, or cater to changing buyer patterns such as the desire for one-stop shopping. Dry cleaners, for instance, have expanded into laundry services, mothproofing, storage, dyeing, and clothing alterations and repairs. Some service firms have effectively expanded their mix by working jointly with companies selling related services. For instance, automobile rental firms have working arrangements with airlines and hotels so that when customers fly to their destination, a car and a hotel room are reserved and waiting.

In some respects, "product" planning is easier for services than for products. Packaging, colour, labelling, and style are virtually nonexistent in service marketing. However, in other respects—branding and standardization of quality, for instance—service industries have greater problems. Branding is difficult because consistency of quality is hard to maintain and because the brand cannot be physically attached to a service.

Standardization of *quality* in a service is an extremely important goal, difficult as it may be. In some fields, such as beauty care and some of the recreation industries, no attempt is made to mass-produce the service. Instead, the sellers offer custom service as required by each customer. Even in these cases, however, the customer wants consistent quality.

It is extremely important for an organization to *design* and *manage* its service quality in such a way that the customers are satisfied.[8] Unfortunately, in many service organizations (transportation firms and retail stores, for example), the people who are actually involved with the customers are often among the lowest-paid employees in those organizations.

In the marketing of services, nowhere is there a greater need for managerial creativity and skill than in the area of pricing. Earlier, we noted that services are extremely perishable; they usually cannot be stored, and the demand often fluctuates considerably. All these features carry significant pricing implications. To further complicate the situation, customers may postpone purchases, or even perform some services themselves (auto and household repairs, for example).

Pricing of Services

These considerations suggest that the elasticity of demand for a service should influence the price set by the seller. Interestingly enough, sellers often do recognize inelastic demand. Then they charge higher prices. But they fail to act in opposite fashion when faced with an elastic demand—even though a lower price would increase unit sales, total revenue, utilization of facilities, and probably net profit.

Certainly, perfect competition does not apply to any extent, if at all, in the pricing of services. Because of the heterogeneity and the difficulty of standardizing quality, most services are highly differentiated. Also, it is virtually impossible to have complete market information. Further, in any given market, such as a neighbourhood, there are often geographic limits within which a buyer will seek a service. Consequently, there is not a large number of sellers. The heavy capital investment required to produce some services (transportation, communications) often limits the freedom of entry considerably.

---

[8]See John A. Czepiel, *Managing Customer Satisfaction in Consumer Service Businesses*, Marketing Science Institute, Cambridge, Mass., report no. 80–109, 1980.

In some service industries, the private seller will establish a price, but it must be approved by a regulatory agency. This regulation of prices, however, need not stifle the opportunity for imaginative, skilful pricing designed to increase profits. Lower rates for long-distance telephoning at night and on Sunday and peak-load electricity pricing are examples of creative pricing to increase market penetration and profits.

In spite of all this, the *basic* methods of price determination now used for services are generally the same as those for products. Cost-plus pricing is used for regulated service industries. It is also used for repair services where the main ingredient is direct labour and the customer is charged on an hourly basis. For other services (rentals, entertainment, legal counselling, management consulting), prices are determined primarily by market demand and competition.

Many of the pricing strategies discussed in Chapter 13 are applicable to service marketing. Quantity discounts, for example, are used by car rental agencies. The daily rates are lower if you agree to rent the car for a week or a month at a time. Cash discounts are offered when insurance premiums are paid annually instead of quarterly. Various professionals, counsellors, and management consultants can use a variable-price policy. Motel or apartment owners offer multiple services (one bedroom, two bedrooms, suites), and they must price each service in relation to the prices of the others. Geographic pricing policies may be involved, although the variable here is time, not freight charges. Mechanics will charge more if they must go out of town, and a doctor will charge more for house calls than for office calls.

Channels of Distribution for Services

Traditionally, most services have been sold directly from producer to consumer or industrial user. No middlemen are used when the service cannot be separated from the seller or when the service is created and marketed simultaneously. For example, public utilities, medical care, and repair services are typically sold without middlemen. Not using middlemen does limit the geographic markets that service sellers can reach. But it also enables the sellers to personalize their services and to get quick, detailed customer feedback.

The only other frequently used channel includes one agent middleman. Some type of agent or broker is often used in the marketing of securities, travel arrangements, entertainment, and housing rentals. Sometimes dealers are trained in the production of the service and then are franchised to sell it. This is the case with some dry-cleaning processes and dance and health studios.

In recent years, some firms have realized that the characteristic of inseparability is not an insurmountable limitation to a seller's distribution system. With a little imagination in management, a service marketer can broaden its distribution considerably. Let's look at some examples, starting with location.

The location of the service seller or the seller's agent should be conveniently accessible to customers, because many services cannot be delivered. Many motels and restaurants have gone out of business when a new highway bypassed their location, thus drawing away the customer traffic. On the other hand, banks have increased their business by installing 24-hour automatic teller services. Dental centres, small medical centres, chiropractors, and optometrists all have opened offices in shopping-centre malls. The retail-store locations for dental centres have been especially successful, and the idea is expanding to all sections of the country. They offer convenience of location, are open long hours, and typically their fees are considerably below the fees charged in a conventional dentist's office.[9] Of greatest consequence, however, is the fact that many people feel more comfortable in a mall setting than in a medical-dental office setting. People who would never visit a dentist in an office building are now prepared to visit one in a mall.

The use of intermediaries is another way to broaden distribution. Some banks have arranged for companies to deposit employees' paycheques directly into their bank accounts. The employer thus becomes an intermediary in distributing the bank's service. Insurance firms have expanded their distribution by setting up vending machines in airports.

When intermediaries are used, both their effectiveness and their market coverage can be expanded by "industrializing" their jobs. Theodore Levitt has suggested several innovative ways to substitute equipment for highly paid service specialists who are humanly limited in the services they can create and market.[10]

The characteristic of intangibility means that physical distribution problems are basically eliminated for most service producers. For example, other than supportive supplies, accountants have no physical inventory to store or handle. However, not all service producers are free from physical distribution problems. For example, a chain of equipment rental stores would have to contend with inventory problems. Sometimes hotels and resorts have a surplus of rooms (inventory), which can result in an unprofitable operation.

Personal selling, advertising, and other forms of promotion are used extensively in the marketing of services. However, it is especially difficult to build a promotional program around intangible service benefits. It is so much easier to sell something that can be seen, felt, and demonstrated.

Personal selling is essential when developing close relationships between the buyer and seller. While point-of-purchase displays of the *services* offered are often impossible, displays of the *results* of using the service can be effective. Many service firms, especially in the recreation-entertainment

Promoting the Service

This agent middleman sells transportation, hotel and motel accommodations, entertainment, and a variety of other services. *(© Van Bucher 1983)*

---

[9]See "Moving the Dentist's Chair to Retail Stores," *Business Week*, January 19, 1981, p. 56.

[10]Theodore Levitt, "The Industrialization of Service," *Harvard Business Review*, September-October 1976, pp. 66–68.

field, benefit considerably from free publicity. Sports coverage by newspapers, radio, and television helps in this matter, as do newspapers' reviews of movies, plays, and concerts. Travel sections in newspapers have helped sell transportation, housing, and other services related to the travel industry.

For years, of course, advertising has been used extensively in many service fields — housing, household operation, transportation, recreation, and insurance, for example. What *is* new is the use of advertising by firms in professional-service industries — lawyers and accountants, among others. Previously, the professional associations in these fields had prohibited advertising on the ground that it is unethical. These associations still try to limit and control the advertising. However, several court and regulatory-agency decisions make it clear that a professional society such as a law society is not immune to federal anti-combines legislation when it attempts to control the advertising activities of its members.[11]

As an indirect type of promotion, physicians, lawyers, and insurance agents may participate actively in community affairs as a means of getting their names before the public. Service firms (banks, utilities, railroads) may advertise to attract new industry. They know that anything that helps the community grow will automatically mean an expanded market for them.

A promotional program in a service company should have three major goals. The first is to portray the service benefits in as appealing a manner as possible. The second is to differentiate its offerings from those of competitors. And the third is to build a good reputation. Because the firm is marketing intangibles, reputation is critical. Advertising campaigns can stress the dependability of the service — its consistent high quality. Ads can also emphasize the courteous, friendly, efficient service.[12]

A service firm's promotional effort can be even more effective if the seller can tie in with something tangible — perhaps a distinctive colour, as used by Howard Johnson or Holiday Inn, or a symbol like Smokey the Bear.

FUTURE OUTLOOK IN SERVICE MARKETING

The Changing Service Environment

The growth in service business in the 1980s has been accompanied by a significant increase in competition in many of the service industries. This competition has been stimulated by several factors. One is the changes in government regulation in some industries — airlines, trucking, banking, and telecommunications, for example. New techniques have opened new service fields — in solar energy and information processing, for example.[13] Technological advances have also brought automation and other "industrial" features to formerly all-hand-labour service fields. Chain-store types of organizations are replacing the small-scale independent in many fields,

---

[11]Marina Strauss, "Law Society's Banning Advertising Liable to Combines Law, Court Told," *The Globe and Mail*, May 26, 1981, p. 8.

[12]See William R. George and Leonard L. Berry, "Guidelines for the Advertising of Services," *Business Horizons*, July-August 1981, pp. 52–56.

[13]See Bruce J. Walker, "Market Challenges for Solar Products," *Business*, March-April 1979, pp. 27–32.

including auto repairs, beauty shops, dental service, and real estate brokerage. Increases in the supply of some service providers (dentists and lawyers, for example) finally are bringing some competition to previously protected fields.

The boom has also been accompanied by a deterioration in the quality of many services. In general, service industries have been plagued by poor management, inefficiency, and low productivity. This inefficiency — and the need to increase productivity — is probably the biggest problem facing service industries in general. The productivity problem also has significant implications for the health of the total economy. Service industries are very labour-intensive compared with manufacturing. Consequently, wage increases in the service sector of the economy have a significant impact on price levels and inflation.

Need for Increased Productivity

Perhaps the key to increasing efficiency in service industries is for management to adopt a manufacturing attitude.[14] The concept of providing a service traditionally conjured visions of personal administration and attendance on others. To improve performance meant simply to try harder, but essentially to continue performing a task in the same old way. In contrast, the idea of manufacturing benefits (or efficiently producing them) enables us to focus on new performance methods. We can apply manufacturing technology, planning, and organization changes to the task at hand — but all this at a price of less humaneness.

Four manufacturing strategies being applied in service industries to increase productivity are mechanization, assembly-line standardization, specialization, and organizational consolidation. The use of *mechanization* to implement hand labour has increased per-worker output in laundry and dry cleaning, for example. Machines have increased service output in commercial dishwashing and floor sanding. *Assembly-line* technology has proven fruitful in such diverse service fields as (1) fast-food retailing (McDonald's hamburgers) and (2) mass physical examinations for corporations and labour unions, using mobile health units and automated test equipment.

Several service firms have made labour more productive by *specialization* of effort. Auto repair firms specialize in brakes, transmissions, or mufflers. *Consolidation* as a means of improving productivity is being practised when Air Canada, CP Air, and Wardair add hotels to their service mix. The development of chain organizations (Ramada Inn, for example) is another useful form of consolidation in service firms.[15]

Automation in a service industry. (*Randy Matusow*)

---

[14]Theodore Levitt, "Production-Line Approach to Service," *Harvard Business Review*, September-October 1972, pp. 41-52; also see Levitt, *op. cit.*

[15]For some additional strategies that service firms can use to increase the mass production and mass marketing of services, see Gregory D. Upah, "Mass Marketing in Service Retailing: A Review and Synthesis of Major Methods,"*Journal of Retailing*, Fall 1980, pp. 59–76. For some marketing strategies seeking to change consumer behaviour in order to increase productivity in service industries, see Christopher H. Lovelock and Robert F. Young, "Marketing's Potential for Increasing Productivity in Service Industries," in *Marketing Consumer Services: New Insights, op. cit.*, pp. 105–121.

Prospects for Growth

There is every reason to believe that services will continue to take an increasing share of the consumer dollar.This forecast seems reasonable even in the face of periods of economic decline. History shows that the demand for services is less sensitive to economic fluctuations than the demand for products. The demand for *business* services should also continue to expand as business becomes more complex and as management further recognizes its need for business-service specialists.

We should temper these optimistic forecasts with some caution, however, because forces both external and internal to service industries could limit growth in these fields. Perhaps the most obvious *external* factor is the customers' alternative of performing a service themselves. Another growth deterrent comes from product manufacturers that produce goods with features that decrease our reliance on service industries. Wash-and-wear shirts are used instead of those that require commercial laundry service, for example, and cable television and VCRs substitute for commercial entertainment.

Internal barriers to future growth in service industries are (1) the small size of the average service firm, (2) the shortage of people with specialized skills, and (3) the limited competition in many professionally dominated service industries, such as accounting and law. These barriers limit internal price competition and sometimes limit entry into the field. But perhaps the overriding internal growth deterrents are (1) the little emphasis on research and development in many service fields, and (2) the general failure to recognize the importance of marketing in every business.[16]

SUMMARY

Services are those separately identifiable, essentially intangible activities that provide want-satisfaction, and that are not necessarily tied to the sale of a product or another service. In the broadest sense, product marketing and service marketing are the same. In actual practice, however, significant differences do exist between product marketing and service marketing.

Service marketing is also worth special attention because of its scope — almost half of what we spend goes for services, and about two-thirds of nongovernmental jobs are in the service field. Not only are services of considerable importance in our economy today, but the prospects are that the service sector will continue to grow faster than the product sector of the economy. Services generally are intangible, inseparable from the seller, heterogeneous, and highly perishable, and they have a widely fluctuating demand. Each of these distinctive characteristics has several marketing implications.

Unfortunately, the growth in services has not been matched by service management's understanding or acceptance of the marketing concept. Service organizations have been slow to adopt marketing programs and tech-

---

[16]For a comprehensive research project on the subject of services marketing, see Eric Langeard, John E. G. Bateson, Christopher H. Lovelock, and Pierre Eiglier, *Services Marketing: New Insights from Consumers and Managers*, Marketing Science Institute, Cambridge, Mass., report no. 81–104, 1981.

niques that, in product marketing, have brought satisfaction to consumers and profits to producers. The development of a program for the marketing of services parallels that for products but takes into account the special character of services.

Probably the biggest problem facing service industries, as we look to their continued growth, is the need to increase productivity. Perhaps the answer lies in adopting processes that have proven successful in increasing output and efficiency in the production of goods. One cost of "industrializing" services, however, will be an increase in the impersonalization of these services.

QUESTIONS AND PROBLEMS

How do you account for the increase in expenditures for services relative to expenditures for products in the last forty years?

2. What are some of the marketing implications in the fact that services possess the characteristic of intangibility?

3. Why are middlemen rarely used in the marketing programs of service firms?

4. Services are highly perishable and are often subject to fluctuations in demand. In marketing its services, how can a company offset these factors?

5. Cite some examples of service marketers that seem to be customer-oriented, and describe what these firms have done in this vein.

6. "Traditionally, marketers of services have *not* been marketing-oriented." Do you agree? If so, how do you account for this deficiency?

7. Present a brief analysis of the market for each of the following service firms. Make use of the components of a market as discussed in Chapters 4 to 7.
   a. Laundry and dry-cleaning firm located in a shopping centre adjoining your campus
   b. Four-bedroom house for rent at a major seashore resort
   c. Bowling alley
   d. Nursing home

8. What are some of the ways in which each of the following service firms might expand its line?
   a. Advertising agency
   b. Telephone company
   c. Automobile repair garage

9. Explain the importance of demand elasticity in the pricing of services.

10. "Personal selling should be the main ingredient in the promotional mix for a marketer of services." Do you agree? Discuss.

11. Present in brief form a marketing program for each of the following services. Your presentation should start with a description of the target market you have selected for the service. Then explain how you would plan, price, promote, and distribute the service.
    a. Chimney cleaning
    b. Home-insulation efficiency surveys
    c. Any service you select

Marketing in Nonbusiness Organizations

Chapter 22

CHAPTER GOALS

In this chapter, we apply many of the concepts and techniques of modern marketing to private, nonbusiness, not-for-profit organizations. After studying this chapter, you should understand:

1. *The exchange concept as applied to nonbusiness organizations*
2. *The wide range of nonbusiness organizations*
3. *The importance of marketing in nonbusiness organizations*
4. *The concept of contributor markets and client markets*
5. *The attitudes of nonbusiness organizations toward marketing*
6. *How market analysis and the marketing mix apply in nonbusiness marketing*
7. *The status of marketing programs in nonbusiness organizations*

To help generate operating funds and to raise its profile in the community, one symphony orchestra organized a lottery, the first prize for which was a Mercedes Benz sedan worth more than $30,000. Several universities and community colleges have advertised new programs directed toward a variety of segments of the student market (part-time, evening, correspondence, etc.). A number of religious organizations conduct rather low-key advertising campaigns on television. Many museums, art galleries, theatre groups, and social agencies (Boy Scouts, YM-YWCA, Big Brothers, etc.) use the same techniques to gain new members and to increase financial support.

Three common threads run through all these real-life situations. First, the organizations are all *nonbusiness* groups, as the term *business* is generally used. Second, they are all *nonprofit* (or, more correctly, *not-for-profit*) organizations — that is, profit is *not* an intended organizational goal. And third, in each situation, *marketing activities* were used to solve key problems.

NATURE AND SCOPE OF NONBUSINESS MARKETING

Basically, the marketing fundamentals for nonbusiness, nonprofit organizations are the same as for the business sector. That is, we want to develop a marketing program strategically planned around a product or service that is effectively priced, promoted, and distributed to satisfy wants in a predetermined market. However, there are important differences in the *implementation* of the marketing program and in nonbusiness management's *understanding* of and *attitudes* toward marketing. The differences tend to limit the marketing activities of nonbusiness, nonprofit organizations, even though these organizations need effective marketing so much.[1]

Nonbusiness Organizations

Organizations may be classified in several different ways. For our purposes, however, three classification bases apply:

1. *Private versus public (government)-owned and -operated.* Most organizations clearly fit in one category or the other, but there are borderline cases. For example, a public university is partially supported by nongovernment funds such as tuition and private donations. A denominational college, on the other hand, may be partially funded by government grants.

2. *Profit-seeking versus not-for-profit.*

3. *Business versus nonbusiness.* Most organizations are easy to categorize on this basis. In some cases, however, the distinction gets fuzzy. Physicians may consider themselves as professionals rather than as business "organizations." A musician may say, "I am an artist," and consider a lucrative performance contract as secondary to the music. But both are really in business.

In this chapter our discussion will be limited to marketing in organizations that are understood to be private, nonprofit, nonbusiness units. Thus we exclude Canada Post, the CNR, and the Ontario Milk Marketing Board. Crown corporations, whether provincial or federal, are generally to be viewed as public business organizations; sometimes nonprofit, other times for profit. This chapter is related to the preceding chapter because most nonbusiness, nonprofit organizations will market *services*, rather than tangible products. Consequently, many of the ideas in Chapter 21 are relevant here.

Types of Nonbusiness Organizations

Private, not-for-profit, nonbusiness organizations number in the thousands and cover a very wide range of activities. The following list of organizational groupings may give you some idea of this broad spectrum.

---

[1]For an analysis of these differences in one field of nonbusiness marketing–social-cause marketing, see Paul N. Bloom and William D. Novelli, "Problems and Challenges in Social Marketing," *Journal of Marketing*, Spring 1981, pp. 79–88. Many of the generalizations developed in this article are equally applicable to marketing in other nonbusiness fields.

- *Educational.* Private schools, high schools, colleges, universities.
- *Cultural.* Museums, zoos, symphony orchestras, opera and theatre groups.
- *Religious.* Churches, synagogues, temples, mosques.
- *Charitable and philanthropic.* Welfare groups (Salvation Army, United Way, Red Cross), research foundations, fund-raising groups.
- *Social cause.* Organizations dealing with family planning, civil rights, stopping smoking, preventing heart disease, environmental concerns, those for or against abortion, or for or against nuclear energy.
- *Social.* Fraternal organizations, civic clubs.
- *Health care.* Nursing homes, health research organizations (Canadian Cancer Society, Canadian Mental Health Association), health maintenance organizations such as The Canadian Save the Children Fund.
- *Political.* Political parties, individual politicians.[2]

The Exchange Concept and Nonbusiness Marketing

In Chapter 1, marketing was broadly defined as an exchange intended to satisfy the wants of all parties involved in the exchange. And marketing consists of all activities designed to facilitate such exchanges. To include a discussion of marketing in nonbusiness organizations is certainly consistent with this broad, exchange-concept definition of marketing. For nonbusiness organizations are also involved in exchanges.

As an example, Great Western Garments (GWG), a business organization, sells to you, through a middleman, a pair of blue jeans in exchange for some money. In a similar vein, your dental clinic, a nonbusiness organization, may provide you with health care in exchange for some money. Your college, another nonbusiness organization, offers an education service to you in exchange for your money and/or your labour.

Markets Involved in Nonbusiness Marketing

A major difference between business and nonbusiness marketing involves the groups with which the particular organization must deal. Business executives have traditionally defined their basic markets as being made up of their present and potential customers. They have thus directed their marketing efforts primarily toward this one group. In contrast, most nonbusiness, nonprofit organizations are involved with *two* major groups

Nonbusiness marketers are involved with two target markets.

[2]For a sample of reports on marketing programs in some of the areas discussed above, see Gary Mauser, "Broadening Marketing: The Case of Political Marketing," *Proceedings* of the Marketing Division, Administrative Sciences Association of Canada (ASAC), vol. 4, part 3, 1983, pp. 201–209; Gordon H. G. McDougall, John D. Claxton, and T. R. Brent Ritchie, "Marketing Energy Conservation: Or What Strategy for the Churchmice and the Hippos?" *Proceedings* of the Marketing Division, ASAC, vol. 2, part 3, 1981, pp. 216–225; Mel S. Moyer, "Marketing Management in Voluntary Organizations," *Proceedings* of the Marketing Division, ASAC, vol. 2, part 3, 1981, pp. 237–245; John A. Quelch, "Marketing Principles and the Future of Preventive Health Care," *Milbank Memorial Fund Quarterly/Health and Society*, vol. 58, no. 2, 1980, pp. 310–347; and Imran S. Curran, Charles B. Wineberg, and Dick R. Wittink, "Design of Subscription Programs for a Performing Arts Series," *Journal of Consumer Research*, June 1981, pp. 67–75.

(markets) in their marketing effort. One of these groups consists of the **contributors** (of money, labour, service, or materials) to the organization. Here the nonbusiness organization's task is that of "resource attraction."[3]

The other major target market is the organization's *clients* — the recipients of the organization's money and/or services. This recipient market is much like that of the customers of a business company. However, nonbusiness organizations — such as churches, Girl Guide companies, nursing homes, symphony orchestras, or universities — are unlikely to refer to their client-recipients as customers. Instead, these organizations will use such terms as *parishioners, members, patients, audience*, or *students*.

This distinction between business and nonbusiness marketing, based on the major markets involved, is significant for this reason: A nonbusiness organization must develop two separate marketing programs — one looking "back" at its contributors, and the other looking "forward" at its clients. Moreover, like businesses, nonbusiness organizations are also involved with several publics in addition to their main markets. A university, for example, must deal with government agencies, environmentalists, mass media, its faculty and staff, and the local community.

Importance of Nonbusiness Marketing

The attention that is finally being devoted to nonbusiness marketing is long overdue and definitely needed. Thousands of these organizations handle billions of dollars and affect millions of people. Often the operation of these organizations is admittedly inefficient. Empty beds in hospitals and empty classrooms constitute a waste of resources we can ill afford. Often a large part of the money collected by a nonbusiness organization goes to cover its administrative expenses, rather than to serve the intended markets. Then there is a dual social and economic loss — donors' gifts are not applied as they intended, and clients are not served efficiently.

The importance of marketing also shows up when nonbusiness organizations fail to do an effective marketing job. Then the result may be additional social and economic costs and wastes. If the death rate from smoking rises because the Canadian Cancer Society and other organizations cannot persuade people of the harm of smoking, we all lose. When anti-litter organizations fail to convince people to control their solid-waste disposal, we all lose. When good museums or good symphony orchestras must cease operating because of lack of contributions and/or lack of attendance, there again are social, cultural, and economic losses.

By developing an effective marketing program, a nonbusiness organization can increase immeasurably its chances of (1) satisfactorily serving both its contributor and its client markets and (2) improving the overall efficiency of its operations.

In the 1980s, three environmental factors in particular are focusing attention on the importance of marketing in nonbusiness organizations. These

[3]See Carole P. Duhaime, Ronald McTavish, and Christopher A. Ross, "Marketing for Development: A Not-for-Profit Perspective," *Proceedings* of the Marketing Division, ASAC, vol. 4, part 3, 1983, pp. 81–91; and Christopher H. Lovelock and Charles B. Wineberg, "Retailng Strategies for Public and Nonprofit Organizations," *Journal of Retailing*, Fall 1983, pp. 93–115.

external factors are forcing even those organizations that have been doing some marketing to develop new strategies to deal with donor markets and client markets. The first major external influence involves the high rates of inflation and unemployment and the generally depressed economic conditions that have plagued the Canadian economy in recent years. Many people find that they are unable to maintain their charitable donations at the same level and now give less to charities and other nonbusiness organizations. Inflation also means, of course, that the donated dollar does not go as far as it once did, and charitable organizations now have to raise far larger amounts of money just to maintain their activities at the same level.[4]

Most nonbusiness organizations that receive their funding in whole or in part from government sources have found that the level of funding to educational, cultural, health-care, and philanthropic groups has decreased. Budgets in such organizations have tightened considerably in recent years. Finally, many nonbusiness organizations that rely heavily on volunteers have had to rethink their approach to recruiting and retaining volunteers. The increase in the number of women in the labour force, combined with generally tight economic conditions, has led to a decrease in the number of unpaid volunteers available. With more women working and fewer people willing to devote their free time to charitable organizations, the task of recruiting volunteers has become a more difficult one.

NONBUSINESS ATTITUDE TOWARD MARKETING

Generally speaking, people in most nonbusiness organizations do not realize that they are "running a business" and should employ business management techniques. It is true that making a profit is *not* the goal of these organizations. Nevertheless, they do need to identify their goals, plan strategies and tactics to reach these goals, effectively execute their plans, and evaluate their performance. Yet only very recently have many nonbusiness organizations started to employ accounting systems, financial controls, personnel management, labour relations, and other business management techniques.[5]

Unfortunately, the acceptance of business management techniques does not often include the use of planned marketing programs. Nonbusiness organizations generally do not seem at all comfortable with marketing.[6] To most of these groups, marketing is limited to some form of promotion, such as advertising or personal selling. These organizations rarely understand the concept of a total marketing program. This involves a planned

---

[4]Diana Swift, "Charity Gets Down to Business," *The Financial Post Magazine*, December 1, 1984, pp. 18–26.

[5]See Lessey Sooklal and James G. Barnes, "Consumer-Oriented Trusteeship for Not-for-Profit Health Care Delivery Systems," *Advances in Health Care Research*, Proceedings of the 1982 Association for Consumer Research Health Care Conference, S. M. Smith and M. Venkatesan (eds.), Salt Lake City, 1982, pp. 59–63.

[6]S. C. Jones and James G. Barnes, *The Marketing of Marketing in Not-for-Profit Organizations: An Organizational Change Perspective*, Working Paper, Faculty of Business Administration, Memorial University of Newfoundland, 1983.

product offering that is effectively priced, promoted, and distributed to provide satisfaction to the various markets (publics). In effect, these organizations still are production-oriented.

Many nonbusiness organizations may speak about marketing and even believe they are practising it. Unfortunately, in many cases they still have a strong production orientation, or at best, a selling orientation. These organizations tend to select — on their own — the products or services that they *think* their customers want (or should want). Then they decide on how to distribute or sell these products. Only at the end of the process do these groups become involved in analysing their markets. This is *not* really a marketing orientation.[7]

In many cases, the people working in nonbusiness organizations tend to have a negative attitude toward marketing. They are apt to think that having a marketing program — and using the term "marketing" — is demeaning and in bad taste. They even seem to feel that it is unethical to use marketing in their organizations.[8]

Perhaps the choice of words is important. The governing body in a church, for example, will not object to "informational notices" (don't call it "advertising") in newspapers or in the Yellow Pages regarding church activities. When church members go to foreign lands to bring new members into the fold, the churches don't call this activity "personal selling." Instead, it is called "missionary work."

Nonbusiness organizations in general seem to face a dilemma. On the one hand, they generally are unaware of what marketing is all about, or they may even have a negative attitude toward it. Yet, on the other hand, these organizations are badly in need of an effective marketing program. Now, taking this latter stand that marketing is needed for an organization's well-being, let's discuss the development of a marketing program for such an organization.

DEVELOPING A STRATEGIC PROGRAM FOR NONBUSINESS MARKETING

The basic structure for planning and developing a marketing program is the same in any organization — private or public, business or nonbusiness, profit or not-for-profit. That is, first we identify and analyse the target markets, and then we develop a strategic marketing mix that will provide want-satisfaction to those markets. Throughout, we use marketing research to help in our decision making.

Target Market Analysis

We really are talking about planning two major marketing programs, one for the contributor market and one for the client market. It is important to pinpoint each market in some detail. Market pinpointing means using market segmentation. A broad (nonsegmented) appeal to the *donor* market is likely to result in a low return. Trying to be all things to all people in the

---

[7]Alan R. Andreasen, "Nonprofits: Check Your Attention to Customers," *Harvard Business Review*, May-June 1982, pp. 105–110.

[8]See Gene R. Laczniak, Robert F. Lusch, and Patrick E. Murphy, "Social Marketing: Its Ethical Dimensions," *Journal of Marketing*, Spring 1979, pp. 29–36.

MARKET
SEGMENTATION IN
POLITICS.

client market is likely to result in being "nothing to nobody" and going broke in the process.

The possible bases for market segmentation for nonbusiness groups are generally the same as those discussed in Chapter 4. In trying to reach its *contributor* market, for example, an organization may segment its appeals by age groups, geographic place of residence, record of past donations, or size of past donations. In effect, segmentation analysis is needed to identify the characteristics of those who donate to the particular organization.[9] Some psychographic (life-style) research may be used to identify contributors on the basis of *why* they donate their money, labour, or materials. People give to nonbusiness organizations for various reasons: (1) They sincerely believe in the organization's work; (2) giving makes them feel good; (3) contributions are tax-deductible; (4) contributing adds to their status in their reference group; or (5) their religious beliefs stimulate giving.

Many nonbusiness organizations typically segment their *client* market, although they probably do not refer to this technique as market segmentation. Our national political parties, as well as some on the provincial level, have become much more sophisticated in developing separate appeals for regional interests, ethnic group interests, organized labour, low income groups, and native peoples. Country clubs develop separate programs for golfers, tennis players, swimmers, and card players. Universities and colleges may segment prospective students on the basis of high-school grade-point average or area of study (technical, liberal arts, professional).

---

[9]See John J. Burnett, "Psychographic and Demographic Characteristics of Blood Donors," *Journal of Consumer Research*, June 1981, pp. 62–66. Also see Leland L. Beik and Scott M. Smith, "Geographic Segmentation: A Fund-Raising Example," in *1979 Educators' Conference Proceedings*, American Marketing Association, Chicago, 1979, pp. 485–488; and William A. Mindak and H. Malcolm Bybee, "Marketing's Application to Fund-Raising," *Journal of Marketing*, July 1971, pp. 13–18.

A decision to employ market segmentation means that the nonbusiness organization must tailor all or part of its marketing program to reach each segment — be it donor or client. Thus the service offering and the promotion may have to be adapted to each major segment.[10]

Careful market analysis requires sophisticated marketing research to identify the various markets. This poses a problem, because most nonbusiness organizations simply are not familiar with marketing research. Fortunately, there are encouraging prospects in this area. Political parties and individual politicians, for example, are frequent users of opinion polls to determine voters' preferences on candidates and issues. Segmentation research also has been used to identify the characteristics of various market segments attending art museums and presentations of the performing arts (opera, concerts, theatres, etc.).[11]

Product Planning

Like a profit-seeking business firm, a nonbusiness organization must decide (1) what products it will offer, (2) what will be the nature of its product mix, and (3) what, if anything, it will do about product attributes such as branding and labelling. In nonbusiness marketing, again, the organization needs two sets of product strategies — one for its contributor market and one for its client market.

Product Offering

In most nonbusiness organizations, the "product offering" to clients typically is a service, an idea, a person (in politics), or a cause. In the case of foundations and charitable organizations, the product offering often is a cash grant — a form of tangible product. Other nonbusiness organizations may offer such tangible products as food and clothing, printed materials, or birth control devices. However, in such cases, the tangible products are incidental to the main services provided by the organization.

The key to determining what its product offering will be is for the organization to decide (1) what "business" it is in and (2) what client markets it wants to reach. If a church views its mission only as providing religious services, its product offering will be relatively limited. On the other hand, if this church views its mission more broadly, it will offer more services to more markets. The church may then provide family counselling services,

A "product" *is* involved, even for the contributor market.

---

[10]See Scott M. Smith and Leland L. Beik, "Market Segmentation for Fund Raisers," *Journal of the Academy of Marketing Science*, Summer 1982, pp. 208–216.

[11]See John E. Robbins and Stephanie S. Robbins, "Museum Marketing: Identification of High, Moderate, and Low Attendee Segments," *Journal of the Academy of Marketing Science*, Winter 1981, pp. 66–76; Margery Steinberg, George Miaoulis, and David Lloyd, "Benefit Segmentation Strategies for the Performing Arts," in *1982 Educators' Conference Proceedings*, American Marketing Association, Chicago, 1982, pp. 289–293; and Michael Bergier and Thomas Muller, "Product Positioning in the Fine Arts: An Application of Perceptual Mapping to the Study of Art Prints," *Proceedings* of the Marketing Division, ASAC, vol. 1, part 3, 1980, pp. 39–48.

day-care services for children, programs for the elderly, religious education courses, and social activities for single people.

Planning the product offering to the contributor market is an even more
difficult task. The organization asks people to donate their money or their
time to a cause. The money or time is the price that contributors pay for
the organization's "product." What is it they are getting for this price? The
benefits they receive in return for their donations must be clearly identified.

Product-Mix Strategies

Several of the product-mix strategies discussed in Chapter 9 can be employed in nonbusiness marketing. Consider, for instance, the strategy of
expanding the product line. Symphony orchestras have broadened their
lines by offering concerts appealing to children, establishing affiliated youth
orchestras, or offering concerts featuring popular music directed to teenagers
and college students. Universities broadened their product mix when they
began to offer programs for part-time adult students, off-campus extension
courses, teleconferencing and correspondence courses, and concentrated
intersessions.

The strategy of *product differentiation* has been employed by several
hospitals and other institutions. Essentially, all hospitals are involved in
the delivery of health care, but many have developed specialties that set
them apart from others. While one hospital may cater to the needs of a
downtown indigent population and will concentrate on the emergency care
normally associated with a downtown hospital, another in a more suburban location will likely deal with obstetrics, child care, and elective surgery.
Similarly, some universities will establish nationally known programs in
the sciences, law, or medicine, while others will nurture a liberal arts
reputation.

The *product life cycle* concept can be applied to nonbusiness marketing.
The Canadian Tuberculosis Association was established many years ago to
fight tuberculosis and to fund research into the development of a cure for
the disease. Later in its life, as effective means were developed to deal with
tuberculosis and the disease was all but eradicated, the association entered
the decline stage of its life cycle. Rather than cease operations, the association changed its name to the Canadian Lung Association and shifted its
emphasis toward the treatment of various diseases related to breathing
and the lungs. In effect, the association had given itself a new lease on life
and had extended its life cycle by embarking upon new challenges within
its mandate to serve the public.

Product Attributes

Nonbusiness groups generally have not done much in the way of using
product strategies such as branding and labelling. The little that has been
done in this area, however, suggests that a nonbusiness organization can
make its marketing more effective by emphasizing product attributes. For

many years, colleges and universities have used nicknames (a form of brand name) primarily for their athletic teams, but also to identify their students and alumni. Most colleges and universities have school colours — another product attribute that helps increase the market's recognition and identification of the school.

Just as packaged-goods manufacturers have developed brand names and trade marks to identify their products, so too have many nonbusiness organizations developed their own distinctive trademarks or logos. The Canadian Lung Association has trademarked its distinctive double-barred Christmas Seal cross and Rotary International's wheel is well known. The trademarks of the Boy Scouts, Girl Guides, the YM-YWCA, and the Salvation Army are recognized and remembered by many people (see Fig. 22-1).

Price Determination

Pricing in many nonbusiness organizations is quite different from pricing in a business firm. First, pricing becomes less important when profit making is not an organizational goal. Also, many nonbusiness groups believe there are *no* client-market pricing considerations in their marketing because there is no charge to the client. The organization's basic function is to help those who cannot afford to pay.

Actually, the products or services received by the clients rarely are free — that is, without a price of some kind. True, the price may not be a monetary charge. Often, however, the client pays a charge — in the form of travel and waiting time, and perhaps of degrading treatment — that a money-paying client-customer would not incur for the same service. Poor children who have to wear donated, second-hand clothes certainly are paying a price if their classmates ridicule these clothes. Or the price may be in the form of embarrassment, as when a couple goes for "free" family-planning counselling or health services. Alcoholics Anonymous and some drug rehabilitation organizations that provide "free" services do exact a price. They require active participation by their clients, and often a very strongly expressed resolve by clients to help themselves.

Some civic and charitable organizations exact rather high "prices" from their members and supporters. For example, joining the Big Brothers organization means that the individual must accept responsibility for acting as a surrogate parent for a child. This not only involves a certain amount of time each week, but requires that the "Big Brother" make a personal commitment, which usually involves a great deal of psychic cost. Similarly, when a blood donor goes to a Red Cross clinic for the first time to donate blood, there are far more than dollar-and-time costs involved.

Some nonbusiness groups *do* face the same general pricing problems we discussed in Chapters 11 to 13. Museums and symphony orchestras must decide on admission prices; fraternal and social organizations must set a schedule for dues; and universities must determine how much to charge for tuition. Essentially, these organizations must (1) determine the base price for their product offering and (2) establish pricing strategies in several areas of their pricing structure.

Figure 22-1
DISTINCTIVE LOGOS
OF NONBUSINESS
ORGANIZATIONS.

Setting the Base Price

Here again we are faced with two market situations — pricing in the contributor market and pricing in the client market.

When dealing with the contributor market, nonbusiness organizations really do not set the price of the donation. That price is set by contributors when they decide how much they are willing to pay for the benefits they expect to receive in return for their gifts. However, the organization may suggest a price. A charitable organization, for example, may suggest that you donate one day's pay or that you donate your time for one day a month.

Some of our discussion regarding the pricing of services (Chapter 21) is appropriate to the client market — for example, in pricing admissions to museums, concerts, or art galleries. But for most nonbusiness organizations, the basic pricing methods used by business firms — cost-plus, balance of supply and demand, market alone — simply are not appropriate. Many organizations know they cannot cover their costs with prices charged to client markets. The difference between anticipated revenues and costs must be made up by contributions.

As yet, we simply have not developed any real guidelines — any methodology — for much of our nonbusiness pricing. It is hoped, however, that some useful ideas will emerge as more and more nonbusiness groups engage in effective marketing research.

One of the most important aspects of pricing that any nonbusiness organization must face involves the reduction of nonmonetary costs. As we have observed above, many nonbusiness organizations make certain nonmonetary demands upon their supporters and members. Volunteer organizations require that their members make a commitment of time. Hospital clinics require that patients invest time in travelling to the clinic and in waiting for service. Some nonbusiness organizations, by their very nature, create certain anxieties in the minds of those with whom they come in contact. All such organizations should do as much as possible to facilitate contact and to reduce these nonmonetary costs. Hospitals can establish remote clinics that take medical service to the people. Libraries often provide book-borrowing services to patients in hospitals. The Canadian Red Cross tries to reduce the anxiety associated with donating blood by creating comfortable facilities and a relaxing environment.

Pricing Strategies

Some of the pricing strategies discussed in Chapter 13 are also applicable in nonbusiness marketing. Discount strategies have widespread use, for example. Some museums offer discount prices to students and to senior citizens. A season ticket for some theatre companies or symphony orchestras costs less per performance than tickets purchased on an individual-performance basis. This is a form of quantity discount.

Considerations regarding one-price versus variable-price policies also are applicable in nonbusiness marketing. Some charitable organizations provide services according to the client's ability to pay — a variable price policy. A one-price policy typically is followed by universities; all students pay the same tuition (in cash or its equivalent in scholarship or hours or labour) for a full load of specialized coursework.

Distribution System

Setting up a distribution system in a nonbusiness organization involves two main tasks. One is to establish channels of distribution back to the contributor market and foward to the client market. The other task, usually the more important one, is to set up a physical distribution system to reach these two sets of publics.

Channels of Distribution

The channels of distribution used in nonbusiness marketing ordinarily are quite simple and short. The nonbusiness organization usually deals directly with its two major publics. That is, no middlemen are used.

When an intermediary is used, ordinarily it is an agent middleman. For instance, to generate increased contributions, a political party or a university may employ an outside fund-raising organization. To reach potential customers, admission tickets to concerts or sporting events may be sold through independent ticket agencies.

FREE OUTDOOR
CONCERTS —
DISTRIBUTING AN
ORCHESTRA'S
PRODUCT TO CLIENTS.
*(Susanne Faulkner
Stevens/Lincoln Center for
the Performing Arts)*

Physical Distribution

The main goal in physical distribution is for the nonbusiness organization to locate itself so as to serve both its contributors and its clients most effectively. The organization should be as accessible to its contributors as possible. That is, if you want people to give you money, make this giving as easy and convenient as possible. Let them pay by cheque, by payroll deduction, on the installment plan, or even by credit card. If the donor is contributing used products, collect them at the donor's residence or at some other choice location. Don't force the donor to haul the stuff across town to a central depository.

Location is also critically important in dealing with client markets. Thus, universities set up branches and offer teleconference and correspondence courses. The Salvation Army and Goodwill Industries generally locate their stores in low-income neighbourhoods. Health-care organizations provide mobile units for lung X-rays, blood-pressure tests, and inoculations. Libraries operate "bookmobiles" and family-planning organizations have satellite (branch) clinics. Big-city museums arrange for portable exhibits to be taken to small towns.[12]

Promotion Program

Promotion is the part of the marketing mix with which many nonbusiness organizations are most familiar. They have regularly used advertising, personal selling, and sales promotion—often very aggressively and effectively—to communicate with both their contributors and their clients. The problem is that these organizations have not integrated their promotional mix

---

[12]For some examples of physical distribution decisions in several nonbusiness fields, see J. Richard Jones and Philip D. Cooper, "The Integration of a Logistical Decision-Making Framework into Nonprofit Marketing," *Journal of the Academy of Marketing Science,* Winter 1981, pp. 28–39.

into a total marketing program. In fact, many nonbusiness groups believe that promotion and marketing are one and the same thing. Obviously this lack of understanding of what marketing is all about has been a major drawback to these organizations.

Advertising

Advertising is used extensively to reach the donor market. Many nonbusiness organizations conduct an annual campaign to collect funds. Mass media (newspapers, magazines, television, radio) frequently are used in these efforts. The media are also used more selectively to solicit funds. Direct mail can be especially effective in reaching segmented donor markets such as past contributors, religious or ethnic groups related to the organizations, or college alumni. Media such as alumni magazines and foreign-language newspapers can also be used to pinpoint donor market segments.

Nonbusiness groups also can use advertising to communicate with client markets. To offset declining enrolments, some universities have conducted advertising campaigns in a variety of media. Some religious organizations, riding a resurgent wave of interest in religion in recent years, have also conducted advertising campaigns for membership, some making very effective use of television. Hospitals, realizing their role not only as providers of health care but also as promoters of an improved level of health in the community, have begun to offer free public counselling sessions to advise people on exercise programs, nutrition and diet, and other matters relating to health. Cultural organizations such as museums, art galleries, and theatre companies regularly advertise to increase attendance.

In some situations, a nonbusiness organization can reach both its contributor and its client markets with the same ad. The Canadian Heart Foundation, the Canadian Cancer Society, or the Canadian Lung Association might advertise, asking you to contribute to its annual campaign. In the same ad, it might urge you to watch your diet, quit smoking, or get a medical checkup.

Personal Selling

Personal selling is frequently used in fund raising efforts. Sometimes a door-to-door campaign is used. At Christmastime, Salvation Army volunteers, with their Christmas Cheer kettles, collect donations in the downtown areas of many cities. And potential large donors often are approached by salespeople.

Many nonbusiness organizations also use personal selling to reach their client public. These personal representatives may not be called salesmen or saleswomen, but that is exactly what they are. For centuries, missionaries of countless religious organizations have recruited new members by personal contact — personal selling. Personal selling also is used to recruit new members for civic organizations (YMCA, Girl Guides, Lions, Rotary).

Universities send "salespeople" (admission officers, alumni, current students) to talk to high-school students, their parents, and their counsellors.

Using sales representatives to reach either contributors or clients poses some management problems for a nonbusiness organization. In effect, the organization has to manage a sales force, including recruiting, training, compensating, supervising, and evaluating performance. Unfortunately, not many nonbusiness organizations think in these terms, nor are they as yet qualified to do this management job.

Sales Promotion

Nonbusiness organizations also have long recognized the value of sales promotion to reach their markets. Many organizations have displays and exhibits (including donation boxes) in local stores and shopping centres, at home and outdoor shows, and at sporting events. Usually, these organizations are not charged for the use of this space.

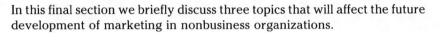

(Ritson, Newfoundland Herald)

IMPLEMEN-TATION OF MARKETING
Interest and Research in the Field

In this final section we briefly discuss three topics that will affect the future development of marketing in nonbusiness organizations.

If nonbusiness marketing is to have a future, it is most important that the people in nonbusiness organizations understand fully (1) what marketing is and (2) what it can do for their organizations. Fortunately, in recent years, people in many different nonbusiness fields have displayed a growing interest in marketing. Books on the topic of nonbusiness or nonprofit marketing are appearing.[13] Several general marketing textbooks, such as this one, devote all or part of a chapter to nonbusiness marketing. Doctoral dissertations and many journal articles are appearing on this subject, and special sessions at professional marketing meetings are being devoted to nonbusiness marketing.

Just a few years ago, research in nonbusiness was initiated mainly by university professors and other people outside the nonbusiness field being studied. Now the marketing research is being generated by people working within various nonbusiness fields. This is a healthy sign for the future.

Measuring Performance

A real managerial challenge for the future is to come up with some valid means of measuring the marketing performance of a nonbusiness organization. At present, this is very difficult, if not impossible, for many of these organizations. A private business can evaluate its performance by using such quantitative measures as net profit, sales volume, or market share.

---

[13]See Philip Kotler, *Marketing for Nonprofit Organizations*, 2d ed., Prentice-Hall, Inc., Englewood Cliffs, N.J., 1982; Ralph M. Gaedeke (ed.), *Marketing in Private and Public Nonprofit Organizations*, Goodyear Publishing Company, Inc., Santa Monica, Calif. 1977; Christopher H. Lovelock (ed.), *Nonbusiness Marketing Cases* (bibliography), Intercollegiate Case Clearing House, Boston, 1979.

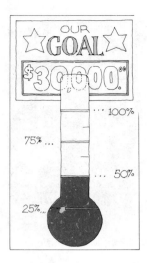

Donations measure only part of the performance of a nonbusiness organization.

For most nonbusiness organizations, however, there are no corresponding quantitative measures.

Nonbusiness organizations can measure the contributions they receive, but that total evaluates only their fund-raising abilities. It does not measure the services rendered to their clients. How do you quantitatively evaluate the performance of, say, the Red Cross? Perhaps by the number of people they house and feed following a disaster, or by the number of blood donors they attract, or by the number of people they train in first-aid and life saving techniques.

Churches, museums, and the YM-YWCA can measure their attendance, but how can we measure the performance of these institutions or the services they provide for their clients? In another area, how does the Canadian Cancer Society or the Canadian Heart Foundation measure its performance? By the decline in death rates from cancer and heart disease? Perhaps, but such a decline may be the result of several factors, including the work of these organizations. When such changes in the incidence of accidents or disease take place, should credit go to the various health and research organizations that may be operating programs in the general area? These are difficult questions to answer.

Managing the Marketing Effort

As stressed throughout this chapter, nonbusiness organizations typically are unfamiliar with marketing, even though they practise some marketing under different names. The marketing activities that they do perform (usually promotion) are not well coordinated, and the people in charge have other duties and titles. In a university, for example, personal selling may be managed by the director of admissions, and advertising may be done through an office of public information. Nowhere in the university will you find anyone with the title of sales manager or advertising manager.

To establish a more formal marketing structure, the organization may set up a group of people to determine where the organization wants to go regarding its marketing effort.[14] These groups can define the organization's marketing goals and identify marketing strategies to reach these goals. Decisions can be made regarding the development of an internal marketing department and the way this department might provide marketing services to the entire organization.

The groups working on such studies should include people with marketing expertise. Many nonbusiness organizations already are using outside marketing specialists. Political parties, health-care organizations, and universities have used marketing-research firms for market analysis and other

---

[14]This organization approach is adapted from Philip Kotler, "Strategies for Introducing Marketing into Nonprofit Organizations," *Journal of Marketing*, January 1979, pp. 41–44; and from S. C. Jones and J. G. Barnes, *The Marketing of Marketing in Not-for-Profit Organizations: An Organizational Change Perspective*, Working Paper, Faculty of Business Administration, Memorial University of Newfoundland, 1983.

purposes. Outside advertising agencies are used to create and produce individual ads or entire campaigns.

As a formal marketing structure develops, the organization may create a new middle-management executive position. Such a position might carry the title of director of marketing. Typically, this will be a staff position — perhaps located in the organization's planning department — with little or no line-operating authority. Eventually, as a sign of marketing maturity, our nonbusiness organization will establish a top-level executive position comparable to that of the vice president of marketing in a business firm.

SUMMARY

The marketing fundamentals apply to private, nonprofit, nonbusiness organizations as well as to firms in the business sector. But the development and implementation of a strategic marketing program are quite different in nonbusiness fields.

The nonbusiness field includes thousands of organizations spanning educational, cultural, religious, charitable, social, health-care, and political activities. Because of the large amounts of money and numbers of people involved in these organizations, marketing is quite important. Yet, many people in nonbusiness organizations tend to be opposed to marketing. They really do not understand what marketing is or what it can do for their organizations.

Most nonbusiness organizations must deal with two major groups (markets) — the *contributors* to the organization and the *client-recipients* of the organization's money or services. Consequently, a nonbusiness organization must develop two separate marketing programs — one to attract resources from contributors and one to serve its clients.

In developing its marketing programs, a nonbusiness organization first must identify and analyse its markets. The use of market segmentation is especially helpful at this stage. Then the organization is ready to develop its strategic marketing mix. The product offering will be determined largely by deciding what business the organization is in and what client markets it wants to reach. Product-mix strategies, such as expansion of mix or product differentiation, may well be used. Pricing in many nonbusiness organizations is quite different from the usual price determination in a business firm. Channels of distribution typically are quite simple in nonbusiness marketing. The main distribution problem is to physically locate the organization so as to make serving both its contributors and its clients as easy and as convenient as possible. In promotion, many nonbusiness organizations have used advertising, personal selling, and other tools extensively, often aggressively, and often quite effectively.

Interest and research in nonbusiness marketing are growing. Both should be of help in implementing nonbusiness marketing programs in the future. Two important problems still to be solved are those of (1) measuring performance in a nonbusiness organization and (2) developing an internal structure to manage the nonbusiness marketing effort.

KEY TERMS AND CONCEPTS

Private versus public organizations 558

Profit versus not-for-profit organizations 558

Business versus nonbusiness organizations 558

Exchange concept in nonbusiness marketing 559

Contributor (donor) markets 560

Client (recipient) markets 560

Importance of nonbusiness marketing 560

The antimarketing attitude 561

Market segmentation in nonbusiness organizations 562

Product differentiation in nonbusiness organizations 564

The marketing mix in nonbusiness organizations:
Product offering 564
Pricing 567
Distribution 568
Promotion 569

Marketing research in nonbusiness organizations 571

Measuring marketing performance in nonbusiness organizations 571

Managing a marketing program in nonbusiness organizations 572

QUESTIONS AND PROBLEMS

1. Are "nonbusiness organizations" and "nonprofit organizations" synonymous terms? If not,
   a. Name some nonbusiness organizations in which profit making is a major goal.
   b. Name some business organizations that are intentionally nonprofit.

2. Distinguish between business and nonbusiness organizations.

3. In this chapter, it is noted that many people in nonbusiness organizations have a negative attitude toward marketing. What suggestions do you have for changing this attitude so that these people will appreciate the value of marketing for their organizations?

4. Identify the various segments of the contributor market for your university.

5. Identify the client markets for:
   a. Your university   c. Your church or other place of worship
   b. The YMCA   d. A museum or art gallery in a large city

6. What are some target markets (publics), other than contributors or clients, for each of the following organizations?
   a. Girl Guides
   b. Community hospitals
   c. Your university

7. What benefits do contributors derive from gifts to:
   a. The Red Cross   c. A symphony orchestra
   b. The Boy Scouts   d. A candidate for a political party

8. What is the product offering of:
   a. A political candidate
   b. Planned Parenthood
   c. An organization opposed to nuclear energy

9. A financial consultant for a Canadian university suggested a change in the university's pricing policy. He recommended that the university discontinue its present one-price policy, under which all full-time students pay the same

tuition. Instead, he recommended that the tuition should vary by faculty within the university. In this way, students majoring in high-cost fields of study, such as Engineering or Biochemistry, would pay higher tuition than students in lower-cost fields, such as History or Economics. Should the university accept this recommendation?

10. Explain how the concept of the marketing mix (product, price, distribution, promotion) is applicable to the marketing of the following social causes:
    a. The use of returnable bottles, instead of the throwaway type
    b. The prevention of heart ailments
    c. A campaign against smoking
    d. Obeying the 100 km/hr speed limit

11. How would you measure the marketing performance of each of the following?
    a. A church   c. The New Democratic Party
    b. Your university   d. A jogging club

12. The performance of a charitable organization may be measured as the percentage of contributions that is distributed among its clients. Explain why you think this is or isn't an effective measure of marketing performance.

13. Assume that your university wants to hire a director of marketing. Prepare a job description for this position, indicating its scope, activities, location within the university's administration, and responsibilities.

Chapter
23
International Marketing

CHAPTER GOALS

As you will see, international marketing entails more than simply marketing in a foreign language. After studying this chapter, you should understand:

1. *The importance of international marketing to Canadian organizations*
2. *Managerial orientations toward multinational operations*
3. *Major organizational structures for operating in foreign markets*
4. *The nature and problems of international marketing research*
5. *The importance of recognizing cultural and environmental differences in various foreign markets*
6. *International marketing programs — product planning, pricing, distribution, and advertising*
7. *The factors affecting balance of trade between countries*

"More than ever before, the economic future of the United States is vested in the marketing process — and future American progress will be determined largely by marketing management's success on the new frontier — the world market."[1] Some people may believe that this quotation overstates the importance of international marketing. But there is no disputing the fact that international trade significantly affects the political and economic health of virtually all nations — the industrialized nations as well as the developing countries in the so-called Third World.

As we move through the 1980s, however, import quotas and other forms of international trade restrictions are a continuing threat to international marketing in several countries. And there is continuing trade friction among the Western European nations, Japan, Canada, and the United States. This is further compounded by the access-to-market and balance-of-payments

---

[1]Ray R. Eppert, "Passport for Marketing Overseas," *Journal of Marketing*, April 1965, p. 6. Although Eppert made this statement in 1965 when president of a large manufacturer of business machines, the point is even more relevant today.

(Erich Hartmann/
Magnum Photos)

problems of many developing countries. Any growth in trade protectionism is extremely unfortunate. History clearly tells us of the damage that national economies can suffer from trade restrictions and trade wars.

Marketing fundamentals are universally applicable. Whether a firm sells in Timmins or Timbuktu, its marketing program should be built around a good product or service, properly priced, promoted, and distributed to a market that has been carefully selected and analysed. However, the strategies used in implementing the marketing programs in foreign countries often are quite different from domestic marketing strategies. Furthermore, for the firm that is interested in international marketing, management must make strategic decisions regarding (1) the company's orientation or degree of involvement in international marketing and (2) the organizational structure for entering and operating in each foreign market.

Different strategies are needed in foreign markets primarily because those markets exist in a different set of environments. Recall that a company operates its marketing program within the economic, political, and cultural environment of each of its markets — foreign or domestic. And none of these environments is controllable by the firm. What complicates international marketing is the fact that these environments — particularly the cultural environment — often consist of elements very unfamiliar to Canadian marketing executives. This includes the American market, about which Canadians in general as well as marketing executives believe they already know a great deal. A further complication is the tendency for people to use their own cultural values as a frame of reference when in a foreign environment.[2]

DOMESTIC MARKETING AND INTERNATIONAL MARKETING

---

[2]K.C. Dhawan, H. Etemad, and R. W. Wright, *International Business: A Canadian Perpective*, Addison-Wesley, Don Mills, Ont., 1981.

IMPORTANCE OF INTERNATIONAL MARKETING

Canadians have long known that their welfare depended to an important degree on their success in world markets. For many years our exports have ranged from 20 to 25 percent of gross domestic product (similar to the United Kingdom) compared with a 4 to 6 percent range for the United States. Currently, more than 25 percent of our GNP is being exported. International marketing's role in trade is a substantial one, and it is the progress we make in international marketing that will substantially affect our future economic welfare. While some people may believe that this is an overstatement of the position of international marketing, we cannot deny the fact that multinational companies have evolved all over the world and firms are still creating new units as well as integrating their domestic and foreign operations into world enterprises. Canadian firms in banking, engineering services, electronics and even provincial marketing boards in hogs, tree fruits, and fish are part of this movement. As the opening sentence in this chapter indicates, Americans feel that their country's progress depends on success in the world market. It this is true for the U.S., with such a small percentage of their gross domestic product involved in foreign trade, it is undeniably true for Canada with five to six times greater reliance on international markets and international marketing.

Among companies in Canada, there seems to be a growing awareness of international marketing opportunities and an increasing willingness to enter foreign markets. As domestic markets become saturated, Canadian producers — even those with no previous international experience — now look to foreign markets as outlets for their productive capacity and sometimes as sources of wider profit margins and higher returns on investments. Naturally, many firms look to the United States for a market and tend not to consider it as foreign.

The world market outside North America sometimes offers greater growth and profit opportunities than the domestic market. The indication of con-

Table 23-1   SHARES OF FREE WORLD EXPORTS: SELECTED COUNTRIES

Period	United States	France	West Germany	Italy	Netherlands	United Kingdom	Japan	Canada
1970	15.4%	6.4%	12.1%	4.7%	4.2%	7.0%	6.9%	5.9%
1975	13.6	6.7	11.4	4.4	4.4	5.6	7.1	4.3
1976	12.8	6.3	11.3	4.1	4.5	5.2	7.5	4.5
1977	11.8	6.4	11.5	4.4	4.3	5.7	7.9	4.3
1978	12.1	6.7	12.0	4.7	4.2	6.0	8.3	4.1
1979	12.1	6.7	11.5	4.8	4.3	6.1	6.8	3.9

Notes:
1. Free world includes all countries except Albania, Bulgaria, Czechoslovakia, East Germany, Hungary, Poland, Romania, Union of Soviet Socialist Republics, People's Republic of China, North Korea, Vietnam, Outer Mongolia, and Cuba.
2. Shares in export markets for total trade are measured as percentages of total exports from the free world. The percentage shares are based on values in U.S. dollars calculated at current exchange rates.
3. World exports are defined as the sums of exports from fifteen major industrial countries.

Source: U.S. Department of Commerce, International Trade Administration, *International Economic Indicators*, vol. VI, no. 4, December 1980.

tinued increases in buying power, gross national product, and capital investment in some foreign nations — despite the effects of the latest recession — makes it almost inevitable that these countries will constitute profitable growth markets (as well as strong competition) for many consumer
and industrial products. A prime example of such newly developing national markets are the NICs — newly industrialized countries. They provide
the real opportunities in the 1980s for increases in Canadian trade as their
economies recovery. In addition to the OPEC countries, the NICs include
South Korea, Malaysia, Brazil, Taiwan, The Phillipines, Hong Kong, and
mainland China.[3]

Canada's position in international markets and its requirements for international marketing are interesting both in terms of our pattern of goods
marketed and in terms of our access to markets.

By 1979, free world exports were more than $1,500.1 billion (U.S.). The
shares of export trade for selected countries shown in Table 23-1 position
Canada as relatively minor in world terms. However, when we view our
trade activity, both export and import, in terms of its importance to us —
as a percentage of GNP — only the Netherlands has a greater involvement
(see Table 23-2). Without question, international activities and events must
be a major concern for us.

Table 23-2   INTERNATIONAL TRADE AS A PERCENTAGE OF GNP:
             SELECTED COUNTRIES

Period	United States	France	West Germany	Italy	Netherlands	United Kingdom	Japan	Canada
				Ratio of Exports to GNP				
1970	4.3	12.7	18.4	14.2	37.0	15.8	9.5	19.6
1975	7.0	15.4	21.4	18.2	42.4	19.2	11.1	20.2
1976	6.7	15.9	22.8	20.0	44.1	20.8	11.9	20.1
1977	6.3	16.6	22.7	21.1	40.9	23.3	11.6	21.3
1978	6.6	16.1	22.0	21.4	38.5	22.7	10.0	23.2
1979	7.5	17.1	22.4	22.3	42.8	22.5	10.2	25.2
				Ratio of Imports to GNP				
1970	4.1	13.5	16.1	16.1	42.2	17.8	9.2	16.3
1975	6.3	15.9	17.8	20.1	43.0	23.2	11.5	21.0
1976	7.1	18.4	19.7	23.3	44.4	25.1	11.5	19.6
1977	7.8	18.4	19.5	22.4	43.6	25.8	10.3	20.3
1978	8.1	17.3	18.8	21.5	41.3	24.9	8.2	21.8
1979	8.7	18.8	20.8	24.0	45.8	25.5	10.9	24.1

Notes: Ratios of exports and imports to GNP or GDP and production are measured in terms of current prices. Production covers
all goods organizing in agriculture, forestry, hunting, fishing, mining, quarrying, and manufacturing — that is, the sum of national
accounts industry components on a value added basis excluding transportation, wholesaling, retailing, other services, and government enterprises. The United States production series for all goods is comparable to that for other countries.

Source: U.S. Department of Commerce, International Trade Administration, *International Economic Indicators*, vol. VI, no. 4,
December 1980.

---

[3]Stuart McEvoy, "Canadian Exports in the 1980s," *The Canadian Business Review*, Summer
1980, p. 38.

Our foreign markets are highly concentrated geographically. It comes as no surprise to see (from Table 23-3) that the United States is our primary foreign customer, taking 72.9 percent of our foreign sales in 1983 and providing us with 71.6 percent of our imports in the same year. Our trade with the rest of the world is small but important. The United Kingdom as a traditional market has decreased in importance as it has become more EEC-oriented in both its importing and exporting.

Not only are our geographic markets highly concentrated, but also our exports are highly concentrated by economic sector. What we sell consists mainly of primary items such as wheat, beef, and other edible products, and raw materials such as ores and concentrates, petroleum and natural gas, and forest products. The detail, shown in Table 23-4, clearly indicates the continuing effect of the Canada–United States Automotive Agreement of 1965 and underlines the importance of this trade in our total. While the agreement has resulted in an increase in manufacturing exports, in the main most of these exports are parent-subsidiary transfers without any international marketing efforts. In all the other areas reported, interna-

Table 23-3   CANADA'S EXPORT AND IMPORT MARKETS

Export Markets

Year	United States	Japan	United Kingdom	Other EEC*	Other
(% of total Canadian exports)					
1975	65.1	6.4	5.5	7.2	15.8
1976	67.3	6.2	4.9	7.0	14.6
1977	69.8	5.7	4.4	6.2	13.9
1978	70.2	5.8	3.8	5.6	14.6
1979	67.9	6.2	4.0	7.1	14.8
1980	63.3	5.8	4.3	8.3	18.4
1981	66.3	5.4	4.0	6.7	17.6
1982	68.2	5.4	3.2	5.7	17.4
1983	72.9	5.2	2.8	4.7	14.3

Import Sources

Year	United States	Japan	United Kingdom	Other EEC*	Other
(% of total Canadian imports)					
1975	68.1	3.5	3.5	6.0	18.9
1976	68.8	4.1	3.1	5.3	18.7
1977	70.4	4.2	3.0	5.6	16.8
1978	70.7	4.5	3.2	6.1	15.5
1979	72.4	3.4	3.1	5.8	15.3
1980	70.1	4.0	2.9	5.2	17.8
1981	68.9	5.1	2.8	5.2	18.0
1982	70.5	5.2	2.8	5.6	15.9
1983	71.6	5.8	2.4	5.5	14.7

*European Economic Community.

Source: Statistics Canada, cat. no. 65-001, Tables 1, 2.

tional marketing activities play a role. The Canadian Wheat Board negotiates country-to-country wheat deals that follow the classic industrial marketing patterns regardless of the "ownership" of the board. The scope of activities involved in international marketing in the categories reported ranges from simple written communication and export to full-fledged, fully developed country operations. In the latter case these operations abroad are the same as they are at home.

Among Canadian companies, there is a continuing and growing awareness of international marketing opportunities. Federal and provincial governments encourage Canadian producers — even those with no previous international experience — to look to foreign markets. Those markets can be outlets for surplus productive capacity, as well as sources of wider profit margins and higher returns on investment.

The world market often offers greater growth and profit opportunities than the domestic market. The buying power and capital investment in many foreign nations means that these countries are profitable markets (as well as strong competition) for many firms. The devaluation of the Canadian dollar in the 1970s, and the accompanying higher valuation of some foreign currencies, also made international marketing more attractive to Canadian firms. These revaluations generally *decreased* the price of Canadian products in foreign markets and *increased* the price of Japanese, European, and American goods in Canada.

International marketing is a two-way street, however. The same expanding foreign markets that offer fine growth opportunities for Canadian firms also have their own producers. These foreign firms are providing substantial competition both in Canada and elsewhere. Canadian consumers have responded favourably, for example, to Japanese radio-TV products (Sony), motorcycles (Honda), cameras (Canon, Nikon), and autos (Datsun, Toyota, Honda). We buy Italian shoes, German autos, Dutch electric razors (Norelco), French wines, Austrian skis, and so on.

Especially strong competition is coming from Japan and the companies in the European Economic Community (EEC), more popularly known as the Common Market. This is a group of nine western European nations (see the following box) that have banded together in a multinational economic union. Competitive challenges are also being encountered from countries in other multinational economic organizations (see box).

A relatively new competitive factor has been the rise of multinational firms headquartered in developing countries (the so-called Third World). The petroleum-exporting countries (members of OPEC) have received the greatest amount of publicity. However, in many industries, significant competition in international markets has come from firms based in Brazil, South Korea, and Taiwan. Furthermore, companies in the developing nations, usually either owned by or strongly supported by governments, are likely to have a growing impact in international business.[4]

---

[4]See David A. Heenan and Warren J. Keegan, "The Rise of Third World Multinationals," *Harvard Business Review*, January-February, 1979, pp. 101–109; and "Looming Threat from the ADCs (Advanced Developing Countries)," *Dun's Review*, March 1979, p. 88.

Table 23-4   MERCHANDISE TRADE DETAIL: EXPORTS 1963–1983

Year	Wheat	Animals and Other Edible Products	Ores and Concentrates	Crude Petroleum and Natural Gas	Other Crude Materials	Lumber	Woodpulp	Newsprint
D	3609					3629	3631	3632
				(Millions of dollars)				
1963	787	675	703	310	414	452	405	760
1964	1,024	817	803	360	453	471	461	835
1965	840	869	863	384	517	490	493	870
1966	1,061	906	934	430	583	474	520	968
1967	742	902	1,016	522	571	505	543	955
1968	684	929	1,262	600	605	656	628	990
1969	473	992	1,138	702	623	697	754	1,126
1970	687	1,181	1,522	855	707	664	785	1,111
1971	833	1,279	1,415	1,038	811	830	798	1,085
1972	927	1,428	1,397	1,315	848	1,174	830	1,158
1973	1,221	1,937	2,000	1,833	1,192	1,599	1,082	1,288
1974	2,065	1,806	2,376	3,914	1,504	1,290	1,889	1,726
1975	2,023	2,124	2,241	4,144	1,581	973	1,835	1,746
1976	1,732	2,563	2,512	3,903	1,872	1,649	2,186	2,003
1977	1,881	2,727	2,730	3,779	2,341	2,387	2,158	2,382
1978	1,913	3,389	2,404	3,763	2,664	3,229	2,181	2,886
1979	2,180	4,134	3,895	5,294	3,350	3,901	3,083	3,222
1980	3,862	4,401	4,210	6,883	3,667	3,353	3,873	3,684
1981	3,728	5,714	4,085	6,875	4,251	2,989	3,819	4,325
1982	4,287	5,939	3,187	7,483	4,108	2,912	3,212	4,080
1983	4,648	5,768	2,897	7,415	4,076	3,964	3,057	4,005

	Fabricated Metals	Other Fabricated Materials	Motor Vehicles and Parts	Other Machinery and Equipment	Consumer Goods and Miscellaneous	Re-exports	Total
			3653				3471
				(Millions of dollars)			
1963	918	572	88	589	127	182	6,980
1964	1,049	680	177	811	147	209	8,303
1965	1,138	738	356	811	157	242	8,767
1966	1,227	823	1,012	956	195	255	10,043
1967	1,368	858	1,739	1,167	234	298	11,420
1968	1,605	975	2,672	1,340	303	373	13,624
1969	1,499	1,087	3,514	1,595	244	428	14,871
1970	1,996	1,311	3,499	1,666	418	419	16,820
1971	1,678	1,406	4,171	1,660	393	422	17,818
1972	1,716	1,700	4,718	2,014	446	479	20,150
1973	2,084	2,171	5,415	2,455	562	583	25,421
1974	2,760	3,030	5,717	2,868	732	767	32,442
1975	2,475	2,855	6,432	3,399	720	780	33,328
1976	3,015	3,375	8,225	3,670	946	825	38,475
1977	3,543	4,458	10,424	3,975	901	870	44,554
1978	4,684	6,175	12,540	5,230	1,201	924	53,183
1979	5,251	8,919	11,900	7,295	1,895	1,324	65,641
1980	8,112	10,323	10,924	8,507	2,648	1,713	76,159
1981	7,735	11,672	13,184	9,968	2,992	2,475	83,811
1982	6,772	10,911	16,507	9,953	2,480	2,706	84,534
1983	7,050	11,911	21,306	9,719	2,609	2,457	90,883

Source: Department of Finance, Canada, *Economic Review*, April 1984, p. 204.

THE MULTINATIONAL ECONOMIC ORGANIZATIONS

EEC (European Economic Community, also known as the Common Market): Belgium, France, West Germany, Netherlands, Luxembourg, Italy, Ireland, Great Britain, Denmark, Greece.

EFTA (European Free Trade Association): Norway, Sweden, Finland, Iceland, Portugal, Austria, Switzerland.

COMECON (Council for Mutual Economic Assistance): Union of Soviet Socialist Republics and other Eastern European communist nations.

OPEC (Organization for Petroleum Exporting Countries): Saudi Arabia, Kuwait, United Arab Emirates, Qatar, Iran, Iraq, Libya, Algeria, Nigeria, Venezuela, Indonesia.

SERA (Latin American Economic System): Twenty-five nations in Central and South America.

THE TOP TEN AND THE BOTTOM TEN MARKETS IN THE THIRD WORLD IN THE 1980s

The Ten Best	The Ten Poorest
1. Mexico	1. Bangladesh
2. Singapore	2. Nepal
3. Taiwan	3. Somalia
4. Venezuela	4. Sierra Leone
5. Yugoslavia	5. Benin
6. Argentina	6. Tanzania
7. Indonesia	7. Haiti
8. Malaysia	8. Uganda
9. Zimbabwe	9. Senegal
10. Nigeria	10. Ghana

These ratings were made by the Grey Advertising Agency. Selection criteria included a country's natural resources, educational level, and political-economic stability. Brazil was not included because it already is considered an excellent market. The Republic of Korea was omitted because of changing governmental policies affecting business.

Source: "Making It in the Third World," *Grey Matter*, vol. 52, no. 1, 1981, pp. 4–7.

The Changing
Scene

As we move through the 1980s, there still are excellent marketing opportunities for companies in multinational operations. *But* the scene has changed. Several situations make international marketing much tougher than it was from 1945 to 1975. Perhaps the most significant occurrences have been the soaring costs of energy and the high inflation rates in many countries. These factors have done much to cut into the profits of many companies.

Another major change has been the shift in international investment patterns that began to take on significant proportions in the late 1970s. Until then, the pattern was for Canadian firms to invest very heavily — in relative terms — in the United States and somewhat in the United Kingdom and other countries. In the late 1970s, the attractiveness of the U.S. market had increased even more and not just for manufacturing firms, but also for real estate developers, service organizations, and the like. The service organizations were also beginning to develop quite well in newly industrialized nations and OPEC countries. The world-wide recession of the early 1980s put a stop to many of these developments. It is only as economic conditions improve that Canadian firms feel comfortable in pursuing such projects.

ALTERNATIVE ORIENTATIONS TOWARD INTERNATIONAL OPERATIONS

Four separate stages may be identified in the evolution of international operations in a firm, and each implies a different set of managerial philosophies.[5] These stages form a conceptual framework that may serve as a starting point for a company in developing its marketing strategies.

Ethnocentric stage (home-country orientation): Foreign operations are treated as secondary to domestic operations. Strategic planning for foreign markets is done in the home office, and marketing personnel are primarily home-country nationals. The marketing mix follows domestic patterns. No major changes are made in the products sold abroad. Promotion and distribution are essentially the same as at home. The ethnocentric position is likely to be adopted by a small company just entering the international market, or by a larger firm whose foreign sales are insignificant. It is also adopted by Canadian firms who see no differences between the operations of Canadian and American markets.

Polycentric stage (host-country orientation): Each foreign country is treated as a separate entity with its own autonomous subsidiary organization. Each of these foreign subsidiaries does its own strategic marketing planning and research. Products are changed to meet local needs. Each subsidiary does its own pricing and promotion. Distribution is through channels and a sales force that are native to the country in question.

Today, most international executives probably view the polycentric position as the most desirable one. In marketing, it is very important to adapt to country-by-country differences, and to employ local nationals in doing a marketing job. Polycentrism, however, is likely to create problems of coordinating and controlling the marketing activities among the several countries. Successful Canadian firms operating primarily in the United States display this kind of an orientation.

Regiocentric stage (regional orientation): A given region is treated as a single market, regardless of national boundaries. Marketing plans and programs are set for the entire region. Personnel can come from anywhere. Standardized products are used throughout the entire region. Distribution channels and promotion are developed on a regional basis to project a uniform image of the company and its products. Only the largest or most sophisticated multinationals would likely operate in this fashion.

[5]This section is adapted from Yoram Wind, Susan P. Douglas, and Howard V. Perlmutter, "Guidelines for Developing International Marketing Strategies," *Journal of Marketing*, April 1973, pp. 14–23.

Geocentric stage (world orientation): The entire world is treated as a single market, so that this stage is essentially an expansion of the regiocentric stage. Those Canadian branches of foreign subsidiaries that receive a "world mandate" from their parent operate in this fashion.

A regiocentric approach is probably more economical and manageable than a worldwide program. From a practical point of view, however, national environmental constraints (laws, currencies, culture, life-style) may severely limit either one of these broad marketing approaches.

STRUCTURES FOR OPERATING IN FOREIGN MARKETS

Once a company has decided to market in foreign countries, management must select an organizational structure for operating in those markets. There are four distinct methods of entering a foreign market. Each represents successively greater international involvement, leading ultimately to a truly multinational operation. The same firm may use more than one of these operating methods at the same time. To illustrate, it may export products to the United States, establish a licensing arrangement in France, and build a manufacturing plant in Singapore (see Fig. 23-1).[6]

The simplest way of operating in foreign markets is by exporting through **export-import agent middlemen**. Very little risk or investment is involved. Also, little time or effort is required on the part of the exporting producer. On the other hand, the exporter has little or no control over its agent middlemen. Furthermore, these middlemen generally are not aggressive marketers, and normally they do not generate a large sales volume.

To counteract some of these deficiencies, management can move to the second stage — exporting through **company sales branches** or other sales subsidiaries located in foreign markets. Bypassing the export-import agent middlemen enables a company (1) to promote its products more aggressively, (2) to develop its foreign markets more effectively, and (3) to control its sales effort more completely. Of course, management now has the time- and money-consuming task of managing a sales force. The difficulty here is that these salespeople are either (1) foreign nationals unfamiliar with the product and the company's marketing practices or (2) Canadian salespeople unfamiliar with the market, even if it is the United States.

As foreign markets expand, management may enter licensing arrangements whereby foreign manufacturers produce the goods. **Licensing** means granting to another producer — for a fee or royalty payment — the right to use one's production process, patents, trademarks, or other assets. **Contract manufacturing** is related to licensing. A Canadian marketer, such as a retail-chain organization, simply contracts with a foreign producer to supply the products that the firm will market in that producer's country. The

---

[6]For suggestions regarding special types of intermediaries that small business firms can use to help them enter and develop foreign markets, see John J. Brasch, "Using Export Specialists to Develop Overseas Sales," *Harvard Business Review*, May-June 1981, pp. 6–8; and S. Tamer Cavusgil and Richard A. Yanzito, "Consulting Services and Trade Co-ops Can Assist Small Firms in Exporting," *Marketing News*, Oct. 17, 1980, p. 1.

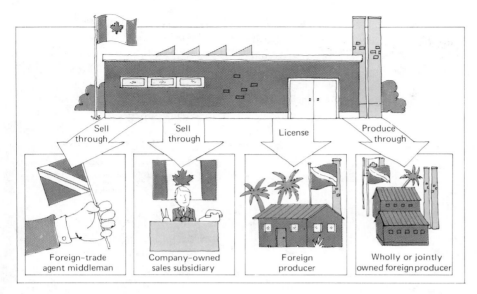

Figure 23-1
THE FOUR BASIC
STRUCTURES FOR
OPERATION IN A
FOREIGN MARKET.

Dylex retail operations are an example of this approach. To distribute either of these two types of foreign-produced output, the marketer may still rely on export-import middlemen. Or the company's own sales branches may be established in major foreign markets.

Licensing offers manufacturers a flexible arrangement with a minimal investment. Yet they still can enjoy the advantages of their patents, research, and know-how. Through licensing or contract manufacturing, producers can enter a market that might otherwise be closed to them because of exchange restrictions, import quotas, or prohibitive tariffs. At the same time, by licensing, manufacturers may be building future competitors. A licensee may learn all it can from the manufacturer, and then proceed independently when the licensing agreement expires.[7] The licensing approach is one that makes sense to Canadian firms who do not necessarily have the scale or resources to deal with a market in substantial terms.

In the fourth method, the company builds or otherwise acquires its own production facilities in a foreign country. The structure can be a *joint venture* or a *wholly-owned foreign subsidiary*. A **joint venture** is a partnership arrangement in which the foreign operation is owned in part by the Canadian company and in part by a company or citizen of the foreign country. The foreign ownership share may be any percentage—more than, less than, or exactly 50 percent. Obviously, when the controlling interest is owned by foreign nationals, the Canadian firm has no real control over any of the marketing or production activities. At the same time, a joint venture may be the only structure (other than licensing) through which a Canadian firm is allowed to enter a given foreign market.

---

[7]For a discussion of conditions under which licensing may be the preferred strategy for operating in a foreign market, see Farok J. Contractor, "The Role of Licensing in International Strategy," *Columbia Journal of World Business*, Winter 1981, pp. 73–83.

Wholly-owned subsidiaries in foreign markets are commonly used by companies that have evolved to an advanced stage of international business. With a wholly-owned foreign subsidiary, a company has maximum control over its marketing program and production operations. This type of international structure, however, requires a substantial investment of money, labour, and managerial attention. The Moore Corporation, Alcan, and Northern Telecom are some domestic firms that use this approach.

This leads us to the final evolutionary stage — one reached by very few companies as yet. This is the stage of the true multinational corporation — the **worldwide enterprise**. Both the foreign and the domestic operations are integrated and are no longer separately identified. The regional sales office in Toronto is basically the same as the one in Paris. Business opportunities abroad are viewed in the same way as those at home. That is, opportunities in Canada are no longer automatically considered to be better. A true multinational firm does *not* view itself as a Canadian firm (Massey-Ferguson), or a Swiss firm (Nestlé), or a Dutch firm (Shell Oil) that happens to have plants and markets in a foreign country. In a true worldwide enterprise, the strategic marketing planning is done on a global basis.[8]

A STRATEGIC PROGRAM FOR INTERNATIONAL MARKETING

Canadian-owned firms that have been very successful in domestic marketing have no assurance whatsoever that their success will be duplicated in foreign markets. A key to satisfactory performance overseas lies in gauging which domestic marketing strategies and tactics should be transferred directly to foreign markets, which ones modified, and which ones not used at all. In other words, foreign markets, too, present the need for strategic marketing planning.[9]

International Marketing Research

A marketing information system would seem to be even more essential in foreign markets than in the domestic market because the risks are so much greater. Yet, in practice, only limited funds are invested in marketing research in foreign countries other than the United States. The basic reason for this disparity is that the costs, relative to the value received, are greater abroad than at home. This situation arises because environmental conditions in foreign markets often have a negative influence on some of the basic elements of marketing research.

Fundamental to marketing research is the idea that problems should be solved in a *systematic, analytical* manner. Unfortunately, an orderly, rational approach runs counter to the instincts of many people throughout the world. In many cultures, the people are guided by factors that either we do not ourselves use or understand or by relatively strong traditional approaches different from our own. None of these is particularly conducive

---

[8]See Thomas Hout, Michael E. Porter, and Eileen Rudden, "How Global Companies Win Out," *Harvard Business Review*, September-October 1982, pp. 98–108.

[9]For an analytical approach to strategic planning for use in environments outside the United States, see Gilbert D. Harrell and Richard O. Kiefer, "Multinational Strategic Market Portfolios," *MSU Business Topics*, Winter 1981, pp. 5–15.

to our type of scientific approach. A second element in marketing research — *customer information* — depends upon the willingness of people to respond accurately when researchers pose questions involving attitudes, buying habits, and motives. In many societies — including our own from time to time — suspicion of strangers, distrust of government, and an individualism that holds that these things are "none of your business" all serve to compound the problems of gathering information.

The scarcity of *reliable statistical data* may be the single biggest problem in some foreign markets.[10] Figures on population, personal income, and production may be only crude estimates. Few studies have been made on such things as buying habits or media coverage. In the design of a research project, the lack of reliable data makes it very difficult to select a meaningful sample. Lack of uniformity makes intercountry comparisons very unreliable.

All these limitations add up to the fact that conducting international marketing research usually poses great difficulties. Moreover, researchers have to be particularly careful to avoid errors caused by language or other cultural differences.[11]

Analysis of Foreign Markets

Nowhere in international marketing is the influence of the cultural and economic environments seen more clearly than in an analysis of market demand. Market demand throughout the world is determined by population, economic ability to buy, and buying behaviour. Also, human wants and needs have a universal similarity. People need food, clothing, and shelter. They seek a better life in terms of lighter work loads, more leisure time, and social recognition and acceptance. But at about this point, the similarities in foreign and domestic markets end, and the differences in cultural and economic environments must be considered.

When analysing consumers' *economic ability to buy* in a given foreign market, management may study the (1) distribution of income, (2) rate of growth of buying power, and (3) extent of available consumer financing. In the emerging economies, large portions of the population have very low incomes. A much different income-distribution pattern — with resulting differences in marketing programs — is found in the industrialized markets of Western Europe, where there are large groups of working classes and a big middle-income market. Thus, many of the products commonly in demand in Belgium or the Netherlands would find very small markets in some African or Asian countries. In Asia, Japan is an exception, of course. Rising incomes in Japan have generated huge markets for travel, sports, and other

---

[10]For sources of secondary data on foreign markets, see Philip R. Cateora, *International Marketing*, 5th ed., Richard D. Irwin, Inc., Homewood, Ill., 1983, pp. 260–263. For an excellent summary of the market opportunities in some forty-three countries, see "SMM's Multinational Marketing Guide," *Sales & Marketing Management*, December 8, 1975, pp. 49–56.

[11]For some interesting, but unfortunate, company experiences in international marketing research, see Charles S. Mayer, "The Lessons of Multinational Marketing Research," *Business Horizons*, December 1978, pp. 7–13.

leisure-time activities. In response, shops in Vancouver, Chicago, London, Paris, and Rome now display window signs saying, "Japanese is spoken here."

Here are some cultural elements that can influence a company's marketing program. The importance of specific elements in marketing varies from country to country.

Family. In some countries the family is an extremely close-knit unit, whereas in other nations the family members usually act more independently. Each of these two situations requires a different type of promotion, and perhaps even different types of products.

Other social groups and institutions. Some cultural differences are illustrated in the boxed material on the following pages.

Educational system. The educational system affects the literacy rate, which in turn influences advertising, branding, and labelling. The brand may become all-important if the potential customers cannot read and must recognize the article by the picture on the label.

Language differences. As Canadians know so well, language differences also pose problems. Literal translations of English-language advertising copy or brand names may result in ridicule of, or even enmity toward, the products. Even some English words have different meanings in Canada, the United Kingdom, and the United States.

Religion. Religion is a major influence on value systems and behavioural patterns.

A few examples illustrate how buying habits are influenced by cultural elements. One-stop shopping is unknown in many parts of the world. In many foreign markets people buy in small units, sometimes literally on a meal-to-meal basis. Also, they buy in small specialty stores. To buy food for a weekend, a *hausfrau* (housewife) in West Germany may visit the chocolate store, the dairy store, the meat market, the fish market, a dry-grocery store, the greengrocer, the bakery, the coffee market, and possibly some other specialty food stores. While this may seem to be an inefficient use of her time, we must recognize that a shopping trip is more than just a chore to be done as fast as possible. It is a useful and enjoyable part of her social life. She will visit with her friends and neighbours in these shops. Shopping in this fashion is simply a foreign version of the bridge club or neighbourhood coffee break. It is only in recent years that, in some Western European countries, large supermarkets have appeared.

In France, if you want bread, go to a *boulangerie*. If you want some pastry, however, you don't go to a bread store. You go to a *pâtisserie*. Fresh meat you get in a *boucherie*. If you want sausage or smoked meats, your best bet is a *charcuterie*. But if you want good fish, try a *poissonerie*. Canned peaches you can get in an *épicerie*. But for fresh peaches, you are better off shopping at the fresh fruit and vegetable stand in the market.

So far in this chapter, we have stressed the significant environmental differences that exist between and within foreign countries. While we do not think of it very often, the same differences exist within Canada on a regional basis. On the horizon, however, we can see a trend toward more

---

SOME CULTURAL CONSIDERATIONS WHEN MARKETING IN THE TWO LARGEST (BY POPULATION) MARKETS IN THE WORLD

ISLAMIC COUNTRIES*

1. Religion is a very important, all-pervasive influence in the daily life of the people. About 20 percent of the world's population is Muslim.
2. Interpersonal relationships are very important. Business relations and friendships frequently are interwoven. For selling in this market, a key factor is the buyer's having *trust* in the seller, or else there's no deal.
3. Men and women are strictly segmented in Muslim society. Outside the home, a woman's position in an Islamic country is light-years away from that of a woman in Canada.
4. It is important to use considerable patience and politeness in your business or personal dealings in these countries.
5. An individual is important first as a person; only secondarily do his experience or qualifications count. "We want to hire Mr. X because he is a fine person who incidentally also happens to be a good designer (or accountant, or secretary, etc.)."

ASIAN COUNTRIES

1. Loyalty is a strong personal value — loyalty to country, company, and family.
2. Be calm, quiet, and *very* patient when dealing with people in these markets.
3. Respect and deference to older people and to authority are deep cultural traits.
4. The Japanese will not say no to you directly, to avoid hurting your feelings. Instead, they use various indirect ways to express a negative reaction.
5. The Japanese try to blend in, rather than stand out. They prefer to rely on consensus in decision making, rather than on one-man rule. There is group cooperation, rather than "rugged individualism."
6. One particularly strong point. People in these markets tend to take a long-run point of view. Unlike many Westerners, Asian businessmen do not look for immediate, short-term profits.
7. The business community operates within a framework of long-term personal relations — it's like an exclusive club. And it is very important to be in harmony with the other person in business dealings.
8. Work is a part of life that is something to be enjoyed. Typically, the "Blue Monday" or "TGIF" (Thank God It's Friday) syndrome has no place in Oriental cultures.
9. Japanese culture and society are very closed to *gaijin* (foreigners) — other Orientals as well as people from Western cultures.

---

*For additional cultural factors with their marketing implications, see Mushtaq Luqmani, Zahir A. Quraeshi, and Linda Delene, "Marketing in Islamic Countries: A Viewpoint," *MSU Business Topics*, Summer 1980, pp. 17–25; and Peter Wright, "Doing Business in Islamic Markets," *Harvard Business Review*, January-February 1981, pp. 34–40.

convergence of tastes, wants, and habits, especially in the Western European countries. Travel, television, and trade are proving to be effective homogenizers of European culture. But—and this should be well understood—a German is still a German, and a Swede is still a Swede. In Europe's uncommon market, there is no such thing as a Mr. and Mrs. European. However, the old order is changing, and we can see increasingly cosmopolitan demands. Pizzerias do business in Germany, lasagna is sold in a Stockholm supermarket. British fish-and-chips are wanted on the Continent, and whisky sales are large in France.

MARKETING PROBLEMS ARE CREATED BY CULTURAL DIFFERENCES

LANGUAGE
Is Chevrolet's Nova a good brand name? In Spanish, *no va* means "it doesn't go."

In Japanese, General Motors' "Body by Fisher" translates as "Corpse by Fisher."

In some languages, Pepsi-Cola's slogan "Come Alive" translates as "Come out of the grave."

In European markets, Gillette's Swivel razors carry the brand name of Slalom—a word that is more familiar and understandable in those markets.

STORE HOURS AND VACATIONS
In Italy, most stores close for lunch from noon to 3:00 P.M., even in the resorts. Generally, the stores close every evening at 7:00 P.M., Saturday afternoon at 1:00 P.M., and all day Sunday.

In Spain, the stores close from 1 to 4 P.M. for lunch.

In Germany, stores are closed at night, Saturday afternoons, and all day on Sundays and holidays. Recent attempts to extend the store hours were met with very strong opposition from unions and most store owners.

In most countries in Western Europe, all workers get four weeks of paid vacation, plus several paid holidays each year.

WHAT TO WEAR WHERE
The Japanese take off their shoes before entering their homes.

Shoes are forbidden in Moslem mosques.

Shorts and halter tops are not permitted in churches, temples, or mosques in many countries.

It may be hot and humid in Jamaica, Bangkok, and other English-influenced places, but men are still expected to wear coats and ties for many occasions.

DESIGN PREFERENCES
In Britain, products like Jell-O are preferred in solid-wafer or cake form.

Germans usually buy salad dressing in tubes.

Product Planning for International Markets

Most companies would not think of entering a domestic market without careful and often extensive product planning. Yet, a Canadian firm typically enters a foreign market with essentially the same product it sells at home. Even when a product is changed expressly for an international market, modification is apt to be minor. A producer may convert an appli-

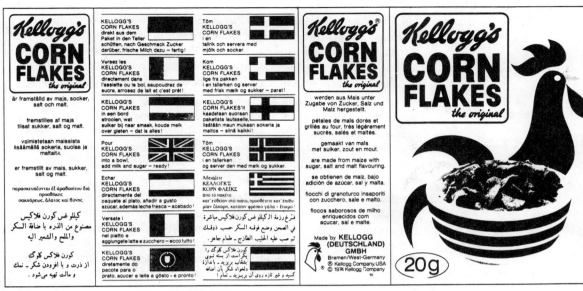

Flags

Swedish	West Germany	Sweden	German
Norwegian	France	Norway	French
Finnish	Netherlands	Finland	Dutch
Danish	Great Britain	Denmark	English
Greek	Spain	Greece	Spanish
Middle-East	Italy	No flag: Middle-East	Italian
Arabic	Portugal	Arabic	Portuguese
Algerian		Algeria	
(Arabic)			

ONE PRODUCT,
ONE MESSAGE,
FOURTEEN
LANGUAGES!

ance for use with 220-volt electrical systems, or paint and package a product to protect it against a destructive tropical climate, for example.

One key to success in planning product strategies has a familiar ring — that is, adapt to the cultural tastes and economic characteristics of the particular foreign market. In Europe, a six-cubic-foot refrigerator is the most popular size, in contrast to the larger units preferred in the United States. True, the cost difference and the existence of smaller kitchens in Europe are decision factors. However, the basic reasons for the Europeans' choice lie in the cultural behaviour patterns of the consumers. As noted earlier, to many European housewives a food-shopping trip is a social event. They go daily and thus do not buy the large quantities that must be stored for several days in the refrigerator. Also, if they have no car, they walk to the store. Because of this, they cannot carry large quantities. As yet, frozen foods are not purchased to any great extent, so large freezer space for storage is not needed.

Warren Keegan has identified five alternative strategies for adapting a product and its promotion (communication message) to a foreign market.[12]

---

[12]The discussion of these strategies is adapted from Warren J. Keegan, "Multinational Product Planning: Strategic Alternatives," *Journal of Marketing*, January 1969, pp. 58–62.

1. *One product, one message — worldwide.* This strategy is appropriate when the same product and the same promotional appeals can be used effectively in all countries and cultures. Pepsi-Cola and Coca-Cola have used this alternative successfully. On balance, however, there probably are more market failures than successes with this approach.

2. *Same product, but modified communications.* This strategy is practical when the same product can be used to fill different needs in foreign markets. Outboard motors that are used for recreation in the United States may be used for commercial fishing or transportation abroad. In this instance, the foreign advertising copy would be quite different, depending upon the product use being promoted.

3. *Product adaptation, communications extension.* With this strategy, essentially the same promotional message is used abroad as at home, but the product is changed to meet local conditions. To illustrate, a soap formula is changed to adapt to local water conditions, appliances are altered for different voltage requirements, and packaging changes are made for different climates.

4. *Dual adaptation.* Both the product and the message are changed to fit the foreign market.

5. *Product invention.* A company develops a new product in response to foreign market demands. For markets with low buying power, one firm "invented backward" by developing an inexpensive, hand-operated washing machine with the tumbling action of an automatic machine.

Branding and labelling are especially important in foreign markets.[13] As suggested earlier, the brand picture may be the only part of the product that a consumer can recognize. Foreign consumers' preference for Swedish, Japanese, French, Canadian, or American products often overcomes nationalistic feelings. So, in many instances a company can use the same brand that is used in the domestic market.[14]

Pricing in International Markets

In earlier chapters, we recognized that determining the base price and formulating pricing strategies are complex tasks, often involving trial-and-error decision making. These tasks become even more complex in international marketing. An exporter faces variables such as currency conversion, a myriad of possible bases for price quotations, and often a lack of knowledge or control of middlemen's pricing.

---

[13]For a report on the information labelling and quality certification programs in Canada and eleven European nations, see John A. Miller, *Labeling Research — The State of the Art*, Marketing Science Institute, Cambridge, Mass., report no. 78–115, 1978, pp. 44–56.

[14]For reports on the influence that country of manufacture has on buyers' perceptions of product quality, see Phillip D. White and Edward W. Cundiff, "Assessing the Quality of Industrial Products," *Journal of Marketing*, January 1978, pp. 80–86. For a report on whether consumers in several foreign markets have the same perceptions of a given product's value, thus allowing market segments to cross national boundaries, see Petr Chadraba and Robert O'Keefe, "Cross-National Product Value Perceptions," *Journal of Business Research*, December 1981, pp. 329–337.

Cost-plus pricing is probably used to a greater extent in export marketing than at home. Consequently, foreign prices usually are considerably higher than domestic prices for the same product. This is so because of additional physical distribution expenses, tariffs, and other export costs.

Sometimes a firm's foreign price is *lower* than its domestic price. The price may be lowered to meet foreign competition or to dispose of outmoded products. Sometimes governments engage in the practice of "**dumping**." That is, government action supports the domestic price at a level above the international market price. Then, when these products are exported, they are sold below the domestic price. Through the years, the surplus production of some raw materials has led to government control of world market prices. For example, individual governments have tried to stabilize the prices of coffee, nitrates, sugar, and rubber. Also, the governments of several countries have established joint agreements covering the prices of such commodities as oil, tin, potash, and cocoa.

Foreign middlemen often are not aggressive in their pricing strategies. They prefer to maintain high unit margins and low sales volume, rather than develop large sales volume by means of lower prices and smaller margins per unit sold. In fact, there is considerable price rigidity in many foreign markets. In some cases, the inflexibility stems from agreements among firms that tend to restrain independent pricing. The rigidity also sometimes results from price-control legislation that prevents retailers from cutting prices at their own discretion.

Combinations among manufacturers and middlemen are tolerated to a far greater extent in many foreign countries than in Canada. This occurs even when the avowed purpose of the combinations is to restrain trade and reduce competition. Probably the best known of these international marketing combinations is the cartel. A **cartel** is a group of companies that produce similar products and that have combined to restrain competition in manufacturing and marketing. Cartels exist to varying degrees in steel and aluminum, fertilizers, electrical products, petroleum products, rayon, dyes, and sulphur.

Another area of pricing practices peculiar to foreign trade relates to price quotations. With respect to shipping, insurance, and related export charges, the three following bases of price quotations are used extensively in foreign trade:

1. *F.O.B. (free on board)*. The f.o.b. point is usually the inland point of departure, or the port of shipment. The buyer pays all shipping charges beyond the f.o.b. point.

2. *F.A.S. (free alongside ship, at port of export)*. The seller pays all charges to deliver the goods to the dock within reach of the ship's tackle, but not on board. All shipping activities, costs, and risk from that point are the responsibility of the buyer.

3. *C.I.F. (cost, insurance, freight at a given point of destination)*. The seller pays all costs up to the arrival of the shipment at the foreign port.

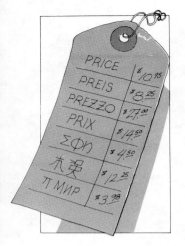

Canadian firms want the price stated in dollars.

Prices may be quoted in Canadian, or often United States, dollars or in the currency of the foreign buyer. Here we become involved in problems of foreign exchange and conversion of currencies. As a general rule, the firm engaged in foreign trade — whether it is buying or selling, exporting or importing — prefers to have the price quoted in its own national currency. Risks from fluctuations in foreign exchange then are shifted to the other party in the transaction. However, whether prices are quoted in the national currency of the importer or the exporter often depends upon the bargaining power of each. One way to get around currency problems, especially when dealing with Eastern Europe or developing nations, is through a barter arrangement in which there is no exchange of money.[15]

DEVALUATION AS AN INTERNATIONAL PRICING STRATEGY

To *devalue* a nation's currency means to reduce its worth relative to the currencies of other nations. Then, products priced in the devalued currency cost less when purchased with other currencies. The effect is the same as reducing the prices of all the exported products of the devaluing nation. With lower international prices, more of these exported products will be purchased, and the devaluing nation will then export more goods. This leads first to a better balance-of-payments position and increased production, and then to increased domestic investment and employment, and a stronger economy.

International Distribution Systems

Understanding the environment in a foreign market helps in understanding the middlemen and the distribution system, because these marketing institutions result from their environment. The perceptive, and thus usually successful, retailers, for example, will capitalize on environmental change by introducing innovations that anticipate trends in the environment. In fact, several European retailers have done a good job of innovating. Within a relatively few years, they have moved from the stage of "mom and pop" stores to a variety of retailing concepts as advanced as anything in North America. These innovative retailers simply leapfrogged several stages of institutional development. In mass retailing, the *hypermarché* in France and the *verbrauchermarkt* in Germany are huge self-service combination superstores operating very profitably and at much lower gross margins than similar North American stores.[16]

Middlemen in Foreign Marketing

Four groups of middlemen operating in foreign trade consist of (1) Canadian foreign-trade middlemen, (2) foreign-trade middlemen located abroad, (3) wholesalers and retailers operating within foreign markets, and (4) manufacturers' sales branches and offices located in foreign countries.

---

[15]See Robert E. Weigand, "International Trade without Money," *Harvard Business Review*, November-December 1977, pp. 26*ff*.; and by same author, "Barters and Buy-Backs: Let Western Firms Beware!" *Business Horizons*, June 1980, pp. 54–61.

[16]See Carolyn Pfaff, "French Supers Expand Arsenals for '80s Fight," *Advertising Age*, February 11, 1980, p. S–1.

HOW ABOUT OPENING GROCERY SUPERMARKETS IN LESS-DEVELOPED NATIONS?

SUPPLY-SIDE PROBLEMS — OPERATING THE STORES

1. Self-service does not work well because the products are not prepackaged, standardized, and graded.
2. Branding, the preselling of products, and mass advertising are in their infancy in many Third World countries.
3. Store equipment is expensive, and the skilled and semiskilled labour needed in supermarkets is costly.
4. Supermarkets must use the same channels of distribution and pay about the same prices as small stores. So the supermarkets cannot offer significantly lower prices or enjoy the economies of scale.
5. The small retailers have considerable political influence, which they use against supermarkets.

DEMAND-SIDE PROBLEMS — CONSUMER BUYING BEHAVIOUR

1. Consumers — especially the low-income ones — must shop daily because they lack refrigeration and storage space.
2. Supermarkets do not provide the easy credit terms and friendly personal relationships found in small stores.
3. Travel costs to reach the supermarkets are high.
4. Product variety and shopping convenience — major benefits provided by a supermarket — generally are not important to shoppers in these countries.
5. Consumers do not perceive that supermarket products are of higher quality.
6. Direct cost savings (through lower prices) are too small to be important to shoppers.

I guess the answer to the opening question is "No, thanks." But do you think we would do any better if we opened a 7-Eleven type of convenience store in these countries?

Source: Arieh Goldman, "Transfer of a Retailing Technology into the Less Developed Countries," *Journal of Retailing*, Summer 1981, pp. 5–29.

For a Canadian producer, the main outlets abroad for manufactured goods are foreign *agents and distributors*. These are firms that act as sales representatives for domestic firms in foreign markets. Agents and distributors differ primarily in two respects: Agents do not take title to the goods, and they normally do not carry inventory stocks. These two types of middlemen are so important in the distribution system that often a manufacturer will grant them exclusive territorial rights. They perform a wide variety of services, including personal selling, advertising, providing market and credit information, making repairs, billing, settling disputes, and collecting invoices. In addition, distributors perform the functions of warehousing and bulk breaking.

Channels of Distribution

The main distribution problem when marketing in a foreign country is to decide whether or not to engage in direct selling and, if so, to what extent.

Middlemen operating *within* foreign countries are, in general, less aggressive and perform fewer marketing services than their North American counterparts. The foreign marketing situation, however, usually argues against bypassing these foreign middlemen. Often the demand is too small to warrant the establishment of a sales office or branch. Also, in many foreign countries, knowledge of the market may be more important than knowledge of the product, even for high-technology products.[17] And sometimes government controls preclude the use of a domestic sales organization abroad. Thus, the middlemen in foreign countries ordinarily are a part of the channel structure.

When foreign middlemen are used, the Canadian seller usually advertises extensively and furnishes point-of-purchase display materials to strengthen the efforts of the middlemen. If the product requires mechanical servicing or installation, the manufacturer must provide reliable repair service. This means training local middlemen, sending in service representatives, or doing both.

Physical Distribution

In foreign marketing, various aspects of physical distribution are quite different from anything found on the domestic scene. Generally, physical distribution expenses account for a much larger share of the final selling price in foreign markets than in domestic markets. Packing requirements, for example, are more exacting for foreign shipment. Problems caused by humidity, pilferage, breakage, and inadequate marking of shipments must be considered. Requirements regarding commercial shipping documents and governmental documents complicate the paperwork in foreign shipping. Marine insurance and the traffic management of international shipments are specialized fields. They involve institutions that are not ordinarily used in domestic marketing.

Bribery in International Distribution

Bribes, kickbacks, and sometimes even extortion payments are facts of life in many international (and sometimes even in domestic) distribution systems. Bribery apparently has existed to varying degrees in buying and selling since time immemorial. However, bribery is not limited to marketing. It is found in many other areas of human interaction. It can start with parents' bribing their children — "If you kids are good today, we'll take you to the park tomorrow."

Bribery is so implanted in many cultures that special slang words are used to designate it. In Latin America, it is called the *mordida* (small bite). It is *dash* in West Africa and *baksheesh* in the Middle East. The French call it *pot de vin* (jug of wine). In Italy there is *la bustarella* (the little envelope)

---

[17]See Dan. T. Dunn, Jr., "Agents and Distributors in the Middle East," *Business Horizons*, October 1979, pp. 69–78.

A NEIGHBOURHOOD
MARKET DISTRICT IN
PARIS.

The shopkeepers are old
friends of most of the
shoppers, who may spend
most of a day on a food
shopping trip. *(Franklin
Wing/Stack, Boston)*

left on a bureaucrat's desk to cut the red tape. In Chicago, Americans speak of *a little grease.*

Bribery in marketing became an international scandal in the mid-1970s. Subsequent political sensitivity resulted in some companies establishing written ethical guidelines. What complicates this situation is the fact that bribery is not a sharply defined activity. Sometimes the lines are blurred between a bribe, a gift to show appreciation, a reasonable commission for services rendered, and a "facilitating" payment to grease the channel of distribution. Realistically, in some foreign markets, a seller must pay a facilitating fee or commission to an agent in order to get in touch with prospective buyers. Without paying such fees to those agents, there is simply no effective access to those markets.[18]

Rather than discuss promotion in its entirety, we limit our discussion to advertising as being illustrative of the strategic problems to international promotion. Advertising is selected because it is probably used by more firms in international marketing than either a company sales force or any sales promotion technique. Many companies without their own international sales force (they use foreign trade middlemen) do advertise internationally.

A controversial issue in international advertising is the extent to which advertising can be standardized in foreign markets. In years gone by, the consensus was that a separate program (copy, appeals, and media) had to

Advertising in Foreign Markets

[18]For more on this problem, see Jack G. Kaikati and Wayne A. Label, "American Bribery Legislation: An Obstacle to International Marketing," *Journal of Marketing,* Fall 1980, pp. 38–43; and Stan Reid and James McGoldrick, "Greasing the Foreign Channel Mechanism," in *1978 Educators' Conference Proceedings,* American Marketing Association, Chicago, 1982, pp. 318–321.

SE PENSATE
A UN REGALO...
PENSATE BULOVA

* 857 39 02 5 Bulova Quartz
impermeabile, acciaio
e laminato oro L. 175.000
** 857 02 21 Bulova Quartz
laminato oro giallo L. 180.000

BULOVA
l'orologio dell'era spaziale

be tailored for each country, or even for regions within a country. While nobody is recommending complete uniformity, today there is much support for the idea of commonality in international ad campaigns. Many companies are using basically the same appeals, theme, copy, and layout in all their international advertising — particularly in the Western European countries. Such standardization of advertising is spurred by the increase in international communications. Hordes of Europeans travel from one country to another while on vacation. Many radio and TV broadcasts from one country reach audiences in another country. The circulation of many European magazines and newspapers crosses national borders.

Perhaps the issue comes down to this point: The goal of advertising is essentially the same at home and abroad, namely to communicate information and persuasive appeals effectively. It is only the media strategy and the specific messages that must be tuned to each country's cultural, economic, and political environment. For some products, the appeals are sufficiently universal and the market is sufficiently homogeneous to permit the use of uniform advertising in several countries. In general, however, each country has its own national identity and characteristics that must be recognized when advertising in the given country.

Attitude of Foreign Markets and Governments toward Advertising

In many countries, the traditionally negative attitude toward marketing in general and toward advertising in particular is a hardship for North American firms. The "build a better mousetrap" theory still prevails to a great extent throughout Europe and the rest of the world. Some foreign consumers feel that a product is of dubious value if it has to be advertised. People in many foreign countries object particularly to hard-sell advertising.

The extent of active consumer discontent and government regulation of advertising does vary considerably from one country to another. Both these forces do exist, however, and they are on the rise in most foreign markets. Many countries already have stringent laws regulating advertising. Where the government regulates the use of radio and television for advertising and where newspapers are government-controlled, this too affects their use as advertising media.[19]

Choice of Media

Essentially the same types of advertising media are available in foreign countries as in Canada, with the exception of television in some markets. Some print media, such as *Reader's Digest*, which is published in Canada and the United States, are also published abroad in foreign languages.

[19]See J. J. Boddewyn, "The Global Spread of Advertising Regulation," *MSU Business Topics*, Spring 1981, pp. 5–13; "Curbs on Ads Increase Abroad as Nations Apply Standards of Fairness and Decency," *The Wall Street Journal*, November 25, 1980, p. 48; and Saeed Samiee and John K. Ryans, Jr., "Advertising and the Consumerism Movement in Europe: The Case of West Germany and Switzerland," *Journal of International Business Studies*, Spring-Summer 1982, pp. 109–114.

Beware When Bearing Gifts in Foreign Lands — and Watch it When it Comes to the Colour

Brazil. Purple is a death colour. Scotch is more popular than bourbon.

England. Apparel and soap are considered a bit too personal. White lilies suggest death, but other flowers are okay.

France. Yellow flowers suggest infidelity. Do not give cutlery.

Hong Kong. White is for funerals, but red is popular in all Chinese-speaking areas.

Italy. Red roses are for your favourite woman. Generally, you don't give handkerchiefs.

Mexico. Yellow flowers are a sign of death.

Russia. Knives and forks are a friendship-cutter.

Saudi Arabia. Give nothing to another person's wife, and don't give anything alcoholic to anyone.

Taiwan. Knives may wound a friendship. Don't give a clock because the word for "clock" sounds like the one for "terminate."

West Germany. If you give cutlery, ask for a coin in payment so you won't cut the friendship. A gift of red roses to a woman means you really care for her.

Source: Business Week, December 6, 1976, pp. 91–92.

Preparation of Advertisements

Most of the mistakes in writing copy and preparing individual advertisements may be traced to lack of intimate knowledge of the foreign market. The wrong colour or a poor choice of words can completely nullify an otherwise good ad. Illustrations are of prime importance in many markets because of illiteracy. They are, of course, effective in all markets, but they must be accurate, believable, and in accord with local cultures. The translation of advertising copy into the appropriate foreign language — especially for radio — is a major problem. Here the advertiser especially needs someone both adept and current (an expatriate often will not do) in the idioms, dialects, and other nuances of the foreign language.

Government Support for International Marketing

In most of the decision-making areas in international marketing, the federal government, as well as many provincial governments, provide contacts, information, guidance, and even financing for Canadian firms. For example, international marketing efforts are aided by the Department of Industry, Trade and Commerce and the Export Development Corporation. The department attempts to assist firms from the research and development stage through to the international marketing of finished products. The Export Development Corporation provides insurance, guarantees, loans, and other financial facilities to help Canadian exporters.

Within the federal department a number of units exist that work on specific problems associated with international marketing. The Office of General Relations is responsible for advance planning of Canada's external trade policies and general policy affecting primary and secondary industry. The Office of Area Relations protects and improves the access of Canadian goods to export markets. The Industry, Trade and Traffic Services Branch deals with shipping problems and trade control, and provides information on Canadian products and companies. The Fairs and Missions Branch coordinates all departmental activities designed to promote the sale of Canadian products and services abroad. The International Defence Programs Branch promotes defence and export trade. The Trade Commissioners Service, with 76 offices in 55 countries, promotes export trade and protects commercial interests abroad. The Publicity Branch supports foreign trade promotion programs. The operational branches within the department (Aerospace; Marine and Rail; Agriculture; Fisheries and Food Products; Apparel and Textiles; Chemicals; Electrical and Electronics; Machinery; Materials; Mechanical Transport; and Wood Products) work to promote the sales of products and services in international markets.

SUMMARY

For countless companies, the marketing opportunities and challenges of the future lie in international marketing. This conclusion seems inevitable as management views its home markets being saturated, its excess productive capacity, its shrinking profit margins, and the intensified competition in Canada coming from both domestic and foreign firms. This broadening of marketing horizons, however, will be a new experience in most cases. Many companies in Canada have never realized that export markets provide them with an opportunity to increase sales volume and profits significantly. Even the increasing competition from foreign imports has usually served only to intensify Canadian sellers' competitive efforts at home, rather than turning their interest to international markets.

But the winds of change are awakening executives to the opportunities in multinational marketing. To make the most of these opportunities a company is urged to think big and plan ahead—clichés, yes, and perhaps trite, but useful admonitions nevertheless. A country-by-country market analysis is becoming increasingly common and is certainly better than going abroad with a one-shot, unplanned approach because some random opportunity has presented itself. Better than a country-by-country analysis, however, is a global planning approach. A company that takes a global system approach is not apt to be blocked later on by some decision made earlier in another country.[20]

This chapter has stressed the notion that a separate marketing plan is needed for each country because of environmental differences. While it is

---

[20]For a step-by-step case example of how one firm went about global planning, plus an evaluation of this approach, see *International Enterprise: A New Dimension of American Business*, McKinsey & Company, Inc., New York, 1962, pp. 21–24.

true that differences between foreign markets are still great, the experiences of a growing number of multinational firms suggest that real benefits can be derived from standardizing some elements of the marketing programs used in different countries.[21]

It is commonly alleged that products manufactured in Canada are being priced out of world markets because of our high cost structure. While this cannot be denied, our labour costs and prices are often offered as excuses, when the truth of the matter is that we have failed to apply our know-how of modern marketing management in foreign countries.[22] While marketing skills and aggressiveness are increasing among foreign firms, Canadian firms do not have a market orientation in their export business. In the past, much emphasis has been placed on production and financial problems in foreign markets.

Let us move for a moment from the micro level of the individual firm to the macro level of the total economy. It is becoming increasingly apparent that the rate of economic growth in less-developed nations will depend largely upon how effective the marketing systems established in these countries are. Typically in these countries (as true earlier in Canada) the economic development effort has been concentrated in production. Now these governments are beginning to recognize the role that marketing can play in their national economic growth. This enlightened attitude offers countless marketing opportunities (but not without attendant problems) to the internationally oriented business firm. Particularly, a marketing executive must understand the government's role in business in each country.[23]

Permeating this chapter has been the theme that marketing management in Canadian firms must become more internationally minded. We conclude with five reasons why it is mandatory to be successful in world marketing.[24]

1. We cannot adequately expand our economy at home without meeting competition abroad.

2. We cannot eliminate large-scale unemployment in this country unless we do smaller-scale employing in other countries.

---

[21]Robert D. Buzzell, "Can You Standardize Multinational Marketing?" *Harvard Business Review*, November-December 1968, pp. 102–113.

[22]Laurence P. Dowd, "Is the United States Being Priced out of World Markets?" *Journal of Marketing*, July 1960, pp. 1–8.

[23]For discussions of the increased attention being paid to marketing and economic growth in emerging economies, see, for example, Charles C. Slater, "Marketing Processes in Developing Latin American Societies," *Journal of Marketing*, July 1968, pp. 50–55; James E. Littlefield, "The Relationship of Marketing to Economic Development in Peru," *Southern Journal of Business*, July 1968, pp. 1–14; Harry A. Lipson and Douglas F. Lamont, "Marketing Policy Decisions Facing International Marketers in Less-developed Countries," *Journal of Marketing*, October 1969, pp. 24–31; in Reed Moyer (ed.), *Changing Marketing Systems*, American Marketing Association, Chicago, 1968, see Lee E. Preston, "Market Development and Market Control," pp. 223–227, and Peter D. Bennett, "Marketing and Public Policy in Latin America," pp. 233–238; and Reed Moyer and Stanley C. Hollander (eds.), *Markets and Marketing in Developing Economies*, American Marketing Association, Chicago, 1968.

[24]Ray R. Eppert, "Passport for Marketing Overseas," *Journal of Marketing*, April 1965, p. 6.

3. To achieve a higher tide of prosperity here, we must be willing to develop trade with those whose prosperity is still at a very low ebb.

4. Balancing our international payment books at home requires filling many more order books abroad.

5. If we are to remain dominant and competitive in our home market, we must compete successfully in the world market.

KEY TERMS AND CONCEPTS

Multinational economic organizations 584

Stages in international operations:
Ethnocentric stage 585
Polycentric stage 585
Regiocentric stage 585
Geocentric stage 586

"Licensing" a foreign manufacturer 586

Contract manufacturing 586

Joint venture 587

Wholly-owned foreign subsidiary 588

Cultural differences as they affect marketing 589

Strategies for matching product and marketing communication 594

Dumping 595

Cartel 595

Pricing terms: f.o.b., f.a.s., c.i.f. 595

Currency devaluation 596

Canadian foreign-trade middlemen 596

Foreign-trade middlemen located abroad 596

QUESTIONS AND PROBLEMS

1. Report on export marketing activities of companies in the province where your school is located. Consider such topics as the following: What products are exported? How many are created by export marketing? What is the dollar value of exports? How does this figure compare with the value of foreign-made goods imported into the province?

2. A luggage-manufacturing company with annual sales over $10 million has decided to market its products in Western Europe. Evaluate the alternative structures this company should consider.

3. Select one product — manufactured or nonmanufactured — for export, and select the country to which you would like to export it. Then prepare an analysis of the market for this product in the selected country. Be sure to include the sources of information you used.

4. If there are foreign students on your campus, interview some of them to determine how their buying habits differ from ours. Consider such patterns as when, where, and how people in their country buy. Who makes the family buying decisions?

5. Many countries unfortunately have a low literacy rate. In what ways might a company adjust its marketing program to overcome this problem?

6. Why should special attention be devoted to labelling and branding when products are sold in foreign markets?

7. If a company used foreign middlemen, it must usually stand ready to supply them with financial, technical, and promotional help. If this is the case, why is it not customary to bypass the middlemen and deal directly with the ultimate foreign buyers?

8. Why do exporters normally prefer to have prices quoted in Canadian or American dollars? Why should foreign importers prefer that quotations be in the currency of their country?

9. "Prices of Canadian products are always higher in foreign countries than at home because of the additional risks, expenses of physical distribution, and extra middlemen involved." Discuss.

10. Study the advertisements in the foreign newspapers and magazines available in your college or city library. Particularly note the advertisements for Canadian products, and compare these with the advertisements for the same products in local newspapers and magazines. In what respect do the foreign ads differ from the domestic ads? Are there significant similarities?

11. Are Canadian manufacturers being priced out of world markets because of their high cost structures?

Case 25
Hoover Furniture Rental Co. Ltd.*

Competitive Strategy in a Service Firm

"I've been in this business for ten years, but I have never seen competition as rough as it has been for the past eight months. Those guys are either offering price concessions, or throwing in extra services, or spending a bundle on special promotions. It seems as if all of a sudden everybody is trying to get a bigger chunk of the market. I just don't know how they can afford such programs. But I do know this—we darned well better come up with a good competitive strategy or else we'll get killed in this market." These words were spoken by Joanna Keuffel, the owner and president of the Hoover Furniture Rental, to two of her executives.

Hoover Furniture Rental was one of six furniture rental firms in an eastern metropolitan area with a population of about one million people. According to Ms. Keuffel, the company had an excellent reputation and was known for its good service and high-quality furniture. Hoover was the only locally owned and operated company of the six. The other five rental firms were branches of large national companies.

The Hoover Company was started about twelve years ago and had grown steadily since then. From time to time the company expanded its warehouse space and its inventory of rental furniture. Last year the gross rental income was about $1.2 million. The company had attracted over 800 new customers last year, over and above about 400 customers who had started renting from Hoover prior to last year.

The company primarily rented furniture for home use. Its stock included a full line of living room, dining room, and bedroom furniture. Lamps and paintings also were available for renting. In addition, Hoover offered a line of office furniture including several styles of desks, filing cabinets, chairs, and credenzas. The company did not carry home appliances or accessories such as dishes or linens.

Joanna Keuffel said that the furniture rental industry really did not become a major operation until the mid-1960s, but it had grown steadily since then. In the 1980s, the industry expects an annual growth rate of 12 to 15 percent in the number of households using rental furniture.

Ms. Keuffel estimated that 75 percent of the furniture rental market were apartment dwellers — either condominium owners or apartment renters. The other 25 percent were home dwellers (again owners or renters) and industrial users. Industry research showed that furniture renters came from a broad spectrum of the population. The age range was from about 18 to 80.

---

*Adapted from case prepared by Michelle Stark, University of Colorado student.

Two particularly good market segments were (1) people being transferred in their jobs — especially if the transfer to a given city was only a temporary move, and (2) people with limited financial resources who did not have enough capital to buy a lot of furniture.

It was generally recognized in the industry that the best way to reach the bulk of this market was through the owners or managers of the buildings. This approach was especially important in the case of apartments and condominium complexes, where one manager controlled the access to many separate housing units.

Consequently, the general promotional technique was for a representative of a furniture rental firm to contact the building manager. The furniture rep (1) explained the services offered by the rental firm, (2) left promotional brochures to be given to prospective renters, and (3) encouraged the manager to refer the housing tenants or owners to the rep's company for their furniture needs.

Beyond that general strategy, however, the different rental firms employed a variety of pricing, services, and promotional strategies. For example, some of Hoover's competitors were paying a commission to building managers for each referral they made. Obviously, this was a significant inducement for a building manager to direct potential furniture renters to the commission-paying firm.

Two of the firms made payments to the building manager when the manager arranged to show, to a prospective tenant, an apartment that had already been fully furnished by the particular rental firm. This allowed the prospective renter to better visualize how the apartment would look with the rental firm's furnishings.

Another strategy was for the apartment complex to set aside one "show" apartment, which a rental firm would then completely furnish at no cost to the owners of the complex. Ms. Keuffel pointed out that this amounted to removing an entire set of household furniture from inventory for an unknown period of time, and sending two employees and a truck to deliver it, set it up, and eventually pick it up — all without receiving any revenue.

Still another promotional strategy was a form of exclusive dealing. The furniture rental company agreed to provide, free of charge, the furniture for an office, a party room, or perhaps the manager's apartment. In return, the manager agreed to refer prospective renters only to that furniture company. The manager would not even display any literature from other rental firms.

Ms. Keuffel then noted that several pricing or promotional strategies were used when the rental company dealt directly with the renting customers. In one case, for example, after a customer had the rental furniture for twenty-four months, the company offered the customer an option to buy this furniture. If the customer wanted to continue renting, the company replaced the old furniture with new pieces at no increase in rental charges.

Also, a variety of competitive policies were employed regarding a security deposit. Some companies did not collect any such deposit. Others collected a deposit, but if the damage exceeded this deposit, the company did not charge for the extra damage.

Furniture delivery and pickup costs also were handled in various ways. Some firms had a specific transportation charge, while other companies provided this service free to customers.

One major competitor offered special deals to institutions and other industrial users. One of these industrial users, for example, was a company that rented furnished condominiums that it owned. Rather than buy the furniture, the owner of this company rented it for all the apartments. The furniture rental firm offered him a particularly attractive package deal for renting the furniture. For one price, the owner had his choice of all the offerings of the furniture rental company—whether the furniture was new or used, expensive or inexpensive.

Keuffel pointed out that the Hoover Company also engaged in variations of some of these practices. However, her company never had gone to the extreme measures adopted by some of her competitors. For example, Hoover offered package deals to industrial users, but not like the lavish (her word) deals offered by some firms. Hoover offered an option to buy after thirty months of rental. But Hoover did not offer to replace the thirty-month rented furniture with new pieces. This company required a substantial security deposit and charged for delivering the furniture. It provided no free furniture for "show" apartments, no commissions for referrals, and no free furniture for building managers.

For some time now, Joanna Keuffel had been aware that the national chains operating in her market were becoming more aggressive in their marketing efforts. She believed that some of them were actually losing money in the local market. However, because they were national chain organizations, their risks were geographically spread. They could recoup in other markets whatever they might be losing in Hoover's market.

The Hoover Company had never engaged in any formal strategic planning. Keuffel felt that this was typical of most small, relatively new firms. However, she believed that the time had come for Hoover to consciously develop a marketing strategy of its own, if the company hoped to continue to operate successfully in the existing competitive environment.

Question

What pricing, service, and promotional strategies should be adopted by the Hoover Company?

Case 26 Ideal Sheen Cleaners*

Revitalizing a Services Marketer in Maturity Stage of Its Life Cycle

Mr. William E. Miller, the owner of Ideal Sheen Cleaners, felt that his company was well into the maturity stage of its life cycle. He also realized that significant changes had occurred in his main market area. Consequently, he was wondering what courses of action he should take to revitalize his firm and to generate further business growth. Mr. Miller was a respected businessman who had been engaged in various aspects of the laundry and dry-cleaning business since 1946 in the area known as the Central City Market.

*Case prepared by Professor Donald W. Scotton and Jeffrey C. Susbauer, Cleveland State University. Used with permission.

Mr. Miller became a self-employed laundry route operator in 1946. He borrowed $200 from a loan-shark relative to purchase a vehicle with which to pick up and deliver laundry to his customers. Of the retail dollar collected from customers, 40 percent was retained by him and the remaining 60 percent was paid to the commercial laundry that cleaned the garments. His ability to generate business depended upon his personality and the price, speed, and quality of the laundry service.

In 1950, Mr. Miller purchased a dry-cleaning and tailor shop at a cost of $1,000. Although this expansion was modest, the services included (1) dry-cleaning and laundry routes, (2) over-the-counter dry-cleaning and laundry services at the store, (3) pressing, and (4) limited garment repairing. Mrs. Miller operated the store while her husband conducted the route service.

Mr. Miller recognized that customers preferred to do business with a shop that cleaned garments on the premises. He also wanted to eliminate the payment of 60 percent of the dry-cleaning revenue to the commercial cleaning plant that was doing the work. Consequently, in 1959 he purchased a dry-cleaning machine. This new machine also reduced the time needed for completing the service.

Over the next several years, the business continued to grow. Modern pressing machines were purchased, and the next-door property was leased to provide needed work space. During this period, commercial bank loans were negotiated with the endorsement of a financially strong co-signer. In 1970, Mr. Miller incorporated his company. By then he also was sufficiently secure financially so that he could establish a line of credit with a bank without a co-signer. About 1970, the company modernized and expanded its dry-cleaning plant on property that had been acquired a few years earlier.

Ideal Cleaners' sales and profits continued to grow until about two years ago. Last year the company's sales were $239,000, down from $263,000 during the preceding year, and the company incurred a net loss of $9,700. In fact, during two of the past three years, the company had incurred a net loss. Furthermore, Mr. Miller predicted that his sales would decline during the current year, and that his firm would again incur a net loss. The latest plant expansion was being utilized at about 50 percent of capacity.

Mr. Miller identified several reasons for the decline in sales and profits. One was that his company had probably reached its sales limit for the existing way of doing business in the Central City Market. This area was populated primarily by poor families. The average income in this area was the lowest in the city. Most of the business was done with consumers. Virtually no dry-cleaning and laundry services were provided for business firms. Another reason was the increasing consumer use of wash-and-wear clothing. Still another factor was the trend toward the casual look that minimized the need for well-cared-for clothes. Finally, for almost a year the company had been losing money on a second shop established in a downtown office building to serve people working in that area.

Mr. Miller recognized that his firm was at a critical point in its business life cycle. He could either accept a decline in growth and profits and eventually close the firm, or seek new ways to revitalize the business. Even though he no longer was a young man and he realized he could probably afford to retire soon, he decided to pursue the second course of action.

He was considering several alternatives by which his company could react to its business maturity and its changed environment. These alternatives included (1) expanding his present services; (2) more deeply penetrating his existing market; and (3) expanding into new markets. Each of these would require (4) expanding his physical plant facilities. These alternatives were summarized as follows:

1.   *Expansion of present services.* Trade association information and his own market surveys indicated five services that Mr. Miller might add to his present line to meet customers' wants.

a.   *Dry cleaning by the kilogram.* This service was being considered because there were different categories of dry cleaning. Dry cleaners who already offered this service charged by the kilogram for garments that required cleaning only and not pressing.

b.   *Easy-care service.* This service provided less finishing and a 40 percent lower price to the customer. The service involved standard dry cleaning and then use of a steam tunnel to remove wrinkles from the garments. At least 30 percent of the garments could be processed *completely* by this method without pressing. The remainder required a minimum of touch-up pressing after passing through the steam tunnel.

c.   *Carpet and upholstery cleaning.* Actually, this service already had been offered by Ideal Cleaners for the past few months on a limited basis. Mr. Miller had attended a one-week training program to get more experience in operating carpet-cleaning machinery and in marketing this service. At this point he was wondering whether to discontinue this service, keep it going at its present modest level, or try to broaden this market considerably.

d.   *Drapery cleaning.* Drapery cleaning would be available to household and business customers. However, it was not possible to promote this service until further expansion of the processing plant was completed.

e.   *Coin-operated laundry.* Plans were considered for the addition of a coin-operated laundry at the main plant. Customer traffic at the retail counter of the plant was supportive of this venture. Again, this plan could not be implemented until plant expansion and financing were arranged.

2.   *Deeper penetration of existing market.* To draw more business from the Central City Market, Mr. Miller was considering plans to:

a.   *Increase sales to existing customers.* Mr. Miller planned to provide additional training for his driver sales force and his retail counter clerks. A part-time employee would be hired to call customers before the route sales rep came. This would enable customers to have sufficient time to consider which garments should be cleaned or laundered. The impact of this was expected to be larger sales and time-savings for route salespeople.

b.   *Attract new customers.* New emphasis was to be devoted to methods for locating prospective customers and informing them of the merits of the Ideal Cleaners' variety of quality services.

c.   *Increase the number of routes.* Mr. Miller believed that the added services would increase business in the present market and require more route and driver salespeople. He planned to delay this action, however, until the new services and sales training had been in operation long enough to have an effect.

3. *Expansion into new markets.* Mr. Miller was thinking about opening new sales routes in the eastern suburbs. He was also considering establishing a retail outlet in a new apartment complex being built downtown. As part of the effort to revitalize downtown, this new complex would appeal to professional people and retired families. The Ideal Cleaners shop would be located in a 75-store shopping mall in the apartment complex.

Mr. Miller estimated that there were at least 4,000 housing units downtown. At an average of $50 per household per year, he could obtain $200,000 in annual sales within the next four or five years. (This volume was impressive compared with his present $240,000 sales in the Central City Market.)

4. *Plant expansion.* An additional plant and new equipment would be required for the planned expansion described above. A building and land next door to the existing dry-cleaning plant was available for purchase. This could house the coin-operated laundry, space to clean rugs and upholstered furniture, added machinery for traditional dry cleaning, and the company's office, which would be moved from its present location. In addition, considerable equipment would be needed. The expansion was estimated to cost approximately $191,000, of which $27,000 would be required for the retail store in the downtown apartment complex.

Question

Evaluate the growth strategies proposed by Mr. Miller to offset the conditions facing his company.

Expanding the Line of Services Marketed

Case 27 Red Cloud Hair Stylists

A little over one year ago, Ms. Laura Chandler and Mr. Harold Siegal founded the Red Cloud Hair Stylists Company in Regina. This company was a hair styling shop — a combination barber shop and beauty shop catering both to men and women. Because of the competitive situation in the hairdressing industry in Regina, the co-owners felt that they needed to do something to differentiate their shop and to increase its sales volume. Consequently, they were considering whether to add a hot tub to the line of services they currently were offering (marketing).

Currently the Red Cloud shop marketed a full line of hairdressing and facial- and skin-care services. The hairdressing services included shampoos, various styles of hair cuts, permanent waves, and hair conditioning. The skin-care services included facials, hair removal, herbal masks, and a cosmetologist's advice regarding makeup. Red Cloud also carried a limited line of hair- and skin-care products — shampoos, conditioners, and makeup.

Sales volume in the Red Cloud shop was running at the rate of $60,000 per year. Sales had increased substantially during the past six months, and the co-owners were predicting that next year's volume would double this year's total. Ms. Chandler stated that the shop clearly was in the growth stage of its life cycle. Sales were lowest in December, May, and June, reflecting the heavy market influence of University of Regina students.

Laura Chandler and Harold Siegal shared the same managerial philosophy. When asked what business they were in, they replied: "We're in the business of making people feel good and look good." They wanted the internal environment in their shop to be friendly and relaxed, so their customers would enjoy coming to Red Cloud.

As they reviewed the competitive situation facing them, Laura and Harold identified over fifty hairdressing shops serving the Regina community. These shops all offered varieties of essentially the same hairdressing services and products. Laura and Harold both felt that Red Cloud's main competitive advantages were their hairdressers, the pleasant atmosphere in their shop, and their location in the downtown area. Red Cloud's main competitive drawback was its newness.

Laura observed that "it takes a while to get established in this business. We have a display in the Yellow Pages, but so do many of the other shops. We have to rely on word-of-mouth advertising from satisfied customers. We get some walk-in trade because of our good location. We run a few ads in the local papers, but I'm not sure they do us much good. We have three excellent hairdressers, but I'm sure all the other shops in town would make the same claim. What we must do is find some way to make us different — to make us stand out. The business is out there. We just have to find some way to attract them to Red Cloud. Competition is tough."

In seeking ways to increase their sales, the co-owners of Red Cloud had considered several alternatives. They already were offering a full line of hairdressing services, so there was no room for service expansion there. They thought about broadening their line of hair-care products, but they were afraid that too many products would only confuse their customers. Adding blow-dryers was another idea, but Red Cloud could not meet the low prices of K Mart, Woolco, and other discount stores. They thought about adding a bar or offering drinks, but they ran into legal complications. One employee suggested installing a sauna in the shop to provide deep-heat conditioning treatment for hair. The suggestion led to the hot-tub idea.

A hot tub is a large wooden tub that is filled with hot water; people relax by soaking in it. Most tubs are made from California redwood. Some people even use old tubs that have been moved from farms or wineries. A heater is used to warm the tub water to anywhere from 35° to 46°C. Tubs range in size from 1.3 to 2 m in diameter and from 1 to 1.3 m in depth. They usually hold six to twelve people.

A new tub ordinarily leaks for a period of time. It usually takes anywhere from one day to two weeks for the tub staves to swell up and seal tightly. After installation, very little maintenance is required. The algae level is controlled by chlorine. About every six months, the sides need to be scrubbed and the filter cartridges cleaned or replaced.

The tubs were sold in completely assembled form or in do-it-yourself kits. Prices for most tubs ranged from $1,350 to $1,900 unassembled. An assembled tub cost about $400 more. Laura anticipated that Red Cloud's initial costs would be about $2,000. This figure would include the tub, installation labour, gas and electric hookups, decking around the tub, and decorations.

Hot tubs usually were installed outdoors, but Red Cloud intended to have an indoor installation. In the back of the shop there was space for both the tub and a dressing room. Outdoor redwood hot tubs became popular in California in the last half of the 1970s, and Laura and Harold thought this popularity might soon spread to other parts of North America.

Very recently redwood tubs had been installed in some cities for public use in health and exercise clubs. Some charged $3.50 or so per half-hour for the use of the tub; others included the use of the tub as part of the total monthly cost of using the club's facilities.

One major concern expressed by both Laura and Harold was whether a hot tub would fit in with the services offered by Red Cloud. Harold asked: "If you wanted to soak and socialize in a hot tub, would you think of going to a hairdressing shop? What will a hot tub do for (or to) our image?" In answer, the women who originally proposed the sauna idea reminded the owners of their stated philosophy — we are in the business of making people feel good and look good.

Laura also raised the question of whether there was an adequate market for a hot-tub service in Regina. She reviewed and updated some of the market analysis she had done prior to opening the Red Cloud shop. She noted that Regina is the provincial capital and the location of the University of Regina. The population of the city and the surrounding area was estimated at 165,000. Per capita income was about 15 percent higher than the national average and was estimated at $9,200 in 1980. Laura described the economic base of Regina as government-education-industrial. The industrial emphasis was on light manufacturing and unemployment was relatively low.

Laura felt that she had a "handle" on the *quantitative* measurements of the Regina market. What worried her were the *qualitative* aspects of this market as they related to the hot-tub service. She wondered what were the consumers' attitudes toward a hot tub.

As Harold put it, "Is Regina ready for a hot tub? I don't want people to think we are opening a massage parlour. I just wish we knew more about the psychology and sociology of this town as they relate to a hot tub in our shop. Maybe we ought to look for some better way to use that space in the back room."

Question

Should the Red Cloud Hair Stylists install a hot tub in their shop?

Strategy in Foreign Markets

Case 28 Pioneer Industries Ltd. *

While his more immediate task in March 1983 was to prepare for negotiations with a Japanese distributor interested in marketing the company's new lockset in the Far East, Steve Corbin, marketing vice-president of Pioneer Industries Ltd., was also anxious to review his company's policies and performance in foreign markets to date. He believed that these markets offered a substantial potential for Pioneer's lockset — a potential that had remained largely unexploited. Corbin felt that high priority should be

---

*This case was written by Professor T. Abdel-Malek of the University of Calgary and was made possible by the cooperation of a company that wishes to remain anonymous. Names and figures were disguised. The case was prepared as a basis for class discussion and is not designed to illustrate correct or incorrect handling of business situations.

given to developing a more effective policy to tap this potential, particularly in view of the low sales volume achieved in the Canadian market and the recent appearance of a competing product.

The Techno Lockset

Pioneer was formed as a private company in 1977, with a capital of $100,000, to produce and market its revolutionary lockset "Techno," which had been invented and developed by Jim MacMillan — now a director in charge of the company's research and development.

Techno was radically different from conventional locksets. Made entirely of thermoplastic, Techno was an injection-moulded lock which had only sixteen parts instead of about seventy-five parts in conventional locks. It required no maintenance, was easy to assemble, was static-electricity free, was adaptable to any style of handle, and could be used for a passage door (not requiring a lock) or for a door where privacy was required. The new lock operated in exactly the reverse manner of conventional sets. In a conventional lock, a complex metal mechanism of many moving parts, and placed in the door itself, was required to retract the bolt. But in the new lock, the latchbolt was on the jamb, and all that was required to operate the lock was a simple spring together with two other moving parts. Closure and forced-entry tests by an independent testing laboratory showed Techno to be highly durable — a fact that enabled the company to issue a twenty-five-year warranty for its lockset.

Production arrangements for the new lock involved no major capital outlays. The company had a set of dies made to the exact specifications of the lockset. The dies were the only equipment owned and controlled by Pioneer. Company policy was to subcontract actual production to one or more of the injection moulding firms with with reputations for strict adherence to quality specifications. A set of dies was estimated to produce 800,000 locksets before it needed replacement, and to cost $15,000 in early 1983.

The Canadian Market

Initially, management was highly optimistic about the sales prospects in the Canadian market. Techno's unique features and apparent superiority to conventional sets in terms of design and durability, low production costs, and the very favourable comments made by the few architectural offices and hardware dealers who were shown samples of the new lock tempted management to press ahead with production arrangements without undertaking a more comprehensive testing of the market. This optimism, however, was gradually dampened by the emergence of three problems. First, the booming building industry was placing contractors under heavy time pressure, which made them reluctant to make the necessary adjustments in the door's standard routing pockets (and incur the extra costs) to fit the new lock, which differed in shape and size from conventional locks. Second, appreciable temperature variability caused a change in the size of the gap between the door and its jamb and, as a result, the new lock was found capable of locking people in when that gap narrowed significantly. Third, Techno locksets were meant for use on interior doors only. The company had no key lock to offer, and it was not technically feasible to develop such a lock in the near future. Although Pioneer had not anticipated any significant problems, most building contractors and particularly apartment builders expressed a preference for using matching locks for interior and main doors. This limited the company's ability to attract sizeable orders from residential building contractors.

Although Jim MacMillan was soon able to solve the lock-in problem caused by temperature variability, by making certain adjustments in the lockset, Pioneer had to find ways of overcoming the other two problems. Thus, instead of selling to building contractors only — a policy that was adopted during the first two years but failed to produce a satisfactory sales volume — the company sought wider distribution by selling also to retail outlets through regional hardware distributors. There were approximately twelve such distributors who serviced over 3,000 retail hardware stores in Canada.

Pioneer initially established a suggested retail price of $4.39 for a passage set and $5.39 for a privacy set. These were in line with prices of good-quality conventional sets. Because Techno's production costs (including packaging) were significantly lower, amounting to about $1.20 per set for a production run of 25,000 sets, the company offered attractive markups of over 35 percent and 50 percent to distributors and retailers respectively, by selling to distributors at $2.15. This price applied to sales to contractors and door manufacturers also. The resulting markups were 5 to 10 percent higher than could be made on conventional sets. However, toward the end of 1972 another plastic lock appeared in the market and was selling to distributors and contractors at $1.35. Although Pioneer believed its lock to have a better quality and a more attractive design, the new lock represented a real threat and the company lowered its distributor's price to $1.59 in February 1983.

Pioneer relied primarily on free publicity articles in local papers and on a brochure sent to potential buyers to promote Techno. In addition, the president and marketing vice-president occasionally paid visits to some of the larger construction firms and distributors. Mr. Corbin felt that the company should reach the ultimate user also, but the tight financial position it was experiencing presently made this difficult to accomplish.

Pioneer's sales force consisted of four salaried salespeople covering various provinces. Except for large orders, personal selling was considered very expensive since several calls were often necessary to close a sale which typically ranged between 300 and 600 sets.

Total sales of Techno in Canada amounted to $50,000 in 1981, its second full year in the market, and $65,000 in the next year. This compared with an estimated $5 million sales of locks to the residential segment in the latter year.

Foreign Markets

From the outset, management believed that an appreciable market potential existed for Techno in many foreign markets, because of its perceived unique advantages. The question was how to go about tapping such potential most effectively in order to gain a share of the estimated $250 million world lockset market. As a preliminary measure, Pioneer obtained patents in twenty-four countries in 1980, including the United States, most West European countries, Japan, India, Australia, New Zealand, Turkey, and the Philippines at a cost of $18,000. In many of these countries, annual fees approximately equal to those paid initially to obtain the patents had to be paid to keep them valid. But this was viewed as a necessary expense to protect Pioneer's future business.

Mr. Corbin pointed out that the world market was dominated by a few large lock manufacturers such as Weiser, Dexter, Yale, Union, and Beaver. These firms not only dominated their home markets but often did an appreciable amount of foreign business also, either through exports or manufacturing and assembly operations abroad.

United States   Soon after Techno was launched into the Canadian market, Pioneer attempted to enter the California market, and appointed a salesperson who operated from Los Angeles. But by the end of 1981 little success was achieved. Consequently, the company withdrew the salesperson and engaged commision agents in California and five other states. They were paid a commission of 7 percent on Pioneer's selling price.

Although Pioneer had expected o sell 50,000 sets during 1982 through agents, actual sales amounted to a few hundred sets only. Mr. Corbin indicated that a 17 percent import duty, price-consciousness on the part of U.S. buyers, and inadequate marketing effort by Pioneer due to its limited resources, were responsible for poor sales.

Australia   The company's interest in the Australian market was enhanced by the favourable appraisal that Techno received from a number of major Australian buyers of locks who had been sent samples of the new lock early in 1980. In view of Australia's import duty of 22½ percent, Pioneer decided to experiment with a licensing arrangement as a means of gaining a firm position in that market. In June 1980, an agreement was successfully negotiated by the president and marketing vice-president with an Australian injection-moulding firm during their trip there. Under the agreement, Pioneer received an initial lump sum of $2,000 and became entitled to a royalty of 8 percent on Techno sales made by the licensee. Sales were expected to reach 30,000 to 50,000 sets in 1981 and to show rapid growth thereafter. Total lockset sales in Australia amounted to $4 million annually in the early 1980s. Techno had the important advantage of being capable of withstanding the hard Australian climate which, not unlike Florida's for example, was very humid, and had high salt-content air and high temperatures — factors that caused metal locks to corrode and fail rapidly and their finish to deteriorate easily.

Nevertheless, Australian sales in 1981 did not exceed 1,500 sets. Moreover, the Australian licensee surprised Pioneer in February 1982 by offering to sell its patent rights to an "improved" Techno lockset, which the Australian firm had developed and registered in Australia recently. Apart from the question of whether or not the licensee's action was appropriate under the existing licensing agreement, Pioneer's inspection of a sample of the improved lockset convinced management that the improvements were of minor significance. A stalemate resulted, and the licensing agreement was terminated by mutual consent a few months later.

United Kingdom   Another market that Techno wanted to enter as early as possible was the U.K. Initially, Mr. Corbin felt that a joint-venture arrangement would be preferable to other means of market entry. An import duty of 22½ percent represented a high barrier to exports. And a licensing agreement was considered less attractive than a joint venture, partly in view of the disappointing Australian experience, and partly because a joint venture offered Pioneer greater control of the marketing effort — control that Mr. Corbin viewed as essential if Techno was to be successfully established in Britain.

The British market was quite large, with annual sales of $15 million in 1980–82. An acute housing shortage prevailed and the government was lending support to efforts aiming at expanding supply and reducing construction costs. Pioneer's management felt that some financial support for a joint venture might be obtained if it succeeded in convincing the government of the advantages which Techno offered, especially its lower costs and its durability. An additional encouragement to enter the British market was the fact that Mr. Corbin had gained many years' experience in it while he was the marketing manager of one of the largest Canadian metal-lock companies prior to joining Pioneer in 1979. His preference for greater control of the marketing effort there was based on his view that many British firms tended to be too conservative in their approach and his belief that a carefully applied North American approach was needed to penetrate the British market.

However, several months of exploration failed to locate appropriate partners or attract government support, and the joint-venture alternative had to be abandoned. Instead, Pioneer was currently attempting to negotiate a licensing agreement with a British injection-moulding firm producing a wide variety of finished and intermediate products sold to several industries including the housing construction industry. In a tentative draft drawn by Pioneer's management, Pioneer proposed to grant the British firm exclusive sales rights in the U.K. and South Africa, provide the necessary technical know-how, and authorize it to use the Techno trademark. Pioneer was also prepared to lend the licensee its moulds for a twelve-week period to produce not more than 240,000 sets; afterwards, the licensee would acquire its own moulds. In exchange, Pioneer proposed to receive a royalty of 10 percent on net sales of 11¢ per set sold, whichever was higher for subsequent sales. Finally, Pioneer asked for a guaranteed minimum royalty of $50,000 per annum for the first two years.

Although this was by no means the company's final offer, Mr. Corbin pointed out that major departures from the proposal were not likely to be acceptable to Pioneer. While awaiting the British firm's reaction, he was pondering what and how many concessions Pioneer should be prepared to make if necessary.

Japan   Pioneer first came in contact with Ako & Co. of Japan during a 1982 trade fair in the United States at which the Techno lock was displayed. Ako was a national distributor for one of the largest paint manufacturers in Japan. It also handled a wide range of plastic materials used in construction and other industries, and generated a total sales volume of $10 million in 1982.

Ako expressed strong interest in the Techno lockset and wanted to explore the prospects of becoming its sole distributor in the Far East. In addition, Ako itself was involved jointly with one of the main construction firms in Japan, in a large modular housing project scheduled to build 16,000 houses per year for the next five years. The company was considering the adoption of Techno locksets for this project, pending the results of a market survey already underway that was using samples received from Pioneer earlier. As a distributor, Ako indicated that other builders were showing interest in Techno, and gave a tentative sales estimate of 20,000 to 30,000 sets per year to start with. Ako also stated that its representative would be in Canada in April 1983, at which time both companies could discuss the terms of an exclusive agency agreement or of a combined technical/agency agreement under which Techno would be assembled in Japan and sold exclusively by Ako in the Far East.

Encouraged by these prospects and by a favourable assessment of Ako as a distributor — an assessment he had just received from the Canadian Trade Commissioner's Office in Tokyo at his request — Mr. Corbin was now beginning to appraise various alternatives in preparation for his meeting with Ako's representative next month. He believed that the Japanese market could provide the sales volume that Pioneer badly needed, but was unable to estimate market potential at this stage and did not know enough about Far East markets. He was convinced that success depended on the effectiveness with which Techno would be promoted by the Japanese distributor, and on effective protection of Pioneer's patent rights against possible infringements through unscrupulous copying of Techno by one or more firms in Japan. Meanwhile, the pros and cons of exporting assembled vs. unassembled locks to Japan had to be considered. If agreement was reached to export Techno unassembled, Pioneer could offer to sell the parts to Ako at around $1.10 per set f.o.b. Ako would pay a 10 percent import duty (instead of 17½ percent on assembled sets), incur about 20¢ to 25¢ per set for freight, assembly and packaging, and could sell to builders for at least $1.95. If large orders could be generated and Pioneer was able to, say, double the size of present production runs, unit costs would drop by about 10 percent.

Mr. Corbin was also not sure whether to offer Ako exclusive agency in Japan only or in the Far East as a whole at present.

Questions

1. Appraise Pioneer's policies and attempts to establish Techno in foreign markets. What changes, if any, would you propose to make these politicies more effective?
2. What terms would you advise Mr. Corbin to offer Ako? Why?

Planning and Evaluating the Marketing Effort

Part 8

PLANNING A COMPANY'S MARKETING PROGRAM, EVALU-
ATING THE MARKETING PERFORMANCE OF A COMPANY,
AND APPRAISING THE ROLE OF MARKETING IN OUR
SOCIETY

Up to this point in the book, we have dealt primarily with the selection of target markets and with the development and management of the four segments of the marketing mix in an individual organization.

Now it is time to tie things together—to take an overview of the firm's *total* marketing program, thus integrating the separate elements of the marketing mix. Our approach in Part 8 will be to apply the *planning* and *evaluation* aspects of the management process to the *total* marketing program. Strategic marketing planning and evaluation in the individual firm are covered in Chapter 24. Then in Chapter 25 we appraise the current position of marketing in the Canadian socioeconomic system.

Chapter 24

Strategic Marketing Planning, Forecasting, and Evaluation

CHAPTER GOALS

This chapter is concerned with two parts of the management of a company's total marketing program—planning and evaluation. After studying the chapter, you should understand:

1. *The nature, scope, and importance of planning in marketing*
2. *Some fundamentals of strategic company planning and strategic marketing planning*
3. *The nature and importance of demand forecasting in marketing*
4. *The major method used in forecasting market demand*
5. *The concept of a marketing audit as a complete evaluation program*
6. *The meaning of misdirected marketing effort*
7. *Sales-volume analysis*
8. *Marketing-cost analysis*

By now, you presumably have acquired a sound foundation in the fundamentals of marketing. With this foundation, we can now revisit the topic of marketing management, which was introduced briefly in Chapter 2. There, marketing management was defined as the process of planning a marketing program, implementing the plans, and evaluating the performance results. In this chapter, we shall discuss strategic planning and performance evaluation as applied to the total marketing effort in an organization. We shall also discuss the forecasting of market demand — an essential ingredient in strategic planning. Our discussion of these topics will be brief, as befits the scope of a beginning course in marketing.

NATURE AND SCOPE OF PLANNING

In simple English, **planning** is drawing from the past to decide in the present what to do in the future. Or, deciding now what we're going to do later, when and how we are going to do it, and who will do it. If we don't have a plan, we cannot get anything done — because we don't know what needs to be done, or how to do it.

As the sign says

PLAN AHEA.

Or, if you don't know where you are going, any road will take you there.

Planning may also be viewed as an extension of input-output theory. Once management forecasts its desired output—that is, sets a goal—then, through careful planning, it can determine what input factors will be needed to attain that goal. To illustrate, assume that the goal is to enter a new geographic market and attain a sales volume of $2 million in this market by the end of the second year. By working backward from that output goal, management can estimate what inputs are necessary, in the form of promotion, production facilities, financing, and personnel, to reach the goal. These inputs can then be organized to attain the goal. Or management may find that the required inputs are beyond the firm's capacity. Then the output goal must be altered—made more modest. Thus, the availability of inputs may actually set limits on output. In essence, planning involves a matching of means and ends, or inputs and outputs.

The concept of planning is not new. However, market and economic conditions in recent years have led to a better understanding of the need for, and value of, formal planning. Truly, any success that management has in increasing the profitability of marketing operations depends in large part upon the nature of its marketing planning. Formal planning is one of the most effective management tools available for reducing risks.

Planning may cover long or short periods of time. **Long-range planning** (for 3, 5, 10, or even 25 years) usually involves top management and special planning staffs. It deals with broad, company-wide issues such as plant, market, or product expansion. **Short-term planning** typically covers a period of one year or less and is the responsibility of lower- and middle-echelon executives. It involves such issues as planning next year's advertising campaign, making merchandise-buying plans in a store, or setting sales quotas for a sales force.

Scope of Planning Activities

The planning activities in an organization may be conducted on three or four different levels, depending upon the size of the organization and the diversity of its products or services. These planning levels are as follows:

1. **Strategic company planning.** At this level, management defines the organization's mission, sets the organization's long-range goals, and decides on broad strategies formulated to achieve the goals. These long-range, company-wide goals and strategies then become the framework within which departmental planning is done. This total-company planning takes into consideration an organization's financial requirements,

production capabilities, labour needs, research and development effort, and marketing capabilities.

2. **Strategic business unit planning.** In large, diversified organizations, a modification of strategic company-wide planning has emerged in recent years. For more effective planning and operation, the total organization is divided into separate product divisions called "strategic business units" (SBUs). Each SBU is, in effect, a separate "business," and each SBU conducts its own strategic "business-wide" planning.

3. **Strategic marketing planning.** At this level, management is engaged in setting goals and strategies for the marketing effort in the organization. In smaller or nondiversified organizations, the SBU planning and marketing planning may be combined into one strategic planning activity. Or, in small, single-business organizations, the top three levels of planning (company, SBU, marketing) may be combined into one planning activity.

   Strategic marketing planning includes the selection of target markets and the development of long-range programs for the major ingredients in the marketing mix — the product, the distribution system, the pricing structure, and the promotional activities. In Parts 3 to 6 of this book, the major ingredients in the marketing mix were considered individually. Realistically, however, planning in all these areas must be done concurrently and must be carefully coordinated, because each element in the mix interacts with every other element.

4. **Annual marketing planning.** The annual marketing plan is one part, covering one time segment, of the ongoing strategic marketing planning process. It is a master plan covering a year's marketing operations for a given product line, major product, brand, or market. Thus, this plan serves as an operational guide to the executives in each phase of the marketing effort for the given product or market.

STRATEGIC COMPANY PLANNING

In Chapter 2, we defined strategic company planning as a managerial process of matching an organization's resources with its marketing opportunities over the long run. This process consists of (1) defining the organization's mission, (2) setting organizational objectives, (3) evaluating the strategic business units (this is called "business portfolio analysis"), and (4) selecting appropriate strategies so as to achieve the organizational objectives (see Fig. 24-1).

The strategic planning process and the resultant company plans are influenced considerably both by external environmental forces and by the organization's internal resources. The external environmental forces are: demography, economic conditions, social and cultural factors, political and legal considerations, technology, competition, and the organization's markets. These forces were first discussed in Chapter 2, and their impact has been seen frequently in our discussion of the four elements in an organization's marketing mix.

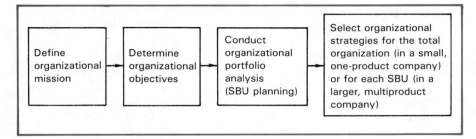

Figure 24-1
THE STRATEGIC
PLANNING PROCESS
FOR THE TOTAL
ORGANIZATION.

Concerning the impact of internal forces, it probably is obvious that management's planning will be influenced by the organization's financial condition, its production facilities, research and development capabilities, and other resources within the firm.

Organizational Mission

The first step in the strategic planning process, as applied to the organization as a whole, is to clearly define the company's mission. For some firms, this step requires only the review and approval of a previously published mission statement. But, for most firms, this step in formal planning really has never been clearly articulated. Or, perhaps at one time, the organization's mission was clear, but personnel changes and changing environmental conditions have caused that previous statement to become irrelevant or inappropriate.

In any event, to start its strategic planning, management must clearly answer the question, "What business are we in?" and further, management may also ask, "What business *should* we be in?" Unless the organization's basic purpose is clear to all executives, any efforts at strategic planning are likely to be ineffective.

An organization's purpose, or mission, should be stated in writing and well publicized. A properly prepared statement of company mission can be an effective public relations tool. The statement should not be too broad or vague — nor should it be too narrow or specific. To say that our mission is "to benefit Canadian consumers" is too broad and vague. To say our business is "to make tennis balls" is too narrow. Neither statement provides sufficient guidance to management.

Traditionally, companies have stated their mission in production-oriented terms: "We make telephones (or furnaces, or skis)." Or management might say, "We are in the railroad business (or in furniture manufacturing)."

Today, in line with the customer-benefit orientation inherent in the marketing concept, organizations are urged to be market-oriented in their mission statements. Thus, instead of making telephones, a company should be marketing communication services. Instead of making furnaces, the company should be marketing home climate control. Not only are these market-oriented statements more attractive to the public, but they also serve to broaden a company's market and extend the company's life. If your mission is to make furnaces, you will be out of the business when furnaces are replaced by heat pumps or solar heating units. But if your mission is to market climate control, then you can discontinue furnace production, switch to alternative energy sources, and continue competing with the new generation of heating and air-conditioning companies.

Organizational Objectives

The next step in the strategic planning process is for management to decide upon a set of objectives that will guide the organization in accomplishing its mission. These objectives can also serve as guides for managerial planning at lower levels in an organization. And, they provide standards for evaluating an organization's performance.

```
    S           R
    P           E
 M E A S U R A B L E
    C   ┌──────┐ L
    I   │GOALS │ I
    F   │MUST  │ S
 C O N S│BE:   │T E N T
    C   └──────┘ I
                C
```

At any level of strategic planning, the objectives should be clearly stated *in writing*. Such statements should avoid meaningless platitudes. Objectives should be action-stimulators, because objectives are achieved by actions that carry out plans.

The organization's objectives should be realistic and mutually consistent. To be effective, each objective should be stated in *specific* terms, and, wherever possible, the objectives should be *quantitatively measurable*. Some examples of objectives that illustrate these criteria are as follows:

Too general. To increase the company's profitability

More specific. To increase the company's return on investment to 18 percent within two years

Not measurable. To improve the company's public image

Measurable. To receive favourable recognition awards next year from at least three consumer or environmental groups

Organizational Portfolio Analysis: Strategic Business Unit (SBU) Planning

Many organizations are so diversified that total-company planning cannot serve as an effective guide for the executives who manage the component divisions of the organization. Certainly in Imasco, for example, the mission, objectives, and strategies in the tobacco division are quite different from those in the retailing division or the land-development division. Most large and medium-sized companies — and even many small firms — are multiproduct, and even multibusiness, organizations. Consequently, for effective planning, the total organization should be divided into separate product groups. Each group would, in effect, be treated as a separate "business," and it would conduct its own strategic "business-wide" planning.

The total organization may then be viewed as a "portfolio" of these businesses. And a key step in strategic planning is an evaluation of the individual businesses in the organization's portfolio. This evaluation is called a **business** (or **product**) **portfolio analysis**. Or, we can use the broader term **organizational portfolio analysis**, to include the use of this planning concept in nonbusiness, nonprofit organizations.

Several years ago, the General Electric Company coined the term "strategic business unit (SBU)" as a title for each individual business in an organization's portfolio. Each SBU may be a major division in an organization, a group of related products, or even a major product or brand. For example, Sears may identify as SBUs its retail-store division, its Allstate Insurance Company, and its automobile rental firm. A large insurance company may treat its life insurance group as one SBU and its fire-casualty-auto group as another.

To be identified as an SBU, a unit should possess these characteristics: (1) it is a separately identifiable business; (2) it has its own distinct mission; (3) it has its own competitors; (4) it has its own executives and profit responsibility; and (5) it can have its own strategic plan.

A portfolio analysis is made to identify the present status of each SBU and to determine its future role in the company. This evaluation also provides guidance to management in designing the strategies and tactics for an SBU. Certainly, management will design different strategies for a profitable, growing SBU than for one that is declining and soon will be eliminated.

The present position and future prospects for SBUs generally are in a state of change. Some are growing; others are declining. Some are profitable, while others are losing money. At the same time, management typically has limited resources to use in supporting its SBUs. Consequently, management needs to know how to allocate these limited resources. Which SBUs should be stimulated to grow, which ones maintained in their present market position, and which ones eliminated? A business portfolio analysis is designed to aid management in this decision making.

Even a small, single-product company can engage in the essence of product portfolio analysis. In such a firm, management would treat the entire organization as a single SBU. Management can analyse the firm's present status and future prospects. This analysis then provides a basis for later designing the organizational strategies for this small company.

Several models have been developed for conducting a business portfolio analysis. Some of the most widely used ones are simply listed here. Any further discussion is outside the scope of this book.[1]

1. A two-way grid on which a product (SBU) is positioned to reflect its market share and the growth rate of its market. This model was developed by the Boston Consulting Group, a well-known management consulting firm.

2. A two-way grid on which the product (SBU) is positioned to reflect the industry's attractiveness and the SBU's strength. This model was developed by the General Electric Company.

3. The Profit Impact of Marketing Strategy (PIMS) model. This model is derived from a large data base gathered from many large companies by the Strategic Planning Institute of Cambridge, Massachusetts. A company can analyse its position in comparison with other firms in the data bank, basing the analysis on market share, marketing expenditures, and several other factors that are related to profitability.

4. Analysing a product (SBU) within the context of its life cycle.

---

[1] For information on methods of product portofolio analysis, see Derek F. Abell and John S. Hammond, *Strategic Market Planning*, Prentice-Hall, Inc., Englewood Cliffs, N.J., 1979; and David W. Cravens, *Strategic Marketing*, Richard D. Irwin, Inc., Homewood, Ill., 1982.

	Present products	New products
Present markets	Market penetration	Product development
New markets	Market development	Diversification

Figure 24-2
ORGANIZATIONAL
STRATEGIES FOR
PRODUCT/MARKET
EXPANSION.

Organizational Strategies

By this point in its strategic planning, presumably the organization has determined where it wants to go — on the basis of its mission statement, its statement of objectives, and its business portfolio analysis. The next step in strategic planning is to design the ways to get there. These are the organizational strategies — the broad, basic plans of action by which an organization intends to achieve its goals and fulfil its mission. We are speaking about selecting strategies (1) for the total organization in a small, one-product company or (2) for each SBU in a larger, multiproduct or multi-business organization.

On the basis of its business portfolio analysis, management can select from among the following four strategic alternatives for the organization in total or for a given SBU:

1. Intensify the marketing effort so as to strengthen and build the SBU.

2. Help the SBU to maintain its present market position.

3. Use the SBU as a cash-flow source to help other SBUs grow or maintain position.

4. Get rid of the SBU.

Most statements of mission and objectives reflect an organization's desire and intention to grow — to increase its revenues and profit. In such cases, an organization may take either of two routes in its strategy design. It can continue to do what it is now doing with its products and markets — only do it better. Or, the organization can venture into new products and/or markets. These two routes, when applied to markets and/or products, result in four major strategic alternatives, which may be displayed in matrix form, as in Fig. 24-2.[2]

The strategy of *market penetration* implies that the company will try to sell more of its present products to its present markets. Supporting tactics might include an increase in advertising expenditures or an increase in the personal selling effort. The strategy of *market development* calls for the company to continue to sell its existing products, but in new markets. Thus, a

---

[2]See H. Igor Ansoff, "Strategies for Diversification," *Harvard Business Review*, September-October 1957, pp. 113–124.

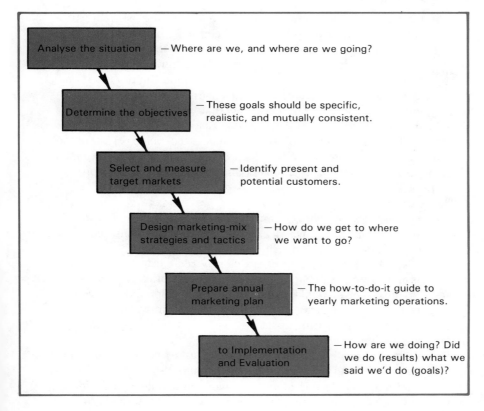

Figure 24-3
THE STRATEGIC MARKETING PLANNING PROCESS.

manufacturer of power tools now selling to industrial users might decide to sell its small portable tools to the consumer market.

A strategy of *product development* means that the organization intends to develop new products to sell to its present customers. A food processor, for example, may introduce a new line of salt-free canned and frozen foods for its existing markets. *Diversification* is a growth strategy that involves adding new, perhaps unfamiliar, products to be sold to new markets. Cigarette manufacturers, for example, have diversified into dog food, beer, soft drinks, and other products and markets that were new to the cigarette firms.

After completing the strategic planning for the total organization or for an SBU, then management can do the planning for each major functional division, such as marketing or production. The planning for marketing (or for any functional division, for that matter) should be compatible with, and guided by, the organizational or SBU mission and objectives.

STRATEGIC MARKETING PLANNING

The planning process in strategic marketing consists of these steps: (1) conduct a situation analysis, (2) determine marketing objectives, (3) select target markets and measure the market demand, (4) design a strategic marketing mix, (5) prepare an annual marketing plan (see Fig. 24-3).

The Planning Process

A *situation analysis* is a review of the company's existing marketing program. By analysing where the program has been and where it is now, management can determine where the program should go in the future. A situation analysis normally includes an analysis of the external environmental forces and the nonmarketing resources that surround the organization's marketing program. These are the same factors (markets, competition, economic conditions, social-cultural forces, etc.) that we have recognized ever since Chapter 2 as being major influences that shape and direct a company's marketing effort. A situation analysis also includes a detailed review of the company's present marketing mix — its product and pricing situation, its distribution system (including suppliers and middlemen), and its promotional program.

The next step in the marketing planning process is to *determine the marketing objectives*. As with organizational objectives, the marketing goals should be realistic, specific, measurable, and mutually consistent. And they should be clearly stated in writing.

The goals at the marketing level are closely related to the company-wide goals and strategies. In fact, a *company* strategy often translates into a *marketing* goal. For example, to reach an organizational objective of a 20 percent return on investment next year, one organizational strategy might be to reduce marketing costs by 15 percent. This organizational strategy would then become a marketing goal.

The *selection of target markets* is obviously a key step in marketing planning. Management should analyse existing markets in detail and identify potential markets. At this point, management should also decide to what extent, and in what manner, it wants to segment its markets. As part of this step in the planning process, management also should forecast its sales in its various markets.

Management next must *design a strategic marketing mix* that enables the company to satisfy the wants of its target markets and to achieve its marketing goals. The design, and later the operation, of the marketing-mix components, constitutes the bulk of a company's marketing effort.

Annual Marketing Plans

Periodically, the ongoing strategic marketing planning process in an organization culminates in the preparation of a series of short-term marketing plans. These plans usually cover the period of a year — hence the name "annual marketing plan." However, in some industries it is necessary to prepare these plans for even shorter time periods because of the nature of the product or market. A separate annual plan should be prepared for each product line, major product, brand, or market.

An annual marketing plan is the master guide covering a year's marketing activity for the given business unit or product. The plan then becomes the how-to-do-it document that guides executives in each phase of their marketing operations. The plan includes (1) a statement of objectives, (2) the identification of the target markets, (3) the strategies and tactics pertaining to the marketing mix, and (4) information regarding the budgetary support for the marketing activity.

In an annual marketing plan, more attention can be devoted to tactical details than is feasible in longer-range planning. As an example, long-range marketing planning may set as a goal the introduction of truly innovative products. The marketing plan for next year, however, may strive to correct an inventory imbalance by strongly promoting one product that is in the declining stage of its life cycle. Or, long-range planning may emphasize the role of personal selling in the promotional mix. The annual plan then might be concerned, for example, with increased college recruiting as a source of salespeople.

The cornerstone of successful marketing planning in a firm is the measurement and forecasting of market demand. The key requirement is the company sales forecast, because it is the basis for all budgeting and all operations in the firm.

FORECASTING MARKET DEMAND

Before we discuss forecasting methods, we need to define several terms, because they often are used loosely in business.

Definition of Some Basic Terms

Market Factor and Market Index

A **market factor** is an item or element that (1) exists in a market, (2) may be measured quantitatively, and (3) is related to the demand for a product or service. To illustrate, the "number of cars three years old and older" is a market factor underlying the demand for replacement tires. That is, the element affects the number of replacement tires that can be sold. A **market index** is simply a market factor expressed as a percentage, or in some other quantitative form, relative to some base figure. To illustrate, one market factor is "households owning appliance X"; in 1983, the market index for this factor was 132 (relative to 1975 equals 100).

Market Potential and Sales Potential

The **market potential** for a product is the total expected sales of that product by all sellers during a stated period of time in a stated market. **Sales potential** (synonymous with **market share**) is the share of a market potential that an individual company expects to achieve.

Thus we may speak of the "market potential" for automatic washing machines, but the "sales potential" (or market share) for one company's brand of machine. In the case of either market potential or sales potential, the market may encompass all of Canada, or even the world. Or it may be a smaller market segmented by income, by geographic area, or on some other basis. For example, we may speak of the *market potential* for washing machines in British Columbia, or the *sales potential* for General Electric washers in homes with incomes of $20,000 or $25,000. The market potential and market share sales potential are the same when a firm has a monopoly in its market, as in the case of some public utilities.

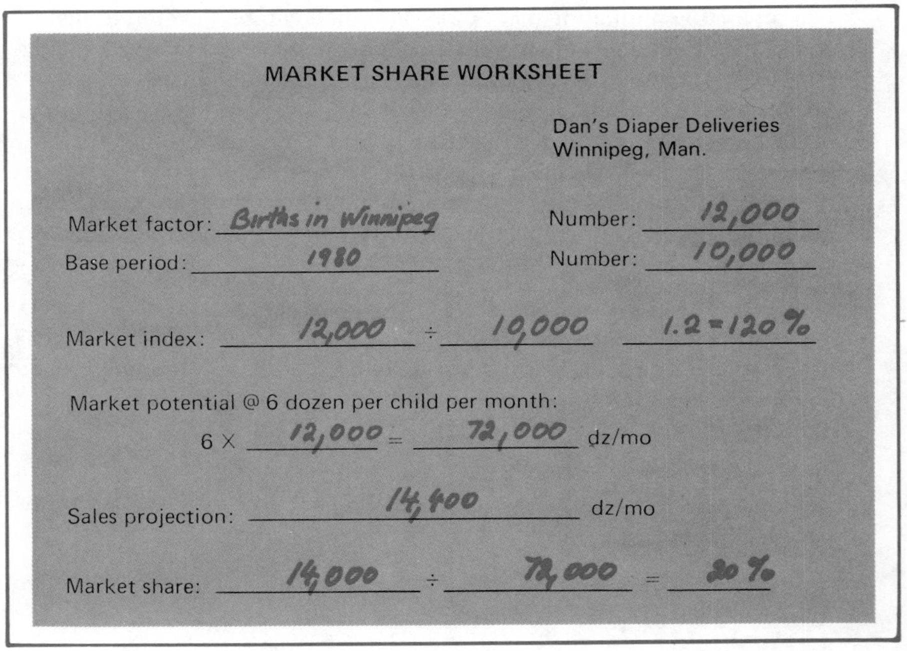

MARKET SHARE WORKSHEET

Dan's Diaper Deliveries
Winnipeg, Man.

Market factor: *Births in Winnipeg* Number: *12,000*

Base period: *1980* Number: *10,000*

Market index: *12,000* ÷ *10,000* *1.2 = 120%*

Market potential @ 6 dozen per child per month:

6 × *12,000* = *72,000* dz/mo

Sales projection: *14,400* dz/mo

Market share: *14,000* ÷ *72,000* = *20%*

**Figure 24-4
BUSINESS
APPLICATION OF
SOME OF OUR
DEFINITIONS.**

Sales Forecast

A **sales forecast** may be defined as an estimate of sales (in dollar or product units) during some specified future period of time, and under a predetermined marketing plan in the firm. A sales forecast can ordinarily be made more intelligently if the company first determines its market and/ or sales potential. However, many firms start their forecasting directly with the sales forecast.

The Sales Forecast and the Marketing Plan The marketing goals and broad strategies — the core of a marketing plan — must be established before a sales forecast is made. That is, the sales forecast depends upon these predetermined goals and strategies. Certainly, different sales forecasts will result, depending upon whether the marketing goal is (1) to liquidate an excess inventory of product A or (2) to expand the firm's market share by aggressive advertising.

However, once the sales forecast is prepared, it does become the key controlling factor in all *operational* planning throughout the company. The forecast is the basis of sound budgeting. Financial planning for working-capital requirements, plant utilization, and other needs is based on anticipated sales. The scheduling of all production resources and facilities, such as setting labour needs and purchasing raw materials, depends upon the sales forecast.

Sales-Forecasting Periods The most widely used period for sales forecasting is one year, although many firms will review annual forecasts on a monthly or quarterly basis. Annual sales forecasts tie in with annual financial planning and reporting, and are often based on estimates of the coming year's general economic conditions.

Forecasts for less than a year may be desirable when activity in the firm's industry is so volatile that it is not feasible to look ahead a full year. As a case in point, many firms engaged in fashion merchandising — producers and retailers alike — prepare a forecast that covers only one fashion season.

A company can forecast its sales by using either of two basic procedures — the "top-down" or the "buildup" approach.

Methods of Forecasting Demand

Using the **top-down** (or **breakdown**) approach, management generally would:

1. *start with a forecast of general economic conditions*, as the basis to
2. *determine the industry's total market potential for a product*; then
3. *measure the share of this market the firm is getting*; the measurements in items 2 and 3 form the basis to
4. *forecast the sales of the product*; the sales forecast, in turn, is the basis for all
5. *budgeting and other operational planning in the firm*.

In the **buildup** technique, managment would generate estimates of future demand in various segments of the market or from various organizational units (sales people or branches) in the company. Then management would simply add the individual estimates to get one total forecast.

Predictions of future market demand — whether they are sales forecasts or estimates of market potential — may be based on techniques ranging from uninformed guesses to sophisticated statistical methods. Marketing executives do not need to know how to do the statistical computations. However, they should understand enough about a given technique to appreciate its merits and limitations. They should also know when each method is best used, and they should be able to ask intelligent questions regarding the assumptions underlying the method.[3]

Here are some of the commonly used methods of predicting demand.

Market-Factor Analysis

This method is based on the assumption that the future demand for a product is related to the behaviour of certain market factors. If we can determine what these factors are and can measure their relationship to sales activity, we can forecast future sales simply by studying the behaviour of the factors.

---

[3]See David L. Hurwood, Elliott S. Grossman, and Earl L. Bailey, *Sales Forecasting*, The Conference Board, New York, report no. 730, 1978; Douglas J. Dalrymple, "Sales Forecasting Methods and Accuracy," *Business Horizons*, December 1975, pp. 69–73; and Vithala R. Rao and James E. Cox, Jr., *Sales Forecasting Methods: A Survey of Recent Developments*, Marketing Science Institute, Cambridge, Mass., report no. 78-119, 1978.

The key to the successful use of this method lies in the selection of the appropriate market factors. It is also important to minimize the number of market factors used. The greater the number of factors, the greater the chance for erroneous estimates and the more difficult it is to tell how much each factor influences the demand. The two procedures used to translate market-factor behaviour into an estimate of future sales are the direct-derivation method and the correlation-analysis technique.

Direct Derivation   As an illustration of the use of this method to estimate *market potential*, suppose that a manufacturer of automobile tires wants to know the market potential for replacement tires in 1986. The primary market factor is the number of automobiles on the road. The first step is to estimate how many cars are likely prospects for new tires. Assume (1) that the seller's studies show that the average car is driven about 15,000 km a year and (2) that the average driver gets about 40,000 km from a set of four tires. This means that all cars that become 2½ years old during 1986 can be considered a part of the potential market for replacement tires during that year. The seller can obtain a reasonably accurate count of the number of cars sold between July 1, 1983 and June 30, 1984. (These are the cars that will become 2½ years old in 1986.) The information sources are provincial motor vehicle licensing agencies or private organizations. In addition, the seller can determine how many cars will become 5, 7½, and 10 years old in 1986. (These ages are multiples of 2½. That is, in 1986, a 5-year-old car presumably would be ready for its second set of replacement tires.) The number of cars in these age brackets times 4 (tires per car) should give a fair approximation of the market potential for replacement tires in 1986. We are, of course, dealing in averages. Not all drivers will get 40,000 km from a set of tires, and not all cars will be driven exactly 15,000 km per year.

The direct-derivation method has much to recommend it. It is relatively simple and inexpensive to use, and it requires little statistical analysis. It is reasonably easy to understand, so that executives who are not statistics-oriented can follow the method and interpret the results.

Correlation Analysis   This technique is a mathematical refinement of the direct-derivation method. When correlation analysis is used, the degree of association between potential sales of the product and the market factor is taken into account. In effect, a correlation analysis measures, on a scale of 0 to 1, the variations between the two series of data. Consequently, this method can be used only when a lengthy sales history of the industry or the firm is available, as well as a history of the market factor.

Correlation analysis gives a more exact estimate of market demand, provided that the method is applied correctly. In direct derivation, the correlation measure is implicitly assumed to be 1.00. But rarely does this perfect association exist between a market factor and the sales of a product. Correlation analysis therefore takes the past history into account in predicting the future. It also allows a researcher to incorporate more than one factor into the formula.

There are at least two major limitations to this method. First, as suggested above, a lengthy sales history must be available. To do a really good job, researchers need about twenty periods of sales records. Also, they must assume that approximately the same relationship has existed between the sales and the market factors during this entire period. And, furthermore, they must assume that this relationship will continue in the next sales period. These can be highly unrealistic assumptions. The other major drawback is that very few marketing people understand correlation analysis and can actually do the necessary computations. Thus a statistical staff may be necessary.

Survey of Buyer Intentions

Another commonly used method of forecasting is to survey a sample of potential customers. These people are asked how much of the stated product they would buy at a given price during a specified future time period. Some firms maintain consumer panels on a continuing basis to act as a sounding board for new-product ideas, prices, and other product features.

A major problem is that of selecting the sample of potential buyers. For many consumer products a very large, and thus very costly, sample would be needed. Aside from the extremely high cost and large amount of time that this method often entails, there is another very serious limitation. It is one thing for consumers to *intend to buy* a product, but quite another for them to *actually buy* it. Surveys of buying intentions inevitably show an inflated measure of market potential.

Surveys of buying intentions are probably most effective when (1) there are relatively few buyers, (2) these buyers are willing to express their buying intentions, and (3) their past record shows that their follow-up actions are consistent with their stated intentions.

Test Marketing

In using this technique, a firm markets its product in a limited geographic area. Then, from this sample, management projects the company's sales potential (market share) over a larger area. Test marketing is frequently used in deciding whether sufficient sales potential exists for a new product. The technique also serves as a basis for evaluating various product features and alternative marketing strategies. The outstanding benefit of test marketing is that it can tell management how many people *actually buy* the product, instead of only how many *say they intend to buy*. If a company can afford the time and money for this method, and can run a valid test, this is the best way of measuring the potential for its product.

These are big "ifs," however. Test marketing is expensive in time and money. Great care is needed to control the test-marketing experiment. A competitor, learning you are test marketing, is usually adept at "jamming" your experiment. That is, by unusual promotional or other marketing effort, a competitor can create an artificial situation that distorts your test results.

To avoid such test-market "wars," some companies are using simulations of test markets. In effect, these marketers are conducting a test market in a laboratory, rather than in the field.[4]

Past Sales and Trend Analysis

A favourite method of forecasting is to base the estimate *entirely* on past sales. This technique is used frequently by retailers whose main goal is to "beat last year's figures." The method consists simply in applying a flat percentage increase to the volume achieved last year or to the average volume of the past few years.

This technique is simple, inexpensive, and easy to apply. For a firm operating in a stable market, where its market share has remained constant for a period of years, past sales alone might be used to predict future volume. On balance, however, the method is highly unreliable.

Trend analysis is a variation of forecasting based on past sales, but it is a bit more complicated. It involves either (1) a long-run projection of the sales trend, usually computed by statistical techniques, or (2) a short-run projection (forecasting for only a few months ahead) based upon a seasonal index of sales. The statistical sophistication of long-run trend analysis does not really remove the inherent weakness of basing future estimates only on past sales activity. Short-run trend analysis may be acceptable if the firm's sales follow a reliable seasonal pattern. For example, assume that sales reach 10,000 units in the first quarter (January–March) and, historically, the second quarter is always about 50 percent better. Then we can reasonably forecast sales of 15,000 units in the April–June period.

---

[4]For a series of articles on the practical aspects of test marketing, see "Test Marketing: What's in Store," special section in *Sales & Marketing Management*, March 15, 1982, pp. 57ff.; and "Test Marketing," *Advertising Age*, February 22, 1982, pp. M-9 to M-40.

Sales-Force Composite

This is a buildup method that may be used to forecast sales or to estimate market potential. As used in sales forecasting, it consists of collecting from all salespeople and middlemen an estimate of sales in their territories during the forecasting period. The total (the composite) of these separate estimates is the company's sales forecast. This method can be used advantageously if the firm has competent, high-calibre salespeople. The method is also useful for firms selling to a market composed of relatively few, but large, customers. Thus, this method would be more applicable to sales of large electrical generators than small general-use motors.

The sales-force composite method takes advantage of the salespeople's specialized knowledge of their own market. Also, it should make them more willing to accept their assigned sales quotas. On the other hand, the sales force usually does not have the time or the experience to do the research needed in forecasting future sales.

Executive Judgement

This method covers a wide range of possibilities. Basically it consists of obtaining opinions regarding future sales volume from one or more executives. If these are really informed opinions, based on valid measures such as market-factor analysis, then the executive judgement is useful and desirable. Certainly all the previously discussed forecasting methods should be tempered with sound executive judgement. On the other hand, forecasting by executive opinion alone is risky. In some instances, such opinions are simply intuition or guesswork.

After the sales forecast and other marketing goals have been determined and the strategies and tactics planned, management is ready to put its marketing plan into action. The activity of operating and directing various parts of a marketing plan — the implementation stage in the management process — is what we have been discussing through much of this book. Now it is time to evaluate the operating results.

As soon as possible after a firm's plans have been set in operation, the process of evaluation should begin. Without evaluation, management cannot tell whether its plan is working and what the reasons are for success or failure. Planning and evaluation thus are interrelated activities. Evaluation logically follows planning and the execution of the plan. That is, planning sets forth what *should be* done, and evaluation shows what *really was* done. Sometimes a circular relationship exists: plans are made, they are put into action, the operational results are evaluated, and new plans are prepared on the basis of this appraisal (see Fig. 24-5).

Previously we have discussed evaluation as it relates to individual parts of a marketing program — the product-planning process, the performance of the sales force, and the effectiveness of the advertising program, for instance. At this point, let's look at the evaluation of the *total marketing effort*.

EVALUATING MARKETING PERFORMANCE

Figure 24-5
THE CIRCULAR RELATIONSHIP AMONG MANAGEMENT TASKS.

The Marketing
Audit: A Total
Evaluation Program

A marketing audit is the essential element of a total evaluation program.[5] An audit implies a review and an evaluation of some activity. Thus, a **marketing audit** is a systematic, comprehensive, periodic review and evaluation of the marketing function in an organization — its marketing goals, strategies, and performance. This audit includes an appraisal of the organization, personnel, and procedures employed to implement the firm's strategies and reach its goals.

To qualify as a complete marketing audit, an appraisal must cover all the marketing areas referred to in the definition — goals, strategies, performance, organization, personnel, and procedure. Obviously a complete audit is an extensive and difficult project.

But the rewards from a marketing audit can be great. Management can identify its problem areas in marketing. By reviewing its strategies, the firm is likely to keep abreast of its changing marketing environment. Successes can also be analysed, so the company can capitalize on its strong points. The audit can spot lack of coordination in the marketing program, outdated strategies, or unrealistic goals. The audit allows management to correctly place responsibility for good or poor performance. Furthermore, an audit should anticipate future situations. It is intended for "prognosis as well as diagnosis. . . . It is the practice of preventive as well as curative marketing medicine."[6]

Misdirected
Marketing Effort

One of the primary benefits of evaluation activities is that they can help correct misdirected or misplaced marketing effort.

The "80-20" Principle

A company does not enjoy the same rate of net profit on every individual sale. In most firms a large proportion of the orders, customers, territories, or products account for only a small share of the profit. This relationship between selling units and profit has been characterized as the "80-20" principle. That is, 80 percent of the orders, customers, territories, or products contribute only 20 percent of the sales or profit. Conversely, 20 percent of these selling units account for 80 percent of the volume or profit. The 80-20 figure is used simply to epitomize the misplacement of marketing efforts. Actually, of course, the percentage split varies from one situation to another.

The basic reason for the 80-20 situation is that almost every marketing program includes some misdirected effort. Marketing efforts and costs are

---

[5]See *Analyzing and Improving Marketing Performance: "Marketing Audits" in Theory and Practice*, American Management Association, Management Report no. 32, New York, 1959; see especially Abe Shuchman, "The Marketing Audit: Its Nature, Purpose, and Problems," pp. 11–19; and Alfred R. Oxenfeldt, "The Marketing Audit as a Total Evaluation Program," pp. 25–36.

[6]Shuchman, *op. cit.*, p. 14.

proportional to the *number* of territories, customers, or products, rather than to their actual sales volume or profit. For example, in a department store, approximately the same order-filling, billing, and delivery expenses are involved whether a mink coat or a necktie is sold. Or a manufacturer may assign one salesperson to each territory. Yet, there may be substantial differences in the potential volume and profit from the various territories. In each case, the marketing effort (cost) is not in line with the potential return.

Reasons for Misdirected Marketing Effort

Many executives are unaware of the misdirected marketing effort in their firms. They do not know what percentage of total sales and profit comes from a given product line or customer group. Frequently executives cannot uncover their misdirection of effort because they lack sufficiently detailed information. The analogy of an iceberg in an open sea has been used to illustrate this situation. Only a small part of an iceberg is visible above the surface of the water, and the submerged 90 percent is the dangerous part. The figures representing total sales or total costs on an operating statement are like the visible part of an iceberg. The detailed figures representing sales, costs, and other performance measures for each territory or product correspond to the important and dangerous submerged segment.

THE ICEBERG PRINCIPLE.

Total sales or costs as presented on an operating statement are too general to be useful in evaluation. In fact, the total figures are often inconclusive and misleading. More than one company has shown satisfactory overall sales and profit figures; but when these totals were subdivided by territory or products, serious weaknesses were discovered. A manufacturer of rubber products showed an overall annual increase of 12 percent in sales and 9 percent in net profit on one product line one year. But management wasn't satisfied with this "tip of the iceberg." When it analysed the figures more closely, it found that the sales change within territories ranged from an increase of 19 percent to a decrease of 3 percent. In some territories, profits increased as much as 14 percent, and in others, they were down 20 percent.

An even more important cause of misplaced marketing effort is the fact that executives must make decisions based on inadequate knowledge of the exact nature of marketing costs. In other words, management lacks (1) knowledge of the disproportionate spread of marketing effort, (2) reliable standards for determining what should be spent on marketing, and (3) what results should be expected from these expenditures.

As an illustration, a company may spend $250,000 more on advertising this year than last year. But management ordinarily cannot state what the resultant increase in sales volume or profit should be. Nor do the executives know what would have happened if they had spent the same amount on (1) new-product development, (2) management training seminars for middlemen, or (3) some other aspect of the marketing program.

The Evaluation
Process

The evaluation process — whether in the form of a complete marketing audit or only an appraisal of individual components of the marketing program — is essentially a three-stage task. In the evaluation process, management's job is as follows:

1. Find out *what* happened — get the facts; compare actual results with budgeted goals to determine where they differ.

2. Find out *why* it happened — what specific factors in the marketing program accounted for the results.

3. Decide *what to do* about it — plan the next period's program and activities so as to improve on unsatisfactory performance and capitalize on the things that were done well.

One effective way to evaluate a total marketing program is to measure the performance results. To do this, two useful tools are available — the sales volume analysis and the marketing cost analysis. These tools are illustrated in the next two sections.

Our discussion of sales volume and marketing cost analyses are built around the Great Western Office Furniture Ltd. (GW)—a hypothetical firm that markets office furniture. This company's market is divided into four sales districts, each with seven or eight salespeople and a district sales manager. The company sells to office-equipment wholesalers and directly to large industrial users. Great Western's product mix is divided into four groups — desks, chairs, filing equipment, and accessories (wastebaskets, desk sets, etc.). Some of these products are manufactured by Great Western, and some are purchased from other firms.

ANALYSIS OF
SALES VOLUME

A **sales volume analysis** is a detailed study of the "net sales" section of a company's profit and loss statement (its operating statement). Management should analyse its *total* sales volume, and its volume by *product lines* and by *market segments* (territories, customer groups). These sales should be compared with company goals and with industry sales.

Sales Results versus
Sales Goals

We start with an analysis of Great Western's total sales volume, as shown in Table 24-1. The company's annual sales doubled (from $18 million to $36 million) during the ten-year period ending in 1985. Furthermore, they increased each year over the preceding year, with the exception of 1982. In most of these years the company met or surpassed its planned sales goals. Thus far, the company's situation is very encouraging. When industry sales figures are introduced for comparison, however, the picture changes. But let's hold the industry-comparison analysis until the next section.

A study of total sales volume alone is usually insufficient, and maybe even misleading, because of the workings of the iceberg principle. To learn what is going on in the "submerged" segments of the market, we need to analyse sales volume by market segments — sales territories, for example.

Table 24-2 is a summary of the planned sales goals and the actual sales results in Great Western's four sales districts. A key measurement figure is the *performance percentage* — the actual sales divided by the sales goal. A performance percentage of 100 means that the district did exactly what was expected of it. Thus, from the table we see that B and C did just a little better than was expected. District A passed its goal by a wide margin, but district D was quite a disappointment.

So far in our evaluation process, we know a little about *what* happened in GW's districts. Now management has to figure out *why* it happened, and what should be done about it. These are the difficult steps in evaluation. In the GW situation, the executives need to determine why district D did so poorly. The fault may lie in some aspect of the marketing program, or competition may be especially strong there. They also should find out what accounts for district A's success, and whether this information can be used in the other regions.

This brief examination of two aspects of sales volume analysis shows how this evaluation tool may be used. In a real business situation, GW's executives should go much further. They should analyse their sales volume by individual territories within districts and by product lines. Then they should carry their territorial analysis further by examining volume by product line and customer group *within* each territory. For instance, even though district A did well overall, the iceberg principle may be at work *within* the district. The fine *total* performance in district A may be covering up weaknesses in an individual product line or territory.

Table 24-1   ANNUAL SALES VOLUME OF GREAT WESTERN, INDUSTRY VOLUME, AND COMPANY'S SHARE IN THE CANADIAN MARKET

Year	Company Volume (in Millions of Dollars)	Industry Volume in Company's Market (in Millions of Dollars)	Company's Percentage Share of Market
1985	36.0	300	12.0
1984	34.7	275	12.6
1983	33.1	255	13.0
1982	30.4	220	13.8
1981	31.7	235	13.5
1980	28.0	200	14.0
1979	24.5	170	14.4
1978	22.5	155	14.5
1977	21.8	150	14.8
1976	18.0	120	15.0

Table 24-2   DISTRICT SALES VOLUME FOR GREAT WESTERN, 1985

District	Sales Goals (in Millions of Dollars)	Actual Sales (in Millions of Dollars)	Performance Percentage (Actual ÷ Goal)	Dollar Variation (in Millions)
A	10.8	12.5	116	+ 1.7
B	9.0	9.6	107	+ .6
C	7.6	7.7	101	+ .1
D	8.6	6.2	72	− 2.4
Total	36.0	36.0		

Market-Share Analysis

Comparing a company's sales results with its goal certainly is a useful form of performance evaluation. But it does not tell how the company is doing relative to its competitors. We need to compare the company's sales with the industry's sales. In effect, we should analyse, preferably in some detail, the company's share of the market. That is, we should analyse its market share in total, and also by product line and market segment.

Probably the major obstacle encountered in market-share analysis is in obtaining the industry sales information in total, and in the desired detail. Trade associations and government agencies are excellent sources for industry sales-volume statistics in many fields.

The Great Western situation is a good example of the usefulness of market-share analysis. Recall from Table 24-1 that GW's total sales doubled over a ten-year period, with annual increases in nine of those years. *But*, during this decade, the industry's annual sales increased from $120 million to $300 million (a 250 percent increase). Thus, the company's share of this market actually *declined* from 15 to 12 percent. Although the company's annual sales increased 100 percent, its market share declined 20 percent.

The next step is to determine *why* Great Western's market position declined. The number of possible causes is almost limitless, and this is what makes management's task so difficult. A weakness in almost any aspect of Great Western's product line, distribution system, pricing structure, or promotional program may have contributed to the loss of market share. It may be that the real culprit is competition. There may be new competitors in the market who were attracted by the rapid growth rates. Or, competitors' marketing programs may be more effective than Great Western's.

Table 24-3   PROFIT AND LOSS STATEMENT AND DISTRIBUTION OF NATURAL EXPENSES TO ACTIVITY COST GROUPS, GREAT WESTERN, 1983

Profit and Loss Statement ($000)		Expense Distribution Sheet ($000)				
		Activity (Functional) Cost Groups				
Net sales	$36,000					
Cost of goods sold	23,400			Ware-housing	Order	Marketing
Gross margin	12,600	Personal Selling	Adver-tising	and Shipping	Processing and Billing	Admini-stration
Operating expenses:						
Salaries and commissions	$2,710	$1,200	$ 240	$ 420	$280	$ 570
Travel and entertainment	1,400	1,040				400
Media space	1,480		1,480			
Supplies	440	60	35	240	70	35
Property taxes	130	16	5	60	30	19
Freight out	3,500			3,500		
Total expenses	9,700	$2,316	$1,760	$4,220	$380	$1,024
Net profit	$ 2,900					

An analysis of sales volume is quite useful in evaluating and controlling a company's marketing effort. A volume analysis, however, does not tell us anything about the *profitability* of this effort. Management needs to conduct a marketing cost analysis to determine the relative profitability of its territories, product lines, or other marketing units. A **marketing cost analysis** is a detailed study of the operating expense section of a company's profit and loss statement. As part of this analysis, management may establish budgetary goals, and then study the variations between budgeted costs and actual expenses.

A company's marketing costs may be analysed:

1. As they appear in the ledger accounts and on the profit and loss statement.
2. After they are grouped into functional (also called activity) classifications.
3. After these activity costs have been allocated to territories, products, or other marketing units.

MARKETING COST ANALYSIS

Types of Marketing Cost Analyses

Analysis of Ledger Expenses

The simplest and least expensive marketing cost analysis is a study of the "object of expenditure" costs as they appear in the firm's profit and loss statement. These figures, in turn, come from the company's accounting ledger records. The simplified operating statement for Great Western on the left side of Table 24-3 is the model we shall use in this discussion.

The procedure is simply to analyse each cost item (salaries, media space, etc.) in some detail. We can compare this period's total with the totals for similar periods in the past, and observe the trends. We can compare actual results with budgeted expense goals. We should also compute each expense as a percentage of net sales. Then, if possible, we should compare these expense ratios with industry figures, which are often available through trade associations.

Analysis of Functional Expenses

For more effective control of marketing costs, they should be allocated among the various marketing functions, such as advertising or warehousing. Then management can analyse the expenses of each of these activities.

The procedure here is to select the appropriate groups, and then to allocate each ledger expense among those activities. (See the expense distribution sheet on the right-hand side of Table 24-3.) In our Great Western example, we have decided on five activity cost groups. Some items, such as the cost of media space, can be apportioned directly to one activity (advertising). For other expenses, the cost can be prorated only after management has established some reasonable basis for allocation. Property taxes, for instance, may be allocated according to the proportion of the total floor space that is occupied by each department. Thus, the warehouse accounts for 46 percent of the total area of floor space in the firm, so the warehousing-shipping function is charged with $60,000 (46 percent) of the property taxes.

A functional cost analysis gives executives more information than they can get from an analysis of ledger accounts alone. Also, an analysis of activity expenses in total provides an excellent starting point for management to analyse costs by territories, products, or other marketing units.

Analysis of Functional Costs by Market Segments

The third and most beneficial type of marketing cost analysis is a study of the costs and profitability of each segment of the market. Common practice in this type of analysis is to divide the market by territories, products, customer groups, or order sizes. Cost analysis by market segment enables management to pinpoint trouble spots much more effectively than does an analysis of either ledger-account expenses or activity costs.

By combining a sales volume analysis with a marketing cost study, a researcher can prepare a complete operating statement for each of the product or market segments. These individual statements can then be analysed to determine the effectiveness of the marketing program as related to each of those segments.

Table 24-4   ALLOCATION OF ACTIVITY COSTS TO SALES DISTRICTS, GREAT WESTERN, 1983

Activity	Personal Selling	Advertising	Warehousing and Shipping	Order Processing and Billing	Marketing Administration
Allocation Scheme					
Allocation basis	Direct expense to each district	Number of pages of advertising	Number of orders to be shipped	Number of invoice lines	Equally among districts
Total activity cost	$2,316,000	$1,760,000	$4,220,000	$380,000	$1,024,000
Number of allocation units		88 pages	10,550 orders	126,667 lines	4 districts
Cost per allocation unit		$20,000	$400	$3	$256,000
Allocation of Costs					
District A — units		27 pages	3,300 orders	46,000 lines	one
District A — cost	$650,000	$540,000	$1,320,000	$138,000	$256,000
District B — units		19 pages	2,850 orders	33,000 lines	one
District B — cost	$606,000	$380,000	$1,140,000	$99,000	$256,000
District C — units		22 pages	2,300 orders	26,667 lines	one
District C — cost	$540,000	$440,000	$1,920,000	$80,000	$256,000
District D — units		20 pages	2,100 orders	21,000 lines	one
District D — cost	$520,000	$400,000	$840,000	$63,000	$256,000

The procedure for making a cost analysis by market segments is similar to that used to analyse functional (activity) expenses. The total of each activity cost (in the right-hand part of Table 24-3) is prorated on some basis to each product or market segment being studied. Let's walk through an example of a cost analysis, by sales districts, for Great Western, as shown in Tables 24-4 and 24-5.

First, for each of the five GW activities, we select an allocation basis for distributing the cost of that activity among the four districts (see the top part of Table 24-4). Then we determine the number of allocation "units" that make up each activity cost, and we find the cost per unit. This completes the allocation scheme, which tells us how to allocate costs to the four districts:

- Personal-selling activity expenses pose no problem because they are direct expenses, chargeable to the district in which they are incurred.

- We allocate advertising expenses on the basis of the number of the pages of advertising that were run in each district. Great Western purchased the equivalent of 88 pages of advertising during the year, at an average cost of $20,000 per page ($1,760,000 ÷ 88).

- Warehousing and shipping expenses are allocated on the basis of the number of orders shipped. Since 10,550 orders were shipped during the year at a total activity cost of $4,220,000, the cost per order is $400.

- Order-processing and billing expenses are allocated according to the number of invoice lines typed during the year. Since there were 126,667 lines, the cost per line is $3.

- The marketing administration cost — a totally indirect expense — is divided equally among the four districts, with each district being allocated $256,000.

Table 24-5   PROFIT AND LOSS STATEMENTS FOR SALES DISTRICTS ($000), GREAT WESTERN, 1983

	Total	District A	District B	District C	District D
Net sales	$36,000	$12,500	$9,600	$7,700	$6,200
Cost of goods sold	23,400	8,125	6,240	5,005	4,030
Gross margin	12,600	4,375	3,360	2,695	2,170
Operating expenses:					
Personal selling	2,316	650	606	540	520
Advertising	1,760	540	380	440	400
Warehousing and shipping	4,220	1,320	1,140	920	840
Order processing, billing	380	138	99	80	63
Marketing administration	1,024	256	256	256	256
Total expenses	9,700	2,904	2,481	2,236	2,079
Net profit in (dollars)	$ 2,900	$ 1,471	$ 879	$ 459	$ 91
(as percentage of sales)	8.1%	11.8%	9.2%	6.0%	1.5%

The final step is to calculate the amount of each activity cost to be allocated to each district. The results are shown in the bottom part of Table 24-4. We see that $650,000 of personal-selling expenses were charged directly to district A, $606,000 to district B, and similarly to districts C and D. Regarding advertising, the equivalent of 27 pages of advertising were run in district A, so that district is charged with $520,000 (27 pages × $20,000 per page). Similar calculations provide advertising activity cost allocations of $380,000 to district B, $440,000 to C, and $400,000 to D.

Regarding warehousing and shipping expenses, 3,300 orders were shipped to customers in district A, at a unit allocation cost of $400 per order, for a total allocated cost of $1,320,000. Warehousing and shipping charges are allocated to the other three districts as shown in Table 24-4.

To allocate order-processing and billing expenses, management determined that 46,000 invoice lines went to customers in district A. At $3 per line (the cost per allocation unit), district A is charged with $138,000. Allocations to the other districts are shown in Table 24-4. Finally, each district is charged with $256,000 for marketing administration expenses.

After the activity costs have been allocated among the four districts, we can prepare a profit and loss statement for each district. These statements are shown in Table 24-5. The sales volume for each district is determined from the sales volume analysis (Table 24-2). The cost of goods sold and gross margin for each district is obtained by assuming that the company gross margin of 35 percent ($12,600,000 ÷ $36,000,000) was maintained in each district.

Table 24-5 now shows, for each district, what the company profit and loss statement shows for the overall company operations. For example, we note that district A's net profit was 11.8 percent of sales ($1,471,000 ÷ $12,500,000 = 11.8 percent). In sharp contrast, district D did rather poorly, earning a net profit of only 1.5 percent of net sales ($91,000 ÷ $6,200,000 = 1.5 percent).

At this point in our performance evaluation, we have completed the "what happened" stage. The next stage is to determine *why* the results are as depicted in Table 24-5. As we indicated earlier, it is extremely difficult to pinpoint the answer to this question. In district D, for example, the sales force obtained only about two-thirds as many orders as in district A (2,100 versus 3,300). Was this because of poor selling ability, poor sales training, more severe competition in district D, or some other reason among a multitude of possibilities?

After a performance evaluation has determined *why* the district results came out as they did, management can move to the third stage in its evaluation process. That final stage is, *what should management do about the situation?* This stage will be discussed briefly after we have reviewed two major problem areas in marketing cost analysis.

Problems Involved in Cost Analysis

Marketing cost analysis can be expensive in time, money, and manpower. In particular, the task of allocating costs is often quite difficult.

Allocating Costs

The problem of allocating costs becomes most evident when activity cost totals must be apportioned among individual territories, products, or other marketing units.

Operating costs can be divided into direct and indirect expenses. (These are sometimes called "separable" and "common" expenses.) Direct, or separable, expenses are those incurred totally in connection with one market segment or one unit of the sales organization. Thus the salary and travel expenses of the sales representative in territory A are direct expenses for that territory. The cost of newspaper space to advertise product C is a *direct* cost of marketing that product. The task of allocating direct expenses is easy. They can be charged in their entirety to the marketing unit for which they were incurred.

Direct costs are
easy to allocate.

The allocation problem arises in connection with indirect, or common, costs. These expenses are incurred jointly for more than one marketing unit. Therefore they cannot be charged totally to one market segment.

Within the category of indirect expenses, some costs are *partially* indirect and some are *totally* indirect. Order filling and shipping, for example, are partially indirect costs. They would *decrease* if some of the territories or products were eliminated. They would *increase* if new products or territories were added. On the other hand, marketing administrative expenses are totally indirect. The cost of the chief marketing executive's staff and office would remain about the same, whether or not the number of territories or product lines was changed.

Any method selected for allocating indirect expenses has obvious weaknesses that can distort the results and mislead management. Two commonly used allocation methods are to divide these costs (1) equally among the marketing units being studied (territories, for instance) or (2) in proportion to the sales volume in each marketing unit.[7] But each method gives a different result for the total costs for each marketing unit.

Indirect costs are
more difficult.

Full-Cost versus Contribution-Margin Controversy

In a marketing cost analysis, two ways of allocating indirect expenses are (1) the contribution-margin (also called contribution-to-overhead) method and (2) the full-cost method. A real controversy exists regarding which of these two approaches is better for managerial control purposes.

In the **contribution-margin approach**, only the direct expenses are allocated to each marketing unit being analysed. These are the costs that presumably would be eliminated if that marketing unit were eliminated. When these direct expenses are deducted from the gross margin of the marketing unit, the remainder is the amount which that unit is contributing to cover total indirect expenses (or overhead).

---

[7]For some recommended bases for allocating functional cost groups to sales territories and to product lines, see Charles H. Sevin, *Marketing Productivity Analysis*, McGraw-Hill Book Co., New York, 1965, pp. 13–15.

In the **full-cost approach**, all expenses — direct and indirect — are allocated among the marketing units under study. By allocating *all* costs, management can determine the net profit of each territory, product, or other marketing unit.

For any given marketing unit, these two methods can be summarized as follows:

Contribution-Margin	Full-Cost
Sales $	Sales $
less	*less*
Cost of goods sold	Cost of goods sold
equals	*equals*
Gross margin	Gross margin
less	*less*
Direct expenses	Direct expenses
equals	*less*
Contribution-margin (the amount available to cover overhead expenses plus a profit)	Indirect expenses
	equals
	Net profit

Proponents of the full-cost approach contend that the purpose of a marketing cost study is to determine the net profitability of the units being studied. They feel that the contribution-margin approach does not fulfil this purpose. The advocates of the full-cost approach point out that management may be deluding itself with the contribution-margin approach. A given territory or product may be showing a contribution to overhead. Yet, after the indirect costs are allocated, this product or territory may actually have a net loss. In effect, say the full-cost people, the contribution-margin approach is the iceberg principle in action. That is, the visible tip of the iceberg (the contribution margin) looks good, while the submerged part may be hiding a net loss.

Contribution-margin supporters contend that it is not possible to accurately apportion indirect costs among product or market segments. Furthermore, items such as adminstrative costs are not at all related to any one territory or product. Therefore the marketing units should not bear any of these costs. These advocates also point out that a full-cost analysis may show that a product or territory has a net loss, whereas this unit may be contributing something to overhead. Some executives might recommend that the losing product or territory be eliminated. But they are overlooking the fact that the unit's contribution to overhead would then have to be borne by other units. Under the contribution-margin approach, there would be no question about keeping this unit as long as no better alternative could be discovered.

So far in our discussion of marketing cost analysis, we have been dealing generally with the first stage in the evaluation process. That is, we have been finding out *what happened*. To conclude this section, let's look at some examples of how management might use the results from a combined sales volume analysis and a marketing cost analysis.

Use of Findings from Combined Volume and Cost Analyses

Territorial Decisions

Once management knows the net profit (or contribution to overhead) of the territories in relation to their potential, there are several possibilities for managerial action. The executives may decide to adjust (expand or contract) territories to bring them into line with current sales potential. Or territorial problems may stem from weakneses in the distribution system, and changes in channels of distribution may be needed. Some firms that have been using manufacturers' agents may find it advisable to establish their own sales forces in growing markets. Intensive competition may be the cause of unprofitable volume in some districts, and changes in the promotional program may be advisable.

Of course, a losing territory might be abandoned completely. An abandoned region may have been contributing something to overhead, however, even though a net loss was shown. Management must recognize that this contribution must now be carried by the remaining territories.

Product Decisions

When the relative profitability of each product or group of products is known, a product line may be simplified by eliminating slow-moving, unprofitable models, sizes, or colours. The salespeople's compensation plan may be altered to encourage the sale of high-margin items. Channels of distribution may be altered. Instead of selling all its products directly to industrial users, for example, a machine-tools manufacturer shifted to industrial distributors for standard products of low unit value, and thereby improved the profitability of these products.

In the final analysis, management may decide to discontinue a product. Before this is done, however, consideration must be given to the effect this will have on other items in the line. Often a low-volume or unprofitable product must be carried simply to round out the line. Customers expect a seller to carry the article. If it is not available, the seller may lose sales of other products.

Decisions on Customer Classes and Order Sizes

By combining a volume analysis with a cost study, executives can determine the relative profitability of each group of customers. If one group shows a substandard net profit, changes in the pricing structure for these accounts may be required. Or, perhaps accounts that have been sold directly should be turned over to middlemen.

A common problem plaguing many firms today is that of the **small order**. Many orders are below the break-even point. The revenue from each of these orders is actually less than the allocated expenses. This is true because several costs, such as billing or direct selling, are the same whether the order amounts to $10 or $10,000. Management's immediate reaction may be that no order below the break-even point should be accepted. Or small-volume accounts should be dropped from the customer list. Actually, such decisions may be harmful. Management should first determine *why* certain accounts are small-order problems and then adopt procedures to correct the situation. Proper handling can very often turn a losing account into a satisfactory one. A small-order handling charge, which customers would willingly pay, might change the profit situation entirely.

SUMMARY

Planning may be defined as drawing from the past to decide in the present what to do in the future. Strategic planning is a major key to a company's success. With regard to the time periods covered, planning may be classed as long-range or short-term. With regard to the organizational level on which it is conducted, we find company-wide planning, strategic business unit planning, strategic marketing planning, and within the last, the annual marketing planning.

Strategic *company* planning is the process of matching an organization's resources with its marketing opportunities over the long run. The organization-wide strategic planning process consists of (1) defining the organization's mission, (2) setting organizational objectives, (3) conducting an organizational portfolio analysis, and (4) designing organizational strategies to achieve the objectives.

Strategic *marketing* planning parallels the strategic planning conducted in finance and production—the other major functional areas in a company. The strategic marketing planning process consists of (1) conducting a situation analysis, (2) setting marketing objectives, (3) selecting target markets, and (4) designing a strategic marketing mix. The annual marketing plan is one part of the ongoing strategic marketing planning process. It is a master plan that covers a year's marketing operations.

The cornerstone of successful marketing planning is the measurement and forecasting of market demand. Management should measure the industry's market potential, and then determine the company's sales potential (market share). The sales forecast is the key controlling factor in all *operational* planning in a firm. There are several major methods for forecasting either the industry market potential or the company's sales potential.

A marketing audit is extremely important in a total marketing evaluation program. Most companies are victims of at least some misdirected marketing effort. That is, the 80-20 situation and the iceberg principle are at work in most firms. This is so because marketing efforts (costs) are expanded in relation to the *number of* marketing units rather than to their profit potential. Fundamentally, companies do not know how much they should be spending for marketing activities, or what results they should get from these expenditures.

Two useful tools for controlling these misdirected marketing efforts are a sales volume analysis and a marketing cost analysis. Given appropriately detailed analyses, management can study its sales volume and marketing costs by product lines and by market segments (sales territories, customer groups). One major problem in marketing cost analysis is that of allocating costs — especially indirect costs — to the various marketing units. But the findings from these analyses are extremely helpful in shaping decisions regarding several aspects of a company's marketing program.

QUESTIONS AND PROBLEMS

1. Why is strategic planning so important to a business or a nonbusiness organization?

2. Prepare a statement of organizational mission for each of the following organizations:
   a. Your school
   b. McDonald's (fast-food service)
   c. Ford Motor Company (car and truck division)
   d. Clairol, Inc. (hair-care products)

3. Explain the difference between organizational objectives and marketing objectives in strategic planning. Give some examples of each.

4. Explain the concept of "business portfolio analysis" in strategic planning.

5. Give some examples, other than those in this chapter, of each of the following product-market growth strategies:
   a. Market penetration
   b. Market development
   c. Product development
   d. Diversification

6. Carefully distinguish between market potential and a sales forecast, using examples of consumer or industrial products.

7. What are some logical market factors that you might use in estimating the market potential for each of the following products?
    a. Central home air conditioners   d. Sterling flatware
    b. Milking machines   e. Safety goggles
    c. Golf clubs

8. How would you determine the market potential for a textbook written for the beginning course in marketing?

9. What are some of the problems a researcher faces when using the test-market method for determining market potential or sales potential?

10. A sales volume analysis by territories indicates that the sales of a manufacturer of roofing materials have increased 12 percent a year for the past three years in the territory comprising the four western provinces. Does this indicate conclusively that the company's sales volume performance is satisfactory in that region?

11. A manufacturer found that one product accounted for 34 to 45 percent of the company's total sales in all but two of the eighteen territories. In each of those two territories, this product accounted for only 15 percent of the company's volume. What factors might account for the relatively low sales of this article in the two districts?

12. Explain how the results of a territorial sales volume analysis may influence a firm's promotional program.

13. What effects may a sales volume analysis by products have on training, supervising, and compensating the sales force?

14. "Firms should discontinue selling losing products." Discuss.

15. Should a company discontinue selling to an unprofitable customer? Why or why not? If not, then what steps might the company take to make the account a profitable one?

Marketing: Societal Appraisal and Prospect

CHAPTER GOALS

We have looked at marketing within the individual firm *and within our economic system. Now, in this final chapter, we shall look more closely at the place of marketing within our social system. After studying this chapter, you should understand:*

1. *The major criticisms of marketing and the phenomenon of consumerism*
2. *Some basic yardsticks for evaluating these criticisms and our marketing system in general*
3. *Government and business responses to consumer discontent*
4. *The emerging societal orientation in marketing and the social responsibilities of marketing management*
5. *Some forces that will shape marketing in the next 10 years*
6. *The broadened, socially responsive marketing concept*

In the first two chapters of this book, we touched on the broader, societal dimension of marketing and examined briefly the role of marketing in the total economy. For the most part, however, we have approached marketing from the viewpoint of the firm, as we discussed the problems facing an individual producer or middleman in managing its marketing activities. Now in this final chapter, we will once again look at marketing from a broader, societal perspective.

First we shall appraise our marketing system by examining (1) the criticisms of the system, (2) the phenomenon of consumerism, and (3) the responses of consumer groups, the government, and business organizations to these criticisms. Then we shall consider some of the societal aspects of marketing management. Finally, we shall look briefly at the future in Canadian marketing.

BASIS FOR EVALUATING OUR MARKETING SYSTEM

The present-day economic system of Canada is a reasonably free market system, but an *imperfect* one. Price is the prime determinant of resource allocation. We call our system imperfect because it is not composed of the

MARKETING:

Does it satisfy consumers' wants — as consumers themselves define or express those wants?

elements basic to the theoretical model of perfect competition. Those elements are great numbers of well-informed buyers and sellers, always acting rationally. Each is so small that one individual's activities have no appreciable influence on total supply, demand, or price. Another imperfection is the structural rigidity of our system. Also, in the interest of the general welfare, the various levels of government often act so as to decrease the free play of market forces.

We shall appraise the Canadian marketing system, using this imperfect economic system as our frame of reference. Before we engage in this evaluation, however, we need to agree on what is the *objective* of the system. Throughout this book we have stressed the philosophy of the marketing concept. The goal of the marketing concept is to develop a customer orientation on the part of management. In line with this philosophy, it seems reasonable to establish as our objective the satisfaction of consumers' wants as they are expressed by the consumers themselves. Then marketing should be appraised on the basis of how well it achieves this goal, that is, how effectively it satisfies consumers' wants. We grant that this is not everyone's idea of the ultimate goal. Some feel that consumers do not know what is good for them — that some group (usually the government) should take over the responsibility for setting standards. Others believe that the social and economic goals should be to ensure energy self-sufficiency, to promote the growth of its underdeveloped regions, or to clean up the environment.

Regardless of how worthy these or other goals may be, our basis for evaluating our marketing system will be: Does it satisfy consumers' wants — as consumers themselves define or express those wants?

CRITICISMS OF MARKETING

For many years, critics of our marketing system have raised a variety of thought-provoking questions and have generated numerous lively discussions. Let us examine their criticisms, try to determine the true nature of these charges, and consider one key question: Does marketing cost too much?

What Are the Criticisms?

We can summarize the major charges against marketing by grouping them in relation to the components of the marketing mix — product, price structure, distribution system, and promotional activities.

The Product

Critics allege that many products are of poor quality or are unsafe. Parts fall off cars, zippers jam, food products are adulterated, trains run late, wash-and-wear clothing really needs ironing, appliances do not perform

Most criticism of marketing concerns personal selling and consumer advertising—probably because these are the most visible aspects of marketing.

as advertised, etc., etc. Also, these products are backed up by confusing and worthless warranties, and repair service is inadequate. Packaging is deceptive, and labels do not carry sufficient information concerning product contents, operating instructions, or care of the product.

Furthermore, heavily promoted product improvements are often trivial. Planned style obsolescence encourages consumers to get rid of products before they are physically worn out. Moreover, too many different types of goods, and too many different brands of each type, are produced. As a result, the buyer is confused and unable to make accurate buying decisions, and much production capacity is wasted in unnecessary duplication.

Price Structure

We hear that prices are too high, or too inflexible, or that they are controlled by the large firms in an industry. Some people feel that price competition has been largely replaced by nonprice competition.

Distribution System

Probably the main objection to the distribution system is that it is unnecessarily complex and includes too many middlemen. This is a two-part charge; there are too many different types of middlemen, and too many of each type.

Promotional Activities

The strongest and most bitter indictments against marketing are in the area of promotional activities — especially personal selling and advertising. Most of the complaints about personal selling are aimed at the retail level. We find that both consumers and businesspeople often are disenchanted with the poor quality of retail selling. Objections are also voiced against the poor services offered by many retailers.

The general criticisms of advertising may be divided into two groups — social and economic. From a *social* point of view, advertising is charged with overemphasizing our material standard of living and underemphasizing our cultural and moral values. Advertising also is charged with manipulating people — making them want to buy things they should not have, cannot afford, and do not need.

A major social criticism of advertising today, and one that has some justification, is that advertising is often false, deceptive, or in bad taste. Exaggerations, overuse of sex and fear appeals, inane claims, excessive numbers of commercials on radio and television, and poor choice of the placement of commercials are examples of this criticism. As with most criticisms in marketing, this one applies to a small segment of advertising. The main offenders are advertisers of a limited number of consumer goods, and the advertising medium causing most of the furor is television. The charge of misleading and offensive advertising is rarely made against advertisers of industrial products or companies that advertise consumer products in trade journals. Most retail display advertising is not subject to this charge, nor is most classified advertising in newspapers and magazines.

Advertising is charged with causing a misallocation of our resources. John Kenneth Galbraith and others have asserted that advertising has contributed significantly to an imbalance of expenditures between the private and the public sectors of our economy. For instance, these people believe that business promotes frills on automobiles when it should be concerned with urban renewal, improving our schools, and eliminating pollution. Furthermore, these critics believe that more of our national output should be diverted from the private to the public sector.

The *economic* criticisms of advertising have taken an interesting turn in recent years.[1] We still hear that advertising costs too much — that it increases the cost of marketing and therefore raises the prices of products. In the past, much criticism was devoted to the competitive nature of advertising and the economic wastefulness of imaginary brand differences. Recently, however, the economic charge drawing the most interest is somewhat the opposite — namely, that advertising leads to restraint of competition, economic concentration, and monopoly.[2]

The line of reasoning behind the economic-concentration complaint goes something like this. (1) The big companies can afford to spend much on advertising to differentiate their products, and thus they are able to acquire a large share of the market; (2) in this way, advertising creates a barrier to market entry by new or smaller firms; (3) a high level of market concentration then results; (4) the firms enjoying this protected position can charge high prices, which in turn lead to high profits.

---

[1]The topic of the economic effects of advertising in Canada is dealt with in O. J. Firestone, *The Economic Implications of Advertising*, Methuen Publications, Toronto, 1967.

[2]For a review of the criticisms of advertising, see Jacques C. Bourgeois and James G. Barnes, "Does Advertising Increase Alcohol Consumption?" *Journal of Advertising Research*, August 1979, pp. 19–29; and James G. Barnes and Chris R. Vaughan, "Taxation of Advertising: The Newfoundland Experience," in *Market Place Canada: Some Controversial Dimensions*, Stanley J. Shapiro and Louise Heslop (eds.), McGraw-Hill Ryerson Limited, Toronto, 1981.

The refutation of the economic-concentration charges was carefully spelled out by Prof. Jules Backman in a study he conducted under the sponsorship of the Association of National Advertisers.[3] He concluded that there is no relationship between advertising intensity and high economic concentration. Nor does there seem to be any link between advertising intensity and (1) price increases or (2) high profit rates. Advertising is highly competitive, not anticompetitive.

In evaluating the charges against marketing, we should be careful to recognize the differences in the nature of the various points. We should understand what fundamentally is being criticized. In a company, is it the marketing department or some other department that is the cause of the complaints? In the economy, is it the marketing system or the general economic system that is being criticized? It is also helpful to know when the critics (1) are misinformed, (2) are unaware of the services performed by the marketing system, or (3) are trying to impose their own value judgements on consumers. That is, the critics may not agree that the goal of the marketing system should be consumer want-satisfaction, as the consumers *themselves* define and express their wants.

In some cases, the criticisms of marketing are fully warranted. They point out weaknesses and inefficiencies in the system and call for improvement. By most people's standards, there are instances of deceptive packaging and of misleading and objectionable advertising. There are weaknesses in marketing, just as there are in any system developed and operated by human beings.

The real key to the evaluation of our marketing system lies in the answers to two fundamental questions. First, is the present system of marketing achieving its goal (that is, satisfying consumers' wants as the consumers themselves express these wants) better than any other known alternative could? The answer is an unqualified yes. Second, is constant effort being devoted to improving the system and increasing its efficiency? Generally speaking, the answer to this question is also a strong yes.

Progress sometimes may seem slow. Companies that operate in a socially undesirable manner even over a short period of time are harmful. Price fixing and objectionable advertising are intolerable and inexcusable. Instances of this nature, though widely publicized, are few relative to the totality of marketing effort. In essence, we are saying that weaknesses exist in marketing and that a continuing effort must be devoted to their elimination. However, at the same time, we should not overlook the improvements in marketing and consumer want-satisfaction over the years. The way to correct existing weaknesses is not to destroy or heavily regulate the existing system.

Many of the censures of marketing can be summarized in the general criticism that marketing costs too much. However, the question of whether marketing costs too much should be analysed and answered from two

Understanding the True Nature of Criticisms

Does Marketing Cost Too Much?

---

[3]Jules Backman, *Advertising and Competition*, New York University Press, New York, 1967.

points of view. The first is within the *macro* context of our total socio-economic system, and the second is within the *micro* context of an individual organization.

In Our Socioeconomic System

It is estimated that the total cost of marketing for all products is about 50 percent of the final price paid by ultimate consumers. Admittedly, marketing costs are a substantial proportion of the total sales value of all products. However, the question of whether marketing costs too much is somewhat academic, because we do not have sufficient information to make comparisons. Even if we had accurate data on marketing costs, we would still have no objective criteria for determining whether these expenses are too high or not high enough. As we noted in Chapter 24, we have not yet developed adequate tools for measuring the return (output) that is derived from a given marketing expenditure (input). To say that marketing costs are too high implies that one or more of the following situations prevail: (1) marketing institutions are enjoying abnormally high profits; (2) more services are being provided than consumers and business people demand; (3) marketing activities are performed in a grossly inefficient manner; (4) consumption is declining; and (5) total costs (production plus marketing) are increasing. Actually, there is no reasonable evidence that any of these conditions exists.

Total marketing costs have indeed risen substantially over the past one hundred years. At the same time, careful studies indicate that these costs have been levelling off for the past three or four decades. Still, it is important that we understand the reasons for this increase in marketing expenses.

Certainly it would be a mistake simply to jump to the conclusion that the cost increase indicates growing inefficiencies in marketing.

Actually, the rise in marketing expense is traceable to several factors, some of which are external environmental influences. As an example, one reason for the increase in the number of people employed in marketing relative to production is simply that the workweek in marketing has been shortened relative to that in production. In the latter part of the nineteenth century, people employed in wholesaling and retailing worked about 66 hours a week. Those employed in production worked about 52. Today, both groups work less than 40. This shift toward equality has meant that relatively more employees were added in marketing.

Another factor is that consumers are demanding more services and more marketing refinements today than in the past. Consumers today demand credit, delivery, free parking, attractive stores, merchandise return privileges, and other services. A related point is the rise in consumer demand for products emphasizing style. And consumers want merchandise assortments covering considerable breadth and depth. Certainly we could cut marketing costs substantially if consumers would buy on a cash-and-carry basis in stores displaying small quantities of standardized merchandise in boxes.

It is a mistake to study the trend in marketing costs alone. A total-cost approach should be adopted. In many instances, a firm can reduce its *total* costs by increasing its *marketing* costs. To illustrate, an increase in advertising expenditures may so expand a firm's market that the unit *production* cost can be reduced more than the *marketing* costs have increased. Thus, the net effect is to reduce total expenses. In another situation, production economies can result when a company locates near sources of raw materials or low-cost power. Yet *marketing* costs (transportation) may be increased in the new location.

It is understandable that productivity in marketing may never match the level attained in manufacturing or agriculture. Marketing offers far fewer opportunities for mechanization. It is one thing to control the input and output of machines. But it is quite another problem when the activity largely involves dealing with people. Until a better system for satisfying consumer wants is proposed, however, we shall continue with the existing system. Its benefits in both the private and public sectors of our economy are considerable by almost any measure used. Business must continue to improve the efficiency of marketing and to seek accurate measures of its cost. Most important of all, business must explain to the Canadian public the essential role marketing plays in our economy.

In an Individual Organization

Unquestionably, in some individual firms, marketing *does* cost too much. In firms that market inefficiently or that are production-oriented in their management and operations, marketing probably costs too much. The high rate of mortality among retail businesses attests, in part, to their inefficiencies in marketing. A high rate of new-product failure raises the cost of marketing in a firm.

Marketing costs undoubtedly are too high—that is, marketing efficiency is too low — in firms that:

1. Do not carry a product mix that customers want;
2. Use obsolete distribution channels;
3. Are totally cost-oriented (ignore demand) in their pricing;
4. Cannot manage a sales force effectively;
5. Waste money with ineffective advertising.

Fortunately, in many firms, marketing does *not* cost too much. These firms have strategically planned and implemented the customer-oriented type of marketing program that has been discussed and advocated throughout this book.

CONSUMERISM: A CRITICISM OF OUR MARKETING SYSTEM

"Consumerism" became a significant social movement in the 1960s, and it shows every indication of continuing in the years ahead. In this section we discuss what consumerism is and why it came to be. Then, in the following section, we consider the responses of government and business to this phenomenon.

Meaning and Scope of Consumerism

We may define consumerism as both (1) a consumer protest against the perceived injustices in exchange relationships and (2) efforts to remedy those injustices. Consumers clearly feel, in exchange relationships between buyers and sellers, that the balance of power lies with the sellers. Consumerism is an expression of this opinion, and an attempt to achieve a more equal balance of power between buyers and sellers. It is, in effect, an extremely important and far-reaching *criticism* of marketing.

Scope of Consumerism

Consumerism today includes three broad areas of consumer dissatisfaction and remedial efforts. The original, and still the major, focus of consumerism involves discontent with direct buyer-seller exchange relationships between consumers and business firms.

The second area of discontent extends beyond business. Consumerism extends to *all* organizations with which there is an exchange relationship. Therefore, consumerism involves such diverse organizations as hospitals, schools, and government agencies (police departments, tax assessors, street maintenace departments, etc.).

The third area of consumerism involves the *indirect* impact that an exchange relationship between two social units (a person, a business, etc.) has on a third social unit. Consumer Jones may buy newsprint from mill A. But in producing the newsprint for that exchange, the mill pollutes the river used by consumer Smith for fishing and swimming. Smith becomes upset and protests. In other words, an exchange between two people or groups has created a problem for a third person or group.

Consumerism Yesterday and Today

Consumerism really is not a new phenomenon. In the early 1900s and again in the 1930s, there was a "consumer movement." Efforts were made to protect the consumer from harmful products and from false and misleading advertising.

The movement that began in the 1960s, however, is different in three ways from earlier consumer movements. First, consumerism is now occurring in a setting of higher incomes and largely filled subsistence needs, in contrast to the harsher economic conditions that surrounded earlier movements. Second, the consumer-movement legislation since the 1960s has been intended first and foremost to protect the consumer's interests. Emphasis in earlier legislation was placed on the protection of competition and competitors.

Third, today's consumerism is much more likely to endure because it has generated an institutional structure to support it. Government agencies have been established to administer the consumer-oriented laws and to protect consumer interests. The social sensitivity of many businesses has increased, and various consumer- and environment-oriented organizations have developed.

Why did consumerism take hold in the 1960s, when the factors of social and economic discontent (pollution, unsafe products, criticisms of advertising, and others) had been with us for some time? It just so happened that a series of issues converged in the mid-1960s to touch off the "social conflagration" that we call consumerism.

Conditions Leading to Consumerism

Broad Cultural Changes

Two broad cultural changes occurred to provide the setting for consumerism. The first was a dramatic shift in the social and economic goals of Canadian consumers as we entered a more advanced stage of cultural and economic developent. In the decades preceding the 1960s, our emphasis was on improving our material standard of living. Today, with our materialistic needs more or less satisfied, we have become more sensitive to social and environmental needs. The second cultural change underlying consumerism was the active role of young people. Compared with previous generations of young adults, today's young people are better educated, more articulate, and more inclined (less afraid) to speak out and take action.

Consumer Discontents and Frustrations

This changing cultural setting converged with a series of highly flammable issues that generated much consumer discontent and frustration. There were economic discontent (inflation), social discontent (unemployment, language issues), and ecological discontent (pollution, diminishing quality of life).

In the business area, discontent was focused on the marketing system as people perceived that their consumer rights were being violated. Consumers were frustrated and indignant because of unfulfilled promises and expectations. Nobody seemed willing to listen to the consumers' complaints or to do anything about them. "We can't get past the computer to deal with real people."

Consumerism in the 1980s

Many people thought that consumerism would decline, and even disappear, once the initial interest and support burned out. On the contrary, however, consumerism has continued through the 1980s, although more slowly and certainly in a different form than in the 1960s and 1970s. Today, there are fewer people marching in the streets, and more people working within the existing political, legal, and social systems in order to bring about change.

One reason why consumerism will not disappear is that many consumer demands of earlier years are now set in legislation. Also, in spite of the remedial progress of the past twenty years, the major areas of consumer discontent today are substantially the same as they were then.[4]

In their research on consumerism, Paul Bloom and Stephen Greyser concluded that consumerism is in the maturity stage of its product life cycle — but, again, showing no signs of decline. Originally, the consumerism "industry" consisted of a few organizations interested primarily in generating regulatory legislation. This industry has evolved into "an enormous web of organizations and institutions, each trying to serve the interests of consumers with its own distinctive set of offerings or brands."[5]

SOME RESPONSES TO THESE CRITICISMS

Significant action-oriented efforts to remedy the conditions leading to consumerism have come from the consumers themselves, from government activities, and from business organizations.

---

[4] See Hiram C. Barksdale and William D. Perreault, Jr., "Can Consumers Be Satisfied?" *MSU Business Topics*, Spring 1980, pp. 19–30; Shelby D. Hunt and John R. Nevin, "Why Consumers Believe They Are Being Ripped Off," *Business Horizons*, May–June 1981, pp. 48–52; "Why Consumers Gripe Louder than Ever," *U.S. News & World Report*, October 5, 1981, pp. 56–57; and James G. Barnes and Lessey Sooklal, "The Changing Nature of Consumer Behavior: Monitoring the Impact of Inflation and Recession," *Business Quarterly*, Summer 1983, pp. 58–64.

[5] Paul N. Bloom and Stephen A. Greyser, *Exploring the Future of Consumerism*, Marketing Science Institute, Cambridge, Mass., report no. 81-102, 1981, p. 7. For the essence of this report, see the authors' article, "The Maturing of Consumerism," *Harvard Business Review*, November–December 1981, pp. 130–139.

For an excellent group of papers dealing with current issues in consumerism and future prospects for the consumer movement, its organizations, and the social environment of marketing, see Paul N. Bloom (ed.), *Consumerism and Beyond: Research Perspectives on the Future Social Environment*, Marketing Science Institute, Cambridge, Mass., report no. 82-102, 1982.

For a discussion of the extent to which consumers are knowledgeable concerning their rights, see John Liefeld, Louis Heslop, and Ann Hammond, "Consumer Knowledge of Their Marketplace Rights," *Proceedings* of the Marketing Division, Administrative Sciences Association of Canada, vol. 3, part 3, 1982, pp. 117–126.

Consumers have reacted in a wide variety of ways to vent their frustrations and to correct what they consider to be injustices. In Canada, consumers have not tended to demonstrate particularly violent responses to marketing programs with which they do not agree. For the most part, consumers are now more willing than ever before to complain at the retail level and to take their complaints to manufacturers and senior officials of companies. In extreme circumstances, there have been occasional boycotts against the products of certain companies and against particular retailers. Consumers as a group have become more politically active since the late 1960s, and organized consumer groups now maintain full-time lobbyists in Ottawa and bring considerable influence to bear on politicians when legislation of interest to consumers is introduced.

Consumers are becoming increasingly, and better, organized in their social and economic protests. In Canada, the major consumer organization is the Consumers' Association of Canada. This association had its origins in 1947, and its membership today numbers more than 100,000. The major objectives of the CAC involve representing the consumer viewpoint to governments. In recent years many other organizations such as church groups, labour unions, and student groups have become involved in consumer issues, whereas in previous years their efforts were in quite different directions.

While consumers have shown themselves to be much more interested today in becoming involved in consumer issues, it is not clear that all consumers have become so interested. Research has shown that consumers who join consumer organizations and who become involved in consumer issues tend to be nonrepresentative of consumers in general. For the most part the consumer activists come from a higher social stratum, tend to be better educated, have higher incomes, and tend to be more cosmopolitan in their outlook on life.[6] Such results suggest that a large mass of consummers have been considerably slower in adopting a consumerist viewpoint. There can be no denying, however, that consumers in general are far more active than they have ever been before, and the results of this activism are quite obvious in the amount of legislation that has been passed in recent years and in the growing strength of consumer organizations in this country.

Consumerism is not likely to fade away; instead, it probably will grow stronger in the coming years. The main reason for this forecast is that today it is politically popular to support consumers. Politicians may generally have been unresponsive to consumer needs in the years prior to the mid-1960s. Since then, however, consumer-oriented activity at both the federal and provincial levels has been carried on at an unprecedented rate. All the provinces and many cities have created some kind of office for consumer affairs.

Responses of Consumers and Consumer Organizations

Government Responses

---

[6]Jacques C. Bourgeois and James G. Barnes, "Viability and Profile of the Consumerist Segment," *Journal of Consumer Research*, March 1979. For a comprehensive study of the consumer movement in the United States, see *Consumerism at the Crossroads*, Sentry Insurance Company, in collaboration with the Marketing Science Insitute, Cambridge, Mass., 1977.

Legislation

Since the mid-1960s, federal and provincial legislatures have been passing for the first time laws whose primary purpose is to aid the consumer. In contrast, very often in the past marketing legislation was generally business-oriented, not consumer-oriented. As we have pointed out earlier, often the intent of such legislation was to protect competition or to benefit some segment of business, and any benefit or protection to the consumer occurred in an indirect manner, if it occurred at all. In contrast, recent years have seen the introduction of a large number of pieces of consumer-oriented legislation at both the federal and provincial levels in Canada.

A significant number of these laws are designed to protect the consumer's "right to safety" — especially in situations where the consumer cannot judge for himself the risk involved in the purchase and use of particular products. In Canada, we have such legislation as the Food and Drugs Act, which regulates and controls the manufacture, distribution, and sale of food, drug, and cosmetic products. A very important piece of legislation, which also protects the consumer's right to safety, is the Hazardous Products Act. This law establishes standards for the manufacture of consumer products designed for household, garden, personal, receational, or child use. Regulations under the Hazardous Products Act require that dangerous products be packaged as safely as possible and labelled with clear and adequate warnings. This law also makes provision for the removal of dangerous products from the marketplace.

One controversial area of product safety legislation is the paternalistic type of law that is intended to protect the consumer, whether or not he or she wants that protection. Thus, it is now mandatory to equip automobiles with seat belts, and in most provinces it is illegal to operate an automobile unless the seats belts are fastened. In effect, somebody else is forcing a consumer to accept what the other person feels is in the consumer's best interests — truly a new and broadening approach to consumer legislation.

Another series of laws and government programs supports the consumer's "right to be informed." These measures help in such areas as reducing confusion and deception in packaging and labelling, identifying the ingredients and nutritional content in food products, advising consumers of the length of life of certain packaged food products, providing instructions and assistance in the care of various textile products, and determining the true rate of interest.

At the federal level, government has passed a number of pieces of legislation designed to provide consumers with more information. Possibly the most important of these is the Consumer Packaging and Labelling Act, which regulates the packaging, labelling, sale, and advertising of prepackaged products. The Textile Labelling Act requires manufacturers of textile products to place labels on most articles made from fabrics. These labels must name the fibres, show the amount of each fibre in the product by percentage, and identify the dealer for whom or by whom the article was made. In addition, federal government programs assist the consumer in providing information on the care of textile products. For example, most textile products sold in Canada today carry care labels, which provide instructions on the washing and ironing of textile products. Similarly, the Canada Standard Sizes program for children's clothing ensures that all children's clothing manufactured in Canada by participating manufacturers is sized in a standard manner so that consumers can feel confident that sizes are standard across manufacturers.

At the provincial level, a number of programs exist that provide information to consumers. For example, all provinces have passed consumer protection legislation, which requires that all consumer lending agencies and retail stores provide consumers with information concerning the true rate of interest that they are paying on borrowed money and on purchases made on credit.

Also at the provincial level there has been considerable interest in recent years in the passage of new consumer-oriented legislation. At the present time all provinces, for example, have on their books a number of laws that offer protection to the consumer. Each province has passed a general Consumer Protection Act, which deals primarily with the granting of credit. All provinces also have legislation that provides for a "cooling off" period during which the purchaser of goods or services in a door-to-door sale may cancel the contract, return any merchandise, and obtain a full refund. In addition, most provinces have legislation that provides for the disposal of unsolicited goods and credit cards received through the mail. All provinces also administer legislation that regulates particular industries such as collection agencies, automobile dealerships, and insurance agents.

The consumer is also protected at both the federal and provincial levels in Canada in the area of misleading and dishonest advertising. The federal Combines Investigation Act contains a number of provisions dealing with misleading advertising; these have been discussed in Chapter 24. Protection is also offered by certain special interest consumer groups in a number of areas. For example, the Province of Quebec, through its Consumer Protection Act, prohibits advertising that is directed to persons under 13 years of age, except under certain limited circumstances.

A development of the late 1970s in many provinces has been the passage of a new form of legislation designed to protect the consumer against certain unfair business practices that had not been covered under legislation existing at that time. This relatively new form of consumer legislation is generally described as "trade practices legislation" since it is intended to prohibit certain unfair, deceptive, or unconscionable trade practices.[7] Trade-practices or business-practices acts are now on the books in Alberta, British Columbia, Manitoba, Newfoundland, Ontario, and Prince Edward Island. The passage of such legislation provides additional protection for Canadian consumers, in that these laws are designed to protect consumers against such illegal practices as advertising that claims that goods are new if in fact

---

[7]Jacob S. Ziegel, "The New Trade Practices Legislation," *Canadian Consumer*, February 1975, pp. 18–20.

they have been reconditioned; representations on the part of service companies that service, parts, replacement, or repairs are needed if in fact this is not so; the sale of products at grossly excessive prices; practices that tend to take advantage of consumers who are unable to protect their own interests because of physical infirmity, ignorance, illiteracy, inability to understand the language of an agreement, or similar factors; and trade practices that tend to subject consumers to undue pressures to enter into the transaction.

These new trade-practices laws have broken new ground in a number of areas. For example, the Alberta legislation provided, for the first time in Canada, for class action suits that may be brought against a supplier on behalf of all wronged consumers. The Alberta law also provides that a court may order corrective advertising by a supplier who has been convicted of an unfair trade practice, and further provides that the court may issue an interim injunction that restrains the company from carrying on certain acts or practices while court action is pending.

Government Regulatory Agencies[8]

One of the most significant responses to the consumer movement on the part of government has been a strengthened and expanded role of regulatory agencies involved in consumer affairs. At the provincial level, Public Utilities Boards hold public hearings and receive briefs from concerned citizens and consumer groups whenever a telephone or hydro company is seeking a rate increase or a change in its services. It has become quite common for organized consumer associations and ratepayer groups to intervene at such hearings as representatives of the consumer interest.

Federally, two major regulatory agencies have emerged as powerful arms of government in recent years. The Canadian Transport Commission regulates all aspects of interprovincial travel and companies that operate nationally, such as Canadian National and the major airlines. Applications for route changes and fare increases must be filed with the CTC, and opportunities are presented at public hearings for consumer groups to make representations. Similarly, the Canadian Radio-Television and Telecommunications Commission (CRTC) regulates the broadcasting industry in this country. This regulatory body has become very much involved in marketing-related areas in recent years. It is responsible for awarding broadcasting licenses to AM and FM radio stations, television stations, and cable television operators. The CRTC also regulates these broadcasters in terms of the content of the programming they use and also administers numerous codes of advertising standards in its role as the agency responsible for regulating broadcast advertising.

---

[8]For an insight into the regulatory process in Canada, see Sylvia Ostry, "Government Intervention in Democratic Economies: A Comparison of Canada and the United States," in *Conference on Canadian–U.S. Economic Relations*, Institute for Research in Public Policy, Montreal, 1978, pp. 1–12; W. T. Stanbury (ed.), *Government Regulation: Scope, Growth, Process*, Institute for Research in Public Policy, Montreal, 1980; and T. Gregory Kane, *Consumers and the Regulators*, Institute for Research in Public Policy, Montreal, 1980.

Also, at the federal level, many government departments play important regulatory roles that have a major impact on the way in which marketers do business. From the point of view of a marketer of consumer products, the two most important would likely be the Department of Consumer and Corporate Affairs and Health and Welfare Canada. Various branches of these departments administer federal regulations and legislation such as the Combines Investigation Act, the Hazardous Products Act, the Consumer Packaging and Labelling Act, and the Food and Drugs Act.

Finally, in all provinces and at the federal level in Canada there exist marketing boards that, to varying degrees, control the production, distribution, and pricing of products. These marketing boards, such as the Ontario Milk Marketing Board, the British Columbia Fruit Board, and the Canadian Egg Marketing Agency, wield considerable power over the marketing of the products that fall under their responsibility. Most of these boards are involved in the distribution of agricultural products and were established to represent the interests of producers. However, through their efforts to promote marketing efficiency, marketing boards also seek to represent the best long-term interests of consumers.[9]

Effectiveness of Government Action

How effective have governmental efforts been in improving the consumer's position? The consumers' answer might start with that cigarette slogan, "You've come a long way, baby," and then would add, "but you still have a long way to go." Just as consumerism started with unrealized expectations from *business* performance, now the consumer is experiencing unrealized expectations from *government's* performance. Although the consumers' position has been greatly improved, the pace of improvement is still too slow to satisfy many consumer advocates. However, many consumers still have decidedly more confidence in government-enforced action than in voluntary business efforts.

Since the late 1970s, the cry for more government regulation and consumer protection has been subsiding. Consumers, economists, and even some politicians are questioning the value of certain health, safety, and other regulations. Soaring costs are being imposed on business, and the regulations of the many federal and provincial regulatory agencies are alleged to add to the rate of inflation. Knowledgeable people outside business are joining business leaders in asking whether the benefits are worth the costs. Often the answer appears to be "no." Consequently, for the first time in many years, pressure is being applied to governments at all levels to "de-regulate." The federal government has appointed a parliamentary task force on regulatory reform, and the Economic Council of Canada has been conducting a major study on the effects of regulation in recent years.

---

[9]Bank of Nova Scotia, "Marketing Boards in Canada," in James G. Barnes and Montrose S. Sommers (eds.), *Current Topics in Canadian Marketing*, McGraw-Hill Ryerson Limited, Toronto, 1978, pp. 216–224; and R. M. A. Loyns, "Marketing Boards: The Irrelevance and Irreverence of Economic Analysis," in Donald N. Thompson et al. (eds.), *Macromarketing: A Canadian Perspective*, American Marketing Association, Chicago, 1980, pp. 196–224.

The major conclusions of the Economic Council study, as stated in an interim report, were that governments should provide advance notice of their intent to impose new regulations; that an assessment of the anticipated costs and benefits (especially of costs to the private sector) should be carried out before new regulations are put in place; and that existing regulatory programs and agencies should be reviewed.[10]

Certainly government regulations protecting consumers' interests are not going to be eliminated. But the regulators are likely to be forced to take a more responsible, realistic, cost-benefit approach than often has been the case in the past.

Business Responses

Business apathy, resistance, or token efforts in response to consumerism simply increase the probability of more government regulation. It is as simple as this today: Consumerism is sufficiently entrenched and well organized so that consumer complaints will be answered. The only question is: Answered by whom — business or government? If business cannot or will not do the job, the only alternative is additional government intervention.

"The reaction of many businessmen who have been caught by consumerism, is like good old Charlie Brown's bafflement when his team lost its 43rd consecutive game: 'How can we lose when we're so sincere?' Good intentions don't impress anyone. The public wants good intentions translated into effective action, and they're going to get it, one way or another."

Source: Elisha Gray II, chairman of Whirlpool Corporation, as quoted in *Newsweek,* July 26, 1971, p. 44.

Yet, unfortunately, a review of the response to consumerism on the part of business indicates that this response has tended to be superficial, negative, unplanned, and uncoordinated, even among large companies. Especially in the early stages of the development of the consumer movement, businesspeople tended to view consumer activism as a passing fad, a problem that would ultimately pass from the scene. Such, of course, has not been the case. In fact, the consumer activism is likely to continue to grow in the future. Businesspeople who continue to ignore its importance or who attempt to rationalize the situation by observing that consumerism does not apply to their particular businesses will do so at their peril.[11]

---

[10]Economic Council of Canada, *Synoposis and Recommendations: Responsible Regulation,* Supply and Services Canada, Ottawa, 1979. See also Leon Courville, *Responsible Regulation Rules versus Incentives?* C. D. Howe Institute, Montreal, 1980; James S. Peterson, *Report of the Special Committee on Regulatory Reform,* Supply and Services Canada, Ottawa, 1981; and J. M. Curtis, "The Ways of Achieving Regulatory Reform," *Canadian Business Review,* Summer 1979, pp. 46–47.

[11]Mel S. Moyer, "Marketing Complaint-Handling Systems," *Proceedings* of the Marketing Division, Administrative Sciences Association of Canada, vol. 4, part 3, 1983, pp. 230–237.

Positive Responses of Individual Firms

The gloomy picture presented above is not the entire story. There is a growing executive awareness of the dangers accompanying a negative response to consumerism. Consequently, we are seeing an increasing number of positive and substantive responses to consumer problems.

Here are just a few examples of how individual firms are responding to consumerism.

- *Better communication with consumers.* Many firms have responded positively to the consumers' "right to be heard." Appliance and insurance companies have established 24-hour "cool lines." This enables customers to call free of charge from anywhere in the country to register a complaint, ask about service, or get product-usage information. Other firms have speeded up and otherwise improved their responses to consumers' written inquires or complaints.

- *More and better information for consumers.* Point-of-sale information has been improved by a number of firms. Manufacturers are publishing instructional booklets on the use and care of their products. In many instances, labelling is more informative now than it was in the past. Many supermarkets have instituted unit pricing.

- *Product improvements.* Companies have introduced many product-safety changes and pollution-reduction measures. Warranties have been simplified and strengthened. Nutritional elements have been added to some foods. In response to increased diet consciousness, food manufacturers have introduced low-salt and sugar-free products.

- *More carefully prepared advertising.* Many advertisers are extremely cautious in approving agency-prepared ads, in sharp contrast to past practices. Advertisers are involving their legal departments in the approval process. They are sensitive to the fact that the CRTC may reject a commercial or the Advertising Standards Council may find that the advertisement violates some particular code of advertising standards. The advertising industry and the media are doing a much more effective self-regulation job than ever before, especially through the Advertising Advisory Board and its Advertising Standards Councils.[12]

Organizing for Effective Response

Many firms have made organizational changes to implement their response programs. Most of these moves have been directed toward establishing an "ombudsman" position — sometimes a high-level executive and sometimes a separate department of consumer affairs. The responsibilities of this position or department typically are (1) to serve as a listening post for consumer inquiries and complaints, and to see that they are answered; (2) to

---

[12]See Mel S. Moyer and John C. Banks, "Self-Regulation in the Canadian Advertising Industry: An Analysis of the Advertising Standards Council," in Donald N. Thompson (ed.), *Problems in Canadian Marketing*, American Marketing Association, Chicago, 1977.

represent the consumers' interests when policies and programs are being formulated; and (3) to ensure that the firm maintains the necessary degree of societal orientation in its planning.

The ombudsman position or department must be an independent unit, preferably reporting directly to the chief executive. Placing the consumer affairs group in the marketing department is ordinarily a mistake. When profit or competitive crises arise, marketing executives too often do not place the consumer's interests foremost in their decision making.

Experience so far shows that consumers' reactions to consumer affairs representatives are mixed. Some programs get high ratings, and others are looked upon simply as "paper consumerism" and "corporate hypocrisy."

Trade Association Responses

Many trade associations have actively responded to consumerism by setting industry standards, stimulating consumer education, and promoting research among the association members. Of course, trade associations have not been neglecting their time-honoured activity as parliamentary lobbyists. In that role they are viewed (1) by businesspeople as seekers of moderation in government antibusiness legislation, but (2) by consumer advocates as negative defence mechanisms striving to defang consumer-oriented legislation.

Limitations to Business Self-Regulation[13]

Generally speaking, the efforts at self-regulation by businesspeople have not been too successful, at least not in the eyes of consumer advocates. Many of the business responses already noted have come only as a result of government prodding.

If an industry depends upon the *voluntary* compliance of its members toward meeting industry standards, the results are likely to be ineffective. For self-regulation to have any real chance of success, an industry must be able to *force* its members to comply with the industry standards. The problem is, however, that any enforcement measure strong enough to be effective (a boycott against an offender, for example), may be considered a violation of the restrictive trade practices provisions of the Combines Investigation Act. One reasonable solution to this problem might involve some form of joint business-government cooperation in the formulation of regulations. For example, the Canadian Code of Advertising Standards was formulated following consumer-government-industry consultation and is administered by the Advertising Standards Council. Similarly, this council administers the Broadcast Code for Advertising to Children on behalf of the Canadian Association of Broadcasters. These and other codes of advertising standards apparently have the support of the federal government, since the government has not yet moved to impose legal regulations in those areas covered by the codes.

---

[13]For a fine analysis of this topic, see Louis L. Stern, "Consumer Protection via Self-Regulation," *Journal of Marketing*, July 1971, pp. 47–53. Also see "When Business Tries to Regulate Itself — ," *U.S. News & World Report*, May 17, 1982, pp. 65–67.

Two additional situations limit the effectiveness of self-regulation. The first is that often it is difficult to get a consensus among industry members regarding an acceptable set of product or promotion standards. The net result is that the industry settles for the least common denominator as the level for its standards. A second limitation is that executives often fail to see anything wrong with various business practices in their industry — practices that are highly criticized by outside observers.

Effective self-regulation by business can serve to balance consumer advocates and governmental action in setting and enforcing industry standards. For business to be effective in this respect, however, it must generate much more confidence among consumers than it does now.

Business Discontent with Consumer Fraud

Discontent is not a one-way street. In growing measure, what might be called a "reverse consumerism" is developing. That is, businesspeople are increasingly concerned and vocal about consumer-initiated fraud against business. Shoplifting, fraudulent redemption of coupons, fraudulent cashing of cheques, and other consumer abuses, especially against retailers, are costing businesses billions of dollars each year.[14]

A SOCIETAL ORIENTATION IN MARKETING

Out of consumerism and our changing consumer goals has emerged a new approach to marketing — a societal orientation. (This point was discussed briefly in Chapter 1.) This new approach — societal marketing — is both a broadening and a logical extension of the managerial systems approach to marketing.

Societal Marketing and Managerial Marketing

Societal marketing is a broadening, but not a replacement, of managerial marketing. In societal marketing, we still must develop a marketing program to plan, price, promote, and distribute products and services to satisfy consumers' wants. But we must also consider the societal consequences of this marketing program. In managerial marketing, for example, we are concerned with marketing automobiles to people. In societal marketing, in addition, we worry about the societal aspects of auto production and use — air pollution and traffic congestion.

In managerial marketing, the criteria for evaluating success are sales volume, costs, and profits. In societal marketing, we consider the social benefits and social costs. By means of a "social audit," we conceptually measure social products (improved safety of workers, reduced use of energy, etc.) and the generating of social wealth.[15] And, when the sales and profit

---

[14]See Robert E. Wilkes, "Fraudulent Behavior by Consumers," *Journal of Marketing*, October 1978, pp. 67–75; this article reports on consumer attitudes and rationale involving fifteen fraud situations and the extent of consumer participation in these situations.

[15]See Raymond A. Bauer and Dan H. Fenn, Jr., "What *Is* a Corporate Social Audit?" *Harvard Business Review*, January–February 1973, pp. 37–48.

criteria conflict with the social criteria, marketing management has a problem that must be solved with an acceptable compromise.[16]

Conflicts in Consumer Goals

The consumers' shift to socially oriented goals is not proving to be easy to implement. As consumers, we have not abandoned our desire for things — but we have complicated our wants with a social concern. Here is the difference, possibly oversimplified, between pre-1970s goals and today's goals. Then, we wanted big cars that would go fast. We paid little attention to air pollution, traffic congestion, depleting oil resources, and polluted streams from mills making steel for autos. Now, we still want autos, but we also want clean air, no traffic jams, clean water, and no dependence on foreign oil resources. Certainly the former goal — a desire for autos only — was much easier to achieve, because the element of *conflict in goals* was largely absent.

The greater the number of target markets (publics) a company must deal with, the more difficult it becomes to satisfy them all. Often, the goals of the different markets are in conflict. One group may want a mill closed because it pollutes the air and water. But another of the target markets wants it kept open because it provides jobs.

In trying to understand this problem of goal conflict, perhaps a key point to keep in mind is that we are dealing with consumers — human beings — with all their attendant contradictions and self-interests. Thus we cry out for safer autos; but, given the opportunity, a large percentage of people would not use their seat belts. We want more energy-generating facilities, but we object when anyone wants to build an oil refinery or a power plant in our town.

Social Responsibilities of Marketing Management

A recurring theme in this chapter has been broadened perspectives in marketing. Continuing in this vein, we now shall focus on the social responsibilities of marketing executives, both in concept and in practice.

What is Social Responsibility?

Marketing executives have a three-fold responsibility — to their firms, to their workers, and to their customers. For their firms, their job is to provide a satisfactory net profit over the long run. To their employees, their responsibility is to provide a good working environment. For their customers, the executive's job is to market want-satisfying goods and services at the lowest reasonable cost.

The substance of social responsibility is much broader, however. It emphasizes the effect of executive actions on the entire social system. Without this broader viewpoint, personal and institutional acts tend to be

---

[16]For a framework to help marketing managers prepare for their part in a company's social audit, see A. H. Kizilbash, Carlton A. Maile, William O. Hancock, and Peter Gillett, "Social Auditing for Marketing Managers," *Industrial Marketing Management*, January 1979, pp. 1–6; and by the same authors, "The Marketing Manager's Role in the Corporate Social Audit," *Bulletin of Business Research* (Ohio State University), April 1978, pp. 4–7.

separated. Marketing executives can lead model personal lives, but they continue to justify their company's pollution of a river because there is no direct personal involvement. To them, river pollution is a public problem to be solved by governmental action.

The concept of social responsibility, however, requires executives to consider their acts within the framework of the whole social system. And the concept implies that executives are responsible for the effects of their acts anywhere in that system. Executives must realize (1) that business does not exist in isolation in our society and (2) that a healthy business system cannot exist within a sick society.

Reasons for Concern About Social Responsibility

Marketing executives should have a high degree of social responsibility simply because it is the morally correct thing to do. While this is simple and beautiful in concept, it is far more difficult to put into operation. Let's look at four points that have a more pragmatic flavor — four practical reasons for social responsibility in business.

To Reverse Declining Public Confidence in Business

The image of business is tarnished — at least in the eyes of many people. To compound the consumerism problems facing business during the 1970s, Canadians were exposed to revelations that business executives (often in very large multinational corporations) had participated in political kickback schemes, payoffs to agents in foreign countries, illegal and unethical gifts, and other unsavoury or illegal acts. Opinion polls tended to show that public confidence in business leadership had declined dramatically as it had in the case of a number of other public institutions, including government, education, and labour unions.

Now the question is, How do we reverse this decline in public confidence? Business leaders must demonstrate in convincing fashion that they are aware of, and will *really* fulfil, their social responsibility. A cosmetic, lip-service treatment will only worsen an already bad situation. Management needs to learn from the mistakes of other firms. Companies must set high ethical standards and then enforce them. Failure to act in this fashion will lead inevitably to further government intervention. Indeed, most of the governmental limitations placed on marketing throughout the years have been the result of management's failure to live up to its social responsibilities. Moreover, once some form of governmental control has been established, it is rarely removed.

Price of Economic Freedom and Flexibility

Marketing executives must act in a socially desirable manner in order to justify the privilege of operating in our relatively free economic system. No worthwhile privilege or freedom comes without a price. Our economic freedoms sometimes have a high price, just as our precious political freedoms do. Moreover, it is very

SOME COMPANIES HAVE ACTED IN A SOCIALLY RESPONSIBLE MANNER; SOME HAVE NOT

FIRESTONE TIRE AND RUBBER COMPANY

Firestone's 500 series of steel-belted radial tires were involved in the deaths of 34 people and hundreds of accidents. The company received thousands of consumer complaints regarding the 500 series tires. The U.S. government said the tire was particularly susceptible to blowouts, tread separations, and other potentially dangerous faults.

The company's response was to lay the blame on the users of the tire — charging that the tire failures were due to consumer neglect and abuse. The company also tried to block the investigations of the tire and sought a court injunction against the release of a survey of tire owners conducted by the National Highway Traffic Safety Administration (NHTSA). The company continued in various ways to delay and generally to "stonewall" the NHTSA investigations. The U.S. government finally forced Firestone to recall about 13 million of its radial tires.

FORD MOTOR COMPANY

Ford Motor Company's Pinto automobile had a gasoline tank that was prone to explode and catch fire when the car was hit hard in the rear end. The car was involved in the burn deaths of several people who otherwise would not have been seriously injured in the accident.

For about eight years the company lobbied against a particular safety standard for motor vehicles that would have required the redesign of the gas tank on the Pinto. The company's successful delaying tactics included (1) inundating the government with technical data that would take the government years to examine, (2) asserting that the drivers, not the cars, were the problem, and (3) asserting that automobile fires were not a major problem. After many years, the company stopped the production of the Pinto.

JOHNSON & JOHNSON

In mid-1982, Tylenol, marketed by the McNeil Consumer Products Company, a division of Johnson & Johnson, was the leading brand of non-aspirin pain relievers. Tylenol's annual sales exceeded $450 million, and the brand accounted for about 17 percent of Johnson & Johnson's net profit. Then tragedy struck. Several people died after taking Tylenol capsules that had been poisoned. Apparently the poison had been injected into a random assortment of capsules some time after the product was shipped from the factory.

Johnson & Johnson's response was speedy and thorough. Within *four days* after the poisonings, the company recalled more than 30 million bottles of Tylenol capsules and tablets. In its accounting records, the company charged off $100 million as a recall expense.

The company was also quite open in its contacts with the media and the public. Toll-free telephone lines were set up to handle over 350,000 calls. Executives appeared on national television, and they talked with the press and the public. All this was done, incidentally, by a company whose former policy was for its executives to stay out of the public eye — that is, to maintain a low public profile.

Within a few months, the company had again distributed its product, this time in a new, tamper-resistant package. The company also has since regained much, if not all, of its former market share.

Source: Elizabeth Gatewood and Archie B. Carroll, "The Anatomy of Corporate Social Response: The Rely, Firestone 500, and Pinto Cases," *Business Horizons,* September–October 1981, pp. 9–16; and news articles.

much in management's self-interest to be concerned with social problems, for these problems affect both the firm and its customers. Also, a concern for the quality of life may very well lead to change, and this change may present opportunities for new business.

The Power-Responsibility Equation The concept that social power begets social responsibility helps to explain why business executives have a major responsibility to society. Marketing executives do wield a great deal of social power as they influence markets and speak out on matters of economic policy. In business, we see many practical applications of the idea of a reasonable balance between power and responsibility. A management axiom holds that authority and responsibility should be matched. Since responsibility is tied to power, we may reason that the avoidance of social responsibility will lead to an erosion of social power. That is, "those who do not take responsibility for their power will lose it."[17]

Marketing Department Represents Company Procter & Gamble put this point nicely in an annual report that is paraphrased here: "When a Procter & Gamble salesperson walks into a customer's place of business — whether calling on an individual store or keeping an appointment at the headquarters of a large group of stores — that salesperson not only represents Procter & Gamble, but in a very real sense, that person is Procter & Gamble."

For marketers who are genuinely interested in working to solve major social problems, there are opportunities for action both within their firms and in their communities. This entire book has been devoted to developing a consumer-oriented, socially responsible marketing program in the firm. In the community, marketing can play an active role in such areas as:

Action Programs Regarding Social Problems

- Hiring and training disadvantaged people
- Contributing to education and the arts
- Urban renewal
- Removing discrimination against women, old people, and minority groups
- Reducing the marketing problems of low-income consumers
- Reducing environmental pollution

In the next section we shall discuss briefly some practical examples of marketing's involvement in the last of these problem areas. But first, note that marketing executives should let the public know about their social-action programs and accomplishments. With all the criticism being heaped on business today, it is not enough just to *do* some good in the social arena. Business executives must start to *tell* people about it instead of hiding their light under a bushel. In the past, many executives went out of their way to

---

[17]Keith Davis, "Understanding the Social Responsibility Puzzle," *Business Horizons*, Winter 1967, p. 49.

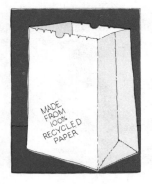

maintain a low profile. Now they are urged to be more visible in their community and in the public media. They should explain what they are doing to improve the quality of life, as well as the standard of living.

Reducing Environmental Pollution

One of the major social problems facing us today is the pollution of our physical environment. Our ecology — the relationship of people to their environment — is being disturbed, and in some cases seriously, by air, water, or noise pollution.

Who Are the Polluters?   Marketing has contributed to the pollution problem. By stimulating a demand for products and by satisfying consumers' wants, marketing has helped to build mountains of solid wastes. Making and using these products pollutes air and water. Promotional efforts in marketing have generated a "throw-away" society and have contributed to a "no-deposit, no-return" behavioural pattern.

However, our ecological problems are far more complex than many people realize. Marketing alone did not cause pollution. Production technology is responsible for air and water pollution from steel mills, chemical plants, paper mills, oil refineries, and utility power plants. Cattle-feed lots and various mining operations contribute their share of wastes. Various government agencies have inadequate control over their own pollution-producing operations — and yet, the critics of business want the government to control pollution. Selfish consumer behaviour adds to the problem. We want clean air, but we won't pay to tune up our auto engines. As a group, we demand highway beautification, but as individuals, we toss trash out the car window and often leave picnic grounds a shambles.

We are dealing with a complex assortment of technological, economic, and even cultural and psychological factors. Furthermore, contrary to the belief held by many critics, pollution is *not* restricted to capitalistic economies and big business. Pollution is a by-product of any industrialized urban society.

Marketing's Contribution to Pollution Reduction   Because of the complexity of ecological problems, effective solutions require cooperation from producers, marketers, and consumers, with the government serving as a coordinating and enforcement agency. The costs of pollution reduction and control are enormously high. Prices will have to be increased to pay for these efforts.

Just as marketing alone did not cause pollution, so too marketing alone cannot cure it. But marketing can and does contribute to the "solution of pollution." To do so is simply a part of our social responsibility. Moreover, there are many profitable business opportunities in pollution abatement. Pollution reduction is *not* limited to shut-down-the mill, don't-drive-your-car, and return-that-bottle type of negative alternatives. Some illustrations of positive efforts by marketers revolve around product planning, channels of distribution, and promotion.

The major polluting industries and many of the lesser culprits provide golden market opportunities for new pollution-control products. A little innovative thinking also helps. As we run out of land for garbage dumps, some cities are generating electricity by using solid wastes for fuel. Marketing is also challenged to develop products that will *not* contribute to solid-waste matter. The disposal of solid wastes is a monumental problem, and one way to cope with it is not to accumulate so much waste in the first place. Thus, biodegradable or recycle products, and returnable or reusable containers, are desirable.[18]

The key to success in recycling is to develop a distribution system that will move waste products from consumers back to a producer who can use them as raw materials in manufacturing new products. Marketing's challenge is to find the incentive needed to stimulate the consumer to start this reverse-channel movement. Marketers can use their skills in promotion and persuasion to urge consumers to conserve our natural resources by using them in a more efficient, less wasteful manner. Promotion also can be used to impress upon consumers the seriousness of our pollution and waste-disposal problems.

From the late 1940s pretty much through the 1960s, the North American economy was booming. The economic growth rate was high. We were amassing mountains of goods to satisfy the pent-up demand of the war years and the Depression of the 1930s. We also were highly successful in our international marketing efforts. At least during the early years of that period, we faced relatively little competition. It was during this period that modern marketing developed and played such an important role in our economic growth.

But the situation changed during the 1970s and the 1980s. The costs of energy soared, the economic growth rate slowed down, and the birthrate declined considerably. We encountered shortages of some resources, and we experienced the worst recession and the highest rate of unemployment since the 1930s. We faced growing competition in international markets. Most of the industrialized nations surpassed us in labour productivity. During this period we also experienced major social changes that carry significant marketing implications.

Now, in the late 1980s, the challenges to marketing management are tremendous. Consumerism will continue as a strong movement, since we still want a better quality of life. We can no longer afford the luxury of a socioeconomic philosophy that is attuned to an economy of unlimited, low-cost resources. Instead, we live in an economy of limited, irreplaceable resources that probably will continue to increase in price.[19]

MARKETING IN THE NEXT TEN YEARS

---

[18]For some examples of new no-waste technologies that are helping companies' profit, growth, and survival, see Michael G. Royston, "Making Pollution Prevention Pay," *Harvard Business Review*, November–December 1980, pp. 6–8*ff.*

[19]See Alan J. Resnik, Harold E. Sand, and J. Barry Mason, "Marketing Dilemma: Change in the '80s," *California Management Review*, Fall 1981, pp. 49–57.

Now, at the end of this book, let's look briefly at a few of the forces that will shape marketing in the next ten years. Three of these forces — government regulation, consumerism, and environmental pollution control — were discussed earlier in this chapter. The remaining forces are (1) the changing consumer and business environment; (2) periods of inflation and recession; and (3) a broadened marketing concept.

Tomorrow's Consumers Will Be Different	Perhaps the most significant prospect is that the markets of the next decade will be quite different from those of today. Consumers will be better educated and more critical. Their goals will be more socially oriented, and they will expect marketers to play a greater role in solving environmental and social problems. Population growth will slow down. The under-30 age group will decline in number, while the 30-to-50 group will increase substantially. The number of two-wage-earner families will continue to increase. Family structures are becoming smaller, less permanent institutions (the divorce rate is rising). There will be further increases in the number of households where people live alone or with an unrelated person. The economic, social, and political role of women will continue to change, with consequent effects on marketing. There will be further movement toward a rental (rather than a product ownership) economy, and growth in the services sector.

Tomorrow's Consumers Will Be Different

Perhaps the most significant prospect is that the markets of the next decade will be quite different from those of today. Consumers will be better educated and more critical. Their goals will be more socially oriented, and they will expect marketers to play a greater role in solving environmental and social problems. Population growth will slow down. The under-30 age group will decline in number, while the 30-to-50 group will increase substantially. The number of two-wage-earner families will continue to increase. Family structures are becoming smaller, less permanent institutions (the divorce rate is rising). There will be further increases in the number of households where people live alone or with an unrelated person. The economic, social, and political role of women will continue to change, with consequent effects on marketing. There will be further movement toward a rental (rather than a product ownership) economy, and growth in the services sector.

Marketing in Periods of Inflation

Inflation presents some real challenges to management in a marketing program — especially in pricing. Management should decide on appropriate strategies and tactics involving the timing and magnitude of price increases. Should the company regularly pass on to its customers the full price increase it faces? Or perhaps a more flexible strategy may be wiser. (A section in Chapter 13 was devoted to pricing in periods of inflation.)

Prices generally are raised during inflation because a firm's costs have increased. So another series of managerial challenges involves ways to control and perhaps reduce some costs. Some firms have engaged in a strategy of product simplication to reduce costs. Others have used a careful marketing cost analysis to identify the high-cost customers, middlemen, and sales territories.

Marketing in a Recession

From time to time in our economic system, we have experienced recessions, and we are likely to encounter them in the future. If the period of economic decline is long and/or deep enough, it will have a major impact on consumer buying power and buying behaviour. People hit by a recession can become discouraged, depressed, scared, and angry. They retrench economically, seeking all possible ways to economize. Their life-styles change. Any significant changes in consumer buying behaviour, of course, have major implications for the marketing programs in countless firms.

Consumers can economize during a recession in several different ways. They will repair existing products themselves rather than buy new ones, or rather than pay somebody else to make the repairs. They will trade down in the articles they do buy. They will shop in lower-priced stores, buy items on sale, and buy lower-priced brands. Economy and durability will replace convenience and status as reasons for buying a given product.[20]

One benefit, if we can call it that, from a recession is that it generally increases our awareness of the importance of marketing. During a recession, we realize we don't have any problems in *making* autos, ski boots, or carpeting, but we surely do have trouble *selling* them. It really is unfortunate that a severe economic decline — a recession — is needed for some people to appreciate the value of marketing.

Earlier in this chapter, we developed the theme that changing cultural values led to consumerism, and subsequently to a societal orientation in the field of marketing. This sequence inevitably leads us to review the marketing concept to determine whether it is compatible with a societally oriented marketing perspective.[21]

Broadening the Marketing Concept

The philosophy of the marketing concept holds that a company should (1) develop an integrated marketing program (2) to generate profitable sales volume (3) by satisfying consumers' wants. The fact that consumerism exists in Canada today means that the marketing concept has to some extent failed. The customer-orientation theme in the marketing concept implies that business should find out what the consumers want and then try to satisfy those wants profitably. Consequently, carried to their logical extremes, consumerism and the marketing concept are mutually exclusive; if one exists, the other does not. Yet, most businesspeople probably would claim that they are consumer-oriented. They look on in wounded surprise at the wave of consumer discontent engulfing them.

Okay, then, what went wrong? Is it simply that the marketing concept has outlived its usefulness and is not compatible with today's societal orientation in marketing? In the opinion of the authors of this book, there is nothing wrong with the marketing concept that a broader interpretation won't cure. It is as viable as it ever was. It is quite compatible with a societal orientation to marketing and with a marketing executive's social responsibility.

However, three things did occur that have hurt the credibility of the marketing concept. The first was that too many marketing executives, while professing wholehearted agreement and support of the philosophy, were in actual practice giving it only token implementation. In some cases, these executives were simply too production- or engineering-oriented to fully comprehend the idea of customer orientation. In other cases, short-run crises have forced operating executives to put their self-interest ahead of consumer satisfaction.

---

[20]See James G. Barnes and Lessey Sooklal, "The Changing Nature of Consumer Behavior: Monitoring the Impact of Inflation and Recession," *Business Quarterly*, Summer 1983, pp. 58–64.

[21]See William S. Sachs and George Benson, "Is It Time to Discard the Marketing Concept?" *Business Horizons*, August 1978, pp. 68–74; Ronald W. Stampfl, "Structural Constraints, Consumerism, and the Marketing Concept," *MSU Business Topics*, Spring 1978, pp. 5–16; and Roger C. Bennett and Robert G. Cooper, "Beyond the Marketing Concept," *Business Horizons*, June 1979, pp. 76–83. Also see A. Parasuraman, "Hang On to the Marketing Concept!" *Business Horizons*, September–October 1981, pp. 38–40.

The two other factors affecting the implementation of the marketing concept revolve around the narrow interpretation of consumer want-satisfaction. Who is a consumer, and what is meant by want-satisfaction? The answers to both these questions have been too narrow and too short-run oriented. Most human beings — whether in the role of producer or consumer — tend to be short-run oriented in most situations. We fail to see the long-run implications of our actions. Thus, we may want certain foods and be satisfied when marketers cater to these wants. But these foods may be fattening and thus bad for us, so there is a negative personal effect on us in the long run.

If the goal is defined as consumer want-satisfaction *in the long run*, then the marketing concept is more in line with the societal perspective of marketing. Of course, the problem of goal conflict crops up here again. To sell us fattening foods is contrary to society's view of socially desirable want-satisfaction. But nonfattening food (while socially desirable and healthy for us) is just not what we want. So the marketer of this food loses our business. Our short-run wants and long-run interests conflict.

Besides extending the *time* dimension in the marketing concept, we need to extend its *breadth*. To view only the direct buyers of a company's product as being the consumers — a view generally held in the past — is too narrow a dimension. We must broaden our definition of target markets to include other groups affected by the direct buyer-seller exchange. Thus, someone may buy an auto and be satisfied with it. But the negative social effects of pollution and traffic congestion from the auto displease other groups. In the broader context, we have not generated customer satisfaction and thus have not successfully implemented the marketing concept.

In summary, the marketing concept can be compatible with a societal perspective of marketing if we define the marketing concept as follows:

THE BROADENED MARKETING CONCEPT IS:

A philosophy whereby a company strives:
- to develop an integrated marketing program
- that generates long-run profitable sales volume
- by satisfying the long-run wants of:
- product-buying customers and
- the other parts of society affected by the firm's activities.

SUMMARY

In this final chapter, we appraised marketing from a broad, societal perspective, in contrast to the individual-company approach followed in the preceding chapters of this book. When evaluating our marketing system, the key point to recognize is the socioeconomic yardstick we used as the basis for the appraisal. We evaluated marketing on the basis of its ability to satisfy consumers' wants *as consumers themselves define or express those wants*. We reviewed some of the common criticisms of marketing, structuring this review around the four components of the marketing mix. Several aspects of the complex question "Does marketing cost too much?" were discussed.

Then we moved to the topic of consumerism. Consumerism is a protest against perceived business injustices, combined with the efforts to remedy these situations. Actually, consumerism is not limited to business alone. It also includes consumers' relations with government and other public organizations in our society. We have experienced consumer movements in the past, but the current one is signicantly different in several respects. Consumerism, as we know it today, stemmed from some broad cultural changes and from consumer discontents and frustrations.

Consumers, individually and in consumer organizations, have responded to perceived injustices. The government, through legislation and the actions of regulatory agencies, also has responded to consumers' cries. Some companies have resisted consumerism, and others have come up with token responses. However, there also have been strong positive responses from a significant number of companies and from trade associations. The current consumer movement shows every indication of continuing into the future.

There is an emerging societal orientation in marketing, and a growing social responsibility on the part of marketing management, for some very practical reasons. A societal orientation is needed to build the public's confidence in business and to justify the privilege of operating in our economic system. A socially responsible attitude is needed if business is to retain its social power. Perhaps the overriding reason for operating in a socially responsible manner is that the alternative is further government intervention. This would be unfortunate, because businesspeople are well qualified to solve many of our social problems.

A review of the past formed the basis for our look into the next decade. In the 1950s and 1960s, our challenge was how to market in a high-growth-rate economy of abundance. In the 1980s, the challenge is how to market during periods of inflation, recession, and increasing competition. In addition, the consumer environment is changing. In line with these prospects, the marketing concept should be modified to a broader, more socially responsive philosophy that will be workable in the society of the next decade.

KEY TERMS AND CONCEPTS

QUESTIONS AND PROBLEMS

1. Some people feel that too much power is concentrated in big business in Canada and that large firms should be broken up. Yet these same people will drive a General Motors car, buy groceries at a large chain supermarket, buy home appliances made by a giant in the industry, wash with a major brand of soap, and brush their teeth with the leading brand of toothpaste. How do you reconcile the behaviour of these people with their opinion concerning big business?

2. "Middlemen make unfairly high profits." Do you agree?

3. Some people believe that there are too many fast-food outlets in their communities. Suggest a method for reducing the number of these retailers. How many should be eliminated in your community?

4. Evaluate the following criticisms of advertising;
   a. It creates a false sense of values.
   b. It costs too much.
   c. It is in bad taste.
   d. It is false, misleading, and deceptive.
   e. It tends to create monopolies.

5. What proposals do you have for regulating advertising?

6. What specific recommendations do you have for reducing the costs of marketing?

7. What information do you think should be included in advertisements for each of the following products or services?
   a. Lipstick
   b. Auto tires
   c. Breakfast cereals
   d. Personal loans

8. What suggestions do you have for an appliance manufacturing company that wants to improve the servicing of its products? An automobile manufacturing company?

9. What is the social and economic justification for "paternalistic" laws — like auto seat-belt regulations — that require us to do something because the government says it is in our best interests?

10. What proposals do you have for resolving some of the consumer goal-conflict situations discussed in this chapter?

11. You are vice president of marketing in a company heavily involved in outdoor advertising. Your company owns billboards and handles the outdoor advertising for many manufacturers. Currently, in your provincial legislature there is a bill pending that would eliminate all outdoor advertising on all major highways in your province. Several key members of the committee considering the bill have received major campaign contributions from your company over the years. Should you tell them that your firm will cut off further financial support if they approve the bill? Assume they do approve the bill. Then what position should your company take at the next election when these legislators seek your campaign contributions?

12. "When a company can sell all it can produce, management should cut expenses by reducing its sales force and advertising expenditures." Discuss.

13. Suggest some pricing and product strategies for a ski manufacturer during an inflationary period.

14. What marketing strategies should be adopted by a retailer of high-priced women's ready-to-wear clothing during a recession?

Case 29
Van der Steen Chocolate Company*

Case for Part 8
Case for Part 8

Designing a Strategic Marketing Mix

Joseph van der Steen had recently inherited the family candy business, located in Oakville, Ontario. While Mr. van der Steen had only limited experience with the manufacture of chocolates in the family kitchens, he had graduated from a business administration program at the local community college, majoring in Marketing. Consequently, he decided, after a detailed analysis of the van der Steen Chocolate Company and consultation with his accountant, to keep the business and to build on the reputation and capital established by his father and grandfather.

The company had a tradition of selling in a limited volume to a select group of customers. Joseph's grandfather had built a loyal following among those who would pay a premium price for beautiful and authentic, old-fashioned, hand-dipped chocolates. All ingredients were natural—real butter and chocolate, fresh-ground vanilla and other favours, authentic maple sugar, and so on. All nutmeats were of premium quality. Recipes and package designs had been virtually unchanged since the family moved from the Netherlands to Canada in 1855.

The candy kitchens and production facilities were located very near the centre of the older downtown area of Oakville, right on the lakeshore highway leading from Toronto to Hamilton. The building and equipment were sturdy, spotless, and in excellent condition, in keeping with the traditions established by the preceding generations of van der Steens. The company also owned a larger building, which was back-to-back with the kitchen building, but it had fallen into disuse. The small staff was expert and loyal, and most had worked for the van der Steen family for many years.

Current production ran from 350 kg per week in July to a high of 600 kg per week in December. Capacity was estimated to be 1,000 kg per week. (But, to reach this level, one or two unskilled workers would have to be added for packing, stock control, and cleaning duties.) Demand had remained relatively stable over the past couple of years despite significant price increases caused by the increasing cost of sugar, chocolate, and packaging supplies.

The van der Steen Chocolate Company sold its candy only to retail customers and only from the company's retail store in the candy-kitchen building. Last month (November), Mr. van der Steen did a little informal marketing research by interviewing 87 customers. He learned that all but 5 were regular, repeat customers, and that 22 were businesspeople buying several packages for business gifts.

---

*Case adapted from the original prepared by Richard J. Jeffries and Ernest F. Cooke. Used with permission.

The family had never advertised in any media; instead, it had depended entirely on word-of-mouth and careful maintenance of customer goodwill. Some investments had been made in packaging, but the basic package designs were virtually unchanged since the turn of the century. They featured Dutch village scenes in pastel colours, and Victorian typefaces.

In planning the first formal marketing program the company had ever developed, Mr. van der Steen first reviewed the competitive situation facing his company. A nearby specialty candy store sold imported chocolates at $30 or more per kilogram. A number of Laura Secord outlets in the Toronto-Oakville-Hamilton area sold their own brand of chocolates at prices starting at $15.95 per kilogram. A specialty chocolate store in a large shopping centre in Toronto sold imported European chocolates at $18 for a 500-gram package or hand-dipped 'home made' chocolates for almost $40 per kilogram. Mr. van der Steen was also checking on the brands and prices for chocolates and other types of candy at major department stores in Toronto and Hamilton.

Mr. van der Steen had learned something about strategic marketing planning in his college marketing courses, and he wanted to put some of that knowedge to work immediately. He estimated that, with a good marketing plan, he could boost sales next year to an average of 1,000 kg per week. At a retail price of $20 per kilogram, this meant a sales volume of about $1 million for the year. This was about twice as much as last year's sales volume.

To reach his objective of doubling his company's sales volume in twelve months, van der Steen realized he would need an effective marketing plan. Part of this plan would involve ways of filling in what he called the company's "summer sales valley." He did decide early that the company would work with a promotional budget of $85,000 for next year.

Questions

Assume that you have been hired as a marketing consultant by Mr. van der Steen to design a strategic marketing plan for van der Steen Chocolates. As part of this plan:

1. Indicate what target market van der Steen should select.

2. Design, in some detail, a marketing mix to reach these markets.

Marketing Arithmetic

Marketing involves people — customers, middlemen, and producers. Much of the business activity of these people, however, is quantified in some manner. Consequently, some knowledge of the rudiments of business arithmetic is essential for decision making in many areas of marketing. Since most students taking this course have already had a beginning course in accounting, this appendix is intended as a review. It contains discussions of three accounting concepts that are useful in marketing: (1) the operating statement, (2) markups, and (3) analytical ratios. Another useful concept — discounts and terms of sale — was reviewed in Chapter 13 in connection with price policies.

THE OPERATING STATEMENT

An operating statement — often called a "profit and loss statement" or an "income and expense statement" — is one of the two main financial statements prepared by a company. The other is the balance sheet. An **operating statement** is a summary picture of the firm's income and expenses — its operations — over a period of time. In contrast, a **balance sheet** shows the assets, liabilities, and net worth of a company at a given time, for example, at the close of business on December 31, 1985.

The operating statement shows whether the business earned a net profit or suffered a net loss during the period covered. It is an orderly summary of the income and expense items that resulted in this net profit or loss.

An operating statement can cover any selected period of time. To fulfil income tax requirements, virtually all firms prepare a statement covering operations during the calendar or fiscal year. In addition, it is common for businesses to prepare monthly, quarterly, or semiannual operating statements.

Table A-1 is an example of an operating statement for a wholesaler or retailer. The main difference between the operating statement of a middleman and that of a manufacturer is in the cost-of-goods-sold section. A manufacturer shows the cost of goods *manufactured*, whereas the middleman's statement shows net *purchases*.

Table A-1

ALPHA-BETA COMPANY, OPERATING STATEMENT, FOR YEAR ENDING DECEMBER 31, 1985

Gross sales			$87,000
Less: Sales return and allowances		$ 5,500	
Cash discounts allowed		1,500	7,000
Net sales			$80,000
Cost of goods sold:			
Beginning inventory, January 1 (at cost)			18,000
Gross purchases		49,300	
Less: Cash discounts taken on purchases		900	
Net purchases		48,400	
Plus: Freight in		1,600	
Net purchases (at delivered cost)			50,000
Cost of goods available for sale			68,000
Less: Ending inventory, December 31 (at cost)			20,000
Cost of goods sold			48,000
Gross margin			32,000
Expenses:			
Sales-force salaries and commissions		$11,000	
Advertising		2,400	
Office supplies		250	
Taxes (except income tax)		125	
Telephone and telegraph		250	
Delivery expenses		175	
Rent		800	
Heat, light, and power		300	
Depreciation		100	
Insurance		150	
Interest		150	
Bad debts		300	
Administrative salaries		7,500	
Office salaries		3,500	
Miscellaneous expenses		200	
Total expenses			27,200
Net profit			$ 4,800

Major Sections   From one point of view, the essence of business is very simple. A company buys or makes a product and then sells it for a higher price. Out of the sales revenue, the seller hopes to cover the cost of the merchandise and the seller's own expenses and have something left over, which is called "net profit." These relationships form the skeleton of an operating statement. That is, *sales minus cost of goods sold equals gross margin*; then *gross margin minus expenses equals net profit.* An example based on Table A-1 is as follows:

	Sales	$80,000
less	Cost of goods sold	− 48,000
equals	Gross margin	32,000
less	Expenses	− 27,200
equals	Net profit	$ 4,800

Sales

The first line in an operating statement records the gross sales — the total amount sold by the company. From this figure, the company deducts its sales returns and sales allowances. From gross sales, the company also deducts the discounts that are granted to company employees when they purchase merchandise or services.

In virtually every firm at some time during an operating period, customers will want to return or exchange merchandise. In a *sales return*, the customer is refunded the full purchase price in cash or credit. In a *sales allowance*, the customer keeps the merchandise, but is given a reduction from the selling price because of some dissatisfaction. The income from the sale of returned merchandise is included in a company's gross sales, so returns and allowances must be deducted to get net sales.

Net Sales

This is the most important figure in the sales section of the statement. It represents the net amount of sales revenue, out of which the company will pay for the products and all its expenses. The net sales figure is also the one upon which many operating ratios are based. It is called 100 percent (of itself), and the other items are then expressed as a percentage of net sales.

Cost of Goods Sold

From net sales, we must deduct the cost of the merchandise that was sold, as we work toward discovering the firm's net profit. In determining the cost of goods sold in a retail or wholesale operation, we start with the value of any merchandise on hand at the beginning of the period. To this we add the net cost of what was purchased during the period. From this total we deduct the value of whatever remains unsold at the end of the period. In Table A-1 the firm started with an inventory worth $18,000, and it purchased goods that cost $50,000. Thus the firm had a total of $68,000 worth of goods available for sale. If all were sold, the cost of goods sold would have been $68,000. At the end of the year, however, there was still $20,000 worth of merchandise on hand. Thus, during the year, the company sold goods that cost $48,000.

In the preceding paragraph, we spoke of merchandise "valued at" a certain figure or "worth" a stated amount. Actually, the problem of inventory valuation is complicated and sometimes controversial. The usual rule of thumb is to value inventories at cost or market, whichever is lower. The actual application of this rule may be difficult. Assume that a store buys 6 footballs at $2 each and the next week buys 6 more at $2.50 each. The company places all 12, jumbled, in a basket display for sale. Then one is sold, but there is no marking to indicate whether its cost was $2 or $2.50. Thus the inventory value of the remaining 11 balls may be $25 or $24.50. If we multiply this situation by thousands of purchases and sales, we may begin to see the depth of the problem.

A figure that deserves some comment is the *net cost of delivered purchases*. A company starts with its gross purchases at billed cost. Then it must deduct any purchases that were returned or any purchase allowances received. The company should also deduct any discounts taken for payment of the bill within a specified period of time. Deducting purchase returns and allowances and purchase discounts gives the net cost of the purchases. Then freight charges paid by the buyer (called "freight in") are added to net purchases to determine the net cost of *delivered* purchases.

In a manufacturing concern, the cost-of-goods-sold section has a slightly different form. Instead of determining the cost of goods *purchased*, the company determines the cost of goods *manufactured* (see Table A-2). Cost of goods manufactured ($50,000) is added to the beginning inventory ($18,000) to ascertain the total goods available for sale ($68,000). Then, after the ending inventory of finished goods has been deducted ($20,000), the result is the cost of goods sold ($48,000).

To find the cost of goods *manufactured*, a company starts with the value of goods partially completed (beginning inventory of goods in process — $24,000). To this beginning inventory figure is added the cost of raw materials, direct labour, and factory overhead expenses incurred during the

Table A-2
_____

COST-OF-GOODS-SOLD SECTION OF AN OPERATING STATEMENT FOR A MANUFACTURER

Beginning inventory of finished goods (at cost)		$18,000
Cost of goods manufactured:		
Beginning inventory, goods in process	$24,000	
Plus: Raw materials $20,000		
Direct labour 15,000		
Overhead 13,000	48,000	
Total goods in process	72,000	
Less: Ending inventory, goods in process	22,000	
Cost of goods manufactured		50,000
Cost of goods available for sale		68,000
Less: Ending inventory, finished goods (at cost)		20,000
Cost of goods sold		$48,000

period ($48,000). The resulting figure is the total goods in process during the period ($72,000). By deducting the value of goods still in process at the end of the period ($22,000), management finds the cost of goods manufactured during that span of time ($50,000).

Gross Margin

Gross margin is determined simply by subtracting cost of goods sold from net sales. Gross margin, sometimes called "gross profit," is one of the key figures in the entire marketing program. When we say that a certain store has a "margin" of 30 percent, we are referring to the gross margin.

Expenses

Operating expenses are deducted from gross margin to determine the net profit. The operating expense section includes marketing, administrative, and possibly some miscellaneous expense items. It does not, of course, include the cost of goods purchased or manufactured, since these costs have already been deducted.

Net Profit

Net profit is the difference between gross margin and total expenses. A negative net profit is, of course, a loss.

MARKUPS

Many retailers and wholesalers use markup percentages to determine the selling price of an article. Normally the selling price must exceed the cost of the merchandise by an amount sufficient to cover the operating expenses and still leave the desired profit. The difference between the selling price of an item and its cost is the **markup**, sometimes referred to as the "mark-on."

Typically, markups are expressed in percentages rather than dollars. A markup may be expressed as a percentage of either the cost or the selling price. Therefore, we must first determine which will be the *base* for the markup. That is, when we speak of a 40 percent markup, do we mean 40 percent of the *cost* or of the *selling price*?

To determine the markup percentage when it is based on *cost*, we use the following formula:

$$\text{Markup \%} = \frac{\text{dollar markup}}{\text{cost}}$$

When the markup is based on *selling price*, the formula to use is:

$$\text{Markup \%} = \frac{\text{dollar markup}}{\text{selling price}}$$

It is important that all interested parties understand which base is being used in a given situation. Otherwise, there can be a considerable misunderstanding. To illustrate, suppose Mr. A runs a clothing store and claims he needs a 66⅔ percent markup to make a small net profit. Ms. B, who runs a competitive store, says she needs only a 40 percent markup and that A must be inefficient or a big profiteer. Actually, both merchants are using identical markups, but they are using different bases. Each seller buys hats at $6 apiece and sets the selling price at $10. This is a markup of $4 per hat. Mr. A is expressing his markup as a percentage of cost — hence, the 66⅔ percent figure ($4 ÷ $6 = .67, or 66⅔ percent). Ms. B is basing her markup on the selling price ($4 ÷ $10 = .4, or 40 percent). It would be a mistake for Mr. A to try to get by on B's 40 percent markup, as long as A uses cost as his base. To illustrate, if Mr. A used the 40 percent markup, *but based it on cost*, the markup would be only $2.40. And the selling price would be only $8.40. This $2.40 markup, averaged over the entire hat department, would not enable A to cover his usual expenses and make a profit.

Unless otherwise indicated, markup percentages are always stated as a percentage of selling price.

Markup Based on Selling Price

The following diagram should help you understand the various relationships between selling price, cost, and markup. It can be used to compute these figures regardless of whether the markup is stated in percentages or dollars, and whether the percentages are based on selling price or cost:

		Dollars	Percentage
	Selling price		
less	Cost	_____	_____
equals	Markup		

As an example, suppose a merchant buys an article for $90 and knows the markup based on selling price must be 40 percent. What is the selling price? By filling in the known information in the diagram, we obtain:

		Dollars	Percentage
	Selling price		100
less	Cost	90	_____
equals	Markup		40

The percentage representing cost must then be 60 percent. Thus the $90 cost is 60 percent of the selling price. The selling price is then $150. [That is, $9 equals 60 percent of the selling price. Then $90 is divided by .6 (or 60 percent) to get the selling price of $150.]

A common situation facing merchants is to have competition set a ceiling on selling prices. Or possibly the sellers must buy an item to fit into one of their price lines. Then they want to know the maximum amount they can pay for an item and still get their normal markup. For instance, assume that the selling price of an article is set at $60 (by competition or by the $59.95 price line). The retailer's normal markup is 35 percent. What is the most that the retailer should pay for this article? Again, let's fill in what we know in the diagram.

		Dollars	Percentage
	Selling price	60	100
less	Cost		
equals	Markup		35

The dollar markup is $21 (35 percent of $60). So, by a simple subtraction, we find that the maximum cost the merchant will want to pay is $39.

It should be clearly understood that markups are figured on the selling price at *each level of business* in a channel of distribution. A manufacturer applies a markup to determine its selling price. The manufacturer's selling price then becomes the wholesaler's cost. Then the wholesaler must determine its own selling price by applying its usual markup percentage based on its — the wholesaler's — selling price. The same procedure is carried on by the retailer, whose cost is the wholesaler's selling price. The following computations should illustrate this point:

Series of Markups

Producer's cost $ 7 ⎱
Producer's selling price $10 ⎰   Producer's markup = $3, or 30%

Wholesaler's cost $10 ⎱
Wholesaler's selling price $12 ⎰   Wholesaler's markup = $2, or 16⅔%

Retailer's cost $12 ⎱
Retailer's selling price $20 ⎰   Retailer's markup = $8, or 40%

If a firm is used to dealing in markups based on cost — and sometimes this is done among wholesalers — the same diagrammatic approach may be employed that was used above. The only change is that cost will equal 100 percent. Then the selling price will be 100 percent plus the markup based on cost. As an example, assume that a firm bought an article for $70 and wants a 20 percent markup based on cost. The markup in dollars is $14 (20 percent of $70). The selling price is $84 ($70 plus $14):

Markup Based on Cost

		Dollars	Percentage
	Selling price	84	120
less	Cost	70	100
equals	Markup	14	20

A marketing executive should understand the relationships between markups on cost and markups on selling price. For instance, if a product costs $6 and sells for $10, there is a $4 markup. This is a 40 percent markup based on selling price, but a 66⅔ percent markup based on cost. The following diagram may be helpful in understanding these relationships and in converting from one base to another.

$$
\begin{array}{lll}
\textit{If selling price } = 100\% & & \textit{If cost } = 100\% \\
\$10 = 100\% \left\{ \begin{array}{l} 60\%\rightarrow \\ 40\%\rightarrow \end{array} \right. & \begin{array}{l} \text{Cost } = \$6.00 \leftarrow 100\% \\ \text{Markup } = \$4.00 \leftarrow\ 66\frac{2}{3}\% \end{array} \left. \begin{array}{l} \\ \end{array} \right\} \$10 = 166\frac{2}{3}\%
\end{array}
$$

The relationships between the two bases are expressed in the following formulas:

$$
(1)\ \%\text{ markup on selling price } = \frac{\%\text{ markup on cost}}{100\% + \%\text{ markup on cost}}
$$

$$
(2)\ \%\text{ markup on cost } = \frac{\%\text{ markup on selling price}}{100\% - \%\text{ markup on selling price}}
$$

To illustrate the use of these formulas, let us assume that a retailer has a markup of 25 percent on *cost* and wants to know what the corresponding figure is, based on selling price. In formula 1 we get

$$
\frac{25\%}{100\% + 25\%} = \frac{25\%}{125\%} = .2,\text{ or } 20\%
$$

A markup of 33⅓ percent based on *selling price* converts to 50 percent based on cost, according to formula (2):

$$
\frac{33\frac{1}{3}\%}{100\% - 33\frac{1}{3}\%} = \frac{33\frac{1}{3}\%}{66\frac{2}{3}\%} = .5\text{ or } 50\%
$$

The markup is closely related to the gross margin. Recall that gross margin is equal to net sales minus cost of goods sold. Looking below the gross margin on an operating statement, we find that gross margin equals operating expenses plus net profit. Normally, the initial markup in a company, department, or product line must be set a little higher than the overall gross margin desired for the selling unit. The reason for this is that, ordinarily, some reductions will be incurred before all the articles are sold. For one reason or another, some items will not sell at the original price. They will have to be marked down, that is, reduced in price from the original level. Some pilferage and other shortages may also occur.

From a study of the operating statement, management can develop several ratios that are useful in evaluating the results of its marketing program. In most cases, net sales is used as the base (100 percent). In fact, unless it is specifically mentioned to the contrary, all ratios reflecting gross margin, net profit, or any operating expense are stated as a percentage of net sales.

ANALYTICAL RATIOS

This is the ratio of gross margin to net sales. In Table A-1, the gross margin percentage is $32,000 ÷ $80,000, or 40 percent.

Gross Margin Percentage

This ratio is computed by dividing net profit by net sales. In Table A-1, the ratio is $4,800 ÷ $80,000, or 6 percent. This percentage may be computed either before or after federal income taxes are deducted, but the result should be labelled to show which it is.

Net Profit Percentage

When total operating expenses are divided by net sales, the result is the operating expense ratio. In Table A-1, the ratio is $27,200 ÷ $80,000, or 34 percent. In similar fashion, we may determine the expense ratio for any given cost. Thus we note in Table A-1 that the rent expense was 1 percent, advertising was 3 percent, and sales-force salaries and commissions were 13.75 percent. Frequently, in its operating statement, a company will add a percentage column at the right. This column will start with net sales being 100 percent and will show, for each item on the statement, the percentage in relation to net sales.

Operating Expense Percentage

Management often measures the efficiency of its marketing operations by means of the **stockturn rate**. This figure represents the number of times the average inventory is "turned over," or sold, during the period under study. The rate is computed on either a cost or a selling-price basis. That is, both the numerator and the denominator of the ratio fraction must be expressed in the same terms, either cost or selling price.

On a *cost* basis, the formula for stockturn rate is as follows:

Rate of Stockturn

$$\text{Rate of stockturn} = \frac{\text{cost of goods sold}}{\text{average inventory at cost}}$$

The average inventory is determined by adding the beginning and ending inventories and dividing the result by 2. In Table A-1, the average inventory is ($18,000 + $20,000) ÷ 2 = $19,000. The stockturn rate then is $48,000 ÷ $19,000, or 2.5. Because inventories usually are abnormally low at the first of the year in anticipation of taking physical inventory, this average may not be representative. Consequently, some companies find their average inventory by adding the book inventories at the beginning of each month, and then dividing this sum by 12.

Now let's assume the inventory is recorded on a *selling price* basis, as is done in most large retail organizations. Then the stockturn rate equals net sales divided by average inventory at selling price. Sometimes the stockturn rate is computed by dividing the number of *units* sold by the average inventory expressed in *units*.

Wholesale and retail trade associations in many types of businesses publish figures showing the average rate of stockturn for their members. A firm with a low rate of stockturn is likely to be spending too much on storage and inventory. Also, the company runs a higher risk of obsolescence or spoilage. If the stockturn rate gets too high, this may indicate that the company maintains too low an average inventory. Often a firm in this situation is operating on a hand-to-mouth buying system. In addition to incurring high handling and billing costs, the company is liable to be out of stock on some items.

Markdown Percentage

Sometimes retailers are unable to sell articles at the originally stated prices, and they reduce these prices to move the goods. A **markdown** is a reduction from the original selling price. Management frequently finds it very helpful to determine the markdown percentage. Then they analyse the size and number of markdowns and the reasons for them. Retailers, particularly, make extensive use of markdown analysis.

Markdowns are expressed as a percentage of net sales and *not* as a percentage of the original selling price. To illustrate, assume that a retailer purchased a hat for $6 and marked it up 40 percent to sell for $10. The hat did not sell at that price, so it was marked down to $8. Now the seller may advertise a price cut of 20 percent. Yet, according to our rule, this $2 markdown is 25 percent *of the $8 selling price.*

Markdown percentage is computed by dividing total dollar markdowns by total net sales during a given period of time. Two important points should be noted here. The markdown percentage is computed in this fashion, whether the markdown items were sold or are still in the store. Also, the percentage is computed with respect to total net sales, and not only in connection with sales of marked-down articles. As an example, assume that a retailer buys 10 hats at $6 each and prices them to sell at $10. Five hats are sold at $10. The other 5 are marked down to $8, and 3 are sold at the lower price. Total sales are $74, and the total markdowns are $10. The retailer has a markdown ratio of $10 ÷ $74, or 13.5 percent.

Markdowns do not appear on the profit and loss statement because they occur *before* an article is sold. The first item on an operating statement is gross sales. That figure reflects the actual selling price, which may be the selling price after a markdown has been taken.

A refinement in the computation of the markdown percentage involves sales allowances. Actually, these allowances are added to markdowns in determining the markdown percentage. The formula is:

$$\text{Markdown \%} = \frac{\text{dollar markdown} + \text{dollar sales allowances}}{\text{total net sales in dollars}}$$

The reasoning here is that, in effect, an allowance is simply a markdown taken after the sale was made. In the hat example above, if the retailer saw that a hat was soiled, it would be marked down by $2. Assume that the retailer did not notice the defect and that the hat was sold for $10. The customer later saw that the hat was soiled and voiced dissatisfaction. The customer kept the hat but was given a $2 allowance. The result is the same in both cases. *Allowances* here should not be confused with *sales returns*, where the customer returns the article and is refunded the full purchase price.

A commonly used measure of managerial performance and the operating success of a company is its rate of return on investment. We use both the balance sheet and the operating statement as sources of information. The formula for calculating return on investment (ROI) is as follows:

Return on Investment

$$\text{ROI} = \frac{\text{net profit}}{\text{sales}} \times \frac{\text{sales}}{\text{investment}}$$

Two questions may quickly come to mind. First, what do we mean by "investment"? Second, why do we need two fractions? It would seem that the "sales" component in each fraction would cancel out, leaving net profit divided by investment as the meaningful ratio.

To answer the first query, consider a firm whose operating statement shows annual sales of $1,000,000 and a net profit of $50,000. At the end of the year, the balance sheet reports:

Assets	$600,000	Liabilities		$200,000
		Capital stock	$300,000	
		Retained earnings	100,000	400,000
	$600,000			$600,000

Now, is the investment $400,000 or $600,000? Certainly the ROI will depend upon which figure we use. The answer depends upon whether we are talking to the stockholders or to the company executives. The stockholders are more interested in the return on what they have invested—in this case, $400,000. The ROI calculation then is:

$$\text{ROI} = \frac{\text{net profit } \$50,000}{\text{sales } \$1,000,000} \times \frac{\text{sales } \$1,000,000}{\text{investment } \$400,000} = 12\frac{1}{2}\%$$

Management, on the other hand, is more concerned with the total investment, as represented by the total assets ($600,000). This is the amount that the executives must manage, regardless of whether the assets were acquired by stockholders' investment, retained earnings, or loans from outside sources.[1] Within this context the ROI computation becomes:

$$\text{ROI} = \frac{\text{net profit } \$50,000}{\text{sales } \$1,000,000} \times \frac{\text{sales } \$1,000,000}{\text{investment } \$600,000} = 8\tfrac{1}{3}\%$$

Regarding the second question, we use two fractions because we are dealing with two separate elements — the rate of profit on sales and the rate of capital turnover. Management really should determine each rate separately and then multiply the two. The rate of profit on sales is influenced by marketing considerations — sales volume, price, product mix, advertising effort. The capital turnover is a financial consideration not directly involved with costs or profits — only sales volume and assets managed.

To illustrate, assume that our company's profits doubled with the same sales volume and investment because management operated an excellent marketing program this year. In effect, we doubled our profit rate with the same capital turnover.

$$\text{ROI} = \frac{\text{net profit } \$100,000}{\text{sales } \$1,000,000} \times \frac{\text{sales } \$1,000,000}{\text{investment } \$600,000} = 16\tfrac{2}{3}\%$$

$$10\% \quad \times \quad 1.67 \quad = 16\tfrac{2}{3}\%$$

As expected, this $16\tfrac{2}{3}$ percent is twice the ROI calculated above.

Now assume that we earned our original profit of $50,000 but that we did it with an investment reduced to $500,000. We cut the size of our average inventory, and we closed some branch offices. By increasing our capital turnover from 1.67 to 2, we raise the ROI from $8\tfrac{1}{3}$ percent to 10 percent, even though sales volume and profits remain unchanged:

$$\text{ROI} = \frac{\$50,000}{\$1,000,000} \times \frac{\$1,000,000}{\$500,000} = 10\%$$

$$5\% \quad \times \quad 2 \quad = 10\%$$

Assume now that we increase our sales volume — let us say we double it — but do not increase our profit or investment. That is, the cost-profit squeeze is bringing us "profitless prosperity." The following interesting results occur:

---

[1] In fact, it has been suggested that the term "assets employed" or "assets managed" be used in the formula instead of "investment" when using the ROI concept as a measure of managerial performance in marketing. See Michael Schiff, "The Use of ROI in Sales Management," *Journal of Marketing*, July 1963, pp. 70–73; and J. S. Schiff and Michael Schiff, "New Sales Management Tool: ROAM (Return on Assets Managed)," *Harvard Business Review*, July–August 1967, pp. 59–66.

$$ROI = \frac{\$50,000}{\$2,000,000} \times \frac{\$2,000,000}{\$600,000} = 8\frac{1}{3}\%$$

$$2\frac{1}{2}\% \times 3.33 = 8\frac{1}{3}\%$$

The profit rate was cut in half, but this was offset by a doubling of the capital turnover rate, leaving the ROI unchanged.

QUESTIONS AND PROBLEMS

1. Construct an operating statement from the following data, and compute the gross-margin percentage:

Purchase at billed cost	$15,000
Net sales	30,000
Sales returns and allowances	200
Cash discounts given	300
Cash discounts earned	100
Rent	1,500
Salaries	6,000
Opening inventory at cost	10,000
Advertising	600
Other expenses	2,000
Closing inventory at cost	7,500

2. Prepare a retail operating statement from the following data and compute the markdown percentage:

Rent	$ 9,000
Closing inventory at cost	28,000
Sales returns	6,500
Gross margin as percentage of sales	35%
Cash discounts allowed	2,000
Salaries	34,000
Markdowns	4,000
Other operating expenses	15,000
Opening inventory at cost	35,000
Gross sales	232,500
Advertising	5,500
Freight in	3,500

3. What percentage markups on cost correspond to the following percentages of markup on selling price?
   a. 20 percent   c. 50 percent
   b. 37½ percent   d. 66⅔ percent

4. What percentage markups on selling price correspond to the following percentages of markup on cost?
   a. 20 percent   c. 50 percent
   b. 33⅓ percent   d. 300 percent

5. A hardware store bought a gross (12 dozen) of hammers, paying $302.40 for the lot. The retailer estimated operating expenses for this product to be 35 percent of sales, and wanted a net profit of 5 percent of sales. The retailer expected no markdowns. What retail selling price should be set for each hammer?

6. Competition in a certain line of sporting goods pretty well limits the selling price on a certain item to $25. If the store owner feels a markup of 35 percent is needed to cover expenses and return a reasonable profit, what is the most the owner can pay for this item?

7. A retailer with annual net sales of $2 million maintains a markup of 66⅔ percent based on cost. Expenses average 35 percent. What are the retailer's gross margin and net profit in dollars?

8. A company has a stockturn rate of five times a year, a sales volume of $600,000, and a gross margin of 25 percent. What is the average inventory at cost?

9. A store has an average inventory of $30,000 at retail and a stockturn rate of five times a year. If the company maintains a markup of 50 percent based on cost, what are the annual sales volume and the cost of goods sold?

10. From the following data, compute the gross-margin percentage and the operating expense ratio:
Stockturn = 9
Average inventory at selling price = $45,000
Net profit = $20,000
Cost of goods sold = $350,000

11. A ski shop sold 50 pairs of skis at $90 a pair, after taking a 10 percent markdown. All the skis were originally purchased at the same price and had been marked up 60 percent on cost. What was the gross margin on the 50 pairs of skis?

12. A men's clothing store bought 200 suits at $90 each. The suits were marked up 40 percent. Eighty were sold at that price. The remaining suits were each marked down 20 percent from the original selling price, and then they were sold. Compute the sales volume and the markdown percentage.

13. An appliance retailer sold 60 radios at $30 each after taking markdowns equal to 20 percent of the actual selling price. Originally all the radios had been purchased at the same price and were marked up 50 percent on cost. What was the gross-margin percentage earned in this situation?

14. An appliance manufacturer produced a line of small appliances advertised to sell at $30. The manufacturer planned for wholesalers to receive a 20 percent markup, and retailers a 33⅓ percent markup. Total manufacturing costs were $12 per unit. What did retailers pay for the product? What were the manufacturer's selling price and percentage markup?

15. A housewares manufacturer produces an article at a full cost of $1.80. It is sold through a manufacturers' agent directly to large retailers. The agent receives a 20 percent commission on sales, the retailers earn a margin of 30 percent, and the manufacturer plans a net profit of 10 percent on the selling price. What is the retail price of this article?

16. A manufacturer suggests a retail selling price of $400 on an item and grants a chain discount of 40-10-10. What is the manufacturer's selling price? (Chain discounts are discussed in Chapter 13.)

17. A building materials manufacturer sold a quantity of a product to a wholesaler for $350, and the wholesaler in turn sold to a lumberyard. The wholesaler's normal markup was 15 percent, and the retailer usually priced the item to include a 30 percent markup. What is the selling price to consumers?

18. From the following data, calculate the return on investment, based on a definition of "investment" that is useful for evaluating managerial performance:

Net sales	$800,000	Markup	35%
Gross margin	$280,000	Average inventory	$75,000
Total assets	$200,000	Retained earnings	$60,000
Cost of goods sold	$520,000	Operating expenses	$240,000
Liabilities	$ 40,000		

Careers in Marketing

Jobs leading to careers in marketing—what are they, where are they, and how do you get one? That's what this appendix is all about. For the past few months, your main concern probably has been to learn enough about marketing to get a good grade in the course. As you studied the various marketing activities, however, at one point or another you might have thought, "I'd like a job like that." Or, as you read about various organizations (manufacturers, retailers, service firms, etc.), you might have said, "I think I'd like to work for an outfit like that." Now perhaps you can devote more attention to the career opportunities that exist in the broad field of marketing.

CHOOSING A CAREER

One of the most significant decisions you will ever make is your choice of a career. Your career decision will have an important influence on your future happiness, self-fulfilment, and well-being. Yet, unfortunately, career decisions often seem to be based on insufficient information, analysis, and evaluation of alternatives.

One key to a wise career decision is to get as much information about as wide a variety of career alternatives as is reasonably possible. By broadening your search, you may discover some interesting fields that you knew nothing about or that you had gross misconceptions about.

At this point, let's look briefly at three key areas that you should analyse in some detail in the course of career selection.

What Do You Want from a Career?

Perhaps this question would be better worded if we asked, "What do you want out of life?" or " What is important to you in life?" To answer these broad questions, you first must answer several more limited ones. For example, are you looking for a career with high financial rewards? How important is the social prestige of the career? Do you want your job and career to be the main thing in your life? Or do you see a career only as the means of financing leisure-time activities? How important are the climate and other aspects of the physical environment in which you live? That is, would you take less money and a less prestigious job in order to live in a pleasant environment? Would you prefer to work for a large company or a small organization? Would you prefer living and working in a small town or in a major urban centre?

Another way to approach the key questions in this section is to identify —in writing—your goals in life. Identify both your short-term goals (three to five years from now) and your long-term goals (ten years or more).

Still another approach is to state your self-concept in some detail. By describing yourself as you see yourself, you may be able to identify various careers that would (or would not) fit your self-image.

What Do You Have to Offer?

Here you have to identify in some detail your strong and weak points. Why would anyone want to hire you? What are your qualifications? What experience — work, education, extracurricular activities — do you have that might be attractive to prospective employers?

A key point to recognize is whether you are more interested in people or in things. In the field of marketing, for example, a people-oriented person might be attracted to a career in personal selling and sales management. A things-oriented person might prefer a job in advertising, marketing research, or physical distribution.

Career Factors to Consider

There are several major factors that you should consider when evaluating a job or career in any given field. To some extent, these issues reflect the first two general topics already discussed in this section.

Will You Be Happy in Your Work?

This is a key factor to consider when evaluating any career. Remember — normally, half or more of your waking hours will be spent at work, commuting to and from work, or doing job-related work at home. So you should look for the job and career that you will enjoy during that big chunk of your waking time.

Also keep in mind that many (and maybe most) of the people in our society do not seem to be happy with their jobs. We speak of "Blue Monday" (the wonderful weekend is finished and I have to go back to work). The saying TGIF (Thank God It's Friday) did not enter our vocabulary because people loved their work.

Does the Career Fit Your Self-Image?

Are the job and career in line with your goals, dreams, and aspirations? Will they satisfy you? Will you be proud to tell people about your job? Will your spouse (and someday your teenage children) be proud of you in that career?

What Demands (Pressures) Are Associated with the Career?

Some people thrive on pressure. They constantly seek new challenges in their work. Other people look for a more tranquil work experience. They do not want a job with constant demands, deadlines to meet, and heavy pressures.

Financial Considerations

How does the starting salary compare with those of other jobs? Consider what the job is likely to pay after you have been there three to five years. Some engineering jobs, for example, have high starting salaries, but you soon hit a salary ceiling. In contrast, some marketing jobs have lower starting salaries, but no upper limits.

Opportunities for Promotion

You should evaluate the promotional patterns in a job or in a firm. Try to find out how long it normally takes to reach a given executive level. Study the backgrounds of the presidents in a number of large companies. Did they come up through engineering, the legal department, sales or marketing, accounting, or some other area?

Travel Considerations

Some jobs involve a considerable amount of travel whether you are an entry-level worker or an executive. Other jobs are strictly in-house, with no travel at all.

Job or Career "Transportability"

Are there similar jobs in many other geographic areas? If you and your spouse both are career-oriented, what will happen, say, to you if your spouse is transferred to another city? Can you also move to that new city and get a job similar to your present job? One nice thing about such careers as teaching, retailing, nursing, and personal selling is that generally these jobs exist in considerable numbers in many different locations.

Qualifications Needed

Determine what qualifications are needed to enter (and later to prosper in) a given field. Then review your own background to see whether there is a close fit between the job requirements and your qualifications.

Supply and Demand Situation

Determine generally how many job openings currently exist in a given field, as compared with the supply of qualified applicants. At the same time, study the future prospects regarding this supply and demand condition. Determine whether a present shortage of workers, or overcrowding in a field, is a temporary situation, or whether it is likely to exist for several years.

WHAT ARE THE JOBS?

Back in the first chapter, we noted that about one-quarter to one-third of all civilian jobs are in the field of marketing. These jobs cover a wide range of activities. Furthermore, this variety of jobs also covers a wide range of qualifications and aptitudes. Jobs in personal selling, for example, call for a set of qualifications that are different from those in marketing research. A person likely to be successful in advertising may not be a good prospect in physical distribution. Consequently, the personal qualifications and aptitudes of different individuals make them candidates for different types of marketing jobs.

In this section we shall briefly describe the major jobs in marketing, grouping them by the title of the job or the activity.

Personal Selling

By far, sales jobs are the most numerous of all the jobs in marketing. Personal selling jobs (1) cover a wide variety of activities, (2) are found in a wide variety of organizations, and (3) carry a wide variety of titles.

You can get some idea of the wide variety of sales jobs by reviewing the seven-part classification of sales jobs back in Chapter 19. Consider the following people: a driver-salesperson for Coca-Cola; a sales clerk in a department store; a sales engineer providing technical assistance in the sales of hydraulic valves; a representative for Canadair selling a fleet of airplanes; a marketing consultant selling his or her services. All these people are engaged in personal selling, but each sales job is different from the others.

Sales jobs of one sort or another are available in virtually every locality. This means you can pretty well pick the area where you would like to live, and still get involved in personal selling.

There are opportunities to earn a *very* high income in personal selling. This is especially true when the compensation plan is straight commission, or is a combination of salary plus a significant incentive element.

A sales job is the most common entry-level position in marketing. Furthermore, a sales job is a widely used stepping-stone to a management position. Many companies recruit people for sales jobs with the intention of promoting some or all of these people into management positions. Personal selling and sales management jobs are also a good route to the top in a firm. This is so because it is relatively easy to measure a person's performance and productivity in selling. Sales results are highly visible.

A sales job is different from other jobs in several significant ways.[1] (1) Salespeople represent their company to customers and to the public in general. The public ordinarily does not judge a firm by its factory or office personnel. (2) Outside salespeople (those who go to the customers, in contrast to those in situations where the customers come to the seller) operate with very little or no direct personal supervision and stimulation. These jobs frequently require a considerable amount of creativity, persistence,

---

[1] Adapted from William J. Stanton and Richard H. Buskirk, *Management of the Sales Force*, 6th ed., Richard D. Irwin, Inc. Homewood, Ill., 1983, pp. 15–17.

and self-motivation. (3) Because of the customer contacts, sales jobs require more tact and social intelligence than do other jobs on the same level in an organization. (4) Salespeople are authorized to spend company money in connection with their travel, entertainment, and other business expenses. (5) Sales jobs frequently involve traveling and require much time away from home and family. (6) Unfortunately, personal selling jobs generally rate low in social status and prestige.

All in all, selling is hard work, but the potential rewards are immense. Certainly no other job contributes as much to the success of an organization. Remember — nothing happens until somebody sells something!

Advertising

As in personal selling, so also in advertising are there many different types of jobs in a wide variety of organizations. However, not nearly so many people are employed in advertising as in personal selling.

Advertising jobs are available in three broad types of organizations. First there are jobs with the *advertisers*. Many of these organizations — manufacturers, retailers, marketers of services — prepare and place their own ads. In some cases, the advertising department is a big operation in these firms. Then there are careers with the various *media* (newspapers, TV stations, magazines, etc.) that carry the ads. And, finally, there are the many jobs with *advertising agencies*, which specialize in creating and producing individual ads and entire campaigns.

Jobs in advertising encompass a variety of aptitudes and interests — artistic, creative, managerial, research, and sales, for example. There is a real opportunity for the artistic or creative type of person. Agencies and advertising departments need copywriters, artists, photographers, layout designers, printing experts, and others to create and produce the ads.

A key position in advertising agencies is that of the account executive. People in this position are the liaison between the agency and its clients (the advertisers). Account executives coordinate the agency's efforts with the clients' marketing programs.

Another group of advertising jobs involves buying and selling the media time and space. Advertisers and agencies also often need people who can conduct consumer behaviour studies and other types of marketing research.

Sales Promotion

The main function of sales promotion is to tie together the activities in personal selling and advertising. Effective sales promotion requires imagination and creativity, coupled with a sound foundation in marketing fundamentals.

One group of sales promotion activities involves retailer in-store and window displays — planning, designing, and creating them. Another area of sales promotion jobs involves direct-mail advertising programs. Still another area deals with trade shows and other company exhibits. Sales promotion activities also include the developing and managing of premium giveaways, contests, sales meetings, product sampling, and other types of promotion.

Marketing Research

Marketing research jobs cover the broad range of activities outlined in Table 3-3 in Chapter 3. People are hired for marketing research jobs by manufacturers, retailers, service marketers, government agencies, and other types of organizations. There also is a large number of specialized marketing research companies. Generally, however, there are fewer jobs in marketing research than in personal selling or in advertising.

Marketing research people are problem solvers. They collect and analyse masses of information. Consequently, they need an aptitude for methodical, analytical types of work. Typically, some quantitative skills are needed. It helps if you understand statistics and feel comfortable using a computer.

Purchasing

The opposite of selling is buying, and here there are a lot of good jobs. Every retail organization needs people to buy the merchandise that is to be sold. Frequently the route to the top in retailing is through the buying (also called merchandising) division of the business. Large retailers have many positions for buyers and assistant buyers. Typically, each merchandise department has a buyer. Consequently, you have a chance to work with the particular products that interest you.

There also are centralized buying offices that buy for several different stores. These resident buying offices typically are in a few large cities.

The purchasing agent is the industrial-market counterpart of the retail-store buyer. Virtually all firms in the industrial market have purchasing departments. People in these departments buy for the production, office, and sales departments in their firms.

Retail buyers and industrial purchasing agents need many of the same skills. They must be able to analyse markets, determine merchandise needs, and negotiate with sellers. It also helps if you have some knowledge of credit, finance, and physical distribution.

Product/Brand Management

In Chapter 8, we briefly discussed the position of product manager in connection with the organizational structure for new-product planning and development. Product managers (sometimes called brand managers) are responsible for planning and directing the entire marketing program for a given product or a group of products.

Early on, product managers are concerned with the packaging, labelling, and other aspects of the product itself. Product managers also are responsible for doing the necessary marketing research to identify the market. They plan the advertising, personal selling, and sales-promotional programs for their products. Product managers also are concerned with the pricing, physical distribution, and legal aspects of the product. All in all, being a product manager is almost like running your own business.

Typically, the job of product manager is a staff position in the organization, rather than a line operating position. Thus, the product manager often has much responsibility for a product's performance. But this person does not have commensurate authority to see that his or her directives and plans are put into effect.

Physical Distribution

A large number of jobs exist in this field, and the prospects are even brighter as we look ahead in the 1980s. More and more firms are expected to adopt the systems approach in physical distribution, to control the huge expenses involved in materials movement and warehousing.

Manufacturers, retailers, and all other product-handling firms have jobs that involve two stages of physicai distribution. First, the product must be moved to the firm for processing or resale. Then the finished products must be distributed to the markets. These physical distribution tasks involve jobs in transportation management, warehousing, and inventory control.

In addition, the many transportation carriers and warehousing firms also provide a variety of jobs that may interest you.

Public Relations

The public relations department in an organization is the connecting link between that organization and its various publics. The department especially must deal with, or go through, the news media to reach these publics. Public relations people must be especially good in communications. In fact, frequently these people have educational backgrounds in communications or journalism, rather than in marketing.

In essence, the job of public relations is to project the desired company image to the public. More specifically, public relations people are responsible for telling the public about the company — its products, community activities, social programs, environmental improvement activities, labour policies, views regarding controversial issues, and so on. The company's position must be stated in a clear, understandable, and above all, believable fashion.

Consumer Affairs and Protection

This broad area encompasses several activities that provide job and career opportunities. Many of these jobs are an outgrowth of the consumer movement discussed in Chapter 25. Many companies, for example, have a consumer affairs department to handle consumer complaints. Several federal and provincial agencies are set up to keep watch on business firms and to provide information and assistance to consumers. Grocery products manufacturers and gas and electric companies regularly hire home economists to aid consumers in product use. Government and private product-testing agencies hire people to test products for safety, durability, and other features.

Other Career Areas

In this brief appendix, it is not possible to list all the careers stemming from marketing. We have, however, covered the major activity areas. You may get additional career ideas from the next section, which deals with the organizations that provide these career opportunities.

WHERE ARE THE JOBS?

In this section, we briefly describe the various companies, institutions, and other organizations that provide jobs in marketing. This section also includes comments on jobs in international marketing and a comparison of job opportunities in large versus small organizations.

Types of Organizations

Literally thousands of organizations provide jobs and career opportunities in marketing. The organizations can be grouped into these categories:

Manufacturing

Most manufacturing firms provide career opportunities in all the activities discussed in the previous section. In their promotional mix, some manufacturers stress personal selling, while others rely more on advertising. Even small companies offer job opportunties in most of the categories we've covered previously.

Large manufacturers typically have good training programs, and many of them come to college and university campuses as part of their job recruiting programs. Starting salaries typically are higher in manufacturing firms than in retailing and the other organizations described below.

Retailing

Retailing firms provide by far more marketing jobs than any other organizational category. Yet careers in retailing typically are not well understood by college students. These students tend to equate retailing with clerking in a department store or filling shelves in a supermarket. Students often perceive that retail pay is low and that retail work hours include a lot of evenings and weekends.

Actually, a career in retailing offers many attractive features. There are opportunities for very fast advancement for those who display real ability. Two factors account for these opportunities: (1) There simply is a shortage of qualified people in retailing; and (2) performance results, such as sales and profits, are quickly and highly visible. So, if you can produce, management will generally note this fact in a hurry.

While the starting pay in many stores is lower than in manufacturing, the compensation in higher-level retailing jobs typically is very good. There are good retailing jobs in virtually every geographic location. Yet, once you are in a job, there is very little travel involved. And, generally speaking, retailing offers you a better opportunity than any other field to go into business for yourself.

Perhaps the main attractions in retailing are less tangible. Retailing can be an exciting field. You constantly are involved with people — customers, suppliers, and other workers. And there are challenges as a merchandise buyer, especially that of finding out what will sell well — what the customers really want.

Of course, retailing is not all fun and games. The hours can be long, and the work is hard. Retailers often can get so involved with their store and their career that they have little time for anything else. Also, the store mortality rate in retailing is high. Competition is fierce, and many stores do not have the financial backing or the managerial abilities needed to survive.

It is easier to get a job or to start a career in retailing than in many other fields. In large stores, there are jobs involving personnel management, accounting controls, and store operations (receiving, credit, and customer service departments). However, the life blood of retailing is the buying and selling of merchandise or services. Consequently, the more numerous and better-paying positions are those of buyer and above in the merchandising end of the business. For many people, the goal is to be a store manager.

Wholesaling

Career opportunities in wholesaling generally are less well understood and appreciated than those in retailing or manufacturing. Wholesaling firms typically do not recruit on campuses, and they generally have a low profile with students.

Yet the opportunities are there. Merchant wholesalers of consumer products and industrial distributors both provide many jobs in buying, personal selling, marketing research, and physical distribution. Manufacturers' agents, brokers, and the other agent middlemen discussed in Chapter 15 also offer jobs and careers. Wholesaling middlemen are increasing in numbers and in sales volume, and their future is promising.

Service Marketing

The broad array of service industries listed in Chapter 21 provides a bonanza of job and career opportuntities in marketing. Many of these firms really are retailers of services. Consequently, all the statements we made earlier about retailing careers are relevant here.

Nonbusiness Organizations

As indicated in Chapter 22, nonbusiness organizations are just beginning to realize that marketing is the key to success. Consequently, it is likely that jobs and careers in many nonbusiness organizations will open up in really large numbers over the next several years. And recall the wide variety of nonbusiness organizations — hospitals, museums, schools, religious organizations, foundations, charities, political parties, and all the others. Truly, these are new opportunities for marketing careers that were nonexistent up to just a few years ago.

Government

Many federal and provincial government organizations hire people for marketing positions. Here we include the major cabinet departments — agriculture, supply and services, health and welfare, trade, energy, and the others. We also include all the regulatory agencies. Government organizations employ people in buying, marketing research, public relations, physical distribution, consumer affairs and protection, and even advertising and sales promotion. Sometimes students tend to overlook the many marketing career opportunities with the government.

Careers in International Marketing

Some students like to travel, and they want to work at least part of the time in foreign countries. They may be interested in careers in international marketing, and they may even major in international business in college. Typically, however, companies do not hire college graduates and assign them to jobs in international marketing. Normally, people are hired for entry-level positions in the domestic divisions of a company's operations. Then, after some years of experience with the firm, an employee may have an opportunity to move into the firm's international divisions.

Usually the only students hired for entry-level positions in international marketing are (1) MBAs from schools with big international programs or (2) foreign students who are hired by Canadian firms to work in the student's home country.

Large versus Small Companies

Should you go to work for a large company or a small firm? Or should you go into business for yourself upon graduation? For over a decade now, more and more students have been saying that they want to work for a small company. They feel there is more freedom of action, more rapid advancement, and less restraint on their life-styles in the smaller firms.

Perhaps so, and certainly no one should discourage you from a career in small business. *But* the authors of this book typically recommend to students (who ask for advice) that they start their careers in a big company. Then, after some years, they can move into a smaller firm. There are three reasons for this recommendation.

1. A large firm is more likely to have a good training program in your chosen field of activity. Most students have little or no practical marketing experience. Consequently, the very fine training programs provided by most large manufacturers, retailers, and major service marketers are critically important to your career.
2. You can learn something about how a big company operates. After all, when you go into a smaller firm, the large companies will be your competitors. So, the more you know about them, the better able you will be to compete with them.
3. After working a while for a big company, you may change your mind and decide to stay with the larger firm after all. On the other hand, let's say that you want to go to a small company after you have worked a few years in a big firm. At that time it will be relatively easy to move from a large company to a smaller one. If you start in a small firm, however, and later want to move into big business, it is not so easy to make such a move.

We have discussed (albeit briefly) the various career fields and the major types of organizations that hire people in these fields. Now let's take a brief look at how you might go about getting a job with one of these organizations.

This entire book and your entire course have been designed to teach you the fundamentals involved in developing and managing a marketing program. These fundamentals are applicable regardless of whether you are marketing a product, service, person, idea, or place. They are equally applicable (1) to large and small organizations, (2) to domestic and international marketing, and (3) to business and nonbusiness organizations.

HOW TO GET A JOB

Now let's see whether we can apply these fundamentals to a program designed to market *YOU*. In other words, we shall now discuss a marketing approach that you can use to get a job and to get started on a career. Here, we are talking about a *marketing* career. This same approach, however, can be used in seeking jobs and careers in any field.

The first step in building a marketing program is to identify and analyse the market. In this case, the market is your future employer. Right now, you don't know exactly who that target market is. So you must research several possible markets, and then eventually narrow down your choice. In effect, we are talking about "choosing a career." Much of what we discussed in the first section of this appendix is applicable here.

Identify and Analyse the Market

The first thing you should do is get as much information as you can regarding various career opportunities in marketing. For information sources, you might start with one or two professors whom you know reasonably well. Then try the placement office in your school, or wherever the jobs are listed. Many companies prepare recruiting brochures for students, explaining the company and its career opportunities.

Newspapers and business journals are another good information source. *The Financial Post* and the business sections of large-city newspapers can be useful. Journals such as *Canadian Business, Stimulus*, and the trade publications in many individual industries are helpful. Sometimes, looking carefully through *Moody's Manual of Investments*, Standard and Poor's *Register*, or even a series of company annual reports can give you ideas of firms you might like to work for. You should exchange information with other students who also are in the job market.

In summary, learn all you can about various firms and industries. Then, from this information search, zero in on the few companies that are your leading choices. You will then be ready to develop the marketing mix that will be effective in marketing yourself to your target markets.

In this case, the "product" you are planning and developing is yourself and your services. You want to make yourself as attractive as possible to your market — that is, prospective employers.

The Product

Start your product planning by listing in some detail your strong and weak points. These will lead into another list — your qualifications and achievements. This self-analysis is something we discussed in the first section of this chapter in connection with choosing a career.

When you are considering your qualifications, it may help to group them into broad categories such as these:

- Education — schools attended, degree earned, grade average, major subjects
- Work experience — part-time and full-time
- Honours and awards
- Extracurricular activities
- Hobbies
- Organizations — membership, offices, committees

Later we will discuss the presentation of your qualifications in a personal résumé (data sheet).

An important aspect of product planning is product differentiation. How can you differentiate yourself from all the other college grads? What did you do that was different, unusual, or exceptional?

Another part of product planning is packaging. When you go for an interview, be sure that the external package looks attractive. People do judge you by your appearance, just as you judge products by the way they look. This means paying attention to what you wear. Are your shoes shined and your fingernails clean? Is your hair well groomed? A good impression starts with prospective employers' first look at you — their first meeting with you.

The Price

"What salary do you want?" "How much do you think we should pay you?" These are a couple of questions a prospective employer may ask you in a job interview. These questions may throw you if you have not done some thinking in advance regarding the price you want for your services.

As part of your marketing program, find out what the market price is for people entering your field. Talk with placement officers, career counsellors, professors, and other students who are in the job market. From these sources, you should get a pretty good idea of starting salaries in entry-level positions. Use this information to decide on at least a range of salaries for yourself, *before* the interview.

Distribution Channel

There are only a few major channels you are likely to use in marketing yourself to prospective employers. The simplest channel is your placement office, assuming there is one on your campus. Most colleges and universities, through their placement offices, play host to companies that send job recruiters to do on-campus interviewing.

Another channel is help-wanted ads in business journals, trade journals, newspapers, and other sources. Perhaps the most difficult, but often the most rewarding, channel is going directly to firms in which you are especially interested. That is, knock on doors or write letters seeking a job interview. Many employers look favourably on people who display this kind of initiative in their job search.

Other than planning and developing an excellent product, the most important ingredient in your marketing mix is a good promotion (or communication) program. Your promotional mix will consist primarily of written communications (a form of advertising) and interviewing (a form of personal selling).

Frequently, your first contact with a prospective employer is a cover letter in which you state briefly why you are writing to that company and what you have to offer. You enclose a personal résumé, and you request an appointment for an interview.

Promotion/ Communication

Cover Letter

In the opening paragraph of your cover letter, you should indicate why you want to work for the firm. Mention a couple of key points regarding the firm—points that you learned from your research. In the second paragraph, you can present a few highlights of your own experience or personality that make you an attractive prospect. In the third paragraph, state that you are enclosing your résumé, and request an appointment for an interview, even suggesting some times or dates.

Résumé

A résumé (also called a personal data sheet) is really a brief history of yourself. You can start with some biographical information such as your name, address, phone number, age, marital status, and physical condition. Then divide the résumé into sections, including education, work experience, and activities that were listed above in the product section.

The final section of your résumé should be your references. List your references by name, also giving their titles and addresses. Make it as easy as possible for the prospective employer to check your references.

It is difficult to overstate the value of a good cover letter and a distinctive résumé. They are critically important elements in your job search. They certainly are two of the most important ads you will ever write.

Interview

Rarely is anyone hired without one or more interviews. In some cases, as when job recruiters come to your campus, the interview is your initial contact with the firm. In other situations, the interviews come as a result of your letter of introduction and your résumé.

The interview is an experience in personal selling—in this case, you are selling yourself. People are often uncomfortable and uptight in interviews, especially their first few interviews. As a result, one good idea is to start by interviewing with companies that you are not especially interested in working for. In effect, these are practice interviews, so if you "blow" one, there is no great loss. These practice interviews also will help you later in handling the tough questions that sometimes are asked. These are questions such as "Why should we hire you?" "Why do you think you are good enough to work for us?" "What kind of a job do you expect to have in five years?"

Your conduct in an interview often determines whether or not you get the job. So be on your toes — be honest in your answers, and try to look relaxed and confident (even though you may not feel that way). Make sure your clothing, grooming, and general appearance are very much in line with the environment of the particular employer.

After the interviews with the company have been completed, write a letter to the interviewers. Thank them for the opportunity to meet them, and state that you hope you will hear from them soon regarding the job.

CONCLUSION — A PERSONAL NOTE

As we said at the beginning of this appendix, choosing a career is one of the most important decisions you will ever make in your life. Certainly, looking for a job upon graduation can be a very exciting experience and yet at times a difficult and worrisome one. We hope that this brief appendix has furnished some ideas that will be helpful in your job search and career decision-making process. But most of all, we hope that you can find a career in which you will be happy.

William J. Stanton
Montrose S. Sommers
James G. Barnes

Glossary

accessory equipment In the industrial market, capital goods used in the operation of an industrial firm. Accessory equipment is shorter-lived than installations and does not materially affect the scale of operations in a company.

administered vertical marketing system A distribution system in which channel control is maintained through the economic power of one firm in the channel.

adoption curve The distribution curve showing when various groups adopt an innovation.

adoption process The stages an individual goes through in deciding whether or not to accept an innovation.

advertisement The nonpersonal message in advertising that is disseminated through media and is paid for by the identified sponsor.

advertising The activities involved in presenting a paid, sponsor-identified, nonpersonal message about an organization and/or its products, services, or ideas.

advertising agency An independent company set up to provide specialized advertising services to advertisers and the advertising media.

advertising appropriation The amount of money allocated for an organization's advertising program for a specific period of time.

advertising media The vehicles (newspapers, radio, television, etc.) that carry the advertising message (the advertisement) to the intended market.

agent middleman An independent business that does not take title to goods but actively assists in the transfer of title.

agents and brokers A broad category of wholesaling middlemen who do not take title to products. The category includes manufacturers' agents, selling agents, commission merchants, auctioneers, brokers, and others.

agribusiness The business side of farming. Usually involves large, highly mechanized farming operations.

AIDA The sales presentation stage of the personal selling process. Consists of steps to attract *A*ttention, hold *I*nterest, arouse *D*esire, and generate buyer *A*ction by meeting the buyer's objections and closing the sale.

annual marketing plan A master plan covering a year's marketing operations. It is one part — one time segment — of the ongoing strategic marketing planning process.

area sample A statistical sample selected at random from a list of geographic areas.

attitude A person's enduring cognitive evaluation, feeling, or action tendency toward some object, idea, or person.

auction company An independent agent wholesaling middleman that (1) provides the physical facilities for displaying products to be sold and (2) does the selling in an auction.

automatic vending The nonstore, nonpersonal selling and delivery of products through coin-operated vending machines.

balance of trade In international business, the difference between the value of a nation's imports and its exports. If exports exceed imports, the country has a favourable balance of trade. When imports exceed exports, there is an unfavourable trade balance.

base price The price of one unit of a product at its point of production or resale. Also called *list price*.

battle of the brands Market competition between manufacturers' brands and middlemen's (store) brands. In recent years, "no-brand" (generic) brands have entered this competitive struggle.

behaviourism An application of the stimulus-response theory of learning. If the same stimulus is constantly repeated, it will strengthen the response pattern.

benefit segmentation A basis for segmenting a market. A total market is divided into segments based on the customers' perceptions of the various benefits provided by a product.

blanket branding A strategy used for branding a group of products. Also called *family branding*.

box store A low-cost, low-price, low-service no-frills supermarket. Offers a limited assortment of staple food products displayed in their original packing boxes. Also called a *warehouse store*.

brand A name, term, symbol, special design, or some combination of these elements that identifies the product or service of one seller.

brand manager A product manager responsible for one or more brands.

brand mark The part of a brand that appears in the form of a symbol, picture, design, or distinctive colour.

brand name The part of a brand that can be vocalized — words, letters, and/or numbers.

breadth of product mix The number of product lines offered for sale by a firm.

break bulk To divide a large quantity of a product into smaller units for resale to the next customer in the distribution channel. This is usually done by middlemen.

break-even point The level of ouput at which revenues equal costs.

broker An independent agent wholesaling middleman whose main function is to bring buyer and seller together and to furnish market information.

business portfolio analysis An evaluation to determine the present status and future roles of a company's strategic business units (SBUs).

buy classes Three typical buying situations in the industrial market — namely, new task, modified rebuy, and straight rebuy.

buyer's market A situation in which the supply of a product or service greatly exceeds the demand for it.

buying decision-making process The steps a buyer goes through in the course of deciding whether to purchase a given item.

campaign In promotion or advertising, a coordinated series of promotional efforts built around a theme and designed to reach some goal.

Canadian Radio-Television and Telecommunications Commission (CRTC) A federal regulatory agency that controls the content of radio and television broadcasts, issues licences to radio, television, and cable TV stations, and regulates broadcast advertising.

canned sales talk A form of sales presentation consisting of a company-provided speech that a sales representative is supposed to deliver verbatim during a sales call.

carload rate (c.l.) The freight rate for shipping a carload of a given product.

cartel A group of companies that have banded together to regulate competition in the production and marketing of a given product.

cash discount A deduction from list price for paying a bill within a specified period of time.

catalogue showroom A retail store that displays the merchandise in a showroom, takes orders out of a catalogue, and fills these orders from inventories stored on the premises.

chain store One in a group of retail stores that carry the same type of merchandise. Corporate chain stores are centrally owned and managed. Voluntary chains are an association of independently owned stores.

channel captain The firm (producer or middleman) that controls a given distribution channel.

channel conflicts Friction in a channel of distribution occurring because the channel members are independent, profit-seeking organizations often operating with conflicting goals. Conflict may occur among middlemen on the same level of distribution (horizontal conflict), or among firms on different levels (vertical conflict).

channel of distribution The route that a product, and/or the title to the product, takes as it moves to its market. A channel includes the producer, the consumer or industrial user, and any middlemen involved in this route.

closing In personal selling, the stage in the selling process when the salesperson gets the buyer to agree to make the purchase.

cognitive dissonance Postpurchase anxiety often experienced by buyers.

cognitive theory of learning A refinement of the stimulus-response theory of learning: Learning is not a mechanistic process but is influenced by mental (thought) processes.

Combines Investigation Act A major piece of federal legislation that prohibits false advertising, misleading sales practices, and other activities that may be in restraint of trade.

COMECON An economic union comprising the U.S.S.R. and other Eastern European communist nations.

commission merchant An independent agent wholesaling middleman used primarily in the marketing of agricultural products. This middleman physically handles the seller's products in central markets and has authority regarding prices and terms of sale.

commission plan A method of compensating a sales force whereby a salesperson is paid for a unit of accomplishment (measured as sales volume, gross margin, or a nonselling activity). It provides much incentive for a sales rep, but little security or stability of income.

communication process A system by which an information source (sender) transmits a message to a receiver.

community shopping centre A shopping *centre* that is larger than a neighbourhood centre but smaller than a regional centre. Usually includes one or two department stores or discount stores, along with a number of shopping-goods stores and specialty stores.

company planning Setting broad company goals and then deciding on company strategies to reach these goals. See *strategic planning.*

concentration In distribution, an activity of middlemen in which the outputs of various producers are brought together. These outputs then are equalized with the market demand and later dispersed to markets.

concept testing The first three stages in the new-product development process — pretesting of the product idea, in contrast to later pretesting of the product itself and the market.

consumer goods Products intended for use by ultimate, household consumers for personal, nonbusiness purposes.

Consumer Packaging and Labelling Act (1974) A federal law requiring that manufacturers place certain information on the packages and labels of consumer products.

consumerism A protest by consumers against perceived injustices in marketing, and the efforts to remedy these injustices.

containerization A cargo-handling system in physical distribution that involves enclosing a shipment in some form of container. The container is sealed after loading and is not opened until it reaches its destination.

contractual vertical marketing system A distribution system in which control is exercised through contracts signed by the producer and/or middlemen members of the channel.

contribution-margin approach In marketing cost analysis, an accounting approach in which only direct expenses are allocated to the marketing units being studied. A unit's gross margin minus its direct costs equals that unit's contribution to covering the company's indirect expenses (overhead).

convenience goods A class of consumer products that people buy frequently and with the least possible time and effort.

convenience store A type of retail outlet that stresses its accessible location, long shopping hours, and the quickness and ease of shopping there.

"cooling-off" laws Provincial laws that permit a consumer to cancel an order for a product — usually within a short period after signing the order.

cooperative advertising An arrangement whereby two different organizations — usually a manufacturer and its retailers — share the cost of an ad.

corporate vertical marketing system A distribution system wherein control is maintained by one company (usually a manufacturer) owning the other (retailing and/or wholesaling) firms in the channel.

correlation analysis A form of the market-factor method of sales forecasting, more mathematically exact than the direct-derivation method.

cost of goods sold A major section in an operating statement, showing calculations to determine the cost of products sold during the period covered by the statement.

cost-plus pricing A major method of price determination. The price of a unit of a product is set at a level equal to the unit's total cost plus a desired profit on the unit.

CRTC See *Canadian Radio-Television and Tele-communications Commission.*

cues Stimuli, weaker than drives, that determine the pattern of responses to satisfy a motive.

culture The symbols and artifacts created by people and handed down from generation to generation as determinants and regulators of human behaviour in a given society.

cumulative quantity discount A discount based on the total volume purchased over a period of time.

dealer Same as a retailer.

decline stage of the product life cycle The stage when sales and profits decline sharply. Management must decide whether to abandon the product or to rejuvenate it in this stage.

demography The statistical study of human population and its distribution characteristics.

department store A large retailing institution that carries a very wide variety of product lines, including apparel, furniture, and home furnishings.

depth of product line The assortment within a product line.

derived demand A situation in which the demand for one product is dependent upon the demand for another product. Found in the industrial market, where the industrial demand is derived from the demand for consumer products.

descriptive label A label that gives information regarding the use, care, performance, or other features of a product.

desk jobber Same as a drop shipper.

devaluation of currency Reduction in the value of one country's currency in relation to the value of the currencies of other nations.

diffusion of innovation A process by which an innovation is communicated within social systems over time.

direct-action advertising Advertising that is designed to get a quick response from the potential customer.

direct derivation A relatively simple form of the market-factor method of sales forecasting.

direct expenses Expenses incurred totally in connection with one market segment or one unit (product, territory) of the company's marketing organization. Also called separable costs.

direct mail An advertising medium whereby the advertiser contacts prospective customers by sending some form of advertisement through the mail.

direct selling A vague term that may mean selling directly from producer to consumer without any middlemen; or, it may mean selling from producer direct to a retailer, thus bypassing wholesaling middlemen. Also called direct marketing or direct distribution.

discount house A general-merchandise retailer featuring self-service and prices that are below list prices or regularly advertised prices.

discount in pricing A reduction from the list price. Usually offered to buyers for buying in quantity, paying in cash, or performing marketing services for the seller.

discount retailing The practice of selling below the list price or regularly advertised price.

discretionary buying power The amount of disposable income remaining after fixed expenses and household needs are paid for.

dispersion In distribution, the middlemen's activities that distribute the correct amount of a product to its market.

disposable personal income Income remaining after personal taxes are paid.

distribution The channel structure (institutions and activities) used to transfer products and services from an organization to its markets.

distribution centre A large warehousing centre that implements a company's inventory-location strategy.

distributor Same as a wholesaler.

diversion in transit A railroad rate concession allowing a shipper to change the destination of its carload-rate rail shipment while the shipment is in transit. The seller pays the carload rate from origin to final destination.

drive A strong stimulus that requires satisfaction. Same as a motive.

drop shipper A limited-function wholesaler that does not physically handle the product. Also called a *desk jobber*.

dumping Selling products in foreign markets below the prices that these goods are sold for in their home markets.

early adopters The second group (following the innovators) to adopt something new. This group includes the opinion leaders, is respected, and has much influence on its peers.

early majority A more deliberate group of innovation adopters that adopts just before the "average" adopter.

economic order quantity (EOQ) A concept in the inventory-control phase of the physical distribution system that identifies the optimum quantity to reorder when replenishing inventory stocks.

economy of abundance An economy that produces and consumes far beyond its subsistence needs.

ego In Freudian psychology, the rational control centre in our minds that maintains a balance between (1) the uninhibited instincts of the id and (2) the socially oriented, constraining superego.

80-20 principle A term describing the situation in which a large proportion of a company's marketing units (products, territories, customers) accounts for a small share of the company's volume or profit, and vice versa.

elastic demand A price-volume relationship, such that a change of one unit on the price scale results in a change of more than one unit on the volume scale. That is, when the price is decreased, the volume increases to the point where there is an increase in total revenue. When the price is increased, demand declines and so does total revenue.

Engel-Kollat-Blackwell theory A comprehensive theory of buyer behaviour.

EOQ See *economic order quantity*.

equalization In distribution, the activity of middlemen that balances the output of producers with the demands of consumers and industrial users.

ethnocentric stage The first stage in the evolution of international operations. A company has a home-country orientation, and foreign operations are treated as secondary to domestic operations. A company simply exports its domestic marketing program with no adjustments for the foreign market.

European Economic Community (EEC) Perhaps better known as the Common Market, an economic union of nine Western European nations (Belgium, France, West Germany, Luxembourg, Netherlands, Italy, Great Britain, Ireland, and Denmark).

European Free Trade Association (EFTA) An economic union of seven Western European nations (Norway, Sweden, Finland, Portugal, Austria, Switzerland, and Iceland).

exclusive dealing The practice by which a manufacturer prohibits its retailers from carrying products that are competitive with that manufacturer's products.

exclusive distribution The practice in which a manufacturer uses only one wholesaler or retailer in a given market.

exclusive territories The practice by which a manufacturer requires each middleman to sell only within that middleman's assigned geographic area.

executive judgement A sales-forecasting method based on estimates made by the firm's executives. Also called *jury of executive opinion.*

"expected" price The price at which customers consciously or unconsciously value a product; what customers think a product is worth.

experimental method A method of gathering primary data in a survey by establishing a controlled experiment that simulates the real market situation.

export-import agent middlemen Middlemen specializing in international marketing. They may be brokers, selling agents, or manufacturers' agents.

fabricating materials Industrial goods that have received some processing and will undergo further processing as they become a part of another product.

fabricating parts Industrial goods that have already been processed to some extent and will be assembled in their present form (with no further change) as part of another product.

facilitating agencies Organizations that aid in a product's distribution, but do not take title to the products or directly aid in the transfer of title. They include such organizations as transportation agencies, insurance companies, and financial institutions, as distinguished from retailing and wholesaling middlemen.

fad A short-lived fashion that is usually based on some novelty feature.

family branding A branding strategy in which a group of products is given a single brand. Also called *blanket branding.*

family life cycle The series of life stages that a family goes through, starting with young single people and progressing through married stages with young and then older children, and ending with older married and single people.

family packaging The use of packages with similar appearance for a group of products.

fashion A style that is popularly accepted by groups of people over a reasonably long period of time.

fashion adoption process The process by which a style becomes popular in a market; sim-

ilar to diffusion of innovation. Three theories of fashion adoption are trickle-down, trickle-across, and trickle-up.

fashion cycle Wavelike movements representing the introduction, rise, popular acceptance, and decline in popularity of a given style.

feedback In the communication process, the element that tells the sender whether and how the message was received.

field (custodian) warehousing A form of public warehousing that provides a financial service for a seller.

fishyback freight service The service of transporting loaded truck trailers or railroad freight cars on barges or ships.

fixed cost A cost that remains constant regardless of how many items are produced or sold.

F.O.B. (free on board) pricing A geographic pricing strategy whereby the buyer pays all freight charges from the F.O.B. location to the destination.

form utility The utility created when a product is produced.

forward dating A combination of a seasonal discount and a cash discount. The buyer places an order and receives shipment during the off-season, but does not have to pay the bill until after the season has started and some sales income has been generated.

franchise system A system wherein one organization (the franchisor) grants a number of independent operators (franchisees) the right to sell the franchisor's products or services, in exchange for meeting certain conditions laid down by the franchisor.

freight absorption A geographic pricing strategy whereby the seller pays for (absorbs) some of the freight charges in order to penetrate more distant markets.

freight forwarder A specialized transportation agency that consolidates less-than-carload or less-than-truckload shipments into carload or truckload quantities. Provides door-to-door shipping service.

full-cost approach In a marketing cost analysis, an accounting approach wherein all expenses — direct and indirect — are allocated to the marketing units being analysed.

full-function wholesaler A merchant wholesaling middleman who performs all the usual wholesaling activities.

functional (activity) costs The grouping of operating expenses into categories that represent the major marketing activities. In a marketing cost analysis, the ledger expenses are allocated to these various activity categories.

functional discount Same as a *trade discount*.

generic product A product packaged in a plain label and sold with no advertising and without a brand name. The product goes by its generic name, such as "tomatoes" or "paper towels."

generic use of brand names General reference to a product by its brand name — cellophane, kerosene, zipper, for example — rather than its *generic name*. The owners of these brands no longer have exclusive use of the brand name.

geocentric stage The most advanced stage in the evolution of international business. The entire world is treated as a single market.

gestalt theory of learning The theory stating that, in learning, people sense the "whole" of a thing rather than its component parts.

grade label Identification of the quality (grade) of a product by means of a letter, number, or word.

gross margin Net sales minus cost of goods sold. Also called gross profit.

growth stage of the product life cycle The stage when sales continue to increase, and profits increase, peak, and start to decline.

Hazardous Products Act (1969) A federal law requiring that manufacturers clearly label and place warning messages and symbols on the containers and packages of products that may be harmful if misused.

horizontal industrial market A situation where a given product is usable in a very wide variety of industries.

horizontal information flow A theory holding that people take their cues from opinion leaders in their own social class.

Howard-Sheth theory A comprehensive theory of buyer behaviour.

human-orientation stage An emerging stage of marketing management that stresses quality of life rather than material standard of living.

hypermarket A very large retail store that sells a very wide variety of products intended to satisfy all of a consumer's routine needs. Also known as a *superstore* or a super-*supermarket*.

iceberg principle The concept that uses the analogy of an iceberg to represent a company's situation. Analysing only total sales and costs is like looking at the tip of an iceberg and can be misleading.

id In Freudian psychology, the part of the mind that houses the basic instinctive drives, many of which are antisocial.

imperfect competition Same as monopolistic competition.

impulse buying Purchasing without planning the purchase in advance.

indirect expenses Costs incurred jointly for more than one marketing unit (product, territory, market). Also called common costs.

indirect-action advertising Advertising designed to stimulate demand slowly over a long period of time.

industrial buying process The series of steps an industrial user goes through when deciding whether or not to buy a given industrial product.

industrial distributor A full-service merchant wholesaler who handles industrial goods and sells to industrial users.

industrial marketing The marketing of industrial goods to industrial users.

industrial products Products intended for use in producing other goods or in rendering services in a business.

industrial users People or organizations who buy products to use in their own businesses or as aids in making other products.

inelastic demand A price-volume relationship such that a change of one unit on the price scale results in a change of less than one unit on the volume scale. That is, when the price is increased, the volume demanded goes down but total revenue increases. When the price is decreased, the volume goes up, but not enough to offset the price increase; so the net result is a decrease in total revenue.

informal investigation The stage in a marketing research study that involves informal talks with people outside the company being studied.

in-home retailing Retail selling in the customer's home. A personal sales representative may or may not be involved. In-home retailing includes door-to-door selling, party-plan selling, and selling by television and computer.

innovation Anything perceived by a person as being new.

innovators The first group — a venturesome group—of people to adopt something new (product, service, idea, etc.).

installations Long-lived, expensive, major industrial capital goods that directly affect the scale of operation of an industrial user.

institutional advertising Advertising designed to generate an attitude toward a company, rather than toward a specific product marketed by that company.

intensity of distribution The number of middlemen used by a producer at the retailing and wholesaling levels of distribution.

intensive distribution A manufacturer sells its product in every outlet where a customer might reasonably look for it. Also known as *mass distribution*.

introduction stage of the product life cycle The stage in which a product is launched into its market with a full-scale production and marketing program. In this stage, sales are low and losses are incurred.

inventory stockturn rate The number of times a company's average inventory is sold during a year.

inverse demand A price-volume relationship such that the higher the price, the greater are the unit sales. Thus, an increase in price results in an increase in unit sales volume.

jobber Same as a wholesaler.

joint venture An operational structure for international marketing in which a firm that wishes to market in a foreign country forms a partnership with an individual firm in the host country.

jury of executive opinion A sales-forecasting method based on estimates made by a firm's executives.

kinked demand curve The type or shape of demand curve existing (1) when prices are determined entirely by market demand or (2) when a "customary" price prevails for a given product. The kink occurs at the level of the market price.

label The part of the product that carries information about the product or the seller.

laggards Tradition-bound people who are the last to adopt an innovation.

late majority The sceptical group of innovation adopters who adopt a new idea late in the game.

leader pricing Temporary price cuts on well-known items. The price cut is made with the idea that these "specials" (loss leaders) will attract customers to the store.

learning Changes in behaviour resulting from previous experiences.

leasing A growing behavioural pattern in the industrial market (as well as in the consumer market) of renting a product rather than buying it outright.

ledger expenses A company's operating expenses as they appear in the usual accounting system. Also called "natural" expenses and "object-of-expenditure" costs.

less-than-carload rate (l.c.l.) A railroad freight rate for shipping a quantity that is less than a carload. This rate is higher than the carload rate.

licensing An arrangement whereby one firm sells to another firm (for a fee or royalty) the right to use the first company's patents or manufacturing processes. This is a common method of entering a foreign market: A company grants (licenses) manufacturing rights to a firm in the foreign country.

limited-function wholesaler A merchant wholesaling middleman who performs a limited number of the usual wholesaling functions.

limited-line store A retailing institution that carries an assortment of products, but in only one or a few related product lines.

list price The official price as stated in a catalogue or on a price list. The price of one unit of a product at the point of production or resale. The price before any discounts or other reductions. Also known as *base price*.

local (retail) advertising Advertising placed by retailers.

logo A symbol used to identify a company and its products and services — usually registered as a trademark of the company.

long-range planning Planning that covers a period of 3, 5, or 10 years, or even longer.

loss leaders See *leader pricing*.

lower-lower class The social class that includes unskilled labourers and workers in nonrespectable jobs.

lower-middle class The social class that includes white-collar workers, such as teachers, salespeople, small-business owners, and office workers.

lower-upper class The social class that includes the socially prominent, newly rich people in a community.

mail interview The method of gathering data in a survey by means of a questionnaire mailed to respondents and, when completed, returned by mail.

mail-order selling A type of nonstore, nonpersonal retail or wholesale selling in which the customer mails in an order that is then delivered by mail or other parcel-delivery system.

management The process of planning, implementing, and evaluating the efforts of a group of people toward a common goal. In this book, the terms "management" and "administration" are used synonymously.

management process Activities involved in planning, implementing, and evaluating a program.

manufacturers' agent An independent agent wholesaling middleman that sells part or all of a manufacturer's product mix in an assigned geographic territory. The agent sells related but noncompeting products from several manufacturers.

manufacturer's brand A brand owned by a manufacturer or other producer. Also called a *national brand*.

marginal analysis A major method of setting a base price. Involves balancing market demand with product costs to determine the best price for profit maximization.

marginal cost The cost of producing and selling one more unit; that is, the cost of the last unit produced or sold.

marginal revenue The income derived from the sale of the last unit — the marginal unit.

markdown A reduction from the original retail selling price, usually made because the store was unable to sell the product at the original price.

market People or organizations with wants to satisfy, money to spend, and the willingness to spend it.

market aggregation A marketing strategy in which an organization treats its entire market as if that market were homogeneous.

market factor An item that is related to the demand for a product.

market-factor analysis A sales forecasting method based on the assumption that future demand for a product is related to the behaviour of certain market factors.

market index A market factor expressed in quantitative form relative to some base figure.

market potential Total expected industry sales for a product in a given market over a certain time period.

market segmentation The process of dividing the total market into one or more parts (submarkets or segments), each of which tends to be homogeneous in all significant aspects.

market segmentation (with multiple segments) A segmentation strategy that involves identifying two or more different groups of customers as target-market segments; the seller then develops a different marketing mix to reach each segment.

market segmentation (with a single segment) A segmentation strategy involving the selection of one homogeneous group of customers within the total market; the seller develops one marketing mix to reach this single segment.

market share One company's percentage share of the total industry sales in a given market.

market-based pricing A pricing strategy in which a company sets the price of its product only in relation to the competitive market price. The firm's costs have no influence at all on this price.

marketing audit A total evaluation program consisting of a systematic, objective, comprehensive review of all aspects of an organization's marketing function. An evaluation of the company's goals, policies, results, organization, personnel, and practices.

marketing concept A philosophy of business based on customer orientation, profitable sales volume, and organizational coordination.

marketing cost analysis A detailed study of the operating expense section of a company's profit and loss statement.

marketing information system (MkIS) An ongoing, organized system for gathering and processing information to aid in marketing decision making.

marketing (macro-societal dimension) Any exchange intended to satisfy human wants or needs.

marketing (micro-organizational definition) Total system of activities designed to plan, price, promote, and distribute want-satisfying goods and services to markets.

marketing mix A combination of the four elements—product, pricing structure, distribution system, promotional activities—that constitute the core of an organization's marketing system.

marketing plan See *annual marketing plan*.

marketing planning Setting goals and strategies for the marketing effort in an organization. See *strategic marketing planning*.

marketing research The systematic gathering and analysis of information relevant to a problem in marketing.

marketing system A regularly interacting group of ideas forming a unified whole. These items include the organization doing the marketing, the thing being marketed, the target market, marketing intermediaries helping in the exchange, and environmental constraints.

markup The dollar amount added to the acquisition cost of a product to determine the selling price.

markup percentage The dollar markup expressed as a percentage of either the selling price or the cost of the product.

maturity stage of the product life cycle The stage wherein sales increase, peak, and start to decline. Profits decline throughout this stage.

merchandise manager An executive position commonly found in retailing. See *product manager*.

merchandising Product planning—getting the right product to the right market, at the right time, at the right price, and in the right colours and sizes.

merchant middleman An independent business that takes title to the product it is helping to market.

message In communication, the information sent from the source to the receiver.

middleman The business organization that is the link between producers and consumers or industrial users. Renders services in connection with the purchase and/or sale of products as they move from producer to their ultimate market.

middleman's brand A brand owned by a retailer or a wholesaler. Also called a *private brand*.

misdirected marketing effort A marketing effort (cost) that is expended in relation to the number of marketing units (products, territories, or customers) rather than in relation to the potential volume or profit from these units.

missionary salesperson A type of manufacturer's sales job that involves nonselling activities such as performing promotional work and providing services for customers. The sales rep ordinarily is not expected or permitted to solicit orders.

MkIS See *marketing information system*.

modified rebuy An industrial purchasing situation between a new task and a straight rebuy in terms of time required, information needed, and alternatives considered.

money income The amount of income a person receives in cash or cheques from salaries, wages, interest, rents, dividends, or other sources.

monopolistic competition A market situation in which there are many sellers. Each seller tries to differentiate its product or its marketing program in some way to suggest that its market offering is distinctive. Also known as *imperfect competition*.

monopoly A market situation in which one seller controls the supply of a product.

motivation The force that activates goal-oriented behaviour.

motive A stimulated need that an individual seeks to satisfy with goal-oriented behaviour.

multiple influence on purchases The situation where the purchasing decision is influenced by more than one person in the buyer's organization.

multiple packaging The strategy of packaging several units of a product in one container in the hope of increasing the product's sales volume.

national advertising Advertising sponsored by a manufacturer or some other producer. Also called general advertising.

national brand A brand owned by a manufacturer or other producer.

neighbourhood shopping centre A small group of stores centring on a supermarket and including other convenience-goods stores and specialty stores. Draws from a market located perhaps within ten minutes by car.

net profit Gross profit minus all operating expenses. Or, sales revenue less both the cost of the goods sold and all operating expenses.

net sales Gross sales less sales returns and sales allowances.

new product A vague term that may refer to (1) really innovative, truly unique products; (2) replacements for existing products that are significantly different from existing ones; and (3) imitative products that are new to the given firm.

new-product development process Developmental stages that a new product goes through. Starts with idea generation and continues through idea screening, business analysis, limited production, test-marketing, and eventually commercialization (full-scale production and marketing).

new task In the industrial buying process, the situation in which a company for the first time considers the purchase of a given item.

nonbusiness organizations A category that covers a wide spectrum of organizations that do not perceive themselves to be in business (even though they really are). Includes such groupings as educational, religious, charitable, social cause, cultural, health-care, and political organizations.

noncumulative quantity discount A discount based on the size of an individual order of products.

nonprice competition Competition based on some factor other than price—for example, promotion, product differentiation, or variety of services.

nonprofit, or not-for-profit, organization An organization in which profit making is not a goal. The organization neither intends nor tries to make a profit.

nonstore retailing A type of retail selling in which the customer does not go to the store.

observational method The method of gathering primary information in a survey by personal or mechanical observation of respondents. No interviewing is involved.

odd pricing Pricing at odd amounts ($4.99 rather than $5, for example) in the belief that these seemingly lower prices will result in larger sales volume. A form of psychological pricing that is also called "penny pricing."

oligopoly A market situation in which only a few sellers control all (or most) of the supply of a product.

one-price policy The pricing strategy by which the seller charges the same price to all customers of the same type who buy the same quantity of goods.

operating ratio A ratio between any two items on an operating statement. Most commonly used are the ratios between some item and net sales.

operating statement The financial statement that shows an organization's revenues and expenses over a period of time. Also called an income statement or profit and loss statement.

operating supplies The "convenience goods" of the industrial market — short-lived, low-priced items purchased with a minimum of time and effort.

opinion leader The member of a reference group who is the information source and who influences the decision making of others in the group.

organizational porfolio analysis Same as *business portfolio analysis*.

packaging The activities in product planning that involve designing and producing the container or wrapper for a product.

party-plan selling A form of in-home retailing in which a personal sales rep makes a presentation to a group of potential customers gathered in a party setting in a person's home. The rep writes orders at this party, and the host or hostess receives a commission based on these sales.

patronage buying motives The reasons why a person or an organization patronizes (shops at) a certain store or some other supplier.

patterned interview A standardized list of questions used by all interviewers when interviewing a group of applicants for a given job.

penetration pricing Setting a low initial price on a product in an attempt to reach a mass market immediately.

percentage-of-sales promotional appropriation A method of determining the promotional appropriation. The amount is set as a certain percentage of past or forecasted future sales.

perception The meaning we attribute to stimuli received through our five senses; or, the way we interpret a stimulus. Our perceptions shape our behaviour.

personal interview A face-to-face method of gathering data in a survey.

personality An individual's pattern of traits that are determinants of behavioural responses.

personal selling The activity of informing and persuading a market on a person-to-person basis (face to face or on the telephone).

personal selling process Activities involved in making a personal sale, starting with presale preparation and including prospecting, the preapproach, the sales presentation, and postsale activities.

physical distribution Activities involved in the flow of products as they move physically from producer to consumer or industrial user.

physical distribution system The concept of treating all physical distribution activities as a total, interacting system, rather than as a series of fragmented, unrelated elements.

piggyback freight service Transporting truck trailers on railroad flatcars.

place utility The utility created by having a product available at the location where a customer wants it.

planned obsolescence As used in this book, the same as *fashion* or *style* obsolescence, in contrast to technological or functional obsolescence. The altering of the superficial characteristics of a product so that the new model is easily differentiated from the old one. The marketer's intention is to make people dissatisfied with the old model.

planned shopping centre A group of retail stores whose activities are coordinated and promoted as a unit to consumers in the surrounding trade area. The centre is planned, developed, and controlled by one organization, typically called a shopping centre developer.

planning The process of deciding in the present what to do in the future.

polycentric stage A host-country orientation in a company's evolution in international business. Each foreign country is treated as a separate entity with its own subsidiary organization that plans and operates its own marketing program.

possession utility The utility created by the transfer of a product's title from the seller to the buyer.

preapproach The stage in the personal selling process when a sales rep learns as much as possible about prospective customers and plans the best way to approach a given prospect.

presentation In personal selling, the activities that involve approaching the customer, giving a sales talk, meeting objections, and closing the sale. This is the AIDA stage in personal selling. See *AIDA*.

pretesting Field-testing a questionnaire, a product, an advertisement (or whatever item is being studied) by trying out the item on a limited number of people, prior to a full-scale market introduction of the item.

price What you pay for what you get. Value expressed in dollars and cents.

price lining A retail pricing strategy whereby a store selects a limited number of prices and sells each item only at one of these prices.

pricing objectives The goals that management tries to reach with its pricing structure and strategies.

primary data Original data (information) gathered specifically for the project at hand.

primary demand The market demand for a general category of products (in contrast to the selective demand for a particular brand of that product).

private brand A brand owned by a middleman.

processing in transit A railroad in-transit shipping privilege. The shipper can unload its product en route, have it processed, and then reload it to the final destination. The carload rate is charged from the original shipping point to the final destination.

product A set of tangible and intangible attributes that provide want-satisfying benefits to a buyer in an exchange. Such attributes include colour, price, packaging, and the reputation and services of the manufacturer and the middleman. A "product" may be a physical good, a service, an idea, a place, an organization, or even a person.

product assortment Full list of products sold by a firm. Same as *product mix*.

product buying motives The reasons for buying a certain product.

product deletion The discontinuance of the marketing of a product; withdrawal of the product from the company's product mix.

product development The technical activities of product research, engineering, and design.

product differentiation A product strategy wherein a company promotes the differences between its products and those of its competitors.

production orientation The first stage in the evolution of marketing management. The basic assumption is that making a good product will ensure business success.

product life cycle The stages of a product goes through from its introduction, through its growth and maturity, to its eventual decline and death (withdrawal from the market or deletion from the company's offerings).

product line A group of similar products intended for essentially similar uses.

product manager An executive responsible for planning the entire marketing program for a given product or group of products.

product mix The full list of products offered for sale by a company.

product planning All the activities that enable an organization to determine what products it will market.

product positioning The decisions and activities involved in developing the intended image (in the customer's mind) for a product in relation to competitive products.

product warranty — express A statement in written or spoken words regarding compensation by the seller if its product does not perform up to reasonable expectations.

product warranty — implied The concept of what a warranty was intended to cover, even though it was not actually stated or written in words.

promotion The element in an organization's marketing mix that is used to inform and persuade the market regarding the organization's products and services.

promotional allowance A price reduction granted by the seller as payment for promotional services rendered by the buyer.

promotional mix The combination of elements that constitute the promotion ingredients in an organization's marketing mix.

prospecting The stage in the personal selling process that involves developing a list of potential customers.

psychic income The intangible income factor related to climate, neighbourhood, job satisfaction, etc.

psychoanalytic theory of personality Sigmund Freud's theory that behaviour is influenced by the action and interaction of three parts of the human mind — the id, the ego, and the superego.

psychogenic needs Needs that arise from psychological states of tension.

psychographics A concept in consumer behaviour that explains a market in terms of demographics, as well as consumers' attitudes and life-styles.

publicity Nonpersonal promotion not paid for by the organization benefiting from it.

public relations A planned effort by an organization to influence some group's attitude toward that organization.

public service advertising Advertising (possibly by a manufacturer or a retailer) that urges people to support some public cause, such as a Red Cross drive or a campaign to drive carefully.

public warehouse An independent firm that provides storage and handling facilities.

quantity discount A reduction from list price when large quantities are purchased; offered to encourage buyers to purchase in large quantities.

questionnaire A data-gathering form used to collect the information in a personal, telephone, or mail survey.

quota sample A nonrandom sample "forced" in some way to be proportional to something.

random sample A sample chosen in such a way that every unit in the whole has an equal chance of being selected for the sample.

raw materials Industrial products that have not been processed in any way and that will become part of another product.

rack jobber A merchant wholesaler who primarily supplies food stores with nonfood items. This middleman provides the display case or rack, stocks it, and prices the merchandise.

readership test An indirect measure of the effectiveness of an ad that measures how many people saw or read the ad.

real income Purchasing power; that is, what money income will buy in goods or services.

recall test An indirect measure of the effectiveness of an ad. Determines how many people remember seeing a given ad.

reciprocity The situation of "I'll buy from you if you'll buy from me." A very controversial buying pattern in the industrial market.

recognition test An indirect measure of the effectiveness of an ad. Determines how many people can identify a given ad.

reference group A group of people who influence a person's attitudes, values, and behaviour.

regiocentric stage A regional orientation in a firm's evolution in international business. A given region (comprising several countries) is treated as a single market. A single marketing program is developed for an entire region.

regional shopping centre The largest type of planned suburban shopping centre (sometimes large enough to be a mini-downtown). Usually includes two or more department stores and many limited-line stores, along with service institutions such as banks, theatres, restaurants, hotels, and office buildings.

reinforcement In learning theory, the positive result of a rewarding (satisfying) behavioural reaction to a drive.

resale price maintenance A pricing policy whereby the manufacturer sets the retail price for a product.

response In learning theory, the behavioural reaction to cues.

retail sale The sale by any organization (producer, wholesaler, retailer, or nonbusiness organization) to an ultimate consumer for nonbusiness use.

retailer A business organization that sells primarily to ultimate consumers.

retailer cooperative chain A retailer-sponsored association of independent stores carrying essentially the same product lines.

retailing Activities related to the sale of products to ultimate consumers for their nonbusiness use.

return on investment (ROI) A measure of managerial performance and operating success in a company. The ratio of net profit to total assets or net worth. Is determined by multiplying the percentage of profit on sales by the rate of asset (or capital) turnover.

salary plan (or straight salary) A sales-force compensation plan that pays a representative a fixed amount per period of time. Provides security and stability of income but generally does not provide much incentive.

sales branch A manufacturer's regional office that carries inventory stocks and performs the services of a wholesaling middleman.

sales-force composite A sales forecasting method based on estimates compiled by the field sales force.

sales forecast The estimate of what a company expects to sell in a given market during a specified future time period.

sales management The managerial efforts involved in planning, implementing, and evaluating the activities of a sales force.

sales office A manufacturer's regional location that does not carry merchandise stocks, but otherwise performs the services of a wholesaling middleman.

sales orientation The second stage in marketing management, wherein the emphasis is on selling whatever the organization produces.

sales potential A company's expected sales of a given product in a given market over some time period.

sales promotion Activities that supplement and coordinate personal selling and advertising. Includes such elements as store displays, trade shows, and product samples.

sales-results test A method of measuring the effectiveness of advertising. Measures the sales volume stemming directly from an ad or a series of ads.

sales volume analysis A detailed study of a company's sales volume over a given period of time.

sample A limited portion of the whole of a thing.

sampling principle The concept that, if a small number of parts (a sample) is chosen at random from the whole (the universe or population), the sample will tend to have the same characteristics, and in the same proportion, as the universe.

SBU See *Strategic Business Unit*.

scrambled merchandising The practice of adding new product lines, quite unrelated to the products usually sold in a given type of store.

seasonal discount A discount given for placing an order during the seller's slow season.

secondary data Information already gathered by somebody else for some other purpose.

selective demand The market demand for an individual *brand* of a product, in contrast to the primary demand for the broad product category.

selective distribution The strategy wherein a manufacturer uses a limited number of wholesalers and/or retailers in a given geographic market.

selectivity in perceptions The process that limits our perceptions. We perceive only part of what we are exposed to, and we retain only part of what we selectively perceive.

self-concept (self-image) The way you see yourself, and also the way you think others see you. The concept includes your actual self-image and your ideal self-image.

seller's market The situation in which the demand for a given item greatly exceeds the supply of that item.

selling Informing and persuading a market about a product or service; synonymous with promotion.

selling agent An independent agent wholesaling middleman who serves as an entire marketing department for a manufacturer. The agent markets the entire output of the manufacturer, and often influences the pricing and design of the products.

services Separately identifiable, intangible activities that provide want-satisfaction and are not tied to the sale of a product or another service.

shopping centre A cluster of retail stores in a limited geographic area. Planned suburban shopping centres typically are planned, developed, and controlled by one organization. Their geographic market may be neighbourhood, community, or regional.

shopping goods Consumer products purchased after the buyer has spent some time and effort comparing the price, quality, colour, etc., of alternative products.

shopping store A type of retail outlet where consumers typicaly compare price, quality, and services with those of other stores before making a buying decision.

short-term planning Planning that typically covers a period of one year or less.

situation analysis The stage in a marketing research study that involves getting acquainted with the organization and its problems by means of library research and interviewing the organization's officials.

skimming pricing Setting a high initial price on a product, hoping to quickly recover new-product development costs.

small-order problem Individual sales orders that are so small as to be unprofitable relative to the cost of filling the orders.

social audit An evaluation of the social benefits and social costs connected with an organization's product.

social class A major division of society based on people's status in their communities.

social (societal) marketing A broadening and extension of managerial marketing. An organization must consider the social and environmental consequences of the production, marketing, and use of its products.

social responsibilities of marketing management Management's broad responsibilities for the effects that executive actions produce on our society.

specialty goods Consumer products with perceived unique characteristics, such that consumers are willing to expend special effort to buy them.

specialty store A retailer that carries only part of a given line of products. Or, in an alternative interpretation, a store that stresses its reputation, quality of merchandise, and abundant and excellent services.

stabilizing prices A pricing goal designed to stabilize prices in an industry. Often found in industries where one firm is a price leader. Other firms price so as to follow the leader and thus not "rock the boat."

stimulus-response theory of learning Learning occurs as correct responses to a given stimulus are reinforced with want-satisfaction, and as incorrect responses are penalized.

stockturn rate The number of times the average inventory is sold (turned over) during a given period of time. It is calculated by dividing net sales by average inventory at retail, or by dividing costs of goods sold by average inventory at cost.

storage The marketing activity that creates time utility. Involves holding and preserving products from the time they are produced until they are sold.

straight rebuy In the industrial market, a routine purchase with minimal informational needs.

Strategic Business Unit (SBU) A separate major product and/or market division in a company. A separate strategic plan is prepared for each SBU.

strategic marketing planning The process of setting marketing goals, selecting target markets, and designing a marketing mix to satisfy these markets and achieve these goals.

strategic planning The managerial process of matching an organization's resources and abilities with its marketing opportunities over the long run.

strategy A broad, basic plan of action by which an organization intends to reach one or more goals.

style A distinctive presentation or construction in any art, product, or activity.

style obsolescence Same as *planned obsolescence*.

subculture A part of a total culture that is reasonably homogeneous with regard to race, religion, nationality, geographic location, or some other factor.

superego In Freudian psychology, the part of the mind that houses the conscience and directs instinctive drives into socially acceptable channels.

supermarket A large, departmentalized, self-service retailing institution offering a wide variety of food products, as well as an assortment of nonfood items. Emphasizes low prices and ample parking space.

superstore A large store carrying all that a supermarket typically carries plus a much wider assortment of the nonfood products that are usually purchased on a routine basis and at a low price. Also called *hypermarket* or *super-super-market*.

survey method A method of gathering data by interviewing a limited number of people (a sample) in person or by telephone or mail.

survey of buyer intentions A method of sales forecasting in which a sample of potential customers is asked about their future plans for buying a given product.

synergism The coordinate action of separate elements so that the total effect is greater than the sum of the effects of individual elements acting independently.

tactic A detailed course of action by which a strategy (or a strategic plan) is to be implemented and activated.

target market A group of customers at whom an organization specifically aims its marketing effort.

target return A pricing goal that involves setting prices so as to achieve a certain percentage return on investment or on net sales.

task or objective method A method of determining the promotional appropriation. First, the organization decides what is to be accomplished, and then calculates how much it will cost to reach this goal.

telephone selling/shopping Selling via telephone. The seller contacts a customer and makes a sales presentation over the phone. Or, the customer contacts the seller and places an order over the phone. It is used in both retailing and wholesaling.

telephone survey or interview A method of gathering data in a survey by interviewing people over the telephone.

teleshopping A form of in-home retailing where the consumer shops with the aid of a television set and possibly a home computer.

test marketing Commercial experiments in limited geographic areas, to determine the feasibility of a full-scale marketing program. The seller may test a new product, a new feature of an existing product, or some other element in the marketing mix.

theme In promotion, the central idea or focal point in a promotional campaign. The promotional appeals are dressed up in some distinctive attention-getting form.

time utility The utility created by having a product available when a customer wants it.

total cost The sum of total fixed costs and total variable costs, or the full cost of a specific quantity produced or sold.

total-cost approach In physical distribution, the optimization of the overall cost–customer service relationship of the entire physical distribution system.

trade association An organization of companies representing a single industry. A trade association often engages in advertising and lobbying on behalf of the industry as a whole.

trade channel Same as a *channel of distribution*.

trade (functional) discount A reduction from the list price, offered by a seller to buyers in payment for marketing activities they will perform.

trademark A brand that is legally protected — essentially a legal term.

trade-practices legislation A series of laws passed by several provinces in the late 1970s with the intention of regulating misleading sales practices, especially at the retail level.

trading down A product-line strategy wherein a company adds a lower-priced item to its line of prestige goods, to reach the market that cannot afford the higher-priced items. The seller expects that the prestige of the higher-priced items will help sell the new, lower-priced products.

trading stamps Stamps that are given to the purchaser of a product or service and that can later be exchanged for merchandise. This is a form of nonprice competition.

trading up A product-line strategy wherein a company adds a higher-priced, prestige product to its line in the hope of increasing the sales of the existing products in that line.

trend analysis A sales-forecasting method that projects future sales on the basis of past trends.

trickle-across concept In fashion adoption, a fashion cycle moves horizontally within several social classes at the same time.

trickle-down concept In fashion adoption, a given fashion cycle flows downward through several socioeconomic classes.

trickle-up concept In fashion adoption, a style becomes popular (fashionable) first with lower socioeconomic classes and then, later, with higher socioeconomic groups.

truck jobber or truck distributor A limited-function wholesaler, usually carrying a limited line of perishable products that are delivered in the jobber's own truck to retail stores. Also called wagon jobber or truck wholesaler.

tying contract A contract under which a manufacturer agrees to sell a product to a middleman only if this middleman also buys another (possibly unwanted) product from the manufacturer.

ultimate consumers People who buy products or services for their personal, nonbusiness use.

uniform delivered price A geographic price strategy whereby the same delivered price is quoted to all buyers regardless of their location. Sometimes referred to as postage-stamp pricing.

unit pricing A form of price reporting where the price is stated per kilogram, per litre, or per some other standard measure — a consumer aid in comparison shopping.

upper-lower class A social class that includes blue-collar workers and the politicians and union leaders whose power base is with these workers.

upper-middle class A social class that includes successful executives in large firms and professionals.

upper-upper class A social class that includes the "old wealth" in a community.

utility The characteristic in an item that makes it capable of satisfying wants.

variable cost A cost that varies or changes directly in relation to the number of units produced or sold.

variable-price policy A pricing strategy in which a company sells similar quantities of merchandise to similar buyers at different prices. The price is usually set as a result of bargaining.

vending See *automatic vending*.

venture team An organizational structure for new-product planning and development. A small group that manages the new product from the idea stage to full-scale marketing.

vertical industrial market A situation where a given product is usable by virtually all the firms in only one or two industries.

vertical marketing system A distribution arrangement whereby a given channel of distribution is treated as a coordinated, integrated unit. Three common types of vertical systems are corporate, administered, and contractual.

voluntary chain A wholesaler-sponsored association of independently owned retail stores carrying essentially the same product lines.

wagon jobber Same as a *truck jobber*.

warehouse store Same as a *box store*.

warehousing A broad range of physical distribution activities including storage, assembling, bulk-breaking, and preparing products for shipping.

wheel-of-retailing theory A theory holding that (1) a new type of retailing institution gains a foothold in the retailing structure by competing on a low-status, low-price, low-service basis; (2) then, to expand its market, this retail institution increases its services and product offerings, thus increasing its costs and prices; (3) this leaves room at the bottom for the next low-price, low-service type of retailer to enter the retailing structure; and (4) the "wheel of retailing" continues to turn as new institutions enter the retail market.

wholesaler A merchant middleman (takes title to the products) whose primary purpose is to engage in wholesaling activities. Also may be called a jobber, industrial distributor, or mill-supply house.

wholesaling All activities involving sales to organizations that buy to resell or to use the products in their businesses.

wholesaling middleman The broad category that includes all middlemen engaged primarily in wholesaling activities.

world enterprise The most advanced form of international marketing structure. Both foreign and domestic operations are fully integrated and are no longer separately identified.

zone delivered pricing A geographic price *strategy* whereby the same delivered price is charged at any location within each geographic zone. Sometimes called parcel-post pricing.

Subject Index

731

Name Index

Howard, Niles, 154
Howell, Roy D., 100
Hughes, G. David, 229
Hunt, Shelby D., 382, 660
Hurwood, David L., 631

Jackson, Donald W., Jr., 415
James, Don L., 333
Jeffries, Richard J., 681
Jolson, Marvin A., 498
Jones, J. Richard, 569
Jones, S.C., 561, 572
Jones, Martin, 130
Jones, Vernon J., 135
Jones, Wesley H., 141
Joyce, Mary, 95

Kaikati, Jack G., 599
Kalbach, Warren E., 87
Kane, T. Gregory, 664
Kassarjian, Harold H., 164
Katz, Elihu, 143
Katz, Gerald M., 230
Keegan, Warren J., 581, 593
Kehoe, William J., 3
Kelley, Eugene J., 14
Kelly, J. Patrick, 233, 526
Kendall, C.L., 279
Kerin, Roger A., 224, 473
Kiechel, Walter III, 104
Kiefer, Richard O., 588
King, John O., 247
Kirpalani, Vishnu H., 134
Kizilbash, A.H., 203, 670
Klompmaker, Jay E., 229
Kluckhohn, Clyde, 125
Koffka, K., 156
Kohler, Wolfgang, 156
Kollat, David T., 165
Kotler, Philip, 3, 571, 572
Krueckeberg, H.F., 270
Krum, James R., 62

Label, Wayne, 599
Laczniak, Gene R., 562
LaGarce, Raymond, 439
LaLonde, Bernard J., 439, 446, 449, 452
Lambert, Douglas M., 443, 449
Lambert, Zarrel V., 343
Lamont, Douglas F., 603
Lamphier, Gary, 390
Langeard, Eric, 554
Laver, James, 257
Lazarsfeld, Paul, 143
Lazer, William, 14, 154
Leighton, David S.R., 134, 135
Leonard, T.L., 128

Levitt, Theodore, 544, 551, 553
Levy, Michael, 333
Levy, Sidney J., 219
Lewin, Kurt, 156
Liefeld, John, 660
Lindhorst, Jurgen W., 393
Lipson, Harry A., 603
Littlefield, James E., 603
Litvack, David S., 390
Litvak, I.A., 335
Lloyd, David, 564
Lovelock, Christopher H., 553, 554, 560, 571
Loyns, R.M.A., 665
Luck, David J., 62
Lunt, Paul, 138
Lusch, Robert F., 562
Lush, Patricia, 270

MacGregor, Robert, 137
Maddox, R. Neil, 128, 144
Mahatoo, W.H., 134
Maile, Carlton, 670
Main, Jeremy, 545
Mallen, Bruce, 134, 137, 335
Marceau, Claude, 87
Marchand, Philip, 92
Marcus, Stanley, 253
Markin, Rom J., 392
Marney, Jo, 270
Martin, W.S., 270
Martineau, Pierre D., 139, 141
Maslow, A.H., 120-21
Mason, J. Barry, 83, 675
Masters, John, 93
Mauser, Gary, 559
Mayer, Alan J., 128
Mayer, Charles S., 589
Mayer, David, 502
McCall, Suzanne H., 95
McCammon, Bert C., J., 423
McDougall, Gordon H.G., 559
McElroy, Bruce F., 341
McEvoy, Stuart, 579
McGoldrick, James, 599
McIntyre, Shelby, 233
McKinnon, Gary F., 526
McMahan, Harry W., 235
McMurry, Robert N., 495, 502
McNair, M.P., 392
McNeal, James U., 130, 262, 470
McTavish, Ronald, 560
McVey, Wayne W., 87
Meeker, Marchia, 138
Mehr, Martin, 277
Miaoulis, George, 564
Michman, Ronald D., 104